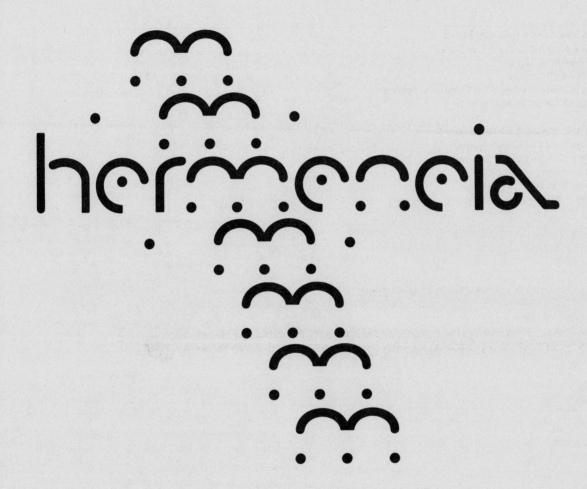

John 1

A Commentary on the
Gospel of John
Chapters 1–6

by Ernst Haenchen

Translated by
Robert W. Funk

Edited by
Robert W. Funk
with
Ulrich Busse

**Fortress
Press**   Philadelphia

Translated from the German *Das Johannesevangelium.*
Ein Kommentar, by Ernst Haenchen, pp. v–341. © 1980
J. C. B. Mohr (Paul Siebeck), Tübingen.

Library of Congress Catalog Card Number 82–48756
ISBN 0–8006–6013–7

Printed in the United States of America
Design by Kenneth Hiebert
Type set on an Ibycus System at Polebridge Press
9614B84   20–6013

Contents
John 1

The name *Hermeneia*, Greek ἑρμηνεία, has been chosen as the title of the commentary series to which this volume belongs. The word *Hermeneia* has a rich background in the history of biblical interpretation as a term used in the ancient Greek-speaking world for the detailed, systematic exposition of a scriptural work. It is hoped that the series, like its name, will carry forward this old and venerable tradition. A second entirely practical reason for selecting the name lies in the desire to avoid a long descriptive title and its inevitable acronym, or worse, an unpronounceable abbreviation.

The series is designed to be a critical and historical commentary to the Bible without arbitrary limits in size or scope. It will utilize the full range of philological and historical tools, including textual criticism (often slighted in modern commentaries), the methods of the history of tradition (including genre and prosodic analysis), and the history of religion.

Hermeneia is designed for the serious student of the Bible. It will make full use of ancient Semitic and classical languages; at the same time, English translations of all comparative materials—Greek, Latin, Canaanite, or Akkadian—will be supplied alongside the citation of the source in its original language. Insofar as possible, the aim is to provide the student or scholar with full critical discussion of each problem of interpretation and with the primary data upon which the discussion is based.

Hermeneia is designed to be international and interconfessional in the selection of authors; its editorial boards were formed with this end in view. Occasionally the series will offer translations of distinguished commentaries which originally appeared in languages other than English. Published volumes of the series will be revised continually, and eventually, new commentaries will replace older works in order to preserve the currency of the series. Commentaries are also being assigned for important literary works in the categories of apocryphal and pseudepigraphical works relating to the Old and New Testaments, including some of Essene or Gnostic authorship.

The editors of *Hermeneia* impose no systematic-theological perspective upon the series (directly, or indirectly by selection of authors). It is expected that authors will struggle to lay bare the ancient meaning of a biblical work or pericope. In this way the text's human relevance should become transparent, as is always the case in competent historical discourse. However, the series eschews for itself homiletical translation of the Bible.

The editors are heavily indebted to Fortress Press for its energy and courage in taking up an expensive, long-term project, the rewards of which will accrue chiefly to the field of biblical scholarship.

The translator and editor of the English edition of this commentary wishes to acknowledge the very considerable contribution of Professor Ulrich Busse and his assistant, Clemens Roggenbuck, to the completion of this translation. Without their help the work would not have progressed so rapidly nor with such improved results.

We are also indebted to the Universitat-Gesamthochschule Duisburg for its support of the editorial assistance of our German colleagues.

The translator and editor also wishes to acknowledge the superb bibliographical and philological help of Professor Karlfried Froehlich of Princeton Theological Seminary and the translation counselling of Professor Burton L. Mack of the Claremont Graduate School.

The translator and editor responsible for this volume is Robert W. Funk of the University of Montana.

January, 1984

Frank Moore Cross
For the Old Testament
Editorial Board

Helmut Koester
For the New Testament
Editorial Board

Rudolf Bultmann's commentary on John is in its way a masterpiece, comparable perhaps only to Karl Barth's *Romans* in this regard. It fused dialectic theology, existentialistic interpretation, the history of religions, source and redaction criticism, each on its growing edge, with "fascinating integration," as Ernst Haenchen put it.[1] Unfortunately Bultmann's brilliant solution was in major respects invalid. Yet the niveau on which he placed Johannine studies is itself an achievement that should not be given up. But who is equipped to dialogue with him at this level with this breadth . . . other than Ernst Haenchen himself, whose review of Bultmann's *John*[2] and the present volume rise to the occasion as few others have.

Ernst Haenchen's point of departure in theological studies had been contemporary philosophy and systematic theology. His fascination with Søren Kierkegaard may account for the fact that he had experienced Adolf von Harnack's dismantling of the history of dogma in the same way as had the dialectic theologians: "Where did that leave God, when finally everything had been delineated in its political, economic and cultural conditionedness in terms of those times?" Haenchen was first Karl Heim's assistant in Tübingen, and then taught systematic theology in Giessen and Münster between the two World Wars. His fragile health (including tuberculosis), a problem since childhood, and a series of military wounds necessitating eleven operations (including the amputation of a leg) during World War I led to a physical collapse in the hardship of World War II that necessitated his living in Davos, Switzerland, from 1944 to 1948. It was against Swiss law to import books printed in Germany, but 'somehow' a copy of Nestle's *Novum Testamentum Graece* crossed the frontier with him, his only reading material for a time in Davos, until Wilhelm Michaelis of Bern supplied him with relevant literature. It was under such impossible circumstances that Haenchen began the intensive exegetical study primarily of the text itself that produced his commentaries on Acts,[3] Mark[4] and ultimately John.

Haenchen's study of John had actually begun while convalescing from his first wounding in Serbia in 1915, when a classmate from Heidelberg sent him his notes from Martin Dibelius' course on John they had been attending when Haenchen was drafted. Then in 1926 he met in Tübingen a student from Marburg, Ernst Käsemann, who shared notes from Bultmann's first course on John. Since Käsemann was writing an essay on "the present status of the Johannine question" to submit in a competition, he and Haenchen began extensive dialogues on Johannine studies which continued for half a century. In 1931 Haenchen had met the systematician

1   "Aus der Literatur zum Johannesevangelium 1929–1956," *TRu*, n.s., 23 (1955) 335.

2   "Das Johannesevangelium und sein Kommentar," *TLZ* 89 (1964) 881–98, reprinted in Ernst Haenchen, *Die Bibel und Wir. Gesammelte Aufsätze* 2 (Tübingen: Mohr-Siebeck, 1968) 206–34.

3   *Die Apostelgeschichte*, KEK (Göttingen: Vandenhoeck & Ruprecht, [10]1956; 7th ed. of Haenchen's

commentary 1977).

4   *Der Weg Jesu: Eine Erklärung des Markus-Evangeliums und der kanonischen Parallelen* (Berlin: Walter de Gruyter, 1966).

Emanuel Hirsch, with whom a lasting friendship also emerged; Hirsch's volume on John[5] became a basic ingredient in Haenchen's Johannine studies in this formative period, even though his dissensus was in this case much more basic than in the case of Käsemann.[6]

Actually, Haenchen did not teach a course on John until World War II, since his chair was not in New Testament. But when most of the faculty as well as students were in military service, apart from those who like Haenchen were invalids, Haenchen was only too glad to respond to student need in choosing his courses. Though he received a medical retirement in 1946, he also taught a course on "Problems of the Gospel of John" in the winter of 1957–1958. But his exegetical work was carried out not primarily from a professorial chair but from a wheel chair, and was made public through publications;[7] his contact with students was largely in terms of assistants who went up and down the stairs in the stacks of the library to locate books for him. One such assistant, Ulrich Busse, carried on after Haenchen's death (1975) by editing the various drafts that Haenchen had been preparing for a generation into the present volume.[8]

With regard to the history of religions, Haenchen's commentary serves in a way to mark the transition from the Qumranian orientation characteristic of much Johannine study in the first decades after World War II to the Nag Hammadi orientation that has become increasingly prominent in recent years. Haenchen quoted Karl Georg Kuhn's enthusiastic statement of 1950, to the effect that in the Dead Sea Scrolls "we reach the matrix of the Gospel of John," but immediately pointed out its inappropriateness: "The Gospel of John has nothing to do with this law piety. . . . Also nothing connects it with the apocalyptic piety of the Qumran congregation."[9] For Haenchen anticipated the sobering of Qumran studies with regard to the Fourth Gospel marked by Herbert Braun's critical sifting of 1962.[10] Thus he

5   *Das vierte Evangelium in seiner ursprünglichen Gestalt verdeutscht und erklärt* (Tübingen: Mohr-Siebeck, 1936); see Ernst Haenchen "Aus der Literatur zum Johannesevangelium 1929–1956," *TRu*, n.s., 23 (1955) 308–9, 312, 326–27.

6   Ernst Käsemann, "Ketzer und Zeuge," *ZTK* 48 (1951) 292–311, reprinted in Ernst Käsemann, *Exegetische Versuche und Besinnungen* 1 (Göttingen: Vandenhoeck & Ruprecht, 1960) 168–87; see Ernst Haenchen, "Neuere Literatur zu den Johannesbriefen," *TRu*, n.s., 26 (1960) 281; Ernst Käsemann, *Jesu letzter Wille nach Johannes 17* (Tübingen: Mohr-Siebeck, 1966, ³1971) = *The Testament of Jesus* (Philadelphia: Fortress Press, 1968); see Ernst Haenchen, "Vom Wandel des Jesusbildes in der frühen Gemeinde," *in Verborum Veritas: Festschrift für Gustav Stählin* (Wuppertal: Theologischer Verlag, 1970) 10 n. 2.

7   There were surveys of recent Johannine research: "Aus der Literatur zum Johannesevangelium 1929–1956," *TRu*, n.s., 23 (1955) 295–335; "Neuere Literatur zu den Johannesbriefen," *TRu*, n.s., 26 (1960) 1–13, 267–91. There were essays on specific topics: "Johanneische Probleme," *ZTK* 56 (1959) 19–54; "Der Vater, der mich gesandt hat," *NTS* 9 (1963) 208–16; "Probleme des johanneischen 'Prologs,'" *ZTK* 60 (1963) 305–34; and "Jesus vor Pilatus (Joh 18:28–19:15) (Zur Methode der Auslegung)," *TLZ* 85 (1960) 93–102. These essays were reprinted in Ernst Haenchen, *Gott und Mensch. Gesammelte Aufsätze* 1 (Tübingen: Mohr-Siebeck, 1965) 78–113, 68–77, 114–43, and 144–56 respectively. A previously unpublished essay on "Historie und Geschichte in den johanneischen Passionsberichten" was included in Ernst Haenchen, *Die Bibel und Wir. Gesammelte Aufsätze* 2 (Tübingen: Mohr-Siebeck, 1968) 182–207. There were also a number of reviews of individual volumes on John (in addition to the review of Bultmann's commentary cited above).

8   See Busse's Preface to the present volume and Ulrich Busse, "Ernst Haenchen und sein Johanneskommentar," *ETL* 57 (1981) 125–43, from which some of the biographical information here cited is derived, as well as from Rudolf Smend, "Ansprache am Sarge Ernst Haenchens. In der Universitätskirche Münster am 6. Mai 1975," *ZTK* 72 (1975) 303–9.

9   Karl Georg Kuhn, "Die in Palästina gefundenen hebräischen Texte und das Neue Testament," *ZTK* 47 (1950) 210, cited by Ernst Haenchen, "Aus der Literatur zum Johannesevangelium 1929–1956," *TRu*, n.s., 23 (1955) 323.

10 "Qumran und das Neue Testament," *TRu*, n.s., 28 (1962) 192–234.

avoided a mistake such as that of W. F. Albright[11] in the history-of-religions classification of John: "The books of the Essenes from the first century BCE provide the closest approach to the Gospels (particularly St. John)," whereas the Nag Hammadi texts (none of which had at that time actually been published!) were ruled to show Gnostics to be "even worse heretics than the Church Fathers supposed": "The supposed forms of mild Gnosticism which might have influenced John simply vanish from the picture." Hence Haenchen considered the Johannine commentary emanating from the Albright school in the Anchor Bible to be "apologetic."

Haenchen for his part recognized in the Gnostic Gospels from Nag Hammadi the opportunity to trace the outcome of the Gnosticizing trajectory in which the Gospel of John is in some way involved, as a new way of casting light on John itself. Thus the 1960's were largely devoted to the study of these Gnostic Gospels,[12] an enterprise which both delayed the composition of the commentary and hence is largely responsible for it not being completed during Haenchen's lifetime, and also gave the commentary, to the extent it *was* completed, its status as being the first to presuppose to this extent the new source material. Haenchen could then with some authority disagree with Bultmann regarding the relation of John to Gnosticism. For whereas Bultmann maintained that "the cosmological dualism of Gnosticism has become in John a *dualism of decision*,"[13] Haenchen disagreed:[14] "We encounter here [in *The Gospel of Thomas*] a Gnostic dualism of decision (that precisely appeals only to words of Jesus!), and have to concede: The concept of 'dualism of decision' says nothing as to whether a text that teaches it is Christian or not."

Of course during the period when Haenchen was writing, not all the Nag Hammadi materials had become available, much less adequately interpreted, a process that is only now in full swing. For example, "the stupendous 'parallels' to the Prologue of the Gospel of John" that Carsten Colpe heralded in Nag Hammadi Codex XIII[15] are not noted, simply because the text had been published in German translation hardly half a year before Haenchen's death.[16] Nor had the all too fragmentary *Dialogue of the Savior* (NH III, 5) become available, which Helmut Koester has used in the context of other apocryphal material to provide a new approach to

11   W. F. Albright, "Recent Discoveries in Palestine and the Gospel of St. John," in *The Background of the New Testament and its Eschatology* [in honor of Charles Harold Dodd], ed. W. D. Davies and D. Daube (Cambridge: Cambridge University Press, 1956) 169.

12   Ernst Haenchen, "Literatur zum Thomasevangelium," *TRu*, n.s., 27 (1961) 146–78, 306–38; *Die Botschaft des Thomas-Evangeliums* (Berlin: A. Töpelmann, 1961); "Spuch 68 des Thomasevangeliums," *Le Muséon* 75 (1962) 19–29; "Neutestamentliche und gnostische Evangelien," composed for the Messina Colloquium on the Origins of Gnosticism (1966), which he was not able to attend due to illness, though the essay was published in *Christentum und Gnosis,* ed. Walther Eltester, BZNW 37 (Berlin: A. Töpelmann, 1969) 19–45. See also his studies on Gnosticism from the 50's: "Gab es eine vorchristliche Gnosis?" *ZTK* 49 (1952) 316–49; "Das Buch Baruch: Ein Beitrag zum Problem der christlichen Gnosis," *ZTK* 50 (1953) 123–58; "Aufbau und Theologie des 'Poimandres,'" *ZTK* 53 (1956) 149–91; all three were reprinted in Ernst Haenchen, *Gott und Mensch. Gesammelte Aufsätze*

1 (Tübingen: Mohr-Siebeck, 1965) 265–98; 299–334; 335–77 respectively.

13   Rudolf Bultmann, *Theologie des Neuen Testaments* (Tübingen: Mohr-Siebeck, 1951) 367 = *Theology of the New Testament,* tr. Kendrick Grobel (New York: Charles Scribner's Sons, 1955) 2: 21.

14   "Das Johannesevangelium und sein Kommentar," *TLZ* 89 (1964) 891.

15   Carsten Colpe, "Heidnische, jüdische und christliche Überlieferung in den Schriften von Nag Hammadi III," JAC 17 (1974) 122.

16   Gesine Schenke, "'Die dreigestaltige Protennoia': Eine gnostische Offenbarungsrede in koptischer Sprache aus dem Fund von Nag Hammadi eingeleitet und übersetzt vom Berliner Arbeitskreis für koptisch-gnostische Schriften," *TLZ* 99 (1974) 731–46. See my review of research, "Sethians and Johannine Thought: The *Trimorphic Protennoia* and the Prologue of the Gospel of John," in *The Rediscovery of Gnosticism,* vol. 2, *Sethian Gnosticism,* ed. Bentley Layton, Studies in the History of Religions [Supplements to *Numen*] 41 (Leiden: E. J. Brill, 1981) 643–62.

the Johannine discourses as developed out of sayings ascribed to Jesus.[17] These are only two of the many instances where the sluggishness of the various Nag Hammadi publication projects is greatly to the detriment of scholarship. But Haenchen did master the three Nag Hammadi texts known as 'Gospels' available in his time, *The Gospel of Truth, The Gospel of Thomas,* and *The Gospel of Philip,* and presupposed them in his commentary on John.

With regard to the sources imbedded in the Gospel of John, Haenchen, like others close to Bultmann such as Käsemann,[18] did not agree that there was a source consisting of non-Christian Gnostic revelation discourses from a Baptist background, but, like Butlmann, did initially assume the existence of a collection of miracle stories, the Semeia Source. In 1966 he said in a letter to me: "The so-called 'Miracles Source' in the sense of 'sign' is in kind a sort of enlarged Mark; it seeks, by narrating miracles that are enlarged over against Mark, to demonstrate the divine sonship of Jesus walking on earth." But already in a letter of 1968 the designation of the source was put in question: "Semeia Source is an unfortunate name, since only the miracle at Cana and the healing of the son of the *Basilikos* are counted as *semeia*; 6:26 is something quite different." Indeed he came to question the unity of the Semeia Source, as reflected in a letter of 1969: "To be sure this does not mean that the Evangelist only had access to a single source. Probably the understanding of the *semeia* as convincing miracles was really the usual thing at that time. Hence it is very questionable to me whether one can, à la Bultmann, reconstruct the texts behind the narrative material (which is all that is now being discussed), the 'source' down to the half-verses. Hence I often have to write 'tradition' without being able to express myself more precisely as to the exact delimitation and origin of this tradition." Hence the non-commitalness of the present commentary in this regard is not indicative of a vascillating uncertainty of a next-to-final revision, but rather of a thoroughly reflected assessment of the state of the matter. Haenchen had a different kind of grandeur from that of Bultmann, namely the self-restraint of not putting in question what has actually been rather solidly achieved by tying it to an all-too-hypothetical global solution. Haenchen's commentary is less dramatic but more durable.

Just as the role of the 'Narrator' behind the 'Evangelist' has been considerably enlarged beyond the dimensions of the Semeia Source and Passion Narrative Source presupposed by Bultmann, the 'Ecclesiastical Redactor' of Bultmann's solution has been upgraded to a 'Supplementer' who composed a considerably larger portion of the Gospel than Butlmann assumed. For, with regard to such 'redaction criticism,' Haenchen appealed less to Bultmann than to his precursor at the opening of the century, Eduard Schwartz. In this regard he made an exception to his normal practice by accepting my offer to procure for him literature not readily available to him: He expressed a desire to examine again Schwartz' "Aporien im vierten Evangelium"[19] and accepted my offer to send him a copy. His assistant prepared for him an index of Johannine passages in Schwartz' work, of which Haenchen sent me

---

17 Helmut Koester, "Dialog und Spruchüberlieferung in den gnostischen Texten von Nag Hammadi," *EvT* 39 (1979) 532–56; "Apocryphal and Canonical Gospels," *HTR* 73 (1980) 105–30; "Gnostic Writings as Witnesses for the Development of the Sayings Tradition," in *The Rediscovery of Gnosticism,* vol. 1, *The School of Valentinus,* ed. Bentley Layton, Studies in the History of Religions [Supplements to *Numen*] 41

(Leiden: (E. J. Brill, 1980) 238–61. *Introduction to the New Testament,* vol. 2, *History and Literature of Early Christianity,* Foundations and Facets (Philadelphia: Fortress Press; Berlin and New York: Walter de Gruyter, 1982) 178–83.

18 Ernst Käsemann, in his review of Bultmann's commentary on John, *Verkündigung und Forschung: Theologischer Jahresbericht, 1942–46* (1947) 186–89.

a copy early in 1969 as an expression of appreciation. Schwartz proposed solving the 'aporias,' the clashes and seams in the text, with the hypothesis that the introduction of the beloved disciple and the dependencies on the Synoptic Gospels are to be understood as secondary expansions of a basic document lacking these traits.

Thus Haenchen moved to the transformation of the 'Semeia Source' and the 'Ecclesiastical Redactor' before and after the 'Evangelist' into three stages of authorship of the Fourth Gospel that were not basically dissimilar in extent and importance. As a result 'Johannine Theology' is no longer, as in Bultmann's *Theology of the New Testament,* limited to the 'Evangelist,' but takes on the shape of tracing the theological contours of the Johannine trajectory or school. Here too Haenchen laid the groundwork for the epoch of Johannine research in which we now stand.[20]

Toward the end of the 60's the Society of Biblical Literature went through a reorganization, part of which involved supplementing the somewhat tedious program of paper after paper with the more lively give-and-take of seminars, consultations and interest groups. On the occasion of the proposal of a 'Gospels Seminar' to initiate this new trend I was asked by the Chair of the Research and Publications Committee, Krister Stendahl, to propose a possible avenue for the future of the study of the Gospels. My resultant presentation on "The Johannine Trajectory" of 19 December 1968 at the SBL meeting in Berkeley became in part an advance announcement of Haenchen's commentary:[21] "Haenchen has been working for a generation toward a commentary on John, which has not yet appeared but which in part is available in manuscript." For I had asked Haenchen to make available to the projected seminar the typescript of the relevant sections, which were duplicated, distributed and discussed at the first session of the Gospels Seminar in New York on 16 December 1969. This appeal from the other side of the Atlantic seemed to be the catalyst that led Haenchen to the third draft of the commentary upon which the present volume is largely based, and to that extent functioned well, not only for that passing occasion, but also for the permanent use to which the present commentary can be put. Indeed mention of the typescript as in the process of preparation heightened the public anticipation of the volume and thus facilitated its posthumous assembly and publication, of which the following comment by Hartwig Thyen in his survey of Johannine research is indicative:[22]

> In the interest of ongoing Johannine interpretation it is urgently to be hoped that the scholarly remains of Ernst Haenchen will be made accessible to the public as soon and as completely as possible. Like [Georg] Richter, Ernst Haenchen is also preparing a Johannine commentary, from whose very promising manuscript there have been quotations here and there in American publications.

It is especially in this context that I want to express my personal satisfaction that Haenchen's *John* is here made available to the English language public.

Claremont, CA
October 1983

James M. Robinson

---

19   Eduard Schwartz, "Aporien im vierten Evangelium," NGG (1907) 1: 342–72; (1908) 2: 115–48; 3: 149–88; 4: 497–560.

20   See the surveys of Johannine research by Hartwig Thyen, "Aus der Literatur zum Johannesevangelium," *TRu,* n.s., 39 (1974) 1–69, 222–52, 289–330; 42 (1977) 211–70; 43 (1978) 328–59; 44 (1979) 97–134; Jürgen Becker, "Aus der Literatur zum Joannesevangelium (1978–1980)," *TRu,* n.s., 47 (1982) 279–301, especially pp. 287–88 concerning the publication of the present volume in German.

21   James M. Robinson, "The Johannine Trajectory," in *Trajectories through Early Christianity* (Philadelphia: Fortress Press, 1971) 236 n. 11.

22   Thyen, *TRu,* n.s., 42 (1977) 212; see also pp. 227 and 242.

The exposition of the Fourth Gospel has continued apace since the death of Ernst Haenchen. In this respect, Haenchen's commentary has suffered the same fate as those of F. L. O. Baumgarten-Crusius, J. H. Bernard, R. H. Lightfoot, and G. Richter. When Ernst Haenchen passed away on 30 April 1975 in his eightieth year,[1] he left behind him several sketches of a commentary on John worked out in detail; these he had worked on intensively for the last twenty-five years. Yet his interest in the Fourth Gospel extends back to his student days. Among his papers were found two manuscripts: one, in his own hand, of a lecture probably given in Münster about the time Bultmann's great commentary on the Gospel of John began to appear in 1937; the other was a joint report on a course of lectures on the Gospel of John given by Martin Dibelius in the summer semester of 1915, also derived from his own hand. Haenchen held Dibelius in the highest esteem as his teacher in the field of New Testament.

Since he was not permitted to complement his commentary on Acts with a commentary on the Gospel of Luke, in 1954 he turned decisively to the Gospel of John. He first undertook a revision of the commentary on John in the *Handbuch zum Neuen Testament.* He worked daily on this commentary until his last days, apart from his illnesses, which constantly threatened his life following a severe injury in World War I, and apart from interruptions occasioned by the revision, from time to time, of his commentary on Acts.

The anticipation aroused by his essays on the Gospel of John and by his work on Gnosticism, which are closely related from the history-of-religions perspective, prompted Frau Haenchen to sort through and organize his papers following his death. Prof. Paul Hoffmann of Bamberg especially encouraged her to put together a manuscript for possible publication. It turned out that all his drafts, although varying in form, conceptually and methodologically followed a scheme that addressed various levels of readers at different times. On occasion he strove for the form of the *Handbuch zum Neuen Testament* (referred to as A in the analysis to follow). In another form he prepared an exposition of the Gospel for a broader audience (B), as he sought to do in his commentary on Mark, *Der Weg Jesu.* Again, he was indebted to the form of his commentary on Acts (C). Since he made use of this form in his final revisions of the John material also (D), it was natural that the commentary should take this final shape.

Since Ernst Haenchen shared with me his rich knowledge of Lucan scholarship, during my doctoral work, there developed between us, during his last years, a teacher-student relationship of the best kind. So I was drawn more and more into the sphere of his Johannine work. From the first assignments, which concerned the gathering of the literature, it was but a short step to the discussions of the Johannine question in all its complexity, which I shared with him mostly in the role of a silent

---

1   Obituary by Rudolf Smend, "Ansprache am Sarge
     Ernst Haenchens. In der Universitätskirche Münster
     am 6. Mai 1975," *ZTK* 72 (1975) 303–9.

listener. In this way I was in a position to provide information regarding the final stage of his thinking, to a certain extent. This made it natural for me to be entrusted with editing the commentary. Professor Hoffmann, to whom I had just been appointed an assistant for NT exegesis in the Catholic Theological Faculty of the University of Bamberg, declared himself ready to free me for this work, to the extent possible, and to guarantee the material conditions.

So the work on the final form of the commentary began in the spring of 1977. Frau Haenchen made preparations by organizing the notes of her husband and by making legible once again several pages of notes written in the shorthand of the old Tübingen Stift. This made it possible to bring the work to an early conclusion. She was also kind enough to make available to me once again all the versions of her husband's work that had been given into the hands of seasoned Johannine scholars. Professor James M. Robinson made his copy available to me, which was identical with a copy given to Professor R. Hamerton-Kelly, Stanford University, and with one found among the papers of Dr. Georg Richter (limited to the first five chapters). Ernst Haenchen had had an intensive exchange of ideas and correspondence with Richter, who unfortunately died much too young in the same year as Haenchen.

A first sifting of Haenchen's papers resulted in the following inventory for the commentary on John.

A §1; §2; §3; §4; §5; §6:1; 1:1–18; 1:19–28; 1:29–34; 1:35–51; 2:1–12; 2:23–25; 3:1–
(1954ff.) 21; 3:22–36; 4:1–42; 4:43–54; 5:1–47; 6:1–15; 6:16–25; 6:60–71; 7:14–52; 8:12–59; 9:1–41; 10:1–42; 11:1–44; 12:1–8; 12:9–11; 12:12–19; 12:36b–50; 13:1–38; 14:1–31; 15:1–17; 15:18–26; 16:1–33; 17:1–26; 20:1–31; 21:1–25.

B §1; §2; §3; §6:1; §6:2; 1:1–18; 1:19–28; 2:1–11; 2:13–25; 4:1–42; 5:1–30; 7:1–52;
(1960ff.) 9:1–41; 11:1–44; 12:12–19; 12:20–36; 13:1–38; 17:1–26; 18:1–40.

C §1; §2; §4; §5; §6:2; §6:3; §6:4; 1:1–18; 1:19–28; 1:29–34; 1:35–39; 1:40–51; 2:1–11;
(1963ff.) 2:13–22; 4:1–42; 4:43–54; 5:1–30; 5:31–47; 6:1–15; 6:16–25; 6:26–51a; 6:51b–59; 7:1–13; 7:14–52; 11:1–44; 11:45–54; 17:1–26; 18:1–27; 18:28–19:16a; 20:1–31; 21:1–25.

D §2; §4; §5; §6:1; 1:19–28; 1:29–34; 2:1–11; 2:13–22; 3:1–21; 4:1–42; 5:1–30; 6:1–13;
(1970ff.) 6:14–25; 11:1–44; 12:1–8; 18:1–27; 18:28–19:16a; 19:16b–42.

In addition to commentary that had been worked out for individual pericopes and parts of the introduction, there were found other essays and sketches on several pericopes (especially on the hymn in the Prologue, 1:1–18) that were indeed complete but which had not been brought to a conclusion. Since, however, Ernst Haenchen had preserved these sketches and bound them together with his finished commentary, it was also possible to take these into consideration in assembling the final version. And so, for example, we were able to create two excurses out of material devoted to the Prologue and to chapter twenty-one. In spite of this welcome fund of materials in general, there were segments of the Gospel of John for which there were only single older versions of commentary that had not undergone revision. Reviews, the commentary, *Der Weg Jesu*, and the lectures of the author were consulted and the older versions augmented in order to bring these segments (7:14–8:59, 12:12–50, and chapters 14-16) up to the latest possible stage of his exposition.

Since a criticial edition of the commentary had not been provided for, the editorial principles were derived from the materials at hand. The author made it evident in C and D that he was striving for the form of his commentary on Acts: translation of the Greek text; references to the literature; detailed comment; overview. This form, consequently, became controlling for the commentary on John. This decision had two consequences: first, the final form of the commentary had been determined. Material designated D in the inventory was to serve as the basis; where that was not available, C was to function as the foundation. At the same time, materials of the A and B type were to be sifted to determine if they contained material useful for the development of the train of thought or the exegetical argument in either the detailed commentary or in the overview. Such material could then be inserted into the final version of the commentary in the appropriate place. Secondly, the pericopes that were available only in an older version had to be reshaped, by using materials already published by the author, to conform to the form and content of the final stage of the author's exegesis, insofar as that could be reconstructed. Thus, the published essays of the author and the commentary, *Der Weg Jesu*, took precedence over the lectures. The latter represent, not the latest stage of his reflection, but the earliest, which was then determined entirely by the commentary of Bultmann that reigned supreme at that time. These lectures are a basic document for the history of the development of the author's views. There is revealed in the later development a gradual—at first hesitant, then increasingly confident—departure from Bultmann's position in which the source theories of Wellhausen and Schwartz play an important role. At the same time, one should not overlook the fact that, in retrospect, Ernst Haenchen was also influenced by the exposition of the Gospel of John by Emanuel Hirsch. It was in relation to these two great commentators of the 20's and 30's that Haenchen worked out his own position, with the help of older scholarship and composition criticism, a variety of redaction criticism, that he helped develop himself and applied so fruitfully in his commentary on Acts.

On the basis of the principle to proceed from the most recent versions of his work and to fall back on earlier versions only in the case of necessity, it becomes immediately evident which parts of his published corpus were especially helpful in completing the commentary. To be mentioned first of all is his article, "Der Vater, der mich gesandt hat."[2] It has been almost completely worked into the commentary. As a consequence, it was not available as a key expression of the author's understanding of the Gospel of John in the crucial introductory section §7: "The Various Christologies in the Gospel of John." It was therefore necessary to revert, in part, to his article, "Vom Wandel des Jesusbildes in der frühen Gemeinde."[3] Beyond these, the following essays were incorporated into the commentary, in part (listed in the order of their importance): "Johanneische Probleme"[4] must be mentioned first, followed by "Probleme des johanneische Prologs";[5] further, "Das Johannesevangelium und sein Kommentar";[6] "Historie und Geschichte in den johanneischen Passions-

2   ["The Father Who Sent Me"], *NTS* 9 (1963) 208–16. In *Gott und Mensch. Gesammelte Aufsätze* 1 (Tübingen: Mohr-Siebeck, 1965) 18–77.

3   ["On the Metamorphosis of the Picture of Jesus in the Early Church"], which appeared in *Verborum Veritas. Festschrift für Gustav Stählin zum 70. Geburtstag*, ed. O. Böcher and K. Haacker (Wuppertal: F. A. Brockhaus, 1970) 9–14.

4   ["Johannine Problems"], *ZTK* 56 (1959) 19–54. In his *Gott und Mensch. Gesammelte Aufsätze* 1 (Tübingen: Mohr-Siebeck, 1965) 78–113.

5   ["Problems of the Johannine Prologue"], *ZTK* 60 (1963) 305–34. In his *Gott und Mensch. Gesammelte Aufsätze* 1 (Tübingen: Mohr-Siebeck, 1965) 114–43.

6   ["The Gospel of John and Its Commentators"], *ZTK* 89 (1964) 881–98. In his *Die Bibel und Wir*.

berichten";[7] "Aufbau und Theologie des Poimandres";[8] "Spruch 68 des Thomas-evangeliums";[9] "Gnosis und Neues Testament";[10] "Literatur zum Codex Jung";[11] and "Statistische Erforschung des Neuen Testaments."[12] Use was also made of the reviews of Ernst Haenchen: Böcher, O., *Der johanneische Dualismus im Zusammenhang des nachbiblischen Judentums;*[13] Dodd, C. H., *Historical Tradition in the Fourth Gospel;*[14] Grundmann, W., *Zeugnis und Gehalt des Johannesevangeliums;*[15] Guilding, A., *The Fourth Gospel and Jewish Worship;*[16] Müller, T., *Das Heilsgeschehen im Johannes-evangelium;*[17] Gögler, R., ed. *Origines: Das Evangelium nach Johannes;*[18] Malinine, M. et al., eds. *De resurrectione (Epistula ad Rheginum): Codex Jung F. XXII ʳ–F. XXV ᵛ;*[19] Schnackenburg, R., *Das Johannes-Evangelium I;*[20] Smith, D. Moody, *The Composition and Order of the Fourth Gospel;*[21] Wiles, M. F., *The Spiritual Gospel.*[22] In spite of all these aids, it has not been possible to give John 12:12–50 and chapters 14–16 the desired form. The material for these sections was insufficient to attempt the reshaping of the older expositions into detailed comment and overview.

To make everything correspond to the basic plan, the editor has frequently written short transitional sentences in order to connect the various versions together. In the editorial process, all quotations were verified and corrected where necessary. Unfortunately, it was not always possible to make citations conform to the most recent edition of particular works.

Although the author had already prepared bibliographies for many individual pericopes and for others had entered appropriate references in his copy of the bibliography of E. Malatesta, *St. John's Gospel: 1920–1965,*[23] it seemed in order to revise the bibliography completely. In accordance with the design of the commentary as such, the bibliography ought to represent the latest stage of scholarship, in this case, to the end of 1979. It seemed worthwhile, moreover, to enlarge the compass of nineteenth century literature inasmuch as many recent commentaries cite literature only back as far as approximately the end of the century and thus overlook the revolutionary battles of the preceding century or present that earlier scholarship only in a limited selection. The editor's judgment in this matter was reinforced by the fact that the author himself was always conscious of the signifi-

Gesammelte Aufsätze 2 (Tübingen: Mohr-Siebeck, 1968) 206–64.

7   ["History and the Historic in the Johannine Passion Narratives"], in *Die Bibel und Wir. Gesammelte Aufsätze* 2 (Tübingen: Mohr-Siebeck, 1968) 182–207.

8   ["Structure and Theology of Poimandres"], in *Gott und Mensch. Gesammelte Aufsätze* 1 (Tübingen: Mohr-Siebeck, 1963) 335–77.

9   ["Saying 68 of the Gospel of Thomas"], *Le Muséon* 75 (1962) 19–29.

10 ["Gnosticism and the New Testament"], RGG³ 2: 1652–56.

11 *TRu* 30 (1964) 39–82.

12 ["Statistical Research on the New Testament"], *TLZ* 87 (1962) 487–98).

13 (Gütersloh: Gerd Mohn, 1965) in *TLZ* 91 (1966) 584.

14 (Cambridge: Cambridge University Press, 1963) in *TLZ* 93 (1968) 346–48.

15 *Eine Studie zur denkerischen und gestalterischen Leistung des vierten Evangelisten,* Arbeiten zur Theologie 7 (Stuttgart: Calwer Verlag, 1961) in *TLZ* 87 (1962) 930.

16 *A study of the relation of St. John's Gospel to the Ancient Jewish Lectionary System* (Oxford: Clarendon Press, 1960) in *TLZ* 86 (1961) 670–72.

17 *Eine exegetische Studie, zugleich der Versuch einer Antwort an Rudolf Bultmann* (Zurich and Frankfurt: Gotthelf-Verlag, 1961) in *TLZ* 88 (1963) 116–18.

18 (Einsiedeln and Köln, 1969) in *TLZ* 87 (1962) 604–5.

19 (Zurich and Stuttgart: Rascher, 1963) in *Gnomon* 36 (1964) 359–63.

20 *Einleitung und Kommentar zu Kap. 1–4,* HTKNT 4 (Freiburg: Herder, 1965) = *The Gospel According to St. John,* vol. 1 (New York: The Seabury Press, 1980) in *TLZ* 93 (1968) 427–29.

21 (New Haven: Yale University Press, 1965) in *TLZ* 91 (1966) 508–10.

22 *The Interpretation of the Fourth Gospel in the Early Church* (Cambridge: Cambridge University Press, 1960) in *TLZ* 86 (1961) 505–6.

23 *A Cumulative and Classified Bibliography of Books and Periodical Literature on the Fourth Gospel,* AnBib 32 (Rome: Pontifical Biblical Institute, 1967).

cance of the scholarship of the preceding century and frequently returned to it, especially to the results of critical work. Since the original bibliography covered the only the period 1920–1965, I have worked the entries up so that they cover, as far as possible, the period 1800–1979, with the help of the research report of H. Thyen,[24] A. Moda,[25] and my own research. In this process the excurses of the commentary and the detailed treatment of specific Johannine problems in the monographic literature were not covered. Also left out of account are the discussions of specific problems in articles, the title of which did not indicate the content. In addition to my work on the bibliography, I am also responsible for the translation from Greek of the following pericopes: John 1:19–34, 12:20–36, 19:1–16a, 16b–42.

I hope that the commentary on the Gospel of John that has come into being reflects, in its many sections, the many-faceted thought of the author and his skill in formulating issues and solutions. At the same time, it ought also to be made clear that, in this commentary, Ernst Haenchen aspired to represent the stance of critical scholarship that can comprehend the unity of the Gospel of John only in its formation. In addition to correcting an overly hasty history-of-religions derivation of the Gospel of John from Gnosticism, that involves posing anew the question of tradition and sources. Only by throwing the switch did it appear to Haenchen that scholarship would strike the right course in solving the riddle of the Fourth Gospel with greater success than it was given to the previous generations of scholars to do. It has been my purpose once again to give voice, without distortion, to the considered words of my revered teacher.

The work was assisted especially by the tireless efforts of Frau Margit Haenchen to bring the life's work of her husband to its fulfillment in this commentary. I am indebted also to the University of Bamberg, which provided the means out of its research funds to finance the preparatory work. Prof. F. H. Kettler, Münster, was kind enough, along with others, to check the patristic quotations. I am grateful to Frau H. Meisner for undertaking the production of the manuscript. I wish to express my thanks also to the students who assisted with proofreading: I. Bouillon, W. Hafner, J. Klinger, L. Klinger, J. Kügler, B. Maier, and C. Roggenbuck.

Bamberg
July 1980

Ulrich Busse

---

24 "Aus der Literatur zum Johannesevangelium," *TRu* 39 (1974) 1–69, 222–52, 289–330; 42 (1977) 211–70; 43 (1978) 328–59; 44 (1979) 97–134.

25 "Quarto Vangelo: 1966–1972. Una selezione bibliografica," *RivB* 22 (1974) 53–86.

1. Sources and Abbreviations

a / New Testament

Matt	Matthew
Mark	
Luke	
John	
Acts	
Rom	Romans
1 Cor	1 Corinthians
2 Cor	2 Corinthians
Gal	Galatians
Eph	Ephesians
Phil	Philippians
Col	Colossians
1 Thess	1 Thessalonians
2 Thess	2 Thessalonians
1 Tim	1 Timothy
2 Tim	2 Timothy
Titus	
Phlm	Philemon
Heb	Hebrews
Jas	James
1 Pet	1 Peter
2 Pet	2 Peter
1 John	
2 John	
3 John	
Jude	
Rev	Revelation

b / Old Testament (LXX, Apocrypha)

Gen	Genesis
Exod	Exodus
Lev	Leviticus
Num	Numbers
Deut	Deuteronomy
Josh	Joshua
Judg	Judges
Ruth	
1 Sam	1 Samuel
2 Sam	2 Samuel
1 Kgs	1 Kings
2 Kgs	2 Kings
1 Chr	1 Chronicles
2 Chr	2 Chronicles
Ezra	
Neh	Nehemiah
Esth	Esther
Job	
Ps(s)	Psalms
Prov	Proverbs
Eccl (Qoh)	Ecclesiastes (Qoheleth)

Cant	Song of Solomon
Isa	Isaiah
Jer	Jeremiah
Lam	Lamentations
Ezek	Ezekiel
Dan	Daniel
Hos	Hosea
Joel	
Amos	
Obad	Obadiah
Jonah	
Mic	Micah
Nah	Nahum
Hab	Habakkuk
Zeph	Zephaniah
Hag	Haggai
Zech	Zechariah
Mal	Malachi
1 Kgdms	1 Kingdoms
2 Kgdms	2 Kingdoms
3 Kgdms	3 Kingdoms
4 Kgdms	4 Kingdoms
Add Esth	Additions to Esther
Bar	Baruch
Bel	Bel and the Dragon
1 Esdr	1 Esdras
2 Esdr	2 Esdras
4 Ezra	
Judith	
Ep Jer	Epistle of Jeremiah
1 Macc	1 Maccabees
2 Macc	2 Maccabees
3 Macc	3 Maccabees
4 Macc	4 Maccabees
Pr Azar	Prayer of Azariah
Pr Man	Prayer of Manasseh
Sir	Jesus Sirach (Ecclesiasticus)
Sus	Susanna
Tob	Tobit
Wis	Wisdom of Solomon

c / Pseudepigrapha (and Related Writings)

2 Apoc. Bar.	*Syriac Apocalypse of Baruch*
3 Apoc. Bar.	*Greek Apocalypse of Baruch*
Apoc. Mos.	*Apocalypse of Moses*
As. Mos.	*Assumption of Moses*
1 Enoch	*Ethiopic Enoch*
2 Enoch	*Slavonic Enoch*
Ep. Arist.	*Epistle of Aristeas*
Jub.	*Jubilees*
Mart. Isa.	*Martyrdom of Isaiah*
Odes Sol.	*Odes of Solomon*
Pss. Sol.	*Psalms of Solomon*
Sib. Or.	*Sibylline Oracles*
T. 12 Patr.	*Testaments of the Twelve Patriarchs*

T. Levi	*Testament of Levi*
T. Benj.	*Testament of Benjamin*
Acts Pil.	*Acts of Pilate*
Apoc. Pet.	*Apocalypse of Peter*
Gos. Eb.	*Gospel of the Ebionites*
Gos. Eg.	*Gospel of the Egyptians*
Gos. Heb.	*Gospel of the Hebrews*
Gos. Naass.	*Gospel of the Naassenes*
Gos. Naz.	*Gospel of the Nazoreans*
Gos. Pet.	*Gospel of Peter*
Gos. Thom.	*Gospel of Thomas*
Prot. Jas.	*Protevangelium of James*

d / Apostolic Fathers

Barn.	*Barnabas*
1 Clem.	*1 Clement*
2 Clem.	*2 Clement*
Did.	*Didache*
Diogn.	*Diognetus*
Herm.	*Hermas*
Man.	*Mandates*
Sim.	*Similitudes*
Vis.	*Visions*
Ign.	*Ignatius*
Eph.	*Ephesians*
Magn.	*Magnesians*
Phld.	*Philadelphians*
Pol.	*Polycarp*
Rom.	*Romans*
Smyr.	*Smyrnaeans*
Trall.	*Trallians*
Mart. Pol.	*Martyrdom of Polycarp*
Pol. Phil.	Polycarp to the *Philippians*

e / Qumran Documents

CD	Cairo (Genizah text of the) Damascus (Document)
Q	Qumran
1QH	*Hôdāyôt (Thanksgiving Hymns)*
1QM	*Milḥāmāh (War Scroll)*
1QpHab	*Pesher on Habakkuk*
1QpNah	*Pesher on Nahum*
1QS	*Serek hayyaḥad (Rule of the Community, Manual of Discipline*
4QTestim	*Testimonia* text from Qumran Cave 4

f / Rabbinic Texts

B.Meṣ.	*Baba Meṣiʿa*
Ber.	*Berakot*
Gen. Rab.	*Genesis Rabbah*
Exod. Rab.	*Exodus Rabbah*
Ketub.	*Ketubot*
Lev. Rab.	*Leviticus Rabbah*
Menaḥ.	*Menaḥot*
Num. Rab.	*Numbers Rabbah*
Midr.	*Midrash*

Cant.	*Canticles*
Lam.	*Lamentations*
Qoh.	*Qohelet*
Ps.	*Psalms*
Sam.	*Samuel*
Pesaḥ.	*Pesaḥim*
Šabb.	*Šabbat*
Sanh.	*Sanhedrin*
Seder Olam	
Rab.	*Seder Olam Rabbah*
Šeqal.	*Šeqalim*
Sukk.	*Sukka*
Taʿan.	*Taʿanit*
Tos.	*Tosefta*

g / Greek and Latin Authors (including Church Fathers)

Aristophanes	
Clouds	*Clouds*
Equites	*Equites*
Ambrosius	
De fide	*De fide ad Gratianum*
Enarr. Ps.	*Enarrationes in Psalmos*
Aristotle	
Pol.	*Politica*
Chrysostom	
Hom.	*Homiliae*
In Joh.	*In Johanneum*
Cicero	
De off.	*De officiis*
Nat.deor.	*De natura deorum*
Clement of Alexandria	
Strom.	*Stromateis*
Cyrillus of Jerusalem	
Hom.	*Homilia in paralyticum*
Euripides	
Bacchae	*Bacchae*
Ion	*Ion*
Eusebius	
H.E.	*Historia ecclesiastica*
Heliodorus	
Aeth.	*Aethiopica*
Hippolytus	
Ref.	*Refutatio omnium haeresium*
Irenaeus	
Adv. haer.	*Adversus haereses*
Isocrates	
Paneg.	*Panegyricus*
Jerome	
Vir. ill.	*De viris illustribus*
Jos.	*Josephus*
Ant.	*Antiquitates Judaicae*
BJ	*Bellum Judaicum*
C.Apion.	*Contra Apionem*
Vita	*Vita*
Justin	Justin Martyr
First Apol.	*First Apology*
Dial.	*Dialogus cum Tryphone*

Longus
    Pastoralia   *Pastoralia*
Maximus (of) Tyre
    Diss.   *Dissertationes*
Orac. Sib.   *Sibylline Oracles*
Origen
    Comm. Joh.   *In Johanneum Commentarius*
    C. Celsum   *Contra Celsum*
Philo (of Alexandria)
    De cher.   *De cherubim*
    De decal.   *De decalogo*
    Det. Pot. Ins.   *Quod deterius potiori insidiari soleat*
    De ebr.   *De ebrietate*
    In Flac.   *In Flaccum*
    De fuga   *De fuga et inventione*
    Leg. all.   *Legum allegoriarum libri*
    De mut. nom.   *De mutatione nominum*
    De post. Caini   *De posteritate Caini*
    De somn.   *De somniis*
    De spec. leg.   *De specialibus legibus*
    De virt.   *De virtutibus*
Philostratus
    Vita Apoll.   *Vita Apollonii*
Pindar
    Pollux   *Pollux*
Plato
    De leg.   *De Leges*
    Ion   *Ion*
Plutarch
    Moralia   *Moralia*
    Pomp.   *Pompey*
    Sera num.   *De sera numinis vindicta*
ps.-Clem.   pseudo-Clementines
    Hom.   *Homilies*
    Recog.   *Recognitions*
Suidas
Theodor of Mopsuestia
    Comm. Joh.   *In Johanneum Commentarius*

h / Periodicals & Reference Works

AB	Anchor Bible
AER	*American Ecclesiastical Review*
AGJU	Arbeiten zur Geschichte des antiken Judentums und des Urchristentums
AGSU	Arbeiten zur Geschichte des Spätjudentums and Urchristentums
AJT	*American Journal of Theology*
AnBib	Analecta biblica
ANF	*The Ante-Nicene Fathers: The Writings of the Fathers down to A. D. 325*, 10 vols., ed. Alexander Roberts and James Donaldson (Buffalo: Christian Literature Publishing Co., 1885–97; reprint Grand Rapids: Wm. B. Eerdmans, 1951–56).
Ang	*Angelicum*
ANQ	*Andover Newton Quarterly*
APOT	*The Apocrypha and Pseudepigrapha of the Old Testament in English, with Introductions and Critical and Explanatory Notes to the Several Books*, 2 vols., ed. Robert Henry Charles Vol. 1, Apocrypha; Vol. 2, Pseudepigrapha (Oxford: Clarendon Press, 1913).
ARW	*Archiv für Religionswissenschaft*
AsSeign	*Assemblées du Seigneur*
ATANT	Abhandlungen zur Theologie des Alten und Neuen Testaments
ATR	*Anglical Theological Review*
AUSS	*Andrews University Seminary Studies*
BA	*Biblical Archeologist*
BBB	Bonner biblische Beiträge
BDF	F. Blass, A. Debrunner, and R. W. Funk, *A Greek Grammar of the New Testament* (Chicago: University of Chicago Press, 1961).
BeO	*Bibbia et oriente*
BETL	Bibliotheca ephemeridum theologicarum lovaniensium
BEvT	Beiträge zur evangelischen Theologie
BFCT	Beiträge zur Förderung christlicher Theologie
BGBE	Beiträge zur Geschichte der biblischen Exegese
BHH	*Biblisch-Historisches Handwörterbuch*, ed. B. Reicke and L. Rost
BHT	Beiträge zur historischen Theologie
Bib	*Biblica*
BibLeb	*Bibel und Leben*
BibS(F)	Biblische Studien (Freiburg, 1895–)
BibS(N)	Biblische Studien (Neukirchen, 1951–)
Billerbeck	H. L. Strack and P. Billerbeck, *Kommentar zum Neuen Testament aus Talmud und Midrasch*, 5 vols. (Munich: C. H. Beck, 1922–28).
BJRL	*Bulletin of the John Rylands University Library of Manchester*
BK	*Bibel und Kirche*
BLE	*Bulletin de littérature ecclésiastique*
BLit	*Bibel und Liturgie*
BR	*Biblical Research*
BSac	*Bibliotheca Sacra*
BT	*The Bible Translator*
BTB	*Biblical Theology Bulletin*
BU	Biblische Untersuchungen
BWANT	Beiträge zur Wissenschaft vom Alten und Neuen Testament
BVC	*Bible et vie chrétienne*
BZ	*Biblische Zeitschrift*
BZNW	Beiheft zur ZNW
CB	*Cultura bíblica*
CBQ	*Catholic Biblical Quarterly*
CJT	*Canadian Journal of Theology*
ConBNT	Coniectanea biblica, New Testament
ConNT	*Coniectanea neotestamentica*
CQR	*Church Quarterly Review*

CurTM	Currents in Theology and Mission	*NorTT*	*Norsk Teologisk Tidsskrift*
EKKNT	Evangelisch-katholischer Kommentar zum Neuen Testament	*NovT*	*Novum Testamentum*
		NovTSup	Novum Testamentum, Supplements
ErJb	*Eranos Jahrbuch*	*NRT*	*La nouvelle revue théologique*
EstBib	*Estudios bíblicos*	*NTApoc*	*New Testament Apocrypha.* Vol. 1: *Gospels and Related Writings,* ed. R. McL. Wilson; tr. A. J. B. Higgins, George Ogg, Richard E. Taylor, and R. McL. Wilson; Vol. 2: *Writings Related to the Apostles; Apocalypses and Related Subjects,* ed. R. McL. Wilson; tr. Ernest Best, David Hill, George Ogg, G. C. Stead, and R. McL. Wilson (Philadelphia: Westminster Press, 1963–1964).
ETL	*Ephemerides theologicae lovanienses*		
ETR	*Etudes théologiques et religieuses*		
EvQ	*Evangelical Quarterly*		
EvT	*Evangelische Theologie*		
ExpTim	*Expository Times*		
FRLANT	Forschungen zur Religion und Literatur des Alten und Neuen Testaments		
Greg	*Gregorianum*		
HeyJ	*Heythrop Journal*	NTAbh	Neutestamentliche Abhandlungen
HibJ	*Hibbert Journal*	NTD	Das Neue Testament Deutsch
HKNT	Handkommentar zum Neuen Testament	NTL	New Testament Library
HNT	Handbuch zum Neuen Testament	*NTS*	*New Testament Studies*
HTKNT	Herders theologischer Kommentar zum Neuen Testament	OBO	Orbis biblicus et orientalis
		PJ	*Palästina-Jahrbuch*
HTR	*Harvard Theological Review*	PTMS	Pittsburgh Theological Monograph Series
IDB	*Interpreter's Dictionary of the Bible,* 4 vols., ed. G. A. Buttrick et al. (Nashville: Abingdon Press, 1962–1976).		
		PW	Pauly-Wissowa, *Real-Encyclopädie der classischen Altertumswissenschaft. Neue Bearbeitung unter Mitwirkung zahlreicher Fachgenossen,* ed. Georg Wissowa (Stuttgart: J. B. Metzler, 1893–).
ITQ	*Irish Theological Quarterly*		
Int	*Interpretation*		
JAC	Jahrbuch für Antike und Christentum	*RB*	*Revue biblique*
JBL	*Journal of Biblical Literature*	*RBén*	*Revue bénédictine*
JJS	*Journal of Jewish Studies*	*RevExp*	*Review and Expositor*
JNES	*Journal of Near Eastern Studies*	*RevistB*	*Revista bíblica*
JPOS	*Journal of the Palestine Oriental Society*	*RevQ*	*Revue de Qumran*
JQR	*Jewish Quarterly Review*	*RevScRel*	*Revue des sciences religieuses*
JR	*Journal of Religion*	*RevThom*	*Revue thomiste*
JSNT	*Journal for the Study of the New Testament*	*RGG*	*Religion in Geschichte und Gegenwart,* ed. Kurt Galling (Tübingen: Mohr-Siebeck, ²1927–1932; ³1957–1962).
JTS	*Journal of Theological Studies*		
KD	*Kerygma und Dogma*		
KEK	Kritisch-exegetischer Kommentar über das Neue Testament	*RHE*	*Revue d'histoire ecclésiastique*
		RHPR	*Revue d'histoire et de philosophie religieuses*
KNT	Kommentar zum Neuen Testament	*RHR*	*Revue de l'histoire des religions*
LCC	Library of Christian Classics (Philadelphia: Westminster Press).	*RivB*	*Rivista biblica*
		RNT	Regensburger Neues Testament
LCL	Loeb Classical Library (Cambridge: Harvard University Press).	*RSPT*	*Revue des sciences philosophiques et théologiques*
LD	Lectio divina	*RSR*	*Recherches de science religieuse*
MPG	Patrologie cursus completus, Series Graeca, ed. Jacques-Paul Migne	*RTP*	*Revue de théologie et de philosophie*
		RUO	*Revue de l'université d'Ottawa*
MPL	Patrologia cursus completus, Series Latina, ed. Jacques-Paul Migne	SANT	Studien zum Alten und Neuen Testament
MScRel	*Mélanges de science religieuse*	SAQ	Sammlung ausgewählter kirchen- und dogmengeschichtlicher Quellenschriften
MTZ	*Münchener theologische Zeitschrift*		
MVAG	Mitteilungen der vorderasiastisch-ägyptischen Gesellschaft		
		SAWW.PH	Sitzungsberichte der Akademie der Wissenschaften in Wien. Philosophisch-historische Klasse
Neot	*Neotestamentica*		
NGG	Nachrichten der Gesellschaft der Wissenschaften in Göttingen		
		SBB	Stuttgarter biblische Beiträge
NKZ	*Neue kirchliche Zeitschrift;* from 1934, *Luthertum*	*SBFLA*	*Studii biblici franciscani liber annuus*

SBLASP	Society of Biblical Literature Abstracts and Seminar Papers	*VT*	*Vetus Testamentum*
SBLDS	Society of Biblical Literature Dissertation Series	WMANT	Wissenschaftliche Monographien zum Alten und Neuen Testament
SBLMS	Society of Biblical Literature Monograph Series	*WTJ*	*Westminster Theological Journal*
SBLSBS	Society of Biblical Literature Sources for Biblical Study	WUNT	Wissenschaftliche Untersuchungen zum Neuen Testament
SBS	Stuttgarter Bibelstudien	*ZDPV*	*Zeitschrift des deutschen Palästina-Vereins*
SBT	Studies in Biblical Theology	*ZHT*	*Zeitschrift für historische Theologie*
Scr	*Scripture*	*ZKG*	*Zeitschrift für Kirchengeschichte*
SE	*Studia evangelica*	*ZKT*	*Zeitschrift für katholische Theologie*
SEÅ	*Svensk exegetisk årsbok*	*ZNW*	*Zeitschrift für die neutestamentliche Wissenschaft*
SHAW.PH	Sitzungberichte der Heidelberger Akademie der Wissenschaften. Philosophisch-historische Klasse	*ZRGG*	*Zeitschrift für Religions- und Geistesgeschichte*
SJLA	Studies in Judaism in Late Antiquity	*ZST*	*Zeitschrift für systematische Theologie*
SJT	*Scottish Journal of Theology*	*ZTK*	*Zeitschrift für Theologie und Kirche*
SNT	Studien zum Neuen Testament	*ZWT*	*Zeitschrift für wissenschaftliche Theologie*
SNTSMS	Society for New Testament Studies Monograph Series		

SPap	*Studia papyrologica*
SPAW.PH	Sitzungsberichte der preussischen Akademie der Wissenschaften. Philosophisch-historische Klasse

i / General Abbreviations

ca.	*circa*, approximately
cf.	*confer*, compare
chap(s).	chapter(s)

SR	*Studies in Religion / Sciences religieuses*
ST	*Studia theologica*
SUNT	Studien zur Umwelt des Neuen Testaments
TBl	*Theologische Blätter*
TBü	Theologische Bücherei
TD	*Theological Digest*
TDNT	*Theological Dictionary of the New Testament*, 10 vols., ed. G. Kittel and G. Friedrich; tr. Geoffrey W. Bromiley (Grand Rapids: Wm. B. Eerdmans, 1964–76).
TGl	*Theologie und Glaube*
THKNT	Theologischer Handkommentar zum Neuen Testament
TLZ	*Theologische Literaturzeitung*
TQ	*Theologische Quartalschrift*
TRE	*Theologische Realenzyklopädie*
TRu	*Theologische Rundschau*
TS	*Theological Studies*
TSK	*Theologische Studien und Kritiken*
TT	*Theologisk Tidsskrift*
TTKi	*Tiddsskrift for Teologi og Kirke*
TToday	*Theology Today*
TTZ	*Trierer theologische Zeitschrift*
TU	Texte und Untersuchungen zur Geschichte der altchristlichen Literatur
TynBul	*Tyndale Bulletin*
TZ	*Theologische Zeitschrift*
UNT	Untersuchungen zum Neuen Testament
VC	*Vigilae christianae*
VD	*Verbum domini*
VSpir	*Vie spirituelle*

ed(s).	editor(s), edited by
e.g.	*exempli gratia*, for example
esp.	especially
ET	English translation
et al.	*et alii*, and others
f(f).	(and the) following (page[s])
i.e.	*id est*, that is
LXX	Septuaginta
MT	Masoretic (Hebrew) Text
n.	note
n.d.	no date
NEB	New English Bible
n.f.	Neue Folge, new series
n.s.	new series
NT	New Testament, Neues Testament
op. cit.	*opere citato*, in the work cited
OT	Old Testament
p(p).	page(s)
par(s).	parallel(s)
Q	Qumran documents
repr.	reprinted
RSV	Revised Standard Version
scil.	*scilicet*, namely: to be supplied or understood
ser.	series
s.v.	*sub verbo* or *sub voce* (under the word or lexical entry)
tr.	translated by, translation
v(v)	verse(s)
vg	Vulgate
viz.	*videlicet*, that is to say, to wit
v (v).l (l).	*variae lectiones*, variant readings

2. Short titles of Commentaries, Studies, and Articles Often Cited

Aland, *Synopsis of the Four Gospels*
Kurt Aland, ed., *Synopsis of the Four Gospels: Greek English Edition of the Synopsis Quattuor Evangeliorum* (United Bible Societies, ³1979).

Barrett, *John*
Charles Kingsley Barrett, *The Gospel According to St. John. An Introduction with Commentary and Notes on the Greek Text* (Philadelphia: Westminster Press, ²1978).

Bauer, *Greek-English Lexicon*
Walter Bauer, *A Greek-English Lexicon of the New Testament and Other Early Christian Literature*, tr. and adapted by William F. Arndt and F. Wilbur Gingrich. Second edition, revised and augmented by F. Wilbur Gingrich and Frederick W. Danker (Chicago and London: University of Chicago Press, 1979) = *Griechisch-Deutsches Wörterbuch zu den Schriften des Neuen Testaments und der übrigen urchristlichen Literatur* (Berlin: A. Töpelmann, ⁴1952, ⁵1958).

Bauer, *Das Johannesevangelium*
Walter Bauer, *Das Johannesevangelium*, HNT 6 (Tübingen: Mohr-Siebeck, ³1933).

Bauer, *Orthodoxy and Heresy*
Walter Bauer, *Orthodoxy and Heresy in Earliest Christianity*, ed. Robert A. Kraft and Gerhard Krodel (Philadelphia: Fortress Press, 1971).

Beginnings of Christianity
F. J. Foakes-Jackson and Kirsopp Lake, eds., *The Beginnings of Christianity*, 5 vols. (Grand Rapids: Baker Book House, 1979).

Belser, *Das Evangelium des heiligen Johannes*
Johannes Evangelist Belser, *Das Evangelium des heiligen Johannes, übersetzt und erklärt* (Freiburg: Herder, 1905).

Bernard, *John*
John Henry Bernard, *The Gospel According to St. John: A Critical and Exegetical Commentary on the Gospel according to St. John*, ed. A. H. McNeile. 2 vols. (New York: Charles Scribner's & Sons, 1929).

Bihlmeyer, *Die apostolischen Väter*
Karl Bihlmeyer, *Die apostolischen Väter*. Vol. 1, *Didache, Barnabas, Klemens I und II, Ignatius, Polykarp, Papias, Quadratus, Diognetbrief*, SAQ, 2, 1 (Tübingen: Mohr-Siebeck, 1924).

Billerbeck
Hermann L. Strack and Paul Billerbeck, *Kommentar zum Neuen Testament aus Talmud und Midrash*, 5 vols. (Munich: C. H. Beck, 1922–61).

Black, *An Aramaic Approach*
Matthew Black, *An Aramaic Approach to the Gospels and Acts* (Oxford: Clarendon Press, ²1954).

Braun, *Jean le théologien*
François-Marie Braun, *Jean le théologien et son évangile dans l'église ancienne* (Paris: J. Gabalda, 1959).

Braun, "Qumran und das Neue Testament"
Herbert Braun, "Qumran und das Neue Testament. Ein Bericht über 10 Jahre Forschung (1950–1959)." *TRu* 28 (1962) 56–61.

Braun, *La Sainte Bible*
François-Marie Braun, *L'Evangile selon Saint Jean*, La Sainte Bible 10 (Paris, 1946).

Brown, *John*
Raymond E. Brown, *The Gospel According to John. Introduction, Translation, and Notes*, 2 vols. Vol. 1, *i–xii*, AB 29 (Garden City: Doubleday, 1966); Vol. 2, *xiii–xxi*, AB 29A (Garden City: Doubleday, 1970).

Büchsel, *Das Evangelium nach Johannes*
Friedrich Büchsel, *Das Evangelium nach Johannes*, NTD 4 (Göttingen: Vandenhoeck & Ruprecht, ²1935).

Bultmann, *Exegetica*
Rudolf Bultmann, *Exegetica. Aufsätze zur Erforschung des Neuen Testaments*, ed. Erich Dinkler (Tübingen: Mohr-Siebeck, 1967).

Bultmann, *History of the Synoptic Tradition*
Rudolf Bultmann, *History of the Synoptic Tradition*, tr. John Marsh (New York: Harper & Row, 1963).

Bultmann, *John*
Rudolf Bultmann, *The Gospel of John: A Commentary*, tr. G. R. Beasley-Murray (Oxford: Basil Blackwell, 1971) = *Das Evangelium des Johannes*, KEK 2 (Göttingen: Vandenhoeck & Ruprecht, ¹⁰1968).

Bultmann, *Theology of the New Testament*
Rudolf Bultmann, *Theology of the New Testament*, vol 2. Tr. Kendrick Grobel (London: SCM Press, 1955).

Burney, *Aramaic Origin*
Charles Fox Burney, *The Aramaic Origin of the Fourth Gospel* (London: Clarendon Press, 1922).

Cullmann, *Peter*
Oscar Cullmann, *Peter—Disciple, Apostle, Martyr. A Historical and Theological Study* (Philadelphia: Westminster Press, 1953, ²1958).

Dalman, *Sacred Sites and Ways*
Gustaf Dalman, *Sacred Sites and Ways: Studies in the Topography of the Gospels*, tr. Paul P. Levertoff (London: S. P. C. K; New York: Macmillan, 1935).

Dodd, *Interpretation of the Fourth Gospel*
Charles Harold Dodd, *The Interpretation of the Fourth Gospel* (Cambridge: Cambridge University Press, 1953).

Dodd, *Tradition*
Charles Harold Dodd, *Historical Tradition in the Fourth Gospel* (Cambridge: Cambridge University Press, 1965).

Edwards, *John*
Richard Alan Edwards, *The Gospel According to St. John* (London: Eyre & Spottiswoode, 1954).

Ewald, *Die johanneischen Schriften*
  Heinrich Ewald, *Die johanneischen Schriften, übersetzt und erklärt*, 2 vols. (Göttingen: Dieterich,
  1861).

Fortna, *Gospel of Signs*
  Robert T. Fortna, *The Gospel of Signs: A Reconstruc-
  tion of the Narrative Source Underlying the Fourth
  Gospel*, SNTSMS 11 (Cambridge: Cambridge
  University Press, 1970).

Godet, *John*
  Frédéric Godet, *Commentary on the Gospel of John*,
  tr. Timothy Dwight (New York: Funk & Wagnalls,
  1886).

Haenchen, *Acts of the Apostles*
  Ernst Haenchen, *The Acts of the Apostles: A Commen-
  tary* (Philadelphia: Westminster Press, 1971) = *Die
  Apostelgeschichte*, KEK (Göttingen: Vandenhoeck &
  Ruprecht, ¹⁴1965).

Haenchen, *Die Bibel und Wir*
  Ernst Haenchen, *Die Bibel und Wir. Gesammelte
  Aufsätze* 2 (Tübingen: Mohr-Siebeck, 1965).

Haenchen, "Johanneische Probleme"
  Ernst Haenchen, "Johanneische Probleme." *ZTK*
  56 (1959) 19–54. In his *Gott und Mensch. Gesammelte Aufsätze* 1 (Tübingen: Mohr-Siebeck, 1965)
  78–113.

Haenchen, "Das Johannesevangelium und sein Kom-
  mentar"
  Ernst Haenchen, "Das Johannesevangelium und
  sein Kommentar." *TLZ* 89 (1964) 881–98. In his
  Die Bibel und Wir. Gesammelte Aufsätze 2 (Tübingen:
  Mohr-Siebeck, 1968) 206–34.

Haenchen, "Petrus-Probleme"
  Ernst Haenchen, "Petrus-Probleme." *NTS* 7
  (1961) 187–97. In his *Gott und Mensch. Gesammelte
  Aufsätze* 1 (Tübingen: Mohr-Siebeck, 1965).

Haenchen, "Probleme"
  Ernst Haenchen, "Probleme des johanneischen
  'Prologs.'" *ZTK* 60 (1963) 305–34. In his *Gott und
  Mensch. Gesammelte Aufsätze* 1 (Tübingen: Mohr-
  Siebeck, 1965) 114–43.

Haenchen, "Der Vater"
  Ernst Haenchen, "'Der Vater, der mich gesandt
  hat.'" *NTS* 9 (1963) 208–16. In his *Gott und
  Mensch. Gesammelte Aufsätze* 1 (Tübingen: Mohr-
  Siebeck, 1965) 68–77.

Haenchen, *Der Weg Jesu*
  Ernst Haenchen, *Der Weg Jesu. Eine Erklärung des
  Markus-Evangeliums und der kanonischen Parallelen*
  (Berlin: Walter de Gruyter, ²1968).

Hahn, *Hoheitstitel*
  Ferdinand Hahn, *Christologische Hoheitstitel. Ihre
  Geschichte im frühen Christentum*, FRLANT 83
  (Göttingen: Vandenhoeck & Ruprecht, 1963).

Heitmüller, "Das Evangelium des Johannes"
  Wilhelm Heitmüller, "Das Evangelium des
  Johannes." In *Die Schriften des Neuen Testaments*,
  ed. Johannes Weiss (Göttingen: Vandenhoeck &
  Ruprecht, 1908) 685–861.

Hirsch, *Frühgeschichte* 1
  Emanuel Hirsch, *Frühgeschichte des Evangeliums*.
  Vol. 1, *Das Werden des Markus-Evangeliums*
  (Tübingen: Mohr-Siebeck, 1941).

Hirsch, *Geschichte der neueren evangelischen Theologie*
  Emanuel Hirsch, *Geschichte der neueren evangelischen Theologie* (Gütersloh: Gerd Mohn, 1960–
  1964).

Hirsch, *Studien*
  Emanuel Hirsch, *Studien zum Vierten Evangelium*
  (Tübingen: Mohr-Siebeck, 1936).

Hirsch, *Das vierte Evangelium*
  Emanuel Hirsch, *Das vierte Evangelium in seiner
  ursprünglichen Gestalt verdeutscht und erklärt*
  (Tübingen: Mohr-Siebeck, 1936).

Holtzmann, *Das Evangelium des Johannes*
  Heinrich Julius Holtzmann, *Das Evangelium des
  Johannes*, rev. Walter Bauer. HKNT 4 (Tübingen:
  Mohr-Siebeck, ³1908).

Jeremias, *Jerusalem*
  Joachim Jeremias, *Jerusalem in the Time of Jesus. An
  Investigation into Economic and Social Conditions
  during the New Testament Period* (Philadelphia:
  Fortress Press, 1969) = *Jerusalem zur Zeit Jesu*
  (Göttingen: Vandenhoeck & Ruprecht, ³1962).

Jeremias, *Jesus als Weltvollender*
  Joachim Jeremias, *Jesus als Weltvollender*, BFCT
  33, 4 (Gütersloh: C. Bertelsmann, 1930).

Jeremias, *Rediscovery of Bethesda*
  Joachim Jeremias, *The Rediscovery of Bethesda: John
  5:2*, New Testament Archaeology 1 (Louisville,
  KY: Southern Baptist Theological Seminary,
  1966).

Käsemann, *New Testament Questions*
  Ernst Käsemann, *New Testament Questions of Today*,
  tr. W. J. Montague and Wilfred F. Bunge (Philadelphia: Fortress Press, 1969).

Käsemann, *The Testament of Jesus*
  Ernst Käsemann, *The Testament of Jesus: A Study of
  the Gospel of John in the Light of Chapter 17*, tr.
  Gerhard Krodel (Philadelphia: Fortress Press,
  1968) = *Jesu letzter Wille nach Johannes 17*
  (Tübingen: Mohr-Siebeck, 1966).

Kümmel, *Introduction*
  Werner Georg Kümmel, *Introduction to the New
  Testament*, tr. Howard C. Kee (Nashville: Abing-
  don Press, 1975).

Kümmel, *NT History and Investigation*
  Werner Georg Kümmel, *The New Testament: The
  History of the Investigation of its Problems*, tr. S.
  McLean Gilmour and Howard C. Kee (Nashville:
  Abingdon Press, 1972) = *Das Neue Testament;
  Geschichte der Erforschung seiner Probleme* (Freiburg:
  K. Alber, 1958).

Lagrange, *Evangile selon saint Jean*
  Marie-Joseph Lagrange, *Evangile selon saint Jean*,
  Etudes bibliques (Paris: J. Gabalda, ²1925, ⁸1947).

Lawlor and Oulton
  Eusebius, *The Ecclesiastical History and The Martyrs*

of Palestine, 2 vols. Tr. Hugh Jackson Lawlor and John Ernest Leonard Oulton (London: S. P. C. K, 1927–28).

Leroy, *Rätsel und Mißverständnis*
Herbert Leroy, *Rätsel und Mißvertändnis. Ein Beitrag zur Formgeschichte des Johannesevangeliums,* BBB 30 (Bonn: Peter Hanstein, 1968) esp. 5f., 183–85.

Lightfoot, *St. John's Gospel*
R. H. Lightfoot, *St. John's Gospel. A Commentary,* ed. C. F. Evans (Oxford: Clarendon Press; London: Cumberlege, 1956).

Loisy, *Le quatrième évangile*
Alfred Loisy, *Le quatrième évangile* (Paris: A. Picard & Fils, 1903, ²1921).

Luthardt, *Das johanneische Evangelium*
Christian Ernst Luthardt, *Das johanneische Evangelium nach seiner Eigentümlichkeit geschildert und erklärt,* 2 vols. (Nuremburg: Gieger, ²1875).

Maier, *Die Texte vom Toten Meer*
Johann Maier, *Die Texte vom Toten Meer,* 2 vols. Vol. 1, *Übersetzung;* Vol. 2, *Anmerkungen* (Munich: E. Reinhardt, 1960).

Metzger, *The Text of the NT*
Bruce M. Metzger, *The Text of the New Testament: Its Transmission, Corruption, and Restoration* (New York and London: Oxford University Press, 1964).

Michaelis, *Einleitung*
Wilhelm Michaelis, *Einleitung in das Neue Testament* (Bern: B. Haller, ²1954).

Nag Hammadi Library
James M. Robinson, ed., *The Nag Hammadi Library in English* (New York: Harper & Row, 1977).

Nestle
Eberhard Nestle and Erwin Nestle, *Novum Testamentum Graece; apparatum criticum recensuerunt,* rev. and expanded by Kurt Aland and Barbara Aland (Stuttgart: Deutsche Bibelstiftung, ²⁶1979).

Noetzel, *Christus und Dionysus*
Heine Noetzel, *Christus und Dionysus. Bemerkungen zum Religionsgeschichtlichen Hintergrund von Johannes 2, 1–11,* Arbeiten zur Theologie 1 (Stuttgart: Calwer Verlag, 1960).

Regul, *Die antimarcionitischen Evangelienprologe*
J. Regul, *Die antimarcionitischen Evangelienprologe,* Vetus Latina, Die Reste der altlateinischen Bibel, Aus der Geschichte der lateinischen Bibel 6 (Freiburg: Herder, 1969).

Ruckstuhl, *Einheit*
Eugen Ruckstuhl, *Die literarische Einheit des Johannesevangeliums* (Freiburg: Paulus, 1951).

Rudolph, *Die Mandäer*
Kurt Rudolph, *Die Mandäer,* 2 vols. Vol. 1, *Prolegomena: Das Mandäerproblem,* FRLANT, n.s., 56; Vol. 2, *Der Kult,* FRLANT, n.s., 57 (Göttingen: Vandenhoeck & Ruprecht, 1960-1961).

Schlatter, *Der Evangelist Johannes*
Adolf Schlatter, *Der Evangelist Johannes. Wie er spricht, denkt, und glaubt. Ein Kommentar zum 4. Evangelium* (Stuttgart: Calwer Veriensbuchhandlung, 1930).

Schnackenburg, *John*
Rudolf Schnackenburg, *The Gospel According to St. John,* 3 vols. Vol. 1, *Introduction and Commentary on Chapters 1–4,* tr. Kevin Smyth (New York: Seabury Press, 1980) = *Das Johannesevangelium,* part 1. HTKNT 4,1 (Freiburg: Herder, 1965); Vol. 2, *Commentary on Chapters 5–12,* tr. Cecily Hastings, Francis McDonagh, David Smith, and Richard Foley (New York: Seabury Press, 1980) = *Das Johannesevangelium,* part 2. HTKNT 4,2 (Freiburg: Herder, 1971); Vol. 3, *Commentary on Chapters 13–21,* tr. David Smith and G. A. Kon (New York: Crossroad, 1982) = *Das Johannesevangelium,* part 3. HTKNT 4,3 (Freiburg: Herder, 1975).

Schwartz, "Aporien"
Eduard Schwartz, "Aporien im vierten Evangelium." NGG (1907) 1: 342–72; (1908) 2: 115–48, 3: 149–88 4: 497–560.

Schweitzer, *The Quest of the Historical Jesus*
Albert Schweitzer, *The Quest of the Historical Jesus: A Critical Study of its Progress from Reimarus to Wrede,* tr. W. Montgomery (New York: Macmillan, 1961) = *Geschichte der Leben-Jesu-Forschung* (Tübingen: Mohr-Siebeck, 1906, ⁶1951).

Schweizer, *Ego Eimi*
Eduard Schweizer, *Ego Eimi. Die religionsgeschichtliche Herkunft und theologische Bedeutung der johanneischen Bildreden, zugleich ein Beitrag zur Quellenfrage des vierten Evangeliums,* FRLANT, n.s., 38 (Göttingen: Vandenhoeck & Ruprecht, ²1965).

Smith, *Composition and Order*
D. Moody Smith, *The Compositon and Order of the Fourth Gospel: Bultmann's Literary Theory* (New Haven and London: Yale University Press, 1965).

Strathmann, *Das Evangelium nach Johannes*
Hermann Strathmann, *Das Evangelium nach Johannes,* NTD 4 (Göttingen: Vandenhoeck & Ruprecht, ¹¹1968).

Tasker, *John*
R. V. G. Tasker, *The Gospel According to St. John,* Tyndale New Testament Commentaries (Grand Rapids: Wm. B. Eerdmans, 1971).

Thüsing, *Erhöhung*
Wilhelm Thüsing, *Die Erhöhung und Verherrlichung Jesu im Johannesevangelium,* NTAbh 21, 1–2 (Münster: Aschendorff, 1960).

Weiss, *Das Johannes-Evangelium*
Bernhard Weiss, *Das Johannes-Evangelium,* KEK 2 (Göttingen: Vandenhoeck & Ruprecht, 1834, ⁹1902).

Wellhausen, *Das Evangelium Johannes*
Julius Wellhausen, *Das Evangelium Johannes* (Berlin: G. Reimer, 1908).

Westcott and Hort

    B. F. Westcott and F. J. A. Hort, *The New Testament in the Original Greek,* 2 vols. (Cambridge and London: Macmillan, 1890–1896).

Wette, *Kurze Erklärung*

    William Martin Leberecht de Wette, *Kurze Erklärung des Evangeliums und der Briefe Johannes,* Kurzgefasstes exegetisches Handbuch zum Neuen Testament 1,3 (Leipzig: Weidmann, ⁴1852).

Wikenhauser, *Das Evangelium nach Johannes*

    Alfred Wikenhauser, *Das Evangelium nach Johannes,* RNT 4 (Regensburg: F. Pustet, ²1957).

Zahn, *Das Evangelium des Johannes*

    Theodor Zahn, *Das Evangelium des Johannes ausgelegt* (Leipzig: A. Deichert, ⁶1921).

Page numbers in [ ], following a reference to an
English translation, denote the original text.

Comprehensive indices for Volume 1 will appear in
Volume 2. An integrated and augmented bibliography
on the Gospel of John will also appear in Volume 2.

Professor D. Ulrich Busse has prepared a biographical sketch of Ernst Haenchen and his work on the
Fourth Gospel; this sketch will appear as an appendix
in the second volume.

The end papers of the Commentary on John are a
reproduction of $\mathfrak{P}^{52}$, which contains a fragment of
John, 18:31–34, 37–38, dating from the early second
century CE. $\mathfrak{P}^{52}$ is the oldest extant fragment of the
New Testament. It is reprinted with the permission of
The John Rylands University Library of Manchester,
England.

Each gospel contains sayings and stories that leave a deep imprint on the reader, passages, for the most part, in which everything is lucid and understandable for the common reader, full of comfort and strength. But there are also passages in each gospel which are difficult to decipher, so to speak, where the reader does not know precisely what is to be derived from them. Nevertheless, such passages can entice the reader to find something new in them ever again, to return to them in order to plumb their mystery, in spite of, indeed because of, their opacity.

The Fourth Gospel possesses this charm perhaps to the highest degree. Its difficulties are enhanced by the fact that the individual questions it poses for us cannot be cleanly separated, but overlap with each other, and can be unraveled only with difficulty, if at all.

The Fourth Gospel commends itself to the reader by virtue of its designation of that mysterious "disciple whom Jesus loved" as its author (21:24), a disciple identified with John son of Zebedee and therefore especially reliable in reporting the words and deeds of the earthly Jesus and yet it contradicts the first three Gospels, the Synoptics, at every turn; it does not agree with them regarding time and place with respect to the activity of Jesus. It commends itself also by virtue of the fact that Jesus speaks about other themes in a different style: synoptic parables are as rare in John as are synoptic miracle stories, although the Johannine miracles, on the other hand, surpass the synoptic stories by far. The "Twelve" have virtually disappeared (except in 6:67), as has the Passover meal (Mark 14:12–25, Matt 26:17–29, Luke 22:7–20; contrast John 13:1f.). And with these belong still other questions: was the mother tongue of the Evangelist really Aramaic, or have we to do with an authentic— with a spoken, colloquial—form of koine Greek? Do we have to reckon with a single voice in the Gospel, or with an earlier written tradition that has been readily supplemented and corrected by a redactor? Is the text transmitted to us so certain that we can depend on it unconditionally, or did it possess a different order at an earlier time (see below, Introduction §4)? Above all, the message of the Fourth Gospel seems to us to deviate so widely from that of Mark, Matthew, and Luke— although all four have the same focal point, Jesus Christ—that there is not even agreement on the last word of Jesus on the cross. Does the Fourth Gospel give us a view of a different Jesus, perhaps one on whom the burden of the earthly life no longers weighs, so that one may conclude with Käsemann that here is a god striding over the earth, not an actual, living man?[1] All these questions and others demand an answer. It is thus self-evident that every exposition of the Fourth Gospel is a venture that requires a correlative degree of reflection and forbearance on the part of the reader.

---

1   *The Testament of Jesus,* 44f.

1. The Fourth Gospel in Early Christian Tradition

Bibliography

Abbot, Ezra
"The Authorship of the Fourth Gospel." In his *The Authorship of the Fourth Gospel and Other Critical Essays Selected from the Published Papers* (Boston: G. H. Ellis, 1888) 9–112.

Aland, Kurt
Studien zur Überlieferung des Neuen Testaments und seines Textes, Arbeiten zur Neutestamentlichen Textforschung 2 (Berlin: Walter de Gruyter, 1967).

Bacon, Benjamin Wisner
"The Elder John, Papias, Irenaeus, Eusebius and the Syriac Translator." *JBL* 27 (1908) 1–23.

Bacon, Benjamin Wisner
"External Evidence." In his *The Gospel of the Hellenists* (New York: Holt, 1933) 7–51.

Bacon, Benjamin Wisner
"Date and Habitat of the Elders of Papias." *ZNW* 12 (1911) 176–87.

Bacon, Benjamin Wisner
"Papias." In the *New Schaff-Herzog Encyclopedia of Religious Knowledge* (Grand Rapids: Baker Book House, 1959) 8: 336–40.

Bacon, Benjamin Wisner
"The Johannine Problem." *The Independent* 57 (1904) 736–37.

Bacon, Benjamin Wisner
"Tatian's Rearrangement of the Fourth Gospel." *AJT* 4 (1900) 770–95.

Bacon, Benjamin Wisner
"An Emendation of the Papias Fragment." *JBL* 17 (1898) 176–83.

Bacon, Benjamin Wisner
"Marcion, Papias and 'The Elders.'" *JTS* 23 (1922) 134–60.

Bacon, Benjamin Wisner
"The Anti-Marcionite Prologue to John." *JBL* 49 (1930) 43–54.

Bacon, Benjamin Wisner
"The Mythical 'Elder John' of Ephesus." *HibJ* 29 (1931) 312–26.

Bacon, Benjamin Wisner
"John and the Pseudo-John." *ZNW* 31 (1932) 132–50.

Bacon, Benjamin Wisner
"The Elder of Ephesus and the Elder John." *HibJ* 26 (1927) 112–34.

Bacon, Benjamin Wisner
"The Elder John in Jerusalem." *ZNW* 26 (1927) 187–202.

Bacon, Benjamin Wisner
"Recent Aspects of the Johannine Problem: I. The External Evidence." *HibJ* 1 (1902/1903) 510–31; 2 (1903/1904) 323–46; 3 (1904/1905) 353–75.

Bartlet, J. Vernon
"Papias' Exposition; Its Date and Contents." In *Amicitiae Corolla, A Volume of Essays presented to James Rendel Harris*, ed. H. G. Wood (London: University of London Press, 1933) 15–44.

Bauer, Walter
Orthodoxy and Heresy in Earliest Christianity, ed. Robert A. Kraft and Gerhard Krodel (Philadelphia: Fortress Press, 1971) = *Rechtgläubigkeit und Ketzerei im ältesten Christentum*, BHT 10 (Tübingen: Mohr-Siebeck, 1934).

Baur, Ferdinand Christian
"Zur johanneischen Frage: 1) Über Justin den Märtyrer gegen Luthardt; 2) Über den Passahstreit gegen Steitz." *Theologische Jahrbücher* 16 (Tübingen, 1857) 209–57.

Baur, Ferdinand Christian
"Die johanneische Frage und ihre neuesten Beantwortungen durch Luthardt, Delitzsch, Brückner, Hase." *Theologische Jahrbücher* 13 (Tübingen, 1854) 196–287.

Bernard, John Henry
"Die Traditionen über den Tod des Zebedäussohnes Johannes." In *Johannes und sein Evangelium*, ed. K. H. Rengstorf (Darmstadt: Wissenschaftliche Buchgesellschaft, 1973) 273–90.

Beyschlag, Willibald
Zur johanneischen Frage. Beiträge zur Würdigung des vierten Evangeliums gegenüber den Angriffen der Kritischen Schule (Gotha: F. A. Perthes, 1876) and *TSK* 47 (1874) 607–723; 48 (1875) 235–87, 413–79.

Bihlmeyer, Karl
Die apostolischen Väter. Vol. 1, *Didache, Barnabas, Klemens I und II, Ignatius, Polykarp, Papias, Quadratus, Diognetbrief*, SAQ, 2, 1 (Tübingen: Mohr-Siebeck, 1924).

Bindemann, E.
"Ueber die von Justinus dem Märtyrer gebrauchten Evangelien." *TSK* 15 (1842) 355–482.

Bludau, Augustinus
Die ersten Gegner der Johannesschriften, BibS(F) 22, 1–2 (Freiburg: Herder, 1925).

Bousset, Wilhelm
Jüdisch-christlicher Schulbetrieb in Alexandria und Rom. Literarische Untersuchungen zu Philo und Clemens von Alexandria, Justin und Irenäus, FRLANT, n.s., 6 (Göttingen: Vandenhoeck & Ruprecht, 1915; Hildesheim and New York: G. Olms, 1975).

Braun, François-Marie
"La 'lettre de Barnabé' et l'évangile de Saint Jean (Simples réflexions)." *NTS* 4 (1957/1958) 119–24.

Braun, François-Marie
Jean le théologien et son évangile dans l'église ancienne (Paris: J. Gabalda, 1959).

Bruce, F. F.
"St. John at Ephesus." *BJRL* 60 (1978) 339–61.

Bruns, J. Edgar
"John Mark: A Riddle Within the Johannine Enigma." *Scr* 15 (1963) 88–92.

Bruns, J. Edgar
"The Confusion between John and John Mark in Antiquity." *Scr* 17 (1965) 23–26.

Bruyne, Donatien De
"Les plus anciens prologues latins des évangiles." *RBén* 40 (1928) 193–214.

Burghardt, Walter J.
"Did Saint Ignatius of Antioch Know the Fourth Gospel?" *TS* 1 (1940) 1–26, 130–56.

Camerlynck, A.
"La question johannique." *RHE* 1 (1900) 201–11, 419–29, 633–44.

Chastand, Gédéon
L'Apôtre Jean et le quatrième évangile. Etude de critique et d'histoire (Paris: G. Fischbacher, 1888).

Corssen, Peter
Die monarchianischen Prologe zu den vier Evangelien (Leipzig: J. C. Hinrichs, 1896).

Corssen, Peter
"Warum ist das vierte Evangelium für ein Werk des Apostels Johannes erklärt worden?" *ZNW* 2 (1901) 202–27.

Dausch, Petrus
Das Johannesevangelium, seine Echtheit und Glaubwürdigkeit, Biblische Zeitfragen 2, 2 (Münster i.W: Aschendorff, 1909).

Davey, D. M.
"Justin Martyr and the Fourth Gospel." *Scr* 17 (1965) 117–22.

Dembowsky, J.
"Das Johannesverständnis des Origenes." Dissertation, Göttingen, 1952.

Dibelius, Martin
"Papias." *RGG²* 4: 892–93.

Dibelius, Martin, ed. and tr.
Der Hirt des Hermas, HNT, Ergänzungsband 4 (Tübingen: Mohr-Siebeck, 1923).

Dix, G. H.
"The Use and Abuse of Papias on the Fourth Gospel." *Theology* 4 (London, 1932) 8–20.

Drummond, James
An Inquiry into the Character and Authorship of the Fourth Gospel (London: Williams & Norgate, 1903; New York: Scribners, 1904).

Ewald, Heinrich
"Ueber die Zweifel an der Abkunft des vierten Evangeliums und der drei Sendschreiben vom Apostel Johannes." *Jahrbücher der biblischen Wissenschaft* 10 (1859/1860) 83–114.

Faure, Alexander
"Das 4. Evangelium im muratorischen Fragment." *ZST* 19 (1942) 143–49.

Ferguson, John
"Philippians, John and the Traditions of Ephesus." *ExpTim* 83 (1971) 85–87.

Gardner, Percy
The Ephesian Gospel (London: Williams & Norgate; New York: G. P. Putnam's Sons, 1915).

Gebhardt, Hermann
Die Abfassungszeit des Johannesevangeliums (Leipzig: A. Deichert, 1906).

Grant, Robert M.
"The Oldest Gospel Prologues." *ATR* 23 (1941) 231–45.

Harnack, Adolf von
Die ältesten Evangelien-Prologe und die Bildung des Neuen Testaments, SPAW.PH 24 (Berlin: G. Reimer, 1928) 320–41.

Heard, R. G.
"The Oldest Gospel Prologues." *JTS,* n.s., 6 (1955) 1–16.

Heitmüller, Wilhelm
"Zur Johannes-Tradition." *ZNW* 15 (1914) 189–209.

Hilgenfeld, Adolf
"Noch einmal Johannes in Kleinasien." *ZWT* 16 (1873) 102–11.

Hilgenfeld, Adolf
"Noch einmal: Petrus in Rom und Johannes in Kleinasien." *ZWT* 20 (1877) 486–525.

Hilgenfeld, Adolf
"Petrus in Rom und Johannes in Kleinasien." *ZWT* 15 (1872) 349–83.

Hillmer, M. R.
"The Gospel of John in the Second Century." Dissertation, Harvard, 1965/1966.

Hofstede de Groot, P.
Basilides am Ausgange des apostolischen Zeitalters als erster Zeuge für Alter und Autorität neutestamentlicher Schriften, insbesondere des Johannesevangeliums, in Verbindung mit anderen Zeugen bis zur Mitte des zweiten Jahrhunderts (Leipzig: J. C. Hinrichs, 1868).

Holtzmann, Heinrich Julius
"Hermas und Johannes." *ZWT* 18 (1875) 40–51.

Holtzmann, Heinrich Julius
"Das Verhältniss des Johannes zu Ignatius und Polykarp." *ZWT* 20 (1877) 187–214.

Holtzmann, Heinrich Julius
"Johannes der Apostel"; "Johannes der Presbyther." In *Bibel-Lexikon. Realwörterbuch zum Handgebrauch für Geistliche und Gemeindeglieder,* ed. Daniel Schenkel (Leipzig: F. A. Brockhaus, 1871) 3: 328–42, 352–60.

Holtzmann, Heinrich Julius
"Papias und Johannes." *ZWT* 23 (1880) 64–77.

Holtzmann, Heinrich Julius
"Barnabas und Johannes." *ZWT* 14 (1871) 336–51.

Howard, Wilbert Francis
"The Antimarcionite Prologues to the Gospels." *ExpTim* 47 (1936) 534–38.

Jaschke, H. J.
"Das Johannesevangelium und die Gnosis im Zeugnis des Irenäus von Lyon." *MTZ* 29 (1978) 337–76.

Jeremias, Joachim
"An Unknown Gospel with Johannine Elements (Pap. Egerton 2)." In *New Testament Apocrypha* 1, ed. R. McL. Wilson; tr. A. J. B. Higgins, George Ogg., Richard E. Taylor, and R. McL. Wilson (Philadelphia: Westminster Press, 1963) 94–97 = "Unbekanntes Evangelium mit Johanneischen Einschlägen (Pap. Egerton 2)." In *Neutestamentliche Apokryphen* 1, ed. Edgar Hennecke and Wilhelm Schneemelcher (Tübingen: Mohr-Siebeck, 1959) 58–60.

Jülicher, Adolf and Erich Fascher
Einleitung in das Neue Testament (Tübingen: Mohr-Siebeck, [7]1931), esp. 397ff.

Köster, Helmut
"Geschichte und Kultus im Johannesevangelium und bei Ignatius von Antiochien." *ZTK* 54 (1957) 56–69.

Kümmel, Werner Georg
Introduction to the New Testament, tr. Howard C. Kee (Nashville: Abingdon Press, 1975), esp. 234–246 = *Einleitung in das Neue Testament* (Heidelberg: Quelle & Meyer, [17]1973), esp. 432, 467–68.

Kürzinger, Josef
"Papias von Hierapolis: Zu Titel und Art seines Werkes." *BZ* 23 (1979) 172–86.

Lagrange, Marie-Joseph
Review of "Les plus anciens prologues latins des Evangiles," by Donatien De Bruyne. *RB* 38 (1929) 115–21.

Larfeld, Wilhelm
Die beiden Johannes von Ephesus, der Apostel und der Presbyter, der Lehrer und der Schüler; ein Beitrag zur Erklärung des Papiasfragmentes bei Eusebius (Munich: C. H. Beck, 1914).

Larfeld, Wilhelm
"Das Zeugnis des Papias über die beiden Johannes von Ephesus." In *Johannes und sein Evangelium,* ed. K. H. Rengstorf (Darmstadt: Wissenschaftliche Buchgesellschaft, 1973) 381–401.

Lietzmann, Hans
A History of the Early Church, 4 vols., tr. Bertram Lee Woolf (Cleveland and New York: World Publishing Co., 1961).

Lightfoot, Joseph Barber
"External Evidence for the Authenticity and Genuineness of St. John's Gospel." In his *Biblical Essays* (London: Macmillan, 1904) 47–122.

Loewenich, Walther von
Das Johannesverständnis im zweiten Jahrhundert (Giessen: A. Töpelmann, 1932).

Loman, Abraham Dirk
Bijdragen ter inleiding op de Johanneische schriften des NTs. Iste stuk: Het getuigenis aangaande Johannes in het Fragment van Muratori (Amsterdam: Loman & Verster, 1865).

Luthardt, Christoph Ernst
Der johanneische Ursprung des vierten Evangeliums (Leipzig: Dörfflung und Franke, 1874).

Luthardt, Christoph Ernst
St. John and the Author of the Fourth Gospel, revised, translated, and the literature much enlarged by Caspar René Gregory (Edinburgh: T. & T. Clark, 1875).

Lützelberger, Ernst Carl Julius
Die kirchliche Tradition über den Apostel Johannes und seine Schriften in ihrer Grundlosigkeit nachgewiesen (Leipzig: F. A. Brockhaus, 1840).

Macaulay, W. M.
"The Nature of Christ in Origin's *Commentary on John*." *SJT* 19 (1966) 176–87.

Martyn, J. Louis
"Clementine Recognitions 1, 33–71, Jewish Christianity and the Fourth Gospel." In *God's Christ and His People. Studies in Honor of Nils A. Dahl*, ed. J. Jervell and Wayne A. Meeks (Oslo: Universitetsforlaget, 1977) 265–95.

Maurer, Christian
Ignatius von Antiochien und das Johannesevangelium, ATANT 18 (Zurich: Zwingli Verlag, 1949).

Mayer, Georg Karl
Die Aechtheit des Evangeliums nach Johannes (Schaffhausen: F. Hurter, 1854).

Metzger, Bruce M.
The Text of the New Testament. Its Transmission, Corruption, and Restoration (New York and London: Oxford University Press, 1964).

Michaelis, Wilhelm
Einleitung in das Neue Testament. Die Entstehung, Sammlung und Überlieferung der Schriften des Neuen Testaments (Bern: B. Haller, ²1954).

Niermeijer, Antonie
Bijdragen Aer verdediging van de echtheit der johanneische Schriften (Schoonk: Van Nooten, 1852).

Nunn, H. P. V.
"The Fourth Gospel in the Early Church." *EvQ* 16 (1944) 173–91, 294–99.

Osborn, Eric Francis
Justin Martyr, BHT 47 (Tübingen: Mohr-Siebeck, 1973).

Overbeck, Franz
"Über zwei neue Ansichten von Zeugnissen des Papias für die Apostelgeschichte und das vierte Evangelium." *ZWT* 10 (1867) 35–74.

Pagels, Elaine H.
The Johannine Gospel in Gnostic Exegesis: Heracleons Commentary on John, SBLMS 17 (Missoula: Scholars Press, 1973).

Paret, O.
Die Überlieferung der Bibel (Stuttgart: Württembergische Bibelanstalt, ⁴1966).

Parker, Pierson
"John the Son of Zebedee and the Fourth Gospel." *JBL* 81 (1962) 35–43.

Perry, Alfred M.
"Is John an Alexandrian Gospel?" *JBL* 62 (1944) 99–106.

Pfleiderer, Otto
"Neue Lösungsversuche zur johanneischen Frage." *Protestantische Monatshefte* 5 (1901) 169–82.

Regul, J.
Die antimarcionitischen Evangelienprologe, Vetus Latina, Die Reste der altlateinischen Bibel, Aus der Geschichte der lateinischen Bibel 6 (Freiburg: Herder, 1969).

Rettig, Heinrich Christian Michael
De quatuor Evangeliorum canonicorum origine, 2 vols. (Giessen: Müller, 1824).

Reuss, Eduard
"Johannes der Apostel und Evangelist." In *Allgemeine Encyklopädie der Wissenschaften und Künste*, Zweite Sektion, Teil 22 (Leipzig: F. A. Brockhaus, 1843) 1–94.

Riggenbach, Christoph Johannes
"Johannes der Apostel und der Presbyter." *Jahrbücher für deutsche Theologie* 13 (1868) 319–34.

Riggenbach, Christoph Johannes
Die Zeugnisse für das Evangelium Johannis (Basel: Bahnmeier's Verlag, 1866).

Riggenbach, D.
"Neue Materialien zur Beleuchtung des Papiaszeugnisses über den Märtyrertod des Johannes." *NKZ* 32 (1921) 692–96.

Roberts, C. H.
An Unpublished Fragment of the Fourth Gospel in the John Rylands Library (Manchester: Manchester University Press, 1935).

Sanday, William M. A.
The Gospels in the Second Century. An Examination of the Critical Part of a Work Entitled "Supernatural Religion" (London: Macmillan, 1876).

Sanday, William M. A.
The Authorship and Historical Character of the Fourth Gospel Considered in Reference to the Contents of the Gospel Itself (London: Macmillan, 1872).

Sanders, Joseph N.
The Fourth Gospel in the Early Church (Cambridge: Cambridge University Press, 1943).

Sanders, Joseph N.
"St. John on Patmos." *NTS* 9 (1962/1963) 75–85.

Sauer, J.
"Die Exegese des Cyrill von Alexandrien nach seinem Kommentar zum Johannesevangelium." Dissertation, Freiburg, 1965.

Schäferdiek, K.
"Theodor von Mopsuestia als Exeget des vierten Evangeliums." *Studia patristica* 10,1 (Berlin: Akademie-Verlag, 1970) 242–46.

Schmiedel, Paul W.
"John, Son of Zebedee." *Encyclopaedia Biblica*, ed. Thomas Kelly Cheyne and J. Sutherland Black (London: A. and C. Black; New York: Macmillan, 1901) 2: 2503–62.

Schneider, Karl Ferdinand Theodor
Die Echtheit des johanneischen Evangeliums nach den Quellen neu untersucht. Erster Beitrag: die äusseren

Zeugnisse (Berlin: Wiegandt & Grieben, 1854–1855).

Scholem, Gershom Gerhard
Major Trends in Jewish Mysticism (New York: Schocken, 1946).

Scholten, Johannes Henricus
Die ältesten Zeugnisse betreffend die Schriften des Neuen Testaments, historisch untersucht (Bremen: H. Gesenius, 1867).

Scholten, Johannes Henricus
Der Apostel Johannes in Kleinasien; Historisch-kritische Untersuchung (Berlin: F. Henschel, 1872).

Schwartz, Eduard
"Über den Tod der Söhne Zebedäi." In *Johannes und sein Evangelium*, ed. K. H. Rengstorf (Darmstadt: Wissenschaftliche Buchgesellschaft, 1973) 202–72.

Schwartz, Eduard
"Noch einmal der Tod der Söhne Zebedäi." *ZNW* 11 (1910) 89–104.

Schwartz, Eduard
"Johannes und Kerinthos." In his *Gesammelte Schriften*, 5 vols. (Berlin: Walter de Gruyter, 1938–1963), 5: 170–82.

Schwartz, Eduard, ed.
Eusebius Kirchengeschichte, Kleine Ausgabe (Leipzig: J. C. Hinrichs, ²1914).

Schweizer, Eduard
"Zu Apg 1,16–22." *TZ* 14 (1958) 46.

Spitta, Friedrich
"Die neutestamentliche Grundlage der Ansicht von E. Schwartz über den Tod der Söhne Zebedäi." In *Johannes und sein Evangelium*, ed. K. H. Rengstorf (Darmstadt: Wissenschaftliche Buchgesellschaft, 1973) 291–313.

Stanton, V. H.
The Gospels As Historical Documents, 3 vols. Vol. 1, *The Early Use of the Gospels;* Vol. 2, *The Synoptic Gospels;* Vol. 3, *The Fourth Gospel* (Cambridge: Cambridge University Press, 1903–1920).

Tayler, John James
An Attempt to Ascertain the Character of the Fourth Gospel; Especially in its Relation to the Three First (London and Edinburgh: Williams & Norgate, 1867).

Thoma, Albrecht
"Justins literarisches Verhältnis zu Paulus und zum Johannesevangelium." *ZWT* 18 (1875) 383–412, 490–566.

Unnik, W. C. van
"The Gospel of Truth and the New Testament." In *The Jung Codex. A Newly Recovered Gnostic Papyrus,* ed. F. L. Cross (London: A. R. Mowbray, 1955) 79–129.

Völker, W.
"Heracleons Stellung zu seiner Zeit im Lichte seiner Schriftauslegung." Dissertation, Halle, 1923.

Volkmar, G.
"Ein neu entdecktes Zeugnis für das Johannes-Evangelium." *Theologische Jahrbücher* 13 (Tübingen, 1854) 446–62.

Volkmar, G.
"Berichtigung zur äussern Bezeugung des Johannes-Evangeliums." *ZWT* 3 (1860) 293–300.

Weiss, Johannes
"Zum Märtyrertod des Zebedäiden." *ZNW* 11 (1910) 167.

Weitzel, K. L.
"Das Selbstzeugnis des vierten Evangelisten über seine Person." *TSK* 22 (1849) 578–638.

Weizsäcker, Karl Heinrich von
"Die Bezeugung des Evangeliums." In his *Untersuchungen über die evangelische Geschichte, ihre Quellen und den Gang ihrer Entwicklung* (Tübingen: Mohr-Siebeck, ²1901) 140–51.

Wetzel, G.
Die Echtheit und Glaubwürdigkeit des Evangeliums Johannes aufs neue untersucht und verteidigt (Leipzig: H. G. Wallmann, 1899).

Wiles, M. F.
The Spiritual Gospel. The Interpretation of the Fourth Gospel in the Early Church (Cambridge: Cambridge University Press, 1960).

Windisch, Hans
Der Barnabasbrief, HNT, Ergänzungsband 3 (Tübingen: Mohr-Siebeck, 1920).

Zeller, Eduard
"Die äusseren Zeugnisse über das Dasein und den Ursprung des vierten Evangeliums. Ein Prüfung der Kirchlichen Tradition bis auf Irenäus." *Theologische Jahrbücher* 4 (Tübingen, 1845) 579–656.

Zurhellen, O.
"Die Heimat des vierten Evangeliums." In *Johannes und sein Evangelium*, ed. K. H. Rengstorf (Darmstadt: Wissenschaftliche Buchgesellschaft, 1973) 314–80.

Copies of the Gospel of John were already in existence at the beginning of the second century.[1] Then about 180 CE there spread abroad, and very quickly, what one may call the early Christian tradition regarding the Fourth Gospel: the Apostle John wrote the Fourth Gospel in his old age. This raises the question: if that is true, why are

---

1 Cf. C. H. Roberts, *An Unpublished Fragment of the Fourth Gospel in the John Rylands Library* (Manchester: Manchester University Press, 1935); K. Aland, *Studien zur Überlieferung des Neuen Testaments und seines Textes,* Arbeiten zur Neutestamentlichen Textforschung 2 (Berlin: Walter de Gruyter, 1967); B.

the Apostolic Fathers so persistently silent about it? Why is the son of Zebedee not named as its author? Why are there no verbatim quotations of the Fourth Gospel? Or are there traces of John to be found in early Christian literature, as some scholars claim?

Some scholars are actually of the opinion that there are such traces of the Fourth Gospel to be found as early as 100 CE. But the agreement of individual words and phrases and reminisences does not constitute evidence. In this connection one must ask whether the Fourth Gospel really presented itself as an ally to an early Christian author in the period in question.

1. 1 Clement

The oldest writing to be considered is *1 Clement.* In the view of Braun,[2] there are more than thirty points of contact between the Johannine literature and *1 Clement.* But this thesis has not gained general consent. Since Braun dates *1 Clement* about 96, as is customary, he cannot very well search there for quotations out of a gospel that, on his own view, was not written until later. Braun helps himself out of this dilemma by proposing that John first gave oral instruction to catechumens. This led to written collections, of which one reached the author of *1 Clement* in Rome. According to Bihlmeyer,[3] *1 Clement* contains eighty-eight allusions to the NT, in addition to 184 quotations from the OT. Of these, however, only one concerns the Fourth Gospel, *1 Clem.* 49.1: "Let him who has love in Christ perform the commandments of Christ."[4] That is reminiscent of John 14:15: "If you love me, you will keep my commandments." But wording and context differ; what they have in common is the general Christian admonition: there is no love of Christ without obedience to his commandments. *1 Clement* is not a real witness for the use of the Fourth Gospel.

2. Ignatius

The relationship of the letters of *Ignatius* to the Fourth Gospel is controversial. Braun points to seventy possible points of contact[5] counts Ignatius among "the most certain witnesses" we have for the use of the Fourth Gospel.[6] On the other hand, he admits that the Apostle John is never mentioned in the Ignatian letters, though Paul is: in his letter to the *Ephesians* (12.2), he calls the Ephesians "fellow-initiates" ($\sigma\nu\mu\mu\acute{\nu}\sigma\tau\alpha\iota$) of Paul, and in Ign. *Rom.* 4.3, Paul is called an apostle along with Peter. This silence regarding John and his Gospel—there is not a single verbatim quotation—is surprising to Braun himself. It is all the more astonishing since Ignatius must have known the son of Zebedee as a contemporary—in the event he lived in the time of Trajan in Ephesus (according to early Christian tradition). So it is not strange that the thesis of Braun is not convincing.

The work of Maurer[7] has received more attention. Maurer proposes to prove that Ignatius makes use of John only at three points: (a) Ign. *Phld.* 7.1//John 3:18 and 8:14; (b) Ign. *Phld.* 9.1//John 10:7, 9; and (c) Ign. *Rom.* 7.3//John 6:33. But none of the three passages offers really conclusive proof for the dependence of Ignatius on the Fourth Gospel. Occasionally an ecclesiastical formula simulates contact with the Gospel of John. The way in which Ignatius understands himself and his situation is reflected in the letters he writes to his congregations on his journey to Rome to suffer martyrdom. All the world has to offer has lost its value for Ignatius—the world is already as estranged from him as it is for a strict gnostic.[8] Ignatius will be fulfilled as a Christian only in martyrdom, for which he yearns.

For the Fourth Gospel, the transition to the kingdom of God transpires at the moment in which a person hears the Christian message and comes to faith. For that reason its language often appears to originate on the far side of this "transition" ($\mu\epsilon\tau\acute{\alpha}\beta\alpha\sigma\iota\varsigma$). Its solemn tranquility contrasts characteristically with the ecstatic speech of Ignatius, which combines the end and triumph of the one condemned to the wild beasts with the constant admonition to hold fast to the leadership of the church, this triad

---

Metzger, *The Text of the NT,* 38f; O. Paret, *Die Über-lieferung der Bibel* (Stuttgart: Württembergische Bibelanstalt, [4]1966).

2 *Jean le théologien,* 1: 179, 393–97.
3 *Die apostolischen Väter,* 1: 156.
4 Tr. Kirsopp Lake, LCL.
5 *Jean le théologien,* 1: 416f.
6 *Jean le théologien,* 1: 291.

7 *Ignatius von Antiochien und das Johannesevangelium,* ATANT 18 (Zurich: Zwingli Verlag, 1949).
8 "Nothing visible is good": Ign. *Rom.* 3.3, tr. Kirsopp Lake, LCL.

of God, Christ, and Church.

Bihlmeyer counts eleven passages in Ignatius that exhibit a relationship with the Fourth Gospel;[9] among them are included the three listed above. Of the remaining eight, only Ign. *Rom.* 7.2 is singled out and marked with an asterisk as a genuine parallel (to John 4:10 and 7:38). Ignatius writes: "My (earthly) love (ἔρως) has been crucified, and there is in me no fire of love for material things (πῦρ φιλόϋλον); but only water living and speaking in me, and saying to me from within, 'Come to the Father.'" Compare John 4:10: ". . . he would have given you living water" and 7:38: "He who believes in me, as the scripture has said, 'Out of his heart shall flow rivers of living water.'" Bihlmeyer goes further back, however, to Zech 14:8: "On that day living waters shall flow out from Jerusalem." By that however, the author does not mean rivers of blessing, but actual rivers that will flow from Jerusalem in the last days. In contrast to all those scholars who assume contact between Ignatius and John, Regul emphasizes:[10] "Ignatius of Antioch is completely silent in his letters to churches in Asia Minor with respect to the apostolic authority of John for this region. That is all the more significant since he was already in the middle of a battle with heretics and would have found it helpful to call on an apostolic authority." . . . "Ignatius does not seem to know that the Ephesians made John into their star apostolic witness following the death of Paul." . . . "But it is absolutely ruled out that Ignatius understood and called himself a disciple of John."[11] Instead, he who was bishop of Antioch calls himself the bishop of Syria (Ign. *Rom.* 2.2), and thereby assumes, in a certain sense, the later position of metropolitan. It is not surprising to find such an official writing letters to all proximate congregations in Asia Minor and preparing the Roman church for his arrival. Unlike Peter and Paul, both of whom suffered martyrdom in Rome, he will certainly not command. They are apostles; he is only a servant. At any rate, he journeys "from Syria to Rome," like Paul, guarded by Roman soldiers, "leopards who become worse for kind treatment."[12] He wrote that after he had begged the Roman church, in chapters 1–4, not to ransom him from authorities and thus not spare him from martyrdom. His journey to Rome for martyrdom must have been the theme, more than anything else, of the Christian church of the east at that time. The problems of the earthly leadership of the church are matters of heartfelt indifference to the spirit-consciousness of the Fourth Gospel. That makes understandable why the Gospel of John is not mentioned in the letters of Ignatius, and why Paul is mentioned: Ignatius is repeating his journey to death. Contacts between the Fourth Gospel and the letters of Ignatius are only apparent.

3. Polycarp of Smyrna

Polycarp of Smyrna lived to a ripe old age; he had witnessed three generations before he mounted the funeral pyre to die in the flames. When the Proconsul Statius Quadratus demanded that he blaspheme Christ in order to save himself, the old man replied: "For eighty and six years have I been his servant, and he has done me no wrong, and how can I blaspheme my King who saved me?"[13] So he died on the second day of the month Xanthicus, on the seventh day before the calends of March, on a "great Sabbath" (*Mart. Pol.* 7.1). Not long before he had traveled to Rome to discuss the Easter controversy with Bishop Anicetus (154–165?). Irenaeus asserts that he converted many heretics while there by referring to the unalterable tradition of the church (*Adv. haer.* 3.4). Irenaeus is admittedly an unreliable witness; he has Polycarp installed by the apostles as bishop in Smyrna, he even holds that he was a disciple of John, who was a disciple of the Lord. Among the anecdotes that Irenaeus relates in this same section of his work is one concerning his meeting with Marcion, whom he calls "the first-born of Satan." This could have grown out of Pol. *Phil.* 7.1. According to this passage, every heretic who does not confess that Jesus has come in the flesh is a "first-born of Satan." The phrase *fraternitatis amatores* ("lovers of the brotherhood") in Pol. *Phil.* 10.1 does not constitute proof that he made use of the Fourth Gospel in this letter otherwise rich in citations. Polycarp pointedly mentions the name of Paul, not John, in his letter to the *Philippians* (3.2, 9.1, 11.3). Paul is "the apostolic authority for him, the authority upon which he calls, the single apostle he refers to by name and whom he more or less makes prominent in relation to the apostles as as group, just as

---

9   *Die apostolischen Väter*, 1: 159.
10   *Die antimarcionitischen Evangelienprologe*, 107.
11   *Die antimarcionitischen Evangelienprologe*, 109.

12   *Rom.* 5.1, tr. Kirsopp Lake, LCL, modified.
13   *Mart. Pol.* 9.3b, tr. Kirsopp Lake, LCL.

in his writing he endeavors to leave the impression that he is a disciple of Paul."[14] He "belonged clearly in the front line of those who fought to advance the legacy of Paul and to place him unambiguously in the anti-heretical front."[15]

4. Epistle of Barnabas

The Epistle of Barnabas is not a genuine letter,[16] much less a letter written by the Barnabas who was Paul's companion; rather, it is a tractate which appears to make use of a book of testimonies (chapters 2–17) and of a set of instructions on "the two ways" (chapters 18–20). Hostile to Judaism with respect to questions of the cult, the author makes ample use of the OT—interpreted allegorically—along with the Synoptics, but not the Fourth Gospel. Two alleged points of contact (6.6, 20.2) derive from Ps 21:19 and Ezek 47:1–12. The name of John the Apostle does not appear and the work lacks a direct quotation from John.

5. Shepherd of Hermas

The so-called *Shepherd of Hermas* was probably written in Rome about 140 CE.[17] The author, who was a brother of the Roman bishop Pius, derives his material from neither the OT nor the NT. The four "visions," the twelve "mandates," and the ten "similitudes" do not grow out of particular passages in the gospels or the letters of Paul. It is thus not surprising that the Gospel of John is not quoted and the name of John not mentioned. The most personal item in the work is the message that a second penance is possible for Christians who sin after baptism. But this message does not grow out of a deeper understanding of the Gospel of John.

6. Bishop Papias of Hierapolis

Bishop Papias of Hierapolis—presumably in the period 130–140—wrote five books called "Exposition of the Sayings of the Lord" (λογίων κυριακῶν ἐξήγησις). Eusebius has quoted some passages from this work in his church

history (*H.E.*). Of particular importance is the passage from the Prologue of Papias which is quoted in *H.E.* 3.39.3. Here the Apostle John is mentioned for the first time in early Christian literature; nevertheless, Papias avoids the title "apostle." The passage runs as follows (divided into sections to simplify the discussion):

> (a) And I shall not hesitate to append to the interpretations [of the words of the Lord] all that I ever learnt well from the presbyters and remember well, for of their truth I am confident.
>
> (b) For unlike most I did not rejoice in them who say much, but in them who teach the truth, nor in them who recount the commandments of others, but in them who repeated those given to the faith by the Lord and derived from the truth itself;
>
> (c) but if ever anyone came who had followed the presbyters, I inquired into the words of the presbyters, what Andrew or Peter or Philip or Thomas or James or John or Matthew, or any other of the Lord's disciples, had said (εἶπεν), and what Aristion and the presbyter John, the Lord's disciples, were saying (λέγουσιν).
>
> (d) For I did not suppose that information from books would help me so much as the word of a living and surviving voice.[18]

From (d) we learn: Papias followed a basic rule that was uncommon at that time: he did not rely on books but on what we would call the "oral tradition." This procedure makes sense, to be sure, only if Papias was able to make inquiries, with the help of the bearers of the tradition, of those materials that mattered to him, viz., the "sayings of the Lord" (λόγια κυριακά) themselves. These included not only individual sayings of Jesus but also longer speeches, in addition to reports of events in the early church (e.g., a report of the death of Judas; s. below).

From (b) it is learned that Papias was conscious of the fact that he did not receive as much material in this way as he did from "the books." Apparently it was no longer easy to trace the chain of tradition all the way back to Jesus himself. Papias accepted this limitation in his

---

14 Regul, *Die antimarcionitischen Evangelienprologe*, 109f.
15 Regul, *Die antimarcionitischen Evangelienprologe*, 110f.
16 H. Windisch, *Der Barnabasbrief*, HNT, Ergänzungsband 3 (Tübingen: Mohr-Siebeck, 1920).
17 Cf. Dibelius, *Der Hirt des Hermas*, HNT, Ergänzungsband 4 (Tübingen: Mohr-Siebeck, 1923) 422.
18 Tr. Kirsopp Lake, LCL.

method becaue he was convinced that he could obtain genuine material, "commandments the Lord himself had given," by this process.

According to (a) and (c) the middlemen for Papias were the "presbyters," although only indirectly. By this Papias did not mean the members of a presbytery under a bishop, nor did he mean all sorts of old men, but a series of revered old men who had been disciples of apostles. Papias avoids the term "apostle" in the passage quoted. That has led to the mistake of identifying the presbyters with the (? twelve) apostles.[19] At all events, Papias names only seven men from the apostolic circle (Andrew, Peter, the brothers Philip and Thomas, James and John, the second pair of brothers, and Matthew); the rest he designates as "any other of the Lord's disciples." It follows, on the basis of the word εἶπεν ("had said") that the first group of men were already dead at the time Papias met followers of the presbyters. We know that James, son of Zebedee, was executed by Herod Antipas in 44 CE (Acts 12:2). Peter probably suffered martyrdom in Rome in 64 CE during the Neronian persecution. There are two differing traditions concerning John, the son of Zebedee. According to one, which was later the only one recognized in the church, John is said to have lived to the time of Trajan (98–117). The other tradition concerning the sons of Zebedee is found in Mark 10:35–40 and Matt 20:20–23. Both report that Jesus predicted the martyrdom of the two brothers. According to Philip Sidetes (middle of the fifth century CE) and Georgios Hamartolos (ninth century), Papias likewise reported this "tradition of martyrdom" in his second book. This squares with the fact that Papias has nothing to say of a gospel attributed to the long-lived son of Zebedee in (c), but rather makes an effort to obtain reports from the presbyters (through disciples) about what the son of Zebedee had said.

On the other hand, Aristion and the elder John lived in the time when the disciples of the presbyters were passing their knowledge along. Eusebius (*H.E.* 3.39.14) indicates to his inquisitive readers that Papias quotes the διηγήσεις ("account") of Aristion and the παραδόσεις ("traditions") of John the Elder in other places in his work. The traditions stemming from these two men were later given the same titles. It is thus likely that these traditions were later written down. However, they have been lost, except for the remnants preserved especially by Eusebius (3.39) and Irenaeus.

This shows, consequently, that Papias knew John the son of Zebedee as a bearer of tradition but not as the author of a gospel. For if Papias sought to learn the words of the son of Zebedee through the presbyters and their disciples, that shows he knew nothing of a gospel composed by him. But he probably believed that John the son of Zebedee was the author of the Apocalypse. The view that he had received a gospel dictated by the son of Zebedee, as asserted in the so-called Anti-Marcionite Prologues, can by no means be reconciled with the proemium of Papias. Moreover, the Gospel of John contains nothing of the doctrine of the millenium (Rev 20:3–7), which Papias piously transmits like many of his contemporaries (cf. Irenaeus and Justin). It is worthwhile to provide an example of that, which shows at the same time what was expected from the "living and abiding voice" at that time. About 180 Irenaeus reports (*Adv. haer.* 5.33.3f.):

As the elders who saw John, the disciple of the Lord, related that they had heard from him how the Lord used to teach in regard to these times, and say: The days will come, in which vines shall grow, each having ten thousand twigs, and in each true twig ten thousand shoots, and in each one of the shoots ten thousand clusters, and on every one of the clusters ten thousand grapes, and every grape when pressed will give five and twenty metretes [1,000 liters] of wine. And when any one of the saints shall lay hold of a cluster, another shall cry out, "I am a better cluster, take me; bless the Lord through me." . . .

And these things are borne witness to in writing by Papias, the hearer of John, and a companion of Polycarp, in his fourth book; for there were five books compiled by him. And he says in addition, "Now these things are credible to believers." And he says that, "when the traitor Judas did not give credit to them, and put the question, 'How then can things about to bring forth so abundantly be wrought by the Lord?' the Lord declared, 'They who shall come to these times shall see.'"[20]

What is presented here as a saying of Jesus transmitted

19   Cf. W. Michaelis, *Einleitung*, 93f.
20   ANF 1: 562f.

by the disciple John, according to Irenaeus and even Papias himself, is in reality a fanciful exaggeration of a late Jewish legend. It is preserved in the Syriac Apocalypse of Baruch (2 Bar 29:5) and reads:

> The earth also shall yield its fruit ten thousandfold and on each vine there shall be a thousand branches, and each branch shall produce a thousand clusters, and each cluster produce a thousand grapes, and each grape produce a cor [or homer = 55 gallons] of wine.[21]

The description of the marvelous future fecundity of the earth in Baruch is itself already a fanciful legend. In the account of John the disciple allegedly transmitted through the elders, it has been fantastically exaggerated. In the version preserved by Papias, however, a dialogue between Jesus and Judas the betrayer has been added. It is evident, on the basis of the dialogue, that Papias would like to believe the legend literally. Whoever does not believe it will not enter the millenium.

The hope fostered by Papias in the unconditional veracity of the oral tradition is thereby refuted. According to Papias, John the son of Zebedee told this story to the elders as an eye- and ear-witness of Jesus. We would then have to reckon with the following chain of tradition: Jesus—John—the elders —their disciples—Papias. At which point did the Baruch legend enter the tradition as an alleged saying of Jesus? We cannot say. At the earliest the unreliability can be attributed to the itinerant (real or alleged) disciples of the elders, who furnished Bishop Papias of Hierapolis with the tradition.

We need not, however, confine the failure of the method of Papias to this passage. Apollinaris of Laodicea preserves another example of tradition stemming from Papias; it concerns the death of Judas.

> Papias, the disciple of John, relates that more clearly in the fourth book of his *Expositions of the Sayings of the Lord:* Judas wanders about in this world as an evil example of godlessness. His body swelled up so much that he could no longer pass through a place that a wagon could get through with ease; he could not even get his head through. His eyelids swelled up so much, as it were, that he could see no light at all, and his eyes could no longer be seen even with the aid of a physician's ophthalmoscope. They were completely em-

bedded in flesh viewed from the outside. . . . Pus and worms flowed through his entire body, both of which already tormented him by virtue of his natural necessities. When he then died, after many plagues and torments, on his own plot of ground, that plot remains desolate and uninhabitated to this day because of the stench; indeed, one cannot pass by that place without holding one's nose.[22]

This horror story of the gruesome end of Judas the betrayer was certainly not transmitted by an immediate disciple of Jesus. It received its stamp from Christian brooding and scribalism[23] and in the weird fantasy that takes delight in revenge. The mention of the ophthalmoscope shows that not even higher learning is sheltered from fantasy. Papias himself would not have invented all these details himself. But he deemed them worth taking up into his work.

Two further traditions that Papias owes to John the Elder and which Eusebius quotes are instructive:

> And the Presbyter used to say this, "Mark became Peter's interpreter and wrote accurately all that he remembered, not, indeed, in order, of the things said or done by the Lord. For he had not heard the Lord, nor had he followed him, but later on, as I said, followed Peter, who used to give teaching as necessity demanded but not making, as it were, an arrangement of the Lord's oracles, so that Mark did nothing wrong in thus writing down single points as he remembered them. For to one thing he gave attention, to leave out nothing of what he had heard and to make no false statements in them."[24]

When the Elder states that Mark lacks "order," he does not necessarily mean to imply that there is another gospel with the putative correct order. It suffices that he knew the tradition recorded in 1 Peter: Peter was in "Babylon" (Rome, cf. Rev 18) where Mark served him. But as Peter's interpreter, Mark knew Peter's preaching only in an arrangement that was not connected to the order of events in Jesus' life.

Matthew was not Papias' regular gospel, as another passage in Eusebius (*H. E.* 3.39.16) indicates:

> This is related by Papias about Mark, and about Matthew this was said, "Matthew collected the oracles (τὰ λογία) in the Hebrew language, and each interpreted them as best he could."

---

21 *APOT* 2: 298.

22 Cf. *Beginnings of Christianity* 5: 22–25; Haenchen, *Acts of the Apostles,* 160, n. 5.

23 Cf. Schweizer, "Zu Apg 1,16–22." *TZ* 14 (1958) 56.

24 *H. E.* 3.39.15f., tr. Kirsopp Lake, LCL.

It is clear that Papias does not have further information about this Hebraic form of Matthew's Gospel. Irenaeus, Clement of Alexandria, and Eusebius (*H. E.* 3.25.5f.) report knowledge of a Hebrew original of Matthew's Gospel. Jerome mentions it often. The most important passage is found in *De viris illustribus* 3, where the text reads:

> Matthew was the first one in Judea to compose the Gospel of Christ in the Hebrew script and language on account of those who came to faith out of Judaism; it is no longer certain who later translated it into Greek. Further, the Hebrew text itself is still to be found in the library at Caesarea, which the martyr Pamphilus assembled with great care. In addition, the Nazarenes in Beroea, a city in Syria, who possess this book, permitted me to make a copy of it. In this copy it is to be noted that the Evangelist follows the original Hebrew text, not the Septuaginta, wherever he introduces witnesses from the OT—whether on his own or on the part of the Lord and Savior.

In his commentary on Matthew, which Jerome wrote five years later, shortly before 398, he writes more cautiously:

> In the gospel that the Nazarenes and the Ebionites use, which we have newly translated from the Hebrew language into Greek, and which is called the authentic Gospel of Matthew by most. . . .

Seventeen years later (*Dialog. adv. Pelag.* 3.2) Jerome writes:

> In the Gospel According to the Hebrews, which is written in the Chaldean and Syrian language, but with Hebrew characters, which the Nazarenes use as the (Gospel) 'According to the Apostle' or, as most presume, 'According to Matthew,' and which is also present in the library at Caesarea. . . .

All these passages suggest that the Greek version of Matthew was earlier translated back from Greek into Aramaic. This back-translation was represented by Jewish Christians, however, as the original form of Matthew. It appears later sometimes to have been used and perhaps also reworked by Jewish-Christian sects under other names. Papias had heard of this Hebrew version of Matthew's Gospel, but had not himself used it; he would hardly have known Hebrew. He then explained the Greek version of Matthew as a translation back into

Greek (from Hebrew). Papias is silent about the Gospel of Luke, the Acts of the Apostles, and the Pauline letters. In general, he is silent about a lot more than he tells us about. For all these reasons, Dibelius describes Papias as the first Christian litterateur.[25] The reason is that he thinks of Mark as Peter's "interpreter," who presided over the final written form of the preaching of Peter. But Luke was more likely the first Christian litterateur, about whom Papias reports nothing. Further, the Presbyter—the particulars about Mark and Matthew derive from him and not from Papias—probably thought of "interpreter" (ἑρμηνεύς) in this case as "translator" of the Aramaic preaching of Peter in question. The proemium of Papias—which Dibelius takes as evidence of the literariness of Papias— was particularly necessary because his method of gathering oral tradition was ununsual for that time and subject to objection.

Papias did not distinguish between the apostles or "the Twelve" and the presbyters in the fragments preserved for us, yet he does not identify them either. Eusebius does not note the absence of the word "apostle," but regards the presbyters as disciples of the apostles. Irenaeus comports himself similarly, occasionally also substituting "disciple of the presbyters" for "presbyter." For Irenaeus the fact that Papias avoids the use of the concept of apostle has the merit of suggesting that his readers were of the opinion that Papias himself had seen and listened to the apostles. Since Irenaeus was also concerned to cite the oldest witnesses that he could, he was happy to refer to Papias as a disciple of John and a comrade of Polycarp.

Walter Bauer, who was misled by the anti-Marcionite prologue to the Gospel of John,[26] viewed Papias in his struggle against Marcion[27] and saw Hierapolis as the easternmost point "that the church in opposition to heretics succeeded in occupying in Asia Minor, or indeed anywhere. Papias offered resistance there with the realization that he was dealing with a superior force. At least, he explains that his perspective, conditioned by his anti-heretical stance with reference to materials of the gospel tradition, set before him the task of excising everything that delights the 'great majority' (οἱ πολλοί). He is convinced that to carry out this plan means to sacrifice the

---

25 *RGG²* 4: 892f.
26 See below.
27 *Orthodoxy and Heresy*, 184–91.

bulk (τὰ πολλά) of the material. But it is also clear to him that what he rejects . . . is foreign in origin and nature (*H.E.* 3.39.3). Since he therefore knows that he is limited in his influence to the minority of Christians in Hierapolis, he quite consciously withdraws to that which he, from his ecclesiastical standpoint, judges to be an authentic apostolic heritage."[28] It appears also to have escaped Bauer that Papias himself did not speak of the apostles. The text does not say that the Christians of Hierapolis, to whom his influence was limited, were in the minority. Although Bauer made a signal contribution by pointing out that there was no "orthodoxy" anywhere at first, after which the church was seduced by heresy, nevertheless his book now threatened to shift the weight entirely.

Papias has reported things over which Eusebius must have shaken his head (he therefore calls him "a small mind" [σμικρὸς τὸν νοῦν] in another passage) and which prompt us to ask whether we should take seriously the traditions he reports.

Eusebius further reports (*H.E.* 3.39.17) that Papias "sets forth another story about a woman accused falsely of many sins before the Lord."[29] This story was taken over from the Gospel of the Hebrews. Rufin has made this woman out to be the woman taken in adultery (John 7:53–8:11) in his translation of Eusebius.[30] But the pericope of the woman taken in adultery (γυνὴ ἐπὶ μοιχείᾳ) was only later inserted into the Gospel of John. The last bit of evidence that Papias knew the Gospel of John thereby vanishes.

In general, it can be said that Papias gives the impression of being a man of the earliest times to whom we owe honor, but with respect to whom we are also to exercise critical judgment. Whether we may refer to him, as Bauer does,[31] as an eager collector of tradition is not so certain. Whenever the possibility presented itself of interrogating a former disciple of the apostles, he gladly seized it; one looks in vain, however, for notes that could have been made and for communications to his readers regarding the names of the witnesses in question.

7. Justin Martyr

Justin Martyr, who was born to pagan-Greek parents in Shechem (Flavia Neapolis/Nablus), sought the truth in various philosophical schools (Stoics, Peripatetics, Pythagoreans, Platonists) until he was finally converted to Christianity, above all by evidence that prophecies had been fulfilled. The Prefect Junius Rusticus had him beheaded on his second stay in Rome, presumably around 165 CE. Only the two so-called *Apologies* and the *Dialogue with Trypho* are preserved of his many writings. Braun has attempted to demonstrate on the basis of eleven passages in the *First Apology* and in the *Dialogue* that Justin had made use of the Gospel of John.[32] However, in all probability, only *First Apol.* 61.4f. appears to be related at all to John 3:1–5, although here the differences are also great. For, Justin writes: "'Unless you are born again you will not enter into the Kingdom of heaven.' Now it is clear to all that those who have once come into being cannot enter the wombs of those who bore them."[33] Loewenich interprets this passage as the strongest possible evidence;[34] however, Justin never discusses the author of the Fourth Gospel. Loewenich regards it as improbable that Justin viewed the Gospel of John as one of the "memoirs of the apostles" (ἀπομνημονεύματα τῶν ἀποστόλων).[35] An apostle John is mentioned in *Dial.* 81.4 as the author of the Apocalypse, which was important to Justin as a scriptural witness on account of his belief in the coming of the millenial kingdom. Justin's doctrine of the sacraments (*First Apol.* 66.2) is reminiscent of John 6:34, 52, but the two are by no means identical. In sum, it cannot be proved that Justin made use of the Gospel of John.[36]

8. Tatian

Justin's pupil, Tatian, who was a Syrian, returned to the East following the death of his master. His work, "Oration to the Greeks," has been preserved; his harmony of

---

28 *Orthodoxy and Heresy*, 190f.

29 *Eusebius*, Lawlor and Oulton, 1: 101.

30 Rufin, *Eusebius, Die Kirchengeschichte (Ecclesiastica historica, griechisch und lateinisch). Die lateinische Übersetzung des Rufinus,* 3 vols. Herausgegeben von Eduard Schwartz. Die lateinische Übersetzung bearbeitet von Theodor Mommsen (Leipzig: J. C. Hinrichs, 1903, 1908, 1909) 1: 293.

31 *Orthodoxy and Heresy,* 184.

32 *Jean le théologien,* 135–39.

33 Tr. E. R. Hardy, *Early Christian Fathers,* LCC 1: 282.

34 *Das Johannesverständnis im zweiten Jahrhundert* (Giessen: A. Töpelmann, 1932) 39–50.

35 *Das Johannesverständnis im zweiten Jahrhundert* (Giessen: A. Töpelmann, 1932) 42 n. 3.

36 Cf. Osborn, *Justin Martyr,* BHT 47 (Tübingen:

the gospels, of which Eusebius[37] knew only that it was still being used by some and that it carried the title "Diatessaron" ($\tau\grave{o}$ $\delta\iota\grave{a}$ $\tau\epsilon\sigma\sigma\acute{a}\rho\omega\nu$ $\epsilon\vec{v}\alpha\gamma\gamma\acute{\epsilon}\lambda\iota o\nu$), was widely disseminated in many versions and often translated down into the fifth century, but was finally lost. Bishops in the East exerted a great deal of effort in replacing this gospel harmony with separate gospels. Tatian's diatessaron is all but lost; a tiny fragment of it was found in Dura Europos in 1933.[38] It is debated whether the Diatesseron was first conceived in Syriac and then translated into many other languages. John 1:5 is quoted in *Oratio ad Graecos* 13.1 as scripture.[39] But that takes us approximately to the year 176 CE, and thus very close to the time of Irenaeus; it would thus not be a fundamentally new piece of evidence.

About 200 CE the situation is suddenly altered: all at once the "ecclesiastical tradition" of the son of Zebedee as the author of the Gospel of John appears. This tradition is present on a broad front: the Muratorian Canon, Iraeneus, Theophilus of Antioch, Polycrates of Ephesus, and somewhat later, Clement of Alexandria.

9. Muratori

The fragment of an index to the canon named for its discoverer and editor, Muratori, has this to say about the Gospel of John:

> The fourth of the Gospels, that of John, (one) of the disciples.
> When his fellow-disciples and bishops urged him, he said: Fast with me from today for three days, and what
> will be revealed to each one
> let us relate to one another. In the same night it was revealed to Andrew, one of the apostles, that, whilst all were to go over (it), John in his own name should write everything down.[40]

One senses that this tradition reflects a compromise. Everything that could lead to the impression that the Gospel of John was composed by John on his own resolve is excluded: John was not prompted to create his Gospel by human requests, but required divine direction. All were to fast for three days and then to relate to each other was had been revealed to each one. But the divine decision came more quickly: already during the first night the apostle was instructed what was to happen: John was to compose the Gospel in his own name, but the others were to check it. Divine revelation determined the method by which the Gospel of John came into being. It carries the name of John alone, yet it was checked by all the other apostles and bishops.

10. Polycrates

In the controversy over the celebration of Easter, Polycrates, bishop of Ephesus, championed the position of the church in Asia Minor, which held to the quartodeciman view, against Bishop Victor. While the church in Rome calls upon the tradition of Peter and Paul, Polycrates argues:

> For indeed in Asia great luminaries ($\sigma\tau o\iota\chi\epsilon\hat{\iota}a$) have fallen asleep. . . . Philip, one of the twelve apostles, who has fallen asleep in Hierapolis, [as have] also his two daughters who grew old in virginity, and his other daughter who lived in the Holy Spirit and rests at Ephesus; and, moreover, [there is] John too, he who leant back on the Lord's breast, who was a priest ($\iota\epsilon\rho\epsilon\acute{v}s$), wearing the sacerdotal plate ($\pi\acute{\epsilon}\tau a\lambda o\nu$), both martyr and teacher. He has fallen asleep at Ephesus.[41]

This passage is invoked as evidence that John, the son of Zebedee, and beloved disciple died and was buried in Ephesus. But Polycrates does not mention that John was the author of the Fourth Gospel. The statement that John was a priest and carried the golden mitre of the high priest shows to what extent the reminiscence has drifted off into legend.

11. Eusebius

Eusebius himself has furnished the following information:

Mohr-Siebeck, 1973) 137.

37 *H.E.* 4.29.6.
38 Dura Europos lies on the west bank of the Euphrates; it was conquered and destroyed by the Sassanids in 256 CE.
39 Kümmel, *Introduction*, 482, 527f.
40 *NTApoc* 1: 43.
41 *Eusebius*, Lawlor and Oulton, 1: 169 (*H.E.* 5.24.2f.).

Cf. n. 29.

Moreover, there was still alive in Asia [at the time of Trajan] and directing the churches there, he whom Jesus loved, apostle alike and evangelist, even John, having returned from his exile on the island after the death of Domitian. And that he survived up to their day—this account is sufficiently accredited by two witnesses, who may be considered worthy of credit . . . : Irenaeus[42] and Clement of Alexandria . . .; the latter mentions Ephesus as the place of John's residence.[43]

12. Irenaeus

Irenaeus, who became bishop of Lyon in 177/178 CE, came from Asia Minor and saw the old Polycarp when he was very young. This information is derived from his letter to Florinus, which Eusebius quotes. In this letter he says:

> These opinions [Valentinian] are not in harmony with the Church . . . These opinions the elders before us, who also were disciples of the apostles, did not hand down to thee. For when I was a boy (παῖς) I saw thee in lower Asia (ἐν τῇ κάτω ᾽Ασίᾳ [he means Smyrna]) in the company of Polycarp, faring brilliantly in the imperial court and endeavouring to secure his favour. . . . I can tell the very place where the blessed Polycarp used to sit as he discoursed, . . . how he would tell of his intercourse with John and with the others who had seen the Lord, how he would relate from memory their words; and what the things were which he had heard from them concerning the Lord, His mighty works and His teaching, Polycarp, as having received them from the eyewitnesses of the life of the Word, would declare altogether in accordance with the Scriptures.[44]

In the continuation of this passage, Irenaeus calls Polycarp the "blessed, apostolic presybter," which indicates that Irenaeus regarded him as one of the presbyters.

Except for a few quotations from them, the letters of Irenaeus have been lost. Extant is his work, *Against Heresies,* in five books, and his shorter work, *Demonstration of the Apostolic Preaching,* which has been preserved only in an Armenian translation. In the preface to his work *Against Heresies,* Irenaeus apologizes for his imperfect Greek style:

> You will not expect from me, a resident among the Celts, and most accustomed to a barbarous language, rhetorical skill, which I have never learned, nor power in writing, I have not acquired, nor beauties of language and style, which I am not acquainted with.[45]

What has gotten dislocated in Irenaeus is knowledge of the times separating events. For example, this is what he says in *Adv. haer.* 5.33.3f.: "The elders who saw John, the disciple of the Lord, related that they had heard from him how the Lord used to teach in regard to these times [the millenial kingdom] and say," and somewhat later, "And these things are borne witness to in writing by Papias, the hearer of John, and a companion of Polycarp."[46] These false chronological intervals go together, to a certain degree, with an incorrect interpretation of John 8:57, where the Jews say to Jesus: "You are not yet fifty years old, and have you seen Abraham?" These words prove that Jesus was for that time a mature man when he taught (maturity came between 40 and 50 years of age). Irenaeus thus derives from John 8:57 that Jesus had already passed 45 years of age, but had not yet reached 50 years. He can then continue: To that "the Gospel and all the elders testify; those who were conversant in Asia with John, the disciple of the Lord, [affirming] that John conveyed to them that information. And he remained among them up to the times of Trajan. Some of them, moreover, saw not only John, but the other apostles also, and heard the very same account from them, and bear testimony as to the [validity of] the statement."[47] If Jesus really did not die on the cross before he was 46 years old, there could have been Christians at the time of the composition of the Gospel of John who had seen him in their youth and the age of the beloved disciple need not have been extremely high.

The two passages from *Against Heresies* quoted above are interesting for other reasons. They show in particular how unreliable is the information that the disciples of the presbyters report to Irenaeus. We have already cited the description of the fecundity of the vines in the millenial kingdom in the passage about Papias, information provided by the presbyters, and we have cited the conversation with Judas that was amplified in the repetition of the story by Papias. Papias and Irenaeus were not the only Christians who lived in such fantasies in the

---

42 Cf. *Adv. haer.* 2.22.5.
43 *H.E.* 3.23.1ff., Lawlor and Oulton, 1: 82.
44 *H.E.* 5.20.4ff., Lawlor and Oulton, 1: 166.
45 *Adv. haer.* Preface 3, tr. E. R. Hardy, LCC 1: 359.
46 ANF 1: 562f.
47 *Adv. haer.* 2.22.5, 6, ANF 1:391f.

middle or toward the end of the second century. Particularly in *Adv. haer.* 4.27ff. Irenaeus speaks frequently of a presbyter from whom he had taken over many doctrines. Thus, *Adv. haer.* 4.27.1 begins with the words: "As I have heard from a certain presbyter, who had heard it from those who had seen the apostles, and from those who had been their disciples. . . ." In the same section, it is said of Solomon: "The Scripture has thus sufficiently reproved him, as the presbyter remarked, in order that no flesh may glory in the sight of the Lord."[48] And he continues: "We ought not, therefore, as that presbyter remarks, to be puffed up, nor be severe upon those of old time."[49] If Gnostics attempt to introduce a second Father, "the elders pointed out that these men are devoid of sense."[50] Further: "Whoever finds fault with God because he permitted the Israelites to take gold and silver vessels with them in their exodus out of Egypt, fails to recognize the righteousness of God and accuses oneself, as the Presbyter said."[51] Of course, Irenaeus occasionally also points directly "to what John, the disciple of the Lord, said in the Apocalypse."[52] And here, too, Irenaeus is reporting a teaching of the presbyter, for he says in what immediately follows: "And the Presbyter refreshed us by such stories and said. . . ."[53] Irenaeus is indebted to him for his typological interpretation of the OT, for example: "The wife of Lot became a pillar of salt that lasts forever; so also the church, the salt of the earth. The old disciple of the apostles spoke this way about the two testaments and showed that they both stem from one and the same God."[54]

During the persecution of Christians in Lyon, in which their bishop Pothinus was beheaded, Irenaeus stayed in Rome. For him Rome remained the model of the steady and reliable congregation. And so he names the Roman bishops from Linus to Eleutherius, who is now the twelfth in succession:

> In this order, and by this succession, the ecclesiastical tradition from the apostles, and the preaching of the truth, have come down to us. And this is most abundant proof that there is one and the same vivifying faith, which has been preserved in the Church from the apostles until now, and handed down in truth.[55]

Irenaeus then continues and tells of a second great authority:

> Polycarp always taught the things he learned from the apostles, and which the Church has handed down, and which alone are true. He was not only instructed by apostles, and conversed with many who had seen Christ, but was also, by apostles in Asia, appointed bishop of Smyrna. . . . To these things all the Asiastic Churches testify, as do also those men who have succeeded Polycarp down to the present time.[56]

This principle of tradition to which Irenaeus constantly points bears a certain resemblance to the principle of tradition in Papias. But Papias sought to preserve the tradition in that he questioned real or alleged presbyters in Hierapolis. In the case of Irenaeus, it was predominantly the bishops and presbyters from whom he sought the right understanding, the correct teaching. An old presbyter appears to have given him special instruction regarding the relation of the two testaments. Irenaeus appears to have had other presbyters as instructors regarding eschatological expectations.

> As the Presbyters say, those who are worthy of heavenly fellowship will enter into heaven: they are those who receive one hundred fold. Those who receive sixty fold, will reside in Paradise, and those who receive thirty fold will dwell in the city described in the Apocalypse.

But Irenaeus not only regarded the disciple John as the author of the Apocalypse, but also as the author of the Gospel of John, and especially discussed the Prologue.

We are indebted to Irenaeus for much; he knew an astonishing amount about the heresies, although he did not always understand what he knew. He had heard about the Gospel of Truth, but had not read it. Who will reproach him for taking courage and consolation in the hope directed to the joy of the millenial kingdom?

---

48   ANF 1: 498f.
49   *Adv. haer.* 4.27.2, ANF 1: 499.
50   *Adv. haer.* 4.28.1, ANF 1: 501.
51   *Adv. haer.* 4.30.1. Cf. ANF 1: 502.
52   *Adv. haer.* 4.30.4. Cf. ANF 1: 504.
53   *Adv. haer.* 4.31.1. Cf. ANF 1: 504.
54   *Adv. haer.* 4.33.3. Cf. ANF 1: 505.
55   *Adv. haer.* 3.3.3, ANF 1: 416.

56   *Adv. haer.* 3.3.4. Cf. ANF 1: 416.

13. Anti-Marcionite Prologues

The so-called anti-Marcionite prologues have been reckoned among the witnesses for the Gospel of John in the second century CE since 1928. It was in that year that Donatien de Bruyne published an essay in the *Revue Bénédictine* entitled, "Les plus anciens prologues latins des Evangiles."[57] There were "prologues," prefaces, to almost every biblical book and they gave the reader information about the person of the author, his addressees, and the occasion of his writing, which led to the composition of the work in question. De Bruyne was of the opinion that he had found, after twenty years of searching, the anti-Marcionite prologues to Mark, Luke, and John; such a prologue has not been found to Matthew. De Bruyne conjectured that Marcion had published his NT (Luke and ten letters of Paul) with a Marcionite prologue provided for each of the letters of Paul. The Roman church responded with a counter edition of its own and added an anti-Marcionite prologue to each of the Gospels; he was convinced that he had found those belonging to Mark, Luke, and John. In the case of the Pauline letters, Marcion's own prologues were inadvertently taken over and used.

Distinguished scholars have agreed with De Bruyne, with modifications: above all, Harnack,[58] but later also Jülicher/Fascher,[59] and Lietzmann.[60] Lagrange,[61] Bacon,[62] and Howard[63] opposed this view, while Grant[64] and Heard[65] likewise had reservations. The corrected text of the anti-Marcionite prologue to John is to be found in Aland.[66]

Haenchen has contested the judgment that the three anti-Marcionite prologues constitute a literary unity or are even similarly constructed, that they stem from a single hand, and that they were directed against Marcion; he also argues that the prologue to John does not offer any exact information about conditions in the second century CE[67] Regul then drew the following conclusions:[68]

(1) The prologues of De Bruynes do not derive from a single hand;

(2) they are not anti-Marcionite in character;

(3) none of the three originated in the second century CE;

(4) the prologue to John has its sole parallels in the *Diversarum haereseum liber* of Filastrius (end of the fourth century CE) and in the Proemium of the Corderius catenae from the seventh century CE;

(5) the prologue is not a reliable witness to conditions in the second century, nor for traditions originating in the second century.

The original text of the so-called anti-Marcionite prologue to John runs:

> *Evangelium Johannis manifestatum et datum est ecclesiis ab Johanne adhuc in corpore constituto, sicut Papias nomine Hieropolitanus, discipulus Johannis carus, in exotericis [id est in extremis] quinque libris retulit; descripsit vero evangelium dictante Johanne recte. Verum Marcion haereticus, cum ab eo fuisset improbatus, eo quod contraria sentiebat, abiectis est ab Johanne. Is vero scripta vel epistulas ad eum pertulerat a fratribus, qui in Ponto fuerant.*

> The Gospel of John was revealed and given to the church by John while he was yet in the body as one Papias of Hierapolis, a dear disciple of John, has reported in the five books of his 'exoterics' [that is, in the last ones]. Indeed, he took down the gospel word for word while John was dictating. But the heretic Marcion was cast out by John after having been disapproved by him because of his opposite opinions. Marcion had, however, carried to John writings or letters from the brethren who dwelt in Pontus.

This text is really difficult to interpret. Even if one substitutes *exegeticis* for *exotericis* or *extremis* with Harnack,

---

57 *RBén* 40 (1928) 195–214.

58 *Die ältesten Evangelien-Prologe und die Bildung des Neuen Evangelienprologe*, SPAW.PH 24 (Berlin: G. Reimer, 1928) 320–41.

59 *Einleitung in das Neue Testament* (Tübingen: Mohr-Siebeck, 71931).

60 *A History of the Early Church*, 4 vols., tr. Bertram Lee Woolf (Cleveland and New York: World Publishing Co., 1961). Relevant to this question: vol. 1.

61 Review of Donatien De Bruyne, "Les plus anciens prologues latins des évangiles," in *RB* 38 (1929) 115–21.

62 "The Anti-Marcionite Prologue to John," *JBL* 49 (1930) 43–54.

63 "The Antimarcionite Prologues to the Gospels," *ExpTim* 47 (1936) 534–38.

64 "The Oldest Gospel Prologues," *ATR* 23 (1941) 231–45.

65 "The Oldest Gospel Prologues," *JTS*, n.s., 6 (1955) 1–16.

66 *Synopsis of the Four Gospels*, 532f.

67 *Acts of the Apostles*, 10–12 n. 1.

68 *Die antimarcionitischen Evangelienprologe*.

one is not done with problems. In his works Papias does not say that he is a "beloved disciple" of John, son of Zebedee. Rather, he writes in the preface to his work: Whenever a disciple of an old time presbyter came through Hierapolis, he inquired what had Andrew or Peter . . . or John . . . said in the words of the presbyter? In plain words: Papias each time asked a disciple of the presbyter about the words of the apostle in the words of the presbyter. At the time of his inquiries, the apostle John was long since dead; he was already dead when the disciple of the presbyter in question learned the words of the apostle from his presbyter. The time in which a disciple of the presbyter was interrogated by Papias lay far in the past: "Whenever a disciple of an old time presbyter came, I used to ask him . . .": Papias did not take notes during these interrogations; he relied on his good memory ($\kappa\alpha\lambda\hat{\omega}s$ $\dot{\epsilon}\mu\nu\eta\mu\acute{o}\nu\epsilon\upsilon\sigma\alpha$) and on the "living voice." That he finally recorded his knowledge in five books is understandable but irrelevant. Bousset[69] once conjectured that the presbyters formed a school that traveled from place to place and gave lessons. One does not derive such an impression from Papias, nor from Irenaeus. He writes constantly of "the presbyter," sometimes of the "old presbyter," who taught him about the unity of the two testaments. If he once called Polycarp the "blessed and apostolic presbyter," he does not thereby identify him with the "old presbyter." For he had only seen Polycarp as a child. It is legend that John, the son of Zebedee, dictated his gospel to Papias. At the time of Papias the Gospel of John already had a long history behind it. The vague way Papias has of expressing himself constitutes the real puzzle.[70] By dispensing with expressions like "the apostle" or "the twelve," he produces the false impression that he was once taught by the apostles and later had his memory refreshed or expanded by one or the other of the wandering disciples of the apostles. In this case, practically two generations of witnesses are shunted aside by a vague expression of Papias and Papias is moved back very, very near Jesus. If

one does not reflect on what kind of abstruse doctrines Papias traces back to this tradition,[71] one succumbs to the error to which Michaelis succumbed and not only him.[72] Marcion appears around 144 CE, when Jesus was long dead, as was the "long-lived John, son of Zebedee," if indeed there was such a person. One ought not to bring a prologue that Regul dates to 400 CE and that knows nothing of the second century into connection with the proem that stems from the second century, merely because the picture of the past has begun to be blurred in it.

One notes that these witnesses reckon with a certain opposition to the Gospel of John, against which they wish to protect it. They explain why the Gospel appeared so late in the list of ecclesiastical writings, why its difference from the Synoptics did not cause it to be depreciated, but constituted its preferred position, and finally why John did not act on his own impulses but had human and divine authorization.

That these apologies were not promulgated without reason is demonstrated by reports of attacks on the Gospel of John from the church. This is the way the reminiscences regarding the "alogoi"—so named by the orthodox opposition—are to be understood; they attribute the Gospel of John to the Gnostic Cerinthus.[73] Evidently the Johannine doctrine of the spirit aroused suspicion. In this context, Bauer mentions, no doubt correctly, the defense against the Roman presbyter Gaius, who composed a "Dialogue with the Montantist Proclus" around 200 CE, involving a polemic against the doctrine of the millenial kingdom in Cerinthus.[74] Hippolytus had attacked Gaius and the alogoi in a work called *On the Gospel and Apocalypse of John*. The Johannine doctrine of the spirit and of the paraclete had prompted the defenders of the anti-Gnostic tradition to train their critical guns on the Gospel of John.

On the other hand, we know that the Gnostic Heracleon, who was a disciple of the Gnostic Valentinus, wrote the first allegorical commentary on the Gospel of

---

69 *Jüdisch-christlicher Schulbetrieb in Alexandria und Rom. Literarische Untersuchungen zu Philo und Clemens von Alexandria, Justin und Irenäus* (Göttingen: Vandenhoeck & Ruprecht, 1915; Hildesheim and New York: G. Olms, 1975) 340.

70 "Words of the presbyter, what Andrew and . . . had said" and the use of $\pi\alpha\rho\grave{a}$ rather than $\dot{\alpha}\pi\grave{o}$ $\tau\hat{\omega}\nu$ $\pi\rho\epsilon\sigma\beta\upsilon\tau\acute{\epsilon}\rho\omega\nu$ [$\pi\alpha\rho\acute{a}$ indicates a more remote connec-

tion than does $\dot{\alpha}\pi\acute{o}$].

71 The miraculous fecundity of things in the millenial kingdom; the wretched death of Judas.

72 See above.

73 Cf. Introduction §2, "The Dismantling of Ancient Johannine Tradition by Modern Criticism."

74 *Orthodoxy and Heresy*, 207f.

John; this work is preserved for us in fifty fragments in the John commentary of his great opponent Origen. This early appropriation of the Gospel of John by Gnosticism precipitated the durable suspicion that the Gospel taught Gnosticism. Only when it was recognized that the Gospel could really be used against Gnosticism did it find its approbation in the "great" church in spite of its differences from the Synoptics. Since it had already been brought into connection with John by the Gnostics, the "great" church was able to build on this tradition.

The form of the beloved disciple was now brought under the cover of the form of the son of Zebedee, who had transmitted the genuine Jesus tradition in superior rivalry with Peter. Since the teaching of Peter apparently lives only in the reminiscences of Mark, it was easier for the Gospel of John to assert itself, although the "beloved disciple" appears only late in the Gospel and then infrequently.

2. The Dismantling of Ancient Johannine Tradition by Modern Criticism

Bibliography

Ballenstedt, Heinrich Christian
Philo und Johannes; oder, Neue philosophisch-kritische Untersuchung des Logos beym Johannes nach dem Philo, nebst einer Erklärung und Uebersetzung des ersten Briefes Johannes aus der geweiheiten Sprache der Hierophanten, 3 vols. (Braunschweig: F. B. Culemann, 1802); *oder, Fortgesetzte Anwendung des Philo zur Interpretation der Johanneischen Schriften; mit besonderer Hinsicht auf die Frage: ob Johannes der Verfasser der ihm zugeschriebenen Bücher seyn könne?* (Göttingen: H. Dieterich, 1812), esp. 2: 3–68.

Bauer, Bruno
Kritik der evangelischen Geschichte des Johannes (Bremen: C. Schünemann, 1840).

Bauer, Bruno
Kritik der evangelischen Geschichte der Synoptiker (Leipzig: O. Wigand, ²1846).

Bauer, Bruno
Kritik der paulinischen Briefe (Berlin: G. Hempel, 1852; Aalen: Scientia, 1972).

Bauer, Bruno
Christus und die Cäsaren. Der Ursprung des Christentums aus dem römischen Griechenthum (Berlin: E. Grosser, 1877; Hildesheim: G. Olms, 1968).

Baur, Ferdinand Christian
"Die johanneischen Briefe. Ein Beitrag zur Geschichte des Kanons." *Theologische Jahrbücher* 7 (Tübingen, 1848) 293–337.

Baur, Ferdinand Christian
Das manichäische Religionssystem nach den Quellen neu untersucht und entwickelt (Tübingen: C. F. Osiander, 1831; Hildesheim: G. Olms, 1973).

Baur, Ferdinand Christian
Die christliche Gnosis; oder, die christliche Religionsphilosophie in ihrer geschichtlichen Entwicklung (Tübingen: C. F. Osiander, 1835; Darmstadt: Wissenschaftliche Buchgesellschaft, 1967).

Baur, Ferdinand Christian
Kritische Untersuchungen über die kanonischen Evangelien, ihr Verhältnis zueinander, ihren Charakter und Ursprung (Tübingen: L. F. Fues, 1847).

Baur, Ferdinand Christian
"Das Verhältnis des ersten johanneischen Briefs zum johanneischen Evangelium." *Theologische Jahrbücher* 16 (Tübingen, 1857) 315–31.

Baur, Ferdinand Christian
"Das johanneische Evangelium und die Passafeier des zweiten Jahrhunderts." *Theologische Jahrbücher* 7 (Tübingen, 1848) 264–86.

Baur, Ferdinand Christian
"Kritische Studien über den Begriff der Gnosis." *TSK* 10 (1837) 511–79.

Baur, Ferdinand Christian
"Das Wesen des Montanismus nach den neuesten

Forschungen." *Theologische Jahrbücher* 10 (Tübingen, 1851) 538–94.

Baur, Ferdinand Christian
"Ueber die Composition und den Charakter des johanneischen Evangeliums." *Theologische Jahrbücher* 3 (Tübingen, 1844) 1–191, 397–475, 615–700.

Baur, Ferdinand Christian
"Zur johanneischen Frage: 1) Über Justin den Märtyrer gegen Luthardt; 2) Über den Passahstreit gegen Steitz." *Theologische Jahrbücher* 16 (Tübingen, 1857) 209–57.

Baur, Ferdinand Christian
"Die johanneische Frage und ihre neuesten Beantwortungen durch Luthardt, Delitzsch, Brückner, Hase." *Theologische Jahrbücher* 13 (Tübingen, 1854) 196–287.

Becker, Heinz
Die Reden des Johannesevangeliums und der Stil der gnostischen Offenbarungsreden, FRLANT, n.s., 50 (Göttingen: Vandenhoeck & Ruprecht, 1956).

Bleek, Friedrich
"Die Zeugnisse und Erscheinungen in der Kirche während des zweiten Jahrhunderts führen entschieden darauf, dass das Johannes-Evangelium schon wenigstens seit dem Anfange dieses Jahrhunderts in der Kirche bekannt und anerkannt war." In his *Beiträge zur Evangelien-Kritik* (Berlin: G. Reimer, 1846) 200–26.

Bousset, Wilhelm
"Ist das vierte Evangelium eine literarische Einheit?" *TRu* 12 (1909) 1–12, 39–64.

Bousset, Wilhelm
"Der Verfasser des Johannesevangeliums." *TRu* 8 (1905) 225–44, 277–95.

Bretschneider, Karl Gottlieb
Probabilia de Evangelii et Epistolarum Joannis Apostoli indole et origine eruditorum iudiciis modeste subiecit (Leipzig: J. A. Barth, 1820).

Bretschneider, Karl Gottlieb
"Einige Bemerkungen zu dem Aufsatze des Herrn D. Goldhorn (...) über das Schweigen des johanneischen Evangeliums von dem Seelenkampfe Jesu in Gethsemane." *Magazin für christliche Prediger* 2,2 (1824) 153–74.

Brown, Raymond E.
The Gospel according to John. Introduction, Translation, and Notes, 2 vols. Vol. 1, *i–xii*, AB 29 (Garden City: Doubleday, 1966); Vol. 2, *xiii–xxi*, AB 29A (Garden City: Doubleday, 1970).

Cludius, H. H.
Uransichten des Christenthums nebst Untersuchungen über einige Bücher des Neuen Testaments (Altona: Hammerich, 1808).

Evanson, Edward
The Dissonance of the Four Generally Received Evangelists, and the Evidence of their Respective Authenticity Examined (Ipswich: G. Jermym, 1792).

Haenchen, Ernst
"Das Johannesevangelium und sein Kommentar." *TLZ* 89 (1964) 881–98. Also in his *Die Bibel und Wir. Gesammelte Aufsätze* 2 (Tübingen: Mohr-Siebeck, 1968) 206–34.

Hirsch, Emanuel
"Stilkritik und Literaranalyse im vierten Evangelium." *ZNW* 43 (1950/1951) 129–43.

Hirsch, Emanuel
Geschichte der neueren evangelischen Theologie, 5 vols. (Gütersloh: C. Bertelsmann, 1949–1954).

Hirsch, Emanuel
Schleiermachers Christusglaube (Gütersloh: Gerd Mohn, 1968).

Hirsch, Emanuel
Das vierte Evangelium in seiner ursprünglichen Gestalt verdeutscht und erklärt (Tübingen: Mohr-Siebeck, 1936).

Hirsch, Emanuel
Studien zum vierten Evangelium (Tübingen: Mohr-Siebeck, 1936).

Horst, Georg Konrad
"Lässt sich die Echtheit des Johannes-Evangeliums aus hinlänglichen Gründen bezweifeln, und welches ist der wahrscheinliche Ursprung dieser Schrift?" *Museum für Religionswissenschaft in ihrem ganzen Umfange* 1 (1803) 47–118.

Horst, Georg Konrad
"Ueber einige anscheinende Widersprüche in dem Evangelium des Johannis, in Absicht auf den Logos, oder das Höhere in Christo." *Museum für Religionswissenschaft in ihrem ganzen Umfange* 1 (1803) 20–46.

Käsemann, Ernst
The Testament of Jesus: A Study of the Gospel of John in the Light of Chapter 17, tr. Gerhard Krodel (Philadelphia: Fortress Press, 1968) = *Jesu letzter Wille nach Johannes 17* (Tübingen: Mohr-Siebeck, 1966).

Käsemann, Ernst
"Aufbau und Anliegen des johanneischen Prologs." In *Libertas Christiana, Friedrich Delekat zum fünfundsechzigsten Geburtstag*, ed. W. Matthias and E. Wolf. BEvT 26 (Munich: Chr. Kaiser Verlag, 1967) 75–99. Also in Käsemann's *Exegetische Versuche und Besinnungen* (Göttingen: Vandenhoeck & Ruprecht, 1964) 2: 155–80.

Kümmel, Werner Georg
The New Testament: The History of the Investigation of its Problems, tr. S. McLean Gilmour and Howard C. Kee (Nashville: Abingdon Press, 1972) = *Das Neue Testament; Geschichte der Erforschung seiner Probleme* (Freiburg: K. Alber, 1958).

Loisy, Alfred
Le quatrième évangile (Paris: A. Picard & Fils, 1903, ²1921).

Oeder, G. L.
De scopo Evangelii S. Joannis Haeres Cerinthi et Ebionis oppositi adversum F. A. Sampe, liber unus. In quo et

Irenaeus atque Calovius contra iniquas criminationes defenduntur (Frankfurt: Schmidt, 1732).

Paulus, Heinrich Eberhard Gottlob
Review of *Probabilia . . .* , by Karl Gottlieb Bretschneider. *Heidelberger Jahrbücher der Literatur* 14 (1821) 112–42.

Paulus, Heinrich Eberhard Gottlob
Commentar über das Evangelium des Johannes. In his *Philologisch-kritischer und historischer Commentar über das Neue Testament, in welchem der Griechische Text . . .* (Lübeck: J. F. Bohn, 1804).

Rudolph, Kurt
Die Gnosis. Wesen und Geschichte einer spätantiken Religion (Göttingen: Vandenhoeck & Ruprecht, 1977).

Schleiermacher, Friedrich
Homilien über das Evangelium des Johannes in den Jahren 1823–1826 gesprochen. Aus wortgetreuen Nachschriften, ed. Ad. Sydow. In his *Sämmtliche Werke,* Zweite Abtheilung, Predigten, vols. 8–9 (Berlin: G. Reimer, 1837 and 1847).

Schleiermacher, Friedrich
Über die Religion. Reden an die Gebildeten unter ihren Verächtern (Berlin: G. Reimer, ³1821).

Schleiermacher, Friedrich
The Life of Jesus, tr. S. MacLean Gilmour. Ed. with an introduction by Jack C. Verheyden. Lives of Jesus Series (Philadelphia: Fortress Press, 1975) = *Das Leben Jesu. Vorlesungen an der Universität zu Berlin in Jahr 1832 gehalten,* ed. K. A. Rütenick (Berlin: G. Reimer, 1864).

Schleiermacher, Friedrich
Einleitung ins Neue Testament. Aus Schleiermacher's handschriftlichem Nachlasse und nachgeschriebenen Vorlesungen, mit einer Vorrede von Dr. Friedrich Lücke, ed. G. Wolde (Berlin: G. Reimer, 1845), esp. 314f., 340.

Schnackenburg, Rudolf
The Gospel according to St John, 3 vols. Vol. 1, *Introduction and Commentary on Chapters 1–4,* tr. Kevin Smyth (New York: Seabury Press, 1980) = *Das Johannesevangelium,* part 1, HTKNT 4,1 (Freiburg: Herder, 1965); Vol. 2, *Commentary on Chapters 5–12,* tr. Cecily Hastings, Francis McDonough, David Smith, and Richard Foley (New York: Seabury Press, 1980) = *Das Johannesevangelium,* part 2, HTKNT 4,2 (Freiburg: Herder, 1971); Vol. 3, *Commentary on Chapters 13–21,* tr. David Smith and G. A. Kon (New York: Crossroad, 1982) = *Das Johannesevangelium,* part 3, HTKNT 4,3 (Freiburg: Herder, 1975).

Schulze, W. A.
"Das Johannesevangelium im deutschen Idealismus." *Zeitschrift für philosophische Forschung* 18 (1964) 85–118.

Schwartz, Eduard
"Aporien im vierten Evangelium." NGG (1907) 1: 342–72; (1908) 2: 115–48, 3: 149–88, 4: 497–560.

Schweitzer, Albert
The Quest of the Historical Jesus: A Critical Study of its Progress from Reimarus to Wrede, tr. W. Montgomery (New York: Macmillan, 1961) = *Geschichte der Leben-Jesu-Forschung* (Tübingen: Mohr-Siebeck, 1906, ⁶1951).

Schweizer, Eduard
Ego Eimi. Die religionsgeschichtliche Herkunft und theologische Bedeutung der johanneischen Bildreden, zugleich ein Beitrag zur Quellenfrage des vierten Evangeliums, FRLANT, n.s., 38 (Göttingen: Vandenhoeck & Ruprecht, ²1965).

Smend, Rudolf
Wilhelm Martin Leberecht de Wettes Arbeit am Alten und am Neuen Testament (Basel: Helbing & Lichtenhahn, 1958).

Spitta, Friedrich
"Julius Wellhausen in seiner Bedeutung für die Evangelienkritik und Geschichte Jesu." In *Archiv der Strassburger Pastoralkonferenz* (Strassburg, 1907) 293–317.

Spitta, Friedrich
"Unordnungen im Texte des vierten Evangeliums." In his *Zur Geschichte und Literatur des Urchristentums* (Göttingen: Vandenhoeck & Ruprecht, 1893) 1: 155–204.

Spitta, Friedrich
"Das Verhältnis von Joh. 6 zum Passah." In his *Zur Geschichte und Literatur des Urchristentums* (Göttingen: Vandenhoeck & Ruprecht, 1893) 1: 216–21.

Spitta, Friedrich
"Johanneische Parallelen." In his *Zur Geschichte und Literatur des Urchristentums* (Göttingen: Vandenhoeck & Ruprecht, 1907) 3, 2: 98–108.

Spitta, Friedrich
Streitfragen der Geschichte Jesu (Göttingen: Vandenhoeck & Ruprecht, 1907), esp. 194ff.

Spitta, Friedrich
Jesus und die Heidenmission (Giessen: A. Töpelmann, 1909) 87ff.

Spitta, Friedrich
Das Johannes-Evangelium als Quelle der Geschichte Jesu (Göttingen: Vandenhoeck & Ruprecht, 1910).

Strauss, David Friedrich
The Life of Jesus Critically Examined, ed. with an introduction by Peter C. Hodgson; tr. George Eliot (Philadelphia: Fortress Press, 1972) = *Das Leben Jesu, kritisch bearbeitet* (Tübingen: C. F. Osiander, 1835 and 1836).

Vogel, Erhard Friedrich
Der Evangelist Johannes und seine Ausleger vor dem jüngsten Gericht (Hof: Grau, 1801).

Weiße, Christian Hermann
Die evangelische Geschichte, kritisch und philosophisch bearbeitet, 2 vols. (Leipzig: Breitkopf & Härtel, 1838).

Weizsäcker, Karl Heinrich von
Das apostolische Zeitalter der christlichen Kirche

(Tübingen: Mohr-Siebeck, ³1902).

Wellhausen, Julius
Das Evangelium Johannis (Berlin: G. Reimer, 1908).

Wellhausen, Julius
Erweiterungen und Änderungen im vierten Evangelium (Berlin: G. Reimer, 1907).

Wendt, Hans Heinrich
Die Johannesbriefe und das johanneische Christentum (Halle: Buchhandlung des Waisenhauses, 1925).

Wendt, Hans Heinrich
Das Johannesevangelium. Eine Untersuchung seiner Entstehung und seines geschichtlichen Wertes (Göttingen: Vandenhoeck & Ruprecht, 1900).

Wendt, Hans Heinrich
Die Schichten im vierten Evangelium (Göttingen: Vandenhoeck & Ruprecht, 1911).

Wendt, Hans Heinrich
Die Lehre Jesu, 2 vols. Vol. 1, *Die evangelischen Quellenberichte über die Lehre Jesu;* Vol. 2, *Der Inhalt der Lehre Jesu* (Göttingen: Vandenhoeck & Ruprecht, 1886–1890).

Wette, Wilhelm Martin Leberecht de
Kurze Erklärung des Evangeliums und der Briefe Johannis, Kurzgefasstes exegetisches Handbuch zum Neuen Testament 1, 3 (Leipzig: Weidmann, ⁴1852), esp. 1: 215–342.

Wette, Wilhelm Martin Leberecht de
"Bemerkungen zu Stellen des Evangeliums Johannis." *TSK* 7 (1834) 924–44.

Wette, Wilhelm Martin Leberecht de
Biblische Dogmatik Alten und Neuen Testamentes; oder, Kritische Darstellung der Religionslehre des Hebraismus, des Judenthums und Urchristenthums (Berlin: Realschulbuchhandlung, 1813).

Wette, Wilhelm Martin Leberecht de
Lehrbuch der historisch-kritischen Einleitung in die kanonischen Bücher des Neuen Testaments (Berlin: G. Reimer, ²1830).

Wilke, Christian Gottlieb
Der Urevangelist; oder, Exegetisch-kritische Untersuchung über das Verwandtschaftsverhältniss der drei ersten Evangelien (Dresden and Leipzig: G. Fleischer, 1838).

Windisch, Hans
"Der johanneische Erzählungsstil." In ΕΥΧΑΡΙΣΤΗΡΙΟΝ. *Studien zur Religion und Literatur des Alten und Neuen Testaments Hermann Gunkel zum 60. Geburtstag, dem 23 Mai 1922, dargebracht von seinen Schülern und Freunden,* ed. Hans Schmidt. FRLANT, n.s. 19 (Göttingen: Vandenhoeck & Ruprecht, 1923) 174–213.

About 180 CE Christendom appeared to be of one mind regarding the Gospel of John. John the son of Zebedee and beloved disciple of Jesus had written it. It was accordingly taken into the circle of canonical gospels. Clement of Alexandria formulated the matter thus: The three synoptic gospels wrote τὰ σωματικά (literally, "bodily," but often translated "the outward facts"); the fourth Evangelist, however, composed the εὐαγγέλιον πνευματικόν ("spiritual gospel").[1] One could then interpret the Gospel of John as a supplement to the Synoptics. But if one took the relative values into account, the Gospel of John had the advantage, since "spiritual" is certainly worth more than "the bodily."

The "Spiritual Gospel," however, concealed an explosion within itself. In the middle of the second century, the Montanist movement arose, first of all in Phrygia. Montanus represented himself as the paraclete promised in the Gospel of John,[2] the "spirit of truth," and proclaimed the imminence of the end of the world. The new Jerusalem would descend on the Phrygian villages Pepuza and Tymion. Connected with the expectation was not only ecstasy, the "new prophecy," but also a severe ethic: one must not flee from persecution; mortal sin is not forgiven; second marriages are not permitted; fasting is intensified. Although the Gospel of John does not propose such an ethic, it fell into discredit because of its references to the paraclete. And the movement continued to spread. In 207 the highly respected rhetorician Tertullian joined the Montanist movement. It gained a footing even in Gaul and also penetrated into Rome.

In *Adv. haer.* 3.11.9, Irenaeus fought a group[3] that went so far in their antithesis to Montanism (and Gnosticism) that they rejected the Gospel of John and the Apocalypse as works of the heretic Cerinthus.[4] Epiphanius gave these people a name of opprobrium, Ἄλογοι ("without reason, without the logos"). The Roman bishop Gaius, whose orthodoxy is beyond dispute, also rejects the Fourth Gospel and the Apocalypse as gnostic-Mon-

---

1 So Eusebius, *H.E.* 6.14.7.
2 14:16f., 26, 15:26, 16:7–11.
3 See Introduction §2, "The Dismantling of Ancient Johannine Tradition by Modern Criticism."
4 Cf. Schwartz, "Johannes und Kerinthos," in his *Zum Neuen Testament und zum frühen Christentum. Mit einem Gesamtregister zum Band I–V*, Gesammelte Schriften 5 (Berlin: Walter de Gruyter, 1963) 170–82.

tanist writings, as Eusebius reports.[5] Perhaps the story, related by Irenaeus also belongs in this context:

> There are also those who heard from him [Polycarp] that John, the disciple of the Lord, going to bathe at Ephesus, and perceiving Cerinthus within, rushed out of the bath-house without bathing, exclaiming, "Let us fly, lest even the bath-house fall down, because Cerinthus, the enemy of truth, is within."[6]

This story is intended to show that John regarded Cerinthus as a heretic. Therefore Cerinthus could not have been the author of the Gospel of John.

Deism

How dangerous the contrast between the synoptic gospels and the Gospel of John could become was made evident when English Deism also gained a following in Germany.[7] Pastors whose writings appeared between 1801 and 1808[8] were not driven by youthful enthusiasms, but were men of fifty or so, who, along with others, could and would no longer remain silent about the inconsistencies they came across in a closing reading of the Gospels. But these first efforts did not precipitate spiritual tremors; they remained relatively unnoticed.

Surprisingly, quite a different destiny befell another book that wanted above all else to avoid sensationalism. Its author, general superintendent K. G. Bretschneider, published his work in Latin in order to make it accessible only to the erudite. What he wrote, moreover, he wanted understood only as a possibility: *Probabilia de evangelii et epistolarum Johannis apostoli indole et origine eruditorum iudiciis modeste subiecit* ("Probable conclusions about the type and origin of the Gospel and Epistles of the Apostle John, modestly submitted to the judgment of the scholarly world"). This book, intended for the professional world, nevertheless contained sentences like this: "It is not possible that both the Jesus of the first three Gospels and the Jesus of the Fourth Gospel are historically true at the same time, since the greatest differences obtain between them not only in the mode of speech, but also in

the way evidence is adduced and in the kind of activity; it is also not possible that the first three Evangelists invented Jesus' teaching, morals, and way of teaching; the author of the Fourth Gospel could quite possibly have concocted his Jesus."[9]

It is to be observed that in this book the synoptic "external facts" ($\sigma\omega\mu\alpha\tau\iota\kappa\acute{\alpha}$) are positively evaluated. Beyond that, the conjecture is expressed that the author could have created the Fourth Gospel out of whole cloth. That amounted to an attack on the canon and the absolute truth of the Holy Spirit.

That attack awakened a storm of protest which the unassuming author had not anticipated. Eighteen counterattacks, essays, and reviews directed against him appeared in rapid succession. After four years Bretschneider gave up and retracted his theses.

F. Schleiermacher

The esteemed F. Schleiermacher was also numbered among his opponents.[10] That was only logical, for he had based his christology entirely on the Gospel of John. He was after a Jesus who was not so divine that nothing remained of his humanity ("docetism"), and not so human that the divine disappeared and a "mere man" remained ("Ebionitism" is what Schleiermacher called this extreme). The Gospel of John seemed to him to present such a Jesus, divine and human at the same time. How far he went in this matter is shown by his treatment of the resurrection. He made use of ideas that appeared in the novel-like life of Jesus by K. H. Venturini,[11] and which later, at the hands of the controversial rationalist, H. E. G. Paulus, provided a model for Schleiermacher.[12] When the disciples took Jesus down from the cross, they detected a spark of life in Him. He was carefully nursed back to life.[13] He recovered enough to be able to undertake further journeys (Emmaus; Galilee in John 21). During these forty days he was able to come together in a "second life" with his followers and tell them what had remained hidden during his "first life." Then he took

---

5 *H. E.* 3.28.2.
6 *Adv. haer.* 3.3.4; ANF 1: 416.
7 Cf. Kümmel, *NT History and Investigation*, and Hirsch, *Geschichte der neueren evangelischen Theologie*, 1: 292–360.
8 Vogel, Horst, and Cludius, among others.
9 *Probabilia de evangelii et epistolarum Johannis apostoli indole et origine eruditorum iudiciis modest subiecit* (Leipzig: J. A. Barth, 1820) vii.
10 Cf. Hirsch, *Geschichte der neueren evangelischen Theologie*, 5: 281–364.
11 Cf. Schweitzer, *The Quest of the Historical Jesus*, 46f. [39].
12 Cf. Schweitzer, *The Quest of the Historical Jesus*, 64 [55].
13 Cf. Josephus, *Life*, 420.

farewell of them in order to die in peace. . . .[14]

Schleiermacher attempted to show, in his doctrine of the "second life of Jesus," that the human Jesus had established the church. He may well have wanted to preclude the possibility of the earthly Jesus falling back into Judaism and the exalted Christ becoming a spirit without flesh and blood[15] or a mere "idea." Schleiermacher's friends remained strangers to all this. They published his lectures on the life of Jesus given in 1832 only in 1864, and then D. F. Strauss provided a worthy and impressive obituary for this lecture series.[16]

D. F. Strauss

This brings up the name of another highly influential theologian of the period. D. F. Strauss received his theological and philosophical training in the Tübingen *Stift* (theological seminary). On a study trip to Berlin in 1831 he became acquainted with Schleiermacher but did not esteem him. Having returned to his post as tutor in Tübingen, he first of all planned to write a "history of the ideas of primitive Christianity as norm for Christian dogma."[17] Fresh from Schleiermacher's lectures on the life of Jesus, a transcript of which he brought back with him from Berlin, he sketched out a preparatory work, a "life of Jesus, critically examined." The two volumes appeared in 1835. In accordance with the Hegelian theme of thesis, antithesis, and synthesis, he set forth supernaturalism as the thesis, out of which rationalism arose as the antithesis. Strauss proposed to develop the "mythical" interpretation as the synthesis (by myth he meant the representation of the idea as an object). Supernaturalism took all miracles on faith, even when human reason resisted strongly. Rationalism explained the miracles away "rationally" at any price. The new, mythical interpretation ought then to solve and reconcile the

two in a higher unity. But in essence it remained an acute, ironic playing off of one gospel against another. Strauss found all four Gospels saturated with "myth," but the fourth, the latest, was saturated to the greatest extent. He hoped to expose everything that was offensive to him as historical dress for primitive Christian ideas—dress that formed an unintentional, poetic saga. Thus, Jesus became a mere man for him: the idea is not wont to lavish all its fullness on one gospel.[18] Christology became anthropology: humanity is the union of the two natures, the true God-man, who is on his way to the realization of the idea.[19] "By faith in this Christ, . . . man is justified before God . . . by the kindling within him of the idea of humanity, the individual man participates in the divinely human life of the species. . . ." "This alone is the absolute sense of Christology."

For Strauss the historical in the gospels was merely the husk of the idea. So he failed to show how the gospels were related to each other in a literary sense and how their historical sequence and development was to be understood. Everything concrete and historical became an idea, with which the church did not know what to do. The Gospel of John suffered the most from this point of view because it was transformed from a cornerstone of faith into a historical picture book delineated in the manner of Hegel.

W. M. L. de Wette

W. M. L. de Wette did not participate in the chase aimed at Strauss. In 1800–1819 he worked in Berlin together with Schleiermacher. In 1809 in a review of a book written by Cludius, he stated with approval that Cludius appeared "not to have that ludicrous preference for the Gospel of John, which prompts many to elevate it above everything in the NT." He espoused the authenticity of

---

14 Cf. Hirsch, *Schleiermachers Christusglaube* (Gütersloh: Gerd Mohn, 1968) 53–79.

15 Cf. Luke 24:39ff.

16 As Schweitzer, *Quest of the Historical Jesus,* 62 [63], says.

17 Inspired by W. Vatke, *Die biblische Theologie,* vol. 1 (Berlin: Bethge, 1835).

18 *The Life of Jesus Critically Examined,* ed. with an introduction by Peter C. Hodgson; tr. George Eliot (Philadelphia: Fortress Press, 1972) 779f. = *Das Leben Jesu, kritisch bearbeitet* (Tübingen: C. F. Osiander, 1835) 2: 739.

19 *The Life of Jesus Critically Examined,* ed. with an introduction by Peter C. Hodgson; tr. George Eliot (Philadelphia: Fortress Press, 1972) 780 = *Das Leben Jesu, kritisch bearbeitet* (Tübingen: C. F. Osiander, 1835) 2: 740.

the Fourth Gospel in 1811, but discovered traces of a reworking—the Lazarus story does not hang together properly. In 1817 he allowed that "the acceptance of the authenticity of this Gospel was not beyond doubt"; yet he assessed the graphic character of the narrative and the purity of the teaching as favorable to authenticity. Later he put the identification of the author of the Gospel with that of 1 John—the authenticity of which appeared certain—into the balance. De Wette's conception of the relationship of the Gospel of John to the Synoptics was formulated this way by Smend:[20] "the Gospel of John presupposes Matthew among the Synoptics, but as the work of an apostle it generally also takes precedence historically and theologically over Matthew." That obviously means that de Wette never reached a firm conclusion on the matter.

F. C. Baur

Those components of a history of the Gospels left unused by Strauss were taken up by his teacher F. C. Baur and expanded into a huge history of Christian dogma.[21] His important early works, *Das manichäische Religionssystem nach den Quellen neu untersucht und entwickelt*[22] and *Die christliche Gnosis oder die christliche Religionsphilosophie in ihrer geschichtlichen Entwicklung*[23] anticipate perspectives that bore fruit only at the hands of Bultmann. His later writings bear more on our theme: *Kritische Untersuchungen über die kanonischen Evangelien, ihr Verhältnis zueinander, ihren Charakter und Ursprung*.[24] The first volume, written in 1844 but improved and expanded, contains the investigation of the Gospel of John. What Baur demands is this: the position of every NT writing within the history of primitive Christianity is to be determined, and every fact contained in that writing is to be assessed in relation to the historical position of that writing. The Johannine question opens up the criticism of the NT gospels for Baur. The Fourth Gospel is not in the same category with the Synoptics. Its author, making free use of tradition upon occasion, sketches the picture of the coming of the Logos, of the one sent by God, who by his appearance confronts everyone he meets with the decision for or against God. He hardens the hearts of the "Jews," so that they act like fanatics and cause him to suffer and die. He frees the disciples from bondage to the world. John and the Synoptics cannot be reconciled. The Synoptics are ignorant of the Johannine outline of the ministry and the message of the Fourth Gospel. All of their differences from the Fourth Gospel arise from this. John no longer contains historical reminiscences. It is therefore impossible to turn its delineation of the historical Jesus into a historical Jesus that is humanly comprehensible and realistic: "It reflects a post-Pauline form of Christian reflection, which fits best into the time when the community was basically severed from Judaism and on its way to the church catholic."[25]

One has to agree with Hirsch: Baur has overstated certain Johannine features. The author of the Gospel of John is neither a poet who creates freely, nor is the entire Gospel written by one and the same hand. Baur dated it much too late (he was unable to anticipate $\mathfrak{P}^{52}$). To this extent Baur did not resolve the Johannine question. Yet he pointed the way to the future, from which his successors deviated to their regret.

Bruno Bauer

Bruno Bauer, who was born only a year later than F. C. Baur, wanted originally to clarify the relationship of John to the Synoptics. But this undertaking led him to ever greater projected works, which remain magnificent ruins. When he habilitated in Berlin in 1834—in those

---

20 *Wilhelm Martin Leberecht de Wettes Arbeit am Alten und am Neuen Testament* (Basel: Helbing & Lichtenhahn, 1958) 156.

21 Cf. Hirsch, *Geschichte der neueren evangelischen Theologie*, 5: 518–53.

22 [The Sources and Development of the Manichean Religion] (Tübingen: C. F. Osiander, 1831; Hildesheim: G. Olms, 1973).

23 [Christian Gnosis or the Christian Philosophy of Religion: Its Historical Development] (Tübingen: C. F. Osiander, 1835; Darmstadt: Wissenschaftliche Buchgesellschaft, 1967).

24 [Criticial Investigations of the Canonical Gospels, Their Relationship to Each Other, Their Character and Origin] (Tübingen: L. F. Fues, 1847).

25 Hirsch, *Geschichte der neueren evangelischen Theologie*, 5: 543.

days he belonged to the Hegelian "Right" and enjoyed the favor of the Minister Altenstein—he was still a defender (1835/1836) of the miracles of Jesus and the divine truth that had become man in Jesus against Strauss. He moved to Bonn in 1840, after which his *Kritik der evangelischen Geschichte des Johannes* appeared. This work marks the beginning of his attempt to understand and resolve the problem of the life of Jesus, not as a historical but as a literary problem. The Fourth Gospel turns out to be unhistorical in the 435 pages of this volume. History was developed out of an idea on the basis of speculation. In its place, Bauer gives the reader the knowledge that the fourth evangelist was an artist. Windisch has renewed this theme in his essay on the Johannine narrative style. But Bauer had already discovered that alongside very successful strands in the Gospel of John at the same time there were artistic miscues.[26] The discourses are full of tautologies. The parable of the good shepherd in John 10 is "a parable that as such is too greatly extended, unclearly expressed, and finally the reflection that forms the whole occasionally passes through quite baldly."[27] Bauer does not inquire whether this interweaving of aesthetically outstanding narratives with discourses that miscarry artistically originated with various sources, the editing, or both. He took the Gospel of John as a whole and saw in the author a thinker who was unable to transpose an idea into history cleanly. When Bauer was denied the *Venia legendi,* by the new Kultusminister Eichhorn, there began a second creative period. He began to investigate the Synoptics, which he assumed were historical writings compared with the Fourth Gospel. Persuaded by Weisse and Wilke that Mark was the first Gospel and that Mark was used by Matthew and Luke, he posed the question whether the oldest witness was not also the literary product of an author, like the Gospel of John. Did not Mark create historical tradition out of general ideas, tradition in which those ideas were to be clothed from now on? Mark was still conscious of the fact that the Jewish people

in the time of Jesus did not entertain a general messianic expectation. The messianic dogma arose for the first time in the Christian community. Jesus of course existed and had reconciled in himself, that is, in his self-consciousness, the contrast between God and man. But he did not appear with the message, "I am he upon whom you wait." Only when he had sacrificed his person to his historical destiny and to the idea for which he lived, and only when he had arisen into the faith of the primitive community as the son of God, did the first christology arise. Bauer still believed in the great personality of Jesus as a historical entity. But he did not rest with that. If there were a historical Jesus who united the divided entities, God and man, in his own self-consciousness, he did not once again separate the two: "I am from above; you are from below." The historical Christ, the man whom faith had exalted to heaven, is no longer a true man, but a man estranged from himself. He has outlived the ancient world and has become the annihilator of the world. On its ruins there remains only the absolute self-conscious, the empty I. This self-alienation of the I must be overcome and is overcome in the knowledge that we are all indebted to the Christian conception for what we know of the historical Jesus. There never was a historical Jesus, as Bauer finally asserts in his work of 1850, *Kritik der paulinischen Briefe*.[28] Yet every religion longs for a founder who redeems that religion. The work of Bauer's old age, *Christus und die Cäsaren*,[29] elevates the philosopher Seneca to the status of the real creator of Christianity, with help from Philo and Josephus. And this, of all things, in an abstruse work with lofty aspirations that became, as Barnikol puts it,[30] "the authoritative book of marxist socialism and communism in a peculiar way through his new friends Marx and Engels," and this in spite of the fact that the aged Bauer with all his radical criticism was a contributor to the newspaper *Kreuzzeitung* and was regarded as a political conservative (in spite of his newly acquired antisemitism).

---

26   *Kritik der evangelischen Geschichte des Johannes* (Bremen: C. Schünemann, 1940) 396–414.

27   *Kritik der evangelischen Geschichte des Johannes* (Bremen: C. Schünemann, 1940) 407.

28   (Berlin: G. Hempel, 1850; Aalen: Scientia, 1972).

29   *Christus und die Cäsaren. Der Ursprung des Christentums aus dem römischen Griechentum* (Berlin: E. Grosser, 1877; Hildesheim: G. Olms, 1968).

30   *RGG*[3] 1: 923.

J. Wellhausen

The next great names that we cannot pass over are those of Wellhausen and Schwartz. They became friends as a consequence of their work on the Gospel of John and together developed a new trend in Johannine studies.

In the introduction to his commentary,[31] Wellhausen gives an account of his methodology and the bases for employing it: "My aim is to correct the regnant exegesis. One does not have the proper distance on the text; one does not approach the text as though one were reading it for the first time; one tunes in anew to old questions. One . . . does not pay sufficient attention to the details in relation to the thread of the discourse; one is not surprised enough at knots and tears in the text. And if one notices problems in the context at all, the apologetes make them disappear by discussing them to death." So much for a sampling of Wellhausen's bitter critique of NT exegesis as he found it. We may now note his suggestion of a new method: "As a point of departure, one must take specific difficulties, insofar as they have been discovered by exegetical work, both those that appear in the didactic sections and those that appear in the historical parts."[32] Wellhausen continues: "A limited textual criticism must be replaced by a comprehensive literary criticism. The task . . . is to distinguish two or more literary layers."[33] Wellhausen provides the reader with examples of his research method: "In my small book,[34] I take as my point of departure the fact that 14:31 is immediately continued in 18:1 and the discourses coming between are out of place. Of even more importance . . . are the two isolated verses 7:3 and 4, according to which Jesus has been at work only in Galilee up to this point; these verses negate the journeys to Jerusalem to observe the feasts and the chronology that depends on those journeys."[35] Finally, Wellhausen notes the characteristic of the Gospel of John that deserves reproach: "The narratives exhibit insertions, swarm with variants, and not infrequently shatter the frame of reference, so that one does not know where one is in the story. How-

ever, individual segments rise from the formless and monotone confusion like stepping stones that represent a continuing line of development, yet that are not unbroken. They stand out from the whole and yet form a kind of backbone for it, so that they could be called the foundational text. The whole is thus . . . a product of a literary process that went through several stages. The foundational text constitutes only the beginning; its scope was greatly extended by infusions of material. The foundational text cannot therefore be called the Gospel of John proper; the former is only an ingredient of the latter. It was by no means preserved intact and complete. One cannot with certainty separate it from the various layers of editorial material. Nevertheless, an attempt must be made to do so at all costs."[36]

Wellhausen's perceptive criticism is hard on the secondary literature of his time. He confesses, of course, that he himself did not achieve his goal. For that reason, one must not pass over in disgust the difficulties and contradictions he perceived. But one may ask oneself whether Wellhausen's failures are not to be attributed to the presuppositions that lay at the base of his work, presuppositions that are understandable for his time. The notion of a foundational text with layers added on top is no longer acceptable, in any case, if one thinks of the "foundational text" as especially valuable historically, and the "layers" on top as theologically inferior. Wellhausen developed his conceptualities and his methodology in his work on the OT. He was an especially distinguished OT scholar and orientalist before he turned to the NT.

E. Schwartz

Schwartz (1858–1940) was a classical philologian and church historian of the highest rank. New Testament problems, especially those he discovered for himself, excited him, but they remained an avocation. His most important contribution to the study of the Gospel of John lies in his "Aporien im vierten Evangelium," which he published in the *Nachrichten der Königlichen Gesellschaft*

---

31 *Das Evangelium Johannes,* 3.
32 *Das Evangelium Johannes,* 4.
33 *Das Evangelium Johannes,* 5.
34 *Erweiterungen und Änderungen im vierten Evangelium* (Berlin: G. Reimer, 1907).
35 *Das Evangelium Johannes,* 5.
36 *Das Evangelium Johannes,* 5.

der Wissenschaften zu Göttingen in 1907 and 1908. Whoever decides to work through these essays closely will want to prepare an index to them, which indicates where the author discusses each verse of the Gospel of John.[37] The essays were not constructed with compelling logic and perspicacity.

In his first essay Schwartz gives the provisional result: "There is only one principal explanation for such confusion: various layers of the narrative interweave and overlay each other."[38] To what extent Schwartz despaired of unraveling these layers, at least temporally, is demonstrated by the complaint in his discussion of chapter 7: ". . . it is not possible to discover the motifs which connect one scene with another; one cannot infer one scene from another. That makes the reconstruction of the oldest form of the Gospel impossible, and one is tempted to lay down one's critical knife dejected and exhausted and leave these segments in the disarray and disorder into which they have fallen as a result of being reworked. But the task of interpreting the text scientifically remains, although these fragments . . . cannot be reassembled."[39]

Wellhausen had been satisfied to make his observations in the form of a short commentary on the individual chapters. Schwartz requires the reader who is interested in his work to look for the specific aporias and to consider their context. At all events, one cannot accuse him of "discussing the problems to death," like most of the commentators of his time. According to Schwartz, at least two editors have made it their aim "to work the synoptic tradition into the Gospel of John."[40] "It is difficult, if not impossible, to give one opinion about the Gospel as a whole."[41] "One effect above all outweighs the other: the carelessness with which the received material was formed, the incredible audacity of the inventiveness that leaves nothing untouched . . . This is not the further expansion of tradition, . . . a highly individualistic poet of the highest conceptive power is here asserting himself; he is presuming to intone an entirely new hymn to the

virtues (ἀρεταί) of his God. . . . He must have written in a time that already lay at some distance from the beginning and yet at a time early enough that he could dare to shunt the synoptic tradition aside, and transform the divinity of Jesus into a poetry of his own, free from dogmatic constraints."[42] "Only in the last stage of the revision of the Gospel was an apostolic origin attributed to it; that presupposes the time in which the attempt was made to interpret apostolic and canonical as identical terms."[43]

F. Spitta and H. H. Wendt

The critical storm subsided with Wellhausen and Schwartz. That this is so is betrayed already by Spitta's book of 1910, *Das Johannes-Evangelium als Quelle der Geschichte Jesu*: "With profound gratitude for the great service Wellhausen and Schwartz have rendered Johannine scholarship,"[44] Spitta still prefers Zahn to Holtzmann: "The person of Jesus exhibits traits here of a purely human sort, which are of overwhelming power and which are in accord precisely with the image that the simple, undogmatic Christian carries in his heart of Jesus."[45] The foundational text stems from the son of Zebedee. An editor has expanded that text by taking over additional materials and reflections of his own. Furthermore, H. H. Wendt only appears to agree with Wellhausen and Schwartz, in spite of the title of his book published in 1911, *Die Schichten im vierten Evangelium*: The discourse layer has priority over the narrative layer.[46] The author of the discourse layer stood very close to the historical Jesus, was even intimate with him. The son of Zebedee "is the author of the literary foundation of this Gospel in all probability."[47]

A. Loisy

The second edition of Alfred Loisy's work on the Fourth Gospel appeared in 1921.[48] It was an improved edition of the work of 1903, which had long been out of print. In the later work, the Fourth Gospel is represented as the centerpiece of the Johannine corpus. For that reason,

---

37 [Haenchen himself prepared such an index. A copy was made available to the translator by James Robinson.—Translator.]
38 "Aporien," 1: 355ff.
39 "Aporien," 4: 497.
40 "Aporien," 4: 559.
41 "Aporien," 4: 557.
42 "Aporien," 4: 558.

43 "Aporien," 4: 559.
44 (Göttingen: Vandenhoeck & Ruprecht, 1910) V.
45 *Das Johannes-Evangelium als Quelle der Geschichte Jesu* (Göttingen: Vandenhoeck & Ruprecht, 1910) VIII.
46 (Göttingen: Vandenhoeck & Ruprecht, 1911) 51.
47 *Die Schichten im vierten Evangelium* (Göttingen: Vandenhoeck & Ruprecht, 1911) 106.
48 *Le quatrième évangile* (Paris: A. Picard & Fils, 1903,

the commentary on 1, 2, and 3 John are included in the 602 pages of the work. The commentary on the Apocalypse he reserved for a second volume.

The discussion of the ecclesiastical tradition about the Gospel of John down to the time of Jerome[49] is followed by a presentation of critical scholarship,[50] which contains a detailed discussion of the secondary literature down to 1920. In the second division, devoted to the Fourth Gospel, the learned author treats the content of the Gospel,[51] followed by its composition,[52] and then by its character,[53] and finally by a discussion of its origin.[54] The commentary on the Gospel of John itself[55] follows upon an introduction to the Johannine epistles.[56]

Loisy indicates the context in which he views the author of the Johannine literature.[57] He was a converted pagan, who had been nourished on a pure strain of Gnosticism; he had perhaps travelled through Palestine, but belonged to the Ephesian congregation, which regarded him highly as a mythical prophet. Although he does not come into prominence as such, he was more of a master of Gnosticism than an apostle of faith. His influence on the circles that understood him was profound. A subsequent generation perhaps suspected that he was leader of a sect and a heretic. Loisy of course went still further. The suspicion arose in the second century that Cerinthus and not John was the author of the Fourth Gospel. At all events, in order to make it acceptable ecclesiastically, it had to be reworked in the spirit of "conventional Christianity" in the second century; this reworking was carried out, in all probability, by more than one hand. The leaders of the Ephesian church did everything that was necessary to see to it that "their" John was honored as an apostolic figure, and even as the beloved disciple of Jesus, and that the improved work was taken up into the canon.

It is curious to what extent Loisy anticipated subsequent scholarship. He regarded the author of the original Gospel as a poet, who treated his material freely; as a non-Jew, who had perhaps come from Antioch and had made a journey through Palestine. In all these points he concurs with Hirsch, who had arrived at comparable conclusions independently. The close connection with hellenistic mysticism is reminiscent of Dodd. His characterization of John as heretic and witness is like a premonition of Käsemann's inaugural address at Göttingen in 1951. The comparison with Valentinus and Marcion surprises the reader, but both of them regarded themselves as good Christians. That applies also to other men who were regarded as heretics in the eyes of the church. To cite an example, a Donatist bishop signed a transcript of a debate with Augustine as *Felix Christianus*.

E. Hirsch

Hirsch saw the author of the original Fourth Gospel as an (anonymous) genius by virtue of God's grace, who gave individual character even to secondary persons by means of brief dialogue and short scenes; this is something that only a dramatic poet of rank succeeds in doing.[58] He was no Semite; some things remind us of Greek tragedy.[59] His language is a willful Greek and not an imitation of the LXX. He wrote in an environment that also spoke Aramaic, in Syrian Antioch.[60] He undertook a journey to Palestine and Jerusalem between 70 and 132 CE as a merchant. What he says about the pool of Siloam in chapter 5 is to be believed,[61] but he did not see the temple, which had been destroyed. He probably came to his mature years only after 70 CE and had no clear recollections of the apostolic times.[62] He wrote the Gospel around 100 CE, and in it he of course made use of the Synoptics.[63] The "ecclesiastical redaction" of the

²1921).

49 *Le quatrième évangile*, 6–18.
50 *Le quatrième évangile*, 18–39.
51 *Le quatrième évangile*, 40–46.
52 *Le quatrième évangile*, 46–55.
53 *Le quatrième évangile*, 55–65.
54 *Le quatrième évangile*, 65–71.
55 *Le quatrième évangile*, 87–529.
56 *Le quatrième évangile*, Division 3; 71–85.
57 *Le quatrième évangile*, 66–68.
58 *Das vierte Evangelium*, 67.
59 *Das vierte Evangelium*, 68, 90.

60 *Das vierte Evangelium*, 71.
61 *Das vierte Evangelium*, 72.
62 *Das vierte Evangelium*, 75.
63 Matthew/Luke: *Das vierte Evangelium*, 301; Mark: 170f.

Gospel took place between 130 and 140 CE.[64] The author also freely shaped the words of Jesus. By and large his Gospel is a free poetic interpretation of history through the eyes of a Christian who believes in Jesus. He wrote down what each character being discribed "had to say" at that time. He has completely blurred the distinction between truth and reality.[65] The Gospel of John is therefore not the account of an eye witness.[66]

His Gospel "is really Pauline."[67] The author alone among those "in the Gentile church . . . understood the Pauline assertion that 'Christ is the end of the law'" (Rom 10:4). The historical contrast between Jesus and law, between Christianity and Judaism, rests on "a primary proposition":[68] Jesus is the obedient son of the Father, who "lives out of his unity with the Father."[69] However, in that case, what is psychologically credible in Jesus has disappeared. Jesus is not the "troubled son" (Gethsemane). The figure of Jesus thus acquires "dreamlike, mythical features."[70] The author is thus on his way to the Christ myth, without being aware of it. He allows Lazarus to remain in the grave for four days, in a way that is surprising to us, so that Jesus can perform something more than a mere healing miracle on him.[71] The Synoptics are necessary supplements to the Gospel of John, as a consequence, since they exhibit the human reality of Jesus.[72] There is manifest in the Gospel of John a super reality viewed poetically, a reality that lays bare the truth of the history of Jesus and the truth of the heart in its encounter with Jesus.[73] The peculiarities and the strengths and weaknesses of Hirsch's exposition of the Gospel of John are made especially clear in the dialogue of Jesus with the Samaritan woman: "This conversation is the most detailed and also the liveliest dialogue in the entire work. . . . The careful delineation of the scene" is a sign that the author has utilized his special craft in creating the entire story. "Whoever does not discern the hand of the poet here is beyond help."[74]

A sign of this craft, according to Hirsch, is the fact that "the Samaritan woman is at once a single woman living in vulgar libertinism and the personification of her people."[75] Hirsch's honored predecessor, H. J. Holtzmann, had already affirmed both of these points.[76] The five gods of the Samaritans have been discovered among the divinities listed in 2 Kgs 17:29ff., which the Assyrians transplanted in the land when it was emptied of most inhabitants in the exile at the end of the Northern Kingdom. Unfortunately, there are really seven in number, not five, and two of them are feminine, and thus not suitable for a masculine role. Josephus has of course simplified the text of the OT and speaks of five peoples and their five gods;[77] that has made allegorization easier. Holtzmann, among others, objected to the tasteless interpretation, according to which the present spouse of the woman points to Yahweh. Moreover, the seven divinities that were worshipped at that time in Samaria by five peoples cannot be reinterpreted as the five successive husbands of the woman of Samaria. Verse 16 certainly is not intended to emphasize that the woman is "a female living in blatant libertinism," but indicates that Jesus is able to perceive persons in a way that cannot be divined by man. The alleged identity of woman and people is thus not involved at all; the woman is all that is left.

Hirsch now writes of the scene at the well: ". . . here we have the loveliest and purest example of the analytical profundity of the author's glimpse into the movement of the human that encounters Jesus, and yet the perspective of the author takes leave of reality. The spiritual event in which the woman's faith comes into being is as clear as crystal."[78] Hirsch of course concedes that such a conversation with the woman could not have taken place. That Jesus is revealed as the fulfiller of all religious yearning and heartfelt needs can "probably be effectively depicted in a such a conversation as profound, but it cannot really happen."[79] That corroborates, at least in part, what Hirsch says of the Evangelist: "What he has written down from a free poetic perspective as Jesus' word is truly Jesus' word for him, revealed to him by the spirit. I

64   *Das vierte Evangelium*, 75.
65   *Das vierte Evangelium*, 77.
66   *Das vierte Evangelium*, 78.
67   *Das vierte Evangelium*, 79.
68   *Das vierte Evangelium*, 80.
69   *Das vierte Evangelium*, 80.
70   *Das vierte Evangelium*, 81.
71   *Das vierte Evangelium*, 82.

72   *Das vierte Evangelium*, 81.
73   *Das vierte Evangelium*, 82.
74   *Das vierte Evangelium*, 146.
75   *Das vierte Evangelium*, 146.
76   *Das Evangelium des Johannes*, 84.
77   *Ant.* 9.288.
78   *Das vierte Evangelium*, 147.
79   *Das vierte Evangelium*, 147.

believe that the distinction between truth and reality was thereby completely eradicated for him."[80]

Hirsch does not see that here the Evangelist is using a received tradition, which he has expanded by additions of his own. The answer of the woman in verse 19b (which some expositors are able to explain only as a diversionary maneuver) serves as the transition from an all-knowing Jesus, a "divine man" ($\theta\epsilon\hat{\iota}os\ \dot{\alpha}\nu\acute{\eta}\rho$), to the theme that is really important for the Evangelist: "The hour comes" (viewed from the standpoint of the Evangelist) "where the true worshippers will worship the Father in spirit and in truth." The Jerusalem temple already lay in ruins when the Gospel of John was composed. That verse 22 is a later insertion is news that has gradually made its way around. The redactor did not find it tolerable that Zion and Gerizim, two places of worship that were connected with a specific locale, are unable to guarantee that form of worship which corresponds to the will of God.

The Evangelist is more prosaic than Hirsch would like to believe. He makes use of received narrative material, but has so decisively altered it that it expresses his own message. It follows from verse 28 that the insertion of the Evangelist ends with verse 27. In his "source," verse 28 followed immediately on verse 18a. The woman's words in verse 29, "Come, see a man who told me all I ever did. Can this be the Christ?" do not take into consideration that in verse 26 Jesus had already revealed to her that he is the messiah. It is precisely at this point that one may discern the technique of the Evangelist: he lets as much as possible of his "source" stand, he inserts his own additions and corrections along the way (e.g., 4:48f.), or he adds them at the end, as in the story of Thomas in 20:29.

Hirsch believed that the Evangelist had completely eradicated the line between truth and reality. Perhaps it is rather the case that he has confused what the text says with his own fantasies. As a result, he has not translated and interpreted the original Gospel, but has indulged himself entirely in setting out his vision of the Evangelist.

H. Windisch and H. Strathmann

Hirsch was not the only one who regarded the author of the Gospel of John as a great poet. Windisch had earlier attributed considerable dramatic powers to the author,[81] and Strathmann likewise emphasizes the poetic facility of the author.[82] In so doing, they take different observations as their points of departure. Chapter 9 especially made a profound impression on Windisch.[83] His depiction of this chapter as a dramatic sequence of scenes could function as the preparation for a modern film script. Strathmann looks at matters differently.[84] The remarkable sacral solemnity, which often threatens to turn into something stiff and awkward, is striking to Strathmann. This is not his judgment about John: "an incomparable poet"; his judgment finally is: "a kerygmatic stylist." John—by whom he means the son of Zebedee—was not a consummate realist, like Canon Edwards[85] endeavors to foist off on the author of the Gospel of John. By contrast, Strathmann is convinced that the Fourth Gospel has nothing to do with realism. Whatever the beloved disciple experienced in association with his master does not come to expression in his representation of the life of Jesus. According to Strathmann, it is difficult to decide whether a scene really reflects an event that was experienced. Strathmann was of the opinion that the Gospel of John—for whose historical inconsistency he had a sharp eye—could only be understood when the disciple sacrificed his own experience to a "kerygmatic stylization." The basis for this strange

80   *Das vierte Evangelium*, 77.
81   "Der johanneische Erzählungsstil," in EYXAPIΣTHPION. *Studien zur Religion und Literatur des Alten und Neuen Testaments Hermann Gunkel zum 60. Geburtstag, dem 23 Mai 1922, dargebracht von seinen Schülern und Freunden*, ed. Hans Schmidt. FRLANT, n.s., 19 (Göttingen: Vandenhoeck & Ruprecht, 1923) 174–213.
82   *Das Evangelium nach Johannes*, 6–10.
83   "Der johanneische Erzählungsstil," in EYXAPIΣTHPION. *Studien zur Religion und Literatur des Alten und Neuen Testaments Hermann Gunkel zum*

60. Geburtstag, dem 23 Mai 1922, dargebracht von seinen Schülern und Freunden, ed. Hans Schmidt. FRLANT, n.s., 19 (Göttingen: Vandenhoeck & Ruprecht, 1923) 181–183.
84   *Das Evangelium nach Johannes*, 23.
85   *The Disciple Who Wrote These Things. A New Inquiry into the Origins and Historical value of the Gospel according to St. John* (London: J. Clarke, 1953) 14.

sounding opinion is to be sought in the simultaneous acceptance of opposing propositions. On the one hand, Strathmann held the old tradition that attributed the Gospel of John to the beloved disciple to be true. By holding to this position, he was entitled to a place in the succession of orthodox exegetes. Strathmann held that the early Christian testimony for the authorship of the Gospel of John was certain.[86] What is to be said to the contrary had become amply clear to him in a passage from Weizsäcker's work on the apostolic age:[87] "There is no power of faith or philosophy great enough to blot out the memory of a real life and replace it with a miraculous image of a divine being. . . . For one of the original apostles that is unthinkable." The transformation of the life of Jesus into a "a tremendous haggadic instruction book,"[88] in the sense of a logos christology, was possible only for someone in the second generation. In accordance with his firm conviction, Strathmann found a way of refuting this line of argumentation: "John's allegiance is not to historicism in his presentation, but to the principle of kerygmatic stylization. . . . No abiding interest attaches to the external side of events, even to persons who had contact with Jesus. . . . If one is inclined to pay too much attention to the details of the reports, then one is tempted to respond with the words of John 6:63: 'It is the spirit that gives life, the flesh is of no avail; the words that I have spoken to you are spirit and life.' The reports of the events of Jesus' ministry are kerygmatically stylized like the discourses, i.e., the way the materials are shaped stands in the service of the kerygma. . . . The shaping of the material is subordinated by him, in artistic freedom, entirely to this task."[89] From this point of view, Strathmann believed that he had the freedom quietly to confess how much there was to be said against the view that the Gospel of John was conceived by an eyewitness: "The figures are mostly stylized, the logic of the discourses baffles psychology, the practical outlook of the Gospel cannot be measured by customary norms." The reports of events, like the discourses, are nothing more than "variations of the forms of proclamation utilized by the Evangelist."

But are they really? This raises a question that one must also pose for Windisch and Hirsch. All three treat the Gospel of John basically as the work of a single hand, even though a redactor may insinuate himself between the lines. Whoever asserts this unity, however, will overlook the inner contradictions that predominate in the Fourth Gospel. We may provide just a few examples: in chapter 9, the reader is given the impression by means of constant repetition that a miracle such as the healing of the man born blind is possible only when God himself stands behind the miracle worker. Miracles are the legitimation of Jesus; whoever denies that is obdurate and inwardly blind. Or, as another example, we may take another great dramatic scene: the resurrection of Lazarus. The Evangelist is able to make use of an artistic and powerful account of an unprecedented miracle, only because, in 11:25–27, he wants to show, by going against the flow of the narrative, what a real resurrection was for him: it is that decisive moment when a man at any time, here and now, comes into fellowship with "the Father" as a result of having been awakened by the message of Jesus. This doctrine, which is hinted at in 5:21f. and is clearly articulated in 5:25, stands in contradiction to the futuristic eschatology found elsewhere. In 5:28f., however, it is again corrected in the direction of a pre-Johannine eschatology, although the author of 5:28f. strives to imitate the style of 5:21 and 5:25f.; minor alterations betray him and he does not succeed. That means, however, that here, as indeed often elsewhere, three hands betray themselves: (1) the hand of the source of the Evangelist; (2) the hand of the Evangelist himself; (3) the hand of the later "conservative" editor, who also introduced the beloved disciple. The source was created by a man who held fast to the tradition and who valued the miracles highly as evidence for the messiahship of Jesus. The redactor replaced the "now-eschatology" with the traditional futuristic eschatology—where the dead rise out of their graves—and again introduced the sacraments. He understands the faithful to be good men and women with good works, and no longer understands them as awakened from death to life. Because Hirsch and Strathmann endeavor to ascribe as much as possible of the Gospel of John to the great poet, in whom, as a consequence, truth and the marvelous are mixed, their standards proved to be unsatisfactory. Whether one

---

86   *Das Evangelium nach Johannes*, 20f.

87   *Das apostolische Zeitalter der christlichen Kirche* (Tübingen: Mohr-Siebeck, ³1902) 517.

88   *Das Evangelium nach Johannes*, 22f.

89   *Das Evangelium nach Johannes*, 23.

regards the "Evangelist" as a Pauline merchant or the son of Zebedee does not much matter anymore.

R. Bultmann

Bultmann's exposition of the Gospel of John is one of the greatest works he has given us. His commentary began to appear as fascicles in 1937 and was finished in 1941. He had written preparatory essays earlier and further publications accompanied the commentary. The impression of the unity of this work helped to give his commentary the influence it came to have: like a mighty tree, it appeared not to permit anything strong and important to prosper in its shadow. This effect did not set in immediately, but once it began, it became clear that Bultmann's commentary on the Gospel of John decisively dominated an entire generation. Already in his essays on the background of the Prologue and on the significance of the newly discovered Manichean and Mandean manuscripts (made available, above all, by M. Lidzbarski), one could perceive a researcher at work who was devoting himself to bringing to light the history of religions background of the Fourth Gospel.[90] The newly discovered writings contained astonishing verbal parallels and perspectives to the Gospel of John, which threw fresh and welcome light on a Gospel that seemed so peculiar to scholars. Bultmann of course knew that these Mandean writings were six hundred years later than the Gospel of John. Yet Bultmann was convinced that the Mandeans were the descendants of the baptist sect that had grown out of the baptismal activity of John. However, his conjectures extended even further: Had the Evangelist himself not been a disciple of John, before he became attached to the Jesus movement? Could he not have been the first one to recognize that the "revelation discourses," including the Prologue, were in fact appropriate only to Jesus? He then translated them from Aramaic into Greek, thereby rendering a great service to the disciples of Jesus. It now appears likely, on the basis of style analysis, that there was a whole series of such "revelation discourses" that are

now scattered over the whole of the Gospel of John. Does the peculiar arrangement and fragmentation—this is the explanation that suggests itself—owe to external forces that have damaged the Gospel of John and have almost completely destroyed the context in chapters 7 and 8 especially?[91] On stylistic grounds it also appears likely that these "revelation discourses," which are reminiscent of the Odes of Solomon, have enriched the first epistle of John.

The "revelation discourses" were not the only source that Bultmann hit upon. Another consisted of the "signs source" ($\sigma\eta\mu\epsilon\hat{\iota}\alpha$ source), which Bultmann isolated in many chapters. But that was not enough: in chapters 18–20, he found yet another source, which was utilized in narrating the passion. Finally, some segments stand out that have contact with the synoptic tradition.[92]

In several respects the "revelation discourses" are, in fact, the most important part of the entire Gospel. That is evident because these discourses, allegedly gnostic and baptist, do indeed set the tone for the Gospel of John. Since the Evangelist takes over the language of the discourses in part, the dividing line between his own formulations and these received discourses is uncertain. Another problem arises in the case of the signs source segments: they do not all contain a reference to the key word, "sign" ($\sigma\eta\mu\epsilon\hat{\iota}ov$). Bultmann characteristically made his decisions regarding sources on the basis of stylistic considerations. Special difficulties lurk in the revelation discourses; in this instance, H. Becker and E. Schweizer have supported Bultmann. In particular, Bultmann's pupil, H. Becker, has endeavored to give examples of the interrelationship of style and source: "It is evident," he writes, "how content has sought a suitable form for itself. Gnosticism, which is essentially dualistic, also produces a dualistic style."[93] He illustrates these assertions by means of some sentences from Excerpt XI in Stobaeus.[94] We have selected No. 18 as an example: "Nothing on earth [is] good, nothing in heaven bad." But these apodictic sentences are not themselves revelation discourses, but

---

90 Bultmann's essays have now been collected and published in the large volume, *Exegetica*, and in the several volumes of his *Glauben und Verstehen: Gesammelte Aufsätze* (4 vols. [Tübingen: Mohr-Siebeck, 1958–1965]; vol. 1 appeared in English as *Faith and Understanding*, ed. with an introduction by Robert W. Funk; tr. Louise Pettibone Smith [London: SCM Press, 1969]).

91 Cf. Bultmann, *John*, 218ff., 222 n. 2 [161f., 164 n. 2].
92 *John*, 428 n. 1 [327 n. 7].
93 *Die Reden des Johannesevangeliums und der Stil der gnostischen Offenbarungsrede*, FRLANT, n.s., 50 (Göttingen: Vandenhoeck & Ruprecht, 1956) 24.
94 A. D. Nock and A. J. Festugière, *Corpus Hermeticum*, 4 vols. (Paris: Les Belles Lettres, 1945–1954) 3: 34ff.

only indices to the content or superscriptions of possible or actual revelatory discourses of the god Hermes Trismegistus. Quite apart from their gnostic content, they are of an entirely different sort: long monologues of a revealer god, who now and then is interrupted by a question or an outcry in admiration on the part a recipient of the revelation. Gnosticism has made use of many literary forms, but not that of the apodictic sentence. The latter are much more at home in wisdom literature. Wisdom is fond of the form—one thinks of the "Sentences of Sextus" in this connection—because it is so easy to remember.

Bultmann regarded John 1:1f. as the perfect model for this style. But nowhere else in the entire Gospel is another verse of comparable artful construction to be found. Bultmann could make his thesis appear plausible only by meddling repeatedly in the text and making it conform in this way to his model. The Prologue may be a composition that is *sui generis*, something that was originally an independent entity, like the Christian hymns in Phil 2:6–11 and Col 1:15–20 may likewise have been. The thesis that the Evangelist was a converted disciple of the Baptist, who viewed the hymn that earlier applied to his first master, John the Baptist, as later fulfilled in Jesus Christ, and who then translated it into Greek and placed it at the beginning of his Gospel, and in the process also misunderstood it, very probably requires correction. The conjecture that the Baptist was venerated as the pre-existent logos by adherents of his sect can perhaps be contemplated from the perspective of the late John book of the Mandeans, but not with respect to what is said about him in the New Testament. He appears in Q (Matt 11:11a and Luke 7:28a) as the proclaimer of the imminent judgment of the world and as the one who administers the eschatological sacrament of baptism, a sacrament that is able save, to those who are repentant. In Mark 9:11–13 and still more clearly in Matt 17:10, he is acknowledged by Jesus as the promised Elijah, who is greater than everyone born of woman. This assertion is of course devalued by the addition in Matt 11:11b and Luke 7:28b: the least Christian is greater than John. Luke devalues him still further in the story of the small Baptist group in Ephesus (Acts 19:1–7), since the baptism of John has to be replaced by Christian baptism, inasmuch as only the latter confers the spirit. In doing so, Luke forgets that he himself has told the story in Luke 3:21 of how Jesus submitted to the baptism of John and thereby received the spirit. In the Gospel of John, the Baptist then denies that he is Elijah: he is only a witness. It is by no means certain that John founded a sect. That is not demonstrated by the parallels with the Qumran sect, nor did the Mandeans live under an eschatological religiosity. At Qumran and among the Mandeans it is a question of baptism frequently repeated, not of one time baptism, like that of John. The disciples of John are mentioned alongside those of Simon and Dositheus in the Pseudo-Clementines, documents that had already passed over into legend. The tradition of the Mandeans sinks completely into the legendary. Becker wrote as early as 1941: "The view that the disciples of John and the Mandeans are essentially identical is untenable, although Bultmann advanced this thesis in his essay . . . as exceptionally probable." In 1960 Rudolph claimed: "The baptism of John and the figure of John must be viewed without any connection at all to Mandeans."[95] He is of the opinion that "The roots of Mandean Gnosis and religion connected with baptism lie in the baptist sects located in the western central region. Here these sects underwent their principal development, on a Jewish base, under the influence of Syrian-gnostic, Iranian (especially Parthian), and, in part, Mesopotamian influence; this development took place already in pre-Christian times. The migration eastward as a consequence of continual Jewish pressure must . . . have taken place in the second century CE (presumably in connection with the Bar Cochba revolution) . . ."[96] "John the Baptist and his disciples had no relation to the Mandeans on the basis of information available to us from the sources."[97] In any case, it follows that the Mandeans were itinerant for a long period, during which they suffered unhappy experiences with Byzantine Chistendom, and eventually settled in the delta region of the Tigris and Euphrates.

This response to the question of sources brought with it a new problem, viz., whether the Gospel of John is to be interpreted as a gnostic document. According to

---

95 *Die Mandäer*, 1: 76.
96 *Die Mandäer*, 1: 251.
97 *Die Mandäer*, 1: 80.

Bultmann, the Gospel of John had indeed taken over the gnostic redeemer myth, but interpreted only in an existential fashion: "John and the Mandeans are in agreement in their understanding of the human self as alienated from the world and delivered over to the powers of the world."[98] But neither the fall of man nor his salvation are cosmic events for the Gospel of John; as a consequence, cosmological instructions are lacking. Salvation occurs in the present existence of man, specifically in his faithful hearing of the revelation.[99] Of what does the revelation consist? "Practically all the words of Jesus in John are assertions about himself and no definite complex of ideas can be stated as their content and claimed to be the 'teaching' of Jesus."[100] "Thus it turns out in the end that Jesus as the Revealer of God reveals nothing but that he is the Revealer. . . . But how is he that? . . . In no other way than that he says that he is it . . ."[101] Jesus' "teaching is not a new teaching because of its conceptual content; for in its content it does not differ from pure Judaism, from pure prophetic teaching. The unheard of thing is that he is speaking now, in the final, decisive hour. What is decisive is not what he proclaims but that he is proclaiming it."[102] "But since John eliminates from the myth its cosmological presuppositions, . . . he appears to retain in his book only the empty fact of the Revelation."[103] This Revelation "does not remain empty. For the Revelation is represented as the shattering and negating of all human self-assertion and all human norms and evaluations."[104] According to Bultmann, "Faith, then, is the overcoming of the 'offense'— the offense that life meets man only in the word addressed to him by a mere man, Jesus of Nazareth. It is the offense raised by a man who claims, without being able to make it credible to the world, that God is encountering the world in him."[105] Further, "the possibility of darkness—illusory self-understanding—is provided by the possibility of light—genuine self-understanding."[106] Consequently, Bultmann understands the Gospel of John as a writing that makes use of the gnostic myth as a medium of expression and understanding, but that has already radically demythologized this myth. "The dualism in John is not the cosmological dualism of Gnosticism, but the expression of a situation calling for decision, in which man stands before God and his revelation."[107]

That lucky moment, however, in which everything seemed to come together just right—observed style, conjectured sources, history of religions atmosphere, existential interpretation—proved to be transitory. The reordering of the text, which was intended to control its disorder, came into question. The Mandean hypothesis was no longer convincing. What was apparently self-evident, viz., that dualistic thought must have been born of a dualistic style, was contradicted by the gnostic texts themselves. To these were added two further tough questions: according to Bultmann, the gnostic "revelation discourses" form the real heart of the Gospel of John. But these revelation discourses are taken to be non-Christian. To be sure, Bultmann had claimed that John only borrowed the language in order to give expression to a different, non-gnostic meaning. But how is the reader to know that this language has to be deciphered in a different code? And finally: does the Gospel of John proclaim a "dualism of decision" that is non-gnostic as such? Such a dualism of decision is to be found in the gnostic Gospel of Thomas; but in the Gospel of John the decision lies with the "Father," who gives some to the son but not others. Further, the answer Bultmann gives to the question of sources gives very little play to the Evangelist's own endeavors: he collects and reworks the material—not without an occasional misunderstanding—and occasionally comments on it. Above all, it is not surprising that some scholars cannot agree entirely with Bultmann where so complicated a source-theory is involved. Among those who cannot are renowned scholars like Dodd and Käsemann. Dodd has not participated in attempts to rearrange the text—even in England some scholars have joined in this enterprise—although he does

---

98 *Exegetica*, 236.

99 *Exegetica*, 237.

100 *Theology of the New Testament*, 2: 63.

101 *Theology of the New Testament*, 2: 66.

102 *Faith and Understanding*, vol. 1, ed. Robert W. Funk; tr. Louise Pettibone Smith (London: SCM Press, 1969) 283 = *Glauben und Verstehen: Gesammelte Aufsätze*, vol. 1 (Tübingen: Mohr-Siebeck, ⁶1966).

103 *Theology of the New Testament*, 2: 67.

104 *Theology of the New Testament*, 2: 67f.

105 *Theology of the New Testament*, 2: 75.

106 *Theology of the New Testament*, 2: 18.

107 *Exegetica*, 237.

not deny his admiration for "the patience and endless ingenuity" of those who do the rearranging. He finds himself satisfied with the received text.[108] Käsemann contests that a "pure humanity" stands at the center of the Johannine interest: "Such a perspective is obliged to operate in abstraction from the mighty works unhesitatingly performed by the Christ of the Fourth Gospel. Indeed, he provides the world with so much to see that the miracles, and in particular the raising of Lazarus, lead to his death."[109] Käsemann is not at all satisfied with Bultmann's interpretation of the Prologue: "The pre-Christian character of the hymn is more than problematical, the Aramaic original incredible, the alleged Baptist hymn a pure hypothesis."[110] Haenchen joins Dodd in his doubt about Bultmann's rearrangement proposals.[111] However, the problem is so difficult that an entire section of this introduction will be devoted to "Disorder and Rearrangement."[112] In addition to the multiple-volume work of Braun,[113] the two substantial commentaries of Brown and Schnackenburg on the Fourth Gospel merit our special attention.

R. E. Brown

Brown discusses the question of authorship in his detailed introduction. He presents his own views of the way the Gospel of John came into being on pages xxxiv–xl.[114] He distinguishes five stages (at least) in the composition of the work. The first stage consists of the formation of a body of tradition concerning the words and deeds of Jesus but independent of the synoptic gospels. The second stage extended over several decades. During this period, the material was sifted and molded into the form and style of the individual narratives and discourses, which later were to become parts of the Gospel of John. This process was presumably influenced by preaching and teaching; the oral tradition was passing into written. In the third stage a continous gospel was created out of the material in stage two. While still in the second stage, a master preacher and teacher had given

shape to the Johannine material, and now arranges the first, Greek edition. Brown refers to this man as the "Evangelist." The fourth stage consists of several editions by the Evangelist, corresponding to his purpose on various occasions (here Brown comes close to the proposals of Wilkens).[115] The fifth stage produces a final edition by the "redactor," who takes up, in part, various versions of existing materials alongside each other. The narration of the public ministry of Jesus ended originally with 10:40–42; the pericope on Lazarus in chapter 11 was then added as the real cause of Jesus' execution. The insertion of the Lazarus story compelled the "redactor" to shift the story of the cleansing of the temple forward to chapter 2. Chapters 11 and 12 were perhaps added in the fourth stage. Liturgical interests have prompted the shift of Jesus' words over the bread and wine at the last supper to chapter 6:51–58. The origins of Johannine material are as early as the first stage and perhaps go back to Jesus himself.[116] At the earliest, the Gospel can have been written after 75 CE, at the latest soon after 100 CE (according to Irenaeus, John lived until the time of the Emperor Trajan, who reigned from 98–117 CE). Thus, one arrives at a date of 75–80 for the first edition, according to Brown, and for the final redaction a date of about 100 CE. The relation of John to his disciples was closer than that of Peter to Mark. The Fourth Gospel was truly written in the spirit of John.

F.-M. Braun and R. Schnackenburg

Schnackenburg was inspired by Braun as regards his own hypotheses concerning the author and conception of the Gospel of John. Braun summaries his views at the end of the first volume: the Gospel of John was not written at a single sitting (as the Prochorus legend represented it: John dictated the entire Gospel word for word to Prochorus while in an ecstatic trance and Prochorus wrote it down word for word). Rather, the preaching of the apostle John (the beloved disciple) crystallized in small literary units. For this purpose he made use of various

---

108 *Interpretation of the Fourth Gospel*, 289f.
109 *New Testament Questions*, 161.
110 *New Testament Questions*, 150.
111 "Das Johannesevangelium und sein Kommentar," 214–16.
112 *Infra*, Introduction §4, "Disorder and Rearrangement."
113 *Jean le théologien.*

114 *John*, vol. 1.
115 "Evangelist und Tradition im Johannesevangelium," in *TZ* 16 (1960) 81–90.
116 *John*, 1: xlviii.

disciples, one after the other, as "secretaries." On each occasion he gave them only the main thoughts and left them to work out the rest. Finally, in view of the situation in Ephesus, John obtained a Jewish Christian who could speak Greek well, and it is to him that we owe the present text directly. After the death of John, this man finished the work, but did not remove all the difficulties. The real author was thus the apostle John. But the Gospel we have does not derive immediately from him, but from the "secretary" who was familiar with Greek Hellenism.[117] At this point Schnackenburg goes beyond Braun: The man who wrote the Gospel was not merely a "secretary," but someone who was independent and worked in his own style. Schnackenburg by no means wishes to deny that he also had at his disposal the oral and written tradition of the apostle John. But he is of the opinion that he also plumbed the words and deeds of Jesus reported by John intellectually (and thus the apostolic interpretation of the saving events) and shaped them in a unified way with a view to his circle of readers. "Thus the evangelist would have been both the spokesman who transmitted the tradition and the preaching of the Apostle John, and a theologian in his own right and teacher of the readers whom he addressed."[118]

Whoever compares Schnackenburg's commentary on the Gospel of John with older Protestant exegesis sees immediately to what extent the exegesis of the two confessions have drawn near each other since the second Vatican council: The Gospel of John—so we also hear now from Schnackenburg—does not intend to provide us with a historical picture (in the modern sense of the word "historical"). Exegesis should not, therefore, strive primarily to recover historical data, as was early often the case, but should concern itself with the theological message of the Gospel.[119] If one considers the decree of the Holy Office of 3 July 1907, "Lamentabili,"[120] and reads the final remark of Schnackenburg in his introduction, he will prefer to advance "cautiously and soberly rather than boldly and unwarily. It [the commentary] aims at

discovering the theological content, though without neglecting the many individual problems which present themselves. Only an exegesis intent upon the literal sense, investigating the text and listening carefully to it, can also bring out the deeper treasures which are contained within the fourth Gospel."[121] One will then also recognize how in modern Catholic scholarship the results of Johannine interpretation are wrested from the conditions laid down in 1907.[122]

E. Käsemann

Käsemann may stand last in the series of significant interpreters of the Gospel of John. In 1966 Käsemann wrote: "The Evangelist whom we call John appears to be a man without definite contours. We can hear his voice, . . . and yet we are unable to locate exactly his historical place. . . . But his voice retains a strange otherworldly quality. . . . Historically, the Gospel as a whole remains an enigma, in spite of the elucidation of individual details."[123] Käsemann describes his impression entirely appropriately, as he does that of the church. But his solution to the riddle does not satisfy either. The ancient church already held as self-evident the view that Käsemann presupposes: each gospel stems from an evangelist. But that certainly does not apply to the Gospel of Matthew or to the Gospel of Luke. In the case of Matthew, one must distinguish three evangelists: Matthew has made use of Mark, the book of miracle stories; he has appropriated the sayings source Q and has thereby allowed Jesus the miracle-worker to recede behind Jesus the teacher of wisdom; and what we call the special material of Matthew is a third factor, without which the Gospel of Matthew would not be the Gospel of Matthew. The same thing applies—*mutatis mutandis*—to the Gospel of Luke.

It is therefore entirely possible that the voices of various "evangelists" confront us out of the Gospel of John. As we will show in what follows, we must reckon with three different authors: (a) the author of the "gospel of

---

117 Schnackenburg, *John*, 1: 101.
118 Schnackenburg, *John*, 1: 102.
119 *John*, 1: 11–13.
120 Cf. Denzinger, *Enchiridion Symbolorum. Definitionum et Declarationum de Rebus Fidei et Morum* (Freiburg: Herder, 1946) 670f.
121 *John*, 1: 217.
122 Cf. especially the studies of G. Richter.

123 *The Testament of Jesus*, 1f. He repeated these assertions in the 1971 edition of the German original.

miracles," which understands the "signs" ($\sigma\eta\mu\epsilon\hat{\iota}\alpha$) as miracles certifying faith; (b) an "evangelist" who interprets the "signs" ($\sigma\eta\mu\epsilon\hat{\iota}\alpha$) as pointers, through Jesus Christ, to the revelation of the invisible God, "the Father of Jesus Christ," pointers whose meaning becomes visible for the first time only through the gift of the spirit at Easter; and (c) an ecclesiastical "supplementer," or redactor, who appends the proclamation of the imminent end of the world, of the sacraments, and of an ethic that conceives of Christians as the elite among good men.

What is proposed here by way of hypothesis can only be ascertained as probable to a high degree by an exposition of the entire Gospel. But before we take up this task, this much can be said in advance: a source such as the "gospel of miracles," briefly described under (a) above, could only have been taken up by the "evangelist" if it were explicable in accordance with its own sense; and if interpretations that are alien to the source he uses are demonstrable as such, at least in many cases; and if, further, the sense of the gospel being employed and its reinterpretation by the evangelist are separable from each other beyond any doubt. In a similar way, the additions of the "supplementer," or redactor, must also be demonstrable as such.

3. The Text of the Gospel of John

Bibliography

Aland, Kurt
  Studien zur Überlieferung des Neuen Testaments und seines Textes, Arbeiten zur Neutestamentlichen Textforschung 2 (Berlin: Walter de Gruyter, 1967).

Birdsall, J. Neville
  The Bodmer Papyrus of the Gospel of John (London: Tyndale Press, 1960).

Birdsall, J. Neville
  "The Text of the Fourth Gospel: Some Current Questions." *EvQ* 29 (1957) 195–205.

Boismard, Marie-Emile
  "Lectio brevior, potior." *RB* 58 (1951) 161–68.

Boismard, Marie-Emile
  "Problèmes de critique textuelle concernant le quatrième évangile." *RB* 60 (1953) 341–71.

Boismard, Marie-Emile
  "Le papyrus Bodmer II." *RB* 64 (1957) 363–98.

Edwards, Sarah A.
  "P[75] and B in John: A Study in the History of the Text." Dissertation, Hartford Seminary, 1974.

Fee, Gordon D.
  "Codex Sinaiticus in the Gospel of John: A Contribution to Methodology in Establishing Textual Relationships." *NTS* 15 (1968/1969) 23–44.

Fee, Gordon D.
  Papyrus Bodmer II (P66): Its Textual Relationships and Scribal Characteristics, Studies and Documents 34 (Salt Lake City: University of Utah Press, 1968).

Fee, Gordon D.
  "The Text of John in the Jerusalem Bible: A Critique of the Use of Patristic Citations in New Testament Textual Criticism." *JBL* 90 (1971) 163–73.

Harnack, Adolf von
  "Zur Textkritik und Christologie der Schriften des Johannes. Zugleich ein Beitrag zur Würdigung der ältesten lateinischen Überlieferung und der Vulgata." SPAW 5,2 (Berlin: G. Reimer, 1915) 534–73.

Kasser, Rudolphe
  L'évangile selon S. Jean et les versions coptes de la Bible, Bibliothèque théologique (Neuchâtel: Delachaux & Niestlé, 1966).

Kieffer, René
  Au delà des recensions? L'évolution de la tradition textuelle dans Jean VI, 52–71, ConBNT 3 (Lund: C. W. K. Gleerup, 1968).

Lejoly, R.
  Annotations pour une étude du papyrus 75, c'est-à-dire du text grec de Jean 1–14, Bodmer XV (Dison: Editions "Concile," 1976).

Martin, Victor and Rudolphe Kasser, eds.
  Papyrus Bodmer XIV–XV. Evangile de Luc et Jean

[Luc chap. 3–24; Jean chap. 1–15] (Cologny-Geneva: Bibliotheca Bodmeriana, 1961).

Martin, Victor, ed.
Papyrus Bodmer II, Supplément. Evangile de Jean, chap. 14–21 (Cologny-Geneva: Bibliotheca Bodmeriana, 1958).

Martin, Victor, ed.
Papyrus Bodmer II: Evangile de Jean chap. 1–14 (Cologny-Geneva: Bibliotheca Bodmeriana, 1956).

Mees, Michael
"Petrus und Johannes nach ausgewählten Varianten von P 66 und S." *BZ* 15 (1971) 238–49.

Mees, Michael
"Sinn und Bedeutung westlicher Textvarianten in Joh 6." *BZ* 13 (1969) 244–51.

Mees, M.
"Unterschiedliche Lesarten in Bodmer Papyrus XV (P75) und Codex Vaticanus aus Joh 1–9." *Augustinianum* 9 (1969) 370–79.

Mees, Michael
"Lectio brevior im Johannesevangelium und ihre Beziehung zum Urtext." *BZ* 12 (1968) 111–19, 377.

Metzger, Bruce M.
"The Bodmer Papyrus of Luke and John." *ExpTim* 73 (1961/1962) 201–3.

Neirynck, Frans et al.
Jean et les Synoptiques. Examen critique de l'exégèse de M.-E. Boismard, BETL 49 (Louvain: University Press, 1979) 23–39.

Nestle, Eberhard
Einführung in das Griechische Neue Testament, ed. Ernst von Dobschütz (Göttingen: Vandenhoeck & Ruprecht, 41923).

Porter, C. F.
"An Analysis of the Textual Variations between P75 and Codex Vaticanus in the Text of John." In *Studies in the History and Text of the New Testament in Honor of Kenneth Willis Clark, Ph. D,* ed. B. L. Daniels and M. J. Suggs. Studies and Documents 29 (Salt Lake City: University of Utah Press, 1967) 71–80.

Rhodes, Erroll F.
"The Corrections of Papyrus Bodmer II." *NTS* 14 (1968) 271–81.

Salmon, V.
Histoire de la tradition textuelle de l'original grec du quatrième évangile avec 64 illustrations (papyrus et manuscrits accompagnés d'une transcription complète) (Paris: Letouzey et Ané, 1969).

Schedl, Claus
"Zur Schreibung von Joh 1, 10A in Papyrus Bodmer XV." *NovT* 14 (1972) 238–40.

Zimmermann, H.
"Papyrus Bodmer II und seine Bedeutung für die Textgeschichte des Johannes-Evangeliums." *BZ* 2 (1958) 214–43.

The text of the Gospel of John is no more immune to alteration than the texts of the other gospels, as the extant textual witnesses demonstrate. Yet the variations are moderate in scope. In chapter 5, only verses 3b and 4 were later insertions, and the pericope of the woman taken in adultery did not belong originally to the text of the Gospel; both facts are demonstrated by the history of the text. John 7:53–8:11 is lacking in the papyri, the oldest uncials, and in the text of the Eastern Fathers. The pericope was later inserted into the Gospel of John at various points and even after Luke 21:38. A similar situation prevails for John 5:3b, 4. Whatever scholars have claimed regarding glosses in the text or additions of a redactor must have happened to the Gospel prior to the publication of the text. That applies also to chapter 21, which is usually called an appendix. This is all important for any literary-critical operations on the text.

In 1881, Westcott and Hort published their great work, *The New Testament in the Original Greek*, in two volumes. The word "papyrus" does not occur in this work; papyri were not yet used in textual criticism. The oldest witnesses used by Westcott and Hort were the uncials B (Vaticanus) and ℵ (Sinaiticus) from the fourth century. In spite of this, Westcott and Hort held the following view: "But enough is already known to enable us to judge with reasonable certainty as to the proportional amount of valuable evidence likely to be buried in the copies as yet uncollated. If we are to trust the analogy thus provided, which agrees with what might have been anticipated from the average results of continued transcription generally, nothing can well be less probable than the discovery of cursive evidence sufficiently important to affect present conclusions in more than a handful of passages, much less to alter present interpretations of the relations between the existing documents."[1] What was decisive for Westcott and Hort was the discrimination of four groups of texts (text-types):

(1) the latest form of the text is the "Syrian" (also

---

1   *The New Testament in the Original Greek*, 77.

called "Byzantine," "Constantinopolitan," "Koine," or, more recently, "majority text"), the last form of which is the Textus Receptus. It is of course not simply a matter of names; Westcott and Hort defined and described these text types exactly and in detail.[2]

(2) The second text-type is the so-called "Western" text. It was also precisely described and thus defined.[3] It may be mentioned here that it arose at a very early date, prior to 150 CE; it shows up already in Marcion, Tatian, Justin, Iraeneus (if not yet in a fully developed form), Hippolytus, and and other Church Fathers. The Western type treats the text in a grammatically free manner, enriches it through additions, harmonizes passages, to mention only a few of its qualities. Its chief representatives are the bilingual (Greek and Latin) manuscript D for the gospels, and Codex Claromontanus (D) for the Acts and the letters.

(3) A further type of text is the "Alexandrian." Its principal representatives are C (Ephraemi Rescriptus), L, the minuscule 33, "the queen of the minuscles," sa and bo (Coptic manuscripts) and the citations of the Alexandrian Church Fathers. This type of text exhibits a refined feeling for language, which betrays itself also in alterations of the text that permit an improvement in language and style.

(4) Westcott and Hort named the fourth type the "neutral" text because they viewed it as the original type that had not been marred by later, inferior readings. The best representative of this type is Vaticanus (B), and the second best is Sinaiticus, a manuscript which its discoverer, Count Tischendorf, saw for the first time in a monastery on Mt. Sinai in 1844 and which he later acquired for the Czar of Russia. Tischendorf regarded it as the best of all New Testament manuscripts, as the designation ℵ indicates (he was unwilling to give it a lower letter of the Roman alphabet, so he gave it the first letter of the Hebrew alphabet). Since ℵ shows Western influence in its text of John (as does B, a fourth century manuscript), Boismard has attempted to show that the concurrence of ℵ and D in John 1–8 gives evidence of a further text-type, which should be given a separate identity along with other text-types.[4]

The work of Westcott and Hort in England meant that the Texus Receptus, which had heretofore reigned supreme, now lost its influence, and the King James Version of 1611, based on a text essentially earlier than that established by Westcott and Hort, faded. Because John W. Burgon, Dean of Chichester, led the passionate and fruitless opposition to the new text, we should not infer that the "old" text, which is attested by the majority of manuscripts, has lost its champions even today.

One thing Westcott and Hort were not able to foresee: the significance of the papyri. Only because of its limited scope can $\mathfrak{P}^{52}$ not serve as evidence that the "neutral" text came to prevail only through recensions about which Jerome wrote in his *Praefatio* to the books of Chronicles:[5]

> *Alexandria et Aegyptus in Septuaginta suis Hesychium laudat auctorem, Constantinopolis usque Antiochiam Luciani martyris exemplaria probat, mediae inter has provinciae Palaestinos codices legunt quos ab Origene elaboratos Eusebius et Pamphilus vulgaverunt; totusque orbis hac inter se trifaria varietate pugnat.*

> Alexandria and Egypt praise Hesychius as the author of their Septuagint; the region from Constantinople down to Antioch endorses the manuscripts of the martyr Lucian; the middle provinces between the two read the Palestinian manuscripts which, based on Origen's labors, Eusebius and Pamphilus made generally available. Thus the whole world is at war on the basis of this threefold variety.

That sounds as though three entities, who dominated the scene, had divided the whole eastern end of the Mediterranean among themselves. But the remark in the first instance meant only for the LXX might also be aimed at the NT text, since Jerome writes in the dedication to Pope Damasus in 382 CE concerning the translation of the gospels:

> *Praetermitto eos codices, quos a Luciano et Hesychio nuncupatos paucorum hominum adserit perversa contentio, quibus utique nec in veteri instrumento [viz., the OT] post LXX interpretes emendare quid licuit nec in novo emendasse; cum multarum gentium linguis scriptura ante translata doceat falsa esse, quae addita sunt.*

> I pass over those manuscripts which are associated with the names of Lucian and Hesychius, and the authority of which is perversely maintained by a hand-

---

2   *The New Testament in the Original Greek,* 134f.
3   *The New Testament in the Original Greek,* 122–24.
4   "Problèmes de critique textuelle concernant le

quatrième évangile," *RB* 60 (1953) 341–71.
5   MPL 28, 1392f. Translation provided by K. Fröhlich.

ful of disputatious persons. It is obvious that these writers could not amend anything in the OT after the labours of the seventy; and it was useless to correct the NT, for versions of the Scripture which already exist in the languages of many nations show that their additions are false.

E. von Dobschütz is of this opinion: "The process of text recension is to be thought of in this way: in general the textual critics concur with the text that is common in the respective church of each, but in doubtful instances, each recensionist follows his own judgment and preference. Accordingly, Hesychius appears to have preferred the lapidary, shorter readings, Pamphilius strove for good Greek expression, and Lucian sought adroitly to weave together the various readings that he discovered in the tradition"[6]

But the rich fund of early papyri, which fortunately contains parts of the Johannine text, has decisively altered the picture of the development of the NT text. At first, $\mathfrak{P}^{45}$ with its strong infusion of "Western" readings permitted us to maintain presuppositions held earlier: the "Western" text dominated the field. The text which later penetrated the recension of Hesychius mentioned by Jerome was formed gradually out of the Western text under Alexandrian influence. Vaticanus and Sinaiticus were accordingly relatively late educated revisions. The discovery of $\mathfrak{P}^{66}$ and $\mathfrak{P}^{75}$ basically altered this picture: $\mathfrak{P}^{66}$ already demonstrates that the "Egyptian" text was in existence as early as the "Western" text, and $\mathfrak{P}^{75}$ reads very much like a precursor of Vaticanus. The statements of Jerome regarding the recensions of Hesychius, Pamphilus, and Lucian are exaggerated: in order to create a text like the Vaticanus, one needed to take only a manuscript like $\mathfrak{P}^{75}$ as a source to produce an edition using the Alexandrian method. The "Western"

text might have come into vogue as early as the second century CE, when the text was still treated with greater freedom. That the "Western" text circulated in two forms (so Boismard), for one of which Tatian is a witness, while D and ℵ offer the second (up to the middle of John 8), and that the Evangelist knew both of them and chose now one and now the other, are hypotheses we regard as improbable. For D and ℵ agree, not only frequently in the first eight chapters of John, but also, for example, in 13:21–14:10. ℵ can be considered an "Egyptian" text only in a very restricted sense; it is a mixed text. As Zimmermann, Schnackenburg,[7] and Aland have emphasized, the evaluation of a text cannot begin with the oldest parchment manuscripts and on that basis pass to the papyri, which are much older, but must in fact begin with the papyri. Whether one can place so high a value on the quotations of the Church Fathers, as Boismard does, is not at all certain. They certainly made use of manuscripts that were older than their own work. But investigations into the texts used by Origen have shown that he appears to have put together and used his own textual apparatus for each of several works on which he was working at the time, without being bothered by the differences among these texts.

It is better not to presuppose a special theory for the text of the Gospel of John; it is sufficient to go into the textual situation as the occasion arises in the course of the commentary on individual verses. That policy especially commends itself in view of the fact that various factors are to be taken into account in assessing the text in particular cases.

---

6   Eberhard Nestle, *Einführung in das griechische Neue Testament*, ed. E. von Dobschütz (Göttingen: Vandenhoeck & Ruprecht, ⁴1923) 26.

7   *John*, 1: 153–71.

4. Disorder and Rearrangement

Bibliography

Bacon, Benjamin Wisner
"Tatian's Rearrangements of the Fourth Gospel."
AJT 4 (1900) 770–95.

Bacon, Benjamin Wisner
"Displacement of John xiv." *JBL* 13 (1894) 64–76.

Bernard, John Henry
*A Critical and Exegetical Commentary on the Gospel
according to St. John*, ed. A. H. McNeile (New York:
Charles Scribner's Sons, 1929).

Bertling, D.
"Eine Transposition im Evangelium Johannis."
TSK 53 (1880) 351–53.

Brinkmann, B.
"Zur Frage der ursprünglichen Ordnung im
Johannesevangelium." *Greg* 20 (1939) 55–82.

Brown, F. J.
"Displacement in the Fourth Gospel." *ExpTim* 57
(1945/1946) 217–20.

Bultmann, Rudolf
"Hirschs Auslegung des Johannes-Evangeliums."
EvT 4 (1937) 115–42.

Church, W. Randolph
"The Dislocations in the Eighteenth Chapter of
John." *JBL* 49 (1930) 375–83.

Clark, Albert Curtis
The Primitive Text of the Gospels and Acts (Oxford:
Clarendon Press, 1914).

Cottam, Thomas
"Some Displacements in the Fourth Gospel."
ExpTim 38 (1926/1927) 91–92.

Cottam, Thomas
The Fourth Gospel Rearranged (London: Epworth
Press, 1956).

Crönert, W.
"Die Überlieferung des Index Academicorum."
Hermes 38 (1903) 357–405.

Easton, Burton Scott
"Bultmann's RQ Source." *JBL* 65 (1946) 143–56.

Flowers, H. J.
"Interpolations in the Fourth Gospel." *JBL* 40
(1921) 146–58.

Hoare, Frederick Russell
The Original Order and Chapters of St. John's Gospel
(London: Burns, Oates & Washbourne, 1944).

Hoare, Frederick Russell
*The Gospel According to St. John Arranged in its Con-
jectural Order* (London: Burns, Oates & Washbourne, 1949).

Holtzmann, Heinrich Julius
"Unordnungen und Umordnungen im vierten
Evangelium." *ZNW* 3 (1902) 50–60.

Howard, Wilbert Francis
*The Fourth Gospel in Recent Criticism and Interpreta-
tion* (London: Epworth Press, [4]1955).

Jeremias, Joachim
"Johanneische Literarkritik." *TBl* 20 (1941) 33–46.

Lewis, Frank Warburton
Disarrangements in the Fourth Gospel (Cambridge: Cambridge University Press, 1910).

Lewis, Frank Warburton
"Disarrangements in the Fourth Gospel." *ExpTim* 44 (1932/1933) 382.

Lewis, G. P.
see: W. F. Howard, *The Fourth Gospel*, 126f., 303.

MacGregor, George Hogarth Carnaby
"How Far is the Fourth Gospel a Unity?" *Expositor*, 8th ser., 24 (1922) 81–110; 25 (1923) 161–85; 26 (1924) 358–76.

MacGregor, George Hogarth Carnaby
"The Rearrangement of John vii and viii." *ExpTim* 33 (1921/1922) 74–78.

MacGregor, George Hogarth Carnaby
The Gospel of John (London: Hodder & Stoughton, 1928).

Moffatt, James
New Translation of the Bible Containing the Old and New Testaments (New York and London: Harper & Brothers, 1935).

Nicklin, T.
"A Suggested Dislocation in the Text of St. John xiv–xvi." *ExpTim* 44 (1932/1933) 382–83.

Norris, J. P.
"On the Chronology of St John V and VI." *The Journal of Philology* 3 (1871) 107–112.

Oke, C. Clark
"At the Feast of Booths. A Suggested Rearrangement of John vii–ix." *ExpTim* 47 (1935/1936) 425–27.

Pierce, F. X.
"Chapter-Rearrangements in St. John's Gospel." *AER* 102 (1940) 76–82.

Power, Albert
"The Original Order of St. John's Gospel." *CBQ* 10 (1948) 399–405.

Redlich, E. Basil
"St John i–iii: A Study in Dislocations." *ExpTim* 55 (1943/1944) 89–92.

Ross, Alexander
"Displacements in the Fourth Gospel." *ExpTim* 58 (1946/1947) 250.

Scott, W. and Ferguson, Alexander Stewart
Hermetica. The Ancient Greek and Latin Writings which contain religious and philosophic teachings ascribed to Hermes Trismegistos, 4 vols. (Oxford: Clarendon Press, 1924–1936).

Smith, D. Moody
The Composition and Order of the Fourth Gospel: Bultmann's Literary Theory (New Haven and London: Yale University Press, 1965).

Spitta, Friedrich
"Unordnungen im Texte des vierten Evangeliums." In his *Zur Geschichte und Literatur des Urchristentums* (Göttingen: Vandenhoeck & Ruprecht, 1893) 1: 155–204.

Thompson, J. M.
"Accidental Disarrangement in the Fourth Gospel." *Expositor*, 8th ser., 17 (1919) 47–54.

Uricchio, N.
"La teoria delle trasposizioni nel Vangelo di S. Giovanni." *Bib* 31 (1950) 129–63; 32 (1951) 567f.

Wilkens, Wilhelm
Die Entstehungsgeschichte des vierten Evangeliums (Zollikon: Evangelischer Verlag, 1958).

Wilson, W. G.
"The Original Text of the Fourth Gospel. Some Objective Evidence Against the Theory of Page Displacements." *JTS* 50 (1949) 59–60.

One senses tensions in the Gospel of John, first of all in relation to the Synoptics, but then also internally. The first sort of tension already became evident in the second century when Tatian created his harmony of the four canonical gospels, the so-called Diatessaron: he had to rearrange some segments of the Gospel of John. Two presuppositions then became evident, as though spontaneously: it was supposed that the evangelists represented the life of Jesus in its chronological context; as a consequence, the (hypothetical) possibility that the gospel segments could be ordered so as to correspond to the sequence of events in Jesus' life was also assumed. In that case, there must originally have been a definite sequence of events and sayings. The possibility that there was a history of the tradition—in itself not always entirely unified—lay just beyond the field of vision, although it was already implied in the acceptance of a plurality of canonical gospels.

Tensions within the Fourth Gospel were likewise felt at an early time, as is shown by the rearrangement of John 18 in Syrus Sinaiticus (sy[s]): verses 13, 24, 14, 15, 19–23, and 16–18 follow each other in that order. That is not an original text, but an attempt to create a more meaningful context by reordering the verses.

Modern criticism has been willing to tinker with the text of the Gospel of John to an ever greater degree. One may work with some sort of notion of the familiar threesome of source(s), evangelist(s), and redactor(s), all three of which one can locate within the evangelist himself, as does B. Wilkens.[1] One then assumes that the manner in which the Gospel arose is what led to its present form. Or, one replaces this view that the development was "normal" although not entirely smooth with a theory of disaster: something happened to the Gospel which produced confusion in the text. This view especially provoked the study of the history of the text. This led to two different attempts to account for the disorder in the Gospel of John.

1. The history of the transmission of the text shows that the pericope of the woman taken in adultery, 7:53–8:11, is lacking in the oldest uncials and the papyri. It was inserted later in various places in the Fourth Gospel and even after Luke 21:38. It does not, therefore, belong to the earliest text. The situation is similar in the case of John 5:3b, 4. This means that the possibility is not foreclosed that insertions were made at other points—at such an early date, to be sure, that the extant textual witnesses betray no traces of them. So the idea arose, especially in the work of Spitta[2] and Wendt,[3] that there was an "original text," which a redactor revised. Wherever a problem appeared in the text the redactor was thought to be responsible, more or less.

2. Another, apparently more objective, attempt to reorder the text also goes back to text-critical observations. A count is made of the letters in the pericope of the woman taken in adultery and then of other pericopes as though they, too, were insertions. That prompts Clark's suggestion, following several earlier attempts, that the original text of John was written in lines of 10–12 characters, and each column contained 167 or 168 characters, which produced 14 to 16 lines per side.[4] The possibility of a further assumption then arose: the Fourth Gospel was written on individual sheets, which were then later combined into a scroll. The joins came loose in the course of time and some sheets were reinserted at the wrong places.

Manuscripts like Vaticanus and Sinaiticus played a dirty trick on researchers in connection with this theory of dislocation. These old unicals were written with extreme care and proportion. That led to the mistaken judgment that the Gospel of John was also written in lines of the same length and on pages of the same depth. More recent discoveries of papyri have taught us better.

Before we explore this new knowledge, we would like to describe two earlier attempts to rearrange the Gospel in detail. The first attempted to show how the sheets in the original text of the Gospel came to be mixed up. The second dispensed with an attempt to reconstruct the process by which the sheets came to be confused. It simply assumed that the text came into the hands of the redactor already disturbed in a variety of ways, owing to external interference. The redactor put it in order as best he could. Bultmann is of the opinion that we must find the courage to rearrange the text with a view to the internal coherence of the text.

The first proposal we wish to report on is that of F. R. Hoare. In 1944 he published a book on which he had worked for sixteen years under the title: *The Original Order and Chapters of St. John's Gospel.*[5] The hypothesis that he develops supposes that the very old apostle John was asked to produce a Greek gospel that would supplement the Synoptics. He consented and dictated his gospel to his secretary following his earlier Aramaic notes. When the Greek version had been completed on loose papyrus sheets, his notes in Aramaic, now being useless, were destroyed. The Apostle now had his secretary prepare a clean copy on one side of unnumbered sheets; the last chapter was added in accordance with a memo-

---

1 *Die Enstehungsgeschichte des vierten Evangeliums* (Zollikon: Evangelischer Verlag, 1958).

2 *Zur Geschichte und Literatur des Urchristentums* 1 (Göttingen: Vandenhoeck & Ruprecht, 1893).

3 H. H. Wendt, *Die Lehre Jesu,* 2 vols. Vol. 1, *Die Evangelischen Quellenberichte über die Lehre Jesu* (Göttingen: Vandenhoeck & Ruprecht, 1886) 5.215–342; H. H. Wendt, *Das Johannesevangelium. Eine Untersuchung seiner Entstehung und seines geschichtlichen Wertes* (Göttingen: Vandenhoeck & Ruprecht, 1900); H. H. Wendt, *Die Schichten im vierten Evangelium* (Göttingen: Vandenhoeck & Ruprecht, 1911). Cf.

Howard, *The Fourth Gospel in Recent Criticism and Interpretation* (London: Epworth Press, [4]1955) 298f.

4 A. C. Clark, *The Primitive Text of the Gospels and Acts* (Oxford: Clarendon Press, 1914).

5 (London: Burns, Oats & Washbourne, 1944).

randum. The Apostle had the clean copy read aloud and approved it.[6] The original copy of the Greek version, having now become useless, was also destroyed. The Apostle was overtaxed by this work and fell into a coma from which he never awakened. Just then the unnumbered sheets of papyrus, which had not yet been made into a continuous scroll, slide to the floor in disarray. The secretary put them in order as best he could and added the second half of verses 24 and 25 of chapter 21.[7]

So much for the romantic account of the origin of the Gospel of John. In order to carry out his reconstruction, Hoare had to assume that each column contained 397 characters in 21 lines of 18–19 characters each. The entire Gospel was comprised of twenty segments (without the pericope of the woman taken in adultery) made up of 2–17 units of this type. Five of these chapters extended to the end of the column, while the other fifteen contained from one to four empty lines to indicate the close of a chapter. The arrangement of Hoare looks this way (the arabic numbers before each chapter refer to the original order, the capital letters indicate the present sequence):

1	(A)	1:1–51	Columns 1–10
2	(C)	4:3b–43	Columns 11–18
3	(B)	2:1–4:3a	Columns 19–32
4	(D)	4:44–5:47	Columns 33–44
5	(F)	7:15–24	Columns 45–46
6	(E)	6:1–7:14	Columns 47–63
7	(G)	7:25–52; 8:12–28a	Columns 64–72
8	(M)	12:34–50	Columns 73–76
9	(H)	8:28b–9:41	Columns 77–91
10	(J)	10:19–11:33	Columns 92–102
11	(L)	12:23b–33	Columns 103–104
12	(K)	11:34–12:23a	Columns 105–114
13	(I)	10:1–18	Columns 115–118
13a	(Z)	7:53–8:11	Columns 118a b c
14	(N)	13:1–19	Columns 119–122
15	(R)	15:17–16:4a	Columns 123–125
16	(O)	13:20–14:14	Columns 126–132
17	(T)	16:15b–23	Columns 133–134
18	(P)	14:13–24a	Columns 135–136
19	(S)	16:4b–15a	Columns 137–138
20	(Q)	14:24b–15:16	Columns 139–143
21	(U)	16:24–21:25	Columns 144–185

Hoare first used the text of Branscheid, then that of Nestle,[8] and finally the edition of Merk.

We now know on the basis of the early papyri $\mathfrak{P}^{52}$, $\mathfrak{P}^{66}$, $\mathfrak{P}^{75}$, and $\mathfrak{P}^{46}$ that there is no question of from one to four empty lines at the end of each chapter. Insofar as $\mathfrak{P}^{66}$ and $\mathfrak{P}^{75}$ mark segments, they employ either a point placed over the line to indicate the end of a segment, or they leave the balance of the line empty after a word completing the meaning of a paragraph or unit, or they move the following line about a character's width to the left. These possibilities of indicating the limits of a segment can also be combined.

In any case, Hoare does not reckon with the codex, but with a papyrus roll. But as early as 1903, in an essay entitled "Die Überlieferung des Index Academicorum," Crönert made some important observations on an open scroll found among a large group of papyrus rolls at Herculaneum (the balance of which were stuck closed by the heat).[9] The copyist had not written on the entire roll, but also not on individual sheets; he had created sections consisting of four or five columns. In so doing he has written right over the seams. The one who pasted the roll together (*Glutinator*) had in some cases placed such segments in the newly created roll in the wrong order. Such errors are easily detected because suddenly one finds an entirely different representative of the Platonic Academy speaking in the text and because at the beginning and end of such segments one finds sentences broken off. Hoare's hypothesis functions only so long as he can assume that empty lines come only at the end of chapters; there are thus no broken sentences to assist in

6   *The Original Order and Chapters of St. John's Gospel* (London: Burns, Oats & Washbourne, 1944) 104.

7   *The Original Order and Chapters of St. John's Gospel* (London: Burns, Oats & Washbourne, 1944) 105.

8   *Novum Testamentum Graecae* (Stuttgart: Deutsche Bibelstiftung, [6]1921).

9   *Hermes* 38 (1903) 357–405.

finding the connections.

In all probability, the Gospel of John was copied onto a codex and not a scroll. $\mathfrak{P}^{52}$ is a fragment of such a codex from the first half of the second century and $\mathfrak{P}^{66}$ and $\mathfrak{P}^{75}$ come perhaps from around 200 CE. $\mathfrak{P}^{75}$ contains the Gospel in a single-quire format: one single quire is inserted into another in forming the codex. The consequence was that the middle protruded considerably and the section Luke 18:18–22:3 was lost because the thread used to sew the quires together was broken. The beginning of Luke is, likewise, preserved only in fragments; the first damaged pages were glued to the first fully preserved page as a kind of substitute cover. The same thing happened to the end of the Gospel of John. From this codex in complete form we possess only John 1:1–13:10. The last pages have been ruined; the sheets on which 14:8–21:25 appeared were glued to the last wholly preserved sheet in order to strengthen it, but they have now been detached, separated, and read. These observations reveal the weak points of a codex that consists of single quires only: the beginning, middle, and end were especially vulnerable.

Owing to $\mathfrak{P}^{66}$, John 1:1–14:15 has been well preserved. The editors have also restored a remarkable amount from fragments of the text. From within the manuscript a quire of four pages that contained John 6:11–11:35 is lacking. This lacuna is preceded by thirty-four pages; pages 39–154 follow. From this it may be deduced that $\mathfrak{P}^{66}$ consists of several quires: signatures 1, 3, and 4 consist of five sheets folded so as to produce twenty pages each. The second signature contains four sheets, the fifth, on the other hand, has eight sheets, or sixteen and twenty-two pages respectively. Originally the codex had 154 pages; forty-six have therefore been lost or are preserved more or less only in fragmentary form. The binding (cf. the bindings on the Nag Hammadi codices) has not been preserved. However, the kind of binding can still be determined.[10] It is especially significant that line length and the number of lines to the page vary considerably. $\mathfrak{P}^{66}$ contains twenty-six lines on its first page, but on page 149 only 14. The number of characters in the first ten lines of the first page vary between twenty-two and thirty-six, but on page 97 they vary between eighteen and twenty-four.

The scribe of $\mathfrak{P}^{75}$ noted that he would not have sufficient room in the second half of his codex. He therefore raised the number of lines from twenty lines in the Nestle text to forty.[11] The entire papyrus contains 144 pages in a 26 x 13 cm. format; $\mathfrak{P}^{52}$, on the other hand, might have a format of 21 x 20. Similarly, $\mathfrak{P}^{66}$ approximates a square page. This shows that we do not know how the first copy of the Gospel of John looked that contained the text known to us. We cannot say what format it had, how long the lines were, and how many lines it had to the column.

Before we pursue further consequences of these new finds, we would like to turn to the second example promised earlier, namely, to the reconstruction of the Fourth Gospel by Bultmann. One would be doing Bultmann an injustice were one to forget that he is by no means the first to try his luck at rearrangement. He had precursors, especially in England. Howard sketches the rearrangement hypotheses of F. W Lewis, James Moffat, G. H. C. Macgregor, J. H. Bernard, and G. P. Lewis in his book, *The Fourth Gospel in Recent Criticism and Interpretation*.[12] Smith rightly recalls these efforts in his outstanding work, *The Composition and Order of the Fourth Gospel*.[13]

Bultmann's theory of rearrangement, however, is unique. He arrives at the following sequence in his commentary:

1:1–21, 25–26, 31, 33–34, 28–30, 35–51
2:1–15
3:1-21, 31–36, 22–30
4:1–54
6:1–27, 34–35, 30–33, 47–51, 41–46, 36–40, 59
5:1–47
7:15–24

10 *Papyrus Bodmer II: Evangile de Jean chap. 1–14*, ed. Victor Martin (Cologny-Geneva: Bibliotheca Bodmeriana, 1956) 12–14.

11 *Papyrus Bodmer XIV–XV: Evangile de Luc et Jean* [Luc chap. 3–24; Jean chap. 1–15] ed. V. Martin and R. Kasser (Cologny-Geneva: Bibliotheca Bodmeriana, 1961) 10.

12 (London: Epworth Press, [4]1955) 111–27, 303.

13 *Composition and Order*, 116–212.

8:13–21
7:1–14, 25–29
8:41–47, 51–53, 56–59
9:1–41
8:12
12:44–50
8:21–25, 28–29
12:34–36
10:19–26, 11–13, 1–10, 14–18, 27–33, 37–42
11:1–57
12:1–33
8:30–40
6:60–71
12:37–43
13:1–31a
17:1–26
13:31b–35
15:1–27
16:1–33
13:36–38
14:1–31
18:1–20, 31
Fragments: 6:28–29; 8:26–27

How is it possible for the text transmitted to us to have arisen from Bultmann's conjectured text? Bultmann rejects the attempt, such as Hoare later undertook, to account for the process in detail. For, as he admits, the orginal order of the text in chapter 6 "cannot be restored with certainty."[14] In the same chapter, "the present text is in a state of disorder, or at least of very poor order, which I can only explain by suggesting that it is the work of an editor who, having found a text which for external reasons had been completely destroyed and so disordered, attempted himself to reconstruct the original order."[15] "Particularly in the middle sections of the Gospel, the editor must have had a text which was highly disjointed and full of omissions."[16] "In my view the only solution is that the section whose conclusion is found in

8:41ff. has been lost (with the exception, that is, of this conclusion). This surely will be no surprise to us, in view of the state of the Gospel. For once it has been accepted that the original text has been disrupted, then the possibility must also be reckoned with that parts of the text have been lost."[17] The redactor "did not create disorder, but attempted to put a disordered text into some sort of order." [18] His job was "to put into order a text that had not yet been published and which, for external reasons, had fallen into disorder."[19] "We cannot say what created the disorder originally (perhaps the confusion of pages)."[20] "As corroboration of the rearrangement theory it may *perhaps* be mentioned that a number of segments that have been displaced are almost exactly the same size, e.g. 3:31–36; 12:33–36, 44–50, and, in addition, the segments in chapters 7 and 8 that have been confused. That would indicate that individual sheets of the work have been mixed up. However, for the whole it is not sufficient to accept the transposition of a page or several pages; the disturbance must have gone much farther, at least in part, as the disorder that prevails within chapters 6 and 10 shows, in my opinion."[21] But in response to the question how the disorder in the present text arose, "it is first of all to be definitely stated that the right of critical observation and the attempt to discover the original order does not depend on the ability to answer this question. But the attempt must be made!"[22] "There are nevertheless some instances in which the transmitted order is meaningless, e.g. the sequence of the farewell discourses, which can be understood merely as the expression of perplexity, or the position of 12:44–50."[23]

B. S. Easton opposes this attempt of Bultmann to reorder the text in his review of Bultmann's work.[24] To be sure, other scholars have reversed chapters 5 and 6[25] or even 3:22–30 and 3:31–36. But assuming that a papyrus roll had been damaged, there would certainly have been broken sentences and words as well. Bultmann does indeed switch sentences far removed from each other,

---

14   *John*, 220 [163].
15   *John*, 220 [162].
16   *John*, 222 n. 2 [164 n. 2].
17   *John*, 315 [238].
18   *John*, 353 n.3 on 8:28 [289 n.1].
19   Bultmann, "Hirschs Auslegung des Johannes-Evangeliums," 117.
20   *RGG*³ 3: 841.

21   Bultmann, "Hirschs Auslegung des Johannes-Evangeliums," 119.
22   Bultmann, "Hirschs Auslegung des Johannes-Evangeliums," 118f.
23   Bultmann, "Hirschs Auslegung des Johannes-Evangeliums," 118f.
24   "Bultmann's RQ Source," *JBL* 65 (1946) 118f.
25   Easton concedes this point.

but always full sentences. How can one account for the fact that 8:12 belongs between 9:41 and 12:44? If the Evangelist wrote short segments on cheap scraps of papyrus without indicating where they went (Easton also reflected on this possibility), then it is impossible to restore the original order of the text.

D. M. Smith has taken up this argument again. [26] One might attempt to support this line of reasoning with the supposition that the redactor had correctly completed incomplete words and sentences in each instance. But such confidence in the ability of the redactor does not square with his failures at other points. It remains a mystery how chapter 9 in the middle of the Gospel and the final section from 18:1 on escaped disturbance, when one considers what we learned from $\mathfrak{P}^{66}$ and $\mathfrak{P}^{75}$, which were especially lightly damaged, and how chapter 6 in its otherwise relatively secure position suffered so much.

Bultmann speaks of the confusion of pages or sheets, which admittedly does not explain everything. He has in mind the manuscript as a whole, one that fell into disorder more or less because of external forces. As a consequence, it did not occur to him that the manuscript may have deteriorated over a long period of time from use; on the contrary, he appears to think that the original manuscript had been damaged by alien, mechanical forces when it fell into the hands of the redactor. But this entails a difficulty that ought to be noted. The Gospel must not have been very heavily damaged, otherwise the redactor would not have noticed that he had in his hand a work of the highest value for the church and that this work was worth making legible and publishing and that it was his duty to do so. If we accept Bultmann's reconstruction of the text, there were indeed some chapters that remained entirely undisturbed, such as chapter 2, chapter 4, chapter 5, chapter 9, chapter 11, chapter 15, chapter 16, chapter 17, and chapters 18–20. That would be something more than half of the Gospel. However, Bultmann thinks these chapters have suffered displacement, in part. But what Bultmann suggests with respect

to displacement and the exchange of pages is not entirely clear, since Bultmann himself says that the displacement of pages will not explain everything. That is, in fact, the case. One need only look over the changes Bultmann introduces into the reconstruction of chapter 1: in place of the present order of 1:1–51, the proposed order is 1:1–21, 25–26, 31, 33–34, 28–30, 35–51. Since the redactor, as Bultmann emphasizes, wanted to create order rather than disorder, he must have come across each of the relatively small segments, verses 1–21, verses 25–26, verse 31, verses 33–34, verses 28–30, and verses 35–51, each as an independent fragment. Such segments were not created, however, by an external derangement of a manuscript. If the joins of a papyrus roll came loose, that would explain nothing, and we get no further with the destruction of the binding of a papyrus codex. Bultmann contributes to the solution with two notions that were not thought through: (1) external deterioration that led, in some chapters, to crumbling;[27] and (2) the confusion of pages, which cannot however be a symptom of old age.

It is therefore not surprising that more recent commentaries on the Gospel of John, like those of Schnackenburg and Brown, discuss the question of rearrangement very cautiously. Schnackenburg admittedly does not contest the fact that sheets were occasionally confused in old writings: Sir 33:16b–36:10 once stood between 30:24 and 30:25, (two signatures of ca. 160 stichoi were displaced),[28] and in 1 Enoch 91:12–17 (8–10 weeks of the ten-week apocalypse) was removed to a position before chapter 93 (weeks 1-7).[29] In the case of John, the dislocation must have occurred already in the original text; in those days one still wrote on papyrus rolls, "and if so, the hypothesis breaks down from the start."[30] Now that is not altogether accurate: dislocations could also take place in the case of papyrus rolls, as Crönert,[31] has shown, as sheets were being glued together. Today it is not at all improbable that Christians made use of the papyrus codex already at the end of the

26 *Composition and Order*, 176.

27 *John*, 220 n. 2 [164 n. 2].

28 According to Alfred Rahlfs, *Septuaginta. Id est Vetus Testamentum graece iuxta LXX interpretes*, 2 vols. (Stuttgart: Deutsche Bibelstiftung, 1935) 2: 429 n.

29 Cf. Schnackenburg, *John*, 1: 53f.

30 Schnackenburg, *John*, 1: 54.

31 "Die Überlieferung des Index Academicorum."

Hermes 38 (1903) 357–405.

first century. On the other hand, the other two objections of Schnackenburg to Bultmann's claims retain their force: the number and length of lines vary widely, so that all calculations having to do with average lines—so much in favor earlier—has become questionable. Beyond that, it is difficult to explain how the deterioration of a manuscript, as Bultmann presupposes, permitted self-contained units to be preserved and then displaced. In order to determine his own position, Schnackenburg[32] reviews the transpositions Wikenhauser affirms: (a) 3:31–36 must originally have followed upon 3:21. Schnackenburg accepts this dislocation, but makes a redactor responsible for it. (b) Chapter 6 stood before chapter 5. A redactor is also guilty of creating this dislocation. (c) 7:15–24 is the continuation of 5:19–47. This is true, but again the redactor is responsible. (d) Schnackenburg rejects the positioning of 10:1–18 between 10:29 and 10:30, as he does (e) the removal of 12:44–50 to another place. Finally, (f) Schnackenburg attributes the insertion of chapters 15–17 to the editorial activity of disciples.

In other words, instead of the fortuitous interchange of sheets or pages, we have here the deliberate rearrangements of a redactor. It then becomes questionable why the redactor made changes for the worse in the text he received. Against the hypothesis that the Evangelist left behind him material that had not been finally put into order, Schnackenburg[33] objects that the Evangelist would not have written on individual sheets but on a roll. Here Schnackenburg becomes the victim of older views of how one composed on rolls.

Brown is still more critical of accidental displacements:[34] one could remove some difficulties in this way, to be sure, but not all of them. Moreover, serious objections remain against any theory of displacement: (1) There is the danger that the commentator will be be commenting on a text that never existed, while the received text did and does exist. (2) The text we have today must have made sense for a contemporary editor. Is it so certain that modern methods can reconstruct a more original order? (3) There is often lacking an explanation of how a particular displacement took place (Brown is also wrong in saying that in a roll the confusion of sheets is not plausible). Surprisingly, Hoare's proposal fares well with Brown[35] because he has not thought it through closely enough. On the whole, however, Brown sticks to the view that theories of accidental displacement create as many problems as they solve.

The time of theories of displacement is gone. They are meaningful when an isolated, coherent segment demonstrably belongs to another context (as in Sirach and 1 Enoch). They lose their cogency when one attempts to make a legible book out of a very difficult text—as in Scott's edition of the Hermetica.[36] That the day of the displacement theory is past is shown by Bultmann himself: in addition to the theory of displacement (that was supposed to smooth out all aporias), there is a four-source theory (revelation discourses, signs source, passion story, other traditions), and then to go with this motley "original text" the distinction between Evangelist and redactor. It is now supposed that in one of these alleged sources ("revelation discourses") there is material for understanding the world in a definite way, viz., a witness for the gnostic revelation myth, which indicates something like the historical locus of this thought. At the same time, this hypothetical source becomes the covert perspective from which the entire Gospel is exegeted. Not only does the history of religions make its claim, but the ground is already being prepared (since 1923, before the close connection with Heidegger) for something like existential interpretation. The theory of displacements is thereby turned into a means (on which one will not reflect very long, as a consequence), which permits the theology of the Gospel of John to be made accessible to modern man.

32 *John,* 1: 55f.
33 *John,* 1: 54.
34 *John,* 1: XXVI–XXVIII.
35 *John,* 1: XVIII.
36 W. Scott and A. S. Ferguson, *Hermetica. The Ancient Greek and Latin Writings which contain religious and philosophic teachings ascribed to Hermes Trismegistos,* 4 vols. (Oxford: Clarendon Press, 1924–1936) 124ff.

5. The Language of the Gospel of John

Bibliography

Abbott, Edwin Abbott
Johannine Grammar (London: A. & C. Black, 1906; reprint Farnborough, England: Gregg International Publishers, 1968).

Abbott, Edwin Abbott
Johannine Vocabulary (London: A. & C. Black, 1905). Reprinted as part one of his *Johannine Grammar* (Farnborough, England: Gregg International Publishers, 1968).

Aland, Kurt
Die Stellung der Kinder in der frühen christlichen Gemeinde und ihre Taufe, Theologische Existenz Heute, n.s., 138 (Munich: Chr. Kaiser Verlag, 1967).

Allis, Oswald T.
"The Alleged Aramaic Origin of the Fourth Gospel." *Princeton Theological Review* 26 (1928) 531–72.

Ball, C. J.
"Had the Fourth Gospel an Aramaic Archetype?" *ExpTim* 21 (1909/1910) 91–93.

Barrett, Charles Kingsley
"The Theological Vocabulary of the Fourth Gospel and of the 'Gospel of Truth.'" In *Current Issues in New Testament Interpretation. Essays in honor of Otto A. Piper,* ed. W. Klassen and G. F. Snyder (New York: Harper, 1962) 210–23, 297–98.

Black, Matthew
An Aramaic Approach to the Gospels and Acts (Oxford: Clarendon Press, 1946, ²1954).

Black, Matthew
"Does an Aramaic Tradition Underlie John i.16?" *JTS* 42 (1941) 69–70.

Blumenthal, M.
"Die Eigenart des johanneische Erzählungsstiles." *TSK* 106 (1934/1935) 204–12.

Boismard, Marie-Emile
"Un procédé rédactionnel dans le quatrième évangile: la Wiederaufnahme." In *L'Evangile de Jean. Sources, rédaction, théologie,* ed. M. de Jonge. BETL 44 (Gembloux: Duculot; Louvain: University Press, 1977) 235–41.

Bonsirven, Joseph
"Les aramaïsmes de S. Jean l'évangéliste?" *Bib* 30 (1949) 405–32.

Bowen, Clayton R.
"The Fourth Gospel as Dramatic Material." *JBL* 49 (1930) 292–305.

Braun, François-Marie
"La reduction du pluriel au singulier dans l'évangile et la première lettre de Jean." *NTS* 24 (1977/1978) 40–67.

Brown, Schuyler
"From Burney to Black. The Fourth Gospel and

the Aramaic Question." *CBQ* 26 (1964) 323–39.

Burchard, C.
"Εἰ nach einem Ausdruck des Wissens oder Nicht-wissens Joh 9:25, Act 19:2, I Cor 1:16, 7:16." *ZNW* 52 (1961) 73–82.

Burney, Charles Fox
The Aramaic Origin of the Fourth Gospel (London: Clarendon Press, 1922).

Burrows, Millar
"The Original Language of the Gospel of John." *JBL* 49 (1930) 95–139.

Buttmann, A.
Review of "Über den Gebrauch des Pronomen ἐκεῖνος im vierten Evangelium," by Georg Eduard Steitz. *TSK* 33 (1860) 505–36.

Cadbury, Henry J.
The Making of the Luke-Acts (London: S. P. C. K, 1968).

Cassem, N. H.
"A Grammatical and Contextual Inventory of the Use of κόσμος in the Johannine Corpus with some Implications for a Johannine Cosmic Theology." *NTS* 19 (1972/1973) 81–91.

Clavier, Henri
"Notes sur un mot-clef du johannisme et de la sotériologie biblique, ἱλασμός." *NovT* 10 (1968) 287–304.

Colwell, Ernest Cadman
The Greek of the Fourth Gospel. A Study of its Aramaisms in the Light of Hellenistic Greek (Chicago: University of Chicago Press, 1931).

Connick, C. Milo
"The Dramatic Character of the Fourth Gospel." *JBL* 67 (1948) 159–69.

Cullmann, Oscar
"Der johanneische Gebrauch doppeldeutiger Ausdrücke als Schlüssel zum Verstädnis des vierten Evangeliums." *TZ* 4 (1948) 360–72. In his *Vorträge und Aufsätze 1925–1962*, ed. K. Fröhlich (Tübingen: Mohr-Siebeck; Zurich: Zwingli Verlag, 1966) 176–86.

Dalman, Gustaf
The Words of Jesus, tr. D. M. Kay (Edinburgh: T. & T. Clark, 1902) = *Die Worte Jesu* (Leipzig: J. C. Hinrichs, 1898, ²1930; reprint Darmstadt: Wissenschaftliche Buchgesellschaft, 1965).

Dibelius, Martin
"The Structure and Literary Character of the Gospels." *HTR* 20 (1927) 151–70.

Dinechin, Olivier de
"Καθώς: la similitude dans l'Evangile selon saint Jean." *RSR* 58 (1970) 195–236.

Driver, Godfrey Rolles
"The Original Language of the Fourth Gospel." *Jewish Guardian* (1923) 1–8.

Dulière, W. L.
La haute terminologie de la rédaction johannique. Les vocables qu'elle a introduits chez les Gréco-Romains: Le Logos-Verbe, le Paraclet-Esprit-Saint et le Messias-

Messie, Collection Latomus 117 (Brussels: Latomus, 1970).

Enslin, Morton Scott
"The Perfect Tense in the Fourth Gospel." *JBL* 55 (1936) 121–31.

Fee, Gordon D.
"The Use of the Definite Article with Personal Names in the Gospel of John." *NTS* 17 (1970/1971) 168–83.

Festugière, A. J.
Observations stylistiques sur l'évangile de S. Jean, Etudes et commentaires 84 (Paris: Klincksieck, 1974).

Fiebig, Paul
"Die Mekhilta und das Johannes-Evangelium." *Angelos* 1 (1925) 57–59.

Fortna, Robert T.
"Theological Use of Locale in the Fourth Gospel." In *Gospel Studies in honor of J. E. Johnson,* ed. M. H. Shepherd, Jr. and E. C. Hobbs. Anglican Theological Review, Supplementary Studies 3 (Evanston, IL, 1974) 58–95.

Freed, Edwin D.
"Variations in the Language and Thought of John." *ZNW* 55 (1964) 167–97.

Gersdorf, Christoph Gotthelf
Beiträge zur Sprachcharakteristik der Schrifsteller des Neuen Testaments. Eine Sammlung meist neuer Bemerkungen (Leipzig: Weidmann, 1816).

Gingrich, Felix Wilbur
"The Gospel of John and Modern Greek." *Classical Weekly* 38 (1945) 145–82.

Glas, S.
Philologia Sacra (Amsterdam, 1694; Leipzig: J. F. Gleditschium, ²1705).

Granger, F.
"The Semitic Element in the Fourth Gospel." *Expositor,* 8th ser., 11 (1916) 349–71.

Gyllenberg, Rafael
"Anschauliches und Unanschauliches im vierten Evangelium." *Studia Theologica Lundensia* 21 (1967) 83–109.

Haenchen, Ernst
"Statistische Erforschung des Neuen Testaments." *TLZ* 87 (1962) 487–98.

Heise, Jürgen
Bleiben. Menein in den johanneischen Schriften, Hermeneutische Untersuchungen zur Theologie 8 (Tübingen: Mohr-Siebeck, 1967).

Hirsch, Emanuel
"Stilkritik und Literaranalyse im vierten Evangelium." *ZNW* 43 (1950/1951) 129–43.

Hobbs, H. H.
"Word Studies in the Gospel of John." *Southwestern Journal of Theology* 8 (1965) 67–79.

Hunkin, J. W.
"Pleonastic' ἄρχομαι in the New Testament." *JTS* 25 (1924) 390–402.

Jeremias, Joachim
"Johanneische Literarkritik." *TBl* 20 (1941) 33–46.

Kalitsunakis, J.
Grammatik der neugriechischen Volkssprache (Berlin: Walter de Gruyter, 1963).

Käsemann, Ernst
"Aufbau und Anliegen des johanneischen Prologs." In *Libertas Christiana, Friedrich Delekat zum fünfundsechzigsten Geburtstag*, ed. W. Matthias and E. Wolf. BEvT 26 (Munich: Chr. Kaiser Verlag, 1957) 75–99. Also in Käsemann's *Exegetische Versuche und Besinnungen* (Göttingen: Vandenhoeck & Ruprecht, 1964) 2: 155–80.

Kilpatrick, George D.
"Some Notes on Johannine Usage." *BT* 2 (1960) 173–77.

Kypke, G. D.
Observationes sacrae in Novi Foederis libros ex auctoribus potissimum graecis et antiquitatibus, 2 vols. (Breslau: Korn, 1755), esp. 1: 347–416.

Lattey, Cuthbert
"The Semitisms of the Fourth Gospel." *JTS* 20 (1918/1919) 330–36.

Lattke, Michael
Einheit im Wort. Die spezifische Bedeutung von 'agape,' 'apagan' und 'philein' im Johannesevangelium, SANT 41 (Munich: Kösel, 1975).

Leroy, Herbert
Rätsel und Mißverständnis. Ein Beitrag zur Formgeschichte des Johannesevangeliums, BBB 30 (Bonn: Peter Hanstein, 1968).

Leroy, Herbert
"Das johanneische Mißverständnis als literarische Form." *BibLeb* 9 (1968) 196–207.

Lewis, Frank Warburton
Disarrangements in the Fourth Gospel (Cambridge: Cambridge University Press, 1910).

Menoud, Philippe-Henri
L'évangile de Jean d'après les recherches récentes (Neuchâtel and Paris: Delachaux et Niestlé, ²1947).

Morgenthaler, Robert
Statistik des neutestamentlichen Wortschatzes (Zurich: Gotthelf Verlag, 1958).

Morris, Leon
"A Feature of Johannine Style." In his *Studies in the Fourth Gospel* (Grand Rapids: Eerdmans, 1969) 293–310.

Moulton, J. H., F. W. Howard, and N. Turner
A Grammar of New Testament Greek, 4 vols. (Edinburgh: T. & T. Clark, 1906–1976) 2: 205–83.

Muilenburg, James
"Literary Form in the Fourth Gospel." *JBL* 51 (1932) 40–53.

Neirynck, Frans et al.
Jean et les Synoptiques. Examen critique de l'exégèse de M.-E. Boismard, BETL 49 (Louvain: University Press, 1979) 41–70.

Nevius, Richard C.
"The Use of the Definitive Article with 'Jesus' in the Fourth Gospel." *NTS* 12 (1965) 81–85.

Odeberg, Hugo
The Fourth Gospel. Interpreted in its Relation to Contemporaneous Religious Currents in Palestine and in the Hellenistic-Oriental World (Uppsala: Almqvist & Wiksells, 1929; reprint Amsterdam: B. R. Grüner; Chicago: Argonaut, 1968).

O'Rourke, John J.
"*Eis* and *en* in John." *BT* 25 (1974) 139–42.

O'Rourke, John J.
"The Historic Present in the Gospel of John." *JBL* 93 (1974) 585–90.

Pernot, M.
"Langue de la Septante." *Revue des études grecques* 42 (1929) 411–25.

Pinto de Oliveira, C. J.
"Le verbe διδοναι comme expression des rapports du Père et du Fils dans le quatrième évangile." *RSPT* 49 (1965) 81–104.

Radermacher, L.
Neutestamentliche Grammatik. Das Griechisch des Neuen Testaments im Zusammenhang mit der Volkssprache dargestellt, HNT 1 (Tübingen: Mohr-Siebeck, ²1925).

Raphael, G.
Annotationes Philologicae in NT (Lüneburg: J. A. Langevak, 1747).

Riesenfeld, Harald
"Zu den johanneischen ἱνα-Sätzen." *ST* 19 (1965) 213–20.

Roberge, Michel
"Notices de conclusion et redaction du quatrième évangile." *Laval théologique et philosophique* 31 (1975) 49–53.

Ruckstuhl, Eugen
"Johannine Language and Style. The Question of their Unity." In *L'Evangile de Jean. Sources, rédaction, théologie*, ed. M. de Jonge. BETL 44 (Gembloux: Duculot; Louvain: University Press, 1977) 125–47.

Ruckstuhl, Eugen
Die literarische Einheit des Johannesevangeliums; der gegenwärtige Stand der einschlägigen Forschungen (Fribourg: Paulusverlag, 1951).

Rudel, W.
"Das Mißverständnis im Johannesevangelium." *NKZ* 32 (1921) 351–61.

Schlatter, Adolf
"Die Sprache und die Heimat des vierten Evangelisten." In *Johannes und sein Evangelium*, ed. K. H. Rengstorf. Wege der Forschung 82 (Darmstadt: Wissenschaftliche Buchgesellschaft, 1973) 28–201.

Schulze, J. D.
Der schriftstellerische Charakter und Werth des Johannes zum Behuf der Specialhermeneutik seiner Schriften untersucht und bestimmt. Voran ein Nachtrag über die Quellen der Briefe von Petrus, Jakobus und

Judas, und über das Verhältnis dieser Briefe zu andern neutestamentlichen Schriften (Weissenfels: In der Böseschen Buchhandlung, 1803).

Schwartz, Eduard
"Das philologische Problem des Johannesevangelium." In his *Gesammelte Schriften*, 5 vols. (Berlin: Walter de Gruyter, 1938–1963) 1: 131–36.

Schweizer, Eduard
Ego Eimi. Die religionsgeschichtliche Herkunft und theologische Bedeutung der johanneischen Bildreden, zugleich ein Beitrag zur Quellenfrage des vierten Evangeliums, FRLANT, n.s., 38 (Göttingen: Vandenhoeck & Ruprecht, ²1965).

Segovia, F.
"*Agape* and *agapan* in First John and the Johannine Tradition." Dissertation, Notre Dame University, 1978.

Seyffarth, T. A.
Ein Beitrag zur Specialcharakteristik der johanneischen Schriften besonders des Johanneischen Evangeliums (Leipzig: C. H. Reclam, 1823).

Seynaeve, Jaak
"Les verbes ἀποστέλλω et πέμπω dans le vocabulaire théologique de Saint Jean." In *L'Evangile de Jean. Sources, rédaction, théologie*, ed. M. de Jonge. BETL 44 (Gembloux: Duculot; Louvain: University Press, 1977) 385–89.

Stange, Erich
Die Eigenart der Johanneischen Produktion. Ein Beitrag zur Kritik der neueren Quellenscheidungshypothesen und zur Charakteristik der Johanneischen Psyche (Dresden: C. L. Ungelenk, 1915).

Steitz, Georg Eduard
"Der classische und der johanneische Gebrauch von ἐκεῖνος." *TSK* 34 (1861) 267–310.

Steitz, Georg Eduard
"Über den Gebrauch des Pronomen ἐκεῖνος im vierten Evangelium." *TSK* 32 (1859) 497–506.

Strachan, Robert Harvey
The Fourth Evangelist: Dramatist or Historian? (London: Hodder & Stoughton; New York: G. H. Doran, 1925).

Süß, W.
Review of *La questione Petroniana*, by E. von Mamorate. *Gnomon* 23 (1951) 312–17.

Swanson, D. C.
"Diminutives in the Greek New Testament." *JBL* 77 (1958) 134–51.

Thackeray, H. St. John
Josephus. The Man and the Historian (New York: KTAV Publishing House, 1967).

Torrey, Charles Cutler
"The Aramaic Origin of the Gospel of John." *HTR* 16 (1923) 305–44.

Turner, Nigel
Grammatical Insights into the New Testament (Edinburgh: T. & T. Clark, 1966) 135–54.

Unnik, W. C. van
"C. F. Burney's Hypothese aangaande de Aramaesche achtergrond van het Johannes-Evangelie." *Vox Theologica* 7 (1935) 123–31.

Vorster, W. S.
"The Gospel of John as Language." *Neot* 6 (1972) 19–27.

Wahlde, Urban C. von
"A Literary Analysis of the *ochlos*-passages in the Fourth Gospel in their Relation to the Pharisees and Jews-material." Dissertation, Marquette University, 1975.

Wahlde, Urban C. von
"A Redactional Technique in the Fourth Gospel." *CBQ* 38 (1976) 520–33.

Wead, David W.
"The Johannine Double Meaning." *Restoration Quarterly* 13 (1970) 106–20.

Wead, David W.
"The Literary Devices in John's Gospel." Dissertation, Basel, 1970.

Wellhausen, Julius
Das Evangelium Johannis (Berlin: G. Reimer, 1908) 133–46.

Wootton, R. W. F.
"The Implied Agent in Greek Passive Verbs in Mark, Luke, and John." *BT* 19 (1968) 159–64.

Zwaan, J. de
"John Wrote in Aramaic." *JBL* 57 (1938) 155–71.

Since the Gospel of John is attributed to John, son of Zebedee, in the ecclesiastical tradition, there has been a strong tendency to assume that it was written in Aramaic or at least in a Semitic form of Greek. But it was not until the twentieth century that this hypothesis found numerous advocates. In his book, *Die Sprache und Heimat des vierten Evangelisten*, Schlatter sought to prove that the Greek of the Gospel of John demonstrates that John thought in and spoke Aramaic.[1] According to Dalman,[2] on the other hand, it cannot be shown that an Aramaic gospel ever existed. The alleged Aramaic original of Matthew, about which Jerome often spoke, is a reverse translation of Greek Matthew back into Aramaic. Dalman even defended the thesis that the Gospel of John

---

1   [The Language and Provenance of the Fourth Gospel], in *Johannes und sein Evangelium*, ed. K. H. Rengstorf (Darmstadt: Wissenschaftliche Buchgesellschaft,

2   1973) 28.

The Words of Jesus, tr. D. M. Kay (Edinburgh: T. & T. Clark, 1902) 57–71 = *Die Worte Jesu* (Leipzig: J. C.

was less Aramaic than the Synoptics. Wellhausen,[3] who was as much at home in the Old Testament as in the New, would have nothing to do with the view that the Gospel of John could have been written only by a Palestinian: "If the Greek of John converges with that of Mark in that they both approximate the common tongue, John diverges in that it is not disguised Aramaic." "On account of the solemnity, it imitates the biblical style with respect to parataxis."[4] "The vocabulary is conspicuously poor." Among 15,416 words used there is a vocabulary (according to Nestle) of only 1,011 words. "One has the impression of pedantry, as in the priestly document. . . . The language verges on corthurnus [the dignified and stilted spirit of ancient tragedy]; it is perhaps hieratic."[5]

C. J. Ball inspired a new approach with his essay, "Had the Fourth Gospel an Aramaic Archetype?"[6] He is to thank for the appearance of C. F. Burney's foundational study of 1922, his well-known book, *The Aramaic Origin of the Fourth Gospel*.[7] Burney presupposes that the Synoptic authors wrote koine Greek, and interprets the abundance of synoptic koine expressions in the Gospel of John as Aramaisms, which he also proposes to identify in mistranslations. At some points he functions occasionally as a precursor—an imperfect one, to be sure—of Matthew Black. J. A. Montgomery was satisfied with an "Aramaic background" of the Gospel of John.[8] C. C. Torrey, on the other hand, vigorously championed an Aramaic original of the Gospel of John;[9] he postulated Aramaic originals behind all four Gospels and Acts 1–15. The reviews of Burney's work by Allis, Driver, and Howard do not of course consent to an Aramaic original of the Gospel of John, but they believe it possible that John made use of a source (oral?) for the words of Jesus. Just how one might envisage an oral source for the logia of Jesus is of course not understandable to every reader.

In the second volume of his *Grammar of New Testament Greek*,[10] Howard adds a detailed appendix: "Semitisms in the New Testament." In his study, "The Original Language of the Gospel of John,"[11] M. Burrows undertakes to renew the question whether there really was an Aramaic original of the Gospel of John, and answers it affirmatively on account of Semitisms and mistranslations. The Greek John is a translation of an original gospel created in Palestine or Syria. J. de Zwaan also champions a translation of the Gospel of John from Aramaic in his "John wrote in Aramaic."[12] The principal evidence, as is usually the case with this thesis, consists of alleged mistranslations. Unfortunately, they do not produce what one expects of them. Sometimes the Aramaic that is presupposed is questionable, sometimes the proposed text is no less difficult than the conjectured "mistranslation." M. Black advances only two examples in his famous work, *An Aramaic Approach to the Gospels and Acts*.[13] In the opinion of Barrett, these examples are comprehensible apart from the acceptance of a mistranslation or a Syriac form: 8:25 (ἔλεγον οὖν αὐτῷ, σὺ τίς εἶ; εἶπεν αὐτοῖς ὁ Ἰησοῦς, τὴν ἀρχὴν ὅ τι καὶ λαλῶ ὑμῖν; "They said to him, 'Who are you?' Jesus said to them, 'Why do I talk with you?'")[14] and 11:33 (Ἰησοῦς οὖν . . . ἐνεβριμήσατο τῷ πνεύματι καὶ ἐτάραξεν ἑαυτόν . . . , "Jesus then . . . was deeply moved in spirit and troubled . . .").[15]

As a consequence, most scholars are today inclined to accept the view that the author indeed wrote in Greek, but that he thought in a Semitic language.[16] The chief witnesses—those to whom one appeals—are Billerbeck 2, Odeberg,[17] and Schlatter, who affirm connections between the Fourth Gospel and Semitic thinking.[18] Schlatter is of the opinion that Palestinians might have spoken both Greek and Aramaic. But that is not entirely certain. Josephus, to whom Schlatter constantly appeals,

Hinrichs, 1898, [2]1930; reprint Darmstadt: Wissenschaftliche Buchgesellschaft, 1965) 45–57.

3   *Das Evangelium Johannes*, 145.
4   *Das Evangelium Johannes*, 146.
5   *Das Evangelium Johannes*, 146.
6   *ExpTim* 21 (1909/1910) 91–93.
7   (London: Clarendon Press, 1922).
8   *The Origin of the Gospel according to John* (Philadelphia: Winston, 1923).
9   "The Aramaic Original of the Gospel of John," *HTR* 16 (1923) 305–44.
10 Vol. 2, *Accidence and Word Formation* (Edinburgh: T.

& T. Clark, 1929).
11 *JBL* 49 (1930) 95–139.
12 *JBL* 57 (1938) 155-171.
13 (Oxford: Clarendon Press, 1946) 7.
14 *John*, 284 in the first edition (1955) of Barrett's commentary; omitted in the second edition.
15 *John*, 399f.
16 Büchsel, *Das Evangelium nach Johannes*, 3; Bauer, *Das Johannesevangelium*, 244; Bultmann, *Theology of the NT* 2: 10; Howard, *The Fourth Gospel in Recent Criticism and Interpretation* (London: Epworth Press, [4]1955) 42; Strachan, *The Fourth Gospel, its Significance and*

was not bilingual. He composed the *Jewish Wars* initially in Aramaic. He had the help of literary Greeks in creating the Greek version of the *Jewish Wars*, and these Greeks were zealous co-workers in the *Antiquities* as well, as Thackeray has demonstrated.[19] And so one may suddenly come across a quotation from Sophocles' *Antigone* in Josephus. Schlatter was satisfied with the evidence that many pasages had been translated back into Johannine Greek from the Mishnah, Talmud, and Tosephta. But that does not yet prove that Johannine Greek is Semitic.

Wellhausen, whose final judgment was reported earlier, added a section devoted to "linguistic matters" to his short commentary on the Gospel of John.[20] In this section he sets out the marks of the Johannine language and its relation to Mark and related literature. He begins with the simple sentence and with the word order of the simple sentence.[21] The fact that the verb mostly precedes and the subject follows in John has often been interpreted as a Semitism. But in distinction from Semitic order, John likes to put the subject at the end of the sentence for special emphasis.[22] "The object, whether a substantive or a pronoun, very frequently occurs before the subject," not infrequently before the governing verb, in clear contrast to Mark. The not infrequent occurrence of a substantival or pronominal genitive also before the governing verb or separated from it is entirely unsemitic. "There is no trace of the construct state in John," such as still shows through in Mark.[23] Only in special cases is there Semitic order when a key term is taken out of a construction and placed in initial position as a nominative absolute or a suspended case and then resumed by a relative pronoun.[24] In sum, the word order is unsemitic for the most part; the initial position of the verb imitates biblical style.[25]

In the second section Wellhausen discusses the coordination of sentences.[26] The period in 13:1–3 goes back to the redactor; it is singular in John. "Parataxis predominates." The biblical style thereby often asserts itself. Unusual but attested in Epictetus is the construction βούλεσθε ἀπολύσω, "do you want me to release" in 18:39. But parataxis differs from that in Mark: "Individual sentences are not continuously connected by καί ('and') and they are not particularly introduced by καί. . . . Certain narrative passages have aphoristic character or are written in lapidary style."

Sections 3–9 treat subordination and conjunctions.[27] "Relative clauses are unusually favored"[28] and often substitute for a participal clause or another brief expression. Attraction to the case of a preceding subject appears more frequently than in Mark. "However, there is no trace of an arthrous noun being governed by a following pronoun in Semitic style."[29] "False relative clauses . . . , which continue the action, appear relatively seldom, whereas they are common in Luke."[30]

Section 4[31] points out: "A determinate participal substitutes more frequently for a conditional relative clause with ὅς ἄν, ὅ τι ἄν, ὅσα ἄν ('if any one, if anything') than in the Synoptics; as a rule with πᾶς ('everyone'), but also without."[32] "An initial participle in the nominative need not be the subject, but can be used absolutely, in that it actually represents a sentence; thus ὁ πιστεύων εἰς ἐμέ κτλ. ('He who believes in me') 7:38" (also 15:2).[33]

Environment (London: SCM Press, [3]1946); and more recently also Käsemann, *New Testament Questions*, 140.

17   *The Fourth Gospel: Interpreted in its Relation to Contemporaneous Religious Currents in Palestine and the Hellenistic-Oriental World* (Uppsala: Almqvist & Wiksells, 1929; reprint Amsterdam: B. R. Grüner; Chicago: Argonaut, 1968) 42.

18   *Der Evangelist Johannes.*

19   *Josephus: The Man and the Historian* (New York: KTAV, 1967) 100ff.

20   *Das Evangelium Johannes*, 133–46.

21   *Das Evangelium Johannes*, 133.

22   E.g. 2:9 ὁ ἀρχιτρίκλινος, "steward of the feast"; 6:3 Ἰησοῦς, "Jesus"; 18:33 "King of the Jews?"; 19:38 "Pilate."

23   That ἐκ σπέρματος Δαυίδ, "out of the seed of David," 7:42, is found only in D is only half right: 𝔓66 also has

this reading, while 𝔓75 does not. It is 𝔓66 that shows Western influence. But these papyri were not yet discovered in Wellhausen's time.

24   Cf. Wellhausen, *Das Evangelium Johannes*, §4, 135f.

25   Wellhausen, *Das Evangelium Johannes*, 134.

26   *Das Evanglium Johannes*, 134f.

27   *Das Evangelium Johannes*, 135–37.

28   *Das Evangelium Johannes*, 135.

29   *Das Evangelium Johannes*, 135.

30   *Das Evangelium Johannes*, 135; also cf. Haenchen, *Acts of the Apostles*, 139 n. 7.

31   *Das Evangelium Johannes*, 135f.

32   *Das Evangelium Johannes*, 135.

33   *Das Evangelium Johannes*, 136.

Section 5:[34] "John's use of temporal ὡς ('while, when, after') is to be distinguished from that of Matthew and Mark but not from that of Luke." Ἕως ("while") appears in 9:4 and 12:36 (so 𝔓⁶⁶, ὡς 𝔓⁷⁵). Ἐπεί ("since") appears as infrequently as it does in the Synoptics.

Section 6:[35] Very characteristic of the Gospel of John "are the correlatives which refer to a pronominal or adverbial relative (= conjunction), or also to a participial or even to a substantive" (1:12, 18, 33; 3:32; 5:11, 36f.; 6:57; 7:18; 10:26; 14:13; but also cf. 11:6; 12:26; 15:19).

Section 7:[36] "Object clauses with a participal as predicate are common," as in 1:36. "On the other hand, the accusative with infinitive is found even less frequently than in Mark. In ὅτι-clauses, . . . the subject can be attracted by the verb in the main clause, . . . as in the Synoptics (3:21, 4:35, 5:42, 9:8)." Such attraction also appears in ἵνα-clauses (15:16). The use of περί ("concerning") is charactertistic of the Gospel of John; in 7:17 and 9:17 it introduces the subject of the subordinate clause by way of anticipation.[37]

Section 8:[38] Indirect discourse is as little preferred by John as it is by the Synoptics. On the other hand, direct discourse is not introduced with ὅτι as often as in the Synoptics.

Section 9:[39] Not only is ὅτι driving the infinitive out, but ἵνα also. "Purpose and result clauses are thus introduced indiscriminately." A ἵνα-clause is occasionally entirely independent, as in 1:8: οὐκ ἦν . . . , ἀλλ᾽ ἵνα μαρτυρήσῃ . . . ("he was not . . . , but in order that he might bear witness . . .").

Sections 10–15 treat verbs.

Section 10[40] is devoted to biblicisms and points of contact with the Synoptics. "Permit, let" and "abandon" can both be represented by ἀφιέναι; θέλειν always appears for βούλεσθαι (except for βούλεσθε . . . ἀπολύσω in 18:39). "Ζῆν means 'to be well'" (4:50–53). Faded ἐκβάλλω appears in 10:4.[41] Ἀπεκρίθη καὶ εἶπεν ("he answered and said") appears often, especially in the early chapters. Ἐρωτᾶν ("to ask") is more frequent than in the

Synoptics (exception: 21:12, where ἐξετάζω appears). "In general, the points of contact are outweighed by the differences":[42] λαμβάνω instead of δέχομαι, λαμβάνειν and τιθέναι for sumere and ponere (probably Latinisms).[43] "Auxiliary ἤρξατο, which is so characteristic of the Synoptics, is found only once in the Gospel of John (13:5) and auxiliary καὶ ἐγένετο does not appear at all."[44] Κηρύσσω and ἰσχύω (= δύναμαι) do not appear. Βουλεύεσθαι means "resolve," not "take counsel" (12:10). Compounds are employed only "if the preposition really contributes to the meaning." The manuscripts often "improve" simple forms by turning them into compounds.

Section 11:[45] The passive with ὑπό appears only in 14:21; impersonal "one" is expressed only by the third person plural active in 15:7.

Section 12:[46] The historical present appears even more frequently than in Mark; the Part. Praes. can also substitute for the Part. Praeteriti (9:8, 25). The perfect active is also popular (3:32; 1:2). "Κέκραγεν in 1:15 and γέγραφα in 19:22 are striking."

Section 13:[47] The periphrastic conjugation is unusual in the active, but very common in the perfect and pluperfect passive. It is always ἔστι γεγραμμένον in place of synoptic γέγραπται.

Section 14:[48] Participles are the subject of this section: An articular participle for the most part represents a generalized subject or a particular subject. It appears without article and in the genitive absolute only in late passages.

Section 15:[49] Finally, the infinitive is being threatened by ὅτι and ἵνα. The substantivized infinite is rare.

Wellhausen treats substantives in sections 16f.[50] "John's nominal vocabulary differs from that of the Synoptics at least as much as does his verbal lexical stock." The term ῥάββι appears in place of διδάσκαλε. Παρρησία means "openness" and not "courage."[51] "The substantivized phrases τὰ ἐπουράνια, τὰ ἐπίγεια, τὰ ἐμά, τὰ ἴδια, τὰ ἄνω, τὰ κάτω are noteworthy."

Section 17:[52] "The article occasionally has generic

---

34   Das Evangelium Johannes, 136.
35   Das Evangelium Johannes, 136.
36   Das Evangelium Johannes, 136f.
37   Das Evangelium Johannes, 137.
38   Das Evangelium Johannes, 137.
39   Das Evangelium Johannes, 137.
40   Das Evangelium Johannes, 137–39.
41   Das Evangelium Johannes, 137f.

42   Das Evangelium Johannes, 138.
43   Das Evangelium Johannes, 49 n. 1.
44   Das Evangelium Johannes, 138.
45   Das Evangelium Johannes, 139.
46   Das Evangelium Johannes, 139.
47   Das Evangelium Johannes, 139.
48   Das Evangelium Johannes, 140.
49   Das Evangelium Johannes, 140.

significance" (2:25, 7:51, 13:5, 15:6). It is lacking rather regularly before determined appelatives; cf. 1:49 (but 3:10), 5:26, 19:7 also. A substantive is made indeterminate by the addition of τις (4:46, 5:5)(not as in Matt 13:28, 52, 18:33, 20:1, 21:33, where ἄνθρωπος appears, or εἷς in the Synoptics: a usage of koine); ἐκ is used with the plural rather than ἀπό (3:25, 7:40).

Section 18:[53] Wellhausen treats pronouns in this section. The object can come before the verb and the genetive before the nominative in John. "It is a peculiarity of Johannine usage . . . that the independent pronouns in the first and second persons" can be used to clarify the subject without giving special emphasis. The use of such pronoun subjects "is to be explained on the basis of colloquial usage," rather than on the basis of Aramaic. The reflexives in the second and third persons, lacking in Semitic languages, are common in the Gospel of John. John makes common use of possessive pronouns also uncommon in Semitic languages. "Ἴδιος functions as the possessive of the third person." Ἐκεῖνος is the favorite demonstrative (koine).

Section 19:[54] Adjectives are rare in the Gospel of John. Ἄλλος always appears in place of ἕτερος. Adverbs derived from adjectives are rare.[55] Τότε is common, but does not mean "thereupon" as it does in Mark. The phrase μετὰ τοῦτο is a peculiarity of John (μετὰ ταῦτα as in Luke). Νῦν varies with ἄρτι.

Section 21:[56] The use of prepositions is gaining ground at the expense of the simple cases (the genitive in particular, but also the dative). The partitive genitive is assisted by the use of ἐκ, the dative by the use of ἐν: 7:4, 16:29, 5:16, 7:22f., 19:31, 6:39, 44, 54, 7:37, 11:24, 12:48. Ἀπό has causal significance only in 21:6. The prepositions εἰς and ἐν are also confused in John; "when" and "where" are also confused with πρός, παρά, and ἐπί. Περί (in regard to) passes over to the meaning of ὑπέρ in 1:30; the latter is often used in the theological sense as it is by Paul. In 8:38 and 11:55 D, πρίν is used as a preposition with the accusative.

Wellhausen was concerned to compare Johannine usage with synoptic and to clarify the relationship of the former to Aramaic. He was occasionally struck by the fact that John and Epictetus concurred. This raises the question that was first clearly perceived and answered by E. C. Colwell: Where is the linguistic usage to be found to which the Johannine usage corresponds?[57]

The answer Colwell gave was: in non-literary koine. The term "koine" is used to designate two different forms of the Greek language in use at that time. "Literary" koine (in contrast to Atticizing Greek) is the written language. "Koine" can also refer to the everyday, spoken language, particularly among common people (the "vulgar" tongue). That does not mean that it was rare. Its characteristics go beyond the limits of Greek and manifest themselves in Latin also, and even in Aramaic. Unfortunately, we have but few witnesses for them: above all, in the comedies, in the humorous sketches in which slaves have a speaking part, but also in the work of Epictetus written in popular style. In reviewing a book of E. von Marmorate, *La questione Petroniana*, W. Süss addressed this problem and offers some observations that are very important for us. The non-literary koine of this period makes use of a newly created indefinite article (earlier *homo* could have meant "the man" as well as "a man"), corresponding to the numeral *unus* (which lives on in French *un* and *une*) and to the Greek εἷς. This εἷς is thus not to be explained on the basis of Aramaic חד, but is rather spoken koine. Instead of *unus*, one could also use *ille*, which then led to French *il* and *ille*. There was a tendency to derive "empty" ἤρξατο (its full meaning is "begin") likewise from Aramaic,[58] but *coepi* is used in Latin—in what corresponds to its non-literary koine—in the same way. Swanson has demonstrated to what extent koine was fond of the so-called diminutives in -ιον, -άριον, -ίδιον, -αρίδιον, -ιδάριον, -ίσκος, ισκη; he has assembled the evidence in perspicuous tables.[59] How important such information is for NT exegesis has been shown in the discussion of the pericope on "the little daughter" of

50 *Das Evangelium Johannes*, 140f.
51 *Das Evangelium Johannes*, 141.
52 *Das Evangelium Johannes*, 141.
53 *Das Evangelium Johannes*, 141f.
54 *Das Evangelium Johannes*, 142.
55 *Das Evangelium Johannes*, §20, 142f.
56 *Das Evangelium Johannes*, 143f.
57 *The Greek of the Fourth Gospel. A Study of its Aramaisms*

in the Light of Hellenistic Greek (Chicago: University of Chicago Press, 1931).

58 Cf. J. W. Hunkin, "Pleonastic ἄρχομαι in the New Testament," *JTS* 25 (1924) 390–402.

59 "Diminutives in New Testament Greek," *JBL* 77 (1958) 134–51.

Jairus: Mark speaks of a θυγάτριον ("little daughter") in 5:23, of παιδίον ("little child") in 5:39, and of κοράσιον ("little girl") in 5:41f. But we learn at the same time that the "little girl" is about twelve years old. She was in that case a נערה and would be marriageable in six months, according to Billerbeck.[60] In his dialogue with J. Jeremias on the question of infant baptism, Aland has quite correctly applied this point.[61] The "ear" (ὠτάριον; 𝔓[66] ὠτίον) of Malchus that Peter cut off in John 18:10 was not a "little ear," but was entirely normal, and the "dogs" of Mark 7:27, Matt 15:26f. were not lap-dogs, but simply dogs without pedigree who waited under the table for scraps. We will discuss these matters further below.

The important essay of J. Bonsirven, "Les aramaïsmes de S. Jean l'Evangeliste?" next requires mention.[62] The insights advanced in this essay are highly significant for our purposes. Bonsirven lays down the following theses for the Gospel of John:

(1) John made use of Greek words to which nothing corresponds in Semitic languages and which therefore appear rarely in the LXX;

(2) John uses Greek words for which only compound expressions occur in Semitic languages;

(3) John employs Greek words which in Semitic possess a sense foreign to the context;

(4) John utilizes Greek words that are (almost) synonymous, without the implication that they conceal different Semitic expressions;

(5) John draws Greek words from a hellenistic vocabulary; and

(6) he made use of the language of non-literary koine precisely at those points where scholars have been inclined to find Aramaisms.

These theses become especially significant in view of the question whether the Fourth Gospel exhibits a unified language. That brings us to the book of E. Schweizer, *Ego Eimi*, which quickly attracted attention in its day. The author is concerned with "the history of religions origin and the theological significance of the Johannine discourses." From the question of the origin of the "ego eimi formula" (chapter 1), to which the Mandean documents then offered the best parallels (chapter 2), Schweizer passes over to the question of Johannine sources in chapter 3. At this point he writes: "There are certain explicit Johannine characteristics, constructions, usages, words that appear within the NT exclusively or almost exclusively in John."[63] If one were to meet these features only in certain sections of the Gospel of John, one would have to assign each of these passages to a particular source. If there were no divisions of this kind, then it would probably be the "final author who either formulated everything himself" or reworked the peculiarities of his source "in his own style." In the second case, we have to reject theories of partition and the "question of sources" is "no longer so decisive."[64]

Schweizer therefore presupposes that one can make inferences from style (style in the sense of the use of certain words and expressions) to the use of particular sources. He makes use of statistics in pursuing his aim. He expresses the results of his study each time in a formula: a + b/c + d. In this formula (a) stands for the frequency of the characteristic feature (whether it is a word or an expression) in the Gospel of John; (b) represents the frequency in the letters of John; (c) stands for the frequency in the balance of the NT; and (d) means the frequency in the synoptic Gospels. The frequency of a word outside the NT is not taken into consideration. Schweizer applies the term "Johannine," then, to a word when it appears frequently in the Gospel of John but rarely or never in the rest of the NT. Where two of these characteristic features appear in one sentence, then all further sentences exhibiting these same two features stem from the same author. The thirty-three Johannine features that Schweizer finally lays out in a list (according to their frequency, which corresponds to their evidential value) encompasses practically the entirety of the Gospel of John, including chapter 21.

J. Jeremias[65] and Menoud[66] have endeavored to sup-

---

60 2: 10.

61 *Die Stellung der Kinder in der frühen christlichen Gemeinde und ihre Taufe*, Theologische Existenz Heute, n.s., 138 (Munich: Chr. Kaiser Verlag, 1967).

62 *Bib* 30 (1949) 405–32.

63 *Ego Eimi*, 87.

64 *Ego Eimi*, 88.

65 "Johanneische Literarkritik." *TBl* 20 (1941) 33–46.

66 *L'évangile de Jean d'après les recherches récentes* (Neuchâtel and Paris: Delachaux et Niestlé, ²1947).

plement Schweizer's work. Finally, E. Ruckstuhl has corrected and extended the work previously done.[67] He has increased the number of features regarded as characteristic of John from thirty-three to fifty. Ruckstuhl really wants to demonstrate that no sources were employed in the Gospel of John and that, as a consequence, the old ecclesiastical tradition according to which John, the son of Zebedee, is the author of the Fourth Gospel is affirmed. To be sure, he has perceptively identified some weaknesses in the work of his predecessors and set those elements aside. Nevertheless, his work suffers from the flaws in the program initiated by Schweizer, as we will now demonstrate. We cannot review all fifty features for lack of space, but we can review the most important. In so doing, it will be shown, among other things, how important the work of Colwell, referred to above, turns out to be.

We will begin with Schweizer's features 3–5: οὖν, τότε οὖν, and ὡς οὖν. For οὖν Schweizer gives the statistics: 138 + 0/ 8 + 0.[68] Τότε οὖν and ὡς οὖν have nothing corresponding in the balance of the NT. In our opinion, one must also include the last two expressions ("now then") in the οὖν-group. But to this is to be said: Οὖν belongs to that group of words which are frequently attested in the spoken, non-literary koine of the period, especially in Epictetus, but also in the "Banquet at Trimalchio's." The frequency of οὖν in the "action-segments" of the Gospel of John and only here is not a feature of Johannine style. What it demonstrates is that οὖν in the "action-segments" of the Gospel of John is a characteristic of spoken, non-literary koine. The appearance of οὖν in these segments is not an individual peculiarity and personal preference on the part of the Evangelist. Its frequent appearance demonstrates, rather, that the tradition of "action-segments" belongs to a particular level of hellenistic Greek. According to R. Morgenthaler, οὖν is found in Mark five times, in Luke thirty-one times, in Matthew fifty-seven times, and in John one hundred and ninety-four times. But, according to Colwell, Epic-

tetus makes use of the word in 1.1–24 (a section about as long as the Gospel of John) one hundred and seventy-three times. Statistics such as these, however, provide only an abstract sense of the relation of NT Greek to a specific development within the Greek language in the Mediterranean basin. A feature of Johannine Greek is not thereby indicated. The appearance of οὖν in John 21 says nothing about the Johannine authorship of this chapter.

The situation is similar for the frequency of ἐκεῖνος in the Gospel of John (number 6 in Schweizer's list).[69] Morgenthaler gives the following numbers for ἐκεῖνος: Mark twenty-three times, Matthew fifty-four times, Luke thirty-three times, John seventy times. Schweizer gives this formula for the frequency of ἐκεῖνος: 44 + 6/ 11 + 0.[70] Ruckstuhl counts ἐκεῖνος forty-seven times in the Gospel of John.[71] The discrepancy in the figures given by Schweizer and Morgenthaler owes to the fact that Schweizer takes into consideration only ἐκεῖνος as an independent personal pronoun in the singular. This ἐκεῖνος is of course used mostly in the Gospel of John to refer to God or Jesus. But ἐκεῖνος is very frequently used by Epictetus in a way that is formally comparable.[72] In a segment that is approximately as long as the Gospel of John, Epictetus uses αὐτός sixteen times, οὗτος seventy-six times, and ἐκεῖνος sixty-four times. For the Gospel of John the comparable figures are: αὐτός eighteen times, οὗτος forty-four times, and ἐκεῖνος fifty-one times. But we do not have in these instances to do with "an unusual word" for which one of the two authors has a personal preference. It is an individual characteristic of neither John nor Epictetus. Ἐκεῖνος is not, therefore, to be put in a list of Johannine characteristics.

Now it is precisely ἐκεῖνος and οὖν that are especially frequent Johannine traits, numerically speaking, according to Schweizer. If one does not count these two, then the features that Schweizer and Ruckstuhl take as characteristic of the Gospel of John, together with the conclusions they draw from them, receive a heavy blow. So far

67 *Einheit*, 180–219.
68 *Ego Eimi*, 90.
69 *Ego Eimi*, 90f.
70 *Ego Eimi*, 91.
71 *Einheit*, 213.
72 Colwell, *The Greek of the Fourth Gospel. A Study of its Aramaisms in the Light of Hellenistic Greek* (Chicago: University of Chicago Press, 1931) 56.

as ἐκεῖνος is concerned, one has the impression that it is preferred equally in the "action-segments" received by the author as tradition and in the dialogues formulated by the Evangelist himself. The Synoptics use ἐκεῖνος quite frequently, but attributively in combination with a substantive. The Gospel of John is of course also familiar with the attributive use of ἐκεῖνος; it appears twenty times. The *Itala* (old Latin tradition)[73] represent independent ἐκεῖνος used in a personal sense mostly with *ille*, but occasionally also with *ipse*. In German we would say simply *er*, or in a more colloquial style, even *der* (in English, "he" and "that one").

Menoud and Ruckstuhl (to give them a say once again) add τὰ Ἱεροσόλυμα (thus the name with article) as a particular Johannine way of saying "Jerusalem"; the formula is: 4 + 0/0. The Gospel of John uses Ἱεροσόλυμα (without the article) eight times (as in the LXX in the canonical writings), as do Mark always (ten times) and Matthew, with the sole exception of 23:37, where, for phonetic reasons (occurrences immediately one after the other), the author chooses to use Ἱερουσαλήμ: "O Jerusalem, Jerusalem, killing the prophets . . ." The article appears with Ἱεροσόλυμα in the Gospel of John in 2:23, 5:2, 10:22, 11:18. That is not sufficient to establish a special preference of the author for the form with article. The name "Jerusalem" appears mostly without the article in the Apocrypha. But in 2 Macc 11:8 one encounters the name with article all of a sudden, and that happens again in 12:9 and 3 Macc 3:16. That shows that the two forms were used interchangeably in the later period, although the anarthrous form predominated, as in the Gospel of John. On this evidence, it is not possible to allege that the arthrous form is Johannine.

As a further "characteristic of John," Schweizer,[74] followed by Ruckstuhl,[75] has identified "unusual word division." There are twelve such instances in the Gospel of John: 4:39, 5:20, 7:22, 7:38, 44, 10:32, 11:15, 12:11, 18:37, 19:20, 21:12. Schweizer has overlooked 17:5

(παρὰ σεαυτῷ . . . δόξασον . . .) and 21:12.[76] But Ruckstuhl has already reminded us that there are examples also in the Acts of the Apostles, and specifically in 19:26 and 27:5. I have pointed to these phenomena earlier in my commentary on Acts[77] and have called attention to some transpositions that separate words that belong together (4:33, 10:28, 11:22, 14:8, 19:26, 21:10). But the book of Acts has many more of these instances than these examples indicate. They appear as early as 1:1, 2, 3, 5 and have had the additional effect of causing the prologue to Acts to be misunderstood. Luke places emphasis on important words within his sentences by means of such transpositions to a much greater degree than does John. Thus, we do not have a peculiarity of John in this case either.

It is also a putative characteristic of John that he replaces the partitive genitive with the preposition ἐκ.[78] In fact, it is a recognized phenomenon of hellenistic Greek. When Schweizer gives the statistics of 31 + 3/26 + 3 for the Johannine use of ἐκ, he is only illustrating what Radermacher says of hellenistic Greek generally: "the language of the NT in general takes pains to avoid the partitive genitive . . . , above all to supplement it with ἐξ, less frequently with ἀπό or ἐν."[79] This development is manifest in the Gospel of John in an advanced stage, no thanks to a special preference on the part of the author for the construction with ἐκ.

Schweizer[80] and Ruckstuhl[81] place special value on the "epexegetical" (explanatory) ἵνα in the Gospel of John: the statistics are 10 (11) + 12/0 (1). What Hirsch has said applies to this usage also: it is not an individual trait, but a hellenistic mode of expression.[82] Here also the Gospel of John reflects the style of its time and does not evidence an individual preference of the author. Pernot believes that very frequent appearance of ἵνα in the Gospel of John demonstrates that the author employs "vulgar" Greek.[83]

The same judgment applies—and this is important—to the frequent connection of sentences by means of

---

73   *Itala. Das Neue Testament in altlateinischer Überlieferung*, ed. A. Jülicher, W. Matzkow and K. Aland, vol. 4, *Johannes-Evangelium* (Berlin: Walter de Gruyter, 1963).

74   *Ego Eimi*, number 32 on 94ff.

75   *Einheit*, 213.

76   Ruckstuhl, *Einheit*, 195.

77   78f.

78   Schweizer, *Ego Eimi*, 92; Ruckstuhl, *Einheit*, 213.

79   *Neutestamentliche Grammatik. Das Griechisch des Neuen Testaments in Zusammenhang mit der Volkssprache dargestellt*, HNT 1 (Tübingen: Mohr-Siebeck, ²1925) 125; cf. BDF §164.

80   *Ego Eimi*, 89.

81   *Einheit*, 213.

82   "Stilkritik und Literaranalyse im vierten Evange-

simple "and" and to asyndeton, equally frequent, and thus to the lack of connective particles linking sentences, phenomena Schweizer[84] and Ruckstuhl[85] view as characteristics of John. Colwell remarks on this matter:[86] Seldom have statistics so little evidential value as in this instance. It is by no means clear when and where one may speak of asyndeton. If, for example, one views coordinated sentences in John 1 as a unity, the number of asyndeta is considerably reduced. Such independent, coordinated sentences take on special significance in chapters 2–4, in chapters 11, 18 and 19: in view of them, one has to speak of one hundred and thirty examples of asyndeta compared with two hundred and forty-seven syndeta. We are not thereby contesting that there are more examples of asyndeta in the Gospel of John than in the Synoptics. But does that go beyond spoken koine? On the basis of about two hundred papyri of the Roman period, no certain conclusions can be drawn; they vary too much in both style and content. In Epictetus 1.14–1.24 one can count two hundred and forty-four examples of asyndetic sentences and only two hundred and twenty syndeta. But this mode of speech in which there are quick changes and sentences aphoristic in character does not yield reliable results. However, where narrative segments do occur in Epictetus, asyndeta are even more frequent than they are in John. It follows that both John and Epictetus are to be contrasted with the Synoptics in this respect.

In most of the cases discussed up to this point, it has been a question of whether a word or usage employed in the Gospel of John reflects the individual style of the author or (non-literary) koine. But in view of Schweizer's list of Johannine characteristics, other questions come into view. For example, in connection with the phrase "on the last day," ($\dot{\epsilon}\nu$) $\tau\hat{\eta}$ $\dot{\epsilon}\sigma\chi\acute{\alpha}\tau\eta$ $\dot{\eta}\mu\acute{\epsilon}\rho\alpha$.[87] The statistics are: $7 + 0/0 + 0$. As Hirsch has already observed, the expression in 7:37 refers to the last day of the feast of Tabernacles and not to "the day of judgment," as in the other six occurrences, and is therefore to be eliminated.

But the other six occurrences do not form a unity either. In 11:24,[88] the Evangelist has the uncomprehending Martha say: "I know that he [Lazarus] will rise again in the resurrection at the last day." In so doing, Martha represents the conception of the future resurrection that was then common, for the most part, in the community. But Jesus immmediately corrects her with the words (11:25f.): "I am the resurrection and the life. He who believes in me, though he die, yet shall he live, and whoever lives and believes in me shall never die." The transformation of the belief in the resurrection that is effected in the Gospel of John thereby becomes evident: the resurrection for the Evangelist is not a future event that takes place at the end of time, but one that occurs in the moment that faith comes into being. The formula that occurs in 6:39, 40, 44, 11:24, 12:48, "and I will raise him up on the last day," shows that one was loath to give up the old conception of the resurrection at the time of the redactor. For that reason, the future expectation that was missed in the text was emphatically restored. A similar correction of 5:25f. appears in 5:28f.

The favorite apologetic ploy, viz., that the Evangelist knew and sympathized with the futuristic eschatology at the end of time, alongside his "present eschatology," overlooks the fact that the context of 11:23–25 has meanwhile become incomprehensible. It is not a question of an individual idiom and of koine usage, but of a theological difference between the Evangelist and his redactor, and therefore a theological problem.

A theological problem is also involved in the Johannine feature introduced by J. Jeremias:[89] "O woman" ($\gamma\acute{\nu}\nu\alpha\iota$) used as a mode of Jesus' address to his mother. Since Jesus addresses his mother only in 2:4 and in 19:26 in this manner, the statistics are: $2 + 0/0$. But the facts are quite different. Jesus also addresses the woman at the well with $\gamma\acute{\nu}\nu\alpha\iota$ (4:21), and in 20:15 he uses the same form of address with respect to Mary Magdalene. This series of instances shows the peculiar distance Jesus maintained between himself and all his female partners

---

lium," *ZNW* 43 (1950/51) 129–43. The reference is to p. 138.

83   *Revue des études grecques* 37 (1927) 128.

84   *Ego Eimi*, 91.

85   *Einheit*, 213.

86   *The Greek of the Fourth Gospel. A Study of its Aramaisms in the Light of Hellenistic Greek* (Chicago: University of Chicago Press, 1931) 10.

87   Schweizer, *Ego Eimi*, 93, features number 24.

88   On this verse see the commentary.

89   Number 27 in Ruckstuhl's list, *Einheit*, 204.

in dialogue, and which permitted him, at the same time, to treat them with courteous matter-of-factness and humaneness, like that he accorded his devoted female disciples and his own mother; this applies even to a stranger like the Samaritan woman.

There is a real parallel to John 2:4 in 7:1–10: Jesus does not permit his brothers to prompt him to act, but always awaits some signal from God that the time and place are right. It is from this deeper unity with the Father that his surprising independence from men flows, although this independence does not preclude concern for the other. The address "O woman" (γύναι) is thus not a mark of Johannine style, but an expression of Johannine theology.

J. Jeremias has introduced the word for "charcoal fire" (ἀνθρακιά) as characteristic number 35.[90] We meet it in 18:18 and 21:9; the statistics are: 2 + 0/0. On it Ruckstuhl remarks: "The word might be unusual," and refers to Mark 14:54 (where φῶς means "fire") and to Luke 22:55 (where the word πῦρ is used). None of these words is characteristic of the style of any of the Evangelists. In John 21:9,[91] the word represents an insertion of the redactor; it is an allusion to the denial scene (18:18), which contributes to its "repetition," since allusion prompts the use of the term previously employed.

In connection with 18:18, one ought to take heed of Cadbury's warning:[92] one ought not to take a word as peculiar to the usage of an ancient author because it is accidently found only in his work. Hapaxlegomena "are more an indication of the limits of our knowledge than of their frequency."

The word "morsel" (ὀψάριον) appears five times in the Gospel of John (6:9, 11, 21:9f., 13; the last three references owe to the imitative policy of the redactor). Schweizer introduces it as a characteristic,[93] and Ruckstuhl lists it as number 39 (Suidas explains it with ἰχθύδιον, "tidbit of fish"). John uses this term in the narrative of the feeding of the 5,000 (on the other hand, the Synoptics use ἰχθύς, "fish"; Mark 8:7 has ἰχθύδιον, "little

fish"). In 21:9f., 13, ὀψάριον is evidently an allusion to the feeding of the 5,000; on the other hand, the word ἰχθύς is connected with the catch of fish in 21:6, 8, 11. It is possible that the Johannine tradition of the feeding has been influenced by the word ὀψάριον in Num 11:22: "Or shall all the fish of the sea (πᾶν τὸ ὄψος τῆς θαλάσσης) be gathered together for them, to suffice them?" The word ἰχθύδιον in Mark 8:7 is no more characteristic of Mark than ὀψάριον is of John.

Ruckstuhl's characteristic number 28 likewise has the statistics of: 2 + 0/0: ἐφανέρωσεν (ἑαυτόν), "manifests (himself)." It appears of course only in the appendix in chapter 21:1. On the other hand, φανερόω (to manifest) appears in 1:31, 2:11, 3:21, 9:3, 17:6, 21:14, in other constructions. The expression in 21:1 concurs with 7:4 as a usage; but in 7:4 it says, "reveal yourself to the world." A personal preference of the Evangelist for this expression is not evident.

The proposed characteristics οὐκ . . . οὐδείς ("not . . . no one"),[94] ἐγγύς ("near"),[95] and ὄχλος ("crowd"; in the plural, only in 7:12) are rejected by Ruckstuhl.[96] Nor does he want to support the double use of ἀμήν ("truly") as a characteristic of John.[97] That may not only be the case because these expressions or words are readily imitated, but also because they probably belong to the language of the later community, which found the single ἀμήν no longer sufficient. The situation with characteristic number 24 in Ruckstuhl's list may be quite comparable, viz., the fixed form of the name, "Simon Peter."[98]

What Schweizer has to say about number 15 in in his list is especially interesting: "The phrase (ἐ)άν (μή) τις is specifically Johannine . . . The relationships expressed statistically are: 24 +4/19 +2, among which two instances in Matthew and Acts are quotations from the OT."[99] Footnote 68 in Schweizer reads: "Five cases of ἄν = ἐάν are specifically Johannine." Ruckstuhl has adopted this characteristic.[100] But let us stay with the footnote for the moment. On such cases BDF rightly remark: "ἐάν . . . is the hellenistic form for 'if'; ἄν is found, however, now

90 Ruckstuhl, *Einheit*, 201.
91 See the commentary on this verse.
92 *The Making of Luke-Acts* (London: S. P. C. K, 1968) 214.
93 *Ego Eimi*, 94.
94 Schweizer, *Ego Eimi*, 93, number 18.
95 Schweizer, *Ego Eimi*, 93, number 19.
96 *Einheit*, 195 and 202.

97 *Einheit*, 198.
98 *Einheit*, 204.
99 Schweizer, *Ego Eimi*, 93.
100 *Einheit*, 213.

and then in NT MSS, thus Jn 12:32 in B, $\mathfrak{P}^{66}$, and $\mathfrak{P}^{75}$; on the other hand, they also read ἐάν, as do D E F G *al.* as well."[101] In 5:19b also, which Ruckstuhl cites,[102] $\mathfrak{P}^{66}$ and $\mathfrak{P}^{75}$ read ἐάν. As BDF emphasize, the uncertainty of the scribe is evident; this accords with the inroads ἐάν has made on the province of ἄν. In view of this situation and the fact that in Acts 9:2 the manuscripts also vacillate, we cannot say that the five examples of footnote 68 are "specifically Johannine," as Schweizer supposes.

The situation is no different with the phrase, ἐάν (μὴ) τις . . . , although the number of instances perhaps requires a special explanation. In any case, they all belong to the discourses of Jesus in the Gospel of John, and then to a solemn form of paraenesis. In Mark and Matthew there corresponds: ὅς (ἐ)άν. . . . In another context, the question has been posed whether the stylistic difference between the Synoptics and John could not have been determined by region. One ought, perhaps, to take these possibilities into consideration here. In that case this further problem would arise: if stylistic features owe to the regional dialects of various authors, do they not also owe to the regional dialects of various scribes?

The first characteristic in Schweizer's list, and therefore the most important, concerns the frequency of ἐμός (possessive pronoun) in the Gospel of John: the statistics are: 39 + 1/34 + 2.[103] Since it is the "revealer" who speaks in the Gospel of John (although this expression is not used), it is virtually a foregone conclusion that the first person singular of the possessive pronoun will appear especially frequently; Schweizer has taken that into account.[104] He therefore takes into consideration only those examples in which ἐμός appears in second attributive position with the article repeated, and then comes to the remarkable result: 29 + 1/0. On this matter, BDF say: "Ἐμός is quite frequent in Jn (koine of Asia Minor? . . .)."[105] But in the first note to §285, they say that the possessive pronoun appears thirty-one times in John in postposition (and not only ἐμός), but when it is emphatic, it takes normal attributive positive before the noun, for example, in John 7:16, "My teaching is not mine" (ἡ ἐμὴ διδαχὴ οὐκ ἔστιν ἐμή). There is probably an error here. The pronoun in postposition with the article carries the greatest emphasis and is often used for just

this reason. The passage quoted by BDF, 7:16, emphasized precisely that Jesus' teaching is not his own, but that of his Father. The formulation ἡ διδ(χ)ὴ ἡ ἐμὴ οὔκ ἔστιν ἐμή ("My own teaching is not mine" or something similar) would put too much emphasis on "my teaching" in contrast to the sense of the context. The high frequency of the pronoun in postposition with the article owes therefore to the fact that the Johannine Jesus speaks as the one who, on the one hand, does not do his own will and does not speak his own word, but does the will of the Father and speaks the word of the Father; everything depends, as a consequence, precisely on hearing and keeping *his* word. All these examples, with the exception of 3:29 where the Baptist speaks, appear in the words of Jesus. It is not a question of an individual preference of the author for a particular expression, but of a suitable expression for the christological relation of the son to the Father, which the other Evangelists have not thought through so carefully. If one bears that in mind, one will see that the phrase "Johannine style" is not in this case unambiguous. It could, for example, imply: this is the style of a particular, individual author (from which one could ultimately draw conclusions regarding sources). But it could also mean the expression of a particular christology, which took shape only gradually and then was crystallized in the Gospel of John. In the Gospel of John, it is predominantly the second; "predominantly" insofar as no other NT author has thought through the christological problem so acutely as the fourth evangelist, who therefore had recourse to this stylistic medium.

We bring this discussion of selected items from Schweizer's and Ruckstuhl's lists to a close with item number 2: the preference of John for the ἵνα-clause, especially for the "epexegetical" (explanatory) ἵνα-clause.[106] Schweizer numbers among these epexegetical clauses "those occurrences of ἵνα that introduce a subordinate clause, which clarifies or explains a demonstrative pronoun appearing in the main clause, and which cannot be interpreted as a final, consecutive, or imperative clause." His results are: 10 (11) + 12/0 (1). These numbers are not enlightening. References in 6:39, 40, 55 do not belong to this group, and neither do the 3 (4)

101 BDF §107.
102 *Einheit*, 208.
103 *Ego Eimi*, 88f.

104 *Ego Eimi*, 88f.
105 BDF §285.
106 *Ego Eimi*, 89.

instances in which ὅτι, and not ἵνα, appears.

On this question Steyer's highly recommended work, *Satzlehre des neutestamentlichen Griechisch*, has this to say: "The NT does not know a pointless use of ἵνα in place of ὅτι. Nevertheless, there is a non-final ἵνα (closely related to the ἵνα of the consecutive clause that precedes, §44.1) in explanatory clauses, which are dependent, for the most part, on demonstratives, and which can be introduced in German, according to preference, by *dass* or *wenn* [and in English, also according to preference, with 'when' or 'if' or a construction with the infinitive]. An example is found in 3 John 4: 'No greater joy can I have than this, to hear (or 'when I hear', or 'if I hear') that my children follow the truth.'[107] This ἵνα sets out the content of the explanatory subordinate clause as thought, not as fact, of course without contesting the factuality of the case."[108] Mark 10:37 seems to us to belong to that use of ἵνα: "Grant us to sit . . . ," Matt 10:25: "It is enough for the disciple to be like his teacher," Matt 8:8: "I am not worthy to have you come under my roof." Schweizer[109] calls on Radermacher,[110] who adduces 1 Cor 9:18 ("otherwise only John"), and Blass,[111] who cites Luke 1:43 as as the sole counter example. Even if one does not admit the synoptic evidence, one cannot cite the epexegetical ἵνα as a characteristic feature of Johannine style, since it appears also in the three epistles of John, which betray different hands (1 John 3:1, 4, 17, 2 John 6,

3 John 4). The third epistle of John exhibits a colloquial newly coined usage in verse 4.

The explanatory ἵνα is of course only a special instance of the development of the language in the koine period: "Ἵνα has gained ground on a broad front: the constructions with ἵνα and ὅτι have developed into serious rivals of the infinitive."[112] We have already indicated above that certain parallel phenomena, corresponding to (non-literary) koine Greek, appear in Latin. That is also the case here. In Latin, *ut* and *quia* or *quod* begin to interchange with the infinitive.[113] The development has been carried further in Modern Greek: "There is no infinitive in Modern Greek; it has been replaced as a rule by νά with subjunctive or by ὅτι or πῶς with the indicative."[114]

Also in the case of number 2 in Schweizer's list, a phenomenon of koine in general is misunderstood as the preference of an individual author. The weaknesses of the attempt to introduce "objective" characteristics of the language of the Gospel of John as arguments against partition into sources thereby become especially evident.

---

107 Cf. John 15:13.

108 G. Steyer, *Handbuch für das Studium des neutestament- lichen Griechisch*, vol. 2, *Satzlehre des neutestamentlichen Griechisch* (Gütersloh: Gerd Mohn, ² 1975) §44.1.

109 *Ego Eimi*, 89 n. 32.

110 *Neutestamentliche Grammatik. Das Griechisch des Neuen Testaments in Zusammenhang mit der Volkssprache dargestellt*, HNT 1 (Tübingen: Mohr-Siebeck, ²1925)

193.

111 BDF §394.

112 BDF §388.

113 BDF §388.

114 J. Kalitsunakis, *Grammatik der neugriechischen Volks- sprache* (Berlin: Walter de Gruyter, 1963) §127.

6. Sources, Composition, Style, and Author

Bibliography

1. The Gospel of John and the Synoptics

Amadon, Grace
  "The Johannine-Synoptic Argument." *ATR* 26 (1944) 107–15.

Anonymous
  "Noch ein Versuch über das Wandeln Jesu auf dem Meere nach Mt 14,24–33; Mk 6,45–51 und Joh 6,16–21." *Magazin für Religionsphilosophie, Exegese und Kirchengeschichte* 12 (1802) 310–33.

Bacon, Benjamin Wisner
  "John and the Synoptists." In his *The Gospel of the Hellenists* (New York: Holt, 1933) 111–19.

Bacon, Benjamin Wisner
  "Lucan versus Johannine Chronology." *Expositor,* 7th ser., 3 (1907) 206–20.

Bailey, John Amadee
  The Traditions Common to the Gospels of Luke and John, NovTSup 7 (Leiden: E. J. Brill, 1963).

Balagué, Miguel
  "San Juan y los Sinópticos." *CB* 12 (1955) 347–52.

Barrett, Charles Kingsley
  "John and the Synoptic Gospels." *ExpTim* 85 (1973/1974) 228–33.

Barton, George A.
  "The Origin of the Discrepancy between the Synoptists and the Fourth Gospel as to the Date and Character of Christ's Last Supper with his Disciples." *JBL* 43 (1924) 28–31.

Bleek, Friedrich
  "Verhältniss der johanneischen Darstellung zur synoptischen in der Erzählung vom Wandeln Jesu auf dem Meere." In his *Beiträge zur Einleitung und Auslegung der heiligen Schrift* (Berlin: G. Reimer, 1846) 102–5.

Bleek, Friedrich
  "Ueber den Monathstag des Todes Christi und des letzten Abendmahles mit seinen Jüngern und die in der Beziehung zwischen Johannes und den Synoptikem stattfindende Differenz." In his *Beiträge zur Einleitung und Auslegung der heiligen Schrift* (Berlin: G. Reimer, 1846) 107–56.

Bleek, Friedrich
  "Ueber die Spuren in den Synoptischen Evangelien, welche für die johanneische Darstellung des äusseren Verlaufes der evangelischen Geschichte, . . . zeugen." In his *Beiträge zur Einleitung und Auslegung der heiligen Schrift* (Berlin: G. Reimer, 1846) 92–99.

Bleek, Friedrich
  "Auslassung der Auferweckung des Lazarus bei den Synoptikem." In his *Beiträge zur Einleitung und Auslegung der heiligen Schrift* (Berlin: G. Reimer, 1846) 100–1.

Blinzler, Josef

Johannes und die Synoptiker, ein Forschungsbericht (Stuttgart: Katholisches Bibelwerk, 1965).

Boismard, Marie-Emile

"Saint Luc et la rédaction du quatrième évangile (Jn iv, 46–54)." *RB* 69 (1962) 185–211.

Borgen, Peder

"John and the Synoptics in the Passion Narrative." *NTS* 5 (1959) 246–59.

Brodie, Louis T.

"Creative Rewriting: Key to a New Methodology." SBLASP 2 (Missoula: Scholars Press, 1978) 261–67.

Broomfield, G. W.

"The Fourth Evangelist and the Synoptic Tradition." In his *John, Peter and the Fourth Gospel* (New York: Macmillan; London: S. P. C. K., 1934) 82–107.

Broomfield, G. W.

"John and Luke." In his *John, Peter and the Fourth Gospel* (New York: Macmillan; London: S. P. C. K., 1934) 108–45.

Brown, Raymond E.

"John and the Synoptic Gospels." In his *New Testament Essays* (Milwaukee: Bruce, 1965) 192–213.

Büchsel, Friedrich

"Johannes und die Synoptiker." *ZST* 4 (1927) 240–65.

Buse, Ivor

"St. John and 'The First Synoptic Pericope.'" *NovT* 3 (1959) 57–61.

Buse, Ivor

"John v, 8 and the Johannine-Marcan Relationship." *NTS* 1 (1954/1955) 134–36.

Buse, Ivor

"St. John and the Marcan Passion Narrative." *NTS* 4 (1957/1958) 215–19.

Buse, Ivor

"St. John and the Passion Narratives of St. Matthew and St. Luke." *NTS* 7 (1960/1961) 65–76.

Calmes, T.

La formazione dei Vangeli: a questione sinottica e il Vangelo di S. Giovanni (Rome: Desclée, 1923).

Cassien, Bishop

"The Interrelation of the Gospels Mt—Lk—Jn." *SE* 1 = TU 73 (Berlin: Akademie-Verlag, 1959) 129–47.

Cerfaux, Lucien

"L'évangile de Jean et 'le logion johannique' des Synoptiques." In his *Recueil Lucien Cerfaux. Etudes d'exégèse et d'histoire religieuse de Monseigneur Cerfaux réunies à l'occasion de son soixante-dixième anniversaire*, vol. 3. Supplement, BETL 18 (Gembloux: Duculot, 1962) 161–74.

Cipriani, Settimio

"La confessione di Pietro in Gv 6,69–71 e suoi rapporti con quella dei sinottici." *San Pietro. Atti della XIX settimana Biblica, Associazione Biblica Italiana* (Brescia: Paideia, 1967) 93–111.

Colwell, Ernest Cadman

John Defends the Gospel (New York: Willett, Clark & Co., 1936).

Cribbs, F. Lamar

"St. Luke and the Johannine Tradition." *JBL* 90 (1971) 422–50.

Cribbs, F. Lamar

"The Agreements that Exist between Luke and John." SBLASP 1 (Missoula: Scholars Press, 1979) 215–61.

Cribbs, F. Lamar

"The Agreements that Exist between John and Acts." In *Perspectives on Luke-Acts*, ed. C. H. Talbert. Special Studies Series 5 (Danville, VA: Association of Baptist Professors of Religion, 1978) 40–61.

Cribbs, F. Lamar

"A Study of the Contacts that Exist between St. Luke and St. John." SBLASP 2 (Missoula: Scholars Press, 1973) 1–93.

Curtis, K. Peter G.

"Three Points of Contact between Matthew and John in the Burial and Resurrection Narratives." *JTS* 23 (1972) 440–44.

Dewey, Kim E.

"Peter's Denial Reexamined: John's Knowledge of Mark's Gospel." SBLASP 1 (Missoula: Scholars Press, 1979) 109–12.

Dodd, Charles Harold

"The Portrait of Jesus in John and in the Synoptics." In *Christian History and Interpretation. Studies Presented to John Knox*, ed. W. R. Farmer, C. F. D. Moule, R. R. Niebuhr (Cambridge: Cambridge University Press, 1967) 183–98.

Dodd, Charles Harold

"Some Johannine 'Herrenworte' with Parallels in the Synoptic Gospels." *NTS* 2 (1955) 75–86.

Dunkel, F.

"Die Berufung der ersten Jünger Jesu: der wunderbare Fischfang bei Lk 5 und Joh 21." *Das heilige Land* 73 (1929) 53–59.

Durand, A. S. 0.

"Jean et ses devanciers." *Etudes* 64 (1927) 129–41.

Fagal, Harold E.

"John and the Synoptic Tradition." In *Scripture, Tradition, and Interpretation. Essays Presented to Everett F. Harrison by His Students and Colleagues in Honor of His Seventy-fifth Birthday*, ed, W. W. Gasque and W. S. LaSor (Grand Rapids: Wm. B. Eerdmans, 1978) 127–45.

Feuillet, André

"Giovanni e i Sinottici." *Studi Cattolici* 13 (1969) 121f.

Flowers, H. J.

"Mark as a Source for the Fourth Gospel." *JBL* 46 (1927) 207–36.

Gardner-Smith, Percival

"St. John's Knowledge of Matthew." *JTS* 4 (1953) 31–35.

Gardner-Smith, Percival
Saint John and the Synoptic Gospels (Cambridge: Cambridge University Press, 1938).

Garvie, Alfred E.
"The Synoptic Echoes and Second-Hand-Reports in the Fourth Gospel." *Expositor*, 8th ser., 10 (1915) 316–26.

Glusman, Edward F.
"The Cleansing of the Temple and the Anointing at Bethany: The Order of Events in Mark 11 and John 11–12." SBLASP 1 (Missoula: Scholars Press, 1979) 113–18.

Glusman, Edward F.
"The Shape of Mark and John: A Primitive Gospel Outline." Dissertation, Duke University, 1978.

Glusman, Edward F.
"Criteria for a Study of the Outlines of Mark and John." SBLASP 2 (Missoula: Scholars Press, 1978) 239–49.

Grant, Frederick C.
"Was the Author of John Dependent upon the Gospel of Luke?" *JBL* 56 (1937) 285–307.

Gümbel, Ludwig
Das Johannes-Evangeliums, eine Ergänzung des Lukasevangeliums: exegetische Studie (Speyer a.R: Verlag der Buchhandlung Nimtz, 1911).

Haenchen, Ernst
"Johanneische Probleme." *ZTK* 56 (1959) 19–54. In his *Gott und Mensch. Gesammelte Aufsätze* 1 (Tübingen: Mohr-Siebeck, 1965) 78–113.

Harrison, Everett F.
"The Christology of the Fourth Gospel in the Relation to the Synoptics." *BSac* 116 (1959) 303–9.

Holtzmann, Heinrich Julius
"Das schriftstellerische Verhältnis des Johannes zu den Synoptikern." *ZWT* 12 (1869) 62–85, 155–78, 446–56.

Jaubert, Annie
"Solution of the Conflict Between John and the Synoptics." In her *The Date of the Last Supper,* tr. I. Rafferty (Staten Island, NY: Alba House, 1965) 95–101.

Johnston, Edwin D.
"A Reexamination of the Relation of the Fourth Gospel to the Synoptics." Dissertation, Louisville, 1955.

Kallas, J. G.
"John and the Synoptics—A Discussion of Some of the Differences between them." Dissertation, University of Southern California, 1968.

Kittlaus, Lloyd R.
"Evidence from Jn 12 that the Author of John knew the Gospel of Mark." SBLASP 1 (Missoula: Scholars Press, 1979) 119–22.

Kittlaus, Lloyd R.
"John and Mark: A Methodological Evaluation of N. Perrin's Suggestion." SBLASP 2 (Missoula: Scholars Press, 1978) 269–79.

Kittlaus, Lloyd R.
"The Fourth Gospel and Mark: John's Use of Markan Redaction and Composition." Dissertation, Chicago, 1978.

Klein, Hans
"Die lukanisch-johanneische Passionstradition." *ZNW* 67 (1976) 155–86.

Kolenkow, Anitra B.
"The Changing Patterns: Conflicts and the Necessity of Death: John 2 and 12 and Markan Parallels." SLBASP 1 (Missoula: Scholars Press, 1979) 123–26.

Lee, Edwin Kenneth
"St. Mark and the Fourth Gospel." *NTS* 3 (1956/1957) 50–58.

Maynard, Arthur H.
"Common Elements in the Outlines of Mark and John." SBLASP 2 (Missoula: Scholars Press, 1978) 251–60.

Mendner, Siegfried
"Zum Problem 'Johannes und die Synoptiker.'" *NTS* 4 (1957/1958) 282–307.

Mensinga, J. A.
"Das Johannes-Evangelium und die Synopsis." *ZWT* 35 (1892) 98–104.

Moe, Olaf
"Spor av Johannes traditionen hos Lukas." *NorTT* 25 (1924) 103–28.

Morris, Leon
"The Relationship of the Fourth Gospel to the Synoptics." In his *Studies in the Fourth Gospel* (Grand Rapids: Wm. B. Eerdmans, 1969) 15–63.

Munro, Winsome
"The Anointing in Mark 14,3–9 and John 12,1–8." SBLASP 1 (Missoula: Scholars Press, 1979) 127–30.

Neirynck, Frans et al.
Jean et les Synoptiques. Examen critique de l'exégèse de M.-E. Boismard, BETL 49 (Louvain: University Press, 1979) 23–29.

Neirynck, Frans
"*Parakypsas blepei:* Lc 24,12 et Jn 20,5." *ETL* 53 (1977) 113–52.

Neirynck, Frans
"*Apälthen pros heauton.* Lc 24,12 et Jn 20,10." *ETL* 54 (1978) 104–18.

Neirynck, Frans
"John and the Synoptics." In *L'Evangile de Jean. Sources, rédaction, théologie,* ed. M. de Jonge. BETL 44 (Gembloux: Duculot; Louvain: University Press, 1977) 73–106.

Onuki, Takashi
"Die johanneischen Abschiedsreden und die synoptische Tradition, eine traditionskritische und traditionsgeschichtliche Untersuchung." *Annual of the Japanese Biblical Institute* 3 (1977) 157–268.

Osty, Emile
"Les points de contact entre le récit de la Passion

dans saint Luc et saint Jean." *RSR* 39 (1951) 146–54.

Parker, Pierson
"Luke and the Fourth Evangelist." *NTS* 9 (1962/1963) 317–36.

Pulligny, J. de
"La première finale du quatrième évangile et l'épisode d'Emmaus dans Luc." *RHR* 95 (1927) 364–71.

Richmond, Wilfrid John
The Gospel of the Rejection. A Study of the Relation of the Fourth Gospel to the Three (London: Murray, 1906).

Riesenfeld, Harald
"Liknelserna i den synoptiska och i den johanneiska traditionen." *SEA* 25 (1960) 37–61. French: "Les paraboles dans la prédiction de Jésus selon les traditions synoptique et johannique." *Eglise et théologie* 22 (1959) 21–29.

Sabbe, M.
"The Arrest of Jesus in Jn 18,1–11 and its Relation to the Synoptic Gospels. A Critical Evaluation of A. Dauer's Hypothesis." In *L'Evangile de Jean. Sources, rédaction, théologie,* ed. M. de Jonge. BETL 44 (Gembloux: Duculot; Louvain: University Press, 1977) 203–34.

Schlatter, Adolf
Die Parallelen in den Worten Jesu bei Johannes und Matthäus (Gütersloh: C. Bertelsmann, 1898).

Schmiedel, Paul W.
The Johannine Writings, ed. Maurice A. Canney (London: A. & C. Black, 1908) = *Johannesschriften des Neuen Testaments,* 2 vols. (Tübingen: Mohr-Siebeck, 1906).

Schmitt, J.
"Le groupe johannique et la chrétienté apostolique." In *Les groupes informels dans l'église* (Strasbourg: C. E. R. D. I. C., 1971) 169–79.

Schnider, Franz and Werner Stenger
Johannes und die Synoptiker. Vergleich ihrer Parallelen, Biblische Handbibliothek 9 (Munich: Kösel, 1971).

Schniewind, Julius Daniel
Die Parallelperikopen bei Lukas und Johannes (Hildesheim: G. Olms, ²1958).

Siegman, Edward F.
"St. John's Use of the Synoptic Material." *CBQ* 30 (1968) 182–98.

Sigge, Timotheus
Das Johannesevangelium und die Synoptiker; eine Untersuchung seiner Selbständigkeit und der gegenseitigen Beziehungen (Münster i.W: Aschendorff, 1935).

Smith, D. Moody
"John 12:12ff and the Question of John's Use of the Synoptics." *JBL* 82 (1963) 58–64.

Smith, Morton
"Mark 6:32–15:47 and John 6:1–19:42." SBLASP 2 (Missoula: Scholars Press, 1978) 281–87.

Smith, Morton
"Collected Fragments: On the Priority of John 6 to Mark 6–8." SBLASP 1 (Missoula: Scholars Press, 1979) 105–8.

Solages, B. de
Jean et les Synoptiques (Leiden: E. J. Brill, 1979).

Soltau, Wilhelm
"Welche Bedeutung haben die synoptischen Berichte des 4. Evangeliums für die Feststellung seines Entstehens?" *ZWT* 52 (1910) 33–66.

Sortino, Placido M. Da
"La vocazione di Pietro secondo la tradizione sinottica e secondo San Giovanni." *San Pietro. Atti della XIX settimana Biblica, Associazione Biblica Italiana* (Brescia: Paideia, 1967) 27–57.

Sparks, H. F. D.
"St. John's Knowledge of Matthew. The Evidence of John 13, 16 and 15, 20." *JTS* 3 (1952) 58–61.

Stamm, R. T.
"Luke-Acts and Three Cardinal Ideas of John." In *Biblical Studies in Memory of H. C. Alleman,* eds. J. M. Myers, O. Reimherr, H. N. Bream. Gettysburg Theological Studies (Locust Valley, NY: J. J. Augustin, 1960).

Steiner, Rudolf
L'évangile de saint Jean dans ses rapports avec les trois autres Evangiles et notamment avec celui de saint Luc. Quatorze conférences faites à Cassel, du 24 juin au 8 Juillet 1909 (Paris: Association de la science spirituelle, 1934, 1945).

Streeter, Burnett Hillman
The Four Gospels. A Study of Origins, Treating of the Manuscript Tradition, Sources, Authorship, and Dates (London: Macmillan & Co., 1924) 393ff.

Tayler, John James
An Attempt to Ascertain the Character of the Fourth Gospel; Especially in its relation to the Three First (Edinburgh: Williams & Norgate, 1867).

Weizsäcker, Karl Heinrich von
Untersuchungen über die evangelische Geschichte, ihre Quellen und den Gang ihrer Entwicklung (Tübingen: Mohr-Siebeck, ²1901) 172–84.

Welch, C. H.
Parable, Miracle and Sign of Matthew and John Considered Dispensationally (London: Berean Publ. Trust, ²1978).

Williams, Francis E.
"Fourth Gospel and Synoptic Tradition: Two Johannine Passages." *JBL* 86 (1967) 311–19.

Windisch, Hans
Johannes und die Synoptiker. Wollte der vierte Evangelist die älteren Evangelien ergänzen oder ersetzen, UNT 12 (Leipzig: J. C. Hinrichs, 1926).

Worsley, Frederick William
The Fourth Gospel and the Synoptists, being a contribution to the study of the Johannine Problem (Edinburgh: T. & T. Clark, 1909).

Zimmermann, Hellmuth
"Lukas und die johanneische Tradition." *TSK* 76 (1903) 586–605.

2. Composition

Barrosse, Thomas
"The Seven Days of the New Creation in St. John's Gospel." *CBQ* 21 (1959) 507–16.

Baur, Ferdinand Christian
"Ueber die Composition und den Charakter des johanneischen Evangeliums." *Theologische Jahrbücher* 3 (Tübingen, 1844) 1–191, 397–475, 615–700.

Blinzler, Josef
"Zum Geschichtsrahmen des Johannesevangeliums." In his *Aus der Welt und Umwelt. Gesammelte Aufsätze* 1, SBB (Stuttgart: Katholisches Bibelwerk, 1969) 94–107.

Briggs, Charles A.
New Light on the Life of Jesus (New York: Charles Scribner's Sons, 1904) 140–58.

Burch, Vacher
The Structure and Message of St. John's Gospel (London: M. Hopkinson, 1928).

Clavier, Henri
"La structure du quatrième évangile." *RHPR* 35 (1955) 174–95.

Deeks, David
"The Structure of the Fourth Gospel." *NTS* 15 (1968/1969) 107–29.

Feuillet, André
"L'heure de Jesus et le signe de Cana. Contribution à l'étude de la structure du quatrième évangile." *ETL* 36 (1960) 5–22.

Fiebig, Paul
"Zur Form des Johannesevangeliums." *Der Geisteskampf der Gegenwart* 64 (1928) 126–32.

Franke, A. H.
"Die Anlage des Johannes-Evangeliums." *TSK* 57 (1884) 80–154.

Girard, Marc
"La structure heptapartie du quatrième évangile." *RSR* 5 (1975/1976) 350–59.

Granskou, David M.
"Structure and Theology in the Fourth Gospel." Dissertation, Princeton, 1960.

Grundmann, Walter
Zeugnis und Gestalt des Johannes-Evangeliums. Eine Studie zur denkerischen und gestalterischen Leistung des vierten Evangelisten, Arbeiten zur Theologie 7 (Stuttgart: Calwer Verlag, 1961).

Hanhart, Karel
"The Structure of John 1,35–4,54." In *Studies in John Presented to Professor J. N. Sevenster on the Occasion of his Seventieth Birthday* (Leiden: E. J. Brill, 1970) 22–46.

Harnack, Adolf von
"Das 'Wir' in den johanneischen Schriften." SPAW.PH 31 (Berlin: G. Reimer, 1923) 96–113.

Hauff, Pfarrer
"Einige Bemerkungen über die Abhandlung von D. v. Baur über die Composition und den Charakter des johanneischen Evangeliums." *TSK* 19 (1846) 550–629.

Herder, Johann Gottfried von
Von Gottes Sohn, der Welt Heiland. Nach Johannes Evangelium. Nebst einer Regel der Zusammenstimmung unsrer Evangelien aus ihrer Entstehung und Ordnung (Riga: J. F. Hartnoch, 1797).

Hönig, W.
"Die Construktion des vierten Evangeliums." *ZWT* 14 (1871) 535–66.

Holtzmann, Heinrich Julius
"Über die Disposition des vierten Evangeliums." *ZWT* 24 (1881) 257–90.

Kammerstätter, J.
"Zur Struktur des Johannesevangliums." Dissertation, Vienna, 1970.

Linder, Gottlieb
"Gesetz der Stoffteilung im Johannes-Evangelium." *ZWT* 40 (1897) 444–54; 42 (1899) 32–35.

Lohmeyer, Ernst
"Über Aufbau und Gliederung des vierten Evangeliums." *ZNW* 27 (1928) 11–36.

Loman, Abraham Dirk
"De bouw van het vierde Evangelie." *TT* 11 (1877) 371–437.

MacGregor, G. H. C., and A. Q. Morton
The Structure of the Fourth Gospel (Edinburgh: Oliver & Boyd, 1961).

McDowell, Edward A.
"The Stuctural Integrity of the Fourth Gospel." *RevExp* 34 (1937) 397–416.

Morris, Leon
"The Composition of the Fourth Gospel." In *Scripture, Tradition, and Interpretation. Essays presented to Everett F. Harrison by His Students and Colleagues in Honor of His Seventy-fifth Birthday,* ed. W. W. Gasque and W. S. LaSor (Grand Rapids: Wm. B. Eerdmans, 1978) 157–75.

Newman, Barclay M., Jr.
"Some Observations Regarding the Argument, Structure, and Literary Characteristics of the Gospel of John." *BT* 26 (1975) 234–39.

Olivieri, Jean and Marie-Joseph Lagrange
"La conception qui domine le quatrième évangile." *RB* 35 (1926) 382–97.

Potterie, Ignace de la
"Structura primae partis Evangelii Johannis (capita III et IV)." *VD* 47 (1969) 130–40.

Quiévreux, François
"La structure symbolique de l'évangile de saint Jean." *RHPR* 33 (1953) 123–65.

Rau, Christoph
Struktur und Rhythmus im Johannes-Evangelium. Eine Untersuchung über die Komposition des vierten Evangeliums, Schriften zur Religionserkenntnis (Stuttgart: Urachhaus, 1972).

Schulz, Siegfried
"Die Komposition des Johannesprologs und die Zusammensetzung des vierten Evangeliums." *SE* 1

= TU 73 (Berlin: Akademie-Verlag, 1959) 351–62.

Schulz, Siegfried
Komposition und Herkunft der johanneischen Reden. BWANT 5 (Stuttgart: W. Kohlhammer, 1960).

Schütz, Roland
"Zum ersten Teil des Johannesevangeliums." *ZNW* 8 (1907) 243–55.

Smith, D. Moody
The Composition and Order of the Fourth Gospel: Bultmann's Literary Theory (New Haven and London: Yale University Press, 1965).

Stange, Erich
Die Eigenart der johanneischen Produktion. Ein Beitrag zur Kritik der neueren Quellenscheidungshypothesen und zur Charakteristik der Johanneischen Psyche (Dresden: C. L. Ungelenk, 1915).

Strachan, Robert Harvey
"The Development of Thought within the Fourth Gospel." *ExpTim* 34 (1922/1923) 228–32, 246–49.

Talbert, Charles H.
"Artistry and Theology: An Analysis of the Architecture of Jn 1,19–5,47." *CBQ* 32 (1970) 341–66.

Temple, Sydney
"A Key to the Composition of the Fourth Gospel." *JBL* 80 (1961) 220–32.

Tenney, Merrill C.
"The Symphonic Structure of John." *BSac* 120 (1963) 117–25.

Thomas, W. H. G.
"The Plan of the Fourth Gospel." *BSac* 125 (1968) 313–23.

Thompson, J. M.
"The Structure of the Fourth Gospel." *Expositor*, 8th ser., 10 (1915) 512–26.

Trudinger, L. Paul
"The Seven Days of the New Creation in St. John's Gospel: Some Further Reflection." *EvQ* 44 (1966) 154–58.

Willemse, Johannes
Het vierde evangelie, Een onderzoek naar zijn structuur (Hilversum: P. Brand, 1965).

3. Sources

Ammon, Christoph Friedrich von
Docetur Johannem Evangelii auctorem ab editore huius libri fuisse diversum (Erlangen, 1811).

Bacon, Benjamin Wisner
"Sources and Method of the Fourth Evangelist." *HibJ* 25 (1926) 115–30.

Bacon, Benjamin Wisner
The Gospel of the Hellenists (New York: Holt, 1933).

Becker, Jürgen
Auferstehung der Toten im Urchristentum, SBS 82 (Stuttgart: Katholisches Bibelwerk, 1976) 117–48.

Becker, Jürgen
"Joh 3,1–21 als Reflex johanneischer Schuldiskussion." In *Das Wort und die Wörter. Festschrift Gerhard Friedrich zum 65. Geburtstag,* ed. H. Balz and S. Schulz (Stuttgart: W. Kohlhammer, 1973) 85–95.

Becker, Jürgen
"Aufbau, Schichtung und theologiegeschichtliche Stellung des Gebetes in Johannes 17." *ZNW* 60 (1969) 56–83.

Becker, Jürgen
"Die Abschiedsreden Jesu im Johannesevangelium." *ZNW* 61 (1970) 215–46.

Becker, Jürgen
"Wunder und Christologie. Zum literarkritischen und christologischen Problem der Wunder im Johannesevangelium." *NTS* 16 (1969/1970) 130–48.

Belle, G. Van
De Sèmeia-bron in het vierde Evangelie. Ontstaan en groei van hypothese, Studiorum Novi Testamenti Auxilia 10 (Louvain: University Press, 1975).

Blauert, H.
"Die Bedeutung der Zeit in der johanneischen Theologie." Dissertation, Tübingen, 1953.

Bousset, Wilhelm
"Der Verfasser des Johannesevangeliums." *TRu* 8 (1905) 225–44, 277–95.

Bousset, Wilhelm
"Ist das vierte Evangelium eine literarische Einheit?" *TRu* 12 (1909) 1–12, 39–64.

Broome, Edwin C.
"The Sources of the Fourth Gospel." *JBL* 63 (1944) 107–21.

Bühner, Jan-A.
Der Gesandte und sein Weg im vierten Evangelium. Die kultur- und religionsgeschichtlichen Grundlagen der johanneischen Sendungschristologie sowie ihre traditionsgeschichtliche Entwicklung, WUNT 2, 2 (Tübingen: Mohr-Siebeck, 1977).

Bultmann, Rudolf
"Hirschs Auslegung des Johannes-Evangeliums." *EvT* 4 (1937) 115–42.

Bultmann, Rudolf
"Zur johanneischen Tradition." *TLZ* 60 (1955) 524.

Carson, Dan A.
"Current Source Criticism of the Fourth Gospel: Some Methodological Questions." *JBL* 97 (1978) 411–29.

Clemen, Carl Christian
Die Entstehung des Johannesevangeliums (Halle: M. Niemeyer, 1912).

Cribbs, F. Lamar
"A Reassessment of the Date of Origin and the Destination of the Gospel of John." *JBL* 89 (1970) 38–55.

Dekker, C.
"Grundschrift und Redaktion im Johannesevangelium." *NTS* 13 (1966) 66–80.

Delff, Heinrich K. H.
Neue Beiträge zur Kritik und Erklärung des vierten

Evangeliums (Husum: C. F. Delff, 1890).

Delff, Heinrich K. H.
Das vierte Evangelium, ein authentischer Bericht über Jesus von Nazareth, wiederhergestellt, übersetzt und erklärt (Husum: C. F. Delff, 1890).

Easton, Burton Scott
"Bultmann's RQ Source." *JBL* 65 (1946) 143–56.

Edwards, H. E.
The Disciple Who Wrote These Things. A New Inquiry into the Origins and Historical Value of the Gospel according to St. John (London: J. Clarke, 1953).

Faure, Alexander
"Die alttestamentlichen Zitate im vierten Evangelium und die Quellenscheidungshypothese." *ZNW* 21 (1922) 99–121.

Fortna, Robert T.
The Gospel of Signs (Cambridge: Cambridge University Press, 1970).

Fortna, Robert T.
"From Christology to Soteriology. A Redaction-Critical Study of Salvation in the Fourth Gospel." *Int* 27 (1973) 31–47.

Fortna, Robert T.
"Christology in the Fourth Gospel. Redaction-Critical Perspectives." *NTS* 21 (1975) 489–504.

Fortna, Robert T.
"Source and Redaction in the Fourth Gospel's Portrayal of Jesus' Signs." *JBL* 89 (1970) 151–66.

Gericke, W.
"Zur Entstehung des Johannes-Evangeliums." *TLZ* 90 (1965) 807–20.

Goodwin, Charles
"How did John Treat his Sources?" *JBL* 73 (1954) 61–75.

Grant, Robert M.
"The Origin of the Fourth Gospel." *JBL* 69 (1950) 305–22.

Hartke, W.
Vier urchristliche Parteien und ihre Vereinigung zur Apostolischen Kirche, I and II, Deutsche Akademie der Wissenschaften zu Berlin, Schriften der Sektion für Altertumswissenschaft 24 (Berlin: Akademie-Verlag, 1961).

Hirsch, Emanuel
See Introduction §2.

Jeremias, Joachim
"Johanneische Literarkritik." *TBl* 20 (1941) 33–46.

Kysar, Robert
"The Source Analysis of the Fourth Gospel—A Growing Consensus?" *NovT* 15 (1973) 134–52.

Làconi, M.
"La critica letteraria applicata al IV Vangelo." *Ang* 40 (1963) 277–312.

Langbrandtner, Wolfgang
Weltferner Gott oder Gott der Liebe. Der Ketzerstreit in der johanneischen Kirche. Eine exegetisch-religionsgeschichtliche Untersuchung mit Berücksichtigung der

koptisch-gnostischen Texte aus Nag-Hammadi, Beiträge zur biblischen Exegese und Theologie 6 (Frankfurt: P. Lang, 1977).

Lindars, Barnabas
Behind the Fourth Gospel, Studies in Creative Criticism 3 (London: S. P. C. K., 1971).

Lindars, Barnabas
"Traditions Behind the Fourth Gospel." In *L'Evangile de Jean. Sources, rédaction, théologie*, ed. M. de Jonge. BETL 44 (Gembloux: Duculot; Louvain: University Press, 1977) 107–24.

Martyn, J. Louis
History and Theology in the Fourth Gospel (Nashville: Abingdon Press, 1968, ²1979).

Martyn, J. Louis
"Glimpses into the History of the Johannine Community. From its Origin through the Period of Its Life in which the Fourth Gospel was Composed." In *L'Evangile de Jean. Sources, rédaction, théologie*, ed. M. de Jonge. BETL 44 (Gembloux: Duculot; Louvain: University Press, 1977) 149–76.

Martyn, J. Louis
"Source Criticism and Religionsgeschichte in the Fourth Gospel." In *Jesus and Man's Hope*, ed. G. Buttrick. A Perspective Book (Pittsburgh: Pittsburgh Theological Seminary, 1970) 1: 247–73.

Nicol, W.
The Sēmeia in the Fourth Gospel. Tradition and Redaction, NovTSup 32 (Leiden: E. J. Brill, 1972).

Noack, Bent
Zur johanneischen Tradition. Beiträge zur Kritik an der literarkritischen Analyse des vierten Evangeliums (Copenhagen: Rosenkilde og Bagger, 1954).

Parker, Pierson
"Two Editions of John." *JBL* 75 (1956) 303–14.

Richter, Georg
Studien zum Johannesevangelium, ed. Josef Hainz. BU 13 (Regensburg: F. Pustet, 1977).

Ruckstuhl, Eugen
Die literarische Einheit des Johannesevangeliums; der gegenwärtige Stand der einschlägigen Forschungen (Fribourg: Paulusverlag, 1951).

Schnackenburg, Rudolf
"Zur Herkunft des Johannesevangeliums." *BZ* 14 (1970) 1–23.

Schwartz, Eduard
See Introduction §2.

Schweizer, Alexander
Das Evangelium Johannes nach seinem innern Werthe und seiner Bedeutung für das Leben Jesu kritisch untersucht (Leipzig: Weidmann, 1841).

Schweizer, Eduard
Ego Eimi. Die religionsgeschichtliche Herkunft und theologische Bedeutung der johanneischen Bildreden, zugleich ein Beitrag zur Quellenfrage des vierten Evangeliums, FRLANT, n.s., 38 (Göttingen: Vandenhoeck & Ruprecht, ²1965).

Smalley, Stephen S.
"Diversity and Development in John." *NTS* 17 (1970/1971) 276–92.

Smend, F.
"Die Behandlung alttestamentlicher Zitate als Ausgangspunkt der Quellenscheidungen im vierten Evangelium." *ZNW* 24 (1925) 147–50.

Smith, D. Moody
"The Milieu of the Johannine Miracle Source: a Proposal." In *Jews, Greeks and Christians. Religious Cultures in Late Antiquity. Essays in Honor of William David Davies,* ed. Robert Hamerton-Kelly and Robin Scroggs. SJLA 21 (Leiden: E. J. Brill, 1976) 164–80.

Smith, D. Moody
"The Sources of the Gospel of John. An Assessment of the Present State of the Problem." *NTS* 10 (1963/1964) 336–51.

Soltau, Wilhelm
Unsere Evangelien, ihre Quellen und ihr Quellenwert vom Standpunkt des Historikers aus betrachtet (Leipzig: H. Dieterich, 1901).

Soltau, Wilhelm
"Zum Johannesevanglium: Die Kritiker am Scheideweg." *Protestantische Monatshefte* 13 (1909) 436–47.

Soltau, Wilhelm
"Das Problem des Johannesevangeliums und der Weg zu seiner Lösung." *ZNW* 16 (1915) 24–53.

Soltau, Wilhelm
"Thesen über die Entwicklung einer johanneischen Literatur." *ZWT* 53 (1911) 167–70.

Soltau, Wilhelm
Das vierte Evangelium in seiner Entstehungsgeschichte dargelegt, SHAW.PH 7 (Heidelberg: C. Winter, ⁶1916).

Spitta, Friedrich
See Introduction §2.

Strachan, Robert Harvey
The Fourth Gospel. Its Significance and Environment (London: SCM Press, ³1946).

Strachan, Robert Harvey
The Fourth Evangelist: Dramatist or Historian? (London: Hodder & Stoughton; New York: G. H. Doran, 1925).

Teeple, Howard M.
"Methodology in Source Analysis of the Fourth Gospel." *JBL* 81 (1962) 279–86.

Teeple, Howard M.
The Literary Origin of the Gospel of John (Evanston,

IL: Religion and Ethics Institute, 1974).

Temple, S.
The Core of the Fourth Gospel (London and Oxford: A. R. Mowbray, 1975).

Thyen, Hartwig
"Entwicklungen innerhalb der johanneischen Theologie und Kirche im Spiegel von Joh 21 und der Lieblingsjüngertexte des Evangeliums." In *L'Evangile de Jean. Sources, rédaction, théologie,* ed. M. de Jonge. BETL 44 (Gembloux: Duculot; Louvain: University Press, 1977) 259–99.

Thyen, Hartwig
"Joh 13 und die kirchliche Redaktion des vierten Evangeliums." In *Tradition und Glaube. Das frühe Christentum in seiner Umwelt. Festgabe für Karl Georg Kuhn zum 65. Geburtstag,* ed. G. Jeremias, H. W. Kuhn, and H. Stegemann (Göttingen: Vandenhoeck & Ruprecht, 1971) 343–56.

Tobler, Johannes Rudolf
Evangelium Johannis nach dem Grundtext getreu wiedergegeben (Schaffhausen: Brodtmann, 1867).

Tobler, Johannes T.
"Über den Ursprung des vierten Evangeliums." *ZWT* 3 (1860) 169–203.

Wahlde, Urban C. von
"The Terms for Religious Authorities in the Fourth Gospel: A Key to Literary Strata?" *JBL* 98 (1979) 231–53.

Weiße, Christian Hermann
Die evangelische Geschichte, kritisch und philosophisch bearbeitet (Leipzig: Breitkopf & Härtel, 1838) 2: 138–304.

Weiße, Christian Hermann
Die Evangelienfrage in ihrem gegenwärtigen Stadium (Leipzig: Breitkopf & Härtel, 1856).

Wellhausen, Julius
See Introduction §2.

Wendt, Hans Heinrich
See Introduction §2.

Wilkens, Wilhelm
"Evangelist und Tradition im Johannesevangelium." *TZ* 16 (1960) 81–90.

Wilkens, Wilhelm
Zeichen und Werke. Ein Beitrag zur Theologie des vierten Evangeliums in Erzählungs- und Redestoff, ATANT 55 (Zurich: Zwingli Verlag, 1969).

Wilkens, Wilhelm
Die Entstehungsgeschichte des vierten Evangeliums (Zollikon: Evangelischer Verlag, 1958).

1. Sources

A gospel as extensive as the Gospel of John cannot have been written without the use of some sources. But what sorts of sources are involved has not yet been determined. Whoever thinks of the author as an eyewitness—perhaps John the son of Zebedee—will be inclined to view such sources as his reminiscences. But it then becomes a question whether he made notes of these reminiscences either during the earthly life of Jesus or shortly thereafter—naturally not in Greek—or whether he was dependent solely on his memory when he conceived his gospel. Various factors play a role in answering this question, factors of which scholars are not always cognizant. Thus, the language of the Gospel is often characterized as "virtually Aramaic," and this leads to the assumption that a young John made notes in Aramaic, which he later utilized in the composition of the Gospel. This is the way Edwards depicts the situation.[1]

Whether the author is an eyewitness is hotly debated. In this connection, there comes into play the differences between John and the Synoptics, along with the points of contact. This leads to the widespread hypothesis that John knew the Synoptics. From this point of view, the discrepancies show that John intended to supplement, correct, or even replace the Synoptics.[2] A great deal of ink has been spilled over these three possibilities. Accordingly, this point of departure, viz., that John knew one, two, or all of the Synoptics, is anything but certain.

In the second century, when the remark of Luke in 1:1 about the "many" who had undertaken a gospel was forgotten, one could get along with so simple a hypothesis, even when one was not attempting to set aside the differences between John and the Synoptics—insofar as they came into view—by means of bold interpretations. That proved to be especially necessary in the case of the date of Jesus' crucifixion. In this case, one sometimes interpreted the Synoptics in relation to John, and sometimes John in relation to the Synoptics. More recent is the information that Jesus held a kind of private passover—either because he observed a different calender (here the differences in Qumran calendar have played a role),[3] or because he was prompted to do so for other reasons.[4] One sees in this connection how complex the issue of sources is, particularly when one takes hold of it with reference to a single point. The question whether Jesus cleansed the temple at the beginning or at the end of his ministry is also much discussed, provided one does not resolve the difficulty by holding that it took place twice, once at the beginning and once at the end.

The way in which one attempts to demonstrate John's use of the Synoptics can take as its perspective an old church tradition that John was the last of the gospel writers to compose his gospel (so Clement of Alexandria). But one could also proceed by referring to the relatively few pericopes in which the Johannine narrative touches the Synoptics: (1) the cleansing of the temple (2:13–21); (2) healing of the official's son (4:46–54); (3) the feeding of the 5,000 (6:1–13), including the story of Jesus walking on the sea (6:16–21); (4) the annointing of Jesus (12:1–8); in addition, there are the points of agreement in the passion narrative. The difficulty that besets any attempt to show a dependence of John on the Synoptics is this: one must accept the view—as Hirsch does—that John not only knew the Synoptics, but that he had their texts in front of him and made use of now this and now that version either verbally or pictorially. How improbable such a method is becomes clear when one reflects on the fact that the Synoptics were not used alongside one another by the church at the end of the first century. Rather, a congregation was probably happy when it had one written gospel in its possession—and that one did not have to be one of the Synoptics.

The recognition that Matthew and Luke made use of Mark, even if in very different ways, plays a certain role in the theory that John made use of the Synoptics. In any case, that John followed a similar method cannot be demonstrated: a reading of John scarcely brings Mark to mind. Rather, the single Evangelist with which John has frequent contact—and that is not close—is Luke.

The determination to undertake a really precise comparative study of the "synoptic" pericopes in the Gospel of John in relation to the corresponding Synoptic passages came late. The pre-eminent study was that of P. Gardner-Smith,[5] followed later by by B. Noack.[6] As these studies show, the Johannine narrative is independent of that represented by the Synoptics, except at a few points where the Johannine version approximates the synoptic.

Beyond this, it remains to observe that there is a great deal of material in the Fourth Gospel (quite apart from

---

1   *The Disciple Who Wrote These Things. A New Inquiry into the Origins and Historical Value of the Gospel according to St. John* (London: J. Clarke, 1953).

2   Cf. Hans Windisch, *Johannes und die Synoptiker. Wollte der vierte Evangelist die älteren Evangelien ergänzen oder ersetzen?* (Leipzig: J. C. Hinrichs, 1926).

3   See especially the work of Jaubert, "Solution of the Conflict Between John and the Synoptics," in her *The Date of the Last Supper,* tr. I. Rafferty (Staten Island, NY: Alba House, 1965).

4   Stauffer: as "a heretic," *Jesus and His Story,* tr. Dorothea M. Barton (London: SCM Press, 1960) 93ff.

5   *St. John and the Synoptic Gospels* (Cambridge: Cambridge University Press, 1938).

6   *Zur johanneischen Tradition. Beiträge zur Kritik an der literarkritischen Analyse des vierten Evangeliums* (Copen-

the discourses), to which there is nothing corresponding in the Synoptics. One is reminded, in the first instance, of the wedding celebration at Cana (2:1–11), which is expressly designated the "first sign" of Jesus, while the healing of the official son appears as the "second sign" (4:54). That suggests a portrayal that is not identical with that of the Synoptics and speaks against the assertion of Noack: John is the first to have put the oral tradition into writing. This hypothesis has come to be regarded as mistaken also for other reasons. In the third place, there is Jesus' encounter with Nicodemus, which is depicted in chapter 3, although very laconically. Fourthly, Jesus encounters the Samaritan woman, which is somewhat elaborately narrated in chapter 4. Fifth is the healing of the lame man at the pool of Bethzatha (5:1–9, 14), and sixth the healing of the man born blind (chapter 9). Finally, there is the raising of Lazarus in chapter 11. This is quite apart from deviations in the passion and resurrection narratives and in chapter 21. Moreover, it may be observed that not only is Nicodemus unknown in the synoptic tradition, but Nathaniel is unknown as well; Peter and Andrew are from Bethsaida according to John 1:44, and not from Capernaum, as one must assume on the basis of Mark 1:29; the sons of Zebedee—apart from chapter 21—are not mentioned, although Thomas appears more frequently by far than in the Synoptics. As a consequence, we must at least assume that John made use of other traditions, in addition to the synoptic tradition, and that these other traditions were written, as we shall see. If, however, one is convinced that in the "synoptic parts" of the Gospel of John, the author did not make use of the Synoptics, the picture with respect to sources takes on an entirely different cast: the Fourth Gospel makes use of traditions that only occasionally touch those of the Synoptics but more strongly deviate from them (one need only recall that the cleansing of the temple appears early in the ministry of Jesus in John, and that John the Baptist and Jesus work alongside each other for a while).

But how should one think of the traditions utilized by John? Wendt had already assumed that the Fourth Gospel had combined two sources: a narrative source and a discourse source. He curiously attributed greater his-

torical reliability to the latter. Bultmann revived that earlier notion but in a new form. He likewise presupposes two sources: a narrative source (which he calls a "signs source") and a discourse source, which he thinks of as a collection of gnostic revelation discourses. Moreover, he also thinks John made use of the Synoptics. While some scholars, Spitta, for example, simply accept the view that the sources of the Fourth Gospel were woven together with great skill without altering their wording, so that there is little left for the redactor to do (so, for example, Macgregor), other scholars, such as Wellhausen and Schwartz, assume that it grew by layers, with an original version as the basis. As it admittedly turned out, this method of tracing layers of additions has not been successful: Schwartz almost despaired because new tensions and aporias always opened up in new layers apparently unified in themselves, with no end in sight.

As inviting as it is to approach the problem of sources in John with a specific theory in view, another method commends itself even more: to begin at a particular place and inquire not only whether John has made use of a source but how he has made use of it. What we mean by that can best be shown by considering John 20:19–29 in detail. The segment John 20:19–23 is strongly reminiscent of Luke 24:36–39. In both cases Jesus suddenly appears in the midst of his disciples on Easter and shows them the nail holes (in John 20:20 the wounds in his side also) and thereby establishes his reality and his identity. But in this Johannine version of the Easter appearance— it is secondary because it takes place in Jerusalem—there appear two sentences that do not show up in the synoptic tradition: "As the Father sent me, even so I send you"— thus turning the disciples (nothing is said of the twelve) into ones sent by himself, just as he is the one sent by his Father. They now take his place in the world, just as he took the place of his Father in the world. There then follows—on Easter day!—the outpouring of the Holy Spirit as he breathes on the disciples just as God breathed the breath of life into the creation. The sentence immediately following, "If you forgive the sins of any, they are forgiven; if you retain the sins of any, they are retained," is reminiscent of Matt 18:18, where, however, it is not the resurrected Jesus speaking. The forgiveness of sins

hagen: Rosenkilde og Bagger, 1954).

plays a remarkably minor role in the Gospel of John: in 1:29, the Baptist calls Jesus the lamb of God that takes away the sins of the world. John 9:41 speaks of sin that remains; in 15:22 it is said that only the revelation of Jesus leads to sin. Finally, sin is given as the ultimate cause of disability in 5:14 and 9:2. The connection of the forgiveness of sin with the outpouring of the Spirit means that we have to do with tradition John has taken over, not with a Johannine composition. The sole sentence typical of John in this segment is verse 21b: "As the Father has sent me, even so I send you." So it seems that John has added only a single sentence—we will verify it momentarily—to a narrative he has taken over; it stipulates for him what the gift of the Spirit brings with it.

The scene with Thomas that follows did not belong originally to the first scene (=20:19–23). For, if the disciples possess the Spirit, then "Thomas, one of the twelve," cannot fall short. This Thomas story stems from a time when the appearance of Jesus in the midst of his own—even if he shows them the evidences of his wounds—was no longer satisfying. The conviction of doubting Thomas was reported in order to quell the most tenacious doubts: according to verse 27, Thomas touches the nail holes with his finger and lays his hand on the wounded side and so comes to faith. John mentions only that Thomas "saw." But that is enough to indicate how he assesses this belief that palpably convinces of its truth: "Blessed are those who have not seen and yet believe." So by means of a single sentence out of the old miracle story—which corresponds in its way to Luke 24:42f.—an indirect picture of true faith has been created, faith that lives only out of the word that the Spirit verifies.

If we may assess the observation made on John 20:19–29, we would have to say that John confines himself, insofar as possible, to correcting the source (which does not at all conform to his views) as simply as possible by short additions, so as to make it bear his own message. That may, in fact, be demonstrated in other instances (e.g. 4:43–54).

Three further passages show that the Gospel of John in its present form was not cast in a single mould. This is most evident in the pericope of the woman taken in adultery (7:53–8:11). It is not found in $\mathfrak{P}^{66}$ and $\mathfrak{P}^{75}$, nor in the old parchment codices ℵ and B. Other manuscripts have indications in their text that this segment does not belong to the Fourth Gospel; still others (f¹ and Armenian texts) place it after John 21:25, the majuscule 225 even after John 7:36, and f¹³ after Luke 21:38. Beyond this, the manuscripts that contain this pericope do not offer a uniform text. All of this points to the fact that this pericope was inserted into the Gospel of John at a late date, at the earliest in the second century, after John had been published.

It is scarcely contested any longer by critical scholarship and others that, in spite of stylistic points of contact, chapter 21 is an appendix to chapters 1–20 and has been added by a foreign hand, although it is present in all manuscripts known to us, unlike the pericope of the woman taken in adultery. The Gospel of John was thus never disseminated without chapter 21. However, it is absurd to think that the disciples returned to their lives as fishermen on the Sea of Galilee after being given the Spirit and commissioned (20:21f.); and, after an obvious conclusion in 20:30f., the additional conclusion in 21:25 looks like an imitation in which an attempt at heightening miscarries. Moreover, there are differences in usage in relation to chapters 1–20. We can discuss the reasons this chapter was added to the Gospel of John only after we have completed the exegesis of chapters 1–20.

There is the least unanimity among scholars regarding the introduction to the Gospel: the so-called Prologue. Linguistic and stylistic differences make it reasonably certain that the author chose an older hymn, originally independent, as the way to introduce his Gospel. Bultmann is of the opinion that the Evangelist, having become a Christian, took an Aramaic hymn derived from the Baptist cult (not without misunderstanding!) and applied it to his new Lord; more recently, Käsemann and Schnackenburg, among others, believe it probable that the author made use of a Christian hymn, which had taken up and developed further motifs out of the Jewish wisdom tradition.

If these observations and conclusions are not wide of the mark, we have to do with sources taken up into the Gospel, in part, and, in part, with later elements added to the Gospel.

Do chapters 1–20 form an internal unity? The answer to that, in my opinion, is no: the Evangelist made use of a source (*Vorlage*) whose theological message differed from his own. Our thesis does not coincide with the earlier view, often discussed, that a basic draft of the Gospel of John was developed by means of further additions. At the basis of our view is the observation that the theology of the Evangelist differs from that of his source. One repeatedly finds narrative segments, like 4:46–54, for example, that intend to establish that Jesus is Son of God by means of his miracles. *The pericope of the healing of the official's son goes back to the synoptic account of the Centurion's servant.* Bultmann correctly saw that.[7] But he made a mistake in assuming that John transformed the story, which he found in the "signs source" (and which in that position was parallel to the synoptic account found in Matt 8:5–13//Luke 7:1–10), into a tale of healing at a distance. He therefore replaced Capernaum with Cana, eliminated the invitation to Jesus to come, and turned the heathen officer into a Herodian court-official, in order to treat the theme of "faith and the sign."[8] The Evangelist does not have the slightest interest in enhancing the miracle by increasing the distance and in eliminating the exemplary faith of a heathen. In Bultmann's analysis, the important thing is the recognition that verse 48, an unrelated insertion, expresses the judgment of the Evangelist regarding the faith awakened by miracles. On the other hand, he overlooks the fact that "he believed the word" ($\dot{\epsilon}\pi\dot{\iota}\sigma\tau\epsilon\upsilon\sigma\epsilon\nu$ $\tau\hat{\omega}$ $\lambda\dot{o}\gamma\omega$) in verse 50 corresponds exactly to faith in the mere word that John desires (for that reason, Hirsch identifies this as the high point of the story), and that the faith created by the affirmation of the miracle in verse 53 corresponds exactly to the faith Jesus depreciates in verse 48.

All these problems disappear when it is recognized that the story, derived from Q and treating exemplary faith (in Matthew heathen faith is extolled, in Luke it appears in a Jewish-Christian form, awkwardly reworked, which emphasizes the service of the Centurion to Judaism), has become in the course of the tradition a pure miracle story, whose focus is no longer the believing Centurion, but Jesus, the miracle worker. But in precisely this form it fits in remarkably well with those miracles, already completely worked out, that the Evangelist had before him in the received tradition; it is with this tradition that he had to deal. He succeeds in doing so by the addition of verses 48f., since the story affirms that

faith comes about, as Jesus predicts in verse 48, as a consequence of the miracle. The problem that we feel in verse 48 (the official does not request a miracle as a condition of his faith, but asks only that his son be healed), is somewhat lessened by this consideration: for John the request for a healing points to a miracle only in the sense of an inner worldly transformation, not in the sense of a new God-relationship. In sum: John left the narrative pretty much as he found it. By the addition of only two verses (48f.), he was able to make the story serve his purpose, since it now suggested the right kind of faith, the kind not dependent on miracles. Had he known the synoptic version as it is found in Matthew, he would have gladly taken over this narrative of right faith. But such a story does not fit well into a gospel designed merely to collect the greatest possible miracles, from which John took this narrative. It thus becomes evident that John has preserved a tradition—even one that resists him—and has revised it by means of a single sentence.

It is very difficult to deal with the question of sources for the passion narrative. Much is to be said for the view that the author also used a written source in this instance; especially since the work of Schniewind,[9] certain points of contact with the Lukan tradition have been recognized. But the part played by the Evangelist may be estimated rather highly. Bultmann posits a special source for the passion narrative. That goes together with the fact that the Johannine passion narrative does not fit into either his alleged signs source or his discourse source. But this line of reasoning suffers from having a third hypothesis built on two uncertain ones.

What we have been able to say up to this point, with some certainty, concerning the sources of John's narrative material, is this: the tradition utilized by John attempts to represent Jesus throughout as someone legitimated by miracles. In contrast, the Evangelist has endeavored to transform this tradition of legitimizing miracles into the doctrine of allusive signs.[10]

2. Composition

In this section two questions must be sharply distinguished, although they are closely related: the question

---

7   *John*, 204 [151].
8   *John*, 206 [152].
9   *Die Parallelperikopen bei Lukas und Johannes* (Hildes-   heim: G. Olms, ²1958).

of sources and the question of the composition of the Gospel. The second presents us at once with that well-known either/or: does the sequence of verses and chapters as we have them now in the present text follow the original sequence? Or has the original order been disturbed? Although numerous exegetes—more recently Barrett in his huge work—have opted for the first possibility, not a few expositors have set out to reconstruct the true sequence of verses and chapters.[11] By way of example, we may offer the order proposed by Macgregor, which leads to a different view of the composition of the Fourth Gospel than that held, for example, by Bultmann. According to Macgregor/Morton,[12] the order of the Gospel originally was: 1:1–3, 13; 3:31–36; 4:43–54; 6:1–21; 5:1–47; 7:15–24; 8:12–20; 7:1–14; 7:25–36; 8:21–59; 7:45–52; 7:37–42; 11:53–12:32; 3:14f.; 12:34; 3:16–21; 12:35–13:35; 16:25–33; 18:1–14; 18:19–24; 18:28–20:31. A first redactor added: 3:22–30; 18:15–18 and 18:25–27. A second redactor added a second source to this document, from which 4:1–42; 6:22–71; 10:1–11:52; 14:1–16; 17:1–26 derive. Some additions of this second redactor include: 1:6–8; 1:15; 7:53–8:11; 13:36–38; and 21:1–25.

As is well known, Bultmann followed a different course. The fact that Bultmann does not discuss the question of authorship and his sources and place in primitive Christianity in detail, but begins his commentary with an exposition of the text, sets him apart from other commentators. One must gather information regarding many introductory questions from occasional discussions in the body of the commentary. So, from preliminary remarks on John 2:1–12,[13] we learn that the Evangelist used a source that contained a collection of miracles. "It is the σημεῖα-source, which in its style is clearly distinguishable from the language of the Evangelist or of the discourse-source, which is the basis of the Prologue and the following discourses; it is equally clearly distinguishable from the miracle stories of the Synoptic tradition."[14] John 1:35–50 forms the introduc-

tion to the σημεῖα-source ("signs-source"), John 20:30f. the conclusion. From the introduction to the Prologue[15] we learn that the Evangelist has taken a hymn from the Baptist community, to which he once belonged, and adapted it to Jesus. The preliminary remarks to 2:13–22 tell us that the Evangelist derived his story of the cleansing of the temple from neither the Synoptics nor the oral tradition, "but from a literary source almost certainly related to the Synoptic accounts."[16] The peculiar thing about this view of the matter is that the Evangelist restricts himself essentially to amplifications that he inserts into the text used by him. But the real focus of the Fourth Gospel comes to rest on the revelation discourses, which the Evangelist has borrowed from non-Christian gnosis. It must also be noted that a redaction took place subsequent to the Evangelist, since otherwise the structure of the Gospel, as Bultmann sees it, becomes incomprehensible.

This structure is very impressive.

A. The Revelation of the Δόξα to the World: Chapters 2–12
   Prelude: 2:1–22

I. The Encounter with the Revealer: 2:23–4:42

II. The Revelation as Κρίσις ("Judgment"): 4:43–6:39, 7:15–24, 8:12–24

III. The Revealer's Struggle with the World: 7:1–14, 25–29, 8:48–50, 54f., 7:30. 7:37–44, 31–36, 37–44, 31, 32–36, 45–52, 8:41–47, 51–53, 56–59, 9:1–41, 8:12, 12:44–50, 8:21–29, 12:34–36, 10:19–21, 22–26, 11–13, 1–10, 14–18, 27–30, 31–39

IV. The Revealer's Secret Victory over the World: 10:40–42, 11:1–57, 12:1–33, 8:30–40, 6:60–71, 12:37–43

B. The Revelation of the Δόξα ("Glory") Before the Community

I. The Revealer's Farewell: 13:1–30, 17:1–26, 13:31–35, 15:1–17, 15:18–16:11, 16:12–33, 13:36–14:31

II. The Passion and Easter: 18:1–20:29
   Appendix: Chapter 21

---

10   [Haenchen is punning: transform the tradition of *beweisenden* miracles into the doctrine of *hinweisenden* signs.—Translator.]

11   See Introduction §4, "Disorder and Rearrangement."

12   *The Structure of the Fourth Gospel* (Edinburgh: Oliver & Boyd, 1961).

13   *John*, 113 [78].

14   *John*, 113 [78].

15   *John*, 13–18 [1–5].

16   *John*, 122 [86].

If this structure goes back to the Evangelist, one cannot really say that he only contributed amplifications. But this structure in the first instance is the attempt of Bultmann to reconstruct the text, as shown by the arrangement of chapters and verses cited above. In support of his attempt Bultmann can point to the many places in the transmitted text where tensions exist; in addition, he presupposes that the Evangelist treats his themes each time in some context.

But the impression that the Gospel of John is an unfinished work arises essentially from the observation that some parts, the story of the man born blind (chapter 9), for example, are very carefully considered and constructed so as to heighten the tension artfully, while other parts, on the contrary, have the effect of being unfinished and rough. That the Evangelist does not consummate the form of the story in chapter 9 is shown by the trajectory of the segment (the same thing applies to the Lazarus story in chapter 11): the story of the man born blind is told so that it necessarily seems to follow that Jesus comes from God or is the Son of Man. For how would he have then performed such a miracle? This compelling conclusion from the standpoint of the "sign," however, is something John sharply resists (e.g. 3:3). The increasing tension so artfully and admirably designed in this chapter is therefore taken over, along with the story itself, from a source. As an author, John is much less sophisticated than Luke, although with very simple means he is able to achieve powerful effects.

We thus have no right to reorder the Gospel arbitrarily, as, for example, Bacon,[17] Macgregor,[18] Bultmann, and Hoare[19] have done, and then to represent this new sequence as the true outline, the original composition of the Gospel, and to interpret everything in accordance with it. Rather, we must first of all attempt to interpret the text just as it stands, with all of its difficulties, and reserve conjectural modifications for cases of extreme necessity, where several indications converge from more than one direction on the same point.

How does the composition of the Gospel of John appear if we assume the traditonal text and its traditional sequence? It is aptly described by Dodd:[20] In the first half, chapters 1–12, the author in general reports "signs," which are subsequently interpreted in discourses of Jesus in relation to their spiritual content. In the second half, in the passion narrative, that was not possible. As a consequence, the discourses are placed before the narrative (so as not to efface the drama); within the passion narrative itself the author interpolates individual explanations where possible.

But beyond these general characteristics, the composition of the Gospel is not at all clear if one approaches it with the demand for a clean sequence and clear separation of themes.

Now, however, let us indicate a two-pronged approach. In the first place, in some instances in which disorder has been conjectured, we are able to discover a completely acceptable context by reflecting on the text more closely. For example, we may take 1:24, which has troubled many exegetes. It can be recognized without great effort that it separates two different segments: Verses 19–23 describe the self-evaluation of the Baptist negatively and positively; he makes no messianic claims for himself, but wants only to be the voice of one preparing the way for Jesus, as Isaiah prophesied. Verses 25–28, on the other hand, treat the further question of how the baptism of John comports with his mission thus understood. The result is: this baptism is merely a water baptism, which does not at all anticipate the really decisive figure already standing by. This lays the groundwork for the next segment, verses 29–34: nothing is said of a baptism of Jesus by John. John has only baptized so as to have the occasion to observe the Spirit descending and abiding on the coming one, who is to baptize with the Spirit. That transpires and John can now testify to it. Verse 24 not only provides a break between two segments, but also makes good sense: In verse 22 the priests and Levites sent from Jerusalem to the Baptist have

17 "John and the Synoptists," in his *The Gospel of the Hellenists* (New York: Holt, 1933) 111–19.

18 *The Structure of the Fourth Gospel* (Edinburgh: Oliver & Boyd, 1961).

19 *The Gospel According to St. John Arranged in its Conjectural Order* (London: Oates & Washbourne, 1949).

20 *Interpretation of the Fourth Gospel*, 289–91.

spoken of those who gave them their commission. In verse 24 they are identified as Pharisees, who appear to John as a kind of official. The statement in verse 24 simply cannot be relocated to a point prior to the answer of the Baptist to the question posed in verse 22 on literary grounds.

Another question is whether difficulties can always be resolved in a comparable way. Thus, 1:31f. is an insertion in all probability. It has been pursued with known methods, viz., it ends with the same expression as the preceding segment: "I myself did not know him." The interpolation in verse 31 presupposes something that is said neither before nor after: John has been commissioned to baptize so that Jesus may be made known to Israel. Moreover, the Spirit is depicted here as a descending dove, as in the Synoptics, and the scene assimilated to that of the synoptic tradition. That is desirable because the baptism of Jesus by John is no longer narrated. The reason is evident: Everything is avoided that gives Jesus a certain dependence on John.

A similar case, in which we again appear to have to do with a gloss, is 4:2. This verse is regarded as a later correction, which reconciles Jesus' baptismal activity with the synoptic account, according to which Jesus did not baptize. But in reality matters are not so simple. It must not be overlooked that, according to John 7:39, the Spirit is to be appear only after the glorification of Jesus; in fact, Jesus brings the Spirit after the resurrection in 20:22. A baptism during the earthly life of Jesus would therefore have been a mere water baptism, not distinguishable from that of John. If, however, the disciples of Jesus practice baptism, the situation is quite different: here they represent the post-Easter community. The Evangelist has often mixed the times in just this way, as, for example, in 4:23, 4:36ff., and 5:25.

We must now disregard such details in order to get at the larger compositional schema. The first question is perhaps that of the so-called Prologue. The view that a converted disciple of John translated it from Aramaic and applied it to Jesus, as Bultmann held, has been generally abandoned today. On the other hand, a comparison of the different "biographically" oriented gospels reveals that each fixes a point in time as the beginning of the salvific events that that Evangelist wants to relate. That point shifts steadily backwards. For Mark it is the preaching and baptism of John. Matthew and Luke move

it further back in two ways: on the one hand, to stories of the miraculous birth and childhood, and, on the other, to the genealogy. But John fixes the point before the creation, which means that it is now insurpassable. But then how is the incarnation to be made comprehensible? First of all, according to an ancient wisdom myth, the "pre-incarnate logos" ("logos asarkos") is depicted in his fruitless activity. The incarnation is necessary because his activity remains futile. He who becomes flesh then establishes his own community. The approximate point at which earlier evangelists begin their story, viz., the appearance of John, is then reached.

It has admittedly not been said that the gospel used by John already contained this prologue. But if one assumes that John himself added 1:1–18, it is also natural to assume that the original draft made use of the "prologue"—although in an abbreviated form. Verses 6–8 have the mistaken perspective that verses 4f. already speak of the "logos incarnate" ($\lambda \acute{o} \gamma o s \; \acute{\epsilon} \nu \sigma \alpha \rho \kappa o s$). However, in the Christian hymn originally—it seems to us that nothing is to be said for a gnostic baptismal hymn—the incarnation of the logos followed because the activity of the "pre-incarnate logos" ($\lambda \acute{o} \gamma o s \; \acute{\alpha} \sigma \alpha \rho \kappa o s$) as such had proved to be fruitless. Only then is 1:14 given its proper weight—in this Bultmann rather than Käsemann is right.

The transition is now made to the theme of the baptism of John. It is represented very differently, to be sure, corresponding to the new christological perspective. The first pericope concerning the Baptist, 1:19–28, is devoted to the testimony he gives about himself, and this goes back essentially in the end to Mark 1:1–13. The Baptist freely admits that he is not the Christ, nor Elijah, nor the prophet—for the Evangelist these concepts are very closely related because together they confer the highest authority—but only the voice crying in the wilderness as foretold by Isaiah. Following a transitional verse, verse 24, which defines more precisely the "the ones sent" ($\pi \acute{\epsilon} \mu \psi \alpha \nu \tau \epsilon s$) of verse 22, a second scene clarifies the meaning of the baptism of John under these circumstances. That does not imply that the messiah, Elijah, and the prophet will baptize. The upshot is: The baptism of John is merely a water baptism, and a mightier one by far will appear immediately after him. It is very difficult to decide whether this pericope was also derived from the underlying source, or whether it is a pure Johannine composition. The answer depends on whether one believes the Evangelist himself created whole scenes without a clue in the tradition. The use of tradition in 3:22f. makes the latter unlikely.

The theme of the superior one to come is further developed in the next pericope, also devoted to the Baptist (1:19–34). Now for the first time clear reference is made to Jesus, who takes away the sins of the world as the lamb of God (a concept foreign to John): He is the mightier one to follow after John. The baptism of Jesus is not mentioned (that also continues a development inaugurated by the Synoptics [Mark 1:14f.]). It is not at all clear whether Jesus' baptism is being presupposed. What sense does it make for him to come to receive a mere baptism in water? The baptism of John, threatened by the complete loss of meaning, now gains its meaning by virtue of the fact that John, in practicing baptism, sees among those present the one upon whom the Spirit descends and abides (this is also a further development of the synoptic tradition). That this occurred is solemnly attested in verse 34. Verses 31f. are presumably an addition strongly assimilated to the synoptic tradition.

John—and probably the gospel of which he made use—now faces the task of making the decisive transition from the theme of "John" to the theme of "Jesus." That is depicted in the next pericope (1:35–51), where two disciples of John go over to Jesus. That five additional disciples of John also switch their allegiance to Jesus completes not only the sacred number of seven, but also gives the author the occasion to show that Jesus has a right to all the traditional christological predicates. Non-synoptic tradition has also been worked into this account.

Following the announcement in 1:50 that the disciples will see greater things than Jesus' marvelous knowledge about Nathaniel, the first Cana pericope (2:1–11) brings the fulfillment of the promise by means of the transformation of water into wine, and that—actually at variance with what precedes—causes the disciples to have faith in Jesus. In the context of the gospel being used, the δόξα ("glory") of Jesus is made evident in his unlimited power in transforming the water into wine. For John himself the miracle does not reflect the replacement of Jewish ritual with Christian worship in Spirit and in truth (so Hirsch), nor does it depict the fullness of the messianic time (thus Nötscher, following Jeremias). The Evangelist rather indicates here that Jesus is not driven by earthly motives, but acts only when the divine hour arrives. This allusion points at the same time to the hour of Jesus' devotion to his own, which will later be consummated in his death on the cross.

The transition in 2:12 sounds like an old Capernaum tradition. The following pericope presents the cleansing of the temple. Its Johannine meaning lies not so much in a cleansing of the Jewish cult—for the Evangelist the Jewish cult is not subject to cleansing—as in the mysterious announcement of the death on the cross. It is important for the composition of John that the cross cast its shadow and its light across the beginning of Jesus activity (2:19 refers in a veiled way to the resurrection!).

Verses 2:23–25, which speak of a faith in Jesus that is not to be trusted—faith that is awakened only by miracles—and which presuppose the performance of many "signs" in Jerusalem, form the transition to the scene with Nicodemus (3:1–21).

In this passage (traditional material—the figure of Nicodemus coming to Jesus by night: cf. 19:39—is used only as an occasion), John shows that the miracles of Jesus as such do not by any means permit the recognition of his divine commission, but that the gift of a basically different, supermundane existence is necessary to be able to see God at work in the wonders of Jesus. We should not be surprised that Jesus' language gradually passes over to the testimony of the post-Easter congregation, if we understand that John deliberately interweaves the times (cf. 4:23, 5:25, and chapter 7). Here also there is veiled reference to Jesus' cross (Moses "raising" the healing serpent in the wilderness), which brings both grace and judgment. Verses 19–21 may be a later addition, traceable to Jesus' rejection of the moral wickedness of the unbelievers.

The Baptist appears for the last time in the next pericope (3:22–36); his discourse passes over into that of the post-Easter community (like that of Jesus to Nicodemus) in verses 31ff. The representation of Jesus as baptizing simultaneously with John and "everyone going out to him" permits the author to show the reader that the Baptist freely and willingly recognizes the absolute superiority of Jesus, the beloved son of God, in whose hands the Father has placed everything. Strictly speaking, 4:1–3 also belongs to this segment. For, as verse 2, which is almost always set aside as a gloss, makes clear, the baptism of the Christian community—superior, of course—stands alongside the baptism of John. Jesus himself did not baptize because the Spirit came only after his exaltation (7:39b). Thus, a baptism practiced by the earthly Jesus could only have been a water baptism, and in that case could not have been distinguished from the baptism of John.

As a consequence, John the Baptist does not appear again in the Gospel of John. It is of course noted in 5:34–36 that John offered testimony on behalf of Jesus, but Jesus no longer claims this testimony. That the testimony of John must have played a certain role in the tradition is demonstrated by 10:41, where his pronouncements over Jesus are recognized by many as true, although he had performed no signs.

Beginning in chapter 4, Jesus occupies the stage center alone. Verses 4–42 clearly demonstrate not only Jesus' omniscience (v 16), and his ability to bestow living water, but John also seizes the opportunity here to elucidate the interweaving of the times before and after Easter (viz., the Jesus who proclaims and the proclaimed Christ), in the mission to the Samaritans (vv 35–38) and elsewhere. He also points out that the Christian worship of God is not bound to a specific geographical location—that was by no means so self-evident to the Jews—but since it lies beyond both Zion and Garizim, it is superior to Judaism and the Samaritan religion alike, the latter half-Jewish and half-heathen. It becomes very clear in this long dialogue dotted with pieces of tradition but conceived as a whole, that the author is never concerned to take up a theme once and exhaust it; rather, he likes to touch on several themes as they are suggested to him by something in the context.

The story of the βασιλικός ("royal official") and his son who lay ill (4:43–54) stems indeed from the synoptic tradition concerning the Centurion from Capernaum. It has undergone a surprising development, and no longer extols exemplary faith but the wonder-working power of Jesus. For that very reason, John was prompted to make clear, in verse 48, that faith awakened by miracles was not authentic faith and not desired by Jesus. If one reflects on that point, the riddle of 4:43–45 is also solved: since the Galileans only believe because they saw Jesus performing signs at the feast in Jerusalem, they do not have faith in the word of Jesus, a faith not borne up by wonders. Their friendly acceptance of Jesus is thus not yet the honor that Jesus really commands from the "own country" (πατρίς).

The structure of chapter 5 is not as clear. An abbreviated, retold miracle story forms the beginning: the healing of the man who had been lame for thirty-eight years at the pool of Bethzatha. A traditional feature, viz., that Jesus had the lame man, now healed, carry his bed (a feature that is a compelling provocation of what follows) leads to an argument between Jesus and the Jews, during the course of which the real contrast is set in bold relief: just as God raises the dead and makes them living, so does the Son—it is to this that the healing points; Jesus raises up the sick and gives them life (cf. "rise" [ἔγειρε] in 5:8). This correlation betweeen Father and Son permits John to describe truly new Christian existence, again with an obvious intermingling of the times. In this existence, man passes from death to life, undergoes the transition "out of death into life" (ἐκ θανάτου εἰς ζωήν). At the same time, it is made evident that Jesus does not act on his own, but only in obedience to the will of the Father. Verses 27–29 may be a later addition which appends the resurrection at the end of days. The theme changes with verse 31: the testimony that Jesus has been giving on his own behalf is defended against the charge that it is not valid as such. In accordance with his station, Jesus accepts no human testimony at all as assurance of his honor— even the testimony of John in this sense does not come under consideration; it is only the testimony of the Father himself that is correlative with his qualities that transcend everything earthly. The final reference to the testimony of Moses could belong to material contained in the tradition.

In 6:1–21, also following a tradition, John narrates the twin miracles of the feeding of the 5,000 and walking on the sea. But they are not understood—as 6:26 emphasizes—in the sense of a sign: the feeding of the multitude really suggests that Jesus is the bread from heaven, the eternal food of fellowship with God, the food that Jesus administers to his own in accordance with the will of God (v 40). His own are those whom the Father draws to himself (v 44). The subsequent reference to the resurrection on the last day may be a later addition; the same thing may be said of verses 54–58, distinguishable from the context by word usage (τρώγω instead of ἐσθίω), with its reference to the necessity of eating or "munching" Jesus' flesh and drinking his blood in the Lord's Supper. That the Spirit alone gives life also means that Jesus' message to those believers brings life from the Father and that this life begins only with the coming of the Spirit.

The discourse about Jesus as the bread from heaven not only causes many disciples to withdraw, but also prompts the question whether the twelve will remain with him. To Peter's confession made in the name of the twelve Jesus answers with the disclosure that one among them is a devil.

The narrative in 7:1–13 makes the reader aware how substantial the opposition to Jesus has already become: the Jews want to kill him; and his own brothers, whose thought and sensibilities belong to the world, remain unbelievers. Nevertheless, the queries regarding Jesus remain active among the Jews.

The following discourse of Jesus extends as far as verse 36. In it Jesus defends the fact that he broke the law by healing on the sabbath; he points out that the Jews themselves are constrained to break the sabbath commandment by circumcising on the sabbath. Here the author may be making use of traditional material. The authentic Johannine comments in this section again touch on various themes—for this reason chapters 7 and 8 seem so incoherent—such as the Father of Jesus whom the Jews do not know, the ineffective persecution, faith based on miracles, the abortive attempt to arrest Jesus, and the order on the part of the Pharisees to arrest Jesus officially. All that provides the background for Jesus to speak for the first time of the fact that he will be with them only a short time longer. This is a riddle the Evangelist uses (7:35) to prompt the Jews to announce the Christian mission to the diaspora among the Greeks, prophetically, against their will.

The discourse of Jesus is continued in 7:37–52, although formally interrupted for the moment, and the theme of the Spirit taken up briefly. The return of the minions of the law to the Pharisees empty-handed provides the occasion for the author to depict the impression Jesus has made on the people and the callousness of the Pharisees, which even Nicodemus cannot penetrate: "the prophet" does not come from Galilee, according to Jewish doctrine.

In 8:12–20, 21–29, and 30–59, themes introduced earlier are repeated in quick succession: Jesus is the light of the world; his self-testimony is valid because in truth it is not only a self-testimony; the Father is hidden from the unbelievers and Jesus is entirely one with him. New in this passage is the note that false faith—the kind that boasts of its own virtues (vv 30ff.)—is turned quickly into hostility toward the gospel of grace. The conflict with the Jews then quickly comes to a head, and Jesus calls them children of the devil (v 44, "your father, the devil"), while Jesus himself comes from eternity and thus from beyond time: Abraham rejoiced to see him.

It would require only a minor offense for the conflict between Jesus and the Jews to flare up. For this purpose John makes use of two pieces of tradition: the story of the healing of the man born blind in chapter 9 and the account of the raising of Lazarus in chapter 11. The perspective on the miracle in chapter 9 indicates that it has been taken from the tradition. Only at the beginning (vv 2–5) and at the conclusion (vv 35–41) has John inserted clarifying statements; in general, however, he has reproduced unaltered the masterfully narrated story of the healing of the blind man and its effect (on the question of source, see above §6.1). This story reveals how perverse the Pharisees are and how anxiety-laden and dejected those dominated by them are (vv 20ff.). The sabbath conflict anticipated in verse 14 does not erupt in this story (it was probably represented in greater detail in the tradition). On the other hand, the situation is thrown into sharp relief at the conclusion: whoever acknowledges Jesus is cast out of the synagogue (v 34). That provides some presentiment of how one may fare with Jesus himself. John has not crowned this narrative with a discourse on "Jesus the light of the world"—that was said already in 8:12 and the reader still has it in mind. It is not the case, in the first half of the Gospel of John, that the appropriate interpretive discourse always follows the marvelous deeds of Jesus. In fact, John's method is freer and richer in variety: he can be satisfied with a suggestion, as in 2:21, but he can also anticipate the interpretation, as in 8:12, and then retain the possibility of adding a second, related clarification to the end, as in 9:40f.

The way in which the discourse of Jesus in chapter 10 follows on the healing miracle story in chapter 9 has rightly occasioned surprise. Bultmann has here again constructed a long, self-contained discourse. But it is not possible to shift about so freely in the case of discourses directed generally to the Jews (10:19). John did not have a miracle story that pointed to Jesus as the good shepherd. He therefore did the next best thing: he employed a discourse with an enigmatic figure of speech (v 6), and then later amplified and interpreted it. It goes without saying that he was already thinking of Jesus in verses 1–5. Nevertheless, one must treat these verses in the first instance as metaphorical and not turn them at once into an allegory. Their subject is—put this way so as not to use the expression straight off—the true shepherd, whose anima (shadowy anti-type) becomes visible as the thief and robber. However, it is the true shepherd who is really being described, who enters in by the door in the sheepfold (it is surrounded by a wall), and is depicted in his trusted relationship to his sheep: he knows each one and each sheep in turn knows him. This relationship of trust does not obtain between a stranger and the sheep: the sheep flee before his strange voice. Verse 2 appears to have provoked an early reader, in a gloss, to view Jesus as the door (not only does sa read "Shepherd" for "door" in v 7, but also $\mathfrak{P}^{75}$; the difficulty was thus sensed at an early date). Verses 7–9 probably belong together; then, in verse 8, by "thieves and robbers" is probably meant the leaders of the revolt in 66–70 CE, who were represented as the saviors of Israel and yet only brought about a terrible bloodbath. Whether there is an allusion in verse 5 to the removal of the Christian congregation to Pella is dubious. The discourse is continued in verse 10 and now turns resolutely to the real theme, the "true shepherd," the "good shepherd," as whose counterpart is introduced not only the wolf but especially the hireling. The discourse on the shepherd indicates not only that Jesus risks his life for "his sheep," but also that he really sacrifices it for them. It cannot be gainsaid that this view of the "sheepfold" leads to a larger unity culminating in "a shepherd and his flock"—the expansion of the Christian church over the entire world that lies beyond his earthly life is only hinted at in 11:52, 12:20, 17:20 and generally affirmed, so to speak, but without giving details and concrete instances (the question of the law has already been settled for John apart from this issue). Jesus' freedom over against death and life is spoken of boldly in verses 17f.; it almost looks as though he resurrects himself from the dead. But it is finally, however, the charge of the Father which lies at its base. The division among the Jews in verses 19–21 is a literary device. In view of the offensive remarks in verse 18, the reader is not to see the demonic at work here. The healing of the blind man is used as a σημεῖον ("sign").

The next scene, the last in view of the publicity

(10:22–39), again treats well-known themes: Jesus' works, the sheep given to him by the Father, his unity with the Father ("and no one shall snatch them out of my hand" corresponds exactly to "no one is able to snatch them out of the Father's hand," vv 28f.), and the vain attempt of the Jews to stone him. The line of reasoning in verses 34ff. could have been taken out of the tradition, inasmuch as it utilizes the OT to a larger degree than is customary for John. Verses 20f. may also contain elements taken from the tradition (emphasis on the miracles of Jesus).

The restoration of Lazarus in chapter 11 provides the event that redeems the catastrophe. The conversation with Martha that the Evangelist inserts into this narrative is decisive for understanding Johannine thought: Jesus contrasts the resurrection on the last day with "I am the resurrection and the life." This discussion reveals the meaning of the resurrection narrative for John: it is only a pointer to the true resurrection, which Jesus brings.

At the same time, this story serves, in verses 45–53, to explain why the Jews have decided to kill Jesus: his miracles would otherwise enlist all Jews in his support and thus bring down the full weight of Roman oppression. It is naive to think that the real relationships are accurately portrayed. It is the tradition taken over by John that is coming copiously to expression. This tradition had already moved the cleansing of the temple to the beginning and created a crisis out of the Lazarus story.

Since Jesus attends the Jewish Passover feast as a matter of course (although John does not report anything of a Passover celebration; Jesus uses them rather as occasions for preaching), he now goes to Jerusalem. In 12:1–11, the author now reports a story well-known to us from the Synoptics in a much more highly developed form, on which he does not comment. Only the connection with the Lazarus story is strongly emphasized. While the account of the anointing comes in Luke at an earlier point (7:36–50), it is found in Matthew and Mark, as in John, during the last days in Jerusalem. By contrast, the Gospel of John does not introduce the entry into Jerusalem until now: 12:12–19. The finding of the ass is dismissed abruptly in verse 14 and is supported only with references to Isa 40:9 and Zech 9:9. Here again the Lazarus story plays a significant role, which is based on material taken by the Evangelist from the tradition.

In 12:20–36, on the other hand, the Evangelist expresses himself by means of a discourse of Jesus. Greek proselytes desire to see Jesus: that is the sign for the Evangelist that the hour of glorification has come, especially in the sense of the hour of death: the grain of wheat must die before it can bear fruit; only when Jesus is lifted up he will draw all of his own to himself (vv 24, 32). With the admonition that Jesus will be with his own only a short time longer (v 35), the certainty of the coming farewell is enhanced for the reader; at the same time, Jesus' act of hiding himself anticipates that farewell (v 37). The verses that follow are derived from tradition: the reproach that they did not believe in Jesus in spite of all the miracles he performed—a reproach that corresponds exactly to the prophecy of Isaiah. Isa 6:9 is always quoted in the NT wherever the enigma of Israel's obstinacy pops up. In any case, this apparent failure is somewhat offset by the observation that many—even of the ἄρχοντες ("rulers")—believed in Jesus but dared not confess it out of fear of the Pharisees (they appear here as the elite corps of the adversaries). A final, brief speech of Jesus (vv 44–50), which touches on the most important themes once again, closes the public ministry.

It is of decisive importance that one not seek to discover the compositional strategy of the Gospel with false expectations. To repeat ourselves, the Evangelist was not a master storyteller nor an overpowering poet. Whenever possible, he was satisfied to take the tradition that came to him and to make that tradition serve his proclamation by as few intrusions as possible. The Evangelist was not interested in a unified style or in a polished narrative; he wanted only to effect the correct teaching, as he understood it. For that purpose, a simple procedure presented itself to him: he took a minimum of miracles from the tradition, which he then had Jesus discuss in his speeches (in chapters 5, 6, 9 and elsewhere). In the case of the passion narrative, the speeches had to precede. The division into two major parts, 1:1–13:30 and 13:31–17:26, permitted the separate handling of two major groups of themes at the same time: Jesus and the world, Jesus and his own. Chapters 18–20 produce the final collision with the world and the "exaltation," including the resurrection, anticipated by the "signs." The passion narrative is not designed especially to awaken sympathy in the reader, but to extol the victor, who has pursued the concern of God, viz., divine love, uninterruptedly, until the last breath. Insofar as Jesus

achieves this victory, his exaltation takes place. Because Jesus is the one the Father has sent in the Gospel of John, and because he speaks the Father's words and does the Father's works, we could also say of this death that the promise of 12:28 is fulfilled: "I have gorified it [my name], and will glorify it again."

3. Style

It will repay us to attack the third problem by means of a brief detour through the synoptic gospels. Mark narrates miracle stories of more than one kind. On the one hand, 7:31–37 and 8:22–26 are constructed along the same lines: Jesus is represented as a "divine man" who heals with various techniques (touching, spittle, gestures, special commands). The miracle stories in 5:1–20 and 9:14–20 are very different in style. With regard to content, it is new that Jesus drives out demons; also new, formally speaking, is the special detail (Matt 8:28–34 is greatly reduced in comparison to Mark 5; Matt 17:14–21 and Luke 9:37–42 reproduce Mark 9 in much shorter form): the details are intended to show how powerful the demons are that Jesus overcomes.

Does it follow from this difference in style that the healing stories of Mark 7 and 8 are from the same source and the stories of demon possession in Mark 5 and 9 from a different source? In other words, is a different style also a certain sign of a special source? Or does each kind of miracle story simply require reproduction in its own or special style? In that case, the form depends on content, and style tells us nothing about putative sources.

Matthew and Luke have left a great deal out of the account of the demon-possessed boy in Mark 9. They do not simply take over their source, but also revise it in accordance with the views of their time. In so doing, even verse 24 (for us theologically highly important) drops out: "I believe; help my unbelief." Perhaps the combination of belief and unbelief in one and the same person shocked the simple reader; one therefore urged upon him the "simple" requirement of faith. There is no evidence of an extra-Markan source in Matthew and Luke. The "thinking in sources" that used to be so popular and that some exegetes still espouse today, overlooks the freedom of the evangelists; they did not intend simply to retell what they found before them, but to narrate what really happened—what really corresponded to the understanding of their own time.

The early picture of the rise of the canonical gospels—each one was written by a particular evangelist (an apostle or disciple of an apostle)—was therefore oversimplified. Whoever recognizes the two-source theory in connection with the Synoptics must also admit that in the first and third gospels there are at least three additional partners in the composition, three additional "evangelists": in the case of Matthew, in addition to Mark, there is QM(atthew) and SM(special [material] of Matthew); in the case of Luke, in addition to Mark, there is QL(uke) and LS(special [material] of Luke). But Matthew and Luke have not simply added these three clusters of material to their own; rather, all four sources have each influenced the other in various ways, linguistically as well as substantively.

Having been enriched by this detour through the Synoptics, let us now turn to the Gospel of John. Here we find a motley conglomeration of styles in the narrative material. Here, too, it is a question of whether this variety in styles reflects various sources, and that also means, whether the Gospel of John does not also have several "evangelists" as its author—as strange as that sounds.

Our first task is to familiarize ourselves with the variety of narrative materials. The first miracle story—the first of the signs that Jesus does—is briefly told: 2:6–10 reports the miracle proper. Although a definite social stratum on a specific occasion is presupposed here, the author is not after realism. Strathman is quite right: "If one reflects on the whole, it is unmistakable that the story evidences a lack of graphicness, is deficient in realism, is impalpable."[21] Verse 11 betrays the reason the story was included: the miracle precipitates faith (also when it is reiterated) and thereby legitimizes Jesus. This interpretation is supported by 2:23 ("Many believed in his name when they saw his signs which he did") and 3:2 ("We know that you are a teacher come from God; for no one can do these signs that you do, unless God is with him").

The second miracle at Cana (4:46bf., 50–53) exhibits the same features. It is again a brief narrative and again precipitates faith in the miracle-worker. But the healing of the lame man at the pool of Bethzatha (5:1–9), the

feeding of the 5,000 (6:1–13), together with the miracle of the walking on the water attached to it, and the healing of the man born blind (9:1, 6f.) are also short, short stories in essence. But only the kernel is brief. For, the Evangelist presents these miracle stories—in contrast to the Synoptics—mostly as graphic symbols that form the basis for the discourses of Jesus to follow. The healing of the lame man becomes the occasion in 5:9c for a conflict over the sabbath, and this leads in turn to a long discourse of Jesus on the relation of the Son to the Father (5:19–47). The situation is about the same in the story of the feeding of the 5,000: it leads up to Jesus' discourse on the true bread, which he himself is (6:35).

But it is not always so easy to determine what the Evangelist has done in reworking the tradition before him. Occasionally, he is content to provide a few hints, as in 4:48f., about how he wants the narrative to be understood. His procedure is basically the same in chapter 11. On the other hand, the Evangelist enriches the story of Jesus and the Samaritan woman by inserting themes of a different consequence. That is the clearest in 4:19–27 ("What is true worship?"). But 4:31–38 probably also goes back to the Evangelist. The story of the healing of the man born blind came to the Evangelist already worked up into a well-crafted composition, a dramatic sequence of scenes. The account of the healing itself (9:3–7) forms only the introduction. The continuation (9:8–12) demonstrates to the neighbors and to those who once knew him that the man healed is really identical with the one born blind, and so shows that an incredible miracle has taken place, something impossible for sinners. The scene with the hearing before the Pharisees (9:13–18a) complicates matters by introducing the motif of the violation of the sabbath. In 9:16 the real problem is pointedly formulated for the first time: "How can a man who is a sinner do such things?" The exchange between the Pharisees and the anxiety-laden parents of the one healed provides a further heightening (9:18b–23); the parents must have feared that they would be excommunicated from the synagogue. In 9:24–34, this destiny befalls the man born blind, who has become ever more courageous and whom the Pharisees have placed in mortal jeopardy. The reunion of Jesus with the man

---

21 *Das Evangelium nach Johannes*, 58.

born blind forms the conclusion; he has now come to complete faith and worship (9:35–38).

This narrative has contributed decisively to the view that the Evangelist is a dramatic poet of the highest order. Hirsch goes the furthest in seeing in the Evangelist something like an early Christian Goethe: "The account may at least be compared poetically with the famous scenes in Goethe's *Egmont.* There is nothing comparable in ancient literature."[22] But Windisch has also expressed a similar judgment, although not so emphatically, in his "Der johanneische Erzählungsstil." He and other exegetes have not noted that the real meaning of the story lies not in the legitimizing miracle, but in the allusion in 9:5: "I am the light of the world." The Evangelist made use of this story, an entirely alien account of a miracle, for the sake of the possiblity of this reference.

The relationship of the Evangelist to received material in chapter 11 is similar and once again variegated. The Lazarus story probably already has behind it a long history in the development of the tradition; that is suggested by the connections with other narratives, especially with those found in Luke: Mary and Martha; the anointing of Jesus; the rich man and poor Lazarus. But that may be ignored here. In its present form, the Lazarus story is the most powerful of all the miracle stories; the synoptic parallels—the daughter of Jairus, the widow's son at Nain—are left far behind by the raising of a corpse already decaying. Here, too, the Evangelist points to a passage often overlooked or misunderstood, viz., 11:20–26, by means of which he comments on the story for the reader. Martha gives expression indirectly to the hopeful request to Jesus to call her brother back to life; God will grant him—of that she is certain—whatever he asks. Jesus promises her that this request will be fulfilled. But the Evangelist now lets Martha suddenly forget what she had asked and what was promised her. She abruptly speaks (11:24) of the (Jewish-Christian) expectation of a general resurrection on the last day. In 11:25 it is made clear why the Evangelist gives the conversation this twist: In sharpest contrast to this futuristic eschatology, Jesus now intones this moving pronouncement: "I am the resurrection and the life; he who believes in me, though he die, yet shall he live, and whoever lives and believes in me shall never die."

Once this context is recognized for what it is, one also recognizes that in a comparable context, viz., chapter 5, a later hand believed it necessary to supply a reference to futuristic eschatology where the original text spoke only of an awakening of the spiritually dead through an encounter with Jesus' proclamation. In 5:21 Jesus has said: "For as the Father raises the dead and gives them life, so also the Son gives life to whom he will." Then Jesus elaborates in verse 24ff. with the words: "Truly, truly, I say to you, he who hears my word and believes him who sent me, has eternal life; he does not come into judgment, but has passed from [spiritual] death to [spiritual] life. Truly, truly, I say to you, the hour is coming, and now is, when the dead will hear the voice of the Son of God, and those who hear will live. For as the Father has life in himself, so he has granted the Son also to have life in himself."

A later hand has inserted verses 5:22f., 27–29, and 30b into this context. By later hand we mean a redactor who edited the Fourth Gospel and appended chapter 21. The activity of the redactor is most evident in 5:28, where "the hour" refers to the day of judgment when all those in tombs will hear the voice of the Son of Man and come forth from their graves.

One should not overlook the fact that the thought of the last judgment is here connected with the key term "Son of Man," and that this judgment is assigned to Jesus as the "Son of Man" in verses 22 and 27. The last judgment will be determined by whether one belongs to "those who have done evil" ($\tau\grave{\alpha}$ $\phi\alpha\hat{\upsilon}\lambda\alpha$ $\pi\rho\acute{\alpha}\sigma\sigma ov\tau\epsilon\varsigma$), who will come forth to the resurrection of judgment, or to "those who have done good" ($\tau\grave{\alpha}$ $\grave{\alpha}\gamma\alpha\theta\grave{\alpha}$ $\pi\rho\acute{\alpha}\sigma\sigma ov\tau\epsilon\varsigma$), who will come forth to the resurrection of life. While the Evangelist has Jesus explain that he gives life to whom he will, in this passage the destiny of man is determined by his deeds. The Evangelist thinks—if one may use a later expression—in predestinarian terms: Only those come to faith whom the Father has given to Jesus; that is especially emphasized in chapter 17 (cf. 6:44). One might be tempted to adopt the view that a necessary paradox is involved: what appears to be a decision of God is, from

22   *Das vierte Evangelium,* 193.

the other side, also to be understood as a decision of man. But, in view of 5:29, that solution will not do. That becomes clear in another passage where "the one doing evil" (ὁ φαῦλα πράσσων) plays an important role, viz., in 3:19–21, which is taken to be an addition. Here the text says that whoever does evil hates the light and does not come to the light lest his evil deeds be exposed as such, etc. The explanation of this contradiction of the Christian message is that a bad conscience prevents the adversaries from joining the Christian community. But whoever has nothing for which to be reproached comes to the light and so becomes a Christian. Christians, on this self-understanding (which is not that of the Evangelist), are men to whom moral exception cannot be taken; those hostile to Christianity, on the other hand, have their lamentable reasons for holding the Christian community at arm's length. John 3:18 indicates how the Evangelist thinks of the judgment: Anyone who rejects God's Son is condemned as a matter of course. Judgment does not ensue at the end of the age, but takes place in the encounter with the proclamation of Christ. The cogency of this view for the Evangelist lies in the fact that the Father, whom no one has ever seen, becomes accessible only in Jesus. Whoever rejects the message of Jesus, misses the only entree to God. Nevertheless, it is not man who takes the real decision; that is unequivocal in 15:16: "You did not choose me, but I chose you." The disciples do not belong to the world, but they do not have themselves to thank for this; on the contrary, Jesus chose them out of the world, as we learn from 15:19.

So far as chapter 21 is concerned, it comes after 20:30f., really *post festum*, as detailed in the commentary. The exposition also demonstrates that chapter 21 was not orginally a unity, but seeks laboriously to combine various motifs and traditions. If a striking usage such as the double "Amen" in 21:19 and chapters 1-20 appears, that says nothing about the identity of the author; something like that is readily imitated. On the other hand, the differences in linguistic usage, adduced by Bultmann,[23] are to be taken seriously: Christians are called brother only here; ἐξετάζω ("inquire") replaces ἐρωτάω ("ask"); ἰσχύειν is used for δύναμαι ("be able"); and ἀπό appears instead of ἐκ ("from"). The hand of the redactor is be-

trayed in such insignificant deviations.

In chapter 21, the action takes place in Galilee; the narrative in John is otherwise localized in Jerusalem, except for the two Cana stories and the feeding narrative (whose locale is admittedly a difficult problem). It is inordinately risky to posit a semeia source. One may distinguish the following uses of σημεῖον ("sign"):

(a) Jesus does many "signs" (miracles): 2:23, 3:2, 6:2, 11:47, 20:30;

(b) a legitimizing "sign" (miracle) is requested in 2:18 and 6:30;

(c) According to 7:21, Jesus has done only one "work," namely, the healing of the lame man in 5:8. The use of "sign" and "work" intersect in some passages.

(d) With reference to 3:2, it is difficult to say whether the Evangelist had a Nicodemus tradition before him in which Nicodemus spoke of "signs" (miracles);

(e) John 4:48f. certainly derives, in my judgment, from the Evangelist;

(f) In 6:14, "sign" (miracle) refers to the feeding of the 5,000 that precedes, as it emerges from "seeing the sign which he had done." On the other hand, in 6:26, Jesus (the Evangelist) disputes that they had "seen signs."

(g) The reference of "do such signs" in 9:16 is to the healing of the man born blind.

(h) Similarly, the raising of Lazarus is spoken of in 12:18 as a "sign" (miracle).

(i) In 7:31, there is reference to greater "signs" in the same sense as in 5:20, where the phrase is "greater works," and as in 1:50, where "greater things" is mentioned. In view of the diversity in the use of σημεῖον ("sign"), it is not possible, in my judgment, to maintain the hypothesis that (almost) all narrative material in John stems from a "signs" source.

In some miracle stories it is evident that older forms in the tradition preceded those versions employed by the Evangelist. As a consequence, the attempt to reconstruct literally the original form of the story in question from the present text encounters greater difficulties than one supposes, for the most part, when undertaking such reconstructions. One thinks, for example, in this connection of the insertion of the sabbath-motif in John 5:9c and 9:14.

---

23 *John*, 700f. [542].

In summary, it may be said:

(1) The Evangelist has not made use of any of the other three canonical gospels in his narrative segments, although respectable scholars like Kümmel and Hirsch are convinced of the contrary.[24]

(2) The Evangelist did not freely create his narrative material, but more or less freely formed it while making use of tradition.

(3) The narrative material was stamped throughout with the point of view that the miracles of Jesus were legitimating and thus designed to awaken genuine faith.

(4) The Evangelist, on the other hand, believes that real events are taking place in the "signs"; but they gain their meaning for Christians only when they point to Jesus as the way to the Father (following the gift of the Spirit).

So far as the discourses are concerned, Bultmann understands them on the whole as the reworking of a discourse source.[25] Fragments of the semeia-source are incorporated here and there. We believe we have demonstrated that the theory of a collection of (gnostic) "revelation-discourses" is untenable.[26] The rich fund of gnostic revelation discourses that have become available in the meantime exhibit an entirely different style: the revealer speaks in long monologues that are interrupted only now and then with brief questions or exclamations on the part of the recipient. While on Bultmann's view the Evangelist often acts only as a redactor, quoting, clarifying, or arranging the alleged revelation discourses, in my opinion, the author expresses himself in the speeches. That does not exclude the possibility that one finds later interpolations in these discourses, on the one hand—one recalls the passage regarding "the ones doing evil" (τὰ φαῦλα πράσσοντες) cited above—or, on the other, that one runs across sayings taken from a tradition

that sounds like synoptic sayings material. The division into narrative and discourse material is all too rough. For example, the material in chapter 1 in the scenes with John the Baptist falls into neither category nor under both. Nor can the hymn of the Prologue be classified as "discourse material."

4. Author

It is entirely possible, on the other hand, that a theologian of the greatest range meets us in the Fourth Gospel; he may have grown up in one of the sects within the sphere of the "great church" (if one may be permitted a phrase that is really fully meaningful only in a later period); it was not until later that a revision made his work accessible to a wider circle in the church. Gnostic formulations in Johannine language inspired gnostics like Heracleon, of the school of Valentinus, to give the Fourth Gospel a gnostic interpretation; this delayed and complicated the recognition of the Gospel. But these difficulties disappeared about the year 200 CE. Origen rightly emphasized how much Heracleon had to deface the text in order to be able to give it a gnostic interpretation. The fourth evangelist was no gnostic. If one takes the style of the Fourth Gospel as a whole, one may say that a diversity of styles are combined. We could then say that the original source, as it may be called—very loosely—contributes in about the same proportions as the Evangelist himself to the whole. The scope of a later redaction is greater, in my judgment, than one was heretofore ready to admit, but in magnitude and significance (with respect especially to the doctrines of futuristic eschatology and the sacraments) it is not to be compared with the first two contributions just mentioned.

---

24 But Connick also, "The Dramatic Character of the Fourth Gospel," *JBL* 67 (1948) 160, who invokes Streeter, *The Four Gospels. A Study of Origins, Treating of the Manuscript Tradition, Sources, Authorship, and Dates* (London: Macmillan, 1924) and Colwell, *John Defends the Gospel* (New York: Willett, Clark & Co., 1936).

25 Cf. Easton, "Bultmann's RQ Source," *JBL* 65 (1946)

143–156.

26 Haenchen, "Das Johannesevangelium und sein Kommentar," 211f.

7. Various Christologies in the Gospel of John

Bibliography

Becker, Jürgen

"Wunder und Christologie. Zum literarkritischen und christologischen Problem der Wunder im Johannesevangelium." *NTS* 16 (1969/1970) 130–48.

Behm, Johannes

"Die johanneische Christologie als Abschluss der Christologie des Neuen Testaments." *NKZ* 41 (1930) 577–601.

Beutler, Johannes

"Psalm 42/43 im Johannesevangelium." *NTS* 25 (1978) 33–57.

Blank, Josef

Krisis. Untersuchungen zur johanneischen Christologie und Eschatologie (Freiburg: Lambertus-Verlag, 1964).

Boismard, Marie-Emile

"La royauté du Christ dans le quatrième évangile." *Lumière et vie* 11 (1962) 43–63.

Boismard, Marie-Emile

"Jesus the Savior According to St. John." In *Word and Mystery. Biblical Essays on the Person and Mission of Christ,* ed. L. J. O'Donovan, S. J. (Glen Rock, NJ, and London: Newman, 1968) 69–85.

Boismard, Marie-Emile

"Jesus, sauveur, d'après saint Jean." *Lumière et vie* 15 (1954) 103–22.

Borgen, Peder

"Some Jewish Exegetical Traditions as Background for Son of Man Sayings in John's Gospel (Jn 3, 13–14 and context)." In *L'Evangile de Jean. Sources, rédaction, théologie,* ed. M. de Jonge. BETL 44 (Gembloux: Duculot; Louvain: University Press, 1977) 243–58.

Boring, M. Eugene

"The Influence of Christian Prophecy on the Johannine Portrayal of the Paraclete and Jesus." *NTS* 25 (1978) 113–23.

Braun, François-Marie

"La seigneurie du Christ dans le monde, selon saint Jean." *RevThom* 67 (1967) 357–86.

Brun, Lyder

"Die Gottesschau des johanneischen Christus." *Symbolae Osloenses* 5 (1927) 1–22.

Bühner, Jan-A.

Der Gesandte und sein Weg im vierten Evangelium. Die kultur- und religionsgeschichtlichen Grundlagen der johanneischen Sendungschristologie sowie ihre traditionsgeschichtliche Entwicklung, WUNT 2,2 (Tübingen: Mohr-Siebeck, 1977).

Christensen, C. R.

"John's Christology and the 'Gospel of Truth.'" *Gordon Review* 10 (1966) 23–31.

Collins, Raymond F.
   "The Search for Jesus. Reflections on the Fourth
   Gospel." *Laval Théologique et Philosophique* 34
   (1978) 27–48.
Coppens, Joseph
   "Les logia johanniques du Fils de l'homme." In
   L'Evangile de Jean. Sources, rédaction, théologie, ed.
   M. de Jonge. BETL 44 (Gembloux: Duculot;
   Louvain: University Press, 1977) 311–15.
Coppens, Joseph
   "Miscellanées bibliques. Le Fils de l'homme johan-
   nique." *ETL* 54 (1978) 126–30.
Creutzig, Hans Erich
   "Zur johanneischen Christologie." *NKZ* (*Luthertum*)
   49 (1938) 214–22.
Dautzenberg, Gerhard
   "Die Geschichte Jesu im Johannesevangelium." In
   Gestalt und Anspruch des Neuen Testaments, ed. J.
   Schreiner (Würzburg: Echter Verlag, 1969) 229–
   48.
Davey, James Ernest
   *The Jesus of St. John. Historical and Christological
   Studies in the Fourth Gospel* (London: Lutterworth
   Press, 1958).
Delling, Gerhard
   Wort und Werk Jesu im Johannes-Evangelium (Berlin:
   Evangelische Verlagsanstalt, 1966).
Dion, Hyacinthe-M.
   "Quelque traits originaux de la conception johan-
   nique du Fils de l'homme." *Sciences ecclésiastiques* 19
   (1967) 49–65.
Dupont, Jacques
   *Essais sur la christologie de saint Jean. Le Christ,
   parole, lumière et vie, la gloire du Christ* (Brugge:
   Editions de l'Abbaye de Saint-André, 1951).
Fennema, David A.
   "Jesus and God According to John. An Analysis of
   the Fourth Gospel's Father/Son Christology."
   Dissertation, Duke University, 1979.
Feuillet, André
   "Les *Ego Eimi* christologiques du quatrième évan-
   gile." *RSR* 54 (1966) 5–22, 213–40.
Fortna, Robert T.
   "Christology in the Fourth Gospel: Redactional-
   Critical Perspectives." *NTS* 21 (1975) 489–504.
Freed, Edwin D.
   "The Son of Man in the Fourth Gospel." *JBL* 86
   (1967) 402–9.
Garvie, Alfred E.
   "Jesus in the Fourth Gospel." *Expositor*, 8th ser., 17
   (1919) 312–20.
Gaugler, Ernst
   "Das Christuszeugnis des Johannesevangeliums."
   In *Christus im Zeugnis der heiligen Schrift und der
   Kirche*, ed. K. L. Schmidt. BEvT 2 (Munich: Chr.
   Kaiser Verlag, 1936) 34–69.
Gnilka, Joachim
   "Der historische Jesus als gegenwärtiger Christus
   im Johannesevangelium." *BibLeb* 7 (1966) 270–78.

Grimm, Carl Ludwig Wilibald
   De joanneae christologiae indole paulinae comparatae
   (Leipzig: Lehnholdiana libraria, 1833).
Haenchen, Ernst
   "Der Vater, der mich gesandt hat." *NTS* 9 (1963)
   208–16. In his *Gott und Mensch. Gesammelte Aufsätze*
   1 (Tübingen: Mohr-Siebeck, 1965) 68–77.
Haenchen, Ernst
   "Vom Wandel des Jesusbildes in der frühen
   Gemeinde." In *Verborum Veritas. Festschrift für
   Gustav Stählin zum 70. Geburtstag*, ed. O. Böcher
   and K. Hacker (Wuppertal: F. A. Brockhaus,
   1970) 3–14.
Hanson, Anthony A.
   "The Jesus of the Fourth Gospel." *New Divinity* 5
   (1974) 20–24.
Harnack, Adolf von
   "Zur Textkritik und Christologie der Schriften des
   Johannes. Zugleich ein Beitrag zur Würdigung
   der ältesten lateinische Überlieferung und der
   Vulgata." SPAW 5,2 (Berlin: G. Reimer, 1915)
   534–73.
Hegermann, Harald
   "'Er kam in sein Eigentum.' Zur Bedeutung des
   Erdenwirkens Jesu im vierten Evangelium." In *Der
   Ruf Jesu und die Antwort der Gemeinde. Exegetische
   Untersuchungen Joachim Jeremias zum 70 Geburtstag
   gewidmet von seinen Schülern*, ed. E. Lohse et al.
   (Göttingen: Vandenhoeck & Ruprecht, 1970)
   112–31.
Higgins, A. J. B.
   "The Words of Jesus According to St. John." *BJRL*
   49 (1966/1967) 363–86.
Howton, John
   "The Son of God in the Fourth Gospel." *NTS* 10
   (1963/1964) 227–37.
Jonge, Marinus de
   *Jesus: Stranger from Heaven and Son of God. Jesus
   Christ and the Christians in Johannine Perspective*, tr.
   J. E. Steeley. SBLSBS 11 (Missoula: Scholars Press,
   1977).
Köhler, H.
   *Von der Welt zum Himmelreich oder die johanneische
   Darstellung des Werkes Jesu Christi synoptisch geprüft
   und ergänzt* (Halle: M. Niemeyer, 1892).
Kunniburgh, E.
   "The Johannine Son of Man." *SE* 4 = TU 102
   (Berlin: Akademie-Verlag, 1968) 64–71.
Lattke, Michael
   "Sammlung durch das Wort. Erlöser, Erlösung,
   und Erlöste im Johannesevangelium." *BK* 30
   (1975) 118–22.
Leroy, Herbert
   "Jesusverkündigung im Johannesevangelium." In
   Jesus in den Evangelien, ed. Josef Blinzler et al.
   (Stuttgart: Katholisches Bibelwerk, 1970) 148–70.
Lindars, Baranabas
   "The Son of Man in the Johannine Christology." In
   Christ and Spirit in the New Testament [Festschrift for

C. F. D. Moule], ed. B. Lindars and S. S. Smalley (Cambridge: Cambridge University Press, 1970) 43–60.

Lütgert, Wilhelm
Die johanneische Christologie (Gütersloh: C. Bertelsmann, 1899, ² 1916).

Mastin, B. A.
"A Neglected Feature of the Christology of the Fourth Gospel." *NTS* 22 (1975) 32–51.

Maurer, Christian
"Der Exklusivanspruch des Christus nach dem Johannesevangelium." In *Studies in John Presented to Professor J. N. Sevenster on the Occasion of his Seventieth Birthday* (Leiden: E. J. Brill, 1970) 143–60.

McPolin, J.
"The 'Name' of the Father and of the Son in the Johannine Writings." Dissertation, Rome, 1971.

Mealand, David L.
"The Christology of the Fourth Gospel." *SJT* 31 (1978) 449–67.

Meeks, Wayne A.
The Prophet King: Moses Traditions and Johannine Christology (Leiden: E. J. Brill, 1967).

Meeks, Wayne A.
"The Man from Heaven in Johannine Sectarianism." *JBL* 91 (1972) 44–72.

Meyer, Heinrich
Die mandäische Lehre vom göttlichen Gesandten mit einem Ausblick auf ihr Verhältnis zur johanneischen Christologie (Breklum: Jensen, 1929). Partial publication from "Mandäische und johanneischen Soteriologie." Dissertation, Kiel, 1929.

Miranda, Juan Peter
Der Vater, der mich gesandt hat. Religionsgeschichtliche Untersuchungen zu den johanneischen Sendungsformen. Zugleich ein Beitrag zur johanneischen Christologie und Ekklesiologie, Europäische Hochschulschriften, series 23. Theologie, vol. 7 (Frankfurt: P. Lang, 1972).

Moloney, Francis J.
The Johannine Son of Man, Bibliotheca di scienze religiose 14 (Rome: Libreria Ateneo Salesiano, 1976, ²1979).

Moloney, Francis J.
"The Fourth Gospel's Presentation of Jesus as 'the Christ' and J. A. T. Robinson's *Redating.*" *Downside Review* 95 (1977) 239–53.

Moloney, Francis J.
"The Johannine Son of Man." *BTB* 6 (1976) 177–89.

Moloney, Francis J.
"The Johannine Son of Man." *Salesianum* 38 (1976) 71–86.

Müller, Ulrich B.
Die Geschichte der Christologie in der johanneischen Gemeinde, SBS 77 (Stuttgart: Katholisches Bibelwerk, 1975).

Murray, John Owen Fargnar
Jesus According to St. John (London: Longmans &

Co., 1936).

Mussner, Franz
"Der Charakter Jesu nach dem Johannesevangelium." *TTZ* 62 (1953) 321–32.

Mussner, Franz
"'Kultische' Aspekte im johanneischen Christusbild." *Liturgisches Jahrbuch* 14 (1964) 185–200. Cf. "Liturgical Aspects of John's Gospel." *Theological Digest* 14 (1966) 18–22. In his *Praesentia Salutis. Gesammelte Studien zu Fragen und Themen des Neuen Testamentes,* Kommentare und Beiträge zum Alten und Neuen Testament (Düsseldorf: Patmos-Verlag, 1967) 133–45.

Pfleiderer, Otto
"Zur johanneischen Christologie, mit Rücksicht auf W. Beyschlag's 'Christologie des Neuen Testaments.'" *ZWT* 9 (1866) 241–66.

Pollard, T. E.
Johannine Christology and the Early Church, SNTSMS 13 (London and New York: Cambridge University Press, 1970).

Potterie, Ignace de la
"L'exaltation du Fils de l'homme (Jn 12,31–36)." *Greg* 49 (1968) 460–78.

Prete, Benedetto
"La missione rivelatrice di Cristo secondo il quarto Evangelista." *Atti della settimana biblica* 20 (1970) 133–50.

Ridderbos, Hermann
"On the Christology of the Fourth Gospel." In *Saved by Hope. Essays in Honor of Richard C. Oudersluys,* ed. J. I. Cook (Grand Rapids: Wm. B. Eerdmans, 1978) 15–26.

Riedl, Johannes
Das Heilswerk Jesu nach Johannes, Freiburger theologische Studien 93 (Freiburg: Herder, 1973).

Robertson, Archibald Thomas
The Divinity of Christ in the Gospel of John (New York: Fleming H. Revell Co, 1916).

Ruckstuhl, Eugen
"Abstieg und Erhöhung des johanneischen Menschensohns." In *Jesus und der Menschensohn. Für Anton Vögtle,* ed. R. Pesch and R. Schnackenburg (Freiburg: Herder, 1975) 314–41.

Ruckstuhl, Eugen
"Die johanneische Menschensohnforschung." In *Theologische Berichte 1* (Zurich and Cologne: Benziger, 1972) 171–284.

Sabugal, S.
"Una contribución a la cristologia joannea." *Augustinianum* 12 (1972) 565–72.

Sabugal, S.
Christos: Investigación exegetica sobre la cristologia joannea (Barcelona: Herder, 1972).

Schenkel, Daniel
Das Christusbild der Apostel und der nachapostolischen Zeit aus den Quellen dargestellt (Leipzig: F. A. Brockhaus, 1879) 174–93, 203–13, 373–97.

Schlier, Heinrich
  "Zur Christologie des Johannesevangelium." In his
  Das Ende der Zeit. Exegetische Aufsätze und Vorträge 3
  (Freiburg: Herder, 1971) 85–88.
Schnackenburg, Rudolf
  "Die Messiasfrage im Johannesevangelium." In
  *Neutestamentliche Aufsätze. Festschrift für Prof. Josef
  Schmid zum 70. Geburtstag,* ed. J. Blinzler, O. Kuss,
  F. Mussner (Regensburg: F. Pustet, 1963) 240–64.
Schnackenburg, Rudolf
  "Der Menschensohn im Johannesevangelium."
  NTS 11 (1964/1965) 123–37.
Schneider, Johannes
  Die Christusschau des Johannesevangeliums (Berlin:
  Furche-Verlag, 1935).
Schulz, Siegfried
  *Untersuchungen zur Menschensohn-Christologie im
  Johannesevangelium, zugleich ein Beitrag zur
  Methodengeschichte der Auslegung des 4. Evangeliums*
  (Göttingen: Vandenhoeck & Ruprecht, 1957).
Segalla, Giuseppe
  "Rassengna di cristologia giovannea." *Studia
  Patavina* 18 (1972) 693–732.
Segalla, Giuseppe
  "Preesistenza, incarnazione e divinità di Cristo in
  Giovanni (Vg e 1 Gv)." *RivB* 22 (1974) 155–81.
Sidebottom, E. M.
  *The Christ of the Fouth Gospel in the Light of First-
  Century Thought* (London: S. P. C. K., 1961).
Sidebottom, E. M.
  "The Ascent and Descent of the Son of Man in the
  Gospel of St. John." *ATR* 39 (1957) 115–22.
Smalley, Stephen S.
  "The Johannine Son of Man Sayings." *NTS* 15
  (1968/1969) 278–301.

Smith, D. Moody
  "The Presentation of Jesus in the Fourth Gospel."
  Int 31 (1977) 367–78.
Smith, T. C.
  "The Christology of the Fourth Gospel." *RevExp*
  71 (1974) 19–30.
Smith, Taylor Clarence
  Jesus in the Fourth Gospel (Nashville: Broadman
  Press, 1959).
Summers, R.
  "The Christ of John's Gospel." *Southwestern Journal
  of Theology* 8 (1965) 35–43.
Sundberg, Albert C.
  "Christology in the Fourth Gospel." *BR* 21 (1976)
  29–37.
Sweeney, T. A.
  "Jesus of the Fourth Gospel." Dissertation, Grad-
  uate Theological Union, 1974.
Tilborg, Sjef van
  "'Neerdaling' en incarnatie: de christologie van
  Johannes. ['Katabasis' and Incarnation in the
  Gospel of John.]" *Tijdschrift voor Theologie* 13
  (1973) 20–33.
Trémel, Y.-B.
  "Le Fils de l'homme selon Saint Jean." *Lumière et
  vie* 12 (1962/1963) 65–92.
Weizsäcker, C.
  "Das Selbstzeugnis des johanneischen Christus."
  Jahrbücher für deutsche Theologie 2 (1857) 154–208.
Wetter, Gillis Petersson
  *"Der Sohn Gottes," eine Untersuchung über den Charak-
  ter und die Tendenz des Johannesevangeliums; zugleich
  ein Beitrag zur Kenntnis der Heilandsgestalten der
  Antike* FRLANT, n.s., 9 (Göttingen: Vandenhoeck
  & Ruprecht, 1916).

How the earthly life of Jesus is understood in the Fourth
Gospel is debatable. Around the turn of the century,
liberal theologians asserted that the Johannine Christ is
represented as God walking about on earth. Bousset,
Heitmüller, J. Weiss, Wetter, and Baldensperger were in
agreement on this point. The very interesting work of
Baldensperger, *Der Prolog des vierten Evangeliums,* contains this sentence on the last page: "one could speak of a
docetic Christology of the Gospel of John."[1] This interpretation of the earthly life of Jesus in the Fourth Gospel
is of course not without its reason: in this Gospel Jesus is
pictured and extolled in many narratives as the great
miracle worker and his miracles are thus conceived as
proof of his divinity.

But these matters are not as simple as they appear at
first. NT scholars are today pretty much agreed that
Matthew and Luke took up almost all of Mark into their
works. To this extent, we could say that each of these
gospels derives from two gospel writers, viz., from one
who provided the greater part of the material, and from
a second who reworked this material, and this is to disregard source Q and the special material each gospel
writer is believed to have used. Thus, a priori there is
nothing against the view that one must also distinguish in
the Gospel of John between the gospel tradition used—
whether this was a written gospel we leave open—and
the interpretation of that tradition. The liberal theologians at the turn of the century unfortunately overlooked this point. There is a great deal to be said for the
view that we are hearing the voices of two theologically

---

1   *Der Prolog des vierten Evangeliums. Sein polemisch-
     apologetischer Zweck* (Tübingen: Mohr-Siebeck, 1898)
     171.

diverging evangelists in the Fourth Gospel.

One may of course ask: how is it possible that the Fourth Gospel took over a tradition or a writing with an entirely different theological posture? The answer to this riddle seems to me to lie in the fact that the Evangelist was convinced by the factuality of those marvelous events that he found reported in his tradition. But he did not want—contrary to his "source"—to understand these miracles as proof of the divinity of Jesus (they are all inner-worldly events), but as signs, as tokens of something quite different. This understanding of $\sigma\eta\mu\epsilon\hat{\imath}\alpha$ ("signs") may be made clearer by reference to Gen 9:13ff. There it is said of the rainbow that God set it in the clouds as a sign that he will never again send a deluge, but that he will remember the covenant with Noah. The LXX translates the Hebrew term אות with $\sigma\eta\mu\epsilon\hat{\imath}ον$ (both mean "sign"). This is the meaning of the term for the Evangelist in the Fourth Gospel. It does not mean proof but pointer.[2] Anyone who experienced the miraculous feeding and then wanted to make Jesus king (6:15) did not really understand the sign precisely as sign (6:26). Otherwise they would have recognized that it pointed to the true salvific event, viz., that Jesus is the true bread from heaven, that he is, as it is put in another passage, the way for us to the Father (14:6). But the Evangelist also makes clear in other passages just how the reader is to understand the miracle stories he narrates. Of that there is a memorable occurrence in the scene with Nicodemus (3:2–4). Nicodemus has just said, "We know that you are a teacher come from God; for no one can do these signs"—the word here signifies "miracle" as in the tradition from which it is taken—"that you do, unless God is with him." To this Jesus responds, "Truly, truly, I say to you, unless one is born anew, he cannot see the kingdom of God." In other words, one cannot see that God is at work in an earthly deed of Jesus, unless God has given him a new life and new eyes. The second miracle at Cana is corrected in 4:48f. by the reproach of Jesus: "Unless you see signs and wonders you will not believe." This reproach has its counterpart in 20:29, where Jesus chides Thomas: "You believe because you have seen me; blessed are those who have not seen and yet believe." Later generations, of course, could no longer see Jesus like his contemporaries; the former had only his word to kindle their faith. In 9:5, the Evangelist's meaning of the healing of the blind is anticipated by this sentence: "So long as I am in the world, I am the light of the world." By way of supplement, he says in 9:39, "For judgment I came into the world, that those who do not see may see, and that those who see may become blind." The real meaning of the raising of Lazarus is provided by 11:25f.: "I am the resurrection and the life; he who believes in me, though he die, yet shall he live, and whoever lives and believes in me shall never die."

In the underlying tradition Jesus is pictured as the great miracle-worker, whose mighty deeds demonstrate and authenticate his divinity. John corrects this perspective embedded in the tradition in a fundamental way, without having to deny the miracles reported by the tradition. For him, their value lies elsewhere. It is not important that Jesus causes a lame man to "rise" (5:8: $\check{\epsilon}\gamma\epsilon\iota\rho\epsilon$), but that he causes the (spiritually) dead to rise (5:21: $\dot{\epsilon}\gamma\epsilon\dot{\iota}\rho\epsilon$, $\zeta\omega\sigma\sigma\iota\epsilon\hat{\imath}$ ["make alive"]), like the Father does. It follows that the time of salvation does not just dawn on the other side of the grave but here and now, at the moment any one whom the Father has given to Jesus hears his word: "Truly, truly, I say to you, the hour is coming, and now is, when the dead will hear the voice of the Son of God, and those who hear will live. For as the Father has life in himself, so he has granted the Son also to have life in himself" (5:25–26). That a later hand, which has often left traces in the Fourth Gospel, has attempted to reverse the meaning again in the direction of the common futuristic eschatology is something one ought to have learned to recognize by now.

It has now become only partially clear what the Fourth Gospel takes the earthly life of Jesus to mean. At least two things have to be said. First: According to John, no one has ever seen the Father (1:18, 5:37b, 6:46). The logos become man—this is the Johannine sense of the earthly life of Jesus—is the visible likeness of the invisible Father. Note well: this is so for the elect, and only for them (14:9). The Evangelist has not used the $\epsilon\dot{\iota}\kappa\acute{\omega}\nu$-formula, which in several respects is dangerous and misleading, but for the most part (close to forty times)

---

2   [It is not a "Beweis" but a "Hinweis," a play on words not reproducible in English—Translator.]

the phrase, "the one the Father has sent." That occurs 23 times with πέμπω ("send"), and 15 times with ἀποστέλλω ("send"); there is no difference in meaning. The passages in which the phrase appears are: 3:34, 4:34, 5:23f., 30, 36f., 38, 6:29, 38f., 44, 57, 7:16, 18, 29, 33, 8:16, 18, 26, 42, 9:4, 10:36, 11:42, 12:44f., 49, 13:16, 20, 14:24, 15:21, 16:5, 17:8, 18, 21, 23, 25, 20:21. This phrase means: Jesus is not here on his own behalf; he is here on behalf of the Father. He does not fulfill his own will but that of his Father: 4:34, 5:30, 6:38, 9:31. On that account, he does not speak his own words but those of his Father: 4:34, (6:63), 7:16, 8:26, 38, 40, 14:10, 24, 17:8. And he does not perform his own works but those of his Father: 4:34, 5:17, 19ff., 30, 36, 8:28, 10:25, 37, 14:10, 17:4, 14. Only on this basis is it possible to understand what Jesus means when he says, "I and the Father are one" (10:30; cf. 17:11, 21f.). The Father remains the one who is fully in charge, so that Jesus can say, without contradicting himself, "the Father is greater than I" (14:28). This expression, "the sent of God," goes far beyond the Jewish concept of שׁלח ("the one sent, an apostle"); it is the most characteristic christological formula in the Fourth Gospel. It has recently been asserted that this phrase interchanges independently with another, that of "to be one with the Father," from which the first receives its special christological meaning. That is simply not the case. The few passages in which Jesus speaks of his oneness with the Father[3] are rather misunderstood if one does not interpret them from the point of view of the phrase "the Father who sent me," which appears extremely often in the Fourth Gospel. Jesus is the divine legate and a legate fulfills his commission all the more thoroughly the more he is simply the expression, the mouth and the hands of his lord. It is then and only then, when he has no political ambitions of his own, but lives entirely in the service of his master, indeed, lives precisely out of this service (4:34), that he is one with his sovereign and has genuine claim to the honor that is due his lord. As a consequence, the Father, who sent him, will not honor anyone who does not honor the Son (5:23, 44, 7:18, 8:50, 54). Jesus does not intend to make himself equal to God, as the Jews imagine (5:18). Yet for us he stands in the place of his lord, the Father, as the one sent, who has devoted himself entirely to his master.

The second thing to be said is this: neither the Jews nor the disciples have seen the Father in him during his lifetime. When John speaks of many coming to faith (2:11, 23, 7:31, 8:30ff.), he immediately emphasizes that it is not true faith (2:24f., 8:40, 47, 59). The position of the disciples is similar: 14:7–9 shows that Philip, although he had been so long in the company of Jesus, had not seen the Father in him. In 16:29ff., Jesus responds to the confident assertion of the disciples that they now believe that he has come from the Father: they will quickly be scattered and leave him alone. In 7:39b the reason for this inability to believe is given: the Spirit has not been given because Jesus was not yet glorified. Only after the resurrection does Jesus breathe the Spirit into his disciples (20:22).

The earthly life of Jesus according to John, as in Paul and in a certain sense also in Mark, is not yet the time when his true being is recognized, although his earthly activity has precisely the purpose, on John's view, of making the Father visible in him. His earthly life achieved this purpose, however, only subsequently: the Spirit led the disciples into all truth. The earthly life of Jesus became transparent in its real sense only after the fact, so to speak, through the Spirit. This meaning is amplified in statements made in the Gospel regarding the "Counselor," the παράκλητος (14:16f., 26, 15:26, 16:5–15). Jesus had already hinted in 8:26 that he had much to say; but only after the exaltation of the Son of Man would they recognize that he was the one whom the Father sent. The role of the Spirit is described more plainly in the farewell discourses: The Spirit of truth will teach the disciples all things (14:26); Jesus still has much to say to them, but they are not yet ready to grasp it.

This now implies that the new picture of Jesus that the Evangelist sketches is itself inspired by the Spirit, which will lead the disciples into all truth (16:13). The doctrine of the Spirit in the Fourth Gospel is not simply a particular piece of tradition that the Evangelist has taken up into his work, along with other pieces; rather, the doctrine of the Paraclete was developed because it corresponded to his personal experience. It is something quite

---

3   In addition to the principal passage, 10:30, there is
     only 17:11, 21f.

different than a mere literary process when the traditional sketch of futuristic eschatology, along with transmitted discourse material, is revamped from the ground up and remodelled into a new conception. Paul of course had also suggested that the resurrected Jesus had not yet fulfilled his purpose. But the eschatological expectations regarding the future remained untouched by that, and were perhaps even strengthened. However, the fourth evangelist has employed the expression of the old anticipation of the parousia in order to express something new, and he could do that only by saying that something new in a new way. In 14:16f. we hear that Jesus will ask the Father to send the Spirit. But in 14:18 he says, "I will not leave you desolate; I will come to you." Finally, in 14:23 Jesus promises the disciples that he and the Father will come and make their home with them. If that is not all a mass of confused traditions, then one can discern the effort of the Evangelist to say the same thing by means of various traditions and to make older tradition understandable to his own generation. That Jesus will return is the customary way of expressing the early expectation of the end. Luke 24:49 and Acts 1:4 perhaps correspond to the statement that Jesus will ask the Father to send the Spirit. The announcement that the Father and Jesus will dwell with the believers (14:23), the second that Jesus will return (14:18), and the third, that the Spirit, the Paraclete, will be sent (14:16) represent the same event in three different modes of speech, so to speak. Which of these is peculiar to the Evangelist? According to John, the Father can appear to us only in the earthly Jesus: the first way of putting the matter thus

means the same thing as the second. For the Evangelist, Jesus returns in the form of the Spirit of truth. In that case, the third expression is for John the most recent and thus as an expression of the experience of the reality that was closest to him. If, however, the center of gravity shifts to the Spirit, to the Paraclete sent to the post-Easter church, to such a degree, then the "earthly Jesus" threatens to become a mere precursor of the Spirit. John has counteracted this threat by recalling that the closest relationship obtains between Jesus and the Spirit: the Spirit "will not speak on his own authority, but whatever he hears he will speak, . . . He will glorify me, for he will take what is mine and declare it to you" (16:13f.). Because the Evangelist proclaims the true meaning of the message of Jesus under the guidance of the Spirit does he really honor Jesus. The Spirit will teach the disciples all things and remind them of everything Jesus told them.

All of this is in accord with 6:63: "It is the Spirit that gives life, the flesh is of no avail; the words that I have spoken to you are spirit and life." Because Jesus spoke this word already during his earthly life—on the view of the Evangelist—his earthly life retains its normative significance. These speeches of course have already been interpreted in a Johannine fashion: the historical Jesus comes to expression as already interpreted.

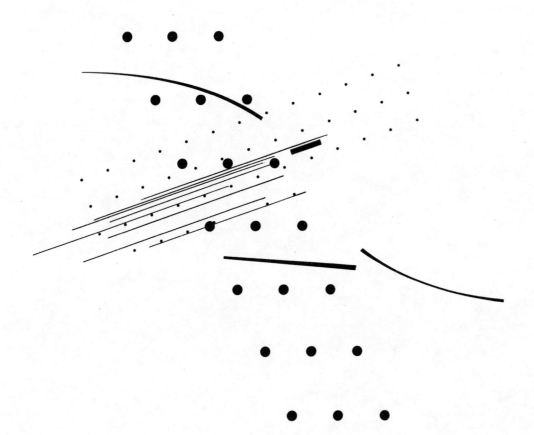

1. Prologue: Introduction

The Prologue to the Gospel of John is difficult to understand. That is certainly not a new observation. And after many centuries of dealing with this text, we are still unable to grasp some of the questions that are necessary to the solution of the problem. It is self-evident to us that this Gospel begins its story at a time prior to the creation. Bultmann has done us the great service of demonstrating, on the basis of style, that the core of the Johannine Prologue is an independent entity, a hymn, that was added to the Gospel as an introduction.[1] But in so doing, Bultmann had to accept the view that the Evangelist thoroughly reworked the hymn and in the process misunderstood his source on a major point: the source speaks of the Logos becoming man only in verse 14, while the Evangelist understands that to have happened already in verse 5. Käsemann asks with some justification whether the Evangelist really understood his source so poorly.[2] But his own attempt to repair the damage—the hymn ended with verse 12—seems to us to make the rupture even worse.

What really prompted the author of this Gospel to preface his work with this hymn? Ever since Harnack's essay, "Über das Verhältnis des Prologs des vierten Evangeliums zum ganzen Werk,"[3] this question has been given serious consideration. Did the Evangelist intend to preface his work with a statement of its leading ideas—as an introduction? But does the Prologue really recite these leading ideas? Did the Evangelist want to make his work palatable to hellenistic readers by making use of the Logos concept? But the Fourth Gospel does not leave the impression that it was written for "a public nurtured in the higher religion of Hellenism."[4] The notion of an overture has also been invoked in this connection: something that attunes the hearer to what is coming.[5] But such an overture appears to be better suited to Wagner than to late antiquity. Introductions of the kind exhibited by the Gospel of Luke were known in late antiquity, of course, but for high literary taste it was possible to open a speech or a writing with an introduction that was only loosely connected to what followed, if it were connected at all. This kind of introduction can be detected occasionally in Philo. But the author of the Gospel of John can be reckoned neither among the authors who were given to historical writing, like Luke, nor among those who liked to surprise the reader by jumping from the introduction to the real theme.

We may thus pose the question anew: why does this Gospel begin with a Prologue like this? If one is seeking an answer to this question, one should not look to the Fourth Gospel alone. The first gospels began with the description of the work of the Baptist. That is demonstrated not only by the beginning of the Gospel of Mark, but also by the "standard sketch" of the gospel indicated by Acts 10:38–40. But things did not stop with this beginning. Indeed, the Markan account of the baptism of Jesus makes his real station already evident, which is then manifested in the miracles of Jesus, in the confessions of the demons, and in the transfiguration—quite apart from the resurrection.

Matthew and Luke have supplemented this testimony to the true office of the Lord, so important to the community. They therefore precede the traditional beginning of the gospel with a kind of preface: the narrative of the miraculous birth and childhood of Jesus. It is thereby made clear to the reader that from the beginning of the earthly life of Jesus, so to speak, this Jesus of Nazareth is not to be confined to the earthly realm.

The Fourth Gospel leaves the other three far behind in a single super leap by starting its account in the time before creation, in eternity. It is difficult to say how such a beginning was viewed. The older gospels offer no model for this move. But a gifted hymnist in the community relieved the Evangelist of this anxiety, provided that he knew how to make use of the gift. Of course, the hymn was not created out of whole cloth. He also reverts to an old legacy,[6] to one that may be very old indeed. There was an old profound and melancholy myth regarding Wisdom. It combined two primordial exper-

---

1   *John*, 13–18 [1–5].
2   *New Testament Questions*, 148.
3   [On the Relationship of the Prologue of the Fourth Gospel to the Work as a Whole], *ZTK* 2 (1892) 189–231.
4   C. H. Dodd, *Interpretation of the Fourth Gospel*, 296.
5   Cf. Heitmüller, "Das Johannes-Evangelium," 716.
6   Cf. Sir 24:1–24; Enoch 42:1f.

iences of man. The first is: this world in which we live was created by divine Wisdom. Wisdom was at the side of God from the beginning, and when he began to create, Wisdom served him as supervising architect. For that reason, everything could and would be truly good. At this point the second primordial experience comes into play: man shuts himself up against the divine Wisdom. No one anywhere wants to know anything of Wisdom. So Wisdom has to wander always further, since no one wants to accept her. The outcome of all this—a melancholy outcome—was that Wisdom returns again to heaven.

The Christian hymnist was able to understand this story. On the basis of 1 Cor 1:21f. we know that Christians told this story: God first of all endeavored, by means of Wisdom, to bring men to acknowledge him. But this endeavor was a failure. Then God undertook to redeem his own by the foolishness of the proclamation of the crucified Christ, who was nevertheless the Wisdom of God. The hymnist thereby discovered the way he had to go: he needed only to substitute the masculine Logos for the feminine Wisdom in order to create a coherent poem. We are not thereby asserting that he was a Paulinist or familiar with the Pauline form of the tradition; while relying on an old tradition (as we will see), he set his own course.

Prologue

Bibliography

Aland, Kurt
"Eine Untersuchung zu Joh 1,3.4. Über die Bedeutung eines Punktes." *ZNW* 59 (1968) 174–209.

Ammon, Christoph Friedrich von
Progr. de prologi Johannis Evangelistae fontibus et sensu (Göttingen, 1800).

Asbeck, M. d'
"La ponctuation des versets 3 et 4 du Prologue du quatrième Evangile et la doctrine du Logos." In *Congrès d'histoire du Christianisme: Jubilé Alfred Loisy,* ed. P.-L. Couchoud (Paris: Les éditions Rieder, 1928) 220–28.

Atal, Dosithée
Structure et signification des cinq premiers versets de l'hymne johannique au Logos, Recherches africaines de théologie 3 (Louvain: Nauwelaerts, 1973).

Ausejo, Serafín de
"Es un himno a Cristo el prólogo de San Juan." *EstBib* 15 (1956) 223–77, 381–427.

Baldensperger, Wilhelm
Der Prolog des vierten Evangeliums. Sein polemisch-apologetischer Zweck (Tübingen: Mohr-Siebeck, 1898).

Barclay, William
"Great Themes of the New Testament—John 1,1–14." *ExpTim* 70 (1958) 78–82; (1959) 114–17.

Barrett, Charles Kingsley
"The Prologue of St. John's Gospel." In his *New Testament Essays* (London: S. P. C. K., 1972) 27–48.

Barrett, Charles Kingsley
"Κατέλαβεν in John 1,5." *ExpTim* 53 (1941/1942) 297.

Becker, Jürgen
"Beobachtungen zum Dualismus im Johannesevangelium." *ZNW* 65 (1974) 71–87, esp., 73–78.

Berger, Klaus
"Zu 'Das Wort ward Fleisch' Joh I,14a." *NovT* 16 (1974) 161–66.

Bergh van Eysinga, G. A. van den
"Zum richtigen Verständnis des johanneischen Prologs." *Protestantische Monatshefte* 13 (1909) 143–50.

Beutler, Johannes
"'Und das Wort ist Fleisch geworden. . . .' Zur Menschwerdung nach dem Johannesprolog." *Geist und Leben* 46 (1973) 7–16.

Black, Matthew
"Does an Aramaic Tradition Underlie John i. 16?" *JTS* (1941) 69–70.

Blank, Josef
"Das Johannesevangelium. Der Prolog: Joh 1,1–18." *BibLeb* 7 (1966) 28–39, 112–27.

Boismard, Marie-Emile
Le Prologue de S. Jean, LD 11 (Paris: Editions du Cerf, 1953).

Boismard, Marie-Emile
"'Dans le sein du Père.' (Jn. I, 18)." *RB* 59 (1952) 23–39.

Bonsack, B.
"Syntaktische Überlegungen zu Joh 1,9–10." In *Studies in New Testament Language and Text. Essays in Honour of George D. Kilpatrick on the Occasion of his Sixty-fifth Birthday,* ed. J. K. Elliott. NovTSup 44 (Leiden: E. J. Brill, 1976) 52–79.

Borgen, Peder
"Observations on the Targumic Character of the Prologue of John." *NTS* 16 (1969/1970) 288–95.

Borgen, Peder
"Logos was the True Light. Contributions to the Interpretation of the Prologue of John." *NovT* 14 (1972) 115–30. In Swedish: "Logos war det sanne lys. Momenter til tolkning av Johannesprologen." *SEÅ* 35 (1970) 79–95;

Bultmann, Rudolf
"Untersuchungen zum Johannesevangelium." *ZNW* 29 (1930) 169–92. In his *Exegetica: Aufsätze zur Erforschung des Neuen Testaments,* ed. Erich Dinkler (Tübingen: Mohr-Siebeck, 1967) 124–97.

Burney, Charles Fox
The Aramaic Origin of the Fourth Gospel (London: Clarendon Press, 1922).

Burrows, Millar
"The Johannine Prologue as Aramaic Verse." *JBL* 45 (1926) 57–69.

Bussche, Henri van den
"De tout être la parole était la vie. Jean 1, 1–5." *BVC* 69 (1966) 57–65.

Bussche, Henri van den
"Il était dans le monde." *BVC* 81 (1968) 19–25.

Cahill, Peter Joseph
"The Johannine *Logos* as Center." *CBQ* 38 (1976) 54–72.

Collantes, Justo
"Un Commentario gnostico a Io I, 3." *Estudios ecclesiásticos* 27 (1953) 65–83.

Collins, Raymond F.
"The Oldest Commentary on the Fourth Gospel." *Bible Today* 98 (1978) 1769–75.

Cranfield, C. E. B.
"John 1:14: 'became.'" *ExpTim* 93 (1982) 215.

Crome, Friedrich Gottlieb
"Ueber Lucas 1,1–4 und Johannes 20,30.31, nebst einem Zusatz über Johannes 1,1–5, 9–14, 16–18, als Beitrag zur Beantwortung der Frage: unter welchen Umständen sind unsere vier canonischen Evangelien entstanden." *TSK* 2 (1829) 754–66.

Cullmann, Oscar
"Ὁ ὀπίσω μου ἐρχόμενος." In *In honorem Antonii Fridrichsen sexagenarii,* ConNT 11 (Lund: C. W. K. Gleerup, 1947) 26–32.

Culpepper, R. Alan
"The Pivot of John's Prologue." *NTS* 27 (1980) 1–31.

Deeks, David
"The Prologue of St. John's Gospel." *BTB* 6 (1976) 62–78.

Demke, Christoph
"Der sogenannte Logos-Hymnus im johanneischen Prolog." *ZNW* 58 (1967) 45–68.

Dewailly, L.-M.
"La parole parlait à Dieu? [Joh 1:1b–2]." *RTP* 100 (1967) 123–28.

Dibelius, Martin
"Im Anfang war das ewige Wort. Zu Joh 1,1–18." *BibLeb* 10 (1969) 237–39.

Dodd, Charles Harold
"The Prologue to the Fourth Gospel and Christian Worship." In *Studies in the Fourth Gospel,* ed. F. L. Cross (London: A. R. Mowbray, 1957) 9–22.

Dörrie, Heinrich
"Der Prolog zum Evangelium nach Johannes im Verständnis der älteren Apologeten." In *Kerygma und Logos. Beiträge zu den geistesgeschichtlichen Beziehungen zwischen Antike und Christentum. Festschrift für Carl Andresen zum 70. Geburtstag,* ed. A. M. Ritter (Göttingen: Vandenhoeck & Ruprecht, 1979).

Dyroff, Adolf
"Zum Prolog des Johannes-Evangeliums." In *Pisciculi; Studien zur Religion und Kultur des Altertums; Franz Joseph Dölger zum sechzigsten Geburtstage dargeboten von Freunden, Verehrern und Schülern* (Münster i.W: Aschendorff, 1939) 89–93.

Eisler, Robert
"La ponctuation du prologue antimarcionite à l'Evangile selon Jean." *Revue de philologie, de littérature et d'histoire anciennes* 56 (1930) 350–71.

Elliot, J. K.
"John 1,14 and the New Testament's Use of *plērēs.*" *BT* 28 (1977) 151–53.

Eltester, Walther
"Der Logos und sein Prophet. Fragen zur heutigen Erklärung des johanneischen Prologs." In *Apophoreta. Festschrif für Ernst Haenchen zu seinem siebzigsten Geburtstag am 10. Dezember 1984,* BZNW 30 (Berlin: A. Töpelmann, 1964) 109–34.

Epp, Eldon Jay
"Wisdom, Torah, Word: The Johannine Prologue and the Purpose of the Fourth Gospel." In *Current Issues in Biblical and Patristic Interpretation. Studies in Honor of Merrill C. Tenney Presented by His Former Students,* ed. Gerald F. Hawthorne (Grand Rapids: Wm. B. Eerdmans, 1974) 128–46.

Feuillet, André
Le prologue du quatrième évangile (Paris: Desclée de Brouwer, 1968).

Florival, Ephrem
"'Les siens ne l'ont pas reçu' Jn 1,11. Regard

évangélique sur la question juive." *NRT* 89 (1967) 43–66.

Franke, A. H.
"Die Anlage des Johannes-Evangeliums." *TSK* 57 (1884) 80–154, esp., 150–51.

Freed, Edwin D.
"Some Old Testament Influences on the Prolog of John." In *A Light Unto My Path. Old Testament Studies in Honor of Jacob M. Myers,* ed. H. N. Bream, R. D. Heim, and C. A. Moore. Gettysburg Theological Studies 4 (Philadelphia: Temple University Press, 1974) 145–61.

Freed, Edwin D.
"Theological Prelude to the Prologue of John's Gospel." *SJT* 32 (1979) 257–69.

Gaechter, Paul
"Strophen im Johannesevangelium." *ZKT* 60 (1936) 99–120, 402–423, esp., 99–111.

Galot, Jean
Etre né de Dieu. Jean 1, 13, AnBib 37 (Rome: Pontifical Biblical Institute, 1979).

Garvie, Alfred E.
"The Prologue to the Fourth Gospel and the Evangelist's Theological Reflexions." *Expositor,* 8th ser., 10 (1915) 163–72.

Gese, Hartmut
"Der Johannesprolog." In his *Zur biblischen Theologie. Alttestamentliche Vorträge.* BEvT 78 (Munich: Chr. Kaiser Verlag, 1977) 152–201.

Glasson, T. Francis
"Jn I, 9 and a Rabbinic Tradition." *ZNW* 49 (1958) 288–90.

Glasson, T. Francis
"A Trace of Xenophon in John i, 3." *NTS* 4 (1957/1958) 208–9.

Green, Humphrey C.
"The Composition of St. John's Prologue." *ExpTim* 66 (1954/1955) 291–94.

Haacker, Klaus
"Eine formgeschichtliche Beobachtung zu Joh 1,3 fin." *BZ* 12 (1968) 119–21.

Haenchen, Ernst
"Probleme des johanneischen 'Prologs.'" *ZTK* 60 (1963) 305–34. In his *Gott und Mensch. Gesammelte Aufsätze* 1 (Tübingen: Mohr-Siebeck, 1965) 114–43.

Haenchen, Ernst
"Das Johannesevangelium und sein Kommentar." *TLZ* 89 (1964) 881–98. In his *Die Bibel und Wir. Gesammelte Aufsätze* 2 (Tübingen: Mohr-Siebeck, 1968) 206–34.

Hambly, W. F.
"Creation and Gospel. A Brief Comparison of Gen 1,1–2,4 and Joh 1,1–2, 12." *SE* 5 = TU 103 (Berlin: Akademie-Verlag, 1968) 69–74.

Hanson, Anthony T.
"John 1,14–18 and Exodus 34." *NTS* 23 (1976/1977) 90–101.

Harnack, Adolf von
"Über das Verhältnis des Prologs des vierten Evangeliums zum ganzen Werk." *ZTK* 2 (1892) 189–231.

Harrison, Everett F.
"A Study of John 1:14." In *Unity and Diversity in New Testament Theology. Essays in Honor of George E. Ladd,* ed. R. A. Guelich (Grand Rapids: Wm. B. Eerdmans, 1978) 23–36.

Hayward, C. T. R.
"The Holy Name of the God of Moses and the Prologue of St. John's Gospel." *NTS* 25 (1978) 16–32.

Hegermann, Harald
"'Er kam in sein Eigentum.' Zur Bedeutung des Erdenwirkens Jesu im vierten Evangelium." In *Der Ruf Jesu und die Antwort der Gemeinde. Exegetische Untersuchungen Joachim Jeremias zum 70. Geburtstag gewidmet von seinen Schülern,* ed. E. Lohse et al. (Göttingen: Vandenhoeck & Ruprecht, 1970) 112–31.

Helderman, J.
"'In ihren Zelten...' Bemerkungen bei Codex 13 Nag Hammadi p. 47: 14–18, im Hinblick auf Joh 1,14." In *Miscellanea neotestamentica* 1, NovTSup 47 (Leiden: E. J. Brill, 1978) 181–211.

Hengel, Martin
Der Sohn Gottes. Die Enstehung der Christologie und die jüdisch-hellenistische Religionsgeschichte (Tübingen: Mohr-Siebeck, 1975), esp. 58, 112ff.

Hengstenberg, E. W.
Ueber den Eingang des Evangeliums St. Johannis (Berlin: Schlawitz, 1859).

Hennecke, Edgar
"Jean 1,3–4 et l'enchaînement du Prologue." In *Congrès d'histoire du Christianisme: Jubilé Alfred Loisy,* ed. P.-L. Couchoud (Paris: Les éditions Rieder, 1928) 207–19.

Hill, David
"The Relevance of the Logos Christology." *ExpTim* 78 (1967) 136–39.

Hodges, Zane C.
"Grace after Grace—John 1:16. Part 1 of *Problem Passages in the Gospel of John.*" *BSac* 135 (1978) 34–45.

Hofrichter, Peter
Nicht aus Blut, sondern monogen aus Gott geboren. Textkritische, dogmengeschichtliche und exegetische Untersuchung zu Joh 1,13–14, Forschung zur Bibel 31 (Würzburg: Echter Verlag, 1978).

Hofrichter, Peter
"'Egeneto anthropos.' Text und Zusätze im Johannesprolog." *ZNW* 70 (1979) 214–37.

Hooker, Morna
"John the Baptist and the Johannine Prologue." *NTS* 16 (1969/1970) 354–58.

Hooker, Morna
"The Johannine Prolog and the Messianic Secret." *NTS* 21 (1974) 40–58.

Ibuki, Yu
    "Lobhymnus und Fleischwerdung. Studien über
den johanneischen Prolog." *Annual of the Japanese
Biblical Institute* 3 (1977) 132–56.

Ibuki, Yu
    "Offene Fragen zur Aufnahme des Logoshymnus
in das vierte Evangelium." *Annual of the Japanese
Biblical Institute* 5 (1979) 105–32.

Irigoin, J.
    "La composition rythmique du prologue de Jean
(I, 1–18)." *RB* 78 (1971) 501–14.

Janssens, Yvonne
    "Une source gnostique du Prologue?" In *L'Evangile
de Jean. Sources, rédaction, théologie,* ed. M. de Jonge.
BETL 44 (Gembloux: Duculot; Louvain: University Press, 1977) 355–58.

Jeremias, Joachim
    *Der Prolog des Johannesevangeliums. (Johannes 1,1–
18),* Calwer Hefte 88 (Stuttgart: Calwer Verlag,
1967).

Jervell, Jacob
    "'Er kam in sein Eigentum.' Zu Joh. 1, 11." *ST* 10
(1957) 14–27.

Käsemann, Ernst
    "Aufbau und Anliegen des johanneischen Pro-
logs." In *Libertas Christiana, Friedrich Delekat zum
fünfundsechzigsten Geburtstag,* ed. W. Matthias and
E. Wolf. BEvT 26 (Munich: Chr. Kaiser Verlag,
1957) 75–99. Also in Käsemann's *Exegetische Versuche und Besinnungen* (Göttingen: Vandenhoeck &
Ruprecht, ³1968) 155–80.

Kehl, M.
    "Der Mensch in der Geschichte Gottes. Zum
Johannesprolog 6–8." *Geist und Leben* 40 (1967)
404–9.

Kemp, I. S.
    "'The Light of Men' in the Prologue of John's
Gospel." *Indian Journal of Theology* 15 (1966) 154–
64.

King, J. S.
    "The Prologue to the Fourth Gospel: Some Un-
solved Problems." *ExpTim* 86 (1975) 372–75.

Kruijf, T. C. de
    "The Glory of the Only Son." In *Studies in John.
Presented to Professor J. N. Sevenster on the Occasion of
his Seventieth Birthday* (Leiden: E. J. Brill, 1970)
111–23.

Kuyper, Lester J.
    "Grace and Truth. An Old Testament Description
of God, and its Use in the Johannine Gospel." *Int*
18 (1964) 3–19.

Kysar, Robert
    "The Background of the Prologue of the Fourth
Gospel. A Critique of Historical Methods." *CJT* 16
(1970) 250–55.

Kysar, Robert
    "A Comparison of the Exegetical Presuppositions
and Methods of C. H. Dodd and R. Bultmann in
the Interpretation of the Prologue of the Fourth
Gospel." Dissertation, Northwestern University,
1967.

Kysar, Robert
    "Rudolf Bultmann's Interpretation of the Concept
of Creation in John 1,3–4. A Study in Exegetical
Method." *CBQ* 32 (1970) 77–85.

Kysar, Robert
    "Christology and Controversy: The Contributions
of the Prologue of the Gospel of John to New
Testament Christology and their Historical Setting." *CurTM* 5 (1978) 348–64.

Lacan, M. F.
    "L'oeuvre du Verbe incarné: le don de la vie." *RSR*
45 (1957) 61–78.

Lamarche, P.
    "Le Prologue de Jean." *RSR* 52 (1964) 497–537.

Lebram, Jürgen Christian
    "Der Aufbau der Areopagrede." *ZNW* 55 (1964)
221–43, esp. 235ff.

Loisy, Alfred
    "Le prologue du quatrième évangile." *Revue d'his-
toire et de littérature religieuses* 1 (1897) 43ff.

Louw, J. P.
    "Narrator of the Father—ἐξηγεῖσθαι and Related
Terms in the Johannine Christology." *Neot* 2
(1968) 32–40.

Martens, R. F.
    "The Prologue of the Gospel of John: An Exami-
nation of its Origin and Emphasis." Dissertation,
Concordia Seminary in Exile, 1974.

McReynolds, Paul R.
    "John 1:18 in Textual Variation and Translation."
In *New Testament Textual Criticism. Its Significance for
Exegesis. Essays in Honour of Bruce M. Metzger,* ed. E.
J. Epp and G. D. Fee (New York and Oxford:
Clarendon Press, 1981) 105–18.

Masson, Charles
    "Le prologue du quatrième évangile." *RTP,* n.s. 28
(1940) 297–311.

Masson, Charles
    "Pour une traduction nouvelle de Jn I:1b et 2."
RTP 98 (1965) 376–81.

Meagher, John C.
    "John 1:14 and the New Temple." *JBL* 88 (1969)
57–68.

Michael, J. Hugh
    "The Meaning of ἐξηγήσατο in St. John i, 18." *JTS*
22 (1921) 13–16.

Michael, J. Hugh
    "The Origin of St. John I.13." *Expositor,* 8th ser.,
16 (1918) 301–20.

Michaels, J. Ramsey
    "Origen and the Text of John 1,15." In *New
Testament Textual Criticism. Its Significance for Exe-
gesis. Essays in Honour of Bruce M. Metzger,* ed. E. J.
Epp and G. D. Fee (New York and Oxford:
Clarendon Press, 1981) 87–104.

Miller, E. L.
"Salvation History in the Prologue of John 1,3–4." Dissertation, Basel, 1981.

Müller, D. H.
"Das Johannes-Evangelium im Lichte der Strophentheorie." SAWW.PH 160 (Wien: Akademie-Verlag, 1909) 1–60, esp. 2–4.

Nagel, Walter.
"'Die Finsternis hat's nicht begriffen' (Joh 1:5)." ZNW 50 (1959) 132–37.

Newman, Barclay M.
"Some Observations Regarding a Poetic Restructuring of John 1,1–18." BT 29 (1978) 206–12.

O'Neill, J. C.
"The Prologue to St. John's Gospel." JTS 20 (1969) 41–52.

Osten-Sacken, Peter von der
"Der erste Christ. Johannes der Täufer als Schlüssel zum Prolog des vierten Evangeliums." Theologia viatorum 13 (1975/1976) 155–73.

Pinto, Basil de
"Word and Wisdom in St. John." Scr 19 (1967) 19–27, 107–25.

Plessis, I. J. du
"Christ as the 'Only Begotten.'" Neot 2 (1968) 22–31.

Pollard, T. E.
"Cosmology and the Prologue of the Fourth Gospel." VC 12 (1958) 147–53.

Potterie, Ignace de la
"De interpunctione et interpretatione versuum Io. 1, 3–4." VD 33 (1955) 193–208.

Prete, Benedetto
"La concordanza del participio erchomenon in Giov. 1,9." BeO 17 (1975) 195–208.

Richter, Georg
"Die Fleischwerdung des Logos im Johannesevangelium." NovT 13 (1971) 81–126; 14 (1972) 257–76. In his Studien zum Johannesevangelium, ed. Josef Hainz. BU 13 (Regensburg: F. Pustet, 1977) 149–98.

Richter, Georg
"Ist en ein strukturbildendes Element im Logoshymnus?" Bib 51 (1970) 539–44. In his Studien zum Johannesevangelium, ed. Josef Hainz. BU 13 (Regensburg: F. Pustet, 1977) 143–48.

Ridderbos, Hermann
"The Structure and Scope of the Prologue to the Gospel of John." NovT 8 (1966) 180–201.

Rissi, Mathias
"John 1,1–18." Int 31 (1977) 395–401.

Rissi, Mathias
"Die Logoslieder im Prolog des vierten Evangeliums." TZ 31 (1975) 321–36; 32 (1976) 1–13.

Rist, John M.
"St. John and Amelius." JTS 20 (1969) 230–31.

Ritschl, A.
"Zum Verständnis des Prologes des johanneischen Evangeliums." TSK 48 (1875) 576–82.

Robinson, J. A. T.
"The Relation of the Prologue to the Gospel of St. John." NTS 9 (1962/1963) 120–29.

Röhricht, R.
"Zur johanneischen Logoslehre." TSK 41 (1868) 299–315; 44 (1871) 503–9.

Sahlin, Harald
"Zwei Abschnitte aus Joh 1 rekonstruiert." ZNW 51 (1960) 64–69.

Sanders, Jack T.
The New Testament's Christological Hymns. Their Historical Religious Background, SNTSMS 15 (London: Cambridge University Press, 1971).

Schlatter, Frederic W.
"The Problem of Jn 1,3b–4a." CBQ 34 (1972) 54–58.

Schlier, Heinrich
"'Im Anfang war das Wort' im Prolog des Johannesevangeliums." Wort und Wahrheit 9 (1954) 169–80.

Schmid, Josef
"Joh 1, 13." BZ 1 (1957) 118–25.

Schmithals, Walter
"Der Prolog des Johannesevangeliums." ZNW 70 (1979) 16–43.

Schnackenburg, Rudolf
"Logos-Hymnus und johanneischer Prolog." BZ 1 (1957) 69–109.

Schnackenburg, Rudolf
"'Und das Wort ist Fleisch geworden.'" Communio 8 (1979) 1–9.

Schneider, Herbert
"'The Word Was Made Flesh.' An Analysis of the Theology of Revelation in the Fourth Gospel." CBQ 31 (1969) 344–56.

Schulz, Siegfried
"Die Komposition des Johannesprologs und die Zusammensetzung des vierten Evangeliums." SE 1 = TU 73 (Berlin: Akademie-Verlag, 1959) 351–62.

Schwank, Benedikt
"Das Wort vom Wort." Erbe und Auftrag 42 (1966) 183–87.

Seeberg, Reinhold
"Ὁ λόγος σὰρξ ἐγένετο." In Festgabe von Fachgenossen und Freunde. A. von Harnack zum siebsigsten Geburtstag dargebracht (Tübingen: Mohr-Siebeck, 1921) 263–81.

Segalla, Giuseppe
"Preesistenza, incarnazione e divinità di Cristo in Giovanni (Vg e 1 Gv.)." RivB 22 (1974) 155–81.

Siegwalt, Gérard
"Introduction à une théologie chrétienne de la récapitulation." RTP 31 (1981) 259–78.

Smith, D. Moody
The Composition and Order of the Fourth Gospel: Bultmann's Literary Theory (New Haven and London: Yale University Press, 1965), esp. 61–63.

Spicq, Ceslaus

"Le Siracide et la structure littéraire du Prologue de saint Jean." In *Memorial Lagrange. Cinquantenaire de l'école biblique et archéologique française de Jérusalem (15 novembre 1890–15 novembre 1940)* (Paris: J. Gabalda, 1940) 183–95.

Stange, Carl

"Der Prolog des Johannes-Evangeliums." *ZST* 21 (1950/1952) 120–41.

Storelli, F.

"Il prologo di Giovanni e il Logos origeniano." *Nicolaus* 5 (1977) 209–18.

Süskind, F. G.

"Etwas ueber die neueren Ansichten der Stelle Joh 1,1–14." *Magazin für christliche Dogmatik und Moral* 10 (1803) 1–91.

Taylor, Jefferson R.

"A Note on St. John i, 18." *ExpTim* 18 (1906/1907) 47.

Theobald, M.

"Im Anfang war das Wort." Textlinguistische Studie zum Johannesprolog, SBS 106 (Stuttgart: Katholisches Bibelwerk, 1983).

Thoma, Albrecht

"Das Alte Testament im Johannes-Evangelium." *ZWT* 22 (1879) 18–66, 171–223, 273–312, esp. 20–28.

Thurneysen, E.

"Der Prolog zum Johannesevangelium." *Zwischen den Zeiten* 3 (1925) 12–37.

Thyen, Hartwig

"Aus der Literatur zum Johannesevangelium." *TRu* 39 (1974) 1–69, 222–52, 289–330; 42 (1977) 211–70; 43 (1978) 328–59; 44 (1979) 97–134, esp. 1: 53ff; 3: 217.

Toit, A. B. du

"On Incarnate Word—A Study of John 1,14." *Neot* 2 (1968) 9–21.

Trudinger, L. Paul

"The Prologue of John's Gospel: Its Extent, Content and Intent." *Reformed Theological Review* 33 (1974) 11–17.

Vawter, Bruce

"'What Came to be in Him was Life' (Jn 1,3b–4a)." *CBQ* 25 (1963) 401–6.

Wagenmann

"Zum johanneische Prolog." *Jahrbücher für deutsche Theologie* 20 (1875) 441.

Weiße, Christian Hermann

Die evangelische Geschichte, kritisch und philosophisch bearbeitet, 2 vols. (Leipzig: Breitkopf & Härtel, 1838) 183–93.

Weizsäcker, C.

"Die johanneische Logoslehre, mit besonderer Berücksichtigung der Schrift: Der johanneische Lehrbegriff, von Dr. B. Weiss." *Jahrbücher für deutsche Theologie* 7 (1862) 619–708.

Wengst, Klaus

Christologische Formeln und Lieder im Urchristentums, SNT 7 (Gütersloh: Gerd Mohn, 1972) 200–208.

Windisch, Hans

Die katholischen Briefe, HNT 15 (Tübingen: Mohr-Siebeck, 1930).

Winter, Paul

"Μονογενὴς παρὰ πατρός." *ZRGG* 5 (1953) 335–65.

Wrede, W.

Review of *Der Prolog des vierten Evangeliums,* by Wilhelm Baldensperger. *Göttingenische gelehrte Anzeigen* (1900) 1–26.

Ziegler, Dr.

"Bemerkungen über das Evangelium des Johannes, und Erklärungen einzelner schwieriger Stellen desselben." *Neuestes theologisches Journal* 9, ed. J. P. Gabler (1802) 15–69, esp. 17–41.

Zimmermann, Heinrich

"Christushymnus und johanneischer Prolog." In *Neues Testament und Kirche. Für Rudolf Schnackenburg,* ed. J. Gnilka (Freiburg and Vienna: Herder, 1974) 220–48.

1

1   **In the beginning was the Logos, and the Logos was with God, and divine [of the category divinity] was the Logos. 2/ He was in the beginning with God; 3/ all things were made through him, and without him was not anything made that was made. 4/ In him was life, and the life was the light of men. 5/ The light shines in the darkness, and the darkness has not comprehended it.**

6   There was a man sent from God, whose name was John. 7/ He came for testimony, to bear witness to the light, that all might believe through him. 8/ He was not the light, but came to bear witness to the light.

9   **The true light that enlightens every man was coming into the world; 10/ he was in the world, and the world was made**

through him, yet the world knew him not;
11/ he came to his own home, and his
own people received him not.

12   But to all who received him, who believed in his
name, he gave power to become children of
God; 13/ who were born, not of blood nor of
the will of the flesh nor of the will of man, but
of God.

14   **And the Word became flesh and dwelt
among us, full of grace and truth; we
have beheld his glory, glory as of the only
Son from the Father, full of grace and
truth.**

15   John bears witness to him, and cried, "This was
he of whom I said, 'He who comes after me
ranks before me, for he was before me.'"

16   **And from his fullness have we all received,
(indeed,) grace upon grace. 17/ For the
law was given through Moses; grace and
truth came through Jesus Christ.**

18   No one has ever seen God; the only Son, who is
in the bosom of the Father, he has made him
known.

■ **1** Like Gen 1:1 LXX, verse 1 begins with ἐν ἀρχῇ ("in the beginning"). That is no mere coincidence; the agreement is intentional. But the differences are much greater than this scarcely accidental congruence: Gen 1:1 narrates an event: God creates. John 1:1, however, tells of something that was in existence already in time primeval; astonishingly, it is not "God." The hymn thus does not begin with God and his creation, but with the existence of the Logos in the beginning. The Logos (we have no word in either German or English that corresponds to the range of meaning of the Greek term)[1] is thereby elevated to such heights that it almost becomes offensive. The expression is made tolerable only by virtue of the continuation in "and the Logos was in the presence of God," viz., in intimate, personal union with God.

In order to avoid misunderstanding, it may be inserted here that θεός and ὁ θεός ("god, divine" and "the God") were not the same thing in this period. Philo has therefore written: the λόγος means only θεός ("divine") and not ὁ θεός ("God") since the logos is not God in the strict sense.[2] Philo was not thinking of giving up Jewish monotheism. In a similar fashion, Origen, too, interprets: the Evangelist does not say that the logos is "God," but only that the logos is "divine."[3] In fact, for the author of the hymn, as for the Evangelist, only the Father was "God" (ὁ θεός; cf. 17:3); "the Son" was subordinate to him (cf. 14:28). But that is only hinted at in this passage because

here the emphasis is on the proximity of the one to the other: the Logos was "in the presence of God," that is, in intimate, personal fellowship with him.

The two prepositions εἰς and πρός with the accusative were originally used only in response to the question "whither?" In Koine they are also used frequently for ἐν and παρά with the dative (cf. 19:25) in response to the question "where?" with the meaning "in" or "at, by, beside."

The Logos therefore was not a substitute for God in the beginning, but lives in and out of this fellowship (1:18, 4:34). But precisely for this reason, viz., that he alone had this primeval union with "God," does he take on added significance. Verse 1c expresses this meaning even more strongly: "and divine (belonging to the category divinity) was the Logos." These statements about him thereby reach their high point, insofar as they concern the realm of that primeval beginning. They impress upon the reader ever more clearly the incomparable station and significance of the Logos.

Bultmann objects to this interpretation: one cannot speak of God (in the Christian sense) in the plural.[4] On the contrary, in the period in which the hymn took its rise, it was quite possible in Jewish and Christian monotheism to speak of divine beings that existed alongside and under God but were not identical with him. Phil 2:6–10 proves that. In that passage Paul depicts just such

---

1   See the Excursus on the pre-Johannine Logos-hymn.   4   *John*, 32f. [16].
2   *De Somn.* 1.229f.
3   Origen, *Comm. in Joh.* 2.2.13–15.

a divine being, who later became man in Jesus Christ, and before whom every knee will one day bow. But it should be noted that the Son will eventually return all authority to the Father (1 Cor 15:28), so that his glory may be complete. Thus, in both Philippians and John 1:1 it is not a matter of a dialectical relationship between two-in-one, but of a personal union of two entities, and to that personal union corresponds the church's rejection of patripassianism.

It goes virtually without saying that the hymn could not have used the terms "messiah" or "son of man" instead of "logos." The "messiah" and the "son of man" of course do not appear until after the creation, and possibly not until the close of the age. It is the case, to be sure, that God had already named the messiah prior to the creation, according to Jewish tradition. But that implies only that the "messiah"—like the sabbath, for example—was already incorporated into the divine plan of creation. And it was impossible, too, to use the term "son." It would have been nonsense to the reader had the hymn begun with the words, "In the beginning was the son." The term "logos" thus does not serve merely as a lure to the Greek reader. The hymn could scarcely have made use of any other diction.

Two words appear to carry the emphasis in each of the clauses in the first verse:

1a   In the beginning was the Word,

1b   and the Word was with God,

1c   and divine (of the category divinity) was the Word. In each case, the second term reappears in the next clause as the lead word: beginning/word; word/God; God/word (ἀρχή/λόγος; λόγος/ὁ θεός; θεός/λόγος). This has prompted Bultmann to speculate that an Aramaic original constructed along the lines of the Odes of Solomon lies behind the hymn.[5] Each couplet consists of two lines that express a single thought (vv 9, 12, 14b); occasionally the second completes the meaning of the first (vv 1, 4, 14a, 16). In other cases, the second line stands in parallelism with the first (v 3), or is the antithesis of the first (vv 5, 10, 11). From this Bultmann concludes that the Evangelist, who was once a disciple of John the Baptist, borrowed a hymn from the Baptist sect and attributed it to Jesus after his conversion and that

prompted him to revise it.[6] Bultmann has to presuppose such a revision; for he can carry through his interpretation only if he presupposes the omission (v 2?) and additions of the Evangelist (vv 9, 10, 11, 12). Beyond that, Bultmann is compelled to assume that the Evangelist misunderstood his source (which spoke of the pre-existent logos in vv 1–5 and 9–12) and interpreted it to refer to the incarnation from verse 5 on. His analysis of form thus turns into a source hypothesis. But Bultmann's views that the Evangelist took over a hymn of the Baptist community and reworked it have not stood up. More recent work on the Prologue reckons only with a Christian hymn; in so doing, it emphasizes that the alleged omissions and additions of the Evangelist do not support the two-member pattern of the source presupposed by Bultmann.[7]

Verse 1 shows, moreover, that a two-member construction does not lie behind it. This verse in its entirety serves the various aspects offered by the recent concept of the logos (λόγος). That occurs in a very subtle fashion, following the pattern a–b; b–c; c–b. This is the only verse in the Gospel of John that structures concepts in so thorough going a fashion. The correspondence is not, in fact, as close as the diction prompts us to suppose. In each of the three clauses we meet the verb form "was" (ἦν). It means something different in each of its occurrences.[8] Verse 1a contains the basic affirmation: In the beginning was the Word, i.e., it *existed* in the beginning. This entity, which in relation to the OT could be said to be new (one could almost use the term "modern" in relation to that generation), existed before the creation and was not therefore created; it shared the highest of all distinctions with "God, the Father" himself: the "Logos" is eternal. Since he becomes incarnate in Jesus, Jesus also shares the divine distinctions. But there was no rivalry between the Logos as θεός and as ὁ θεός (in English the distinction is expressed by "divine" and "God"); the new (Christian) faith does not conflict with the old monotheistic faith. That becomes clearer in verse 1c: "and divine (in essence) was the Logos." In this instance, the verb "was" (ἦν) simply expresses predication. And the predicate noun must accordingly be more carefully observed: θεός is not the same thing as ὁ θεός ("divine" is not the same

5   *John*, 15–18 [2–5].

6   *John*, 16–18 [3–5].

7   Recent work includes that of Schnackenburg, Brown,

Demke, Haenchen, Käsemann.

8   Cf. Brown, *John*, 1: 4.

thing as "God"). That contains a christology of the subordination of the son, albeit still covertly. It is precisely for this reason that the believer sees the Father in the son: the son does not speak his own words, he does not do his own works, he does not effect his own will, but subordinates himself entirely to the words, work, and will of the Father. There is still much to be said about this christology that exaltation (δόξα) lies in humility and obedience and triumph in death on the cross.

When Bultmann objects that one should then expect θεῖος ("divine") instead of θεός ("god"),[9] he overlooks the fact that θεῖος says less than what is here affirmed of the Logos and would either make use of a literary Greek entirely foreign to the Gospel of John, or express a different meaning. The "neutral" expression, τὸ θεῖον, is necessary, for example, in the Areopagus speech (Acts 17:29), in order to designate "the divine" in the language of the Greek enlightenment. 2 Peter, which is relatively late, speaks again in 1:3f. of "divine power" (θεία δύναμις) and "divine nature" (θεία φύσις). Windisch correctly points out with regard to these verses that they are imbued with the outlook and expressions of hellenistic piety, and as parallels to "divine power" (θεία δύναμις) he points to Acts 8:10, Plato, *De leg.* 3.691e, and Aristotle, *Pol.* 4(7).4, and other passages.[10] 2 Peter 1:4 "partakers of his divine nature" (θείας κοινωνοὶ φύσεως) concurs with Philo, *De decal.* 104, "sharing in a divine nature" (θείας ... φύσεως ... μετεσχηκότων), and refers to all Christians. 2 Peter thus exhibits a later and different theology in relation to the Gospel of John. There is no precise form parallel to 1:1 in the whole of the Gospel of John.

In contrast to the interpretation advocated by us, Bultmann advances a quite different theological reading. In a certain sense Bultmann acknowledges the tension between the statements in 1b and 1c: "Whereas the statement ὁ Λόγος ἦν πρὸς τὸν θεὸν could have made us think that we were concerned with the communion of two divine persons, the statement is pushed to its opposite extreme: θεὸς ἦν ὁ Λόγος. But this, too, is at once

protected from any misunderstanding, as it were, by revoking what has just been said and repeating the πρὸς τὸν θεόν ['with God'] ..."[11] There is no attempt to go back behind the statement: "The Logos was in the presence of God." "But is the intention really to express the mythological idea of the existence in the beginning of two divine persons, either alongside each other, or the one subordinate to the other? ... The status of the Λόγος is one of equality with God: he was God."[12] In expounding John 1:1f. in this way, the real concern of Bultmann appears to be that one cannot speak of God as though he were an "objective" entity, but one can speak of him only insofar as he reveals himself. If, however, this revelation consists in the revealer, who is wholly man, asserting that he is the God whom he reveals, and reveals nothing beyond that, then Bultmann does not agree with John. For John has Jesus say in his "I am" sayings, "I am the bread of life," etc., and these sayings are not spoken in his own name, but in the name of the Father. This matter will be examined more closely in the commentary on chapter 5.

■ **2** Verse 2 exhibits a different character. Bultmann therefore conjectures that verse 2 replaces a mythological statement in the alleged sectarian source.[13] Käsemann rightly objects to this view: "What would the Evangelist have been correcting in v. 2, when he took no offense at v. 18b, than which there could scarcely be anything more mythologically formulated?"[14] He then concludes that verse 1 is a triplet, and asks: "should we not do well to let this postulate (already erected by Burney)[15] of a consistent couplet pattern go by the board, and the textual changes it necessitates can go with it?"[16] It is true that the couplet dominates as far as verse 12; but that may not yield a rigid pattern. In any case, Schnackenburg, too, denies that this verse belongs to the original hymn because it adds nothing new and it cannot be understood as a verse with two key words.[17] But that is not in itself sufficient reason to ascribe the verse to the Evangelist. It remains a general question whether it

9 *John*, 33 [17].

10 *Die katholischen Briefe*, HNT 15 (Tübingen: Mohr-Siebeck, 1911, ²1930) 85.

11 *John*, 34 [17].

12 *John*, 33 [16].

13 *John*, 34f. [17f.].

14 *New Testament Questions*, 142.

15 *The Aramaic Origin of the Fourth Gospel* (London:

Clarendon Press, 1922) 40ff.

16 Käsemann, *New Testament Questions*, 142.

17 *John*, 1: 227.

makes sense to divide this hymn into segments of two and three lines. The other hymns in the NT cannot be resolved into such couplets and triplets. Phil 2:6–11, Col 1:15–20, and 1 Cor 13 support the view that such hymns exhibit what is often a marvelous rhythmical prose. Under these circumstances it is not certain that an alien hand has intruded itself when one verse is longer than an adjoining verse.

Verse 2 encapsulates what was important in 1a–c and therefore pinpoints it for the reader: "This one (the Logos) was in the beginning with God." The first subsection of the hymn is thereby brought to a close and the relationship between the Logos and "God" clarified. This shows the reader what position was being occupied, who was originally divine, but then became flesh in order to bring the message from the Father, whom no one has ever seen.

Of course one can object to such expressions as are found in verses 1f. on the grounds that they are "mythological" or "mythic." In that case, one must expound them differently, as Bultmann does, by demythologizing them.[18] But then the same objection can be raised against Paul: he speaks in Phil 2:6ff. of the one "who, though in the form of God, emptied himself, in taking the form of a servant," and in 2 Cor 8:9, he speaks of the Christ as the one "who though rich became poor." The Gospel of John says nothing about an "emptying" ($\kappa\acute{\epsilon}\nu\omega\sigma\iota\varsigma$) of course, but it does indeed speak of the glory he will again acquire when he is "raised up," a glory he possessed on the basis of God's love before the foundation of the world (17:24). This "myth" is found in all the writings of the NT; the Easter experience caused it to be expressed pervasively in the Christian proclamation. The view that verses 1 and 2 are intended to express a paradoxical state of affairs by oscillating between two assertions[19] does not necessarily commend itself. It is possible that a kind of "heavenly prelude" is being suggested here, if the poet who created the hymn placed any value on such a localization.

■ **3** Verse 3 begins a new subsection. After he has clearly stated the relationship of the Logos to God in verses 1f., the "poet" comes now to speak of the task of the Logos, the task on which everything to follow is based: he becomes the intermediary in the creation, a role played by Wisdom in late Judaism. Bultmann interprets "everything that was made through him" to refer to the world of men: "everything" ($\pi\acute{\alpha}\nu\tau\alpha$) is only a matter of liturgical style.[20] But the text contradicts that. The text emphasizes the all-encompassing role of the Logos as mediator. The emphatic statement, "and without him was not anything made that was made," makes sense only if it refers to the creation in its entirety and not just to humankind. The material world did not come into existence through the Logos, according to Gnosticism; over against the $\kappa\acute{o}\sigma\mu o\varsigma\,\nu o\eta\tau\acute{o}\varsigma$, the primary, spiritual world, the material world was worthless and base. According to the commentary of the Valentinian gnostic Heracleon (ca. 150 CE),[21] the real creator of the world is the inferior figure, the Demiurge. The Logos provides only the impulse to create. That is the explanation for $\delta\iota\acute{\alpha}$ ("through"), which is to be distinguished from $\grave{\alpha}\phi'\,o\mathring{v}$ ("from which something is created") and from $\mathring{v}\phi'\,o\mathring{v}$ ("by whom something is created").[22] The spiritual world—Heracleon calls it the Aeon and what is in the Aeon—was not created by the Logos; it was already present prior to his activity as agent. Ptolemaeus, who was also of the Valentinian school, assists in a somewhat different way, as Irenaeus reports:[23] the Logos gave essence and form to all the Aeons. But there is something else more important than this particular item: Ptolemaeus attempts to find the answer to the fundamental question about the origin of the spiritual world in the Prologue to the Gospel of John—which he traces back to John, the disciple of the Lord. In this process he proceeds on the basis of a scheme already created prior to him, viz.: those powers that form the highest circle of the $\kappa\acute{o}\sigma\mu o\varsigma\,\nu o\eta\tau\acute{o}\varsigma$ ("the spiritual world"), the Ogdoad, arose, in turn, one out of the other. At the pinnacle stands the Father, God. The

---

18 *John*, 32f. [16].
19 Bultmann, *John*, 34 [17].
20 Bultmann, *John*, 36–38 [19f.].
21 The fragments of Heracleon's commentary on John are collected and translated in Robert M. Grant, *Gnosticism. A Sourcebook of Heretical Writings from the Early Christian Period* (New York: Harper & Brothers, 1961) 195–208. The fragments are preserved by

Origen.
22 Origen, *Comm. in Joh.* 2.14.
23 *Adv. haer.* 1.8.5, tr. in R. M. Grant, *Gnosticism: A Sourcebook of Heretical Writings from the Early Christian Period* (New York: Harper & Brothers, 1961) 182f.

"beginning" (ἀρχή), of which John 1:1 speaks, is an Aeon, in which a second Aeon is already found. On the basis of the gnostic understanding, verse 1a is to be translated: "In the 'beginning' existed the Logos" (which is also an Aeon, a high, spiritual power). The "beginning," the "arche," occupies a middle position between the Father, from whom it was derived as the first creation, and the Logos, to which it, the "arche," gave rise. The "beginning," the "arche," is also called "Son," the only begotten (μονογενής) and "God." We learn that there were other beings beyond the Logos in this system: at the same time as the Logos came into being, the balance of the Aeons emerged from the "beginning," to which the Logos then gave form. What, then, is the next Aeon in the line, the one that is contained in the Logos and emerges from him? Verse 3 gives the answer, if the phrase, "that which has come into being," is construed with what follows: "in him (the Logos) was the life" (ζωή). The life is the syzygy (the pair) of the Logos; in accordance with this gnostic scheme, two Aeons at a time are especially closely linked.

The author of the hymn therefore stands in opposition to Gnosticism. For the gnostic the material world was base. Nor was it self-evident for the gnostic to say that the spiritual world, which was elevated above the material world, was created by the Logos. Gnosticism therefore contradicts the assertion that the All (the universe) was created by the Logos. The terms "creation" (κτίσις) and "to create" (κτίζειν) are avoided in the Prologue, as indeed in the Gospel of John generally. The passive construction, "all things were made through him" (πάντα δι' αὐτοῦ ἐγένετο) appears to be especially suited to describe the intermediary role of the Logos. For the Gospel of John the real creator is "God" (17:24). In contrast to all gnostic doctrine, the hymn proclaims that simply everything came into being through the Logos—humankind does not exist in a vacuum, but in the All, and this All was created "through" the Logos. It therefore makes sense to speak of the coming into being of the All prior to the coming into being of humankind.

■ 4 In the twenty-fifth edition of Nestle, verse 4 still begins with "In him" (ἐν αὐτῷ). In the twenty-sixth edition, it begins with "That which came into being" (ὃ γέγονεν), incorrectly in my judgment. Aland proposes to detach the phrase from verse 3 and move it to verse 4. He defends this proposed change in a detailed article.[24] With the help of numerous citations from the manuscripts and from quotations drawn from gnostic texts and the Church Fathers, he seeks to prove: the attribution of ὃ γέγονεν to verse 3 "began to be carried out in the fourth century in the Greek Church. This transfer arose in the conflict with the Arians, and functioned to guard the doctrines of the church. Its secondary character is unmistakable. The change was unknown in the West."[25] Aland appears to us to be correct in affirming that the phrase ὃ γέγονεν is attested by the gnostics and by the Eastern Church. Only when these words proved to be a danger in the fight with the Arians were they attached to verse 3 (they appear to attest a becoming on the part of the Logos). But that does not exclude the possibility that one thereby restores the original reading. The situation in the manuscripts is as follows: 𝔓⁶⁶ and 𝔓⁷⁵*, as well as B and ℵ, have no punctuation marks from verse 1 to the conclusion of verse 5. In Kasser's edition of 𝔓⁷⁵,[26] a period appears before ὃ γέγονεν. The facsimile edition reveals that the period was sandwiched in between the letters later. Now many later manuscripts have a mark of punctuation before ὃ γέγονεν.[27] But that merely shows that the non-gnostic textual tradition has taken over the gnostic punctuation (not, however, the gnostic interpretation). In the opening lines of the hymn, the gnostics (Valentinians, Naassenes, Peratikoi) saw described the origin of the powers of the Ogdoad, which form the uppermost circle of the "spiritual world" (κόσμος νοητός), the highest spiritual powers. They arose, each one from another (see further above). The words in verse 1, "In the beginning was the Logos," were interpreted as follows: in the "beginning," that is, in the only begotten, the Logos was concealed. What came into being in him, in

24 "Eine Untersuchung zu Joh 1,3.4. Über die Bedeutung eines Punktes," *ZNW* 59 (1968) 174–209.

25 Aland, "Eine Untersuchung zu Joh 1,3.4. Über die Bedeutung eines Punktes," *ZNW* 59 (1968) 203.

26 *Papyrus Bodmer XIV–XV: Evangile de Luc et Jean* [Luc. chap. 3–24; Jean chap. 1–15], ed. Victor Martin and Rudolphe Kasser (Coloquy-Geneva: Bibliotheca Bodmeriana, 1961).

27 From C* to syᶜ; see the appartus in Nestle.

the Logos, was the "life" ($\zeta\omega\acute{\eta}$), his pair (syzygy). They read their doctrine of the emanations into verses 1ff. in this way. It is clear that they misused the Greek text.

Ambrosius shows how the exegesis of the Roman Church interpreted this text with its gnostic punctuation. Indeed, he read: *Quod factum est in ipso, vita est* ("what came into being in him is life"), but he then interpreted "in him" ($\dot{\epsilon}\nu$ $\alpha\dot{\upsilon}\tau\hat{\omega}$) as instrumental, as *per eum* ("through him").[28] In that way agreement with "through him" ($\delta\iota'$ $\alpha\dot{\upsilon}\tau o\hat{\upsilon}$) in verse 3 was achieved. Later he switched to the reading of "most of the scholars and faithful," which connected $\mathring{o}$ $\gamma\acute{\epsilon}\gamma o\nu\epsilon\nu$ to verse 3.[29] Origen distinguishes what the Logos himself is from what comes into being through him in relation to humankind, viz., light and life.[30] To the phrase, "the one coming into the world" ($\dot{\epsilon}\rho\chi\acute{o}\mu\epsilon\nu o\nu$ $\epsilon\dot{\iota}\varsigma$ $\tau\grave{o}\nu$ $\kappa\acute{o}\sigma\mu o\nu$) in verse 9, he adds the following by way of interpretation: "the true and spiritual world," thus the $\kappa\acute{o}\sigma\mu o\varsigma$ $\nu o\eta\tau\acute{o}\varsigma$. One misconstrues the facts when one connects $\mathring{o}$ $\gamma\acute{\epsilon}\gamma o\nu\epsilon\nu$ to verse 4 by invoking the oldest manuscripts, to say nothing of the fact that one does not thereby achieve a meaningful text. Bauer has shown that,[31] and Bultmann, too, has demonstrated it in spite of himself. He interprets verse 4, which begins for him with $\mathring{o}$ $\gamma\acute{\epsilon}\gamma o\nu\epsilon\nu$, to mean that both the beginning of the world "and its continuing existence are attributed to the Logos."[32] But there is no mention of "continuing existence" in the text. Bultmann offers two interpretations of the Greek text: (a) "What has come to be—in him (the Logos) was the life (for it)." The additions in parentheses indicate that the text does not provide what the interpreter seeks. (b) "What has come to be—in it he (the Logos) was the life."[33] That is a style foreign to the hymn. In fact, if verse 4 begins with $\mathring{o}$ $\gamma\acute{\epsilon}\gamma o\nu\epsilon\nu$, it means: "What has come into being—in it is the life." That means: when $\mathring{o}$ $\gamma\acute{\epsilon}\gamma o\nu\epsilon\nu$ is combined with verse 4, verse 4 has nothing to say about the Logos. One must therefore connect $\mathring{o}$ $\gamma\acute{\epsilon}\gamma o\nu\epsilon\nu$ with verse 3, since hardly anyone today admits a gnostic interpretation. The Naassenes of course used the clever ploy of reading out of the phrase

"and without him was not anything made that was made" ($\kappa\alpha\grave{\iota}$ $\chi\omega\rho\grave{\iota}\varsigma$ $\alpha\dot{\upsilon}\tau o\hat{\upsilon}$ $\dot{\epsilon}\gamma\acute{\epsilon}\nu\epsilon\tau o$ $o\dot{\upsilon}\delta\grave{\epsilon}$ $\acute{\epsilon}\nu$): "The Nothing that came into existence apart from him is the material world."[34] This world was created, according to the Naassenes, by Chaos and the fiery God Esaldaios (= El Shaddai). But verse 4 means something entirely different: In the Logos was the true, divine life (as in the Father), the spirit, and this life of the Logos was the light of men. That means: this light does not remain the hidden possession of the Logos, but is accessible to every man, and could and would enlighten every one who comes into the world. Whoever lives in harmony with God—and that alone is true life—whoever knows himself to be secure in God and is given his goal by God (expressed in gnostic terms: "whoever knows whence he comes and whither he goes," viz., from and to God), for him the darkness can no longer obscure the way to life. Umbrage, doubt, mistrust, despair are unknown to him. Furthermore, he has no further doubt about the riddle of his way to life (cf. 16:23).

■ **5** Verse 5 opens a new subsection. In verse 4, life is designated as the light of men; we now learn that the light shines in the darkness and the darkness has not comprehended it. The present tense of "shines" ($\phi\alpha\acute{\iota}\nu\epsilon\iota$) is a puzzle; it is followed immediately by the aorist, "has not comprehended" ($\kappa\alpha\tau\acute{\epsilon}\lambda\alpha\beta\epsilon\nu$). It is of course the case that one always lights a light whenever it is dark. But this generalization does not say enough with regard to this verse.

If one interprets verse 5 from the point of view of verses 6–8, verse 5 is to be related to the incarnation of Jesus. In fact, the interpretation of the ancient church is generally invoked for the first mention of the Logos becoming man in verse 5. But in so doing, the probability that the ancient church has taken over the gnostic punctuation of verse 4 (as early as $\mathfrak{P}^{75}$) is not considered; but, above all, no consideration is given to the fact that the ancient church is anything but critical. For the church it was decisive that John the Baptist is treated in verse 6.

---

28 *Enarr. in Ps 36.35*; MPL 14.1030 D–1031 A.
29 *De fide* 3.6; MPL 16.6226 D.
30 *C. Celsum* 6.5.
31 *Das Johannesevangelium*, 12f.
32 *John*, 39 [21].
33 *John*, 39 [21].
34 Hippolytus, *Ref.* 5.8.5. Cf. Grant, *Gnosticism: A Sourcebook of Heretical Writings from the Early Christian Period* (New York: Harper & Brothers, 1961) 106f.

On that basis, the church unavoidably interpreted verse 5 to refer to the incarnation of the Logos. Once one views verses 6–8 as a later addition, as modern scholarship does, there is no reason to read verse 5 as a reference to the incarnation. If the original hymn meant the incarnation (that would be a decisive event), then one ought at least to expect a clearer allusion to it, and not just the present tense of "shines" ($\phi\alpha\acute{\iota}\nu\epsilon\iota$), which proves nothing. Exegetes have expended an enormous amount of energy in attempting to explain this tense. For, one really ought to expect an aorist here, as the designation of the event of the incarnation, just as it appears, in fact, in verse 14. In the normal course of events, one would expect the mention of John the Baptist prior to that of Jesus in any tradition based on Mark. The effort is occasionally made to interpret verse 9 as a description of the incarnation; but this effort is shattered on the fact that neither the imperfect "was" ($\mathring{\eta}\nu$) nor the periphrastic imperfect "was coming" ($\mathring{\eta}\nu \ldots \grave{\epsilon}\rho\chi\acute{o}\mu\epsilon\nu\sigma\nu$; in the event one construes the verb with the participle) is suited to describe the beginning of such an event. Yet Käsemann affirms "that the portrayal of Jesus Christ as appearing in history begins at v. 5."[35] He very strongly emphasizes the point: "There is absolutely no convincing argument for the view that vv. 5–13 ever referred to anything save the historical manifestation of the believer."[36] Since the text of the hymn appears to have been widely disseminated only with verses 6–8 already inserted, verse 5 in this context could of course have been understood only as a reference to the incarnation. It is improbable that the Evangelist himself misunderstood his source in this way;[37] it is just as unlikely that Bultmann's further suggestion[38] is correct: "Verses 5–13 give a suggestive description of the appearance of Jesus Christ in history," which is then followed, in verses 14–16, by a concrete description.[39] Käsemann has rightly argued against an alleged misunderstanding on the part of the Evangelist.[40] But his solution, viz., that verses 5 and 14 are parallel to each other, is no more convincing.

The arguments to be marshaled against these views are, first, that there is no indication why the Logos really became flesh. Second, it is striking that this event is reported in the present tense, while the reaction of the darkness is depicted immediately following in the aorist. Käsemann does not think the verb in verse 5 is timeless,[41] but asserts that "the excellent parallel in I John 2.8 has a present 'sound.'"[42] Käsemann thereby overlooks the fact that, although 1 John 2:8 indeed makes use of the vocabulary of the Gospel, it nevertheless reflects an apocalyptic expectation of the imminent end to a high degree: "because the darkness is passing away and the true light is already shining." The text certainly speaks of the present, but it does so in such a way that what is said is that the imminent end is in the process of coming to realization. Such ardent expectation of the end ("Little children it is the last hour!" 1 John 2:18) has nothing to do with the Gospel of John.

Furthermore, in the third place, Käsemann has taken over the view from Bultmann "that the Evangelist provided the hymn which he had before him with an epilogue—i.e., vv 14–18."[43] If, then, the "the ring of the present," which Käsemann detects, does not offer the desired solution, what does the present tense of "is shining" ($\phi\alpha\acute{\iota}\nu\epsilon\iota$) imply? We are of the opinion that it expresses an indefinite but very long duration of time, during which the state of affairs represented by "is shining" ($\phi\alpha\acute{\iota}\nu\epsilon\iota$) persisted, while the aorist "did not comprehend" ($\sigma\mathring{\upsilon} \kappa\alpha\tau\acute{\epsilon}\lambda\alpha\beta\epsilon\nu$) expresses an opinion regarding the failure of this activity. Verse 5 therefore has to do—if we may make use of these later concepts—with the fruitless activity of the Logos in the generations prior to the the incarnation of the Logos. The hymn does not tell us why this failure occurred. It does not describe a fall into sin, like the story of Adam and Eve with its consequences, such as are depicted in 4 Ezra 7:11f.: "For it was for their sakes I made the world; but when Adam transgressed my statues, then that which had been made was judged[44] and then the ways of this world

35 *New Testament Questions*, 144.

36 *New Testament Questions*, 150.

37 Bultmann, *John*, 45ff. [26ff.] thinks he did.

38 Here he refers to Harnack, "Über das Verhältnis des Prologs des vierten Evangeliums zum ganzen Werk," *ZTK* 2 (1892) 220.

39 *John*, 45ff. [26f.].

40 *New Testament Questions*, 144ff.

41 Contrary to Bultmann, *John*, 27f. and n. 2 [12 n. 6].

42 *New Testament Questions*, 150f.

43 *New Testament Questions*, 152.

44 Paul presupposes something comparable in Rom 8:20.

became narrow and sorrowful and painful and full of perils coupled with great toils."[45] The hymn thus does not speak of things like that, nor does it speak of a coming apocalyptic turn of events, but depicts the situation prevailing between creation and incarnation only in the briefest terms—a description that is continued in verses 9–11.

■ **6–8** Verses 6–8 are striking by virtue of their contrasting, more prosaic, and biblical cast. Ruckstuhl seeks vainly to demonstrate that these sentences were composed in verse.[46] The segment is reminiscent of the narrative style found in the OT, for example, in 1 Sam 1:1. Whoever attributes these verses to the Evangelist, like Bultmann does, must also assume that the Evangelist no longer understood the hymn. This much is correct about that view: the interpolator in fact took verse 5 as a early reference to the incarnation of the Logos. But that presented him with a difficulty: an account of John the Baptist had to be given prior to the appearance of Jesus. Verses 6–8 are now to rectify this apparent deficiency. Actually, the Baptist should have been mentioned even before the Logos was mentioned; but there was no opportunity to do so between verses 4 and 5. The first occasion came following verse 5, although even there the words about the Baptist strike one as misplaced. The compelling proof that verses 6–8 are secondary is the fact that in verses 19–28 the significance of the Baptist as the forerunner is presented and expounded in a detailed scene. Of course, verses 6–8 also intend to subordinate John to Jesus: the Baptist is not himself the light, but is to bear witness to the light. But the allusion to Mal 3:1 and 4:6 (which have also influenced Mark 9:12 and Matt 17:11) has caused the Baptist to be given the task of leading everyone to faith (in Jesus; v 7). That does not comport with either the content or the theology of the Gospel of John. And assigning this aim to the preaching of John the Baptist does not agree either with the significance the Fourth Gospel attributes to the Baptist. In order to be able to ascribe verse 7 to the Evangelist nevertheless, Bultmann is obliged to make do with this bit of information: "The fact that *all* men are to be brought to faith by the Baptist, shows that the Evangelist was not thinking of the historical situation of the Bap-

tist's preaching, but that he was referring to his witness as it was constantly re-presented through the tradition and which in this way retains its actuality."[47] Now of course in verse 15 the Baptist together with his testimony is made an honorary member of the Christian community, as we will see. But what reader could have been expected to discover in verse 7 the meaning that Bultmann alleges is there? As elegant as Bultmann's solution is, it is a makeshift. We believe it to be much more likely that here we find an echo of a synoptic tradition, a very old one that went beyond Mark 1:5: John the Baptist is to put all things right as the returning Elijah promised in Mal 3:2. In that case, John 1:19–28 has a quite different ring to it. Jesus speaks of the witness of the Baptist in 5:33f., but in such a way that it becomes clear that 1:19–28 is echoed. Of course, Jesus does not invoke this testimony, since he depends solely on the testimony of the Father, which will come only with the appearance of the Spirit.

Who, then, thought it necessary to insert verses 6–8? Scholars do not assume that the Evangelist had the hymn before him in an expanded form. Both Bauer[48] and Bultmann[49] assume that the Evangelist himself inserted the troubling verses: "One has to suppose that in oral recitation the 'comments' would be distinguishable by the tone of the speaker."[50] That is conceivable only if the Evangelist himself recited the text. A silent or an audible reader of the written text would not know that verses 6–8 were to be understood as "comments" and therefore to be read with a different emphasis. But in that case one must reckon with the possibility that the redactor who added chapter 21 to the Gospel is also the author of these verses.

Hirsch conjectures that the redactor moved verses 6–8 from their original position (before 1:19) to their present place; he "wanted to distinguish clearly between the cosmological and the soteriological functions of the Logos (i.e., between creation and redemption), and to prevent 1:9–13 from being interpreted in relation to the pre-incarnate Logos."[51] The redactor assumed that everything from verse 9 on referred to the incarnate Logos. According to Hirsch, this revision, among others, took place between CE 130 and 140 because the phrase

---

45   *APOT* 2: 580f.
46   *Einheit*, 43–54.
47   *John*, 51 [31].

48   *Das Johannesevangelium*, 15.
49   *John*, 48f. [29].
50   *John*, 16 n. 3 [3 n. 4].

"in his own name" in John 5:42 refers to Bar Kochba. On the basis of $\mathfrak{P}^{52}$, we know today that this dating is in error;[52] the Gospel of John in its present form was in existence as early as about 100 CE. But at that time, the themes of the history of dogma in the second century had not become sufficiently critical to support Hirsch's hypothesis. In addition, and here we come to the point that is finally decisive, verses 6–8 are comprehensible only where they stand between verses 5 and 9 because of the way in which they speak of the "light."

What, then, prompted the addition of verses 6–8? The redactor, like Käsemann and others today, took verse 5 to describe the earthly appearance of Jesus. In that case, it is necessary to say something about John the Baptist, the forerunner prior to that, as in the synoptic Gospels and in Acts 10:37. It goes without saying that the redactor took into consideration what is said about the light in verses 5 and 9 and the general tendency of the Fourth Gospel to depreciate the Baptist by comparison with Jesus. Nevertheless, he had a somewhat different image of the Baptist in mind than the one held by the Evangelist: he had in view the picture of the witness who would lead everyone to faith.

It is necessary, to be sure, to speak first of John the Baptist and only then of Jesus. But if one does not wish to remodel the hymn entirely, it is not possible to introduce the Baptist into the hymn prior to verse 5. The reader can easily try that experiment for himself or herself. The appropriate occasion is immediately after verse 5, and since both verses 5 and 9 (which originally followed immediately on v 5) discuss the "light" ($\phi\hat{\omega}s$), it was necessary to depict the Baptist in his relation to the "light." The lack of skill that characterizes the way in which the redactor permits verses 8 and 9 to clash shows us that he was not a particularly deft author, and he repeats this clumsy process again in verse 15.

■ **9–11** Verses 9–11 continue the discussion of the subject indicated in verse 5, without adding specific details. They emphasize only what is really incomprehensible: the world that came into being through the Logos (in this case the world of humankind is intended) has flatly rejected him, as one refuses a strange tramp. The pattern of the Wisdom myth again becomes evident. The hymn does not provide an explanation for this incomprehensible condition of the world, unlike Gnosticism; it only depicts it lamentably and accusingly. "He was," so verse 10 continues, "in the world, and the world was made through him"—it should therefore have recognized and accepted him. But no: "yet the world knew him not. He came into his own, and his own people did not receive him." Just as one slams the door in the face of an unwelcome strange bum, so goes it with divine Wisdom, with the divine Logos: one does not open oneself to him. Man does not know that he mediates being to the world; he is like a stranger with whom one does not have social intercourse. The words "he was the true light" (which do not go with v 8 at all) and "coming into the world" are so widely separated that "coming into the world" ($\dot{\epsilon}\rho\chi\dot{o}\mu\epsilon\nu o\nu$ $\epsilon\dot{\iota}s$ $\tau\dot{o}\nu$ $\kappa\dot{o}\sigma\mu o\nu$) is taken to refer to "every man," since in early Judaism "every one coming into the world" was synonymous with "every one." There is no cause to strike "man" ($\ddot{a}\nu\theta\rho\omega\pi o\nu$) with Bultmann,[53] since the result is not a verse with two emphases. On the other hand, there is no basis, in my opinion, for rejecting the whole of verse 9. Käsemann speaks of the interpretation of Ruckstuhl, according to which the Logos is the light of all men "inasmuch as their life of reason and will, i.e., all their natural spiritual activities, is produced by his working," and rejects this interpretation for the reason that verse 5b speaks "not only of not apprehending but of not comprehending."[54] But Käsemann himself gives no real explanation for the assertion of verse 9 that the Logos enlightens every man coming into the world. It is thus not surprising that he raises the question himself whether this verse is not finally an addition of the Evangelist, without telling us how we are then to understand it.[55] If verse 9 does concern the pre-incarnate Logos, then Ruckstuhl's interpretation is not so impossible, although it becomes inadequate the moment one understands the Logos as mediator of redemption. In that case, "enlightens" ($\phi\omega\tau\dot{\iota}\zeta\epsilon\iota$) must mean the proffering of the knowledge of salvation, as does "shines" ($\phi a\dot{\iota}\nu\epsilon\iota$) earlier in verse 5. The history of the text gives us no reason to eliminate the verse from the hymn altogether, and the combination of "light" ($\phi\hat{\omega}s$) in verse 5 and "true light" ($\phi\hat{\omega}s$ $\dot{a}\lambda\eta\theta\iota\nu\dot{o}\nu$) in verse 9 contains nothing suspicious. The

---

51 *Studien*, 45.

52 See the Introduction §3, "The Text of the Gospel of John."

53 *John*, 52 n. 2 [32 n. 6].

54 *New Testament Questions*, 143.

55 *New Testament Questions*, 151.

incarnation of the Logos makes it comprehensible that the comprehensive activity of the Logos and his complete rejection by the "world" (κόσμος), by "his own things" (τὰ ἴδια) or by "his own people" (οἱ ἴδιοι), are so strongly emphasized, as it is announced in verse 14. For the Logos did not give up in the face of this rejection. On the contrary, he now does the highest, the final, thing that was still possible: he becomes man himself, in order to be received by humankind.

■ **12** The two verses 12 and 13 do not go well with either verse 11 or verse 14. Occasionally, to be sure, the sharp contrast between "received not" (οὐ κατέλαβον) in verse 11 and "all who received" (ὅσοι δὲ ἔλαβον) is taken to be a specifically Johannine expression of the contrast between faith and lack of faith,[56] but the notion of a small number is not implied in "all who" (ὅσοι). That becomes evident by virtue of the fact that ὅσοι in the Gospel of John is almost always preceded by "all" (πάντες, πάντα). Otherwise, only "whoever" (ὅστις) would be involved; it is customarily combined with ἄν (a particle of mood) in the Gospel of John and in any case does not have the secondary sense of a small number.[57]

What does "received" (ἔλαβον) mean? This term can really only have the sense of "believe." That goes with what immediately follows: "who believed in his name." But if it is now said of the believers in verse 12b that to them "he gave power to become children of God," then another possibility appears to be indicated, one that goes beyond the status of the believers. The "children of God" would then be more than those who "believe in his name" (a community formulation that is used also in 2:23 and 3:18 and that appears in 1 John 3:23 and 5:13 as well). But the Gospel of John provides no suggestion of a grade of Christian beyond that of the simple believer. That means these expressions seem to have been piled up

without their having been thought through.[58]

■ **13** The generations of interpreters who have labored over this verse strengthen the impression that it, like verse 12, has not been thought through. It continues the description of those who believe in Jesus: they are born not of blood (αἱμάτων)[59] and not of the will of flesh nor of the will of man, but of God. Taken literally, these words express the virgin birth for all Christians. It is not therefore surprising that this verse has been made to refer to Jesus only by two minor alterations (ὅς instead of οἵ and ἐγεννήθη instead of ἐγεννήθησαν, i.e., by replacing the plural in each case with a singular). The weak and late attestation of this reading indicates that it was an attempt to correct the text.[60] The verse was probably intended to say simply that true Christians do not owe their existence as such to natural procreation, to any earthly conditions whatever.[61]

Understood in this way, there is nothing objectionable in this verse, precisely from the point of view of the Gospel of John—if it were connected to verse 14. Unfortunately, that is not the case. Verse 13 does not make it at all comprehensible that the Logos became flesh nor why it became flesh (σάρξ in this instance means "men," not as something hostile to God but as an entity qualitatively distinct from God). The redactor,[62] taking over the language of these verses, does not expect something impossible of Christians and is not asserting that they lack human parents. He only wishes to emphasize—again by piling up all possible expressions—that one does not become Christian by a natural process of procreation, but by virtue of an act of God, which alone can call man to true life. It is thus merely the awkwardness of the redactor that has caused theologians so much trouble. Precisely because he uses as many expressions as possible, without permitting the sense of these expressions to

---

56 Bauer, *Das Johannesevangelium*, 21, even interprets "all who" (ὅσοι) to imply: "one can count them."

57 Cf. 2:5, 8:25, 14:13, 15:16, 21:25.

58 Cf. Haenchen, "Probleme," 139.

59 Cf. Bultmann, *John*, 60 n. 2 [38 n. 2]: a Greek expression that appears as early as Euripides, *Ion*, 693: ἄλλων τραφεὶς ἐξ αἱμάτων = a son sprung from strange blood.

60 Cf. Schmid, "Joh 1,13," *BZ* 1 (1957) 118–25.

61 Haenchen came later to regard this meaning as a thought specifically characteristic of the Evangelist. That permits us to suppose that he would not have

attributed this insertion to the Evangelist, although he had earlier identified it as belonging to the redactor. [Editor]

62 The redactor is a "supplementer"; see further the end of Introduction §2, "The Dismantling of Ancient Johannine Tradition by Modern Criticism."

emerge cleary, has he created a riddle in this passage and forced interpreters to take refuge in the hypothesis that here the Evangelist is speaking "indirectly." Once one treats this passage as an insertion, the structure of the hymn emerges and the work of the redactor becomes evident.

■ **14** If verse 14 is connected with verse 11, these difficulties disappear. The author of the hymn could profess that the pre-incarnate Logos, who has heretofore been ineffective, has now undertaken a final act, of which neither paganism nor Judaism had the slightest premonition: the Logos seized a final possibility and has become like those that he has always intended to help. The weakness of Käsemann's proposal is that he (like others) does not understand the new as such and is thus not able to account for it. Bultmann, on the other hand, recognizes the fundamental shift in verse 14.[63] However, he is troubled by the difficulty that comes with his aim to explain the text "as a whole," not necessarily in its historical and literary evolution, but in its present form, including verses 6–8 and 12–13.

It is correct to say that the old Wisdom myth offers little material for this part of the hymn.[64] Käsemann thinks it especially significant that the style of the hymn changes with verse 14. That observation is correct. Our proposal takes that into account: the author of the hymn is now describing something that he did not derive from the old Wisdom tradition, but that the community itself had experienced. At any rate, connections and agreements are not entirely lacking. The term "dwelt" ($\grave{\epsilon}\sigma\kappa\dot{\eta}\nu\omega\sigma\epsilon\nu$)—the Logos pitched his tent in the midst of the human world—corresponds to the "live, dwell" ($\kappa\alpha\tau\epsilon\sigma\kappa\dot{\eta}\nu\omega\sigma\alpha$) of the wisdom myth: in Sir 24:8 it is said of Wisdom that it received a "dwelling" ($\sigma\kappa\dot{\eta}\nu\omega\mu\alpha$), a homestead, in Jacob. In 2 Cor 5:1 earthly existence is also spoken of as "the earthly tent we live in" ($o\grave{\iota}\kappa\dot{\iota}\alpha \ \tauo\hat{v} \ \sigma\kappa\dot{\eta}\nuo\upsilon\varsigma$), and in 5:4 it is referred to simply as "tent" ($\sigma\kappa\hat{\eta}\nuo\varsigma$). Moreover, the stylistic break is not as harsh as Käsemann would have us believe: the chain-like inter-

twining extends further. The word "glory" ($\delta\delta\xi\alpha$) in verse 14c is repeated in verse 14d; "full of" ($\pi\lambda\dot{\eta}\rho\eta\varsigma$) in 14 reappears in "fullness" ($\pi\lambda\dot{\eta}\rho\omega\mu\alpha$), verse 16; and "grace and truth" ($\chi\dot{\alpha}\rho\iota\varsigma \ \kappa\alpha\grave{\iota} \ \grave{\alpha}\lambda\dot{\eta}\theta\epsilon\iota\alpha$) in verse 14e appears a second time in verse 17. The reuse of earlier terms thus continues beyond verse 14, quite apart from the repetition of "only begotten" ($\mu o\nu o\gamma\epsilon\nu\dot{\eta}\varsigma$) and "Father" ($\pi\alpha\tau\dot{\eta}\rho$) in verses 14 and 18; verse 18 might not have belonged to the orignal hymn, but it has been assimilated to it stylistically. The author of the hymn therefore wishes to say that the Logos pitched his tent in the midst of the human world and took up his abode there: he became a man among men, a person among persons. Of course, he did not win all men to himself by so doing. The "we" that praises his deed is a Christian community.

How "the Logos becomes flesh" we do not of course learn. There is no parallel to the Pauline "he emptied himself" (Phil 2:7), and one is not simply to be imported into the Prologue[65] (although it does appear in John 17:5). In John 1:45, Jesus is designated the son of Joseph from Nazareth, and Philip, who makes the statement, is not corrected. There is no hint of a virgin birth. Evidently "how" the Logos became flesh did not concern the author (or the Evangelist).

The problems that lurk here are evident in the hymn in Phil 2:6ff. The danger of docetism in fact presents itself in the Philippians hymn, a problem that the Gospel of John avoids;[66] the expressions in the hymn in Philippians that signal the danger are: "in the likeness of men" ($\grave{\epsilon}\nu \ \grave{o}\mu o\iota\dot{\omega}\mu\alpha\tau\iota \ \grave{\alpha}\nu\theta\rho\dot{\omega}\pi\omega\nu$)[67] and "being found in human form" ($\sigma\chi\dot{\eta}\mu\alpha\tau\iota \ \epsilon\grave{\upsilon}\rho\eta\theta\epsilon\grave{\iota}\varsigma \ \grave{\omega}\varsigma \ \grave{\alpha}\nu\theta\rho\omega\pi o\varsigma$).

Of course, the question is how the author of the hymn understood the words "we have beheld his glory," and how they were conceived by the person who designed the gospel that is today customarily known as the "signs source" and who prefaced that gospel with this hymn. It is possible that they both understood "glory" ($\delta\delta\xi\alpha$) to refer to the miracles done by Jesus. In this passage, the same expression could have meant three different things

---

63 *John*, 60f. [38f.].
64 This remained the view of Haenchen, "Johanneische Probleme," 131.
65 Käsemann, *New Testament Questions*, 160; in this Käsemann is entirely correct.
66 Käsemann views the matter differently, *The Testament of Jesus*, 26.
67 Ἀνθρώπου is a meaningless variant; it is not meant to

indicate the station of the primal man, but simply the humanity of him who became flesh.

when employed by the three persons involved—the poet who composed the hymn, the author of the source of the Fourth Gospel, and the primary Evangelist himself.[68] We cannot make out how the poet who composed the hymn came to terms with the contrast between the Mosaic law and grace and truth. The contrast between "grace" ($\chi\acute{\alpha}\rho\iota\varsigma$) and "law" ($\nu\acute{o}\mu o\varsigma$) is alien to the Fourth Gospel; the word "grace" ($\chi\acute{\alpha}\rho\iota\varsigma$) appears only in 1:14 and 1:16f. The interpretation of the Gospel of John by Hirsch, in spite of many important observations, is therefore in error, since he makes this contrast his point of departure.[69]

The term "only begotten" ($\mu o\nu o\gamma \epsilon\nu\acute{\eta}\varsigma$), which appears first in John 1:14, means the only (and therefore especially beloved) son, who enjoys a privileged position. It is elaborated by the addition of "from the father" ($\pi \alpha\rho\grave{\alpha}$ $\pi \alpha\tau\rho\acute{o}\varsigma$), which in classical usage would indicate which side of the family is involved.[70] It is a necessary addition in this instance, since the simple genetive would have led to misunderstanding: "only begotten of the father" ($\mu o\nu o\gamma \epsilon\nu o\hat{\nu}\varsigma \pi \alpha\tau\rho\acute{o}\varsigma$) would apparently have referred to the "only father."

■ **15** Verse 15 breaks into the train of thought that is not resumed until verse 16; it introduces an unexpected word about the Baptist and a pronouncement by him. It is peculiar from a temporal perspective: "John bears witness to him and cries:[71] 'This is he of whom I have said, "The one who comes after me ranks before me, for he preceded me."'" This saying is best understood from the point of view that John has apparently been incorporated into the community; as a member of the community he is perpetually present. On the other hand, nothing was communicated by this saying prior to this point. "This was he" ($o\hat{\upsilon}\tau o\varsigma \hat{\eta}\nu$) recalls that the appearance of the Baptist belongs to the past. Apart from the verb ($\hat{\eta}\nu$), the saying has its closest parallel in John 1:30;

the expression "the one who comes after me" ($\acute{o}$ $\acute{o}\pi\acute{\iota}\sigma\omega$ $\mu o\upsilon$ $\acute{\epsilon}\rho\chi\acute{o}\mu\epsilon\nu o\varsigma$), however, appears earlier in 1:27. In this verse, the Baptist is subordinated to Jesus, without impinging on their harmony; there is no trace of a strong opposition to the disciples of the Baptist. John 1:15 is intended to show that the well-known prophecy of the Baptist has been fulfilled. The apparent disadvantage of Jesus that he began his work only after John had begun his is without force, since Jesus, who comes from eternity, always precedes and exceeds the Baptist. The "we" of the community and its witness is apparently to be further strengthened by having an apparent opponent of Jesus join in the chorus of witnesses for Jesus.

■ **16** The original train of thought is "For,[72] from his fullness have we all received, grace upon grace." The meaning of "upon" ($\acute{\alpha}\nu\tau\acute{\iota}$) is of course controversial. Bultmann[73] and Barrett[74] explain it by pointing to Philo, who uses the expression in the sense of "we are overwhelmed with grace again and again."[75] The community that speaks this way is conscious of living out of grace that is forever being renewed; that is explained by the $\acute{o}\tau\iota$-clause in verse 17.

■ **17** In this verse "grace and truth" are contrasted with the law that came into being through Moses in a way that does not appear elsewhere in the Gospels. Grace and truth have come through Jesus Christ. That is to be interpreted specifically: in Jesus grace has become visible and effective as a divine reality. Bultmann assumes that the hymn goes back to an Aramaic cultic hymn of the Baptist movement, and so contests that verse 17 belonged originally to the hymn and ascribes it to the Evangelist.[76] But Schnackenburg, who accepts the hypothesis that we have here a Christian hymn, surprisingly does not want to admit that the name of Christ appears in the hymn. Rather, he thinks verses 17f. are

---

68 Editor: and by the redactor?

69 *Das vierte Evangelium*, 101–6.

70 BDF §237(1).

71 Present perfect: BDF §341.

72 This $\acute{o}\tau\iota$ must not be omitted as secondary, as many exegetes do; it is explanatory of the phrase "we saw his glory," and of the expression "full of grace and truth."

73 *John*, 78 and n. 2 [53 and n. 1].

74 *John*, 168f.

75 *De post. Caini* 145: "and storing them [gifts] up for the future gives others in their stead [$\acute{\alpha}\nu\tau$' $\acute{\epsilon}\kappa\epsilon\acute{\iota}\nu\omega\nu$],

and a third supply to replace the second, and ever new in place of earlier boons, sometimes different in kind, sometimes the same." Tr. F. H. Colson, LCL, vol. 2.

76 *John*, 78f. [53].

additions of the Evangelist, because the name appears so abruptly here, as it does in 17:3.[77] But the solemn naming of the one sent from God in 17:3 does not prove that the name in 1:17 betrays the hand of the Evangelist. And one must certainly not invoke 1 John 1:3, 2:1, 3:23, 4:2, 15, 5:6, 20, as Schnackenburg does.[78] For in these passages, what is the high point of the hymn has become a set, ecclesiastical formula. "Style and content" do not suggest, as Schnackenburg thinks, that the Evangelist is speaking in the passage in question. To the contrary, it is the most natural thing in the world if the hymn closes with the name of the one it is praising.

■ **18** The naming of Jesus Christ in verse 17 has made it possible for the Evangelist to add the last verse of the Prologue as a transition to the "real" gospel, to scenes of the activity of the Baptist and Jesus, which begin with 1:19. Following what we have discussed earlier under the heading of "divine" and "God," one is led to expect "God" (ὁ θεός) here. But the Evangelist does not call Jesus "God"; the apparent exception in 20:28 is to be explained differently.[79] He therefore does not need to write "God" in this passage. That no one up to the present has seen God at any time (except the son) is reaffirmed in 5:37 and 6:46. God is not an entity in the world. His voice cannot be heard and man cannot catch sight of his form. For that we should be sad and glad at the same time. Glad, since otherwise God would be an object within the world, although perhaps an especially imposing one. But he would not be the one who could be the bread of life and the light of the world for us, but would himself require these things. Yet, at the same time, God's invisibility causes us much anxiety. For this thought constantly threatens to intrude upon us: this God that no one can see, whose existence one cannot demonstrate, would not exist at all. All talk of him would be merely mythological, a fantasy, pious poetry. It is therefore a great gift when he sends somebody who is not in our situation vis-à-vis God, but to whom God is accessible. The clause "who is in the bosom of the Father" (ὁ ὢν εἰς κόλπον τοῦ πατρός)[80] does not imply, as Käsemann, among others, interprets it,[81] that Jesus lies continually on the bosom of the Father in spite of the fact that he has become man and therefore his human form is in appearance only and thus a docetism. In support of a double existence of Jesus on earth and in heaven, Brown points to 3:13,[82] where Jesus speaks of himself as the Son of man "who is in heaven." But the attestation for the words "who is in heaven" is weak and late and might have been drawn from 1:18. Another elaboration of 3:13 is "he who is from heaven"; it is still more weakly attested. The participle ὤν ("being" = "who is") expresses the past since Greek has no special participial form for the past tense.[83] At the same time, however, the words of the community are meanwhile present (cf. 17:5) become future, where Jesus will again be at the side of the Father in the glory he once had (17:24). If the incarnation were only apparent, God would be invisible afterwards as before. There would be no place where we could see him. Johannine logic requires that he who has rested on the bosom of the Father and who has come to know him intimately has brought us a message. A docetic redeemer would make fools of us all.

This verse contains a very difficult textual problem: what is the correct form of the phrase? ℜ Θ *pl* latt sy [c] read "the only son" (ὁ μονογενὴς υἱός); 𝔓[75] ℵ[1] 33 Cl and the gnostics read "the only God" (ὁ μονογενὴς θεός); 𝔓[66] B C* L sy[p] Ir Or, however, have "only God" (μονογενὴς θεός). Hirsch proposes to derive all of these variants from an original ὁ μονογενής ("the only").[84] The text was elaborated in various ways so as to exclude a misinterpretation with reference to the gnostic Aeon. Schnackenburg does indeed think that is possible, but he finally decides in favor of "the only son" (ὁ μονογενὴς υἱός).[85] That may in fact be the best reading in view of the context.

Since the hymn casts a backward glance at the earthly life of Jesus, there is a abiding tension between the

---

77 *John*, 1: 276f.

78 *John*, 1: 276f.

79 See *ad loc.*

80 The preposition εἰς does not express direction, but is a hellenistic usage; in classical usage the phrase would be παρὰ τῷ.

81 *The Testament of Jesus*, 70.

82 *John*, 1: 276f.

83 Cf. the contrived form in Rev 1:4, 8, 4:8, 11:17, 16:5: ὁ ὢν καὶ ὁ ἦν.

84 *Studien*, 3.

85 *John*, 1: 278, 280.

"Prologue" and the narrative of the "gospel" which begins with 1:19: "Prologue" and Gospel overlap. But in distinction from Matthew and Luke, the "Prologue" does not fall into the category of infancy story.

Overview

The Johannine Prologue has been investigated with increasing intensity during the last one hundred years. It becomes ever more apparent that in this segment the most varied problems, which can be distinguished from each other only with the greatest difficulty, demand attention. It is striking that the Fourth Gospel begins with a prologue unlike anything known to the Synoptics. For, the mention of the Baptist in the Prologue (verses 6–8, 15) stems from a later hand. It was really a hymn directed to Jesus Christ, the Logos become flesh, the highest form of heavenly being after God. Harnack forced scholarship to inquire after the relationship of the Prologue to the rest of the Gospel.[86] His own answer went: the Prologue is intended to introduce the hellenistic reader to the Gospel. Dodd accepted this answer in his book of 1953.[87] Harnack took under consideration and then rejected a second answer: the Prologue is a summary of the Gospel; an English interpreter, Hoskyns, also decided for this view.[88] To these Käsemann objects: "The Prologue is therefore neither a summary of the Gospel nor a pedagogic introduction for the Hellenistic reader. . . . It bears witness to the presence of Christ . . . as the Creator of eschatological sonship to God and of the new world."[89]

The second question that the Prologue poses for modern scholarship concerns its position in the history of religions: is it to be approached through the OT? The simplest explanation based on an approach through the OT consists in accepting the view that the Logos is the personified "he says" ($\epsilon \hat{\iota} \pi \epsilon \nu$) of Gen 1:3, 6, 9, 11, 14, 20, 24, 26 (LXX). But it is alien to Jews to personify the "he says" ($\epsilon \hat{\iota} \pi \epsilon \nu$) in a hypostasis that is distinguished from God (see the Excursus).

A third question concerns the verses that were added at a later time. Brown gives the following list of scholars and what they accept (and reject) for comparative purposes:[90]

Bernard	1–5	10–11	14		18
Bultmann	1–5	9–12b	14	16	
De Ausejo	1–5	9–11	14	16	18
Gaechter	1–5	10–12	14	16	18
Green	1, 3–5	10–11	14a, d		18
Haenchen	1–5	9–11	14	16–17	
Käsemann	1, (2?), 3–5	10–12			
Schnackenburg	1, 3–4	9–11	14	16	

Brown himself decides for verses 1–5, 10–12b, 14, 16. He sees verses 12c–13 and 17–18 as later clarifying additions. The final redactor added 6–9 and 15.

Finally, Demke has designated a song of the "heavenly ones" (vv 1, 3–5, 10–12b), recited in a worship service in the community, and its response, the confession of the "earthly ones," of the congregation (vv 14, 16), as the source of the Evangelist, without telling us who the "heavenly ones" are.[91] We learn only that the "heavenly ones" are not the Logos or God.[92]

The question arises out of this juxtaposition of confusing and opposing opinions: is the Evangelist responsible for the problem? Or did he find the Prologue in this form, or is it the responsibility of a redactor? The Prologue takes on a different cast in relation to the way in which one attempts to solve these three problems. Two issues may serve to illustrate.

It is self-evident for Bultmann that verse 17 is not original, because he is reckoning with a hymn belonging to the community of the Baptist. Other scholars object to verse 17 on the grounds that the mention of Moses and Jesus Christ are not appropriate to the style, or that the mention of the Mosaic law weakens the mention of Christ's name. This verse is a part of the original hymn, in my judgment, although in other passages a redactor has inserted new information into the original text. Yet everyone agrees that the hymn has undergone expan-

---

86   "Über das Verhältnis des Prologs des vierten Evangeliums zum ganzen Werk," *ZTK* 2 (1892) 189–231.
87   *Interpretation of the Fourth Gospel*, 292–96.
88   *The Fourth Gospel*, ed. Francis Noel Davey (London: Faber and Faber, 1940, ²1947) 137.
89   *New Testament Questions*, 165.
90   Brown, *John*, 1: 122.
91   "Der sogenannte Logos-Hymnus im johanneischen Prolog," *ZNW* 58 (1967) 64.
92   "Der sogenannte Logos-Hymnus im johanneischen Prolog," *ZNW* 58 (1967) 61 n. 111.

sion. That prompts us to ask: how did this divergence arise?

On the other hand, Bultmann saw,[93] as did Heitmüller,[94] that the Prologue was an introduction in the sense of an overture to the Gospel, an overture that emphasized motifs from the Gospel, and that sought to stimulate the questions only in relation to which the Gospel could be understood. From the point of view of the history of religions, the Prologue belongs to the Baptist movement, which had been influenced by Gnosticism; Bultmann had developed this bold interpretation in his early writings.[95] He was able to draw upon the works of Reitzenstein and Lidzbarski. The works of Reitzenstein that were particularly important were: *Poimandres*; *Das mandäische Buch des Herrn der Größe und die Evangelien*; *Das Iranische Erlösungsmyterium*; and *Die Vorgeschichte der christlichen Taufe*. He drew upon the following works of Lidzbarski: *Das Johannesbuch der Mandäer*; *Mandäische Liturgien*; and *Ginzā: der Schatz oder das große Buch der Mandäer*.

Bultmann made full use of these sources in his great essay of 1925.[96] These sources strengthened his conviction "that the Mandeans arose as the baptismal sect that had its origin in the activity of John the Baptist along the Jordan." That is the only way of explaining that among the Mandeans "flowing water suitable for baptism" is called "Jardna" (=Jordan).[97] "The hatred for Judaism . . . and the relation to Jerusalem, the destruction of which functions as a sign of the final judgment" appeared to Bultmann to be explicable only if the Mandeans took their rise prior to the destruction of Jerusalem. Johannine Christianity represented an older type of Christianity than did the Synoptics. The appearance and proclamation of Jesus perhaps appear much stronger in the context of the gnostic baptist movement; the Jewish-Christian community known from the synoptic tradition may perhaps have been a judaizing reaction. The more original primitive Christian baptismal practice might have been more strongly inclined to hellenization than the primitive community. "We do not need to resort to mystical 'Easter complexes,' in order to understand the contexts of Palestinian and hellenistic Christianity. Naturally, all of this is to be understood as an hypothesis." Bultmann in fact modified even this hypothesis at many important points at a later time.

These presuppositions of Bultmann, which also incorporated his later perspectives, were threatened from the start. It is indeed probable that the Mandaeans were first a baptismal sect in the region east of the Jordan. But the identification of them with "the disciples of John" rested on an all too optimistic interpretation of the so-called Johannine book of the Mandeans. How difficult was the existence of a sect in the wilderness has only now been recognized by virtue of the excavations at Qumran. But John the Baptist has been connected with Qumran too hastily. His baptism was a sacrament of repentance once for all in view of the imminent end of the world.[98] There is no mention of repeated ritual washings therefore in the case of John. We have no indication that he founded a sect permanently located with him at the Jordan. The term "sect" is not to be used of those baptized by him, in the same sense as it applies to the community at Qumran: it has not been demonstrated that his disciples remained with him following their baptism. Nor is there evidence that the beheaded Baptist was honored at an early time as a divine being and was the object of hymns of praise. From the account in Acts 19:1–7 there is little to be gleaned beyond the fact that Luke appears to presuppose a one-time baptism practiced by disciples of John at that time, but nothing is said of repeated ritual baths. In the decade of the twenties, we had not yet gained a sense of how difficult it is to reconstruct an account of the itinerant Mandeans and of the influences to which they were exposed during this time until they finally found a miserable refuge in the marshy region of the Tigris and Euphrates.

Still missing at that time were the advances made by Lady Drower, R. Macuch, and K. Rudolph. Rudolph is

93   *John*, 24–31 [9–15].
94   "Das Evangelium des Johannes," 716.
95   See the bibliography for the Excursus on the pre-Johannine hymn, below.
96   "Die Bedeutung der neuerschlossenen mandäischen und manichäischen Quellen für das Verständnis des Johannesevangeliums," *ZNW* 24 (1925) 100–146. In his *Exegetica*, 55–104.
97   This article is now found in his *Exegetica*, 55–104.
98   Bultmann so interprets it as early as his *Jesus and the Word*, tr. Louise Pettibone Smith and Erminie Huntress Lantero (New York: Charles Scribner's Sons, 1958) 23ff.

of the opinion: "John did not found a real community." "The baptism of John and the figure of John must for once be interpreted completely without regard to any connection with the Mandeans."[99] Rudolph conjectures that "the roots of Mandean Gnosticism and a religion connected with baptism" are to be found "among the baptismal sects of the west central region." "Here Mandeanism took its primary shape under Syrian-gnostic, Iranian (especially Parthian), and partly Mesopotamian influence, on a Jewish base, and did so already in pre-Christian times. The migration to the east as a consequence of constant Jewish pressure must have followed in the second century CE (presumably in connection with the Bar Kochba revolution) . . ."[100] "John the Baptist and his entourage did not have any relationship to the Mandeans according to the sources available to us for examination."[101]

Macuch published an essay, entitled "Alter und Heimat des Mandäismus nach neuerschlossenen Quellen," already in 1957. Lady Drower had acquired a document from the Mandeans, *Diwan Haran Gawaita*, in which it says in lines 4–8: "The inner Haran has accepted him, that city, where the Nasoraeans are, because there was no access for the Jewish rulers. Artabanus was king over them. Therefore 60,000 Nasoraeans separated themselves from the sign of the seven (= planets) and went into the mountains of Media, a place where no tribes ruled over them. They then built the temple and lived in the vocation of life and in the power of the highest king of light until they came to the end." Macuch interprets this text as follows: Under the reign of King Artabanus III in Hauran, the Mandeans, under pressure from the Jews, escaped from Jewish influence about 37 CE and migrated from Palestine to Mesopotamia. In that case, the Mandaeans emigrated to Mesopotamia at a very early time. At this point, the story of the Mandeans grows hazy in the mists of the legendary.

According to Bultmann, the Evangelist himself was first a disciple of John before he became a Christian. He then reinterpreted an Aramaic hymn consisting of couplets to refer to Jesus Christ. However, that disturbed the inner unity of the hymn. The Evangelist did not understand that the hymn spoke first of the pre-incarnate Logos and only with verse 14 did it refer to the incarnate Logos. As a consequence, he took verse 5 to refer already to the incarnation and inserted the prosaic passage, found now in verses 6–8. Other interpretive glosses are also to be laid to his account.[102] Belonging to the hymn originally were only verses 1, 3–5, 9–12b, 14–16.[103] Verse 2 replaces a more mythological pronounced sentence of the source.

Käsemann subjected all this to a thorough-going critique and came up with an entirely different reading of the Prologue.[104] He praised Bultmann for interpreting verse 5 as referring to the Logos incarnate. But the (Christian) hymn consisted only of verses 1, (2?), 3f., and 5, and (9?) 10–12. The Evangelist provided the hymn with an epilogue in verses 14–18, in which verse 14a, as the transitional sentence, takes up what has already been expressed. The real purpose of the incarnation is to make God present; the Logos is always designated as the creator, although the hymn clearly enough refers to him only as the mediator. We must now consider all these questions further.

Each of the four canonical Gospels begins at the point at which its author took the story of salvation to begin.[105] For Mark that lay in the appearance of John the Baptist. Luke proceeds in a different manner: Luke 1:1–4 is a literary proemium, which reports on the tradition, on his predecessors, and on his own purpose. Only then does the author return to the customary beginning point, which has been enriched, however, by the narration of the marvelous infancy stories of John the Baptist and Jesus. Matthew, on the other hand, traces the genealogy of Jesus back to Abraham and so connects the OT with the NT history of salvation. The so-called Prologue of the Gospel of John goes far beyond these possibilities

99 *Die Mandäer*, 1: 73.

100 *Die Mandäer*, 1 251.

101 *Die Mandäer*, 1: 80.

102 *John*, 16 [3f.].

103 *John*, 16–18 [3–5].

104 *New Testament Questions*, 139–44.

105 Cf. Wikenhauser, *Das Evangelium nach Johannes*, 40 and Barrett, *John*, 149.

in reverting to the primordial beginning in Gen 1:1. Of course, he also leaves even this beginning far behind. For, according to John 1:1, the Logos existed already before all creation in the presence of God. Since the Logos was already there before the creation (cf. John 17: 5, 24), he did not belong among the things created. The Gospel of John thus opens with a "heavenly prelude." The evident effort to locate the commencement of the history of salvation at an ever earlier date and thus finally to embrace everything has reached its final goal in this prelude. However, it is not simply a matter of an abstract extension of this history "backwards" until it reaches its ultimate limits, through which the community would be confident that from the outset its place in God's plan of salvation had been anticipated and provided for. In this way, rather, Jesus Christ, whom the community honors as its lord, comes into view in another dimension of his work, as it were, a dimension that, up to this point, has not become evident. The trends are thereby plotted for the development of christology over the next few centuries.

Verses 1–18, viewed formally—we propose to set verses 6–8, 12f., and 15 aside provisionally—form a hymn dedicated to a heavenly being, who became man on our behalf. This hymn has parallels in Col 1:15–20 and Phil 2:6–11; 1 Cor 13 is also an early Christian hymn that differs in theme, to be sure. These hymns were not written in two or three member verses, but in a kind of rhythmical prose.

The hymns in Colossians and Philippians tell of a heavenly being, like John 1:1–17, who has come down to earth for the redemption of humankind. The heavenly being that is called the Logos in John 1:1, 14 is connected with the Gospel proper in 1:18; for its part, the Gospel proper now opens with John the Baptist.

Certain clues make it probable that this hymn existed originally as an independent entity, although not in its present form. Those clues include:

1. The diction: the Logos appears in the Gospel of John only in 1:1 and 1:14, and never after that. The concepts "full, fullness" ($\pi\lambda\acute{\eta}\rho\eta\varsigma$, $\pi\lambda\acute{\eta}\rho\omega\mu\alpha$) are used only in 1:14 and 1:16. The contrast between the Mosaic law and the grace that came through Jesus Christ is met only in 1:17. The word "grace" ($\chi\acute{\alpha}\rho\iota\varsigma$) is found in the Gospel of John only in 1:14, 16f. This examination indicates that the Prologue makes use of a set of concepts that is independent of the Gospel.

2. John 1:1–17 is also formally distinguished from the balance of the Gospel. These verses are not constructed in accordance with the strict requirements of meter (the careful construction of 1:1 is not repeated), but on the order of free verse. These are interspersed, of course, with prose insertions by another hand (vv 6–8, 12f., 15), as indicated above in the detailed commentary. One can call the rhythmical part of the Prologue a hymn, in which the community celebrates its lord.

3. The Prologue extends from the existence of the Logos prior to the creation of the world to his activity as a man. However, the Prologue is not joined to what follows without seam; it overlaps with the story of the Baptist (which begins in 1:19).

4. The transitional verse, 1:18, connects the Prologue with the Gospel as a whole.

Bultmann has rightly emphasized that "the figure of Wisdom, which is found in late Judaism, and also in the OT itself, does seem to be related to the Logos-figure in the Johannine Prologue."[106] More recent scholarship, however, has rejected Bultmann's view that the original hymn was non-Christian and has come to the conviction that we have a hymn of the Christian community before us.[107] It treats the appearance of Jesus Christ on earth. But the (unknown) author of this hymn viewed the appearance of Jesus Christ on earth as the concluding event in a long, miraculous story, which had its beginning in eternity.

The author, in my judgment, went back to a Wisdom tradition for the first part of the hymn, a tradition known in various forms in late Judaism. The oldest pertinent form known to us is in Enoch 42:1ff. This form could even go back to a still earlier, non-Jewish form (in this conjecture we concur with Bultmann): according to this version, the feminine consort and assistant of the primal god, his "Thought" or $\check{\epsilon}\nu\nu\sigma\iota\alpha$, brought forth the creation in accordance with his will. This conception was not gnostic. The world did not arise by virtue of a power hostile to God, as in dualistic systems of Gnosticism.

---

106 *John*, 22 [8].
107 Käsemann, *New Testament Questions*, 141f.; Schnackenburg, *John*, 1: 230f.; Brown, *John* 1: 21; Haenchen, "Das Evangelium und sein Kommentar," 209–314.

Accordingly, there is no explicit mention of a primal fall. But bitter experience showed again and again that humankind did not know how properly to engage the world created by the divine Thought. The form of the Wisdom tradition in Enoch 42:2 corresponds to this view: "Wisdom went forth to make her dwelling place among the children of men;/And found no dwelling place:/Wisdom returned to her place,/ And took her seat among the angels."[108] This version is a lament full of melancholy over the maliciousness of humankind that does not grant Wisdom a space in which to dwell.

A different, presumably later kind of Wisdom tradition in early Judaism is found expressed in Sir 24:2–24: Wisdom came forth from the mouth of the Most High and wandered vainly through the whole earth seeking a place of rest. Then the Creator finally gave her a permanent abiding place in Israel. In this fashion, Judaism appropriated that melancholy lament about homeless Wisdom for itself and thereby transformed the expression of lamentation into that of pride. For, the Wisdom that became at home in Judaism was nothing other than the Torah, the "instruction" or the Law, that Israel had received from its God and according to whose wise commandments it ordered its life. Billerbeck calls attention to numerous sayings of the rabbis on the Law in which the Law is identified with Wisdom.[109] Kittel remarks: "The Rabbis increasingly, and from an early period, identified wisdom with the Torah."[110]

This hymn to Wisdom also found a place in the Christian understanding of things. Here we may ignore the allusions to Wisdom found in the Synoptics (Luke 7:35, Matt 11:19, Luke 11:49, 13:34, Matt 23: 24–46) and in Paul (1 Cor 1:21–24, Rom 1:19f.) and in which Jesus is more or less identified with Wisdom. Only the author of the Prologue actually made use of the figure of Wisdom by taking it over as the basis for the first half of the hymn. Of course, Wisdom ($\sigma o \phi \acute{\iota} a$) as a feminine form could not then be identified with the figure that subsequently becomes man. There is evidence, however, especially in Philo, that the form of the Logos was virtually identical in substance with that of Wisdom. For Philo, the Logos was the highest of the Powers ($\delta \upsilon \nu \acute{a} \mu \epsilon \iota \varsigma$) of God, which sometimes appear as relatively independent powers, and sometimes as mere aspects of God; it almost appears as if the later Kabbalistic doctrine of the Sefiroth were being anticipated.[111] Philo of course conceives of the Logos (which he occasionally calls "divine" [$\theta \epsilon \acute{o} \varsigma$], but never "God" [$\acute{o} \theta \epsilon \acute{o} \varsigma$]) as the highest angel and as the highest idea at the same time (occasionally even as a "second god" [$\delta \epsilon \acute{\upsilon} \tau \epsilon \rho o \varsigma \theta \epsilon \acute{o} \varsigma$]). Here OT, Platonic, and Stoic concepts come together in a bewildering unity. Thus, for the author of the Prologue, the Logos, which was already an agent in the creation, could appear in the place of Wisdom, which in Judaism could be represented as mediator of the creation. The destiny of the Logos was thus borrowed entirely from that of Wisdom. The world created through the Logos was not intended to know him, as verses 3–5, 9–11 indicate. If one may designate the position of the Logos at this stage of his history with an expression of the later church, one can speak here of the (futile) activity of the pre-incarnate Logos, of the Logos not yet become flesh. The term Logos, which is basically not translatable into German or English, approximates the significance of the heavenly Wisdom.

Like the underlying hymn to Wisdom, the author refuses to depict a "fall of man." That interest would have diverted him from the configuration he wanted to depict. He was therefore content with two facts: (1) The All or universe was brought into being by God through the agent of creation, and (2) the human world closed its mind to everything to which it was indebted. The Logos found himself in the position of a light that shone in the darkness. It was not his fault that things came to the pass they did: he was the true light that enlightens every man who comes into the world. Consequently, in verse 4 it says: "In him was life, and the life was the light of man." Since the life is identified with light in the second part of the verse, it cannot refer to the animal, the physical life. It must rather be a matter of the divine vitality, which the Logos possesses and can transmit. It must be the life of the Spirit. On this basis, it is possible to understand that it can be identified with the light of man. Yet it cannot be the light of human reason. It must be a higher light: the light of the knowledge of God.

It was precisely this gift of which the Logos was not relieved, as the much debated verse 5 shows. Many

108 Tr. R. H. Charles, *APOT*.
109 Billerbeck, 2: 353–58; 3: 126–33.
110 *TDNT* 4: 136.

111 Cf. Gershom G. Scholem, *Major Trends in Jewish Mysticism* (New York: Schocken Books, 1946) 212–21.

exegetes, from ancient times to Käsemann,[112] have thought to find in this verse a depiction of how the Logos became flesh. What can be adduced in support of this view—in addition to the numerous exegetes who so understand it—is merely the present tense: "And the light shines in the darkness," which is of course immediately superceded by an aorist: "and the darkness has not comprehended it." Now it is indeed extremely common for a light to shine in the darkness; one does not light a light on a bright day. But this common experience is employed in verse 5 in order to indicate something more profound: the Logos offers this light to the darkness. But the darkness makes no use of it. Verse 9 appears to support this interpretation: "He was the true light, which enlightens everyone who comes into the world." The present tense of "enlightens" (φωτίζει) corresponds precisely to the words "shines" (φαίνει) in verse 5. The point of course is not that the Logos gives reason to everyone who is born. Rather, now as earlier, the light has to do with "knowledge of God." In that case, "enlightens" cannot imply that the light really enlightens everyone. The light can shine and shine, but man is able to close himself off to that knowledge of God.

It is evident that what is involved is not a single event, but an event that is repeated ever and again: the present tense in verse 9 expresses this repetition, this duration. That the Logos incarnate is not at work here is beyond dispute. It is a fundamental mistake, from a purely grammatical perspective, to confuse the imperfect in verse 9 ("he was," ἦν) with the aorist in verse 14 ("And the Logos became flesh"). The subject of the hymn in verses 5, 9–11 is the Logos not yet become flesh. But the pre-incarnate Logos was not received. The human world, which owes its existence to him, did not recognize him (in v 10 the neuter becomes masculine). He was an unwelcome stranger, whom one turns away at the door. His own received him not.

Up to this point, the representation is determined by the old hymn to Wisdom. Now, however, there is something to be said that was unknown to the resignation of the old pagan story and to the Jewish praise of Wisdom in the Torah: the Logos neither returns to heaven nor becomes a book; rather, he becomes man. An entirely palpable man, who pitches his tent among "us" (the community that proclaims him)[113] and whose glory we beheld. His glory was a glory like the beloved son of the Father (God) has. He possesses a character that can be described with the words "grace and truth" (truth means divine reality). The grace and truth of the Logos incarnate is not rejected, unlike the light of the pre-incarnate Logos in verses 10f.: "For, from his fullness we have all received, grace upon grace." This statement is amplified by setting it over against its counterpart: "For the law was given through Moses; grace and truth came through Jesus Christ." The Christian hymn comes to a close with this explicit reference, finally, to the name of him who became flesh. Verse 18 connects the hymn to the Gospel that follows: No one has ever seen God—God is not visible for man and eludes his perceptive powers. "The only Son, who is in the bosom of the Father, alone has made him known." The Logos becoming flesh and the gospel go together. In verse 18, the earthly activity of Jesus ("he has made known," ἐξηγήσατο) is combined with the heavenly reality of the "only son" (μονογενὴς υἱός).

It is now time to return to verses 6–8, 12f., and 15, which we temporarily bracketed out. We may begin with verses 6–8, which most modern interpreters regard as a later addition. These verses describe the sending and mission of the Baptist. As in the Synoptics, one really ought to speak first of John the Baptist as forerunner, and only then of his confirmation candidate, Jesus. To this order there corresponds, in John 1, the two sections, verses 19–28, in which the central role is played by the Baptist, and verses 29–51, where Jesus takes center stage. This agrees precisely with the synoptic order. Yet verses 1–4 speak clearly of the Logos, which, as the pre-incarnate Logos (to use the categories of later doctrine), precedes the Logos incarnate. So long as the hymn was used in relation to its own context, there was no need to mention the Baptist. His mention would even have disturbed and disrupted the hymn. The situation is changed, however, when the hymn is employed as an introduction to the Gospel. In that case, the Baptist would no longer represent the beginning; the Logos would (vv 1–17); the Baptist is the subject of verses 19–

---

112 *New Testament Questions*, 144.
113 This feature could stem from the picture of Wisdom. See above, on verse 14.

28, Jesus of verses 29ff. That means, however, that two different sketches have been superimposed: the first begins in eternity and leads through the Logos becoming flesh to the contemporary community. In this version, the fate of the Logos is the real theme; there is no place in this sketch for the Baptist. The second sketch is different: in this version, the activity begins on earth, as it were, at the Jordan with the Baptist, and then passes over to Jesus. If one uses the hymn as an introduction to the Gospel, there arises a tension between these two outlines. This permits us to detect that the hymn does not come to an end before the Gospel "proper," but is projected beyond the Gospel into the time of the congregation that is celebrating the return of Jesus to heaven, where he is once again with the Father. One could say that in a certain sense the hymn encompasses the entire Gospel that it serves to introduce.

The second sketch, which probably corresponds to verses 19–51, is the older. It remains entirely in the realm of the earthly: it begins with the Baptist, whom the Jews interrogate about whether he is the Expected One, and then makes the transition to Jesus; there is always a certain distance between John and Jesus, so that there is really no place for a baptism, only for an announcement. And, as this section is presented to us, it is not old; the Baptist defers humbly to Jesus, at whom he may only look and to whom he may only bear witness. If one may use a modern phrase in this connection, that is a defamiliarization of the old tradition.

Whoever inserted verses 6–8 into the Logos hymn no longer understood the contexts just discussed. He did not see that the Baptist has become superfluous in this Prologue, that the decisive transition from the story of the Baptist to the story of Jesus no longer transpires, but that the leap is from eternity into time, as verse 14 depicts it. Because the lack of reference to the Baptist in the Prologue struck him as an error, he felt compelled to rectify the omission by the addition of verses 6–8. And, of course, he did not reinstate the order of events that he had in mind. He then had to accept the view that verse 5 describes the appearance of Jesus, who could only "really" come after John, the forerunner. And everyone, from the Church Fathers to Ernst Käsemann, who does not comprehend the meaning and structure of the hymn and who therefore thinks he finds a reference to the incarnation of Jesus in verse 5, inevitably comes to grief on the allegedly completed form of the Prologue.

The redactor who added these verses understood, of course, that the baptism could not come in the Prologue, and that therefore the Baptist could only be described as a witness, in accordance with the subsequent representation in verses 19–51, through whom everyone would of course be led to faith in Jesus. This corresponds to the picture sketched in Mal 4:5f.: "Behold, I will send you Elijah the prophet before the great and terrible day of the Lord comes. And he will turn the hearts of fathers to their children and the hearts of children to their fathers . . ." But the redactor did not understand that the activity of the pre-incarnate Logos was further described in verses 9–11, but now made these verses refer to the Logos become flesh, too. In that case, the insertion does not suit the context: the Logos incarnate, the Galilean Jesus, did not experience only rejection.

The redactor or "supplementer" was thus compelled to make a second addition: verses 12f. Not everyone—this is the way the redactor thinks (he corrects by supplementing since he does not dare strike anything)—has rejected Jesus; he has indeed gathered a community who has accepted him. Of this community he now asserts: (a) Jesus gave the members of the community power to become children of God; (b) they believe in his name (a favorite expression in the Christian community); (c) the members were born not of blood nor of the will of flesh nor of the will of man, but of God. That is not to be taken to mean that they all owe their existence to a virgin birth, but to a new birth from God (3:3)—the last redactor was thinking of Christian baptism in this connection. The consequence of this insertion is that verse 14, strictly speaking, now becomes meaningless: the insertion presupposes what is first expressed in the hymn in verse 14b, in different terms, to be sure. And it causes the incarnation in verse 14a to come too late, after Jesus has already begun to work.

This now applies also to the third passage in which the redactor makes an insertion: verse 15. It is evident that this verse disrupts the context: "full of grace and truth" ($\pi\lambda\eta\rho\eta\varsigma$ $\chi\alpha\rho\iota\tau\sigma\varsigma$ $\kappa\alpha\iota$ $\alpha\lambda\eta\theta\epsilon\iota\alpha\varsigma$) is clearly continued by "For, from his fullness . . ." ($\delta\tau\iota$ $\epsilon\kappa$ $\tau\sigma\hat{\upsilon}$ $\pi\lambda\eta\rho\dot{\omega}\mu\alpha\tau\sigma\varsigma$ . . .). In addition to the fact that it interrupts the context, verse 15 is also puzzling by virtue of the fact that the present tense, "John bears witness, . . ." is followed by the past tense: "This was he of whom I said." If, however, one considers the intention of the redactor, all three puzzles are solved at the same time. The testimony of John belongs, for the redactor, to the testimony of the community. For that reason, he puts it in the present tense: "John bears witness and cries"; but this testimony in the present is to be distinguished from the earlier words of the Baptist. For the redactor, the words of John and the entire earthly life of Jesus lie in the past. Consequently, he cannot say: "This is he of whom, . . ." as he does in verse 30, but: "This was he of whom I said." The way in which the Baptist is here incorporated into the Christian community contrasts with the view of the Evangelist: the redactor can treat the Baptist impartially in a more positive manner.[114] That he thereby breaks the connection between verses 14 and 16 would not be so bad, were it not also for the fact that in so doing he also obscures a second item: the chain-like connection of the verses with each other does not come to an end with verse 12; this feature of the hymn reasserts itself and shows that the hymn continues.

We should now take one final glance back along the path we have followed. We have taken as our point of departure the assumption that we share with many others, viz., that the Fourth Gospel began with a hymn. But in the long run we could not accept Bultmann's view that this hymn is a translation of an Aramaic text, whose lines, each consisting of two emphatic words, orginally were written in praise of the Baptist. Too much violence is required to put the text into this form, and the gnostic hymn to the Baptist is lost, for us, along with the Aramaic version consisting of couplets. In its place we have, in concert with Käsemann and Schnackenburg, a Christian hymn before us. But we must also finally part company with them. For we think that they, too, require too much of this Christian hymn: verses of identical length, although strophes of two lines and some of three members are now also accepted. But we recall that the other early Christian hymns known to us are comparable rather to the free rhythm of Hölderlin: constructions

with wonderful rhythm, but no strophes of the sort found in the Choruses of Greek tragedy; expressions on each occasion following their own structure and each line its own length, without, however, collapsing into the formlessness of colloquial prose. It was not difficult to discover—it was indeed long ago discovered—that the first half of the hymn makes use of material from an old myth of Wisdom, in which Wisdom wanders in vain through every land. It was once a sad pagan myth full of grief about this chaotic world, which has no place for Wisdom. Then the hymn was taken over by Judaism and put in the service of the Torah: the Torah is Wisdom, which has now found a resting place in Israel. But now the Christian hymn could attribute fresh purpose to this pointless wandering of Wisdom or now, rather, of the Logos: the Logos became man and discovered a believing community, whose praise constitutes the second strophe, full of joy at the grace and truth to be found here. While prior to this time, there was only the law given through Moses, there is now grace and truth through Jesus Christ. Since he who connected the hymn with the Gospel following portrayed Jesus Christ as the one who truly announces the presence of the unseen Father, he combined the hymn with the narrative of that announcement.

We come to the last problem that the Prologue presents to us. The hymn to Wisdom that is used in the Prologue provided an expression for early christology. It taught that God's agent in creation, the Logos, had long sought a hearing among men, but in vain. The Christian hymn then showed that this Logos, undiscouraged, having become man, founded his community, which received grace upon grace from him. Verse 18, the transitional verse, indicates that the Logos brought news of the God whom no one had ever seen and thereby establishes the authority and reliability of the following narrative. The hymn and the Prologue say nothing of the death and resurrection of Jesus. Precisely for that reason is it suitable as a foreword to the story of the

---

114 Editor: In his last version (s. the commentary on verse 14) Haenchen reckoned with a more complicated history of the tradition than he reflected in his essay, "Probleme des johanneischen Prologs." The redactor could now also have been the author of the source of the Fourth Gospel, i.e., the so-called "Signs Source." But since he does not express himself unequivocally in any of the many revised versions following the appearance of the essay referred to above, the question must remain open. One may assume as the point of departure that he attributes verses 6–8 and verse 15 to the redactor. Verses 12 and 13, like verse 18, could, however, stem from the Evangelist.

earthly life of Jesus, at whose end it is then possible to speak of the death and resurrection of Jesus.

This hymn to Christ was not the only hymn that the young movement possessed and with which it indicated the mystery of the form of Christ. Each hymn in Col 1:15–20 and Phil 2:6–11 contains in its second half the apocalyptic counterpart to the primordial existence of the heavenly being that became man; this apocalyptic counterpart is lacking in the Prologue to the Gospel of John and not by chance. For in this Gospel it is the encounter with the message of Jesus on each occasion that now consitutes the decision regarding salvation and judgment.

According to 1:14, this encounter is possible only because the heavenly being has been transmuted into human existence. The insignificant word "became" ($\dot{\epsilon}\gamma\acute{\epsilon}\nu\epsilon\tau o$) describes this transmutation and confronts us with the mystery that determined the development of christological and trinitarian doctrine in the ancient church. The "parallel" hymns in Philippians and Colossians are each placed in a new environment, which thereby colors their meaning. In Philippians, for example, the hymn appears clearly in a paraenetical context and underscores obedience and service as characteristics of the Christian posture. Here, in the Prologue to the Gospel of John, there is no such reference. For that reason, the mystery of the incarnation—the $\mu\epsilon\tau\acute{a}\beta a\sigma\iota\varsigma$ $\epsilon\grave{\iota}\varsigma$ $\ddot{a}\lambda\lambda o$ $\gamma\acute{\epsilon}\nu o\varsigma$—especially stands out.

If one is of the opinion, like Käsemann in his recent work, *The Testament of Jesus*, that the Fourth Evangelist was not only exposed to the danger of docetism, but fell prey to a naive and therefore not yet mature and basically unacknowledged form of docetism, so that for him the label "unreflected docetism" is apt, then of course no such thing as a transmutation from one form to another ($\epsilon\grave{\iota}\varsigma$ $\ddot{a}\lambda\lambda o$ $\gamma\acute{\epsilon}\nu o\varsigma$) follows, and incarnation and exaltation merely means "a change of location"; in that case, Jesus would be the God who walks on the face of the earth, as Käsemann repeatedly asserts.[115] But John 17:5 contains the petition of Jesus to the Father to glorify him with the glory that he possessed in the presence of the Father before the foundation of the world. This one who has become man thus did not possess this glory in his present state. As a consequence, his prayer to the Father in chapter 17 is not to be interpreted as a "naive docetism" any more than is Jesus' death on the cross. The Gospel of John thus in its own way teaches a kind of kenosis, which is connected with this heavenly being becoming man.

Whether the Gospel of John was as "naive" as it appears to many interpreters is dubious, although the reflection of the Evangelist in 1:14 is not ostentatious. After all, 1:45 speaks of "Jesus, the son of Joseph from Nazareth," without this statement later being corrected. There is no hint of a virgin birth in the Gospel of John, such as Matthew and Luke relate in various forms. That might lead to the conclusion that the full humanity of Jesus is consistently expressed, while in Matthew and Luke that is not the case. One ought therefore to stop and reflect before calling the Gospel of John "gnosticizing."

Of course, that transmutation "into another genus" ($\epsilon\grave{\iota}\varsigma$ $\ddot{a}\lambda\lambda o$ $\gamma\acute{\epsilon}\nu o\varsigma$) has become all the clearer, yet the Prologue does not betray how the Evangelist understood it. Was such a "transmutation" not as incredible for the Evangelist and his time as it is for us? Against that view it can be said: all the history of religions parallels that one can adduce know nothing of the Logos becoming flesh in the form of a particular, actual man. The doctrine of the spirit in the Gospel of John, as it is indicated in the farewell discourses, points, however, to the way in which the Evangelist engaged this question.

---

115 *The Testament of Jesus*, 8f., 66, etc.

Bibliography

Aall, A.
Der Logos. Geschichte seiner Entwickelgung in der griechischen Philosophie und der christlichen Literatur, 2 vols. Vol. 1, *Geschichte der Logosidee in der griechischen Philosophie;* Vol. 2, *Geschichte der Logosidee in der christlichen Literatur* (Leipzig: O. R. Reisland, 1896 and 1899).

Ballenstedt, Heinrich Christian
Philo und Johannes; oder, Neue philosophisch-kritische Untersuchung des Logos beym Johannes nach dem Philo, nebst einer Erklärung und Uebersetzung des ersten Briefes Johannes aus der geweiheten Sprache der Hierophanten, 3 vols. (Braunschweig: F. B. Culemann, 1802).

Ballenstedt, Heinrich Christian
Philo und Johannes; oder, Fortgesetzte Anwendung des Philo zur Interpretation der Johanneischen Schriften; mit besonderer Hinsicht auf die Frage: ob Johannes der Verfasser der ihm zugeschriebenen Bücher seyn könne? (Göttingen: H. Dieterich, 1812).

Bormann, K.
"Die Ideen-und Logoslehre Philons von Alexandrien." Dissertation, Köln, 1955.

Bousset, Wilhelm
Kyrios Christos. A History of the Belief in Christ from the Beginnings of Christianity to Irenaeus, tr. John E. Steely (Nashville: Abingdon Press, 1970), esp. 385–99 = *Kyrios Christos. Geschichte des Christusglaubens von den Anfängen des Christentums bis Irenaeus* (Göttingen: Vandenhoeck & Ruprecht, [5]1965), esp. 304–16.

Bréhier, Emile
Les idées philosophiques et religieuses de Philon d'Alexandrie. (Paris: A. Picard & Fils, 1907; Librairie philosophique J. Vrin, [2]1925).

Bultmann, Rudolf
"The Concept of the Word of God in the New Testament." In his *Faith and Understanding* 1, ed. Robert W. Funk; tr. Louise Pettibone Smith (London: SCM Press, 1969) 286–312 = "Der Begriff des Wortes Gottes im Neuen Testament." In his *Glauben und Verstehen: Gesammelte Aufsätze* 1 (Tübingen: Mohr-Siebeck, [6]1966) 268–93.

Bultmann, Rudolf
"Untersuchungen zum Johannesevangelium." *ZNW* 29 (1930) 169–92. In his *Exegetica: Aufsätze zur Erforschung des Neuen Testaments,* ed. Erich Dinkler (Tübingen: Mohr-Siebeck, 1967) 124–97.

Bultmann, Rudolf
Jesus and the Word, tr. Louise Pettibone Smith and Erminie Huntress Lantero (New York: Charles Scribner's Sons, 1958).

Bultmann, Rudolf
"Der religionsgeschichtliche Hintergrund des

Prolegs zum Johannes-Evangelium." In his *Exegetica: Aufsätze zur Erforschung des Neuen Testaments,* ed. Erich Dinkler (Tübingen: Mohr-Siebeck, 1967) 10–35.

Bultmann, Rudolf
"Die Bedeutung der neuerschlossenen mandäischen und manichäischen Quellen für das Verständnis des Johannesevangeliums." *ZNW* 24 (1925) 100-146. In his *Exegetica: Aufsätze zur Erforschung des Neuen Testaments,* ed. Erich Dinkler (Tübingen: Mohr-Siebeck, 1967) 55–104.

Clark, G. H.
The Johannine Logos, An International Library of Philosophy and Theology, Biblical and Theological Studies (Nutley, NJ: Presbyterian & Reformed, 1972).

Cohn, Leopold
"Zur Lehre vom Logos bei Philo." In *Judaica. Festschrift zu Hermann Cohens siebzigstem Geburtstag* (Berlin: Bruno Cassirer, 1912) 303–31.

Colpe, Carsten
Die religionsgeschichtliche Schule. Darstellung und Kritik ihres Bildes vom gnostischen Erlösermythus, FRLANT, n.s., 60 (Göttingen: Vandenhoeck & Ruprecht, 1961).

Conzelmann, Hans
"Die Mutter der Weisheit." In his *Theologie als Schriftauslegung. Aufsätze zum Neuen Testament,* BEvT 65 (Munich: Chr. Kaiser Verlag, 1974) 167–76. Also in *Zeit und Geschichte. Dankesgabe an Rudolf Bultmann zum 80. Geburtstag im Auftrage der Alten Marburger und in Zusammenarbeit mit Hartwig Thyen,* ed. Erich Dinkler (Tübingen: Mohr-Siebeck, 1964) 225–34.

Daniélou, Jean
Philon d'Alexandrie (Paris: A. Fayard, 1958).

Dillon, John M.
The Middle Platonist. A Study of Platonism, 80 B. C. to A. D. 220 (London: Duckworth, 1977).

Dix, G. H.
"The Heavenly Wisdom and the Divine Logos in Jewish Apocalyptic." *JTS* 26 (1924/1925) 1–12.

Dürr, L.
Die Wertung des göttlichen Wortes im Alten Testament und im antiken Orient, zugleich ein Beitrag zur Vorgeschichte des neutestamentlichen Logosbegriffes, MVAG 42,1 (Leipzig: J. C. Hinrichs, 1938).

Epp, Eldon Jay
"Wisdom, Torah, Word: The Johannine Prologue and the Purpose of the Fourth Gospel." In *Current Issues in Biblical and Patristic Interpretation: Studies in Honor of Merrill C. Tenney Presented by his Former Students,* ed. Gerald F. Hawthorne (Grand Rapids: Wm. B. Eerdmans, 1975) 128–46.

Fascher, Erich
"Vom Logos des Heraklit und dem Logos des Johannes." In his *Frage und Antwort. Studien zur Theologie und Religionsgeschichte* (Berlin: Evangelische Verlagsanstalt, 1968) 117–33.

Fascher, Erich
"Der Logos-Christus als göttlicher Lehrer bei Clemens von Alexandrien." In *Studien zum Neues Testament und zur Patristik, Erich Klostermann zum 90. Geburtstag dargebracht,* TU 77 (Berlin: Akademie-Verlag, 1961) 193–207.

Goldberg, A. M.
Untersuchungen über die Vorstellung von der Schekhinah in der frühen rabbinischen Literatur—Talmud und Midrash, Studia Judaica 5 (Berlin: Walter de Gruyter, 1969).

Goodenough, Erwin Ramsdell
By Light, Light. The Mystic Gospel of Hellenistic Judaism (New Haven: Yale University Press, 1935 ²1969).

Greiff-Marienburg, A.
"Platons Weltseele und das Johannesevangelium." *ZKT* 52 (1928) 519–31.

Grether, O.
Name und Wort Gottes im Alten Testament (Giessen: A. Töpelmann, 1934).

Hadidan, Yervant H.
"Philonism in the Fourth Gospel." In *The Macdonald Presentation Volume, a Tribute to Duncan Black Macdonald, consisting of articles by his former students, presented to him on his seventieth birthday, April 9, 1933* (Princeton: Princeton University Press, 1933) 211–22.

Haenchen, Ernst
"Aufbau und Theologie des Poimandres." In his *Gott und Mensch. Gesammelte Aufsätze* 1 (Tübingen: Mohr-Siebeck, 1965) 335–77, esp. paragraphs 5 and 9.

Hamerton-Kelly, Robert G.
Pre-existence, Wisdom, and the Son of Man. A Study of the Idea of Pre-existence in the New Testament, SNTSMS 21 (New York: Cambridge University Press, 1973).

Hamp, Vinzenz
Der Begriff "Wort" in den aramäischen Bibelübersetzungen. Ein exegetischer Beitrag zur Hypostasen-Frage und zur Geschichte der Logos-Spekulationen (Munich: Neuer Filser-Verlag, 1938).

Harris, J. Rendel
"Athena, Sophia, and the Logos." *BJRL* 7 (1922/1923) 56–72.

Harris, J. Rendel
"The Origin of the Prologue to St. John's Gospel." *Expositor,* 8th ser., 12 (1916) 147–60, 161–70, 314–20, 388–400, 415–26.

Harris, J. Rendel
"Stoic Origin of the Fourth Gospel." *BJRL* 6 (1921/1922) 439–51.

Hayward, Robert
Divine Name and Presence: The Memra (Totowa, NJ: Allanheld, Osmun, 1981).

Hayward, Robert
"Memra and Shekhina: A Short Note." *JJS* 31 (1980) 210–13.

Hegermann, Harald
Die Vorstellung vom Schöpfungsmittler im hellenist-ischen Judentum und Urchristentum, TU 82 (Berlin: Akademie-Verlag, 1961).

Heinemann, Isaak
Philons griechische und jüdische Bildung. Kulturver-gleichende Untersuchungen zu Philons Darstellung der jüdischen Gesetze (Breslau: M. & H. Marcus, 1932).

Heinisch, P.
Personifikationen und Hypostasen im AT und Alten Orient (Münster: Aschendorff, 1921).

Heinrici, C. F. Georg
Die Hermesmystik und das Neue Testament, Arbeiten zur Religionsgeschichte des Urchristentums 1,1 (Leipzig: J. C. Hinrichs, 1918).

Heinze, M.
Die Lehre vom Logos in der griechischen Philosophie (Oldenburg: F. Schmidt, 1872).

Hellwag, J.
"Die Vorstellung von der Präexistenz Christi in der ältesten Kirche." *Theologische Jahrbücher* 7 (Tübingen, 1848) 144–61, 227–63.

Holtzmann, Heinrich Julius
"Der Logos und der eingeborene Gottessohn im 4. Evangelium." *ZWT* 36 (1893) 385–406.

Jendorff, B.
Der Logosbegriff. Seine philosophische Grundlegung bei Heraklit von Ephesos und seine theologische Indienst-nahme durch Johannes den Evangelisten, Europäische Hochschulschriften, Series 20; Philosophie 19 (Frankfurt and Bern: P. Lang, 1976).

Jeremias, Joachim
"Zum Logos-Problem." *ZNW* 59 (1968) 82–85.

Jervell, Jacob
Imago Dei. Gen 1, 26f. im Spätjudentum, in der Gnosis und in den paulinischen Briefen, FRLANT, n.s., 58 (Göttingen: Vandenhoeck & Ruprecht, 1960), esp. 52–70.

Jonas, Hans
Gnosis und spätantiker Geist, 2 vols. Vol. 1, *Die Mythologische Gnosis*, FRLANT, n.s., 33 (Göttingen: Vandenhoeck & Ruprecht, 1934); Vol. 2, *Von der Mythologie zur mystischen Philosophie*, FRLANT, n.s., 45 (Göttingen: Vandenhoeck & Ruprecht, 1954), esp. 2: 44–49, 70–121.

Kahn, C. H.
"Stoic Logic and Stoic Logos." *Archiv für Geschichte der Philosophie* 51 (1969) 158–72.

Kanavalli, P. S.
"The Concept of Logos in the Writings of John and Justin." Dissertation, Munich, 1969.

Keferstein, Friedrich
Philos Lehre von den göttlichen Mittelwesen. Zugleich eine kurze Darstellung der Grundzüge des philonischen Systems (Leipzig: W. Jurany, 1846).

Kleinknecht, Hermann
"Logos." *TDNT* 4: 77–91.

Koschorke, Klaus
"Eine gnostische Paraphrase des johanneischen Prologs." *VC* 33 (1979) 383–92.

Krebs, Engelbert Gustav Hans
Der Logos als Heiland im ersten Jahrhundert; ein religions- und dogmengeschichtlicher Beitrag zur Erlö-sungslehre. Mit einem Anhang: Poimandres und Johannes; kritisches Referat über Reitzensteins religions-geschichtliche Logosstudien (Freiburg: Herder, 1910).

Kroll, Josef
Die Lehren des Hermes Trismegistos (Münster, i.W: Aschendorff, 1914), esp. 55ff.

Küchler, Max
Frühjüdische Weisheitstraditionen. Zum Fortgang weisheitlichen Denkens im Bereich des frühjüdischen Jahweglaubens, OBO 26 (Fribourg: Universitäts-verlag; Göttingen: Vandenhoeck & Ruprecht, 1979).

Lagrange, Marie-Joseph
"Vers le logos de saint Jean." *RB* 32 (1923) 161–84, 321–71.

Langkammer, H.
"Zur Herkunft des Logostitels im Johannes-prolog." *BZ* 9 (1965) 91–94.

Leisegang, H.
"Logos." PW 13.1 (1926) 1035–81.

Lidzbarski, Mark, ed.
Das Johannesbuch der Mandäer, 2 vols. in 1 (Giessen: A. Töpelmann, 1905–1915).

Lidzbarski, Mark, ed. and tr.
Ginza; Der Schatz oder das Große Buch der Mandäer, Quellen der Religionsgeschichte 13 (Göttingen: Vandenhoeck & Ruprecht; Leipzig: J. C. Hinrichs, 1925).

Lidzbarski, Mark, tr.
Mandäische Liturgien, Abhandlungen der könig-lichen Gesellschaft der Wissenschaften zu Göttingen, Philologisch-historische Klasse, 17/1 (Berlin: Weidmann, 1920).

Lieske, A.
Die Theologie der Logosmystik bei Origenes, Münster-ische Beiträge zur Theologie 22 (Münster i.W: Aschendorff, 1938).

Long, A. A., ed.
Problems in Stoicism (London: University of London, The Athlone Press, 1971).

Lovelady, E. J.
"The Logos-Concept of John 1,1." *Grace Journal* 4:2 (1963) 15–24.

Mack, Burton L.
Logos und Sophia: Untersuchungen zur Weisheits-theologie im hellenistischen Judentum, SUNT 10 (Göttingen: Vandenhoeck & Ruprecht, 1973).

Macuch, R.
"Alter und Heimat des Mandäismus nach neuer-schlossenen Quellen." *TLZ* 82 (1957) 401–8.

Macuch, R.
"Anfänger der Mandäer." In *Die Araber in der Alten Welt*, ed. F. Altheim and R. Stiehl (Berlin: Walter de Gruyter, 1965) 76–190, esp. 107–9.

Martens, R. F.
"The Prologue of the Gospel of John: An Examination of its Origin and Emphasis." Dissertation, Concordia Seminary in Exile, 1974.

McNamara, Martin
"*Logos* of the Fourth Gospel and *Memra* of the Palestinian Targum (Ex 12:42)." *ExpTim* 79 (1968) 115–17.

Meyer, Heinrich
Die mandäische Lehre vom göttlichen Gesandten mit einem Ausblick auf ihr Verhältnis zur johanneischen Christologie (Breklum: Jensen, 1929). Partial publication of "Mandäische und johanneische Soteriologie." Dissertation, Kiel, 1929.

Middleton, R. D.
"Logos and Shekina in the Fourth Gospel." *JQR* 29 (1938/1939) 101–33.

Miller, E. L.
"The Logos of Heraclitus: Updating the Report." *HTR* 74 (1981) 161–76.

Moeller, H. B.
"Wisdom Motifs and John's Gospel." *Bulletin of the Evangelical Theological Society* 6 (1963) 92–100.

Moore, George Foot
"Intermediaries in Jewish Theology: Memra, Shekinah, Metatron." *HTR* 15 (1922) 41–85.

Mühl, M.
"Der λόγος ἐνδιάθετος und προφορικος von der älteren Stoa bis zur Synode von Sirmium 351." *Archiv für Begriffsgeschichte* 7 (1962) 7–56, esp. 33–43.

Mühlenberg, Ekkehard
"Das Problem der Offenbarung in Philo von Alexandrien." *ZNW* 64 (1973) 1–18.

Niedner, Christian Wilhelm
"De subsistentia τῷ θείῳ λόγῳ apud Philonem Judaeum et Joannem Apostolum tributa." *ZHT* 11 (1849) 337–81.

Odeberg, Hugo
The Fourth Gospel. Interpreted in its Relation to Contemporaneous Religious Currents in Palestine and the Hellenistic-Oriental World (Uppsala: Almqvist & Wiksells, 1929; reprint Amsterdam: B. R. Grüner; Chicago: Argonaut, 1968).

Paul, Ludwig
"Ueber die Logoslehre bei Justin Martyr. Artikel II." *Jahrbücher für Protestantische Theologie* 17 (1891) 124–48.

Pollard, T. E.
"Logos and Son in Origen, Arius and Athanasios." *Studia Patristica* 2 (1957) 282–87.

Prümm, K.
Der christliche Glaube und die altheidnische Welt. Vol. 1, *Der religionsgeschichtliche Hintergrund des johanneischen Logos* (Leipzig: J. Hegner, 1935), esp. 227–52.

Pulver, M.
"Die Lichterfahrung im Johannesevangelium, im Corpus Hermeticum, in der Gnosis und der Ost-

kirche." *ErJb* 10 (1943) 253–96.

Reitzenstein, R., and H. H. Schaeder
Studien zum antiken Synkretismus aus Iran und Griechenland (Leipzig: B. G. Teubner, 1926; reprint Darmstadt: Wissenschaftliche Buchgesellschaft, 1965), esp. 69–103.

Reitzenstein, Richard
Poimandres. Studien zur griechisch-ägyptischen und frühchristlichen Literatur (Leipzig: B. G. Teubner, 1904; reprint Stuttgart: B. G. Teubner, 1966).

Reitzenstein, Richard
Das mandäische Buch des Herrn der Grösse und die Evangelien, SHAW.PH 12 (Heidelberg: Carl Winter, 1919).

Reitzenstein, Richard
Die Göttin Psyche in der hellenistischen und frühchristlichen Literatur, SHAW.PH 10 (Heidelberg: Carl Winter, 1917).

Reitzenstein, Richard
Das iranische Erlösungsmysterium (Bonn: A Marcus & E. Weber, 1921).

Reitzenstein, Richard
Die Vorgeschichte der christlichen Taufe (Leipzig: B. G. Teubner, 1929).

Réville, Jean
La doctrine du logos dans le quatrième Evangile et dans les oeuvres de Philon (Paris: G. Fischbacher, 1881).

Ringgren, Helmer
Word and Wisdom. Studies in the hypostatization of divine qualities and functions in the ancient Near East (Lund: Olssons boktr, 1947).

Robinson, James M.
"Sethians and Johannine Thought: The *Trimorphic Protennoia* and the Prologue of the Gospel of John." In *The Rediscovery of Gnosticism,* 2 vols., ed. Bentley Layton. Studies in the History of Religions [Supplement to *Numen*] 41. Vol. 1, *The School of Valentinus;* Vol. 2, *Sethian Gnosticism.* (Leiden: E. J. Brill, 1980–1981) 643–62.

Rudolph, Kurt
Die Mandäer, 2 vols. Vol. 1, *Prolegomena: Das Mandäerproblem,* FRLANT, n.s., 56 (Göttingen: Vandenhoeck & Ruprecht, 1960); Vol. 2, *Der Kult,* FRLANT, n.s., 57 (Göttingen: Vandenhoeck & Ruprecht, 1961).

Schaeder, Hans Heinrich
"Der 'Mensch' im Prolog des IV. Evangeliums." In *Studien zum antiken Synkretismus aus Iran und Griechenland,* ed. H. H. Schaeder and R. Reitzenstein (Leipzig: B. G. Teubner, 1926; reprint Darmstadt: Wissenschaftliche Buchgesellschaft, 1965) 306–50.

Schencke, Wilhelm
"Die 'Chokma' (Sophia) in der jüdischen Hypostasenspekulation: ein Beitrag zur Geschichte der religiösen Ideen in Zeitalter des Hellenismus." In *Videnskapsselskapets skrifter* 2: *Hist.-filos. Klasse,* 1912, no. 6 (Kristiana: Dybwad, 1913).

Schimanowski, G.
"Präexistenz und Christologie. Untersuchungen zur Präexistenz von Weisheit und Messias in der jüdischen Tradition." Dissertation, Tübingen, 1981.

Scholem, Gershom Gerhard
Major Trends in Jewish Mysticism (New York: Schocken, 1946).

Schulz, Siegfried
"Die Bedeutung neuer Gnosisfunde für die neu-testamentliche Wissenschaft." *TRu* 26 (1960) 209–66, 301–34 (esp. with reference to Lady Drower).

Siegfried, Carl
Philo von Alexandrien (Jena: H. Dufft, 1875), esp. 219–29.

Soulier, Henry
La doctrine du Logos chez Philon d'Alexandrie (Turin: V. Bona, 1876).

Stemberger, Günter
"'Er kam in sein Eigentum.' Das Johannes-evangelium im Dialog mit der Gnosis." *Wort und Wahrheit* 28 (1973) 435–52.

Strachan, Robert Harvey
The Fourth Gospel. Its Significance and Environment (London: SCM Press, ³1941) 90–96.

Thomas, J.
Le mouvement baptiste en Palestine et Syrie (150 av. J.-C.–300 ap. J.-C.) (Gembloux: Duculot, 1935).

Thyen, Hartwig
"Die Probleme der neueren Philo-Forschung." *TRu* 23 (1955/56) 230–46.

Urbach, Efraim Elimelech
The Sages, their Concepts and Beliefs, tr. Israel Abrahams (Jerusalem: Magnes Press, Hebrew University, 1973), esp. 1: 37–65.

Völker, W.
"Heracleons Stellung zu seiner Zeit im Lichte seiner Schriftauslegung." Dissertation, Halle, 1923.

Wennemer, Karl
"Theologie des 'Wortes' im Johannesevangelium. Das innere Verhältnis des verkündigten *logos theou* zum persönlichen *Logos*." *Scholastik* 38 (1963) 1–17.

Wolfson, Harry Austin
Philo. Foundations of Religious Philosophy in Judaism, Christianity, and Islam, 2 vols. (Cambridge: Harvard University Press, ²1948).

Yamauchi, Edwin M.
"Jewish Gnosticism? The Prologue of John, Mandean Parallels and the Trimorphic Proten-noia." In Festschrift G. Quispel (Leiden: E. J. Brill, 1981) 467–97.

Yamauchi, Edwin M.
"The Present Status of Mandaean Studies." *JNES* 25 (1966) 88–96.

Zeller, Eduard
Die Philosophie der Griechen in ihrer geschichtlichen Entwicklung, 3 vols. (Leipzig: O. R. Reisland, 1903–1922), esp. 3,2: 417–34.

The Johannine Prologue was never easy reading, not even when one took the Apostle John to be the author. But the difficulties began to multiply when historical criticism arose and the history of religions began its detailed comparisons. Zahn's commentary on the Gospel of John is a good example of the defensive posture vis-à-vis the history of religions method and its results.[1] Zahn was convinced that John, the son of Zebedee, was the author of the Fourth Gospel and its Prologue. Zahn sharply rejected the history of religions explanation of the Prologue (Philonic doctrine of the Logos; the doctrine of Wisdom in late Judaism):[2] "The step ladder on which the Evangelist is supposed to have climbed up to his alleged doctrine of the Logos, according to a hypothesis which is never quite defunct, lacks not only the rungs, but has no foundation on which to rest; it hangs in the air and ends in fog."[3] . . . "Christ as a human, as a person appearing in the world is . . . the word of God per se, therefore the perfect word, which God has spoken to the world."[4] But

"John does not fasten onto the title of Logos as though this were more than a human attempt to express succinctly what God has given to mankind by sending his son."[5] Two things escape Zahn's notice. First, the Prologue uses the term Logos only of the being that has not yet become man. Secondly, if "Logos" is only a "human attempt," then so is "Son of God." It follows that it could be a severe obstacle for Zahn if the hellenistic or late Jewish expressions in Philo about God and his Logos—as human expressions—turn out to be as valuable as the biblical categories.

Just how dangerous it is to reject the history of religions approach to the Prologue is indicated in a similar way in the work of Hirsch.[6] One ought not to ask the Evangelist: "What do you think about all the other ideas that men at that time have expressed about the divine word of creation, about the Stoic philosophical doctrine of the World Reason (logos), which is the order of the world . . . and about the speculations peculiar to Jewish

1 *Das Evangelium des Johannes.*
2 *Das Evangelium des Johannes,* 100ff.
3 *Das Evangelium des Johannes,* 104.
4 *Das Evangelium des Johannes,* 108.
5 *Das Evangelium des Johannes,* 109.
6 *Das vierte Evangelium,* 103ff.

theologians regarding the word, speculations that make the Jewish bible more palatable to the tastes of pagan speculation? He gives no answers to such questions." Of course he doesn't answer such questions. The answers to such questions in a history of religions context can only be inferred in retrospect from the text itself, and it is possible to do so. Hirsch explains "in the beginning" ($\dot{\epsilon}\nu$ $\dot{\alpha}\rho\chi\hat{\eta}$) as follows: "The author wants . . . to say: in Jesus the first day of creation dawns miraculously over us once again." Hirsch thereby forgets, as does Zahn, that there is no reference to the Logos become flesh in 1:1, only to the pre-incarnate Logos. In place of the "orthodox" interpretation of Zahn, there appears a pietistic expression that is alien to the Prologue. Instead of advancing explanations that are alien to the text, it is therefore worthwhile to take a short detour so as not to exclude the history of religions "parallels" from consideration without further ado.

We are then presented with a new task. We must attempt to determine more precisely the locus of this hymn in the history of religions.

It seems to be clear that an exposition of the segment treating the Logos should take this word as its point of departure and seek to establish the meaning of the term in this passage. It has long been taken for granted that its meaning goes inseparably together with its provenance. The attempt is often made to derive the Logos in the Johannine Prologue from the OT, or from Greek philosophy, or, finally, from early Judaism or Gnosticism. Bultmann has performed the service of clarifying the situation on most points.[7] He has spoken out against the earlier popular supposition that the Johannine Logos is the "he said" ($\epsilon\hat{\iota}\pi\epsilon\nu$, וַיֹּאמֶר), become a person, in the creation narrative of the LXX. In the first place, there is no mention of the creation in John 1:1f. In the second place, Judaism never took that "and God said" ($\epsilon\hat{\iota}\pi\epsilon\nu$) as a person standing alongside God. The designation in the Talmud מֵימְרָא (= word) always appears as the *Memra* of Yahweh or of Adonai. To be sure, the word of God is occasionally poetically personified in the OT (e.g. LXX Ps 32:6 [33:6]: "By the word of the Lord the heavens were made, and all their host by the breath of his mouth"; Ps 106:20 [107:20]: "He sent forth his word,

and healed them").[8] Wis 18:15f. (LXX) goes the furthest in this direction: "Thy all-powerful word leaped from heaven, from the royal throne, into the midst of the land that was doomed, a stern warrior carrying the sharp sword of thy authentic command, and stood and filled all things with death, and touched heaven while standing on earth." In this passage, of course, it is not God's creative word that is being depicted, but his curse, which brings the plagues on the Egyptians. For that purpose a terrible angel of vengeance is useful—but only as a poetic figure. The Logos of John 1:1 is patently of a very different sort.

This use of Logos is no more to be understood on the basis of Hellenism than it is out of the OT or the Targums. As H. Kleinknecht demonstrates,[9] the word logos was assigned a surprisingly large number of meanings in Hellenism. We propose to adduce only the most important. Etymologically logos has the basic meaning of "gathering" and "gleaning" in the selective sense. As a mental activity, it was first of all used in the sense of "counting" or "reckoning." Since the critical and the counting nuances resonate together in the term, logos acquires the sense of "enumerating, narrative, speech, language, sentence, word"; then it also means the subject matter that appears in speech. From logos as "account, reckoning, result of reckoning" comes the meaning in a more metaphysical sense of: "principle, law, or reason," and, on the other side, as an economic or commercial term: "cash account, account." Finally, as a mathematical concept logos connotes: "proportion, relation," and thus the rational relation of things to each other, the sense, the order, the measure. Conceived subjectively, it has the meaning of man's ability to think, human reason, the spirit, ideas, since the time of Democritus. It is impossible to represent this full range of meaning in a single German word (in the masculine gender, since that's what logos is in Greek) or in a single English term. But it does not stop here. Heraclitus also uses the term in the sense of revelation as the pointing out of something that man ought to recognize and understand, as the power of the insight with which man understands himself and his place in the world, in which a logos, a recognizable law, prevails, which now also becomes the norm of life. In Hellenism the term designates, as Kleinknecht further indi-

---

7   *John*, 20–31 [6–14].

8   Also cf. Ps 32:4 [33:4], 147:4, 7 [147:15, 18]; Isa 40:8, 55:11.

9   *TDNT* 4: 77–91.

cates, the order and meaning of the world, the cosmic law of reason, and thus also the principle that creates the world. As the "cosmic law" (λόγος ὀρθός)—the world may have a "law" (νόμος) just as individuals may have a law—it gives men the power of knowledge. Logos received its loftiest meaning in Stoicism: it is the world reason that orders the event, with which the reason of individual men concurs (if they follow their rational selves). This logos, which does not exist alongside matter or above it but is matter's principle of order, has nothing in common with John 1:1.

Neither Hermes[10] nor the Egyptian god Toth have anything to do with John 1:1, although they are once designated as word. They stand in the twilight of personified concepts in which many traditions are intermingled. Neoplatonism likewise developed a doctrine of the Logos, according to which the Logos is a shaping power that gives form and life to things and is thus connected with "form" (μορφή) and "life" (ζωή). About the logos in Philo and the mystery religions something will be said later. Although the hellenistic concept of the logos is reminiscent of the Johannine Logos in certain respects, the two remain very deeply divided: it is impossible on the hellenistic view for the logos to become an individual person.

All this goes to show that neither the OT nor Hellenism provides the key for understanding the Johannine concept of the Logos.

Bultmann has pointed to a further possibility, viz., to Gnosticism, insofar as its original dualistic system is taken into account, and to the systems of Neopythagoreanism and Neoplatonism, which belong to the Greek tradition and which hold more tenaciously to the unity of the world.[11]

In both the Greek and the gnostic systems, the Logos appears as an intermediary between God and the world. This intermediary is intended to make comprehensible how it was possible for a (material) world to arise in the face of a fully transcendent deity. The man to whom this thought appeals feels that he is a stranger in the world, that he really belongs to the divine realm of light.[12] Since the Logos is the basis not only for the existence of mortal souls in the world, but also for their deliverance, he is not only creator, but also savior, σωτήρ. In contrast to the Stoic doctrine of the Logos, here the Logos does not permit man to be incorporated into the world, but prompts him to be separated from the world and to find his true home in the domain beyond this world. In a certain sense the Logos thereby annuls the act by which the world arose; it amounts to a kind of eschatology as the self-dissolution of the world.[13] The Logos descends into the material world in human form; his mortal body deceives the demonic world powers. He is identified with Jesus in Christian-gnostic systems of thought. But, according to Bultmann, the idea of the redeemer becoming man has not "in some way penetrated Gnosticism from Christianity; it is itself originally Gnostic, and was taken over at a very early stage by Christianity, and made fruitful for Christology."

"This figure appears under different names. . . . It is called δεύτερος θεός ['second god'], υἱὸς θεοῦ ['son of god'], μονογενής ['only begotten'], εἰκὼν τοῦ θεοῦ ['image of god'], occasionally δημιουργός ['demiurge'], and is also termed Ἄνθρωπος, ['archetypal man']. But almost without exception" it is also called Logos, although νοῦς (reason) may take its place, "especially in the philosophical authors." "This figure appears as a mythological person in Gnosticism proper," often, of course, "attenuated or divided" into several entities, whereby occasionally "the Redeemer, who has become man (in Jesus), is distinguished from the cosmic Logos."[14] The basic ideas of this view of the Logos are found from the first century onwards "in both the religio-philosophical literature of Hellenism . . . and in the Christian Gnostic sources."[15] Furthermore, Bultmann invokes Ignatius, the Odes of Solomon, and the Mandean writings. But Bultmann asserts "that decisive ideas of the Gnostic myth—

---

10 Cf. the book of J. Kroll, *Die Lehren des Hermes Trismegistos* (Munster: Aschendorff, 1914) 55ff. which has meanwhile been surpassed; also see my essay, "Aufbau und Theologie des Poimandres," in *Gott und Mensch. Gesammelte Aufsätze* 1 (Tübingen: Mohr-Siebeck, 1967) 335–77, especially sections 5 and 9.

11 *John*, 24–31 [9–15].

12 Cf. H. Jonas, *Gnosis und spätantiker Geist*. Vol. 2, *Von der Mythologie zur mystischen Philosophie*, FRLANT, n.s., 45 (Göttingen: Vandenhoeck & Ruprecht, 1954), esp. 44–49, 70–121.

13 Cf. especially the *Treatise on Resurrection* found among the Nag Hammadi documents.

14 *John*, 26f. [10f.].

15 *John*, 27 [11].

and in particular the idea of the intermediary, that mediates divine powers to the world—are of pre-gnostic origin"[16] and are intended to explain the rise and structure of the world.[17] Gnosticism in its dualistic form probably first took up the figure of the intermediary, according to Bultmann,[18] and transformed it for its own purposes. Christianity took up the idea of the soteriological intermediary, as it was finally worked out; this is the case already in Paul (Rom 5:12ff.; 1 Cor 15:43f.). The source used by the Fourth Gospel belonged to early oriental Gnosticism, which had not reflected on the origin of the world that was hostile to god (the idea of the primordial fall does not appear), but which, in the Odes of Solomon, was modified owing to the OT belief in God.[19] There is no speculation regarding the egress of the Logos from the Father; the conceptual meaning of the word logos as "word" has become unclear.[20] A pre-existence of the souls of men and of their belonging to a unity with a Being of Light (archetypal man) is not mentioned. But, according to Bultmann, there are traces of that to be found in John 3:4.[21] The Johannine Logos is both creator and revealer; the world is understood as darkness that is hostile to God in its actual condition.[22]

In view of this intelligence, it is a question whether one ought not to strike out on a different course, one that does not take the concept of the Logos as its point of departure, but begins with the ideas of the Prologue (though this may also be contested). Bultmann has already emphasized that "the figure of Wisdom, which is found in Judaism, and also in the OT itself, does seem to be related to the Logos-figure in the Johannine Prologue."[23] One must of course observe in this connection that the Wisdom myth (the one that Philo knew already) has a history of its own. In one form, it treats of a feminine consort of the Primal God,[24] to whom the creation is attributed, either directly or indirectly. According to Prov 8:22ff. God formed ($\check{\epsilon}\kappa\tau\iota\sigma\epsilon\nu$) Wisdom before the creation, or even begot ($\gamma\epsilon\nu\nu\hat{q}$) it. She was his craftsman ($\dot{\alpha}\rho\mu\acute{o}\zeta o\upsilon\sigma a$) at his side. As a skilled workman ($\tau\epsilon\chi\nu\hat{\iota}\tau\iota s$) she has taught man (Wis 7:21); she is a particle of divine power, a reflection of the invisible light (7:25). God created all things through the Logos and formed man through Wisdom (9:1f.). Ben Sirach says something similar (Sir 1:4, 24:3ff.).[25] The Isis-aretology probably offers the closest model for this. But Judaism and the Isis cult probably took over an older myth. But in view of the fact that man did not know what to do with the world that was created good, the myth was modified and assumed the form we find in Enoch 42:1: When Wisdom found no dwelling place among men, she returned to heaven and took her place among the angels. In this older form the myth had a ring of melancholy, a sense of resignation: divine Wisdom had created the world, but men wanted nothing to do with such Wisdom. For that reason, life became as miserable as we know it to be. Judaism was of course not satisfied with this doctrine of Wisdom: it was believed that Wisdom itself was to be discerned in the Torah. Jesus Sirach accordingly interprets the story as follows (24:2–22): Wisdom, who came forth from the mouth of the Most High, wandered in vain through the whole earth looking for a resting place. But then the Creator gave her a permanent dwelling

16 *John*, 27 [11f.].
17 Bultmann, *John*, 27 [11], appeals to Reitzenstein, *Studien zum antiken Synkretismus aus Iran und Griechenland* (Leipzig: B. G. Teubner; reprint Darmstadt: Wissenschaftliche Buchgesellschaft, 1965) 69–103, in support of this view. But cf. C. Colpe, *Die religionsgeschichtliche Schule. Darstellung und Kritik ihres Bildes vom gnostischen Erlösermythus*, FRLANT, n.s., 60 (Göttingen: Vandenhoeck & Ruprecht, 1961).
18 *John*, 28 [12].
19 *John*, 29 [13].
20 *John*, 29 [13f.].
21 *John*, 30 [14].
22 *John*, 31 [15].
23 *John*, 22f. [8f.].
24 Known to us from Gnosticism, but also from Philo, *Leg. All.* 2.49, *De ebr.* 30, *De Virt.* 2.62.
25 On this cf. Conzelmann, "Die Mutter der Weisheit," in his *Theologie als Schriftauslegung. Aufsätze zum Neuen Testament*, BEvT 65 (Munich: Chr. Kaiser Verlag, 1974) 167–76. Also in *Zeit und Geschichte. Dankesgabe an Rudolf Bultmann zum 80. Geburtstag im Auftrage der Alten Marburger und in Zusammenarbeit mit Hartwig Thyen*, ed. E. Dinkler (Tübingen: Mohr-Siebeck, 1964) 228ff.

place in Israel: Wisdom now makes her home in Israel and in the Torah.

Scholars have long failed to recognize that the first half of the Prologue is not only quite similar to the Wisdom myth, it even borrows from it, albeit it in modified form. This failure occurred for various reasons. In the first place, in verses 1 and 14 it is not Wisdom that is spoken of, but the Logos. Secondly, the two Jewish variations of the Wisdom myth do not appear to parallel the first half of the hymn closely with respect to content. Thirdly, misled by the gnostic interpretation and its consequent punctuation, scholars have not perceived the structure of the Christian hymn and have made its true sense undecipherable by virture of allegedly necessary additions. Finally, the question has not been asked why the author of the Christian hymn—who was not the Evangelist—had any reason at all to borrow from the hymn to Wisdom.

With respect to the first point: it is clear that it was not possible to speak of Wisdom ($\sigma o \phi \iota a$) becoming man in Jesus (although Paul once refers to Christ in 1 Cor 1:24 as "the power of God and the wisdom of God"): Wisdom was always represented as God's female partner. Fortunately, however, there was a male counterpart to Wisdom: the Logos. The Logos played a role quite comparable to that of Wisdom, for example, in the thought of Philo (which was drawn from many sources) and could therefore readily appear in her place. The Logos soon appears as the highest of the divine powers ($\delta v v \acute{a} \mu \epsilon \iota s$)— the powers could represent various aspects of the deity in Philo, or they could also be independent beings, of course subordinate to God. Again, he conceived them as angels along Old Testament lines (so that the Logos became the highest of the angels), but in other passages, he makes them identical with the Platonic Ideas. As the representative of Wisdom, the Logos can become the World Reason ($\kappa \acute{o} \sigma \mu o s$ $v o \eta \tau \acute{o} s$), which the Stoics saw at work in the ordering of the world. Philo could occasionally refer to so high a power as "divine" ($\theta \epsilon \acute{o} s$, which means God but not literally, in distinction from "God" proper, $\acute{o}$ $\theta \epsilon \acute{o} s$).

With respect to the second point, it may be said that verses 1–5 and 9–11 (and thus the first half of the original "Prologue") in fact constitute the exact counterpart to the Wisdom myth in the form mentioned first above. That was not noted because the later insertions in

verses 6–8 and 12f. were not recognized as such, with the result that the train of thought of the "Prologue" was not perceived clearly.

That brings us to the third point. It has not been observed that the gnostic interpretation of verses 3 and 4 led to incorrect punctuation, which then affected subsequent non-gnostic interpretation.

The fourth point is the most important of all: interpreters took into consideration only the parallel between Wisdom as the divine assistant in the creation and the intermediary activity of the Logos in the creation, and overlooked the fact that the Christian hymnist was fully justified when he also incorporated into his hymn the fruitless activity of Wisdom on earth. For he asked himself—so far as we know, he was the first to do so— why it was that the redemptive incarnation came so late in the course of events. So long as Christians entertained thoughts of the apocalyptic expectation, it appeared plausible that the birth, death, and resurrection of Jesus were to come only in the last generation before the turn of the ages: it was precipitated by these events. As soon as the apocalyptic hope died out, there was no longer an answer to the question why the incarnation did not come earlier. In this case, however, only the myth of the fruitless activity of Wisdom wandering about on earth could come to the rescue: God's solicitous concern for man does not come just at the last moment, but was actually continuous through all the preceding generations. But man wanted to have nothing to do with it. And that is precisely what may now be said about the Christian understanding of the Logos: as pre-incarnate Logos he constantly sought his own, but without success. At this point, however, the Christian hymnist was able to surpass the old Wisdom myth: according to the Jewish tradition, Wisdom returned again to heaven as a result of her despair and took her place among the angels; the hymn of praise of the Christian community could proclaim a different and happy turn of events: the Logos became flesh and as man discovered the community that now gives thanks to him as the emissary of God's revelation. The second half of the Christian hymn to the Logos is thereby given: Verses 14 and 16f.

It goes without saying that the second half of the hymn could not derive its material from the Wisdom myth alone in the way that the first half had. The so-called Prologue is therefore neither an introduction aimed at

139

the hellenistic reader (cf. Harnack and Dodd), nor is it a summary of the Gospel (cf. Hoskyn and Schlier), nor is it an overture that serves as a prelude to emphasize various motifs from the Gospel and thus confirms the reader (cf. Heitmüller and Bultmann). Instead, it depicts the history of salvation from its beginning in eternity to the earthly work of Jesus. In this fashion the story of Jesus' words and deeds in 1:19ff. are made to connect up, although not entirely smoothly.

2. The Confession of John

Bibliography

Baldi, D.
"Betania in Transgiordania." *Térra Santa* 22 (1947) 44–48.

Bammel, Ernst
"The Baptist in Early Christian Tradition." *NTS* 18 (1971) 95–128.

Braun, François-Marie
"L'arrière-fond judaïque du quatrième évangile et la communauté de l'alliance." *RB* 62 (1955) 5–44.

Braun, Herbert
"Entscheidende Motive in den Berichten über die Taufe Jesu von Markus bis Justin." In his *Gesammelte Studien zum Neuen Testament und seiner Umwelt* (Tübingen: Mohr-Siebeck, 1967) 168–72.

Braun, Herbert
"Qumran und das Neue Testament. Ein Bericht über 10 Jahre Forschung (1950–1959)." *TRu* 28 (1962/1963) 97–234; 29 (1963/1964) 142–76, 189–260; 30 (1964/1965) 1–38, 89–137. Reprinted as *Qumran und das Neue Testament* (Tübingen: Mohr-Siebeck, 1966).

Buse, Ivor
"St. John and 'The First Synoptic Pericope.'" *NovT* 3 (1959) 57–61.

Buzy, Denis
"Béthanie au-delà du Jourdain." *RSR* 21 (1931) 444–62.

Cullmann, Oscar
"Ὁ ὀπίσω μου ἐρχόμενος." In *In honorem Antonii Fridrichsen sexagenarii, ConNT* 11 (Lund: C. W. K. Gleerup, 1947) 26–32.

Dalman, Gustaf
Sacred Sites and Ways: Studies in the Topography of the Gospels, tr. Paul P. Levertoff (London: S. P. C. K.; New York: Macmillan, 1935) 81–98 = *Orte und Wege Jesu* (Gütersloh: C. Bertelsmann, 1919) 75–95.

Dibelius, Martin
Die urchristliche Überlieferung von Johannes dem Täufer, FRLANT 15 (Göttingen: Vandenhoeck & Ruprecht, 1911).

Freed, Edwin D.
"*Egō Eimi* in John 1:20 and 4:25." *CBQ* 41 (1979) 288–91.

Galbiati, Enrico
"Esegesi degli Evangeli festivi: La testimonianza die Giovanni Battista (Giov. 1,19–28)." *BeO* 4 (1962) 227–33.

Garofalo, S.
"Preparare la strada al Signore." *RivB* 6 (1958) 131–34.

Glasson, T. Francis
"John the Baptist in the Fourth Gospel." *ExpTim* 67 (1956) 245–46.

Goguel, Maurice
  Au seuil de l'Evangile Jean-Baptiste (Paris: C. Payot, 1928), esp. 80–85.
Goguel, Maurice
  "Les sources des récits du quatrième évangile sur Jean-Baptiste." *Revue de théologie et de questions religieuses* 21 (1911) 12–44.
Grensted, L. W.
  "I Cor. x. 9; John i. 22." *ExpTim* 35 (1923/1924) 331.
Haenchen, Ernst
  "Probleme des johanneischen 'Prologs.'" In his *Gott und Mensch: Gesammelte Aufsätze* 1 (Tübingen: Mohr-Siebeck, 1965) 135–38.
Holzmeister, U.
  "'Medius vestrum stetit, quem vos nescitis' (Jn I,26)." *VD* 20 (1940) 329–32.
Iersel, B. M. F. van
  "Tradition und Redaktion in Joh 1 19–36." *NovT* 5 (1962) 245–67.
Jonge, Marinus de
  "Jesus as Prophet and King in the Fourth Gospel." *ETL* 49 (1973) 160–77, esp. 160, 163–69.
Keck, Leander E.
  "John the Baptist in Christianized Gnosticism." In *Initiation*, ed. C. J. Bleeker (Leiden: E. J. Brill, 1965) 184–94.
Kraeling, Carl H.
  John the Baptist (New York and London: Charles Scribner's Sons, 1951), esp. 8f.
Krieger, Norbert
  "Fiktive Orte der Johannestaufe." *ZNW* 45 (1954) 121–23.
Kuhn, Karl G.
  "The Two Messiahs of Aaron and Israel." In *The Scrolls and the New Testament*, ed. K. Stendahl (New York: Harper & Brothers, 1957) 54–64.
Lohmeyer, Ernst
  Das Urchristentum. Vol. 1, *Johannes der Täufer* (Göttingen: Vandenhoeck & Ruprecht, 1932) 26–31.
Maerten, T.
  "Le troisième dimanche de l'Avent (Jn 1,19–28; Phil 4,4–7)." *Paroisse et liturgie* 44 (1962) 710–16.
Martyn, J. Louis
  "We Have Found Elijah." In *Jews, Greeks, and Christians. Religious Cultures in Late Antiquity. Essays in Honor of William David Davies*, ed. Robert Hamerton-Kelly and Robin Scroggs. SJLA 21 (Leiden: E. J. Brill, 1976) 181–219.
Modersohn, E.
  "Des Täufers Selbst- und Christuszeugnis (Joh 1,19–24)." *Heilig dem Herrn* 31 (1940) 157–59.
Mommert, Carl
  Aenon und Bethania, die Taufstätten des Täufers (Leipzig: E. Haberland, 1903).
Muilenburg, James
  "Literary Form in the Fourth Gospel." *JBL* 51 (1932) 40–53.

Niccacci, Alviero
  "La fede nel Gesù storico e la fede nel Cristo risorto (Gv 1,19–51//20,1–19)." *Antonianum* 53 (1978) 423–42.
Overbeck, T. G.
  Neue Versuche über das Evangelium Johannis (Gera: Beckmannsche Buchhandlung, 1784).
Parker, Pierson
  "Bethany beyond Jordan." *JBL* 74 (1955) 257–61.
Payot, Christian
  "L'interprétation johannique du ministère de Jean-Baptiste." *Foi et vie* 68 (1969) 21–37.
Proulx, P. and Alonso Schökel, L.
  "Las Sandalias del Mesías Esposo." *Bib* 59 (1978) 1–37.
Redford, J.
  "Preparing the Way: John the Baptist." *Clergy Review* 66 (1981) 193–200.
Richter, Georg
  "Bist du Elias? (Joh 1,21)." *BZ* 6 (1962) 79–92, 238–56; 7 (1963) 63–80. Now in his *Studien zum Johannesevangelium*, ed. Josef Hainz. BU 13 (Regensburg: F. Pustet, 1977) 1–41.
Richter, Georg
  "Zur Frage von Tradition und Redaktion in Joh 1,19–34." In his *Studien im Johannesevangelium*, ed. Josef Hainz. BU 13 (Regensburg: F. Pustet, 1977) 288–314.
Sahlin, Harold
  "Zwei Abschnitte aus Joh 1 rekonstruiert." *ZNW* 51 (1960) 64–69.
Schnackenburg, Rudolf
  "Die Messiasfrage im Johannesevangelium." In *Neutestamentliche Aufsätze. Festschrift für Prof. Josef Schmid zum 70. Geburtstag*, ed. J. Blinzler, O. Kuss, F. Mussner (Regensburg: F. Pustet, 1963) 240–64, esp. 245–50.
Trocmé, Etienne
  "Jean-Baptiste dans le quatrième évangile." *RHPR* 60 (1980) 129–51.
Velena, J. H.
  "Adventsonthulling, Jo 1,26b." *Homiletica et biblica* 23 (1964) 266–69.
Voigt, Simão
  "Topo-geografia et Teologia del Battista nel IV Vangelo." *SBFLA* 27 (1977) 69–101.
Weifel, W.
  "Bethabara jenseits des Jordan (Joh 1, 28)." *ZDPV* 83 (1967) 72–81.
Williams, Francis E.
  "Fourth Gospel and Synoptic Tradition: Two Johannine Passages." *JBL* 86 (1967) 311–19.
Wink, Walter
  "John the Baptist in the Gospel Tradition." SNTSMS 7 (London: Cambridge University Press, 1968) 87–106.
Zahn, Theodor
  "Zur Heimatkunde des Evangelisten Johannes." *NKZ* 18 (1907) 265–94, 593–608; 19 (1908) 31–39, 207–18.

19 And this is the testimony of John, when the Jews sent priests and Levites from Jerusalem to ask him, "Who are you?" 20/ He confessed, he did not deny, but confessed, "I am not the Christ." 21/ And they asked him, "What then? Are you Elijah?" He said, "I am not." "Are you the prophet?" And he answered, "No." 22/ They said to him then, "Who are you? Let us have an answer for those who sent us. What do you say about yourself?" 23/ He said, "I am the voice of one crying in the wilderness, 'Make straight the way of the Lord,' as the prophet Isaiah said." 24/ Now they had been sent from the Pharisees. 25/ They asked him, "Then why are you baptizing, if you are neither the Christ, nor Elijah, nor the prophet?" 26/ John answered them, "I baptize with water; but among you stands one whom you do not know, 27/ even he who comes after me, the thong of whose sandal I am not worthy to untie." 28/ This took place in Bethany beyond the Jordan, where John was baptizing.

■ **19** Verse 19 is connected to the Prologue and to the transitional verse 18 by means of a narrative "and" (καί). According to Hirsch,[1] 1:6–8 originally came before 1:19.[2] According to Barrett,[3] 1:19–28 is linked by allusion to 1:6–8: the ὅτε-clause ("when") describes the occasion on which the Baptist makes the confession. This clause does not suggest a date on which the confession took place, but emphasizes the very official nature of the situation: the Jews sent a delegation. But 1:6–8 does not by any means intend a single act of confession; rather, this confession is the sole and abiding task of John.

The delegation consists of priests and Levites. They appear in the Gospel of John only here; by contrast frequently in the OT and often in 1QS,[4] and also of course in the Mishnah.[5] The fact that priests and Levites come is not to be explained on the basis that questions of purification are involved.[6] For the question put to John is: "Who are you?" The religious significance of the scene is rather to be emphasized. According to Zahn,[7] the Levites escort the delegation on a precarious journey as members of the temple police. Levites, according to the Mishnah, stand night watch in twenty-one locations in the outer perimeter of the temple precincts; it is clear that they cannot have been involved in escorting a priestly delegation of this kind. But whether the Evangelist knew anything more precisely about the temple guard is as uncertain as whether he has the temple guard in mind in 7:32 and 45f. when he refers to the "servants of the high priests and Pharisees" (note "Pharisees").[8] The official inquiry, "Who are you?" is intended to provide the occasion for the Baptist's confession that the narrator has designed for the reader. That is shown by the triple, formal repetition of the question; that makes sense only in an idealized scene, not in a historical one. The word μαρτυρία ("witness") stands at the beginning as a theme or leitmotiv.

■ **20** John immediately understands the question "Who are you?" in its relevant sense. He answers with a solem-

---

1   *Studien*, 45.
2   This supposition is improbable; see on 1:6–8 above.
3   *John*, 171.
4   See F.-M. Braun, "L'arrière-fond judaïque du quatrième évangile et la communauté d'alliance," *RB* 62 (1955) 22f.
5   H. Braun, "Qumran und das NT," 97–234.
6   Bultmann, *John*, 87 [80].
7   *Das Evangelium des Johannes*, 112.
8   Jeremias, *Jerusalem*, 209f., interprets differently.

nity that appears ostentatious at first blush. But one must not eliminate the first "he confessed," used absolutely, and its negative counterpart, "he did not deny," as additions, as does Hirsch.[9] On the contrary, the question is put and answered solemnly because it concerns the most important matter, in the judgment of the narrator. From 4:25 we learn that the meaning of ὁ χριστός as "the messiah" is presupposed as well known. The Jews also understand the term in 10:24 in this sense. Of course, the Fourth Gospel understands ὁ χριστός in a deeper sense than as the messiah of the Jews, yet it is Jews who pose the question here. The ὅτι that is used here to introduce direct discourse betrays the colloquial koine of the Fourth Gospel.[10]

■ **21** The continuation of the questioning by the emissaries presupposes that the figures now mentioned by them, "Elijah" and "the prophet," do not carry as much significance as "the messiah"; nevertheless, they express a particularly high rank. Both are designated figures of the messianic age.[11] The words προφήτην . . . ὡς ἐμέ ("the prophet . . . like me") in Deut 18:15 LXX are understood by some parties in contemporary Judaism as the designation of a particular prophet in the end time. At an earlier time, in support of this view one could only invoke the evidence of the Pseudo-Clementines, which prefer to refer to Jesus as "the prophet" ("the prophet" *Hom.* 11.25f., 13.14;—"the true prophet" 8.10, 10.3;—ὁ τῆς ἀληθείας προφήτης ["the prophet of truth"] 3.11, 11.19, 12.29;—μόνος ἀληθὴς προφήτης ["only true prophet"] 3.21;—in 3.53, Deut 18:15 is expressly interpreted with reference to the special prophetic mission). But the view of the *Pseudo-Clementines* that the true prophet was revealed in Adam and then repeatedly in subsequent times shows us that a Jewish Christianity with a gnostic strain is finding expression here. On the other hand, 1QS 9.11 ("until the coming of the prophet and the messiahs of Aaron and Israel") demonstrates that in the sectarian document from Qumran, in addition to the priestly and royal messiahs ("anointed ones"), "a new prophetic law-

giver" was expected for the end time.[12] In 4QTest 5–8,[13] Deut 18:18f. is included in a collection of messianic passages. In John 6:14f. "the prophet who is to come into the world" is identified with the messianic king. The same applies to John 7:52, if one reads ὁ προφήτης ("the prophet") with 𝔓⁶⁶ and 𝔓⁷⁵, which is probably original.

The prophetic movement in the syncretistic milieu, which Bauer invokes,[14] does not come into consideration, nor is John 9:17 relevant here.

H. Braun[15] has discussed the various modern hypotheses regarding the relation of our text to the Qumran texts in a very detailed and pertinent study. His conclusions are: the Qumran prophet of the end time is not identical with one of the messiahs; but such a connection appears in John 6:14 and 7:52. Of course, whether that applies to 1:21 also[16] may be doubted: Elijah is not identified with the χριστός ("the messiah"). An old Jewish-Christian tradition has probably been used, one that speaks of Elijah and "the prophet" as forerunners of the messiah. It is not stipulated that the narrator views these three figures as of equal rank.[17] The composition of the passage might well be understood as follows: John is first asked whether he lays claim to the highest authority, that of the Christ. When he has denied that, he is asked whether he wants to be one of the lesser figures of the messianic age; he does not lay claim to that authority either!

The wording of the first question is variously transmitted. Bultmann[18] regards τί οὖν σύ ("What then are you?") as original. Bauer[19] reads, probably correctly, τί οὖν ("What then?") followed by the further question: "Are you Elijah?" (following 𝔓⁶⁶ [which reads τίς "who?" for τί "what?"] and 𝔓⁷⁵ C 33).

■ **22–24** Hirsch[20] writes: "the fabric of the dialogue would be more closely woven were one to follow v 21 with v 25; vv 22–24 thus may be attributed to the redactor. The need to assimilate this account to that of the Synoptics could readily explain the addition as the work of the 'redactor'." But he nevertheless contents

9   *Studien*, 45f.
10   Cf. BDF §470.
11   On the identification of John and Elijah in Mark and Matt, see the Overview below.
12   Cf. Kuhn, "The Two Messiahs of Aaron and Israel," in *The Scrolls and the New Testament*, ed. K. Stendahl (New York: Harper & Brothers, 1957) 63; and especially on this passage, J. Maier, *Die Texte vom Toten*

Meer, 2: 32f., with bibliography.
13   On which see Maier, *Die Texte vom Toten Meer*, 2: 165.
14   *Das Johannesevangelium*, 32f.
15   "Qumran und das NT," 196–202.
16   As Braun intends ("Qumran und das NT," 197).
17   Contrast Braun, "Qumran und das NT," 197.
18   *John*, 88 n. 3 [60 n. 5].
19   *Das Johannesevangelium*, 32.

himself with excising verse 24. Bultmann,[21] on the other hand, goes further and strikes verses 22–24. He is of course not satisfied with that, but adopts further additions and rearrangements (see on vv 26f. below). Van Iersel[22] undertakes a modest critique of Bultmann's reconstruction, while Ruckstuhl[23] and Smith[24] undertake a sharper critique. We are unable simply to take over either Bultmann's hypothesis or the criticisms of his opponents,[25] but will seek to chart our own course.

At first glance, verses 22–24 appear to come exactly at the right place.[26] John has thrice explained who he is not. Following three negative answers a positive response appears necessary: he should now state who he really is. The quotation from Isa 40:3 appears in a form unlike any employed by the Synoptics, and verse 24 may be explained as transitional.

Neither Bultmann nor his critics note where the real difficulty lies: the words σὺ τίς εἶ ("Who are you?") in verse 19 have an entirely different meaning from τίς εἶ ("Who are you?") in verse 22. The phrase in verse 19 means (as John immediately perceives): "Are you the Christ?" It introduces the first of the three questions and answers that show that John does not stand on the same level with Jesus and certainly not above him. *The Baptist* has no independent significance. If now in verses 22–24 the question regarding the positive significance of John is raised and answered, this answer contradicts the inner trajectory of the pericope. Since the first declarations of John are in response to the question, "You are . . .?" (to which, in each instance, a negative answer follows), the question "Who are you?" should also readily have elicited positive information. For the redactor, to whom we also wish to ascribe verses 22–24, it is not a matter simply of a positive answer as such, but of introducing the well-known quotation from Isa 40:3 that should not be omitted from the representation of John. But this citation, in the form employed by the Synoptics (following the LXX), could no longer be used in response to the question, "Who are you?" in verse 21. Rather, it had to be assimilated to that question. The consequence is the bold rephrasing: "I am the voice of one crying" (a proclaimer).

■ **24** Verse 24 might have been intended to form the transition to verses 25ff. A few peculiarities also argue against the originality of this verse. The ἐκ is unusual. One expects ἀπό instead, in accordance with hellenistic Greek usage.

The reading οἱ ἀπεσταλμένοι ("those sent") in ℜ W Θ vg *pl* shows that the difficulty was sensed at an early date. The delegation of priests and Levites was thus turned into Pharisees. That is highly improbable, because the Pharisees were a lay movement.

If verses 22–24 are a later addition, then the question regarding the character of verses 19–21 is posed in an even more pointed way: are these verses to be understood as an independent unity, or are they merely preparation for the question to follow about baptism? The answer appears to be given with the observation that the narrator introduces the confession of John in verse 21 in an especially solemn manner. The first three questions are thereby so strongly emphasized that one cannot conceive them merely as preparation for the question regarding baptism. The significance of the Baptist as a person and of his baptism were pressing problems for the contemporary Christian community; they had to be prepared to answer both questions.

■ **25** With this verse a second theme is introduced. Up to this point it has been pointed out that John possesses no authority such as belongs to the Christ, Elijah, or "the prophet." The question is thereby made acute: what then gives John the right to baptize? This does not imply that the narrator intends for the Christ, Elijah, and the prophet to be understood as baptizers. No trace of such a tradition is to be found. The baptism that John administers to those who are permitted to escape the baptismal fires of judgment by virtue of their repentance—this "eschatological sacrament" is without parallels in the history of religions. Even the ablutions practiced in

20   *Studien*, 46.
21   *John*, 84f. [57f.].
22   "Tradition und Redaktion in Joh 1 19–36," *NovT* 5 (1962) 245–67.
23   *Einheit*, 149–59.
24   *Composition and Order*, 119–25.
25   See also Fortna, *Gospel of Signs*, 171–73.
26   So also Schnackenburg, *John*, 1: 192.

Qumran, which are sometimes connected with the baptism of John, have nothing to do with this sacrament. Of course, the Fourth Gospel also no longer recognizes the original sense of the baptism of John and does not suspect that the Christian community, in all probability, took over the practice of baptism from converted disciples of John, just as it did fasting (cf. Mark 2:18–22).

The reading προφήτης ("prophet," without article) in Δ *pc* shows that the meaning of "the prophet" was quickly forgotten. Of course, Acts 3:22 understands ὁ προφήτης ("the prophet") still in the messianic sense.

■ **26f.** According to the present text, John answers that he baptizes "with water." That is apparently intended to mean "only with water," and thus a baptism unaccompanied by a bestowal of the Spirit. Acts 19:2 supports this view; in the Baptist's sect there seems not to have occurred the kind of ecstatic events that might be taken as evidence of spirit possession. Bultmann,[27] however, deletes the words "I baptize with water" as he does verse 27; further, he strikes ἐν ὕδατι βαπτίζων ("baptizing with water") in verse 31, ἐν ὕδατι ("with water") and ὁ βαπτίζων ἐν πνεύματι ἁγίῳ ("the one baptizing with the Holy Spirit") in verse 33. Verses 31 (in an abbreviated form) and 33 are made to follow on an abbreviated verse 26; verse 33 ends with οὗτος ἐστιν ("this is [the one]"). Bultmann brings the pericope to an end with verses 34, 28–30. We shall return to this point in the discussion of verses 29–34. Bultmann appears to let himself be led here, as often elsewhere, by the assumption that the Fourth Evangelist originally collected everything that relates to a theme into one passage. But the text prompts the query whether the Fourth Evangelist does not employ another narrative strategy: he often comes back, without hesitating to repeat, to the same theme, and at first only hints at what he later spells out. Hirsch[28] believes the ascription of verses 25–27 to a redactor is unnecessary: "the question regarding the basis of baptism is natural after John sweepingly denies the presuppositions that alone would have constituted a call (at least in the understanding of the church in the post-Apostolic period) to a fully empowered baptism, and the answer of John that his baptism is an unempowered baptism of water . . . corresponds 'well' to the picture of John

painted by the Evangelist." We have demonstrated earlier that this question is not at all natural when one considers the meaning of the question "Who are you?" in verse 21.

Whoever strikes ἐγὼ βαπτίζω ἐν ὕδατι ("I baptize with water") in verse 26 following Bultmann ends up with a very dubious context, since now, in answer to the question of the emissaries "Why do you baptize?" (v 25), this answer would follow: "Among you stands one whom you do not know." This drives Bultmann to all the deletions and rearrangements mentioned above. If what was said earlier regarding the narrative technique of John is correct, the combination of the water baptism of John and the reference to the coming one stands as an initial enigmatic hint for the hearer and reader. This Johannine sketch is not far removed from the corresponding Lukan picture. Luke does not know of an official delegation to John, but does know of the expectation and unexpressed question of everyone whether John is the Christ (Luke 3:15). Luke has John answer this question in a way similar to the Fourth Evangelist by referring to the fact that he baptizes with water (only) and that a mightier one comes whose sandals he is not worthy to untie. Of course, there follows in Luke 3:16c the announcement of a baptism with the Spirit that derives from source Q.

What the emissaries can do with the response of John is a matter of indifference to the narrator: their questions have provoked the answers which are important to him. The phrase "among you stands one" takes notice of Jesus, who appears, so to speak, in the penumbra of the scene; more will be said about him in the next pericope.

The ὁ in ὁ ὀπίσω ("the after . . .") has been omitted in B ℵ* by haplography; 𝔓66 and 𝔓75 do not yet exhibit this error. The manuscripts E F G N *pc* have incorrectly inserted the mention of baptism with the Spirit into 1:27.

■ **28** The mention of place serves to close the scene, as in 6:59 and 8:20. At the same time, it gives the appearance of John, hitherto completely indeterminate (vv 19–27), a spatial frame of reference.

Unfortunately, the place name is not uniformly transmitted. 𝔓66 and 𝔓75 as well as B ℵ* it vg syᵖ bo Heracleon attest Βηθανία ("Bethany"), which we prefer with Schnackenburg[29] and Brown.[30] Origen[31] found this

27   *John*, 85 [58].
28   *Studien*, 46.

name "in nearly all manuscripts." Since he could find no place known by this name on the Jordan, he substituted Βηθάβαρα ("Bethabara") (attested by Π Ψ 33 sy^sc sa Eus). The form Βηθάραβα ("Betharaba") is read by א² sy^hms. Βαθάραβα appears to be a scribal error, but there is a place by that name some four kilometers west of the Jordan. Hirsch,[32] to whom $\mathfrak{P}^{66}$ and $\mathfrak{P}^{75}$ were not yet available, explains the situation thus: originally verse 28 lacked a designation of place (otherwise it would have been repeated in 10:40); a regional name must have stood there, something like τῇ Ἀραβία ("in Arabia"). Out of this a copyist created Βηθάραβα. Βηθανία and Βηθάβαρα are attempts to turn the tradition into a possible place name. Hirsch thus conjectures a highly improbable geographical designation on the basis of a mere supposition that flies in the face of the entire tradition. Moreover, Βηθάβαρα could reflect a local tradition about the place where John baptized.[33]

That a name is mentioned shows that some sort of tradition regarding the baptismal locale had been accepted. This does not certify the scene with the emissaries. Bethany "beyond the Jordan" is obviously to be distinguished from the place of the same name known to Christians (thus probably Bethany near Jerusalem).

Overview

Only about three years separate two works that can be used to illustrate the difference between two generations of scholars: the "conservatives" of the nineteenth century and the liberal, critical scholars of the early twentieth.

In his commentary of 1908,[34] Zahn treats the Fourth Gospel as a completely reliable historical work. How does this presupposition affect the exposition of our pericope? Zahn[35] reflects: "It is as improbable as it is unattested that 'John' should have lived for months at a time, through all the changes in seasons and weather, in the blazing hot Ghor, day and night always under the open sky, . . . or in caves along the valley rim . . . ; thus he and his regular disciples cannot have failed to have had

quarters from which they could reach the Jordan without a significant loss of time. . . . If the emissaries from Jerusalem did not find him upon their arrival at the Jordan where he . . . customarily baptized, they would not have begrudged a journey of two-three hours to seek him out in his permanent quarters." Why this display of fancy clad in realism? It is a matter of linking the Baptist located at the Jordan with a Bethany not to be found in the vicinity of the Jordan. Zahn identifies it with a place mentioned in Josh 13:26 (13:27 LXX) בטנים. That he had to represent it with a τ and not with a θ he accounts for on the basis that the son of Zebedee dictated his work to a Greek! This place name derived from the book of Joshua Zahn identifies with Betonim (Khirbet Batneh) located about ten kilometers from the Jordan. He then has the Baptist cheerfully journey with his disciples twenty kilometers each day in the "blazing hot Ghor."

Martin Dibelius treats John 1:19–34 quite differently in his 1911 book:[36] "We must not seek historical references in this passage, for apart from the reminiscence of a saying of the Baptist in 1:26f., also reported by the Synoptics, and apart from the allusion to the baptism of Jesus by John . . . , which the Evangelist nevertheless appears to take care to avoid, the single historical item in the entire pericope is probably only the originally close tie between the two movements, Johannine and Christian. . . . In the first scene, the author has John say: I am only a voice, I am not the messiah, indeed, I am not even a forerunner. . . . From the mighty forerunner, to whom one must grant a special, if now also antiquated, honor because he came historically *before* the gospel, there emerges a figure *alongside* Jesus, an attendant phenomenon of the gospel, whose value consists solely in his selfless testimonial."

The development in the evaluation of the Baptist suggested here, whose beginning may still be deduced from Matt 3:11//Luke 3:16 (Q), comes to its culmination in John 1:27. We propose to investigate that next.

John really felt himself to be the forerunner of an

29   *John,* 1: 295f.
30   *John,* 1:44f. n. 28.
31   6.40.240.
32   *Studien,* 4 n. 28.
33   Barrett, *John,* 175.
34   ⁶1921.
35   *Das Evangelium des Johannes,* 119.
36   *Die urchristliche Überlieferung von Johannes dem Täufer,*

FRLANT 15 (Göttingen: Vandenhoeck & Ruprecht, 1911) 108f.

incomparable figure of might and superiority, whose shoelaces he was not even worthy to untie. This mighty figure could not have been Yahweh himself. One cannot compare man with God. But was the Coming One a human being for John? The sayings found in Matt 3:12//Luke 3:17 exclude that possibility: "His winnowing fork is in his hand, and he will clear his threshing floor and gather his wheat into the granary, but the chaff he will burn with unquenchable fire." What is thus described is not a man but a heavenly being, who will come to bring judgment by *fire*. And the moment of this judgment is near: "Even now the ax is laid to the root of the trees"—just as the woodsman measures his swing by touching his ax to the spot to which he intends to deliver the mighty blow—"every tree therefore that does not bear good fruit is cut down and thrown into the fire" (Matt 3:10//Luke 3:9). This is a demand for eschatological repentance in the final hour; for the one who comes to repentance there is an "eschatological sacrament," which John was called to administer: baptism in the Jordan. Whoever does not receive baptism (in water) he will baptize with fire!

The *historical* Jesus also came to this John to be baptized, along with many others. This produced the result that the early Christian tradition began with the baptism of John, as Mark shows. Two further factors facilitated this assimilation of the John tradition. In the first place, John was conscious of his role as forerunner of the world judge soon to come. As soon as the post-Easter Christian community became certain that the risen Jesus would return as this expected world judge, they necessarily saw in John the precursor of Jesus. For another thing, they thought they had found a biblical allusion to John in Isa 40:3: "the voice of a proclaimer in the wilderness: prepare the way of the Lord." Here it appears to be said in unmistakable terms that someone would preach in the wilderness to prepare the way of the Lord, viz., Jesus.

It is thus overlooked that this verse was really to be understood differently—with reference to the return of the Jews from their Babylonian exile: "A voice cries: In the wilderness prepare the way of the Lord, make straight in the desert a highway for our God." If one refers this text to John, the one baptizing in the Jordan

simultaneously becomes a proclaimer in the wilderness. But still other difficulties present themselves: John appeared *first* and Jesus was baptized by him. That appears to be evidence of a certain superiority of John over Jesus, and the canonical gospels from Mark to John show how the effort was made to efface that "appearance." John's preaching of repentance (Matt 3:7b–10, 12//Luke 3:7b–9, 17), taken over by Matt and Luke from Q, is missing in Mark, and thus the central metaphors of the ax that is laid at the root of the trees, and the thresher who will winnow the wheat and burn the chaff with unquenchable fire. And while it might have read in Q: "I have baptized you with water, but he will baptize you with fire!", in Mark a new contrast appears: "I have baptized you with water, but he will baptize you with the Holy Spirit." That may have led to the combination of "Holy Spirit" and "fire" in Matt 3:11// Luke 3:16, while according to Q, those who are not baptized by John in water will be baptized by fire. In any case, Matt 3:7//Luke 3:7 (with complete verbal agreement) shows that those desiring baptism were convinced of the saving power of John's baptism.

The fact of Jesus' baptism by John began to produce embarrassment for Christians, as Matt 3:14f. shows clearly: when Jesus presented himself for baptism, John at first declined by saying that it was necessary for him to be baptized by Jesus and not the reverse. But the real difficulty had not at that time become evident to Christians: "We have good reason," writes Käsemann,[37] "not to forget that the baptism of Jesus by John belongs to the indubitable happenings of the life of the historical Jesus. For its significance is that Jesus began with the same burning expectation of the End as the Baptist, and that he therefore had himself 'sealed' from the imminent judgment of wrath and incorporated into the holy remnant of the people of God." Although the concepts "seal" and "holy remnant" are imported from other contexts, the observation of Käsemann is correct: Jesus went to the Jordan in response to the conditions of repentance proclaimed by the Baptist and had himself baptized in order to escape the coming wrath (cf. Luke 3:7b//Matt 3:7b). But he then did not continue the conduct and the preaching of the Baptist in his own proclamation: he did

37 *New Testament Questions*, 112.

not baptize (contrary to John 3:22) and he neither practiced nor commanded his disciples to practice penitential fasting like John, so that he was accused of being "a glutton and a drunkard" (Luke 7:33f.), and he based his refusal in fact on a metaphor (Mark 2:19) that indicated that for him the anticipation of the coming of God was occasion for jubilant rejoicing and not for the anxiety of judgment associated with John. Something must therefore have happened—which is probably reflected in the baptismal narrative (Mark 1:9–11 pars.)—between Jesus' journey to the Jordan and the beginning of his own preaching, that made him certain that the way willed by God was quite different than John saw it. To this extent the community was correct when they were not only convinced that the Baptist was merely a forerunner, but also that a significant "qualitative difference" separated him from Jesus.

The Fourth Gospel provides the final correction in the picture of John handed down in the tradition. He represents John as a "witness" for Jesus and furthermore allows that John aspired to be no more than a humble and selfless witness. The Fourth Gospel therefore does not call John the "Baptist," as Mark (1:4) and Matt (3:1) do, and beyond that does not report the baptism of Jesus by John. It remains to discuss, at the appropriate point, the report in John 3:22–36 that John and Jesus baptized simultaneously.

The first and most detailed of the three scenes with John in chapter one presents us with the question: to what extent is there a firm tradition, to what extent is it a matter of only certain basic convictions and concepts contained in the tradition that an author has taken and arranged in a more or less coherent composition? The following observations support the second possibility: the three questions and answers comprising the dialogue between the Jewish emissaries and John form an extraordinarily sensitive structure. John is first asked whether he claims the highest authority, that of the Christ; then the lesser authority of Elijah comes into play (which was still conferred on John in the older tradition: Mark 9:11–13//Matt 17:10–13) and finally the palest authority, that of the "prophet." There follows upon these three questions—if our own analysis of verses 22–24 is correct—the question of the baptism of John. That question is less emphatic than the first, as the order of the whole indicates. The fact that John baptized was recognized, of course, and could not be contested. It is even used in 3:22ff. in order to show how fully John subordinates himself to the "bridegroom" as a true friend. There was no room in this tradition for the apocalyptic words of the primitive Christian Baptist tradition from Palestine. What John says about Jesus (1:29, 36) is of a different order. But there is something which should not be expressly mentioned: the fact that John had baptized the Lord. This comprises the essential content of the first scene. In one respect the first scene is similar to those that follow: in spite of many particulars of place and person—priests and Levites from Jerusalem, Bethany— the scene does not lose its vague and indefinite character. That does not owe to a weakness of the author, but to the fact that he only tells what is important to him. It is not his aim to describe the "historical" concretely.

3. The Testimony of John

Bibliography

Ashbey, G.
"Lamb of God." *Journal of Theology for Southern Africa* 21 (1977) 63–65; 25 (1978) 62–65.

Barrett, Charles Kingsley
"The Lamb of God." *NTS* 1 (1954) 210–18.

Barrosse, Thomas
"The Seven Days of the New Creation in St. John's Gospel." *CBQ* 21 (1959) 507–16.

Blakeway, C. E.
"Behold the Lamb of God." *ExpTim* 31 (1919/1920) 364–65.

Bogaert, M.
"Jn 1,19–28." *AsSeign* 5 (1966) 41–54.

Boismard, Marie-Emile
"La première semaine du ministère de Jésus selon S. Jean." *VSpir* 94 (1956) 593–603.

Buse, Ivor
"St. John and 'The First Synoptic Pericope.'" *NovT* 3 (1959) 57–61.

Carey, G. L.
"The Lamb of God and Atonement Theories." *TynBul* 32 (1981) 97–122.

Cousar, Charles B.
"John 1:29–42." *Int* 31 (1977) 401–6.

Dodd, Charles Harold
Review of *Theologisches Wörterbuch zum Neuen Testament, Lieferungen 1–7, JTS* 34 (1935) 280–85.

Frisch, M. J. F.
Vollständige biblische Abhandlung vom Osterlamme überhaupt (Leipzig: Breitkopf, 1758), esp. 600–655, 671–963, 1002–1166.

Gabler, J. P.
Meletemata in locum Joh 1,29 (Jena, 1808–1811).

Giblet, Jean
"Pour rendre témoignage à la lumière (Jean I, 29–34)." *BVC* 16 (1956/1957) 80–86.

Gilchrist, E. J.
"And I knew him not." *ExpTim* 19 (1907/1908) 379–80.

Hahn, Ferdinand
"Beobachtungen zu Joh 1,18.34." In *Studies in New Testament Language and Text. Essays in Honour of George D. Kilpatrick on the Occasion of his Sixty-fifth Birthday,* ed. J. K. Elliott. NovTSup 44 (Leiden: E. J. Brill, 1976) 24–37.

Howton, John
"The Son of God in the Fourth Gospel." *NTS* 10 (1963/1964) 227–37.

Jeremias, Joachim
"Ἀμνὸς τοῦ Θεοῦ - παῖς Θεοῦ (Jn I:29, 36)." *ZNW* 34 (1935) 117–23.

Joüon, Paul
"L'Agneau de Dieu (Jean I, 29)." *NRT* 67 (1940–1945) 318–21.

Leal, Juan
"Exegesis catholica de Agno Dei in ultimis viginti et quinque annis." *VD* 28 (1950) 98–109.

May, E. E.
Ecce Agnus Dei A Philological and Exegetical Approach to John 1:29, 36, Studies in Sacred Theology, 2nd ser., 5 (Washington: The Catholic University of America Press, 1947).

Mozley, A. D.
"St. John i. 29." *ExpTim* 26 (1914/1915) 46–47.

Negoistsa, Athanase and Constantin Daniel
"L'Agneau de Dieu et le Verbe de Dieu (Ad Jo i 29 et 36)." *NovT* 13 (1971) 24–37.

O'Neill, J. C.
"The Lamb of God in the Testaments of the Twelve Patriarchs." *JSNT* 2 (1979) 2–30.

Plessis, P. J. du
"Zie het Lam Gods." In *De Knechtsgestalte van Christus. Studies door collega's en oud-leerlingen aangeboden aan Prof. dr. Herman Nicolaas Ridderbos*, ed. H. H. Grosheide et al. (Kampen: Kok, 1978) 120–38.

Potterie, Ignace de la
"Ecco l'Agnello di Dio." *BeO* 1 (1959) 161–69.

Richter, Georg
"Zu den Tauferzählungen Mk 1,9–11 und Joh 1,32–34." *ZNW* 65 (1974) 43–56; Also in his *Studien zum Johannesevangelium*, ed. Josef Hainz. BU 13 (Regensburg: F. Pustet, 1977) 315–26.

Roberge, Michel
"Structures littéraires et christologie dans le quatrième évangile: Jean 1,29–34." In *Le Christ hier, aujourd'hui et demain. Colloque de christologie tenu à l'Université Laval*, ed. R. Laflamme and M. Gervais (Québec: Les Presses de l'Université Laval, 1976) 467–78.

Roberts, J. H.
"The lamb of God." *Neot* 2 (1968) 41–56.

Sahlin, Harald
"Zwei Abschnitte aus Joh 1 rekonstruiert." *ZNW* 51 (1960) 64–69.

Stanks, T.
"The Servant of God in John I 29.36." Dissertation, Louvain, 1963.

Taylor, E. K.
"The Lamb of God." *Clergy Review* 48 (1963) 285–92.

Trudinger, L. Paul
"The Seven Days of the New Creation in St. John's Gospel: Some Further Reflection." *EvQ* 44 (1972) 154–58.

Virgulin, Stephen
"Recent Discussion of the Title, Lamb of God." *Scr* 13 (1961) 74–80.

Watt, A. C.
"John's Difficulty in Knowing the Christ—'and I knew him not.'" *ExpTim* 19 (1907/1908) 93–94.

Weise, M.
"Passionswoche und Epiphaniewoche im Johannesevangelium. Ihre Bedeutung für Komposition und Konzeption des vierten Evangeliums." *KD* 12 (1966) 48–62.

Williams, J.
"Proposed Renderings for Some Johannine Passages." *BT* 25 (1974) 351–53.

1

29 The next day he saw Jesus coming toward him, and said, "Behold, the Lamb of God, who takes away the sin of the world 30/ This is he of whom I said, 'After me comes a man who ranks before me, for he was before me.' 31/ I myself did not know him; but for this I came baptizing with water, that he might be revealed to Israel." 32/ And John bore witness, "I saw the Spirit descend as a dove from heaven, and it remained on him. 33/ I myself did not know him; but he who sent me to baptize with water said to me, 'He on whom you see the Spirit descend and remain, this is he who baptizes with the Holy Spirit.' 34/ And I have seen and have borne witness that this is the Son of God."

John 1:29–34 is to be clearly distinguished from the preceding section. In the earlier passage, only the enigmatic word about the mightier one points cryptically to Jesus without naming him. Now Jesus himself appears and his name is mentioned. But he still utters no word. The reader will hear his voice only in the next segment. In these three pericopes we thus have—as Strathmann[1] has already observed—a dramatic heightening, which would be destroyed were one to collapse the first two scenes into one, as Bultmann[2] proposes to do. In 1:19–28 John officially professes his task as Jesus' witness; now the Baptist appears before us with his testimony. He makes known to his auditors that Jesus is the lamb of God, that he cancels the sins of the world, that he comes from eternity and that he is the Son of God. The only purpose of John's commission to baptize with water is to recognize that Jesus as the recipient and bearer of the Spirit also baptizes with the Spirit. The baptism of John thereby acquires a sense other than the one suggested by verse 26a.

■ 29 "The next day" seems to indicate, along with the temporal notices in verses 35, 39, 43, 2:1, a special period of time. Barrosse[3] takes them to mean "the days of a new creation." Boismard,[4] on the other hand, sees here "a holy week." Such edifying interpretations of course transgress Wellhausen's ironic remark:[5] "Upon the next, and then the next, and once more the next day there follows here the third."

Such a series of times is meaningful only if it begins with the day of the Jewish delegation which is also the day of Jesus' baptism. Zahn[6] suggests that John baptized Jesus before the emissaries appeared. One can point to 1:16 and 1:32 in support of this view. But such an inference is not only uncertain but out of place. The Fourth Gospel avoids mentioning the baptism of Jesus by John. With this silence the difficulty disappears that the baptizer has a higher rank than the one baptized (cf. Matt 3:14f.). Whoever disdains this explanation of the silence of the Gospel of John has to explain why the baptismal

day is presumed to be the starting point of a temporal period but remains unspecified. Also these temporal notices could presumably be only markers indicating that a new scene is beginning (but cf. also the local notice in v 28). Such temporal and local notices can simply be used as compositional devices to indicate segments.

It has not yet been determined to whom John is speaking. Not to the emissaries! By their interrogation they have prompted John to express his own self-depreciation very clearly and (without naming a name) to point to Jesus who is so superior to him. In verse 28 they exit the scene. The disciples of John are not a possible candidate either. They have not yet been mentioned; when they hear these same words in verse 36, they follow Jesus immediately. Actually, the readers of the book are being addressed. For this reason the setting can remain indefinite. To what extent this is so is made evident by the fact that Jesus comes to John without meeting him. The mention of the arrival of Jesus has compositional significance: it provides motivation for the word John now pronounces over him. In the Fourth Gospel, Jesus does not have a conversation with John, as he does in Matt 3:14ff.; John is a witness and speaks only about Jesus, not with him.

Because the scene lacks concrete particulars, the saying about the lamb of God floats freely in narrative space. It sounds like the OT. But which OT passage does the author have in mind? None of the passages mentioned in Billerbeck,[7] TDNT,[8] and Dodd,[9] is really suitable. Lev 16:7 speaks of a "scapegoat," which allegedly takes away sins. But it is a goat and not a lamb. According to 1 Cor 5:7f. and John 19:36, Jesus functions as the true paschal lamb, at least in some Christian congregations. The paschal lamb of course does not remove sin, although its blood causes the angel of death to pass over. Jeremias[10] refers to Isa 53:7, perhaps prompted by Burney,[11] and thinks the Aramaic word טליא involves a play on its double sense of (a) lamb and (b) servant, boy. The original phrase would have been טליא דאלהא = παῖς

1   Das Evangelium nach Johannes, 46f.
2   John, 85 [58].
3   "The Seven Days of the New Creation in St. John's Gospel," CBQ 21 (1959) 507–16.
4   "Les traditions johanniques concernant le Baptiste," RB 70 (1963) 5–42.
5   Das Evangelium Johannes, 13.
6   Das Evangelium des Johannes, 115.

7   2: 363–70.
8   1: 342–45.
9   Tradition, 269–71.
10 TDNT 1: 339; "'Αμνὸς τοῦ Θεοῦ (Jn I:29, 36)," ZNW 34 (1935) 117–23.
11 Aramaic Origin, 107f.

θεοῦ ("servant of God"). But an Aramaic original is not likely and the Targum on the Prophets shows that Aramaic עבדא was readily available for the Hebrew term עבד.[12] We do not therefore need recourse to a translation error and do not need to accept an allusion to Isa 53:7, where the servant of God is compared to a sheep standing dumb before its shearers. The discussion in the Overview will go into these matters more precisely.

This much may now be said: the narrator has constructed a new picture of the significance of Jesus out of various traditions, in which Jewish materials had a part. "To take away the sin of the world" is not really appropriate to the christology of the Evangelist. In his view, Jesus has come only for those whom the Father has given to him (John 6:39, 17:12). Thus Martin Luther's famous dictum: *Non enim absolute pro omnibus mortuus est Christus* ("Christ did not die for all absolutely"). So verse 29 is to be taken as a piece of a "source" and probably not only this verse.

The word ἁμαρτία "sin" is likewise not a basic concept in the message of the Evangelist.

■ **30** On this verse Bultmann remarks:[13] "Naturally this relates, not to the saying in verse 15, which is contextless, but, as in v 15, to a scene which the Evangelist has not described but assumes to be familiar. The reference, of course, is to the parallel saying in the synoptic tradition, which the editor has inserted at verse 27." In my judgment, verse 15 and not verse 27 derives from a redactor. Verse 27 ("the one who comes after me") appears to have served as the pattern for the first part and verse 30 ("who was before me, because he existed before me") for the second part. Verse 15 is by no means "contextless" in the sense in which the redactor has inserted it there; rather, the redactor incorporates John into the witnessing community.

But why, following the saying about Jesus as the lamb of God, does the narrator direct the attention of his readers to the saying of John (v 30) that he had already spoken once before? References to scenes reported only by the Synoptics are not otherwise characteristic of the Fourth Gospel; Bultmann's solution therefore seems not so natural to us as it does to him. Consequently, if the narrator is not pointing to a scene foreign to his work, the logic of verse 30 suggests that this saying had already found expression but without expressly naming Jesus. That means: the allusion is to verse 27, which is now taken up and developed further (and thus not by a redactor). What is new in verse 30—it is something different in the Synoptics—is the solution to a problem that had not yet become so conspicuous in the Synoptics. They saw the superiority of the one proclaimed by John in his position as eschatological judge and not, as in verse 30, in Jesus' pre-existence. Nevertheless, verse 30 has a further function: it does not only provide for a connection with the preceding pericope but with the next verses. While verse 29, which announces the appearance of Jesus, spoke only of Jesus, verse 30 brings the train of thought back to the relation between John and Jesus. The question remains open, nevertheless, why John only now manifests specific knowledge of Jesus. In our judgment, the compositional aim of the author comes to expression in this way: he permits the revelation to emerge step by step.

■ **31** appears to provide an answer to the preceding question but in a very remarkable form. For the sentence, "I myself did not know him; but I came baptizing with water, that he might be revealed to Israel," is at first glance contradictory—how can John make someone manifest whom he does not yet know? Insofar as the ignorance of John is concerned, one thinks of the conviction attested by Justin[14] and reported in John 7:27 as the opinion of the authorities: "When the Christ appears, no one will know where he comes from." Here, however, where John rejects identification with Elijah (1:21), the interest lies elsewhere: the water baptism of John has the function of making Jesus known to Israel. But since it is not said in the Johannine report that John baptized Jesus,

---

12 Bultmann, *John*, 96 n. 3 [66 n. 7]; Dodd, Review of *Theologisches Wörterbuch zum Neuen Testament, Lieferungen* 1–7, *JTS* 34 (1935) 280–85.

13 *John*, 97 [67] (translation amended).

14 *Dial.* 8.3 "But Christ—if He has indeed been born, and exists anywhere—is unknown, and does not even know Himself, and has no power until Elias come to anoint Him, and make Him manifest to all" (ANF 1: 199).

it is not clear how the sending of John as the Baptist is to fulfill that purpose.

■ **32** Verse 32 seeks to explain the preceding point, without speaking about the baptism of Jesus: John testifies that he saw the Spirit descending from heaven as a dove and abiding on Jesus. Behind this report lies the representation, known to us from the Synoptics, of an objective, visible event that John perceived (Matt 3:16ff.). Such a representation does not comport with the Prologue of the Fourth Gospel, according to which Jesus is the logos become flesh.[15] Moreover, it is surprising that what appears to be a parallel follows in verses 33f.

■ **33** As in verse 31, the narrative is resumed with the words, "I myself did not know him, but. . . ." A repetition of this type readily arouses the suspicion that one has to do with an insertion or an addition. Yet verse 33 is quite readily understood: the One who sent John to baptize with water said to him: he upon whom you see the Spirit descend and remain is he who baptizes with the Holy Spirit. Why is the designation "God" replaced by ὁ πέμψας με ("the one sending me")? Presumably not because Jesus occasionally speaks of his own sending in this way (e.g., in 5:30)—the Fourth Gospel seeks to set Jesus off from John!—but rather because a special sending of John by God is not to be enunciated so openly.

The difficulty remains, however, of combining the doctrine of the logos with a baptismal account similar to the Synoptics. There is a further difficulty: Jesus is said to baptize with the Holy Spirit, in contrast to John, who baptizes only with water. But according to the Evangelist (7:39, 20:22), the outpouring of the Spirit comes only after the resurrection; the genuineness of the reference to "water" in 3:5 and 19:34 is contested. If "baptism with water" and "baptism with the Spirit" (1:33) form a contrasting pair in 1:19–34, that contrast was probably taken over by the Evangelist (1:26, 31, 33) but not created by him. In 3:22f., where Jesus and John baptize simultaneously, no mention is made of this contrast, nor is there any contrast implied in 4:1. The Evangelist states in 5:26 that the Son has life in himself—and gives life—just as does the Father. That is the real Johannine equivalent to the notion that Jesus baptizes with the Spirit.

■ **34** Verse 34 brings this scene to a close. John testifies that he saw the Spirit descending and abiding on Jesus (the notion that the Spirit is a visible object is also very likely alien to the Evangelist) and he offers the correlative testimony that Jesus is the "Son of God." As a consequence, "Son of God" must be the equivalent of "baptizer with the Spirit."

Nevertheless, P[5vid] ℵ* b e ff[2] sy[sc] Ambros read ἐκλεκτός ("elect") (cf. Luke 23:35), and many exegetes prefer this reading because, with this designation, this chapter contains seven honorific titles for Jesus: (1) lamb of God, (2) elect, (3) rabbi, (4) messiah, (5) son of God, (6) king of Israel, and (7) son of man. Schnackenburg[16] cites a conjecture of Jeremias[17] to the effect that the earlier reading ἐκλεκτός ("elect") was replaced in the fourth century CE by υἱὸς τοῦ θεοῦ ("son of God") in the fight against adoptionism. Meanwhile, the discovery of 𝔓[66] and 𝔓[75] (beginning of the third century CE), contradict this conjecture. These manuscripts offer υἱὸς τοῦ θεοῦ ("son of God") as do A B D Θ al sy[h] bo also. Barrett's reference[18] to Isa 42:1 Ἰσραὴλ ὁ ἐκλεκτός μου,. . . ἔδωκα τὸ πνεῦμα μοῦ ἐπ᾽ αὐτόν ("Israel, my elect,. . . I bestow my Spirit on you") can be understood, contrary to his intention, as an explanation of why Christian scribes like to read ἐκλεκτός ("elect") in this context.[19]

Overview

It is rather readily recognized what it is in the three scenes with John (1:19–28; 1:29–34; 1:35–39) that tempts interpreters to make the most daring alterations and rearrangements of the text. First of all, intrusive traces of the synoptic tradition are perceived here and there. But this "synoptic text" always has its own peculiarities. Further, the contrast between water baptism and Spirit baptism appears to play a decisive role; the theme words, however, are widely separated from each other: we meet the first in verse 26, the second in verse 33. Thirdly, it is asserted that the sole function of John's baptism is to make manifest to John *who* among the crowd of coming ones is really the one who comes after him. In so doing, the outpouring of the Spirit is turned into a visible event, a conception that cannot be attributed to the Evangelist (John 20:21f.). Moreover, if John had witnessed the gift of the Spirit to the appointed

15   Bauer, *Das Johannesevangelium*, 38f.
16   *John*, 1:305f.
17   Article on "παῖς θεοῦ," *TDNT* 5: 687, n. 260.
18   *John*, 178.
19   On "Son of God," see Hahn, *Hoheitstitel*, 280–333; for the Fourth Gospel, esp. 329f.

one, he himself would have ceased baptizing. But he continues to baptize as though nothing had happened. This idea, consequently, has not been thought through to its logical conclusion: among the many doublets that strike exegetes, only the double mention of "And I myself did not know him, but . . ." in verses 31 and 33 and the twofold mention of the descending Spirit in verses 32 and 33 may be noted.

All this makes it understandable when Schwartz lets a sigh escape in his "Aporien im vierten Evangelium"[20] — however, before he comes to our pericope: "One is tempted, exhausted and discouraged, to lay the critical knife aside and leave these passages in the confusion and dismay into which they have fallen as a result of their revision." That characterizes the mood of the last great literary critic of the Fourth Gospel, and it was consistent that he would not include these "Aporien" ("Problems")—comprising all of 169 pages—in his collected works. In a certain sense, that is a pity. For alongside hypotheses that seem to us impossible, these now as good as forgotten "Problems" contain very remarkable insights. So Schwartz and others discovered the freedom with which the tradition is reworked theologically in the Fourth Gospel—without regard to casualties—until everything fits into the picture—at least almost everything.

His observation must be combined, to be sure, with others regarding the compositional techniques of the Fourth Gospel before one has the prospect of finding one's way through the labyrinth. To these belongs the observation that the narrator suggests pictures of definite situations but does not completely fill them in. John and the Jesus going out to meet him yield such a picture. This situation alone confronts the reader; all the trimmings are missing. The essentials are not presented to us in motion, but appear in a "snapshot," so to speak. It does not amount to an encounter, a verbal exchange with Jesus, the two do not exchange a single word, and only the word of John provoked by the appearance of Jesus is reported: "Behold, the Lamb of God, who takes away the sin of the world." This pronouncement on the meaning of Jesus, his task and his being, is intended for the reader.

It was heard and very profoundly determined the picture of the Fourth Gospel in the church, with the comforting ring and fervor that emanated or seemed to emanate from its message: the congregation hoped for the consoling and healing presence of such a savior. Moreover, it happens that one is not aware of the cool austerity with which the picture of Jesus meets us in the discourses of the Fourth Gospel. The picture of the lamb that takes away the sin of the world and the picture of the exalted one who will draw all his own to himself prove to be related at bottom. That also explains how the Evangelist can also take over from his "source(s)" texts that are alien to his thoughts.

Great freedom is exercised in this pericope in making use of a series of traditional figures in depicting the testimony of John. The narrative is not so tasteless as to make Jesus into a "scapegoat." But this function in ancient Israel is attributed to Jesus. John is not here claiming the fulfillment of an OT prophecy. The "scapegoat" does not indeed take away the sin of the world (as was believed), but only the sin of Israel. The lamb, which is spoken of here rather than the goat, recalls the paschal lamb. The meaning of that which protects or saves is connected with this figure. But Acts 8:32f. shows that the sheep of Isa 53:7, the one that is dumb before its shearer, is understood as representing the silent, suffering Jesus. The various forms of the portrait of Jesus are kaleidoscopically reflected in verse 29, in which all the details subconsciously work together to form a new image in its own right.

This reshaping of the tradition takes place with such mastery, such bold freedom, that the reader, who has been gratefully attentive to this quality of the narrator, is full of hope, and now wants to open up more of the text in a similar manner, in compelling power. But that is not so cheaply purchased. John was long aware—so we learn in verse 33—that it was his task to bear witness to one coming after him who greatly surpassed him. But he could not anticipate what human shape would be taken by the one sent from eternity—he can, of course, anticipate to the extent of verse 30: he does not know him and yet he knows of his call to serve as a witness. That we now understand. But the manner and means by which

---

20   4: 497.

John came to this recognition is alien to the reader: supposedly God prompted the baptismal activity of John so that, among the multitudes flooding out to him, he could discern the one upon whom the Spirit descended and abode. That again recalls the Synoptics and their account of the baptism. But more important is the audacity with which the Baptist makes everything subservient to the one thing to which the Fourth Gospel also knows itself to be duty bound. All meaning attached to John—which at that time was still visible through the murky medium of the Baptist sect—disappears as misunderstanding and distortion. That is the way it turns out—we must admit—and not without violence: the Baptist movement kindled by John possessed its own strength, which prompted Jesus to leave his home and his region and become a pilgrim to the Jordan. Whoever views the meaning of the Fourth Gospel in the light of the wealth of information available about the time of Jesus must be shocked by the historical sketch presented in this passage—if he is willing to admit it. But the narrator does not choose to paint the past in the many hues of its historical dress, but intends to exhibit the lines connecting the great individual figures as he saw them.

Verses 1:31f. have represented the new interpretations of the baptism of John so laconically and opaquely that a later hand, in our judgment, develops the allusions of verse 31 more fully and clearly, by means of a clarifying supplement, in verses 33f., without, however, obscuring what is to be clarified. If this conjecture is valid, then the contrast between baptism with water and baptism with Spirit disappears from the original conception. It basically does not fit. The narrator understands the baptismal activity of John only as a means by which John comes to a recognition of Jesus. He has already said what Jesus is recognized to be (the lamb of God . . . , v 29). But in later times, in which Christians boasted of their baptism as accompanied by the gift of the Spirit (although it was no longer accompanied by an ecstatic outpouring of the Spirit), verse 33 was uttered with deep conviction.

This brief passage permits a glimpse into the metamorphosis that took place in the Christian church of the first century CE. It shows, at the same time, how both gain and loss are joined. Insofar as the Spirit that accompanies baptism is distinguished from visions and ecstasies, to this extent does the sacrament of baptism become independent of the experience that befalls the faithful in that connection (or is even denied them). This sacrament is thereby separated from the rites of the mysteries to which some think it is related (even modern investigators). But then the dangerous possibility arises that the sacrament of baptism will be devalued as a ticket into a "club" that one inherits at birth.

4. Disciples of John Go Over to Jesus

Bibliography

Agnew, F.
"Vocatio primorum discipulorum in traditione synoptica." *VD* 46 (1968) 129–47.

Cribbs, F. Lamar
"St. Luke and the Johannine Tradition." *JBL* 90 (1971) 422–50, esp. 433–35.

Cullmann, Oscar
The Johannine Circle, tr. John Bowden (Philadelphia: Westminster Press, 1976) = *Der johanneische Kreis* (Tübingen: Mohr-Siebeck, 1975).

Dauer, Anton
Die Passionsgeschichte im Johannesevangelium, SANT 30 (Munich: Kösel, 1972), esp. 35f.

Dodd, Charles Harold
Historical Tradition in the Fourth Gospel (Cambridge: Cambridge University Press, 1965), esp. 302–12.

Hahn, Ferdinand
"Die Jüngerberufung Joh 1,35–51." In *Neues Testament und Kirche. Für Rudolf Schnackenburg,* ed. J. Gnilka (Freiburg: Herder, 1974) 172–90.

Hanhart, Karel
"'About the Tenth Hour' . . . on Nisam 15 (Jn 1:35–40)." In *L'Evangile de Jean. Sources, rédaction, théologie,* ed. M. de Jonge. BETL 44 (Gembloux: Duculot; Louvain: University Press, 1977) 335–46.

Hornung, A.
"Nachfolge im Lichte der Apostelberufungen." *Claretianum* 10 (1970) 79–108.

Hulen, Amos B.
"The Call of the Four Disciples in John I." *JBL* 67 (1948) 153–57.

Spaemann, Heinrich
"Stunde des Lammes. Meditationen über die ersten Jüngerberufungen (Joh. 1, 35–51)." *BibLeb* 7 (1966) 58–68.

Wulf, F.
"'Meister, wo wohnst du?' (Joh 1, 38)." *Geist und Leben* 31 (1958) 241–44.

Zimmermann, Heinrich
"'Meister, wo wohnst Du?' (Joh 1,38)." *Lebendiges Zeugnis* (1962) 49–57.

1

35 **The next day again John was standing with two of his disciples; 36/ and he looked at Jesus as he walked, and said, "Behold, the Lamb of God " 37/ The two disciples heard him say this, and they followed Jesus. 38/ Jesus turned, and saw them following, and said to them, "What do you seek?" And they said to him, "Rabbi**

(which means Teacher), where are you staying?" 39/ He said to them, "Come and see." They came and saw where he was staying; and they stayed with him that day, for it was about the tenth hour.

The call of the first disciples follows upon the encounter with John (and the baptism, which is not narrated), in two scenes. The two scenes are fundamentally different from the synoptic reports. The first disciple to be won over appears to be Andrew, while the second remains shrouded in mystery. Exegetes, especially the earlier ones, believed that the second, however, was to be identified with John, son of Zebedee (although his brother, James, is mentioned neither here nor elsewhere in the Fourth Gospel, except for chapter 21), or with that "disciple whom Jesus loved" who is John himself (although he is not spoken of explicitly here). Peter is then led to Jesus by Andrew, and receives the name Cephas, the meaning of which the Evangelist knows. On the next day, Andrew finds Philip, who is also from Bethsaida, and then Nathanael, who is not mentioned in the Synoptics. The way in which these disciples address Jesus shows that they proleptically represent the believing community. There are various indications that the Evangelist is here making use of a report that has been transmitted to him. The call of the disciples is the means of clarifying the christological significance of Jesus. The concepts of the entire older tradition are thereby taken up: he is the one who is expected as the definitive emissary of God and known by various designations. John closes this section with a picture representing the abiding affinity of the "Son of Man" with God, a picture which transcends all previous christological statements.

■ **35** "The next day" again opens a new scene. The narrator continues to employ the same method: he indicates only what is most important. That gives the story an air of mystery: the reader feels that more is being said than what is explicitly stated in the text. John is standing there with two of his disciples; he is not represented as a baptizer of the masses as in Matt 3:5, 7. "Two out of . . ." is equivalent to "two of . . .": ἐκ is common in koine for the partitive genitive. As a consequence, one must not assume from the construction that other disciples were present. If only a pair out of a whole band of disciples

follow John's suggestion, that would be a paltry result. One must also not assume, with many of the older exegetes, that the two disciples were present on the previous day; in that case one misunderstands the entire sequence of scenes.

■ **36** This time Jesus does not come out to John (as in v 29), but "walks around" (the narrator does not like verbal repetition). But this construction serves the same purpose: it prompts the abbreviated repetition of words from verse 29 (the reader knows what the whole formula means). Zahn[1] construes as follows: Jesus "spent the night in the vicinity (v 38) and still does not betray his intention to leave the territory of the Baptist (v 43). Does he intend to join the Baptist as disciple, like other Galileans? And does he now await an invitation to do so? John himself appears surprised . . . ." Here an ingenious and at times pedantic imagination attempts to fill in the blanks that, in his judgment, are found in the text: everything is reckoned down to the last penny.

Ἐμβλέψας ("look at") is not to be distinguished in sense from βλέπει in verse 29: the narrator likes variety. Although it is not clear, in fact, why Jesus walks around (apart from the fact that it accounts for the action), John does not exhibit surprise, but discretely nods to the two disciples as he pronounces Jesus the lamb of God.

■ **37** They hear, understand the order, and follow it: they follow Jesus. Here ἀκολουθεῖν ("follow") is only the precursor of real discipleship. In this regard Braun[2] asks: " The two disciples follow Jesus. Curiosity aroused? More or less consciously enchanted by the person of Jesus? Mysterious action of grace? Who will plumb this mystery?" All these are questions foreign to the narrator; he is thus unable to respond to them.

■ **38** Jesus turns and asks them what they want. Everything is concrete,[3] but everyday. This has prompted exegetes such as Büchsel[4] to comment: "To tell this story makes sense only if the Evangelist conceals the beloved disciple behind the unnamed companion of Andrew (v 40). If he is here narrating his own story, and if the first

1   *Das Evangelium des Johannes,* 129.
2   *La Sainte Bible,* 10: 324.
3   Not "picturesque"; Zahn, *Das Evangelium des*

Johannes, 30.
4   *Das Evangelium nach Johannes,* 41.

readers knew that, it is best to understand that he did not want to forego the opportunity to report these events that had an incomparable significance for him in spite of their simplicity." Such an apologetic evaluation forgets that concreteness does not guarantee historicity and that everydayness can have an entirely different meaning here.[5] Godet[6] elucidates Jesus' question "What do you seek?" with the words: "He knows at what the yearning of Israel, the sighing of mankind, is aimed." That turns the question into a sham and converts the everyday into an allegory with a deep meaning. The mode of address of the disciples ("rabbi," literally, "my great one"; cf. phrases such as "my Lord") treats the one addressed as someone deserving respect, not as "a theologian authorized to teach." The question of the disciples regarding Jesus' place of abode ($\mu\acute{\epsilon}\nu\epsilon\iota\nu$) challenges the exegetes in a variety of ways: "Since the two disciples had already seen Jesus on the previous day"—about which the text says nothing—"they assume that he must have had a shelter for the night nearby"[7] "and since he gives no indication of an intention to leave, they ask him about the quarters he occupies." To this Schwartz[8] responds in exasperation: "Were hotels erected there to accommodate the hordes that poured out to John?" He then conjectures that here there is a remnant of the genuine call of disciples which took place at the permanent home of Jesus. But the narrator does not picture John as being beseiged by masses of people and therefore does not have the two disciples request an uninterrupted "private interview." The rule that one must not transpose the narratives of one gospel into another gospel as a matter of course is often forgotten.

■ **39** Jesus answers their question with a common expression constituting a polite invitation. The language of the ordinary is retained, to the regret of many exegetes. The perception, which is understandable, that "it must have involved more than a simple visit," leads exegetes to supply what is apparently missing out of their own repertoire. It is innocent enough when Bengel[9] praises the simplicity of Jesus' room (following the lead of 2 Kgs 4:10). It is more serious when Belser[10] conjectures that Jesus related the story of his three temptations, which had just taken place, to the two of them. How wise the narrator was when he did not make the attempt to describe the "blessed hours" in more detail (in which case the profound would have been lost in the superficiality of the everyday) will be known to every minister who has undertaken to improve upon the narrator at this point. We are not saying, to be sure, that the author approached his task with the presuppositions of a modern author. Jesus' invitation, "Come and see," can perhaps have possessed the overtones of a call for him. That would not be an allegory in the ordinary sense, but a writing or painting rich in background, out of which the beholder himself strives to form a picture. In any case, our narrator was not given to many words and the worn cliche.

The "tenth hour" has given exegetes trouble. In accordance with the common way of reckoning in the gospels, the expression means "the fourth hour" of the afternoon. But then is it not already approaching dusk in the east? The temporal designation (always introduced in the Fourth Gospel with $\acute{\omega}\varsigma$ "about") marks the end of the narrative unit, not the end of the visit.

Overview

This segment especially demonstrates how important are the presuppositions of exegesis, presuppositions that appear obvious to us but often remain subconscious. Earlier exegetes were looking for a historically reliable report, especially in the form of an eyewitness account. If one presupposes that type of report, then one looks at every graphic detail in the text as proof of the historical exactness of the account. When such concrete features are missing, one is tempted to supply them, either by logical deductions, or by recourse to the presentations of other gospels, or even simply by virtue of a lively imagination. If one proceeds in this fashion, then the character

5 See the Overview.
6 *John*, 97.
7 Zahn (*Das Evangelium des Johannes*, 130 n. 35) proposes the southeastern perimeter of the Oasis of Fasail, in the Wadi Mellaha.
8 "Aporien," 4: 527.
9 *D. Joh. Alberti Bengelii Gnomon Novi Testamenti* (Stuttgart: Steinkopf, [8]1887) 1: 433.
10 *Das Evangelium des heiligen Johannes*, 61.

of the text is unintentionally altered. It is the obligation of exegesis, however, to clarify *the text* that lies before us, in all its ambiguity.

Our detailed comment endeavored to show that this segment (and the three scenes with John generally) does not strive to depict a definite event in stenographic exactness, but leaves it to the reader to seize the meaning of what is only hinted at. The more detail a verse contains, the greater the temptation to employ the earlier method of exegesis. The more one makes clear everything that the text does *not* say, the more dubious becomes the undertaking. Is it not curious that the two disciples apparently forsake their former master without so much as a word of farewell? That Jesus remains at the baptismal site so long, even though there is no mention of his baptism? That John no longer appears as a baptizer, but only as a witness on behalf of Jesus? That the two disciples inquire after the μονή ("abode") of Jesus? That we do not learn what they are to begin after this day (many exegetes have them—deliberately—spend the entire night with Jesus)? And so on. It would be a hopeless enterprise were we to go into all these questions which apparently do not interest the narrator at all.

Neither does the author intend to represent the emergence of the apostolic circle, as is occasionally suggested—the two disciples remain anonymous in this pericope. It has already been noted that the Twelve play no special role in the Fourth Gospel. The author is concerned rather with the rise of the congregation and at the same time with the relation of John and his disciples to Jesus. (That the mission commences in 1:40–51 is almost a matter of course, for church and mission go very closely together in early Christianity.) This relationship is reflected indirectly in an ordinary story of a visit, during which apparently no questions of faith are touched upon. The Christian readers understand this indirect communication: the two disciples—they represent the congregation—learn where Jesus is "at home," and it becomes clear that here the real transition from John to Jesus takes place. The saying of John in 3:30, "He must increase, but I must decrease," stands as the unexpressed motto over this scene.

The three scenes (1:19–28 without vv 22–24; 1:29–34; and 1:35–39) have proved to be very carefully constructed compositions, which is all to the author's literary credit. But would a "source" have been composed in this way, would narratives in this kind of form have been transmitted in the tradition? We believe that to be very unlikely. The tradition regarding John in Mark and Q has a very different cast. Only in the special Matthean material does critical reflection become audible (3:14f.), however without serious disruption. The two verses in question are not of the oldest tradition.

The question of an old source or old tradition in these scenes can probably be posed only in this way: one must bear firmly in mind the difference between the Synoptics and John so far as the relationship between John and Jesus is concerned. In the Synoptics Jesus begins to proclaim as John disappears for ever behind the walls of Machaerus (cf. Mark 6:14–29 with pars.). In the Fourth Gospel the two men continue to work alongside one another (cf. John 3:22–36). Who is correct? The synoptic account or the Johannine version?

In his book, *Jesus and His Story*,[11] Ethelbert Stauffer decides for the Johannine sketch and accounts for the cleansing of the Temple at the beginning of Jesus' activity as follows: Jesus was still understood as a disciple of the Baptist and, carried along by the sympathy of the common people for his master, he cleanses the Temple. This interweaving of the Synoptics and the Fourth Gospel seems to us to be methodologically inadmissible and is discredited by the fictitious combinations to which it invites us. The Johannine picture of the inauguration of the work of Jesus comes from a time when the beginnings of the "narratives of Jesus" started to lose their contours and so, having become free forms, were capable of serving as the means of expressing the Christian gospel.

---

11 *Jesus and His Story,* tr. Dorothea M. Barton (London: SCM Press, 1960). See chap. 4: "Jesus and the Baptist's Movement," 59–69.

5. The Call of the First Disciples

Bibliography

Barrett, Charles Kingsley
"Das Fleisch des Menschensohns (Joh 6,53)." In
Jesus und der Menschensohn. Für Anton Vögtle, ed. R.
Pesch and R. Schnackenburg (Freiburg: Herder,
1975) 342–54.

Betz, Otto
"Kann denn aus Nazareth etwas Gutes kommen?"
Wort und Geschichte [Festschrift for K. Elliger], ed.
H. Gese and H. P. Rüger (Neukirchen: Neu-
kirchener Verlag, 1973) 6–16.

Borsch, Frederick H.
The Christian and Gnostic Son of Man, SBT, 2nd ser.,
14 (Naperville, IL: Allenson, 1970).

Brown, Raymond E.
*Peter in the New Testament: A Collaborative Assessment
by Protestant and Roman Catholic Scholars* (Minnea-
polis: Augsburg; New York: Paulist, 1973), esp.
129–47.

Coppens, Joseph
"Les logia johanniques du Fils de l'homme." In
L'Evangile de Jean. Sources, rédaction, théologie, ed.
M. de Jonge. BETL 44 (Gembloux: Duculot;
Louvain: University Press, 1977) 311–15.

Cousar, Charles B.
"John, 1:29–42." *Int* 31 (1977) 401–6.

Cullmann, Oscar
"Πέτρα," "Πέτρος, Κηφᾶς." *TDNT* 6: 95–112.

Dieckmann, Hermann
"'Der Sohn des Menschen' im Johannesevangelium." *Scholastik* 2 (1927) 229–47.

Dion, Hyacinthe-M.
"Quelque traits originaux de la conception johannique du Fils de l'Homme." *Sciences ecclésiastiques*
19 (1967) 49–65.

Enciso Viana, Jesús
"La vocación de Natanael y el Salmo 24." *EstBib* 19
(1960) 229–36.

Freed, Edwin D.
"The Son of Man in the Fourth Gospel." *JBL* 86
(1967) 402–9.

Fritsch, J.
"'. . . videbitis . . . angelos Dei ascendentes et des-
cendentes super Filium hominis' (Jn 1,51)." *VD* 37
(1959) 3–11.

Haenchen, Ernst
"Petrus-Probleme." *NTS* 7 (1961) 187–97. In his
Gott und Mensch. Gesammelte Aufsätze 1 (Tübingen:
Mohr-Siebeck, 1965) 55–67.

Hahn, Ferdinand
"Die Jüngerberufung Joh 1,35–51." In *Neues
Testament und Kirche. Für Rudolf Schnackenburg,* ed.
J. Gnilka (Freiburg: Herder, 1974) 172–90.

Hahn, Ferdinand
"Sehen und Glauben im Johannesevangelium." In

Neues Testament und Geschichte. Historisches Geschehen und Deutung im Neuen Testament. Oscar Cullmann zum 70. Geburtstag, ed. H. Baltensweiler and B. Reicke (Zurich: Theologischer Verlag; Tübingen: Mohr-Siebeck, 1972) 125–41.

Hanhart, Karel
"The Structure of John 1,35–4,54." In *Studies in John Presented to Professor J. N. Sevenster on the Occasion of his Seventieth Birthday* (Leiden: E. J. Brill, 1970) 22–46.

Iber, G.
"Überlieferungsgeschichtliche Untersuchung zum Begriff des Menschensohns im Neuen Testament." Dissertation, Heidelberg, 1953.

Jacobi, Bernhard
"Über die Erhöhung des Menschensohnes. Joh 3, 14.15." *TSK* 8 (1835) 7–70.

Jeremias, Joachim
"Die Berufung des Nathanael." *Angelos* 3 (1928) 2–5.

Kuhli, Horst
"Nathanael—'wahrer Israelit'? Zum angeblich attributiven Gebrauch von ἀληθῶς in Joh 1,47." *Biblische Notizen* 9 (1979) 11–19.

Kunniburgh, E.
"The Johannine 'Son of Man.'" *SE* 4 = TU 102 (Berlin: Akademie-Verlag, 1968) 64–71.

Lentzen-Deis, Fritzleo
"Das Motiv der 'Himmelsöffnung' in verschiedenen Gattungen der Umweltsliteratur des Neuen Testaments." *Bib* 50 (1969) 301–27.

Lindars, Barnabas
"The Son of Man in the Johannine Christology." In *Christ and Spirit in the New Testament* [Festschrift for C. F. D. Moule], ed. B. Lindars and S. S. Smalley (Cambridge: Cambridge University Press, 1973) 43–60.

Mehlmann, John
"Notas sobre Natanael—S Bartolomeus, Joh 1,45–51." *Revista di Cultura Biblica* 5 (1961) 337–42.

Menoud, Philippe-Henri
"'Le fils de Joseph.' Etude sur Jean I, 45 et IV, 42." *RTP* 18 (1930) 275–88.

Michaelis, Wilhelm
"Joh 1,51, Gen 28,12 und das Menschensohn-Problem." *TLZ* 85 (1960) 561–78.

Michaels, J. Ramsey
"Nathanael under the Fig-tree (Jn 1:48; 4:19)." *ExpTim* 78 (1966/1967) 182–83.

Moloney, Francis J.
The Johannine Son of Man, Biblioteca di scienze religiose 14 (Rome: Libreria Ateneo Salesiano, 1976, ²1979).

Moloney, Francis J.
"The Johannine Son of Man." *BTB* 6 (1976) 177–89.

Moule, C. F. D.
"A Note on 'Under the Fig-tree' in John i. 48, 50." *JTS,* ns. 5 (1954) 210–11.

Mussner, Franz
Petrus und Paulus—Pole der Einheit. Eine Hilfe für die Kirchen. Quaestiones Disputatae 76 (Freiburg: Herder, 1976) esp. 40–49.

Neyrey, Jerome H.
"The Jacob Allusions in John 1:51." *CBQ* 44 (1982) 586–605.

O. L. in Schlesien
"Nathanael." *ZWT* 16 (1873) 96–102.

Painter, John
"Christ and the Church in John 1,45–51." In *L'Evangile de Jean. Sources, rédaction, théologie,* ed. M. de Jonge. BETL 44 (Gembloux: Duculot; Louvain: University Press, 1977) 359–62.

Potterie, Ignace de la
"L'Exaltation du Fils de l'homme." *Greg* 49 (1968) 460–78.

Quispel, G.
"Nathanael und der Menschensohn (Joh 1, 51)." *ZNW* 47 (1956) 281–83.

Riedl, Johannes
"Wenn ihr den Menschensohn erhöht habt, werdet ihr erkennen." In *Jesus und der Menschensohn. Für Anton Vögtle,* ed. R. Pesch and R. Schnackenburg (Freiburg: Herder, 1975) 355–70.

Ruckstuhl, Eugen
"Abstieg und Erhöhung des johanneischen Menschensohnes." In *Jesus und der Menschensohn. Für Anton Vögtle,* ed. R. Pesch and R. Schnackenburg (Freiburg: Herder, 1975) 314–41.

Ruckstuhl, Eugen
"Die johanneische Menschensohnforschung." In *Theologische Berichte 1,* ed. J. Pfammatter and F. Fürger (Zurich and Cologne: Benziger, 1972) 171–284.

Schnackenburg, Rudolf
"Der Menschensohn im Johannesevangelium." *NTS* 11 (1964/1965) 123–37.

Schnackenburg, Rudolf
"Die Messiasfrage im Johannesevangelium." In *Neutestamentliche Aufsätze. Festschrift für Prof. Josef Schmid zum 70. Geburtstag,* ed. J. Blinzler, O. Kuss, F. Mussner (Regensburg: F. Pustet, 1963) 240–64.

Schulz, Siegfried
Untersuchungen zur Menschensohn-Christologie im Johannesevangelium, zugleich ein Beitrag zur Methodengeschichte der Auslegung des 4. Evangeliums (Göttingen: Vandenhoeck & Ruprecht, 1957).

Sidebottom, E. M.
"The Son of Man as Man in the Fourth Gospel." *ExpTim* 68 (1956/1957) 213–35, 280–83.

Sidebottom, E. M.
"The Ascent and Descent of the Son of Man in the Gospel of St. John." *ATR* 39 (1957) 115–22.

Smalley, Stephen S.
"Johannes 1,51 und die Einleitung zum vierten Evangelium." In *Jesus und der Menschensohn. Für Anton Vögtle,* ed. R. Pesch and R. Schnackenburg (Freiburg: Herder, 1975) 300–13.

Smalley, Stephen S.
  "The Johannine Son of Man Sayings." *NTS* 15 (1968/1969) 278–301.
Spaeth, H.
  "Nathanael: Ein Beitrag zum Verständnis der Composition des Logos-Evangeliums." *ZWT* 11 (1868) 168–213, 309–43.
Trémel, Y. B.
  "Le Fils de l'homme selon saint Jean." *Lumière et vie* 12 (1962/1963) 65–92.
Windisch, Hans
  "Angelophanien um den Menschensohn auf Erden. Zu Joh 1, 51." *ZNW* 30 (1931) 215–33.
Windisch, Hans
  "Joh 1, 51 und die Auferstehung Jesu." *ZNW* 31 (1932) 199–204.

1

40 **One of the two who heard John speak, and followed him, was Andrew, Simon Peter's brother. 41/ He first found his brother Simon, and said to him, "We have found the Messiah" (which means Christ). 42/ He brought him to Jesus. Jesus looked at him, and said, "So you are Simon the son of John? you shall be called Cephas" (which means Rock). 43/ The next day Jesus decided to go to Galilee. And he found Philip and said to him, "Follow me." 44/ Now Philip was from Bethsaida, the city of Andrew and Peter. 45/ Philip found Nathanael, and said to him, "We have found him of whom Moses in the law and also the prophets wrote, Jesus of Nazareth, the son of Joseph." 46/ Nathanael said to him, "Can anything good come out of Nazareth?" Philip said to him, "Come and see." 47/ Jesus saw Nathanael coming to him, and said to him, "Behold an Israelite indeed, in whom is no guile " 48/ Nathanael said to him, "How do you know me?" Jesus answered him, "Before Philip called you, when you were under the fig tree, I saw you." 49/ Nathanael answered him, "Rabbi, you are the Son of God You are the King of Israel " 50/ Jesus answered him, "Because I said to you, I saw you under the fig tree, do you believe? You shall see greater things than these." 51/ And he said to him, "Truly, truly, I say to you, you will see heaven opened, and the angels of God ascending and descending upon the Son of man."**

■**40** A new segment begins abruptly. One of the two unnamed disciples of verse 35 becomes the known figure of Andrew. Papias[1] names Andrew before Peter and Philip; only with the fourth name do the two lists deviate: John mentions Philip, Papias names Thomas. Here apparently a tradition that displaces Peter from first

1   Eusebius, *H.E.* 3.39.4.

position in the synoptic list makes its appearance. Peter appears in third position owing to the two disciples who were called first; this, too, does not agree with Papias. Since the second disciple remains unnamed, his historicity may be doubted. Because Andrew is the brother of Peter, it is natural that Andrew should first of all seek and "find" him—we do not learn where he and Philip stay: the story is extremely abbreviated—apart from the Nathaniel episode. It is necessary that personal names appear in verses 40–51 because now the formation of the first circle of disciples is described, if only by way of suggestion. In verse 35 the names of the two disciples would only have distracted from the two central figures, Jesus and John. The emergence of the circle of disciples is of course not clearly developed (the Fourth Gospel does not speak of apostles; were it to do so, all the disciples would be included: 20:19–22).

The narrator is indifferent to the question where the two disciples spent the night, as he is to where the "finding" took place. One thinks of the vicinity of John's activity. In any case, the Fourth Gospel says nothing about the baptism of John, other than that it is effected (only) with water. It is wise not to press the narrator for more on geographical references than he explicitly provides.

■ **41** The third word of this verse already precipitated questions at an early time. In the ancient church, $\pi\rho\hat{\omega}\tau os$ led to the welcome supposition that the as yet unnamed companion of Andrew, for his part, brought his own brother to Jesus. Unfortunately, that is not stated but only inferred from the reading $\pi\rho\hat{\omega}\tau os$. The ancient church saw in this a concealed self-reference of the modest author (John, the son of Zebedee), without stopping to ask whether modesty and concealed self-references comport with each other. Of course the unnamed companion of Andrew—if one permits the thought patterns of the early church—could also be James, the other son of Zebedee, who is almost always named before his brother John in the Gospels; only in Luke 8:51 and 9:28 do the readings vary. James was apparently the more energetic of the two brothers and consequently fell victim to the persecution of Herod Aggripa (Acts 12:2). However, the reading $\pi\rho\hat{\omega}\tau ov$ is

better attested, and one cannot base any great conjectures on $\emph{ἴδιos}$: it is often used in koine without emphasis. And $\pi\rho\hat{\omega}\tau ov$ could mean: the next thing that happened was the following: Andrew found his brother Simon. In that case Andrew would not be obligated to find additional followers. Moreover, verse 43 interrupts the pattern: a newly acquired disciple always, for his part, finds yet another follower.

The plural is not often noted: "We have found . . . ," which is repeated in verse 45 in the mouth of Philip. It is perhaps to be explained as the "we" of the congregation in process of formation, which is used each time by the named disciple as a representative of that body.

The Graecized word $M\epsilon\sigma\sigma\acute{\iota}as$ (*mashiach*, meaning "anointed one, messiah") is translated for the reader with the term "Christ" ($X\rho\iota\sigma\tau\acute{o}s$).

$\Pi\rho\hat{\omega}\tau os$ is attested only by $\aleph$* $\Re$ W *al.* $\mathfrak{P}^{66}$ and $\mathfrak{P}^{75}$, along with B A Θ f^1 f^{13} *al* sa bo, read: $\pi\rho\hat{\omega}\tau ov$. Both readings present difficulties. For that reason, the reading *mane* ($\pi\rho\omega\acute{\iota}$, "early in the morning") arose at an early time; this Latin word almost certainly goes back to a Greek word, although unattested in the manuscript tradition. Thus it is here a case of a clarifying conjecture.

■ **42** Jesus looks at the one brought to him and says: "You are Simon, the son of John" (Hebrew: יוחנן). In Matt 16:17, however, Jesus addresses him as "Simon, son of Jonah." On this Jeremias remarks:[2] "Apart from the prophet Jonah there is no instance of Jona(h) as an independent man's name prior to the 3rd century A. D." On the other hand, Jonah occasionally appears in the LXX for Hebrew Jochanan. From that Jeremias would like to conclude that Jonah in Matt 16:17 is an abbreviation of Jochanan. But that conclusion is uncertain because the ordinary shortening of Jochanan is pronounced יוחא or יוחי. It is possible that the less common name Jonah was replaced by the more common "Jochanan" (John). The Fourth Gospel would then be following another tradition here (see v 40). Whether the narrator is of the opinion that Jesus speaks this word out of his omniscience—after all, he had already been conversing with Andrew, the brother of Peter–is not entirely certain. In contrast, certainty does apply to the second part of the pronouncement of Jesus: "You shall be called Cephas (which means

2   *TDNT* 3: 407.

Peter)." In Matt 16:18 we find one pronouncement with reference to the present, "You are Peter," combined with a second one with reference to the future: "On this rock I will build my church." In John 1:42, the verb is in the future: "You shall be called Cephas": a name of honor is conferred on the disciple at the beginning of Jesus' ministry.[3] This disciple may have borne the name שמעון (Acts 15:14 and in some manuscripts of 2 Pet 1:1 represented by Συμεών); however, it is entirely possible that he also had the genuine Greek name Σιμών (attested already in Aristophanes, *Clouds*, 351). The Aramaic word כפא, Greek equivalent Κῆφας, means the rock, which denotes a trait; πέτρα refers rather to stones; yet the distinction is not strictly maintained. Since πέτρα is a feminine form in Greek, the name of the disciple was interpreted as Πέτρος. According to Mark 3:16, Jesus conferred this name of honor on Peter at the time of the call of the Twelve, according to Matt 16:18 at Caesarea Philippi. In fact, however, Matt uses the name Peter as early as 4:18 and 10:2 in the phrase "Simon named Peter." He presupposes that in 16:18 and interprets the name thus: "Peter is the rock on which I will build my church."[4] Because the name appears in the Fourth Gospel already in 1:42, Cullmann writes:[5] "From these variations, . . . we conclude that in the process of transmission the memory of the moment in which Jesus gave Peter the title had become lost; the same is true of the setting of many other stories in the Gospels." Since the leadership of the church is not turned over to Peter until 21:15–17 ("feed my sheep"), while prior to this time he plays no especially praiseworthy role, verse 42 is to be taken as a reflection of a pre-Johannine tradition that the narrator did not want to overlook.

■ **43** "The following day" indicates a certain break in the narrative. The subject of the verb is not named. It is sometimes thought to be Andrew, who finds a "second" in the person of Philip. It is more likely, however, that Jesus is the subject; he is the principal participant. In that event, the pattern, one disciple who is "found" finds another, is not employed. Why Jesus' intention to go to Galilee is mentioned here is not entirely clear; preparation for 2:2 could be the reason. Philip is the only disciple in the Fourth Gospel who is expressly called to discipleship by Jesus himself. Jesus' command, "Follow me," sounds synoptic (Mark 2:14 in the call of Levi), but is not for that reason derived from the Synoptics.

■ **44** Verse 44 is intended to clarify how it came about that Andrew, Peter, and Philip are called one after the other: they all came from the same town, Bethsaida, which lay east of the mouth of the Jordan. They could therefore have appeared as a group for John's baptism, although only Andrew is designated a disciple of John. The house of Simon and Andrew stood in Capernaum, however, according to Mark 1:29, a few kilometers west of the point at which the Jordan empties into the Sea of Gennesaret. Strathmann[6] has attempted to reconcile the two places by suggesting that Peter married into a family in Capernaum. Such an accommodation of data drawn from Mark and John—one that overlooks Andrew—is most probably dictated by apologetic aspirations. The continuation of the narrative makes it clear that here the Fourth Gospel is following a non-Markan tradition, and probably a less reliable one.[7] It is true that Jesus stays a few days in Capernaum, according to John 2:12, with his mother, his brothers, and the disciples, and this is the place where the βασιλικός ("official") lives. But it is in this city that the great defection of most of Jesus' disciples takes place at a later time (John 6:66); it is no contradiction that Capernaum, according to Matt 11:23, is utterly depraved— ἕως Ἅδου καταβήσῃ ("you will be brought down to Hades")—because of its unbelief.

■ **45** The "finding" goes on. This time Philip finds Nathanel, who is apparently known to him. The Synoptics know nothing of Nathanel; he comes from Cana in Galilee, according to John 21:2. Instead of "Messiah," we read now of "him of whom Moses in the law and also the prophets wrote" —Law and Prophets together denote "sacred scripture." A specific OT text is not mentioned.

---

3   On this cluster of problems, cf. Cullman, *TDNT*, vol. 4, and especially his book, *Peter—Disciple, Apostle, Martyr. A Historical and Theological Study* (Philadelphia: Westminster Press, 1953, ²1958). Since Cullmann offers hypotheses that are in part opinionated, caution is advised (cf. the critical review of Haenchen, "Petrus-Probleme," 55–67).

4   Haenchen, *Der Weg Jesu*, 300–03.

5   *Peter*, 21.

6   *Das Evangelium nach Johannes*, 52f.

7   In spite of Dodd, *Tradition*, 309f.

The precise designation of Jesus as "Jesus, son of Joseph, from Nazareth," permits us to recognize the point at which, according to this tradition, objections to Jesus were lodged: it was not against Joseph as his father.

■ **46** Nathanel expresses this doubt: he is dubious about anyone who comes from *Galilean* Nazareth. John 7:52 is a correlative text. Matt and Luke have attempted in various ways to reconcile the two traditions of Jesus' origins: the Nazareth and the (later) Bethlehem traditions. The parents of Jesus, according to Luke 2:4, live in Nazareth, but Jesus was born in Bethlehem as a consequence of special circumstances. Later, the parents return to Nazareth with Jesus (2:9). In contrast, in Matt 2:11 Joseph owns a house in Bethlehem, to which the stars guide the Magi. Only after they return from Egypt (Matt 2:23) do the parents settle down in Nazareth. The tradition utilized by Luke is relatively later than that of Matthew, where Nazareth does not figure in the story until late. Here John could offer the oldest tradition.[8] Philip answers (as does Jesus in v 29) with the common expression:[9] "Come and see." His own experience will contradict the objections of the Jewish tradition. Seeing is emphasized especially in this segment: in verses 46–48 seeing forms something like a chain of catchwords of a formal sort, although the content of the narrative hangs together very closely. As in 4:48, the emphasis here on one's own seeing makes it evident that Christians must see for themselves; it is not enough merely to hold that the Christian message is true.

■ **47** When Nathanael comes to Jesus, the response of Jesus reveals that the hearts of all men are open to him. The commentaries rightly emphasize that here the true Israelite, in whom there is no guile, is to be distinguished from the Jews, who are the enemies of Jesus and his disciples in the Fourth Gospel (20:19, 26).

■ **48** The question of Nathanael: "How do you know me?" prompts the answer of Jesus and reveals that Jesus possesses supernatural knowledge, like a θεῖος ἀνήρ ("divine man"). It is unimportant whether Nathanael meditated under the fig tree or even taught there. The point has to do only with the knowledge of Jesus thus made manifest. Dodd[10] points to Sus 51–59, where the question of the kind of tree becomes decisive for the

evaluation of the testimony of eyewitnesses; Moule[11] points to the same passage.

■ **49** The response of Nathanael is the homage he pays to Jesus as the result of his conviction. "Rabbi" denotes the earthly station of Jesus; "Son of God" and "King of Israel" announce his supernatural rank and his significance for the chosen people.

■ **50** Up to this point, Jesus has revealed only the kind of knowledge attributed at that time to a "divine man" (θεῖος ἀνήρ). Now he promises that Nathanael will see even greater things.

■ **51** The introductory words, "And he said to him," prompt the reader to understand what follows as a continuation of the conversation with Nathanael. However, what follows is introduced by "Truly, truly, I say to you" (plural), which is elsewhere used in the Fourth Gospel to introduce the longer monlogues of Jesus addressed to two or more people. The promise itself, "You will see heavens open, and the angels of God ascending and descending upon the Son of man," is an allusion to Jacob's vision at Bethel (Gen 28:12). But the ladder, on which the angels move up an down, has disappeared. The saying as a whole is a figurative expression of the continuous relationship Jesus has with the Father during his earthly sojourn. That does not imply that he lingers on the bosom of the Father or that his existence on earth is evanescent as in docetism.[12] The picture of the mediating angels is deliberately chosen so that it permits Jesus' dwelling on earth to possess complete earthly reality.

Overview

In the Fourth Gospel the story of how Jesus finds the first disciples and how they find him reveals its special character in comparison with Mark 1:16–20 and Luke 5:1–11. In Mark two brief episodes follow one another. In the first, Jesus meets the fisherman Simon and his brother Andrew on the Sea of Galilee, into which they are casting their nets, and says to them: "Follow me and I will make you become fishers of men." He then meets the brothers James and John, who are in their boat mending nets, and he calls them. They immediately leave their father Zebedee in the boat with the hired servants and

8   See the Overview.
9   Billerbeck, 2: 371.
10   *Tradition*, 310 n. 2.

11   "A Note on 'Under the Fig-tree' in John i. 48, 50,"
     JTS, ns. 5 (1954) 210–11.
12   So Käsemann, *The Testament of Jesus*, 26, 70.

follow Jesus. There can be no doubt that even these scenes already stylized are abbreviated and condensed into what is absolutely essential. Nevertheless, upon closer examination, there is adequate concrete detail: how a strange, commanding figure tears two brothers away from their life as fishermen and causes them to follow him. Mark also narrates the call of Levi with comparable brevity: he leads Levi away from the tax office (2:13f.). These are the only two calls he reports. It would appear that Mark knew old stories of the call of only five disciples. Then, in Mark 3:16–19, the list of the "twelve apostles" is completed, following another tradition.

In 5:1–11, Luke has woven the two stories of Mark 1:16–20 into a single dramatic event. The disciples are prepared for the call by first hearing Jesus preach and then by experiencing the miraculous catch of fish, which wins Peter to faith: he is then declared to be a fisher of coming generations.

Although these two accounts of Mark and Luke differ between themselves, they nevertheless form a unity in comparison with the Johannine account. Place and manner of call, number and sequence of names in the latter are scarcely reminiscent of the synoptic type of story.

If one examines the Johannine narrative in 1:23–51 more closely, it proves to have been composed by putting three small segments together. The first, 1:35–39, speaks of two unnamed disciples of the Baptist who transfer their allegiance to Jesus. The second, verses 40–45, depicts Andrew, Peter, and Philip becoming disciples of Jesus. The coherence of the three segments rests on v 44 where the disciples are all said to come from Bethsaida, a "fishing village."

The second segment is connected to the first in that one of the two anonymous disciples of the first scene is now identified, in the second, as Andrew. The narrator is satisfied, in verses 35–39, that John (indirectly) permits two of his disciples to switch their allegiances to Jesus. The expectation that John would precipitate a mass defection of his disciples to Jesus is avoided by the simplest of narrative techniques: John's glance at the two disciples indicates the trajectory of the plot. In so doing the narrator makes use of a tradition, traces of which we later find in Papias. This identification, however, paves the way for difficulties: the second anonymous disciple, who is irrelevant to the second scene, becomes the object of inquiry and thus leads to speculation about the two sons of Zebedee. Strictly speaking, Peter would not be the second but the third disciple to come to Jesus; the anonymous companion of Andrew should be counted ahead of him. But whether or not he is introduced into the context of the second segment, it is not at all certain whether Andrew or this anonymous disciple is the first disciple, indeed, whether there really was a first disciple to whom the narrator wants to point. The second scene thus touches upon a non-synoptic, pre-Johannine tradition, which is found later in Papias (although in the context of a list of the twelve apostles). But only the appendix is used: Nathanael is missing from the list.

The third scene is connected with the second in that Philip "finds" Nathanael. The scene with Nathanael breaks the pattern heretofore established that the pronouncement "Jesus is the Messiah," or something like that, meets with no resistance at all. It is precisely Nathanael, although he is truly an "Israelite," who raises an objection to Jesus' origin in Nazareth. This objection—which rejects faith in the man from Nazareth on the basis of Jewish tradition—is overcome by Jesus himself as a result of his marvelous knowledge.

The third scene, which has an entirely different atmosphere than the first two, may stem from a pre-Johannine tradition. It reflects the apologetic of Jewish Christianity in the face of Judaism. That a "true Israelite" of all people raises an objection of this kind against Jesus makes it all the more significant that he is now persuaded by Jesus. Perhaps this episode ended at one time with verse 49, the fervent recognition of Jesus by Nathanael.

The observation that in verse 48 Jesus actually exhibits only a marvelous kind of knowledge of the sort that one generally attributes to magicians really suits the theology of the tradition here being utilized (we meet it again in John 4:10f.). Verse 50 with the ironic question posed by Jesus ("Because I said to you, I saw you under the fig tree, do you believe?") and the promise ("You shall see greater things than these") could be a correction of the Evangelist. Or should one rather ascribe verse 51, which announces the one essential thing in an unforgetable picture, to the Evangelist? It is very difficult to identify a single verse of the Fourth Gospel by source.

Hirsch[13] reads "teacher" (διδάσκαλε) in verse 34 and so finds seven epithets: lamb of God, the elect of God, the teacher, the messiah, the Son of God, the king of Israel, and the son of man. He asserts of these seven names: "They have some kind of basis and reason in Israelite hope and piety. Jesus is the fulfillment of the last, the hidden one, which lives in the Israelite quest for God. But he is the fulfillment that shatters Judaism and the Law." This interpretation goes together with the Pauline front, which Hirsch also finds in the Fourth Gospel. But there is no basis for διδάσκαλε, "teacher," in the Israelite hope. It may rather be said that here all the names that were used in the Christian congregation to honor Jesus are collected together, and that here, where the embryo of this fellowship was formed, they are used to express what this congregation found in Jesus by way of gift and promise. As a consequence, "rabbi" is in a certain sense the earliest of the names with which the pre-Easter band of disciples already honored Jesus. The other names, however, have lost their peculiar force in John, "Son of God" alone excepted. Put more precisely: the real name for Jesus in the Fourth Gospel is "the Son," a name that singles him out with respect to the entire Jewish tradition; this name makes sense, to be sure, only in his own mouth and cannot be a mode of address for the celebrating congregation. Thus far in chapter one, the principal name that is the expression of the rank and office of Jesus in the Fourth Gospel still remains concealed.

On the other hand, something quite different clearly emerges this early in the Gospel of John: Jesus is unique.

The Baptist is therefore sacrificed to this uniqueness; he can no longer be the baptizer of Jesus, but must resign himself to the role of witness. It is to his credit, therefore, that he leads his disciples to Jesus with his testimony. The question is whether this is a piece of early Christian polemic against the Baptist, or whether by this comportment John does not take the final step that leads to faith. At first glance that is a fanciful idea. Yet, as we will see, Jesus is not one for himself, but exists for the Father and that existence is his glory. That comes clearly to expression for the first time in 5:19f.

A final word regarding narrative technique: in retrospect, it is evident how one thing follows logically on another. From 1:19 on the trajectory of events emerges. In literary terms that means: we have before us a consciously created composition. Everything that is derived from or inspired by another tradition is blended together. It is very improbable that the author is transcribing a source. The hope of Schwartz and Wellhausen to uncover an underlying source of the highest historical value is thus disappointed. But also unfulfilled is the hope of Noack[14] that here, for the first time, oral tradition of the greatest antiquity has taken written shape. It is very likely the case that here theological reflection is at work in a way that is not to be found in the synoptic tradition, at least not to the same degree. Theological reflection is joined to poetic facility so as to set what is critical graphically in relief. As a consquence, scenes poor in historical information but unequalled in expressive power remain implanted in the memory of the reader.

---

13 *Das vierte Evangelium*, 119.
14 *Zur johanneischen Tradition. Beiträge zur Kritik an der literarkritischen Analyse des vierten Evangeliums* (Copenhagen: Rosenkilde og Bagger, 1954).

6. The Wedding at Cana

Bibliography

Alfaro, Juan I.
"La mariología del Cuarto Evangelio. Ensayo de teología bíblica." *RivB* 41 (1979) 193–209.

Amerding, Carl
"The Marriage in Cana." *BSac* 118 (1961) 320–26.

Anne-Etienne, Sr.
"Une lecture communautaire de la Bible." *Foi et vie* 77 (1978) 79–86.

Bächli, Otto
"'Was habe ich mit Dir zu schaffen?' Eine formelhafte Frage im A. T. und N. T." *TZ* 33 (1977) 69–80.

Baumann, Emile
"Zur Hochzeit geladen." *PJ* 4 (1908) 67–76.

Besser, W. F.
"Über Joh 2, 4." *TSK* 18 (1845) 416–25.

Boismard, Marie-Emile
Du baptême à Cana, LD 18 (Paris: Editions du Cerf, 1956) 133–59.

Braun, François-Marie
La mère des fidèles (Paris: Casterman, ²1954) 47–74.

Brown, Raymond E.
"The 'Mother of Jesus' in the Fourth Gospel." In *L'Evangile de Jean. Sources, rédaction, théologie,* ed. M. de Jonge. BETL 44 (Gembloux: Duculot; Louvain: University Press, 1977) 307–10.

Bussche, Henri van den
"Het wijnwonder te Cana (Joh 2,1–11)." *Collationes Gandavenses* 2 (1952) 113–253.

Busse, Ulrich and Anton May
"Das Weinwunder von Kana (Joh 2, 1–11). Erneute Analyse eines 'erratischen Blocks.'" *Biblische Notizen* 12 (1980) 35–61.

Cassel, P.
Die Hochzeit von Kana, theologisch und historisch in Symbol, Kunst und Legende ausgelegt. Mit einer Einleitung in das Evangelium Johannis (Berlin: F. Schulze's Verlag, 1883).

Ceroke, Christian P.
"The Problem of Ambiguity in John 2, 4." *CBQ* 21 (1959) 316–40.

Charlier, Jean-Pierre
Le signe de Cana. Essai de théologie johannique (Brussels: La Pensée Catholique, 1959).

Collins, Raymond F.
"Cana (Jn. 2:1–12)—The First of His Signs or the Key to His Signs?" *ITQ* 47 (1980) 79–95.

Cortés, J. B.
"The Wedding Feast at Cana." *TD* 14 (1966) 14–17.

Dequeker, L.
"De bruiloft te Kana (Jo., II 1–11)." *Collectanea Mechliniensia* 52 (1967) 177–93.

Derrett, J. Duncan M.
"Water into Wine." *BZ* 7 (1963) 80–97.

Dillon, Richard Joseph
"Wisdom, Tradition and Sacramental Retrospect in the Cana Account (Jn 2,1–11)." *CBQ* 24 (1962) 268–96.

Dinkler, Erich
"Das Kana-Wunder. Fragen der wissenschaftlichen Erforschung der Hl. Schrift. Protokoll der Landessynode der Ev. Kirche im Rheinland," (January 1962) 47–61.

Feuillet, André
Johannine Studies, tr. Thomas E. Crane (Staten Island, NY: Alba House, 1964) 17–37 = *Etudes Johanniques*, Museum Lessianum Section biblique 4 (Paris: Desclée de Brouwer, 1962), esp. 11–33.

Feuillet, André
"La signification fondamentale du premier miracle de Cana (Jo II, 1–11) et le symbolisme johannique." *RevThom* (1965) 517–35.

Feuillet, André
"L'heure de Jésus et le signe de Cana. Contribution à l'étude de la structure du quatrième évangile." *ETL* 36 (1960) 5–22.

Gaechter, Paul
"Maria in Kana (Jo. 2, 1–11)." *ZKT* 55 (1931) 351–402.

Galbiati, Enrico
"Nota sulla struttura del 'libro dei segni' (*Gv.* 2–4)." *Euntes docete* 25 (1972) 133–44.

Geoltrain, P.
"Les noces à Cana. Jean 2, 1–12. Analyse des structures narratives." *Foi et vie* 73 (1974) 83–90.

Geyser, A.
"The Semeion at Cana of the Galilee." In *Studies in John Presented to Professor J. N. Sevenster on the Occasion of his Seventieth Birthday* (Leiden: E. J. Brill, 1970) 12–21.

Grassi, Joseph A.
"The Wedding at Cana (John II 1–11): A Pentecostal Meditation?" *NovT* 14 (1972) 131–36.

Harsch, H. and G. Voss, eds.
Versuche mehrdimensionaler Schriftauslegung. Part 2, *Gesprächsmodell: Joh 2,1–11* (Stuttgart: Katholisches Bibelwerk; Munich: Chr. Kaiser Verlag, 1972) 72–140.

Heine, R.
"Zur patristischen Auslegung von Joh 2,1–12." *Wiener Studien* 83, n.s., 4 (1970) 189–95.

Hennig, J.
"Was ist eigentlich geschehen? Joh 2,11." *ZRGG* 15 (1963) 276–86.

Kopp, C.
Das Kana des Evangeliums. Palästinahefte des deutschen Vereins vom Heiligen Lande 28 (Köln: Bachem, 1940).

Léonard, Jeanne-Marie
"Notule sur l'Evangile de Jean. Le récit des noces de Cana et Esaie 25." *ETR* 57 (1982) 119–20.

Leroy, Herbert
"Das Weinwunder in Kana. Ein exegetische Studie zu Jo 2,1–11." *BibLeb* 4 (1963) 168–75.

Lindars, Barnabas
"Two Parables in John." *NTS* 16 (1969/1970) 318–29.

Linnemann, Eta
"Die Hochzeit zu Kana und Dionysios oder das Unzureichende der Kategorien." *NTS* 20 (1974) 408–18.

Lohmeyer, Ernst
"Über Aufbau und Gliederung des vierten Evangeliums." *ZNW* 27 (1928) 11–36.

Mackowski, Richard M.
"Scholar's Qanah. A Re-examination of the Evidence in Favor of Khirbet-Qanah." *BZ* 23 (1979) 278–84.

Meyer, Paul W.
"John 2:10." *JBL* 86 (1967) 191–97.

Michaud, Jean-Paul
"Le signe de Cana dans son contexte johannique." *Laval théologique et philosophique* 18 (1962) 239–85.

Michel, Otto
"Der Anfang der Zeichen Jesu." In *Die Leibhaftigkeit des Wortes. Theologische und seelsorgerliche Studien und Beiträge als Festgabe für Adolf Köberle zum 60. Geburtstag*, ed. O. Michel and Ulrich Mann (Hamburg: Furche-Verlag, 1958) 15–22.

Michl, Johann
"Bemerkungen zu Jo. 2, 4." *Bib* 36 (1955) 492–509.

Moloney, Francis J.
"From Cana to Cana (Jn. 2:1–4:54) and the fourth Evangelist's concept of correct (and incorrect) faith." *Salesianum* 40 (1978) 817–43.

Müller, Ludolf
"Die Hochzeit zu Kana." In *Glaube, Geist, Geschichte. Festschrift für Ernst Benz zum 60. Geburtstag*, ed. G. Müller and W. Zeller (Leiden: E. J. Brill, 1967) 99–106.

Nicol, W.
The Sēmeia in the Fourth Gospel. Tradition and Redaction, NovTSup 32 (Leiden: E. J. Brill, 1972).

Olsson, Birger
Structure and Meaning in the Fourth Gospel. A Text-Linguistic Analysis of John 2:1–11 and 4:1–42, tr. Jean Gray. ConBNT 6 (Lund: C. W. K. Gleerup, 1974).

Parkin, V.
"'On the Third Day There Was a Wedding in Cana of Galilee' (John 2.1)." *Irish Biblical Studies* 3 (1981) 134–44.

Pesch, Rudolf
"Das Weinwunder bei der Hochzeit zu Kana (Joh 2,1–12)." *TGl* 24 (1981) 219–25.

Preisker, Herbert
"Johannes 2, 4 und 19, 26." *ZNW* 42 (1949) 209–14.

Ramos-Regidor, J.
"Signo y Poder—A proposito de la exegesis patristica de Jn 2,1–11." *Salesianum* 27 (1965) 499–562; 28 (1966) 3–64.

Rissi, Mathias
"Die Hochzeit in Kana Joh 2,1–11." In *Oikonomia. Heilsgeschichte als Thema der Theologie. Oscar Cullmann zum 65. Geburtstag gewidmet,* ed. F. Christ (Hamburg: Reich, 1967) 76–92.

Rottmanner, O.
"Joh 2,4: Eine mariologische Studie." *TQ* 74 (1892) 215–45.

Ruegg, U.
"Zur Freude befreit: Jesus auf der Hochzeit zu Kana." In *Die Wunder Jesu,* ed. Anton Steiner and Volker Weymann (Basel: F. Reinhardt Verlag; Zurich: Benziger, 1978) 147–66.

Schmidt, Karl Ludwig
"Der johanneische Charakter der Erzählung vom Hochzeitswunder in Kana." In *Harnack-Ehrung. Beiträge zur Kirchengeschichte ihrem Lehrer Adolf von Harnack zum seinem 70. Geburtstag* (Leipzig: J. C. Hinrichs, 1921) 32–43.

Schnackenburg, Rudolf
Das erste Wunder Jesu (Johannes 2, 1–11) (Freiburg: Herder, 1951).

Schulz, A.
"Das Wunder in Kana im Lichte des Alten Testaments." *BZ* 16 (1924) 93–96.

Serra, A.
Contributi dell'antica letteratura giudaica per l'esegesi di Giovanni 2, 1–12 e 19, 25–27, Scripta Pontificiae Facultatis Theologicae "Marianum" 31, n.s., 3 (Rome: Herder, 1977).

Smith, Morton
"On the Wine-God in Palestine (Gen 18; Jn 2 and Achilles Tatius)." In *Salo Wittmayer Baron Jubilee Volume on the Occasion of his Eightieth Birthday,* ed. Saul Lieberman and A. Hyman (Jerusalem: American Academy for Jewish Research; New York: distributed by Columbia University Press, 1974) English section, 2: 815–29.

Smitmans, Adolf
Das Weinwunder von Kana. Die Auslegung von Jo 2, 1–11 bei den Vätern und heute, BGBE 6 (Tübingen: Mohr-Siebeck, 1966).

Spicq, Ceslaus
"Il primo miracolo di Gesú dovuto a sua Madre." *Sacra Doctrina* 18 (1973) 125–44.

Stauffer, Ethelbert
"Die Hochzeit zu Kana." In *Neue Wege im kirchlichen Unterricht,* ed. K. Frör. Hilfsbücher für den kirchlichen Unterricht 1 (Munich: Chr. Kaiser Verlag, 1949) 49–61.

Temple, Sydney
"The Two Signs in the Fourth Gospel." *JBL* 81 (1962) 169–74.

Theissen, Gerd
Urchristliche Wundergeschichten. Ein Beitrag zur formgeschichtlichen Erforschung der synoptischen Evangelien. SNT 8 (Gütersloh: Gerd Mohn, 1974).

Thyen, Hartwig
"Auf neuen Wegen dem Rätsel des vierten Evangeliums auf der Spur? Überlegungen zu dem Buch von Birger Olsson." *SEÅ* 40 (1975) 136–43.

Toussaint, Stanley D.
"The Significance of the First Sign in John's Gospel." *BSac* 134 (1977) 45–51.

Vanhoye, Albert
"Interrogation johannique et exégèse de Cana (Jn 2,4)." *Bib* 55 (1974) 157–67.

Walter, N.
"Die Auslegung überlieferter Wundererzählungen im JE." In *Theologische Versuche* 2, ed. J. Rogge et al. (Berlin-Ost: Evangelische Verlagsanstalt, 1970) 93–107.

Williams, Francis E.
"Fourth Gospel and Synoptic Tradition: Two Johannine Passages." *JBL* 86 (1967) 311–19.

Windisch, Hans
"Die johanneische Weinregel." *ZNW* 14 (1913) 248–57.

Worden, T.
"The Marriage Feast at Cana (John 3.1–11)." *Scr* 20 (1968) 97–106.

Zehrer, F.
"Das Gespräch Jesu mit seiner Mutter auf der Hochzeit zu Kana (Joh 2, 3f.) im Licht der traditions- und redaktionsgeschichtlichen Forschung." *BLit* 43 (1970) 14–27.

2

1 On the third day there was a marriage at Cana in Galilee, and the mother of Jesus was there; 2/ Jesus also was invited to the marriage, with his disciples. 3/ When the wine failed, the mother of Jesus said to him, "They have no wine." 4/ And Jesus said to her, "O woman, what have you to do with me? My hour has not yet come." 5/ His mother said to the servants, "Do whatever he tells you." 6/ Now six stone jars were standing there, for the Jewish rites of purification, each holding two or three measures. 7/ Jesus

said to them, "Fill the jars with water." And they filled them up to the brim. 8/ He said to them, "Now draw some out, and take it to the steward of the feast." So they took it. 9/ When the steward of the feast tasted the water now become wine, and did not know where it came from (though the servants who had drawn the water knew), the steward of the feast called the bridegroom 10/ and said to him, "Every man serves the good wine first; and when men have drunk freely, then the poor wine; but you have kept the good wine until now." 11/ This, the first of his signs, Jesus did at Cana in Galilee, and manifested his glory; and his disciples believed in him. 12/ After this he went down to Capernaum, with his mother and his brothers and his disciples; and there they stayed for a few days.

■ 1 "On the third day": reckoned from the scene featuring Nathanael. Because Jesus was still in the region of the Jordan in the previous scene, the phrase "on the next day," used hitherto, would not be satisfactory. "Cana in Galilee": the reader will of course know where Jesus is now headed. Wikenhauser[1] takes this to refer to Khirbet Cana (l4 km north of Nazareth) or to Khirbet Kenna (7 km northeast of Nazareth).[2] One normally used γάμος in the plural for a marriage celebration.[3]

Earlier exegetes trace the presence of Mary (never referred to in the Fourth Gospel by name) at the wedding celebration to friendship or the rôle of a relative;[4] or, they assume that the family of Jesus had moved to Cana.[5] The narrator reports only what is absolutely essential and does not concern himself with needless details of the sort that those of us enamored of historical detail would very much like to know.

■ 2 Who invited Jesus is one of those details about which the narrator is completely indifferent. According to Braun,[6] Nathanael had invited the small group while they were still near the Jordan (note 2l:2). Zahn[7] thinks that Jesus and his disciples made their way to Nazareth, learned that his mother and brothers were at a wedding celebration in Cana, and then went to join them. Brown[8] mentions the possibility that the invitation came from Nathanael. But how could he issue an invitation to a wedding in Cana while still at the Jordan? It is a mistake to interpret every detail of the narrative historically in this way. Zahn writes,[9] quite correctly, "What John provides are sketches," but then he unfortunately adds: "which manifest vivid perceptions and recollections."

■ 3 The narrator is also not concerned with why the wine fails (read ὑστερήσαντος οἴνου with P[66] and P[75] rather than the longer text found in ℵ* it syh[mg]), although some interpreters are. With Bultmann, one can only regard the theory that the seven-day wedding celebration[10] had already lasted several days and the wine supply was taxed by the tardy invitation of Jesus and his disciples[11] as a bizarre interpretation.[12] As the reaction of Jesus shows,[13] the remark of Mary contains an unspoken request to remedy the situation. Not, to be sure, in the form of sending a disciple to buy additional wine or even in the sense of Mary admonishing Jesus and the disciples to leave the celebration.[14] Rather, Jesus is expected to perform a miracle. That this is counted as the first of the "signs" in the Fourth Gospel rests on the fact that the

1   Das Evangelium nach Johannes, 72.
2   Billerbeck, 2: 400.
3   Bauer s. v.
4   So Wikenhauser, Das Evangelium nach Johannes, 73.
5   So Ewald, Die johanneischen Schriften, 145.
6   La Sainte Bible, 327.
7   Das Evangelium des Johannes, 148.
8   John, 1: 98.
9   Das Evangelium des Johannes, 161.
10 Judg l4:10–18; Tob 11:18; Tos. Ber. 2.10, Zuckermann p. 4, 7.
11 B. Weiss, Das Johannes-Evangelium, 110.
12 Bultmann, John, 115 n. 6 [80 n. 7].
13 R. E. Brown, John, 1: 99.
14 Zahn, Das Evangelium des Johannes, 154; B. Weiss, Das Johannes-Evangelium, 110; Bultmann, John, 116 n. 2

story did not circulate originally in this context (see below on v 11).

■ **4** Verse 4 has occasioned much concern, especially for Catholic exegetes, because it creates difficulties for Mariology. The address "woman" (γύναι) (translated by Luther with *Weib*, which today is misleading) contains nothing really disparaging. But it is nevertheless surprising that Jesus addresses his mother here (and in 19:26) in the same terms as he does the Samaritan woman in 4:21 and Mary Magdalena in 20:13. This form of address becomes more understandable, as does his way of putting his refusal, "what have you to do with me?" (τί ἐμοὶ καὶ σοί) (1 Ki 17:18, etc.), in the light of Jesus' further response: "My hour has not yet come." That means: Jesus does not permit himself to be prompted to act by any human agent, even when that agent is his own mother; he is driven by the will of the Father alone.[15] When Jesus then performs what is requested of him in a few minutes or a few days later, that is no contradiction in the eyes of the Evangelist. It has nothing to do with a temporal interval, but with the fact that Jesus will only heed the divine call (7:13, 30). All such acts of surrender to the will of the Father culminate, however, in the final act of surrender to the Father's love in the exaltation on the cross (15:13, 13:1, 19:30). Every "sign" performed earlier is an anticipation, a preview of the final one.

■ **5** The mother of Jesus does not waver in her conviction that he will help by performing some sort of deed. The narrator does not explain how Mary achieved her authority in the wedding party. It is only important to him that the servants be prepared to follow what must have been to them an incomprehensible order issued by a guest. He no doubt had in mind the activity indicated in verse 7, which could not have been executed by a single individual.

■ **6** Verse 6 depicts the conditions of the miracle that is to come. It will certainly not consist merely of changing a little water into wine. Rather, an enormous amount of water will be changed into wine. But where can such a large amount of water be found in the home that is the scene of the wedding? The story assumes that six stone jars were standing there, each one of which held two to three μετρηταί ("measures") or about 80 to 100 liters (18 to 27 gallons) (one measure = 39.39 liters or about nine gallons). Exceedingly large stone jars are also mentioned in Jewish literature. Storage jars holding up to 50 liters were used for oil, wine, and corn (1 gallon = 3.785 liters). However, we nowhere have any indication that six stone jars of such unheard of capacity would have stood ready in a house (or its courtyard?) for the purposes of purification. This exaggeration owes to the narrator's desire to represent a miracle of transformation of super proportions in this story.

■ **7** Jesus now instructs the servants to fill the stone jars. They must therefore have been partially and even entirely empty.[16] The jars are now filled to the brim with drinking water, which has been fetched from somewhere nearby. That was by no means a simple undertaking, since it would have been necessary to carry water weighing several hundredweight (the maximum would be up to 700 kilograms or more than 1500 lbs.). The story appears to reckon with the maximum case. For only if the jars were entirely empty and then filled to the brim with water is it certain that a prodigous amount of water was actually changed into wine (see v 9).

■ **8** It goes without saying that these stupendous jars, whose content alone would have weighed up to 200 lbs., could not have been carried to the "steward of the feast." Only a sample is presented to the ἀρχιτρίκλινος ("steward of the feast"). Brown[17] thinks it possible that only this sample of the water was changed into wine, but he agrees that such a possibility contradicts the intention of the narrator. For the logic of the narrative suggests that this wine would have to be served to others in the course of the wedding party. Moreover, it would not have been necessary to have emptied the stone jars and filled them with fresh water had only a small amount of water been transformed into wine. Strathmann[18] is entirely correct

---

[80 n. 7].

15 Cf. e.g., 5:19, 30; 7:6; 8:25, on which see Lightfoot, *St. John's Gospel,* 101, and Haenchen, "Der Vater," 68–77.

16 B. Weiss, *Das Johannes-Evangelium,* 112.

17 *John,* 1: 100.

18 *Das Evangelium nach Johannes,* 58.

when he asserts that all (apologetic) attempts to soften the extent of the miracle are inappropriate: "for example, Jesus wanted to provide the married couple with an extensive supply . . . or a suggestive illusion took place or the narrator has exaggerated the amount." Strathmann[19] thereby unhesitatingly recognizes "that a remarkable shadowy illusiveness, indeed, unreality, is inherent in the account." "Neither the steward of the feast nor the bridegroom nor the guests note what has transpired. Nobody thanks the one who provided the wine. The provider himself disappears without a word."[20]

To these difficulties are to be added another, viz., that there are no good parallels to the position of the ἀρχιτρίκλινος ("steward of the feast") here presupposed. Billerbeck[21] can only point to the ἡγούμενος ("leader") mentioned in Sir. 32:1f., whom others chose to be master of the feast. The συμποσιάρχης ("toastmaster") was in any case one of the guests in Greek usage. Heliodorus (third century CE) speaks[22] it is true, of ἀρχιτρίκλινος and οἰνοχόοι ("cupbearer").[23] That would point to a "head waiter," who has responsibility for the oversight and management of the festival. The "steward of the feast" in this narrative appears to fall between the two possibilities: a guest or head waiter (slave or servant).

■ 9 At all events, this man, who knows nothing of the miracle but understands wine, attests the outstanding quality and superiority of the new wine (the servants could bear witness to the miracle but no one asks them). When he wants to summon the bridegroom in order to give his testimony on this point, he does not find him in the banquet hall. But details are again not provided in order not to detract from the decisive thing: the irrefragable assertion that the new wine is incomparably better.

■ 10 The maxim introduced in this context is admittedly unknown beyond this passage.[24] Billerbeck[25] mentions *Num. Rab.* 16 (181[b]), according to which merchants show inferior goods first and only then the superior. This is not a real parallel. Windisch[26] refers to a passage in a fragment of Pseudo-Theopompus. But in this passage is reproached only the bad habit of the Spartans in serving their guests first good and then inferior wine. Brown[27] believes it overcritical to hold the view that the Evangelist himself created this alleged maxim *ad hoc*. But this verse need not go back to the Evangelist. For another thing, the situation presupposed by the "maxim" is not a real situation: a marriage celebration of this kind lasts not only a couple of hours during which the guests gradually become drunk and unable to judge the quality of the wine. Rather, the festival is extended over several days; during this period some guests leave and others arrive. Neither group is able to certify that the wine has been switched.

■ 11 "This Jesus did as the first sign in Cana of Galilee" sums the story up and characterizes it. For this construction Bauer[28] points to Isocrates:[29] ἀλλ᾽ ἀρχὴν μὲν ταύτην ἐποιήσατο εὐεργεσιῶν ("But he did this first of the good deeds"). The word σημεῖον, which is used to translate the Hebrew term אות ("sign") in the LXX (e.g., Exod 4:8f., Isa 7:11, 14) might have been understood as "miracle" in the tradition embodied in this story. But the Evangelist takes it as "pointer" and thus as indicating something quite different; it is in this sense that he understands it as "sign." It is possible that the story originally ended with the complement to the effect that the "steward of the feast" had served the good, new wine. But then the story was inserted into a larger context (cf. 4:54), the limits of which are difficult to determine. The note that Jesus' disciples have only now come to faith (ἐπίστευσαν) is not congruent with 1:40–49 where various confessions of faith are given. The attempts of some exegetes to do away with this tension—the disciples came to a deeper understanding of the person of Jesus[30]—does not suit the underlying tradition, but at best matches the meaning of the tradition that the Evangelist found tolerable.

The transmission of the first words in verse 11 exhibits variants. 𝔓[66c] 𝔓[75] H A Θ *al* read: ταύτην ἐποίησεν ἀρχὴν

19 *Das Evangelium nach Johannes,* 58.
20 *Das Evangelium nach Johannes,* 57f.
21 2: 407f.
22 *Aeth.* 7.27.7.
23 Bauer s. v.
24 It is certainly not merely a "remark . . . meant humorously," as Schnackenburg (*John,* 1: 334 [337]) supposes.
25 2: 409.
26 In "Die johanneische Weinregel [Jn. 2:10]," *ZNW* 14 (1931) 248–57.
27 *John,* 1: 100.
28 *Das Johannesevangelium,* 45.
29 *Paneg.* 10.38, ed. Blass.
30 Schnackenburg, *John,* 1: 337.

κτλ. ℵ^c 𝕽 insert the article before ἀρχήν; 1241 puts ἀρχήν before ἐποίησεν. The reading offered by ℵ^c 𝔓⁶⁶ is more important (transmitted with variation in word order): ταύτην πρώτην ἀρχήν κτλ. The Latin witnesses indicate that the reading must have been widespread. Thus, f* *hoc primum fecit initium signorum Jesus;* q: *hoc primum initium fecit Jesus signum;* b: *hoc primum signum;* foss: *primum signorum.* Fortna[31] holds the reading of ℵ* 𝔓⁶⁶ to be original, i.e., to go back at least to John. It could not be—on account of the gender of πρώτην—a conflation; the variants are explained by assuming that the scribes have sought to improve the text in a variety of ways. But, in my opinion, it could be a conflation: the ταύτην led a scribe to suppose that the text continued with πρώτην, which he then added; he then saw that manuscript from which he was copying contained ἀρχήν, which he added without striking πρώτην. Such errors are common. But it is also possible that the primary text of 𝔓⁶⁶* contained ταύτην τὴν ἀρχήν and the scribe misread την for πρώτην.

■ **12** Verse 12 is a transitional verse: Jesus cannot go from Cana down to Jerusalem. Matt 4:13 indicates that there was a tradition of Jesus' sojourn in Capernaum (cf. John 6:59).

The phrase μετὰ τοῦτο is not to be distinguished from μετὰ ταῦτα ("after this").[32]

The word αὐτοῦ is lacking after ἀδελφοί in 𝔓⁶⁶* and 𝔓⁷⁵, as well as in B *pc.* This may be viewed, from the Catholic point of view, as support for the thesis that the ἀδελφοί of Jesus were not his blood brothers, but were either children of an earlier marriage of Joseph (so Epiphanius) or sons of Joseph's brother or Mary's sister (so Jerome). Brown[33] quotes Bernard[34] with approval: "It is difficult to understand how the doctrine of the Virginity of Mary could have grown up early in the second century if her four acknowledged sons were prominent Christians, and one of them bishop of Jerusalem." The brothers are named in Mark 6:3: James, Joses, Judas, and Simon. Yet Mark 3:20f., 31–35 compared with Luke 8:19–21[35] is sufficient to show that human ideals can get along very well with traditions that are clearly alien to each other.

Overview

We would like to postpone for the moment the question of the sources of this story, of its aim, of what it really wants to say to us. That will later prove to be useful. We shall first inquire into the structure of the story, into its composition, in the form in which it presents itself to us in the transmitted text. This narrative, connected only vaguely to what precedes by the words "on the third day," begins abruptly: there was a wedding in Cana of Galilee (this was not the only village by that name!) and the mother of Jesus—she is not given the name Mary in the Fourth Gospel—was there. Whether she was there for a longer period or had only just arrived the author leaves open, as he does her relation to the wedding family (legend has been very active in filling in the alleged lacunae in the narrative, e.g., Mary was an aunt of the bridegroom).[36] Since she was not with Jesus at the Jordan, she could not have come with him to Galilee. So the narrator has her standing ready, as it were, in Cana. But Jesus, together with his disciples, was also invited. It is of interest neither to the reader or to the narrator how the invitation came to Jesus at the Jordan. So, the narrator can tell his story in this free style apart from unimportant details. For that reason, he does not need to tell us why the supply of wine gave out. Earlier exegetes have answered that question, each in his own way. This sudden emergency is the redeeming moment. It appears that the time for the mother to step in has come: she calls her son's attention to the fact that the guests have no more wine. Büchsel[37] is of the opinion that "Jesus obviously did not appreciate the dilemma, if he noticed it at all." The narrator does not concern himself with such reflections. He does not want interest to be diverted to such details at the decisive moment. The reader also anticipates that Jesus will proceed to perform a miracle in response to this indirect request. But then comes the

31   *Gospel of Signs,* 35.
32   Cf. Bultmann, *John,* 121 n. 6 [85 n. 6].
33   *John,* 1: 112.
34   *John,* 1: 85.
35   On which see Haenchen, *Der Weg Jesu,* 139–45.
36   Brown, *John,* 1: 98.
37   *Das Evangelium nach Johannes,* 44.

surprise: Jesus gruffly refuses and follows his "No!" with the puzzling words: "My hour has not yet come." That is not a retarding moment in the ordinary literary sense. Nor does it have anything to do with the rejection of the request of the Syrophoenician woman, which Brown recalls.[38] In Mark 7:24–30//Matt 15:21–28, Jesus' "No" is given for entirely different reasons than here: it is solely a case of Jesus acting when God wills (5:19). Jesus' mother is not discouraged—at least not according to the received text. She says (with words that are reminiscent of Gen 41:15) to the servants: do whatever he tells you. That obviously presupposes an unusual yet expected command of Jesus, which he immediately issues. The reader thereby understands that the narrator must go into one matter in detail. Somewhere in the house there are six enormous stone water jars of the kind required for Jewish rites of purification. The narrator does not tell us more about these jars, but there now transpires what the presupposition of the miracle anticipates: Jesus commands the servants to fill the jars up to the brim. That certifies that the unheard of volume of water is really there to be turned into wine. The phrase, "they filled them up to the brim," summarizes an action that takes considerable time. For the anticipation of the reader must not be overtaxed. The water jars are now full, and Jesus has the steward of the feast draw a sample out of any one of the jars, which the narrator now knows to be full of costly wine. The steward of the feast cannot know that; his praise of the wine gains objectivity precisely for that reason. On the other hand, the servants must know (there must be witnesses present): they put water into the jars and took wine out. How good the wine is can only be indirectly represented: the steward of the feast calls the bridegroom and reproaches him for having held back this noble wine for so long. One should not expect the bridegroom to respond,[39] "Where did this wine come from?" On the contrary, the miracle remains shrouded in mystery (in spite of the witnesses). Even the servants do not really know how Jesus achieved the transformation.

But the reader has seen enough and now understands completely that the disciples believe on Jesus as a result of this miracle.

When the structure of the story is clarified in this way, questions over which many exegetes have been exercised cease to be cogent. How could Jesus' mother have been invited before him?[40] Could he have been invited from the Jordan to Cana at a time when no one anticipated that he would not appear alone but be accompanied by newly acquired disciples?[41] The idle question about why the wine gave out just then is not to be answered, as B. Weiss does,[42] by suggesting that unexpected guests arrived. Jesus' gruff refusal of Mary's request (see above on v 4) has caused some Catholic exegetes grief. Since the later Christian diaconate appears to Schwartz to be concealed in the διάκονοι ("servants"), he[43] wants to leave it to the guests to fill the water jars. Criticism is no mean thing, but when it is overdone, it can become ludicrous. It goes without saying that we do not learn how long the celebration had been going on when the new wine is brought out or that the bridegroom thanks Jesus.[44] The decisive event has occurred and should not be depreciated by insignificant particulars.

What questions remain? Prior to the Enlightenment miracle stories were no problem for the reader; they could serve as proof. Lessing then insisted that we do not have the miracle itself before us, but only an account of a miracle, which arouses questions or awakens the wish to be rid of the miraculous in an acceptable manner. This Dodd[45] seeks to achieve by supposing that the miracle story grew out of a metaphor. It perhaps began, "A man gave a wedding feast . . ." and ended with "you have kept the good wine back until now." Well and good. But then it would have been necessary for Jesus to tell of a wine miracle between that beginning and that ending, and who could have performed that deed? Dodd's further assumption, that the story of the coin in the fish's mouth (Matt 17:24–27) arose from a parable of Jesus, is shattered on the same objection.

38   *John,* 1: 99.
39   Cf. Strathmann, *Das Evangelium nach Johannes,* 58.
40   Schwartz, "Aporien," 4: 512 n. 1.
41   Zahn, *Das Evangelium des Johannes,* 154; B. Weiss, *Das Johannes-Evangelium,* 110.
42   *Das Johannes-Evangelium,* 109.
43   "Aporien," 4: 512.
44   So also Strathmann, *Das Evangelium nach Johannes,* 58.
45   *Tradition,* 227f.

Schwartz[46] and others have asked whether Mary originally appeared in the story. Verse 4 exhibits the language and patterns of the thought of the Evangelist (cf. 7:6). However, whoever omits verse 1b and verses 3 (after καὶ ὑστερήσαντος οἴνου, "When the wine failed") through 5, must move verse 6 up to follow the first phrase of verse 3 and thus create an inexplicable foreshortening. It is better to consider another possibility: the text originally went from λέγει ἡ μήτηρ τοῦ Ἰησοῦ ("the mother of Jesus says") to verse 5 to τοῖς διακόνοις ("to the servants"). In that case, the mother of Jesus would be assigned the entirely honorable task of helping prepare for a miracle of Jesus in the underlying tradition. Is it possible to conceive of the rudiments of a mariology at that early date? One need only recall passages like Luke 1:26–35 or 2:19 to be able to answer yes to such a question. It is a long step, to be sure, from Mary as as assistant in preparing for a miracle of Jesus to the doctrine of Mary as the mediator of all grace, and the Fourth Evangelist has not made this step exactly easy with verse 4. In support of the effort to reconstruct a source briefer in compass one could adduce the following: in accordance with the present text, which has been expanded by the Evangelist, the reaction of the mother of Jesus in verse 5 is strange: did not Jesus forbid her interference in this matter in any form? Moreover, the Evangelist corrects the tradition in a way similar to the correction found in the brief insertion in 4:48f.

It is incontestable that the Evangelist and the narrator of the underlying story have not simply made the whole thing up. Tradition is therefore involved. But what kind? Jeremias[47] argued in 1930 that "The picture of the wedding celebration in contemporary literature and in the NT is exceptionally familiar. The wedding celebration will take place in the days of the Messiah, as it says in *Midr. Rab.*[48] In the NT also the wedding is the symbol of the coming time of salvation and the reunion of the Messiah and the congregation. . . . Even now, says Jesus—and that is the overpowering boldness of his word

regarding the reigning messianic expectation—even now the joyous celebration is dawning in my lowliness. . . ."[49] "The key to understanding the story of the wedding at Cana is also to be found here (John 2:1–11). When it is said there that 'he revealed his glory and his disciples came to faith in him,' that is meant in the sense of the Evangelist . . . : the disciples understood what Jesus intended to say by that, viz., that he changes water into wine and that he brings to them as his first sign the waxing of the time of salvation."[50] Bultmann objects:[51] "The wine of the marriage at Cana does not come from the OT expectation of salvation but from the Dionysus cult in Syria" (on this point, see below). But Noetzel[52] points out that the rabbinic interpretations and calculations are built on Gen 49:11f. and that they quote the apocalypse 2 Bar (Syriac);[53] the latter is discussed in detail in the Introduction §1, "The Fourth Gospel in Early Christian Tradition." The result is that each vine in the millenium will produce ten trillion hectolitres of wine or about 264,000,000,000 gallons! By comparison, the 5 to 7 hectolitres (about 132 to 184 gallons) of our pericope is a very modest indication of the superabundance to come. To be sure, this legend does not refer to a changing of water into wine. This legend is not to be considered a source for this pericope any more than is the passage in the blessing of Jacob, which the Rabbis like to include in such reckonings.

Others—among whom Bultmann[54] may be mentioned—prefer to derive the story from pagan tradition: "There can be no doubt that the story has been taken over from heathen legend and ascribed to Jesus. In fact the motif of the story, the changing of the water into wine, is a typical motif of the Dionysus legend. In the legend this miracle is the miracle of the epiphany of the god, and was therefore dated on the night of the 5th to 6th of January." The ancient church still understood that when it "held that the 6th of January was the date of the marriage at Cana." For the Evangelist this story is the symbol of the "divinity of Jesus as the Revealer." Bult-

46 "Aporien," 4: 512.
47 *Jesus als Weltvollender,* 21–29.
48 Ed. Stettin (1864) 15.30 on Exod 12:2 (43ª.29).
49 Jeremias, *Jesus als Weltvollender,* 24.
50 Jeremias, *Jesus als Weltvollender,* 29.
51 *John,* 120 n. 1 [84 n. 1].
52 *Christus und Dionysus,* 45.
53 Billerbeck, 4: 810.
54 *John,* 118f. [83].

mann appends this note:[55] "It is very likely that the Evangelist could find support for his interpretation in an earlier tradition. Even according to Philo the Logos (represented by Melchisedek) gives to the souls ἀντὶ ὕδατος οἶνου ['wine instead of water'] (*Leg. All.* 3.82), and is called the οἰνοχόος τοῦ θεοῦ ['cup-bearer of God'] (*Som* 2.249)."

Philo does not, however, state that the logos changes water into wine, and the "*sobria ebrietas*" ("sober intoxication") of the spirit symbolized by the wine goes together with the bacchanalian revelries only *e contrario*. The Greek tradition does not claim that Dionysus turns water into wine. The *Bacchae* of Euripides graphically describes the penetration of the orgiastic Dionysus cult into Greece. "And one of them took her thyrsus [a light stick of reed or fennel, with fresh strands of ivy twined around it] and struck it on the rock; and from the rock there gushed a spring of limpid water; another struck her wand down into the earth, and there the god made a fountain of wine spring up; and any who wanted milk had only to scratch the earth with the tip of her fingers, and there was the white stream flowing for her to drink; and from the ivy-bound thyrsus a sweet ooze of honey dripped."[56] Plato has shown (*Ion* 534a) that all these wonderful practices take place in the minds of the maenads and do not occur in the "objective" world. The authentic poets, he says, are like "the bacchants, [who,] when possessed, draw milk and honey from the rivers but not when in their senses. So the spirit of the lyric poet works. . . ."[57] The ecstatic frenzy that seized the women and maidens was domesticated by the state and the priesthood; they turned it into a state cult that was observed on prescribed days.[58] Noetzel reports, following Pausanias (VI 26.1f.): "In ancient times the women of Elis invoked the god with the music of flutes and the miracle of the wine bubbling up was the sign that he had appeared. . . . Later we find there an edifice and a priesthood to manage the miracle itself." With respect to the traditions of the Dionysus miracle cited by Bultmann

(Naxos, Teos, Andros, Nysa) Noetzel says:[59] "All these miracles tales . . . are relatively late and show that a time had come when mythic poesis was very popular and produced a wide variety." It is astonishing that the motif of transformation, which played no role in the Dionysus cult, was taken from the Cana miracle "in order to justify biblically an Epiphany celebration that derived from a practice of the Egyptian Osiris cult."[60] One does well to abandon the history of religions view that the Cana story is allegedy derived from the cult of Dionysus.

Finally Hirsch[61] chooses the distinction between wine and Jewish water for purification as the point of departure for his exposition of the pericope: "The story itself connects the water vessels with the prescriptions of the Jewish law concerning clean and unclean. If one holds to the contrast between spirit and law, the profound metaphorical meaning of the story is sufficient, in accordance with the author's style. The purity connected with the law disappears into the gift of the Holy Spirit. The figurative relationship is probably to be understood in the most general sense as the contrast between the Jewish religion of law and the Christian religion of spirit and truth. In that case, the miracle is clearly a figurative representation of what comes as a result of the death of Jesus."

All of these sorts of interpretations have one thing in common: they believe the event as narrated meant little to the Evangelist. Not that he held that the miracle never took place,[62] but that it was only "symbolic." But if Jesus causes water to be turned into wine here, that wine would have been drunk like any other wine, and Lazarus, who was raised from the dead, also died again later (cf. John 12:10). That means: these miracles leave mankind within the sphere of this world and do not basically alter the character of life. But that is precisely what Jesus intends, on the view of the Gospel of John. For that reason, the "hour" of Jesus is the central event for the Evangelist. For this was the hour in which Jesus gave himself completely to the fulfillment of the Father's will,

---

55 *John*, 119 n. 5 [83 n. 5].

56 Tr. Philip Vellacott, *Euripides: The Bacchae and Other Plays* (Harmondsworth, Middlesex: Penguin Books, 1954) 203.

57 Tr. Lane Cooper, in *The Collected Dialogues of Plato*, ed. Edith Hamilton and Huntington Cairns (Princeton: Princeton University Press, 1963) 220.

58 On this cf. the excellent study of Noetzel, *Christus*

und Dionysus.

59 *Christus und Dionysus*, 15.

60 Noetzel, *Christus und Dionysus*, 37.

61 *Das vierte Evangelium*, 122–27.

62 As Bultmann (*John*, 120 n. 4 [83 n. 4]) conjectures.

and the hour, at the same time, when the way of Jesus to the cross opened the way to the Father—also for us. At this point there came into view what was hidden and inaccessible in the world. All the "signs" of Jesus in the Gospel of John point to this last hour and to that extent anticipate it. Whoever believes in Jesus knows what really occurs in that particular hour: salvation is made accessible in Jesus. The Evangelist may have understood the Cana story in the light of 1:16f. of the Prologue: "And from his fullness have we all received, grace upon grace." That the author refers to the purification of the Jews is evident from 1:17: "For the law was given through Moses; grace and truth came through Jesus Christ." In 1:50, "you shall see greater things than these," there is reference to that uncanny knowledge of Nathaniel's past. In Cana, one of these greater things becomes evident. In the older rites of purification man attempted to make himself clean before God. But now, in the "hour," comes the new, the new hour of God: man does not take his own impurity away; "the lamb of God" does (1:29, 36). Because God shows himself as the great giver, his Lordship appears in power. That becomes concrete in the Cana story. But only he can see it whose vision is not fixed on the rapture of the wedding celebration. We have a better cause for joy than the wedding celebration as such: Jesus goes to the Father and thereby opens the way for us. The Evangelist does not go into the matter at this point. He merely paints a picture before our eyes. He will often discuss the matter, in one way or another. But this is the center of the Johannine gospel, which is here expressed for the first time.

7. The Cleansing of the Temple

Bibliography

Bjerkelund, Carl J.
"En tradisjons- og redaksjonshistorik analyse av perikopene om tempelrendelsen." *NorTT* 69 (1968) 206–16.

Braun, François-Marie
"L'expulsion des vendeurs du Temple (Mt. xxi, 12–17, 23–27; Mc. xi, 15–19, 27–33; Lc xix, 45–xx, 8; Jo. ii, 13–22)." *RB* 38 (1929) 178–200.

Braun, François-Marie
"In spiritu et veritate." *RevThom* 52 (1952) 245–74, esp. 249–54.

Buse, Ivor
"The Cleansing of the Temple in the Synoptics and in John." *ExpTim* 70 (1958/1959) 22–24.

Bussche, Henri van den
"Le Signe du Temple (Jean 2, 13–22)." *BVC* 20 (1957/1958) 92–100.

Carmichael, J.
Leben und Tod des Jesus von Nazareth (Munich: Szczesny Verlag, ²1965).

Cullmann, Oscar
"L'opposition contre le temple de Jérusalem, motif commun de la théologie johannique et du monde ambiant." *NTS* 5 (1958/1959) 157–73.

Derrett, J. Duncan M.
"Fresh Light on the Lost Sheep and the Lost Coin." *NTS* 26 (1979) 36–60.

Dubarle, A.-M.
"Le signe du temple [Jn. 2:19]." *RB* 48 (1939) 21–44.

Eisler, Robert
The Messiah Jesus and John the Baptist, ed. A. H. Krappe (London: Methuen, 1930).

Eppstein, Victor
"The Historicity of the Gospel Account of the Cleansing of the Temple." *ZNW* 55 (1964) 42–58.

Freed, Edwin D. and R. B. Hunt
"Fortna's Signs-Source in John." *JBL* 94 (1975) 563–79, esp. 570–73.

Giblet, Jean
"Le Temple de l'Eternelle Alliance, Joh 2,21s." *Eglise vivante* 9 (1957) 122–25.

Haenchen, Ernst
"Johanneische Probleme." *ZTK* 56 (1959) 19–54, esp. 34–46. In his *Gott und Mensch. Gesammelte Aufsätze* 1 (Tübingen: Mohr-Siebeck, 1965) 78–113, esp. 93–105.

Haenchen, Ernst
Der Weg Jesu. Eine Erklärung des Markus-Evangeliums und der kanonischen Parallelen (Berlin: Walter de Gruyter, ²1966) 382–89.

Hiers, Richard H.
"Purification of the Temple: Preparation for the

Kingdom of God [Mk 11:15–17]." *JBL* 90 (1971) 82–90.

James, M. R.
"Notes on Apocrypha." *JTS* 7 (1906) 562–68, esp. 566.

Kolenkow, Anitra B.
"The Changing Patterns: Conflicts and the Necessity of Death: John 2 and 12 and Markan Parallels." SBLASP 1 (Missoula: Scholars Press, 1979) 123–26.

Léon-Dufour, Xavier
"Le signe du temple selon saint Jean [Jn. 2:13–22]." *RSR* 39 (1951/1952) 155–75.

Martin, R. A.
"The Date of the Cleansing of the Temple in Joh 2,13–22." *Indian Journal of Theology* 15 (1966) 52–56.

Mendner, Siegfried
"Die Tempelreinigung." *ZNW* 47 (1956) 93–112.

Moulton, Harold K.
"*Pantas* in John 2:15." *BT* 18 (1967) 126–27.

Power, E.
"Jo. 2. 20 and the Date of the Crucifixion." *Bib* 9 (1928) 257–88.

Roth, C.
"The Cleansing of the Temple and Zechariah." *NovT* 4 (1960) 174–81.

Sabbe, M.
"Tempelreiniging en Tempellogion." *Collationes Brugenses et Gandavenses* 2 (1956) 289–99, 466–80.

Safrai, S.
The Pilgrimage at the Time of the Second Temple (Tel Aviv: Am Hasserfer Publisher Ltd., 1965) [in Hebrew].

Schille, Gottfried
"Prolegomena zur Jesusfrage." *TLZ* 93 (1968) 481–88.

Selong, G.
The Cleansing of the Temple in Jn 2,13–22 with a Reconsideration of the Dependence of the Fourth Gospel Upon the Synoptics. Dissertation, Louvain, 1971.

Simon, Marcel
"Retour du Christ et reconstruction du Temple dans la pensée chrétienne primitive." In *Aux sources de la tradition chrétienne. Mélanges offerts à M. Maurice Goguel à l'occasion do son soixante-dixième anniversaire* (Paris: Delachaux & Niestlé, 1950) 247–57.

Trocmé, Etienne
"L'expulsion des marchands du Temple [Mt 21:12–17]." *NTS* 15 (1968/1969) 1–22.

Vogels, Heinrich Josef
"Die Tempelreinigung und Golgotha (Joh 2:19–22)." *BZ* 6 (1962) 102–7.

White, H. J.
"On the Sayings Attributed to Our Lord in John II,19." *Expositor*, 8th ser., 17 (1919) 415–23.

2

13 The Passover of the Jews was at hand, and Jesus went up to Jerusalem. 14/ In the temple he found those who were selling oxen and sheep and pigeons, and the money-changers at their business. 15/ And making a whip of cords, he drove them all, with the sheep and oxen, out of the temple; and he poured out the coins of the money-changers and overturned their tables. 16/ And he told those who sold the pigeons, "Take these things away; you shall not make my Father's house a house of trade." 17/ His disciples remembered that it was written, "Zeal for thy house will consume me." 18/ The Jews then said him, "What sign have you to show us for doing this?" 19/ Jesus answered them, "Destroy this temple, and in three days I will raise it up." 20/ The Jews then said, "It has taken forty-six years to build this temple, and will you raise it up in three days?" 21/ But he spoke of the temple of his body. 22/ When therefore he was raised from the dead, his disciples remembered that he had said this; and they believed the scripture and the word which Jesus had spoken.

■ **13** As in 11:55, the temporal proximity of the Passover of the Jews prompts Jesus to go up to Jerusalem, which was situated on the central ridge of the hill country. The verb "go up" (ἀναβαίνω) was the common expression for this pilgrimage. But in the Gospel of John Jesus does not behave like a pilgrim. We never hear that he participates in the Jewish cult. For the Fourth Gospel, the "Passover of the Jews," and the feast of Tabernacles in 7:2, the feast of Dedication in 10:22, and the "feast of the Jews" that is not further specified in 5:1, are not Christian worship services, but feasts that no longer concern Jesus and his disciples. The Gospel of John makes it clear to the reader at this point, where one of the great Jewish festivals is mentioned for the first time, how strongly Jesus objected to them. According to the Fourth Gospel, the feasts in the Jerusalem temple merely offer Jesus an occasion for his own proclamation. They prompt him to speak to the Jews gathered together about his own significance. The narrator does not employ these feasts as historical milestones by which one might reckon the duration of his public ministry. But because the Johannine tradition referred to several Passover feasts for the reason mentioned above, and others, the Evangelist has connected the story of the cleansing of the temple with the first of the Passovers he mentions: Jesus could not have waited until the end of his ministry to effect his protest in word and deed against this kind of worship.

■ **14** Reference to the "temple" (ἱερόν) follows upon the mention of Jerusalem (as in Mark 11:11, 15). Commentators think that the narrator makes reference to the extraordinarily large "Court of the Gentiles," which stretched south and north from the inner court and the temple proper (v 19: ναός). But none of the evangelists uses this designation, "Court of the Gentiles," and it is uncertain how exact their notions of the Jewish temple were. It had lain in ruins more than twenty years before the Gospel of John was written. It is by no means certain that the evangelists (or the authors of their "sources") had the latest archaeological data at their disposal.

According to verse 14, in addition to pigeons (the offering of the poor: Lev 5:7, 12:8), one also purchased oxen and sheep in the "temple." The more expensive oxen were rarely used as private offerings.[1] The two young bullocks presented by the priests as community sacrifices on Passover morning (Lev 1:1–17; Jos. *Ant.* 3.224ff.; Philo, *De Spec. leg.* 1.162f.) were of course not available for purchase in the temple beforehand. The tradition that R. Baba ben Buta (a contemporary of Herod the Great) once drove 3,000 head of small livestock from the steppe of Qedar to the temple hill in order to depress the inflated price is reported as one individual case that is greatly exaggerated in number.[2]

The number of pilgrims and Passover sacrifices was greatly exaggerated. Josephus asserts that 255,600 sacrificial animals were counted once in the 60's CE[3] On the assumption that at least ten persons belonged to each Passover group (not "on average" but "at least"), Josephus arrives at a figure of 2,700,000 participants in the Passover meal. Jeremias[4] has estimated the number of pilgrims at 125,000, and then adds: "We shall probably not have to increase or decrease that number by more than half." An additional note inserted into the third edition[5] raises the question whether the total number of participants in the feast, 180,000 (pilgrims and residents) is not still too high. It is certain that it is and by quite a bit. In 1965, Safrai[6] takes earlier estimates back to more modest and realistic numbers: one could possibly speak of some ten thousand pilgrims. According to *Pesaḥ.* 8.3,[7] it was sufficient when each participant received a piece of the Passover lamb the size of an olive. Thus a single lamb would be sufficient for twenty or more participants. One should not therefore agree that there were enormous flocks in the lower precincts of the Herodian temple, as Schlatter conjectures.[8] In all probability, most groups of pilgrims brought their own lambs with them; the others could acquire their Passover lambs in Jerusalem from the tenth of Nissan on. Whether such lambs could also be obtained in the market on the Mount of Olives remains a

---

1   See *Šeqal.* 5.3 in Billerbeck, 1: 851.
2   *p. Jom Tob* 2.61ᶜ, 13; Billerbeck, 1: 852.
3   *BJ* 6.420, 423–25.
4   *Jerusalem,* 77–84, especially 83f.
5   *Jerusalem,* 84.
6   *The Pilgrimage at the Time of the Second Temple* (Tel Aviv: Am Hassefer Publisher Ltd., 1965) 71–74.
7   Cf. Billerbeck, 4.1: 46.

8   *Der Evangelist Matthäus: Seine Sprache, seine Zeit, seine Selbständigkeit* (Stuttgart: Calwer Verlag, [1929] ⁶1963) 612.
9   Cf. *Ta'an.* 4 69ᵃ.37; Billerbeck, 1: 851.

question.[9] The main hypothesis proposed by Eppstein in this connection seems to us to be dubious: the high priest Caiaphas fell out with the Sanhedrin in the year 30 CE ("priests opposed to rabbis") and withdrew the meeting room in the Chamber of Hewn Stone from the Sanhedrin. When the owners of the market on the Mount of Olives mentioned above made a room in it available to the Sanhedrin for use as a meeting room, Caiaphas took revenge on these merchants and permitted their competitors to keep their animals in the Court of the Gentiles itself for the first time in history. Thus Jesus was confronted with a scene that he had not seen on his earlier visits to the temple. But Caiaphas was not the only Sadducee in the Sanhedrin (if he was a Sadducee at all); in addition to him members of the family of the high priest were represented, and the "Elders," the second group in the Sanhedrin, were probably predominantly "orthodox" Sadducees. The scribes in the Sanhedrin did not possess their power by virtue of their numbers, but because the people stood behind them.

Money changers (who, in any case, set up their tables in the "Court of the Gentiles" only a few days before Passover) were necessary because the temple tax was not to be paid with Roman or Greek money (on account of the human image appearing on them, which the Law forbade). Since Judea had lost its right to coin money as a Roman province, one made use of Tyrian money, which carried only the designation of the value of the Shekel. The surcharge of the money changers amounted to only 2.12%. In the case of a temple tax of a didrachma per person, that would amount to only a few pennies (perhaps as little as 4%). Noisy bargaining was not practiced. According to *Seqal.* 5.3,[10] one could purchase, for example, a drink-offering at a fixed price in accordance with a thoroughly organized system (also payable in Tyrian coin). Exegetes who represent the commercial activity in the "Court of the Gentiles" as a kind of activity typical of a county fair have come to this view not on the basis of archaeological evidence, but because they could account for the action of Jesus only on the assumption of an unseemly huckster in the temple.

■ **15** Since one cannot drive animals merely with one's hands, Jesus made "a kind of whip" (read ὡς φραγέλλιον

with 𝔓⁶⁶ and 𝔓⁷⁵) out of the cords with which the animals had been tethered. He did not use it against people, but drove the animals out with it. The exegetes Wellhausen,[11] Hirsch,[12] and Bauer,[13] among others, want to strike the words "the sheep and the oxen" in verse 15—and thus to eliminate the mention of sheep and oxen in verse 14 also—as an alleged late addition, but that is unecessary. If the word "all" refers to both a neuter and a masculine plural, the masculine gender (here: τοὺς βόας, "the oxen") determines the gender of πᾶς ("all"), which results in πάντας. The construction τε ... καί ("both ... and"), of course, appears only here in the Gospel of John. But it can have been taken over from the source. In that case, it would be unnecessary to strike the sheep and the oxen and the words "those who sold pigeons," as Hirsch proposes. Such an emendation would have as its consequence, moreover, that, after pouring out their coins and overturning their tables, Jesus would have demanded of them: "Take your things and get out!" And he would have done this although he had already driven out the money changers earlier, according to Hirsch's reconstruction. On this view, Jesus—and this is important—does not attack the money changers with his whip (as some artists and also commentators have represented it), but put a stop only to the exchange of money.

𝔓⁶⁶ and 𝔓⁷⁵ read τὰ κέρματα, as does B. It is thus not necessary to read the collective singular κέρμα with ℵ ℜ Θ *al* as Bauer does.[14] Κατέστρεψεν in ℵ Φ *pc* is probably a late reading. 𝔓⁶⁶ offers ἀνέτρεψεν, as do B Θ *al;* Bauer prefers the reading ἀνέστρεψεν (A L), which is now also attested by 𝔓⁷⁵.

■ **16** It is consonant with this picture that Jesus does not also proceed against those who were selling pigeons, but only orders them to remove the cages and pigeons. The picture that the narrator is painting of Jesus is thus far consistent. The only difficulty lies in conceiving how he drove out the animals—where did he drive them?—at the same time as he attacked the money changers. In the Overview we will consider to what extent this picture is historical. The affirmation, "You shall not make my Father's house a house of trade," is directed against all the groups mentioned above. But in the interests of the

---

10 Billerbeck, 1: 851.
11 *Das Evangelium Johannes,* 15.
12 *Studien,* 47.
13 *Das Johannesevangelium,* 47.
14 *Das Johannesevangelium,* 47.

composition, the weightiest item is placed at the end. The Evangelist does not take this affirmation to mean that Jesus rejects commercial activity in sacred precincts: there are no sacred precincts for the Johannine Jesus, neither on Gerizim nor in Jerusalem (John 4:21). What the Johannine Jesus rejects is the delusion that man can buy God's favor with sacrifices. Verse 16 can also have been derived from the source. But it was thereby intended, if we understand it correctly, to say something different, viz., the fulfillment of the thing indicated in Zech 14:21: "And there shall no longer be a trader in the house of the Lord of hosts on that day." The quotation, however, is not made especially evident as such, nor is its fulfillment.

■ **17** This lack of clarity might have prompted the insertion of verse 17.[15] Jesus' action appears to lack a biblical base. As a consequence, verse 10 is taken from Ps 69, which is interpreted christologically, and interpreted to mean: Jesus' behavior follows from his zeal for the house of God (therefore as a cleansing of the temple, not its destruction) and that would bring about his destruction ($\kappa\alpha\tau\alpha\phi\acute{\alpha}\gamma\epsilon\tau\alpha\iota$: third singular future of $\kappa\alpha\tau\epsilon\sigma\theta\acute{\iota}\omega$, "to consume").[16] From this addition it follows that the disciples, who have not been mentioned up to this point in the story, were reminded of Ps 69:9 by Jesus' action and understood that Psalm as a prophecy. This addition, which separates verse 16 from verse 18, need not have arisen subsequently, but could have been present already in the source of the Evangelist. In contrast to the Synoptics, this indirect prooftext is not, however, attributed to Jesus but to the disciples; it cannot be used as an immediate addition to Jesus' words.

■ **18** "The Jews" (in Mark 11:27 the chief priests, the scribes, and the elders are mentioned; in Matt 21:23 it is "the chief priests and elders of the people"; in Luke 20:1 "the chief priests and the scribes with the elders") pose the question of authority in a way that requires a legitimating sign. The Johannine tradition thus parts company with the Synoptics at this point, for the Synoptics

introduce John the Baptist and his baptism into the conversation. At the same time, "the Jews" appear as representatives—as often in the Gospel of John—of the world that is alienated from God. The miracle at Cana appears to have been forgotten. The continuation of the dialogue in John is possible only on that assumption.

■ **19** Verse 19 presents the saying of Jesus regarding the destruction of the temple, reflected in various forms and attributed to Jesus in Mark 14:57f., Matt 26:60f., Acts 6:14, Mark 15:29, and Matt 27:40: "Destroy this temple, and in three days I will raise it up." This saying is ambiguous and the author makes deliberate use of this ambiguity. The Jews understand his saying in the sense that he promises, as legitimation of his action in the temple, to rebuild the temple in three days were the Jews now to destroy it. We thus encounter one of those "Johannine" misunderstandings that show: the world proves to be incapable of understanding his words.

■ **20** The answer of the Jews demonstrates that they actually misunderstand Jesus in this crass way. They offer as evidence against Jesus: the construction of the temple has been going on for forty years. The matter is so phrased that it sounds like the entire time was devoted to its completion. According to Josephus,[17] the Herodian temple was begun in 20/19 BCE; it was completed shortly before the war with Rome.[18] If this scene may be used to date the events,[19] it would have taken place on Passover of the year 28.

The datum "46 years" has contributed to the discussion of Jesus' age. For, since Christians identified Jesus' body with the temple, they took this to be an indication of his age. Moreover, the numerical value of the word "Adam"—Jesus is the second Adam—is 46 years.[20] But Irenaeus was already aware of such speculations and even knew their sources. According to Irenaeus,[21] the presbyters had some information that had come to them through John, the disciple of the Lord, to the effect that Jesus was 40–50 years old when he taught in his prime. And that fits well with our verse: if one thinks of the

---

15   Cf. Haenchen, "Johanneische Probleme," 103.
16   Cf. BDF §74(2).
17   *Ant.* 15.380.
18   Billerbeck, 2: 411f.
19   Schnackenburg, *John*, 1: 366; Brown, *John*, 1: 117.
20   Augustine, *Joh. tract.* XCC 36.107f. and 12.
21   *Adv. haer.* 2.22.5.

construction time of the temple as 46 years up to this time and, correlatively, identifies Jesus' answer with his age, it follows that he was then 46 years old. If the temple of his body were destroyed, Jesus would raise it up again in three days: he would be raised up again after three days. It is also possible that in the background stood the attempt to render impossible gnostic speculations regarding the number 30, the years of Jesus' life, and the number of gnostic aeons.

Jesus was still born under Herod the Great, who died 4 BCE. He therefore was presumably some years older when he began his ministry than the 30 years attributed to him by Luke. That could have supported the tradition derived from John 8:57 ("You are not yet fifty years old").

The word ἐγείρω ("raise") has an active sense. But in John 10:18 Jesus says that he has the power to lay down his life and the power to take it up again. That agrees exactly with 2:19 and his ἐγερῶ ("I will raise . . ."): Jesus will raise himself up again.[22]

■ **21** Verse 21 casts light on the mysterious saying of Jesus: Jesus did not speak of the Herodian temple, but of the temple of his body. So long as Jesus lives on earth, God is present in him—and him alone—while for the Jews the presence of God is connected with the temple on Zion. Thus, to interpret Jesus' words literally: if the Jews kill him—and he knows they will, and he assents to his passion just as he does to the betrayal of Judas in John 13:27—then he will "raise up" his body (again) on the third day, will rise again (not, to be sure, with the mortal body in which he lived during his life). It is entirely possible that Jesus has answered the question of the Jews regarding his authority from the Christian point of view: his resurrection will legitimate his deeds. That, of course, still lies in the future. And that is not the miraculous proof demanded by the Jews with whom he is speaking. But the source could well have argued along that line. That there was such an understanding of the resurrection as legitimation in the time of the Gospels is proved by Matt 12:40. In this passage Jesus responds to the demand for a sign on the part of the Jews with the conundrum: the Son of man will be in the belly of the earth three days and three nights, just as Jonah was in the belly of the whale. For the Christian reader this form of legitimation does not come any later than the saying of Jesus about the temple in the source being used in the Gospel of John. The Evangelist himself did not, of course, look at the matter this way (see 3:2). For him, the outpouring of the Spirit through the resurrection of Jesus produces a true relationship to God for the first time and, at the same time, true understanding through the disciples. The condemnation of false Jewish worship found in verse 16 ("God cannot be bought") would thus have been supplemented positively: Jesus' exaltation brings us to God, not our sacrifices. But whether the Evangelist brought these widespread aspects of his thought together the context does not permit us to determine with compelling clarity.

■ **22** Jesus' disciples comprehended the meaning of his puzzling words in 2:19 only after the resurrection, and they attributed faith to this saying (faith carries understanding with it). In any case, the phrase, "the scripture and," presents a difficulty. It could not refer to a specific text (ἡ γραφή is used to denote a specific passage; αἱ γραφαί means the holy scripture) because such a text (which speaks of three days) does not apear in the passage. Schnackenburg[23] imagines a logion regarding the resurrection ("within three days"), although it is not cited. The passage envisaged will therefore be Psalm 69:10 mentioned in verse 17. But in this Psalm only the death of Jesus is involved—even interpreted christologically—and it requires an unusual stretch of the imagination, as Schnackenburg's further effort shows, to derive an allusion to the resurrection from this Psalm. Thus, the phrase, "the scripture and," is an addition that rates the words of Jesus on par with "holy scripture"— the OT was the only "sacred scripture" that Christianity recognized at first.

With Jesus' action in the temple the Evangelist has in mind only Jesus' rejection of Jewish worship. The question of the Jews is aimed at the justification for this reform, and the justification consists entirely of the authentic worship in Spirit and in truth that Jesus can and does reveal. The event is comprehensible only on this interpretation; and so is the strangely weak reaction

---

22 Editor: In another version of the author's notes we find just exactly the opposite interpretation: "The word ἐγείρω has an active sense. But in 10:18 Jesus says he has the power ἐγεῖραι. This does not appear to fit: Jesus is raised up!"

23 *John*, 1: 367.

of the Jews to Jesus' intervention in the temple service, as the Gospel of John reports it.

Overview

The Gospel of John comes into contact with the synoptic tradition for the first time at this point: Mark 11:11, 15–17, 27–33//Matt 21:12f., 23–27//Luke 19:45f., 20:1–8. It will pay us to compare these three versions and to investigate whether the history of this segment of tradition comes into view. There is the further question of whether and how the Johannine version of this history fits into the picture. Only then may we ask after the historical value of this tradition in general and of the Johannine version in particular. Finally, the modern critical resolution of this question itself constitutes a problem, which will take us down to the current views of this pericope.

The four related stories have more in common than one perceives at first glance. Each time a Passover is involved (only then were the tables of the money changers, in fact, set up in the Court of the Gentiles—this designation is of course not used in any of the accounts). The real action consists of a violent intervention in the ordinary course of temple business in this period. Jesus' words explain and, at the same time, justify his course of action. Finally, it comes to a discussion of his authority.

Mark 11:11 offers a singular piece of information: Jesus does not begin cleansing the temple immediately after he enters Jerusalem and the sacred precinct; he only looks around at everything. The commentators are rather perplexed about this item, if they devote attention to it at all. According to Holzmann,[24] everything was "new" for Jesus; also according to Wellhausen,[25] Jesus had not often been in the temple. Taylor[26] has Jesus go only as far as the Court of the Israelites. Papyrus Oxyrhynchos 840 with its controversy dialogue between Jesus and a high priest named Levi in the temple[27] has occasionally tempted a scholar to state that the Fourth Gospel is "exceptionally well informed" for reasons that are both good and bad, and then to explain the words, "he looked around at everything." The supposition that Jesus visited the precincts of the temple area reserved for priests or even the high priest alone is even more precarious. If one prefers not to turn Jesus into a tourist who exploits every opportunity, one can pass that off only as messianic occupation of the temple. Of course there is no hint in the text of such a thing.

The actual report of the cleansing of the temple begins in Mark 11:15. It is reported here, to the consternation of some scholars, that Jesus (acting alone; nothing is said about the disciples) drives out buyers and sellers, overturns the tables of the money changers and the seats of those who sell pigeons (not a word is said about resistance on the part of those affected), and does not permit anyone to carry a (water) jar through the large temple square (v 16). Verse 17 contains the words that justify such action: "My house shall be called house of prayer for all peoples" (Isa 56:7, Jer 7:11; a so-called "mixed citation"). In their contexts, however, these two citations mean something quite different that has nothing to do with our scene: the passage from third Isaiah does not perhaps propose to abolish sacrifices and replace them with prayer, but presupposes that the Gentiles who join with Israel might also enter the temple in the endtime and that their offerings will be as pleasing to God as those of the Jews. "House of Prayer" (בית תפלה) is thus not being contrasted here with sacrifices. The second part of the "mixed citation" also has a different meaning in its original context: Jer 7:11 means that one steals, commits murder, commits adultery, swears falsely, makes sacrifices to Baal, runs after other gods, and then goes into the temple in the presence of God and hopes to be saved. "Has this house, which is called by my name, become a den of robbers in your eyes?" (Jer 7:11). "Den of robbers" refers to a place where one goes with the booty, after having stolen and robbed, and feels safe. In pointing to this "biblical basis," Mark and his community

---

24 "Das schriftstellerische Verhältnis des Johannes zu den Synoptikern," *ZWT* 12 (1869) 161.

25 *Das Evangelium Marci* (1905, ²1909) 88.

26 *The Gospel According to St. Mark* (London: Macmillan, ²1966) 457.

27 Cf. Jeremias, "Unbekanntes Evangelium mit johanneischen Einschlägen (Pap. Egerton 2)," in *NTApoc* 1: 92–94.

indicate to us how they attempt to account for Jesus' activity. Here Christians, like the Jews before them, have not paid attention to the context and have seized on one sentence or another or even on a phrase. It is possible that Mark understood the phrase "for all nations" to refer to the great external "Court of the Gentiles," so called, and that he represents the situation in such a way that the money changers and those who sold pigeons carried on their business there. Matthew and Luke omit the phrase, "for all nations," and thus achieve a sharp contrast between "house of prayer" and "den of robbers." Luke was evidently not entirely comfortable in describing precisely an action of Jesus involving violence; he has omitted these features, as a consequence, while Matthew retains them as a matter of course.

The Gospel of John, on the other hand, has depicted the action of Jesus in detail: it speaks of the sale of oxen and sheep; it has Jesus make ready a kind of whip and drive "them all" out, oxen and sheep; it has Jesus pour out and overturn the coins and tables of the money changers. The sellers of pigeons receive the gentlest treatment: they are to take their pigeons away, and no one is to turn "my Father's house" into a marketplace. There is certainly no such saying in the OT. The final verse alone could have been influenced by a passage from the OT, viz., by Zech 14:21, where to a good and happy future belongs: "And there shall no longer be a trader in the house of the Lord of hosts on that day."

The final verses of the Johannine pericope (2:18–21) make it clear that the true temple is the body of Jesus. The action against the Jerusalem temple (in which the Jews want to buy God's favor) is actually based on the contrast between Jewish and Christian worship (with this cf. 4:21–23). But that means: the Johannine tradition indeed reports Jesus' violent action against the merchants and money changers in greater detail than the Synoptics and thereby offers a form of the story that is more developed; but Jesus' action has attained another meaning: the Jewish cultus must give way to Christian

worship in Spirit and in truth (so 4:23). It is not a matter of a "cleansing of the temple," but of the abolition of the temple cultus altogether. That cultus came to an end with the destruction of Jerusalem and the temple in 70 CE at the latest, and the narrator knows it only in that state.

And for the other question: is there a historical reality behind the synoptic and Johannine accounts of the incident in the temple, and, if so, what is it? The first subordinate question is this: is the Synoptic dating of the event (the cleansing of the temple at the beginning of the passion of Jesus) to be preferred to the Johannine (at the beginning of the public ministry) or not? Braun,[28] Lagrange,[29] and Taylor,[30] still support the superiority of the Johannine account. But the majority of scholars, among whom there are also Catholic exegetes like Schnackenburg[31] and Brown[32] (Catholic exegetes tend to treat the matter cautiously), prefer the Synoptic date.

No matter how one decides this question, one must also ask whether a historical event lies behind these reports at all. Each Evangelist is certainly convinced that he is reporting an actual occurrence. Nevertheless, the significance of the event was the main concern of them all. The elucidation of the historical event, as we undertake it, is more in the nature of a subordinate enterprise.

That has complicated efforts of modern historical-critical work to elucidate the historical background of the two types of story. Research first had to go through a long and painful process to free itself from the notion that the way of representing things, say, in Mark 11:15–19 and 11:27–33 or John 2:13–22, was something like a documentary film. Criticism had still not really dawned with Zahn and Bernhard Weiss. Zahn[33] pictures the event like this: hundreds of oxen and sheep were collected in the outer courts and halls around the temple area. Jesus made a whip "out of cords or strips of leather which would have been easy to find on the floor" and drove "the cattlemen together with their cattle . . . out of the temple area through porches and gates surrounding

28 *La Sainte Bible,* 10: 330f.
29 *L'Evangile selon Saint Jean,* 64f.
30 *The Gospel According to St. Mark* (London: Macmillan, ²1966) 461f.
31 *John,* 1: 370.
32 *John,* 1: 118.
33 *Das Evangelium des Johannes,* 169.

it." Zahn did not notice how absurd it was to have Jesus drive large herds entirely out of the temple area, together with their owners—where did he drive them, really? When did Jesus find the time to turn to the money changers and sellers of pigeons (Zahn has depicted the treatment of both groups with an ardent pedantry)? He did not consider this in his eager efforts to reproduce the scene. In the view of B. Weiss,[34] "the Synoptic tradition . . . has erroneously" misplaced "the unforgettable incident" at the end of Jesus' public ministry. "All historical probability speaks for the account" of the Fourth Gospel. "On his last festival pilgrimage, where Jesus . . . already proclaimed the downfall of the city and the temple, the cleansing of the temple was a pointless provocation. . . . On the other hand, Jesus could not have inaugurated his public activity more suitably . . . than by bearing witness against the dislocation and poisoning of the practice of national piety by common greed, and bearing that witness at the center of common life in a theocracy."

The turn in scholarship is already evident in Lohmeyer:[35] the narrative is scarcely to be labeled a historical report, but is a paraenetical example with teaching appended. Historically speaking, the incident can hardly be brought clearly into view: "for it is difficult to imagine how Jesus cleaned out the entire temple square alone" and why neither the temple guard nor the Roman police in the tower of Antonia intervened. "The action of Jesus could have taken place only in the Court of the Gentiles . . . and signals a revolutionary act vis-à-vis the Sanhedrin." Did the Sanhedrin have to restrain itself because of the people, who supported Jesus, or because of the Roman government? Did Jesus act in order to prepare for the end of the age by performing an eschatological deed?

For Hirsch[36] the resolution of the question is much simpler. The Pre-Markan report of the eyewitness account of Peter lies at the base of the narrative; the verses Mark 11:15b, 16, 18 are, in part, later additions.

The reproach that the worship of God has been commercialized governs the free recasting. "To adjust the story a little with deft hands and listen to the words that belong to the story with the ears of the Spirit—that was all (the Evangelist) did." The cleansing of the temple "is something entirely unique, something that does not fit Jewish logic; at best one could call it an authoritative act of the kind typical of the prophets. It is not essentially an act of violence employing armed followers, but the act of a man of God himself that produces paralyzing fright and unresisting timidity. Its effect lies in the inner shock delivered to those concerned. It does not therefore require helping hands to be told; what there is of helping hands is of little consequence for the event." It becomes clear in Mark 11:17 that one cannot get by with such a psychologizing interpretation: Jesus does not permit (imperfect of duration) anyone to carry a vessel through the sacred temple precinct. That is the point of view of a Pharisee: one must not treat the sacred temple precinct as a profane domain (the same thing applies to the synagogue) by using it as a shortcut.[37] Since the temple buildings practically divide the great Court of the Gentiles into a northern and a southern region, which a single person could not have overseen and controlled, surveillance would have been possible only by a guard made up of Galilean pilgrims stationed at all the gates of the Court. Some exegetes assist by supplying an enthusiastic crowd of messianic pilgrims from Galilee, who could have served perhaps as the helping hands of Hirsch. But would the pilgrims have been so enthusiastic when Jesus and his disciples made it impossible for them to present the temple tax, an offering of doves, and to participate in the Passover meal, especially since Jesus had not prepared them for such a deed by appropriate preaching and thus made it comprehensible. It actually turns out that the Christian community attempted, in different ways at various times, to find a "biblical meaning" in the stories about an action of Jesus.

In Mark 11:18 the chief priests and scribes hear of

---

34 *Das Johannes-Evangelium*, 100.

35 *Das Evangelium des Markus, übersezt und erklärt*, KEK 1,2 (Göttingen: Vandenhoeck & Ruprecht, 1932, [16]1963) 235–37.

36 *Frühgeschichte*, 1: 121–28 and *Das vierte Evangelium*, 127–33.

37 Billerbeck, 2: 27.

Jesus' deed without daring to proceed against him, on account of the people. The question of the chief priests regarding the authority of Jesus is separated from the cleansing of the temple by sayings about the fig tree, faith, and forgiveness (vv 21–25), separated to such an extent that the question, "By what authority are you doing these things?" hangs in the air. When Jesus poses the counter question whether the baptism of John is from "heaven" (= God), they respond: "we don't know." Because every answer presents them with a dilemma—here the narrator reconstructs what is in the priests' minds—Jesus evades the necessity of giving out information about his authority by means of this adroit, loaded question. But was it really impossible for the council to respond to Jesus' counter question? The chief priests could rightly have replied: If you appeal to the baptism of John, why do you not baptize yourself? Or, put differently: even if John were authorized by God to practice baptism, that has nothing to do with the question whether Jesus' violent attack was sanctioned by God or not. This entire scene looks much more like Christians reflecting very cleverly in their imaginations on how Jesus could have exercized his authority and power without his opponents being able to respond at all. It was as certain for Mark that "everybody" regarded John as a prophet as it was that Christian baptism was concerned with the will of Jesus.

Luke has not only gotten rid of the encumbrance involved in the story of the fig tree. That story is neither consistent in itself—it was not the time for figs, Mark 11:13b—nor is it suitable as proof of the power of God in prayer. Luke also drops the concrete descriptions of Jesus' behavior. Jesus no longer turns over tables of money changers and seats of merchants and he drives no cattle out. In the Lukan account, the story of the question about authority is now certainly proximate to the the story of the cleansing of the temple. As a consequence, Luke has detached the question of authority from the cleansing of the temple and connected it to the teaching of Jesus: the interrogators can now question Jesus on "one of those days."[1]

This amelioration of what offends in the story does not, however, set historical critics and their imaginations at ease. That opens up a dangerous course for Hirsch,[38] as it does for Zahn. If one, for instance, has Jesus "strike one or the other of the [money changers'] tables," as Zahn does,[39] "so that the coins that were sorted and stacked up on the table are mixed up and roll onto the ground," and if one then has Jesus overturn "the tables themselves in order to complete the disruption," one then gives the reader an impression that the narrator did not at all intend. How little Zahn[40] understands the Evangelist at this point is demonstrated by his interpretation of John 2:17: "The violent demeanor of Jesus also appears to the disciples to be that of a Zealot and thus dangerous." It is not surprising that R. Eisler could sketch out a plot in 1930[41] in which Jesus launches an unfortunate attack on the temple and is quashed by Pilate (tower of Siloam, Luke 13:4; Carmichael[42] did not read Eisler's book without profit). No one of the Gospel writers came upon the idea of ascribing a zealotic misunderstanding to the disciples, even though sayings open to such a misunderstanding were part of the tradition, such as: "I have not come to bring peace, but a sword" (Matt 10:34//Luke 12:51). The Fourth Gospel was conceived in a community for which the temple cultus (it was then no longer in existence) was still something reformable and for which the realm of the king Jesus was not of this world.

Is there now a historical kernel anywhere in the story? Jesus carries out "the cleansing of the temple" alone in all four accounts. How are we to account for that? M. R. James has called attention to the translation of the Bible in verse, known as *Aurora*,[43] made by Peter of Riga (in the late twelfth century) with many notes. This appears in the cleansing of the temple: In the gospels used by the Nazareans it is said that rays came out of Jesus' eyes, through which the opponents of Jesus were struck dumb.

38   *Das vierte Evangelium*, 130f.
39   *Das Evangelium des Johannes*, 169f.
40   *Das Evangelium des Johannes*, 171.
41   *The Messiah Jesus and John the Baptist*, ed. A. H. Krappe (London: Methuen, 1930).
42   *Leben und Tod des Jesus von Nazareth* (Munich: Szczesny Verlag, ²1965).
43   "Notes on Apocrypha," *JTS* 7 (1906) 562–68, espe-

cially 566.
44   *Comm. in Mt* 9.9.

James speculates that these remarks go back to Jerome,[44] to a passage that ends with the words: *Ignem enim quiddam atque sidereum radiabat ex oculis eius, et divinitatis majestas in his countenance.* Jerome does not of course mention a gospel used by the Nazareans. But James nevertheless does not consider it out of the question that Jerome knew such a source. In fact Jerome is here borrowing from Origen.[45] Origen interprets the story of the cleansing of the temple purely symbolically in his commentary on John (the temple stands for the church)[46] and indicates that this story could not have taken place in a literal sense (if one does not care to salvage it as ἡ θειοτέρα τοῦ Ἰησοῦ δύναμις, "the holy power of Jesus"), especially since Jesus would have acted questionably from a moral point of view and the merchants and money changers would have been confident of the justice of their position. But the moral shock-effect of Jesus' action has also not become more comprehensible as a result. One has also to presuppose a sense of guilt—if only the minimum—on the part of the money changers and those who sold pigeons, as Hirsch has actually already done. But these people were not only licensed by the temple authorities, they had no reason to have a bad conscience with respect to their occupation—without which the payment of the temple tax and the temple cultus could not be carried out.

Earlier we referred to Lohmeyer's conjecture[47] that "the story is not a historical report, . . . but a paraenetical example with appended teaching." It then remains to inquire why the community historicized what is really a paraenetical example story in passing it on. To this question one may respond with the suggestion that the Evangelists transmitted numerous such (diverging) fragmentary sketches of Jesus.[48] There comes to mind that story which (indirectly) ascribes to Jesus a positive

response to the question of the temple tax (Matt 17:24–27); the story that attributes to Jesus a positive response to an offering in the temple (Matt 5:23–24); his approval of the money offering to the temple (Mark 12:41–44//Luke 21:1–4); in addition to which there is the prediction of the destruction of the temple (Mark 13:1–4//Matt 24:1–3//Luke 21:5ff.), the desecration of the temple (Mark 13:14//Matt 24:15), the lament over the judgment of Jerusalem (Matt 23:37–38//Luke 13:34–35, including the mention of the οἶκος, "house"), and the lament over the daughters of Jerusalem (Luke 23:27–31). The sayings about the destruction and rebuilding of the temple form another group (Mark 14:58, Matt 26:61, Mark 15:29, Matt 27:40, John 2:19, Acts 6:14; cf. Acts 7:47, 17:24).

The images of Jesus suggested by each of these sayings are not simply to be covered over: on the contrary, they provide various aspects of the picture of Jesus in the Gospels (of varying historical worth). One can not agree that these variations are simply to be traced back to the difference between Jewish and Gentile Christians. Such a simple scheme would not do justice to the manifold character of early Christian tradition and preaching. One is reminded also of the saying imputed to Jesus regarding fecundity in the millennial kingdom, to which we were able to point earlier as a further development of the Syrian Apocalypse of Baruch.[49]

The sayings of Jesus were not always transmitted as isolated logia, but were also embedded in graphic scenes, out of which one cannot reconstruct a unified historical overview. But various OT sayings about the "temple" (ναός; Isa 56:7, Jer 7:11, Zech 14:21) very likely played an important role in the formation of these scenes, to say nothing of Psalms interpreted christologically.

---

45 I am indebted to my esteemed colleague, Prof. Kettler, for this friendly tip; I am obligated to him for much besides.

46 Cf. Book X.25, §§143–51, pp. 197f.

47 *Das Evangelium des Markus, übersezt und erklärt*, KEK 1,2 (Göttingen: Vandenhoeck & Ruprecht, 1932, [16]1963) 237.

48 Cf. Schille, "Prolegomena zur Jesusfrage," *TLZ* 93

(1968) 481–88.

49 See Introduction §1, "The Fourth Gospel in Early Christian Tradition," s.v. Bishop Papias.

8. Jesus Performs Many Miracles

Bibliography

Guthrie, Donald
"The Importance of Signs in the Fourth Gospel."
Vox evangelica 5 (1967) 72–83.

Hodges, Zane C.
"Untrustworthy Believers—Joh 2,23–25." *BSac*
135 (1978) 139–52.

Richter, Georg
"Zum sogenannten Taufetext Joh 3,5." In his
Studien zum Johannesevangelium, ed. Josef Hainz.
BU 13 (Regensburg: F. Pustet, 1977) 327–45.

Stanley, David M.
"Israel's Wisdom Meets the Wisdom of God."
Worship 32 (1958) 280–87.

Stauffer, Ethelbert
"Agnostos Christos. Joh 2,24 und die Eschatologie
des vierten Evangeliums." In *The Background of the
New Testament and its Eschatology* [in honor of
Charles Harold Dodd], ed. W. D. Davies and D.
Daube (Cambridge: Cambridge University Press,
1956) 281–99.

Topel, L. John
"A Note on the Methodology of Structural Analysis in John 2:23–3:21." *CBQ* 33 (1971) 211–20.

Tsuchido, Kiyoshi
"The Composition of the Nicodemus-Episode,
John 2,23–3,21." *Annual of the Japanese Biblical
Institute* 1 (1975) 91–103.

2

23   **Now when he was in Jerusalem at the
Passover feast, many believed in his
name when they saw his signs which he
did; 24/ but Jesus did not trust himself to
them, 25/ because he knew all men and
needed no one to bear witness of man;
for he himself knew what was in man.**

This short passage is often identified as an addition of the
Evangelist.[1] But it is a question of what one means by the
Evangelist. Whoever thinks of him as a redactor of a
higher order, as Bultmann does, must have different
reasons for doing so than the one who holds the view
that the Evangelist is a theologian of the greatest range,
for whom, however, it is of no consequence to retain
something of the tradition if he can somehow bring that
something into agreement with his own view. That the
pericope contains Johannine expressions[2] does not imply
that it contains no tradition. Certainly the pericope is
unusually colorless. Among those to whom reference is
being made here, Nicodemus is probably also to be
included. To this extent, these verses form not only a

---

1   E.g. Wellhausen, *Das Evangelium Johannes,* 16 and
Bultmann, *John,* 130 [91f.].
2   See Brown, *John,* 1: 126f.

kind of conclusion to the preceding scene (in continuing the situation), but also preparation for 3:1–21.

■ **23** Jesus is still in Jerusalem. The repetition of ἐν ("in") three times is excessive. The phrase "at the Passover" (ἐν τῷ πάσχα) might be regarded, with Hirsch,[3] as an addition of the redactor; it is intended to give precise identification to the feast. According to the preceding story, Jesus had performed no miracles in Jerusalem, if one does not consider the cleansing of the temple as one, and that of course is not warranted by the text. In any case, the faith of many based on the signs they have now seen (θεωρέω and even βλέπω have replaced ὁράω in the present tense) is conceived by the Evangelist as preparation for the story of Nicodemus: 3:2 corresponds to the faith based on miracle; it appears that for the Evangelist this does not say much for their faith (cf. 3:3). "Believed in his name" (John 1:12, 2:23, 3:18, Matt 18:6, Mark 9:42; John customarily says "believe in him" or "believe in me") appears to be an expression of the community in the sense of to perceive or acknowledge someone as sent from God. This does not speak unqualifiedly for the Evangelist as author. But here the miracles intended as signs identify Jesus only as a "divine man" (θεῖος ἀνήρ), of which there were many at that time. The tradition available to the Evangelist depicts Jesus throughout in this manner. The miracles legitimate him. Verse 23 may thus be understood as a kind of summary. In a similar way, 4:45 speaks of Galileans who saw everything that Jesus did in Jerusalem. Also in 7:31 many miracles that Jesus did in Jerusalem are reckoned with, while 7:3 seems to presuppose that Jesus had only performed miracles in Galilee up to this point. In 11:47 and 12:37 many signs are attributed to Jesus, and they are mentioned again in 20:30. If these "summaries" were already contained in the "gospel" used by the Evangelist, then its character as a "gospel of miracles" would have been further heightened: then the major individual miracles narrated would merely have been especially impressive examples of the miracle-working power of Jesus. The

Evangelist could have taken over such "summaries" as easily as he did individual miracles, if he understood the former as pointers just as he did the later.

■ **24** "But Jesus did not trust himself to them": this usage appears rarely in Greek.[4] The word-play works with various meanings of πιστεύω ("believe, trust"). The phrase might mean: "He did not trust them"; perhaps even: "He did not make himself known to them." Thus Stauffer:[5] "Again and again he avoided revealing his secret" (ἐπίστευεν: imperfect). Verse 24 has nothing to do with the late Jewish speculation regarding the hidden messiah who lives as a beggar before the gates of Rome.

■ **25** Verse 25 awkwardly explains verse 24b. Bultmann[6] takes this fussiness of language as evidence that the Evangelist himself composes this sentence. But the style of the Evangelist differs; the narrator does not intend, of course, to represent Jesus as one of the "divine men" (θεῖοι ἄνθρωποι), many of whom boasted of their omniscience, like Apollonius of Tyana or the Mandean Manda d'Hayye,[7] but as the all-knowing son of God (but cf. the suggestion found already in Mark 2:8). Schwartz[8] thinks the singular "man" points to the betrayer; but the text offers no support for this suggestion.

Overview

Did this pericope, which can be understood as a transition and introduction to the Nicodemus scene, already have this sense in the source? It is difficult to accept the view that it did, for in that case the Nicodemus scene had a different content. That would not be impossible, since the figure of Nicodemus appears again in 19:39 with an illusion to 3:1f.[9] Schwartz[10] remarks on the many "signs" (σημεῖα): "It is to be noted that the 'many signs' occur only in speeches and explications or in the explanation inserted in 12:37, never in the narrative itself, as is often the case in the Synoptics; they are even presupposed by the Synoptics and, in the Fourth Gospel, do not belong to the tightly woven series of miracles that is graduated until it reaches a climax in the resurrection of the dead."

3   *Studien*, 48.
4   Wettstein (*Novum Testamentum Graecum editionis receptae cum Lectionibus variantibus . . . necnon commentario pleniore . . . opera studio Joannis Jacobi Wetstenii*, 2 vols. [Amsterdam, 1751, 1752] 1: 849) mentions a passage in Eustathius; Bauer (*Das Johannesevangelium*, 50) a further one in Plutarch: "This person seems to me to show sense in trusting himself to a good man

rather than to a strong place" (Plutarch's Moralia, LCL, vol. 3, tr. F. C. Babbitt [1931] 181D).
5   *Jesus and His Story*, tr. Dorothea M. Barton (London: SCM Press, 1960) 61.
6   *John*, 131 n. 4 [92 n. 5].
7   Bauer, *Das Johannesevangelium*, 50.
8   "Aporien," 1: 352 n. 3.
9   On Naqdemon ben Gorgion, mentioned several

Perhaps one ought rather to say: the mention of "many signs" in 12:37 and 20:30 may well have been taken over by the Evangelist, but was not created by him. For him, the single miracle in 7:21 is sufficient: Jesus heals the paralytic by the pool of Bethzatha. The few miracles the Evangelist has taken over are not meant to serve the legitimation of Jesus, to demonstrate his divine being.

They can only point to his divine being as events which refer to an entirely different dimension. For that reason the Evangelist does not require numerous miracles; they only prove something for those who have not yet perceived the "qualitative distinction" between the divine and human spheres. That will be made clear by the scene with Nicodemus which now follows.

times by the rabbis, cf. Billerbeck, 2: 413–17.

10   "Aporien," 2: 121 n. 1.

9. Jesus and Nicodemus

Bibliography

A. On 3:1–21

Balembo, Buetubela
"Jean 3,8: L'Esprit-Saint ou le vent naturel?" *Revue Africaine de Théologie* 4 (1980) 55–64.

Ballenstedt, Heinrich Christian
Philo und Johannes, 3 vols. (Braunschweig: F. B. Culemann, 1802; Göttingen: H. Dieterich, 1812), esp. 1 (1802) 97–118; 2 (1812) 69–94.

Bauer, Johannes
"Πῶς in der griechischen Bibel." *NovT* 2 (1958) 81–91.

Beauvery, R.
"Accueillir le dessein d'amour que Dieu révèle en Jésus (Jn 3,14–21)." *Esprit et vie* 80 (1970) 113–16.

Becker, Jürgen
"Joh 3,1–21 als Reflex johanneischer Schuldiskussion." In *Das Wort und die Wörter. Festschrift Gerhard Friedrich zum 65. Geburtstag*, ed H. Balz and S. Schulz (Stuttgart: W. Kohlhammer, 1973) 85–95.

Belleville, L. L.
"Born of Water and Spirit: John 3:5." *Trinity Journal* (1981) 125–41.

Bietenhard, H.
Die himmlische Welt im Urchristentum und Spätjudentum, WUNT 2 (Tübingen: Mohr-Siebeck, 1951), esp. 82ff.

Billerbeck, Paul
"On John 3:21." 2: 429.

Bligh, John
"Four Studies in St. John, II: Nicodemus." *HeyJ* 8 (1967) 40–51.

Böcher, Otto
"Wasser und Geist." In *Verborum Veritas. Festschrift für Gustav Stählin zum 70. Geburtstag*, ed. O. Böcher and K. Haacker (Wuppertal: F. A. Brockhaus, 1970) 197–209.

Bojorge, Horacio
"La entrada en la tierra prometida y la entrada en el Reino. El trasfondo teológico del diálogo de Jesús con Nicodemo (Jn 3)." *RevistB* 41 (1979) 172–86.

Braun, François-Marie
"'La vie d'en haut' (Jo. III,1–15)." *RSPT* 40 (1956) 3–24.

Büchsel, Friedrich
"Κρίνω." *TDNT* 3: 933–41.

Carpenter, J. W.
"Water Baptism." *Restoration Quarterly* 54 (1957) 59–66.

Cullmann, Oscar
"Der johanneische Gebrauch doppeldeutiger Ausdrücke als Schlüssel zum Verständnis des 4. Evangeliums." *TZ* 4 (1948) 360–72.

Dalman, Gustaf
   The Words of Jesus, tr. D. M. Kay (Edinburgh: T. & T. Clark, 1902) = *Die Worte Jesu* (Leipzig: J. C. Hinrichs, 1898, ²1930; reprint Darmstadt: Wissenschaftliche Buchgesellschaft, 1965).

Fowler, R.
   "Born of Water and the Spirit (Jn 3:5)." *ExpTim* 82 (1971) 159.

Gaeta, Giancarlo
   Il dialogo con Nicodemo. Per l'interpretazione del capitole terzo dell'evangelo di Giovanni. Studi Biblici 26 (Brescia: Paideia, 1974).

Goppelt, Leonhard
   "Taufe und neues Leben nach Joh. 3 und Röm 6." *Stimme der Orthodoxie* 4 (1970) 51–53; 5 (1970) 36–41.

Gourbillon, J.-G.
   "La parabole du serpent d'Airain et la 'lacune' du Ch. III de l'évangile selon s. Jean." *RB* 51 (1942) 213–26.

Graf, J.
   "Nikodemus (Joh. 3,1–21)." *Tübinger theologische Quartalschrift* 132 (1952) 62–86.

Hahn, Ferdinand
   Christologische Hoheitstitel. Ihre Geschichte im Frühen Christentum, FRLANT 83 (Göttingen: Vandenhoeck & Ruprecht, 1963) 112–25.

Hodges, Zane C.
   "Problem Passages in the Gospel of John, Part 3: Water and Spirit—John 3:5." *BSac* 135 (1978) 206–20.

Hoyt, H. A.
   "The Explanation of the New Birth." *Grace Journal* (1967) 14–21.

Ibuki, Yu
   "Καὶ τὴν φωνὴν αὐτοῦ ἀκούεις. Gedankenaufbau und Hintergrund des dritten Kapitels des Johannesevangeliums." *Bulletin of Seikei University* 14 (1978) 9–33.

Jonge, Marinus de
   "Nicodemus and Jesus: Some Observations on Misunderstanding and Understanding in the Fourth Gospel." *BJRL* 53 (1971) 337–59.

Krenkel, Max
   "Joseph von Arimathäa und Nikodemus." *ZWT* 8 (1865) 438–45.

Krummacher, E. W.
   "Bezieht sich Joh 3,5 auf die heilige Taufe?." *TSK* 31 (1859) 507–11.

Meeks, Wayne A.
   "The Man from Heaven in Johannine Sectarianism." *JBL* 91 (1972) 44–72.

Meinertz, Max
   "Die 'Nacht' im Johannesevangelium." *TQ* 133 (1953) 400–407.

Mendner, Siegfried
   "Nikodemus." *JBL* 77 (1958) 293–323.

Menken, G.
   Über die eherne Schlange und das symbolische Verhältniß derselben zu der Person und Geschichte Jesu (Frankfurt, 1812).

Michaelis, Wilhelm
   Die Sakramente im Johannesevangelium (Bern: Buchhandlung der Evangelischen Gesellschaft, 1946).

Michel, M.
   "Nicodème ou le non-lieu de la vérité." *RSR* 55 (1981) 227–36.

Neyrey, Jerome H.
   "John III—A Debate over Johannine Epistemology and Christology." *NovT* 23 (1981) 115–27.

Nötscher, F.
   Zur theologischen Terminologie der Qumran-Texte. BBB 10 (Bonn: Peter Hanstein, 1956) 112f.

Pesch, Rudolf
   "'Ihr müsst von oben geboren werden': Eine Auslegung von Jo 3,1–12." *BibLeb* 7 (1966) 208–19.

Plessis, I. J. du
   "Christ as the 'Only begotten.'" *Neot* 2 (1968) 22–31.

Potterie, Ignace de la
   "Naître de l'eau et naître de l'Esprit. Le texte baptismal de Jn 3,5." *Sciences ecclésiastiques* 14 (1962) 417–43.

Potterie, Ignace de la
   "Structura primae partis Evangelii Johannis (capita III et IV)." *VD* 47 (1969) 130–40.

Potterie, Ignace de la
   "Ad dialogum Jesu cum Nicodemo (2,23–3,21). Analysis litteraria." *VD* 47 (1969) 141–50.

Potterie, Ignace de la
   "Jesus et Nicodemus: de necessitate generationis ex Spiritu (Jo 3,1–10)." *VD* 47 (1969) 193–214.

Potterie, Ignace de la
   "Jesus et Nicodemus: de revelatione Jesu et vera fide in eum (Jo 3,11–21)." *VD* 47 (1969) 257–83.

Richter, Georg
   "Zum sogenannten Tauftext Joh 3,5." *Münchener theologische Zeitschrift* 26 (1975) 101–25. Also in his *Studien zum Johannesevangelium,* ed. Josef Hainz. BU 13 (Regensburg: F. Pustet, 1977) 327–45.

Richter, Georg
   "Zum gemeindebildenden Element in den johanneischen Schriften." In his *Studien zum Johannesevangelium,* ed. Josef Hainz. BU 13 (Regensburg: F. Pustet, 1977), esp. 392–94.

Ritt, Hubert
   "'So sehr hat Gott die Welt geliebt . . .' (Joh 3,16)— Gotteserfahrung bei Johannes." In *"Ich will euer Gott werden . . . ." Beispiele biblischen Redens von Gott,* SBS 100 (Stuttgart: Katholisches Bibelwerk, 1981) 207–26.

Roberts, R. L.
   "The Rendering 'Only Begotton' in John 3:16." *Restoration Quarterly* 16 (1973) 2–22.

Robinson, D. W. B.
   "Born of Water and Spirit: Does John 3:5 Refer to Baptism?" *Reformed Theological Review* 25 (1966) 15–23.

Roustang, F.
"L'entretien avec Nicodème [Jn 3:1–15]." *NRT* 78 (1956) 337–58.

Sasse, Hermann
"Κόσμος." *TDNT* 3: 891–92, 894–95.

Schlatter, Adolf
Der Evangelist Johannes (Stuttgart: Calwer Vereins-buchhandlung, 1930) 1183–84 on John 3:1.

Schnackenburg, Rudolf
"Die Sakramente im Johannesevangelium." *Sacra Pagina. Miscellanea biblica congressus internationalis catholici de re biblica,* 2 vols., ed. J. Coppens, A. Descamps, and E. Massaux. BETL 12–13 (Paris: J. Gabalda; Gembloux: Duculot, 1959) 2: 235–54.

Schweizer, Eduard
Erniedrigung und Erhöhung bei Jesus und seinen Nachfolgern, ATANT 28 (Zurich: Zwingli Verlag, ²1962) 179f.

Schweizer, Eduard
"Zum religionsgeschichtlichen Hintergrund der Sendungsformel Gal 4,4; Röm 8,38; Jo 3,16f.; Jo 4,9." In his *Beiträge zur Theologie des Neuen Testaments. Neutestamentliche Aufsätze* (Zurich: Zwingli Verlag, 1970) 83–96.

Scognamiglio, R.
"Se uno non nasce da acqua e da spirito." *Nicolaus* 8 (1980) 301–10.

Sjöberg, Erik
"Neuschöpfung in den Toten-Meer-Rollen." *ST* 9 (1959) 131–36.

Smith, C. Hughes
"Οὕτως ἐστιν πᾶς ὁ γεγεννημένος ἐκ τοῦ πνεύματος." *ExpTim* 81 (1969/1970) 181.

Spicq, Ceslaus
"Notes d'exégèse johannique: la charité est amour manifeste." *RB* 65 (1958) 358–70.

Spriggs, G. D.
"Meaning of 'Water' in John 3:5." *ExpTim* 85 (1974) 149–50.

Stählin, Gustav
"Ὀργή." *TDNT* 5: 430–34.

Steinmeyer, F. L.
Beiträge zum Verständniss des johanneischen Evangeliums. Vol. 4, *Das Nachtgespräch Jesu mit dem Nikodemus* (Berlin: Wiegandt & Grieben, 1889).

Thomas, J. D.
"A Translation Problem—John 3:8." *Restoration Quarterly* 24 (1981) 219–24.

Thüsing, Wilhelm
Die Erhöhung und Verherrlichung Jesu im Johannes-evangelium, NTAbh 21, 1–2 (Münster: Aschen-dorff, 1960).

Topel, L. John
"A Note on the Methodology of Structural Analysis in John 2:23–3:21." *CBQ* 33 (1971) 211–20.

Tsuchido, Kiyoshi
"The Composition of the Nicodemus-Episode, John 2,23–3,21." *Annual of the Japanese Biblical Institute* 1 (1975) 91–103.

Usteri, J. M.
"Exegetische und historisch-kritische Bemer-kungen zum Gespräch Jesu mit Nikodemus, Joh. 3, 1–21." *TSK* 63 (1890) 504–51.

Vellanickal, M.
The Divine Sonship of Christians in the Johannine Writings, AnBib 72 (Rome: Pontifical Biblical Institute, 1977) 163–213.

Vergote, A.
"L'exaltation du Christ en croix selon le quatrième évangile." *ETL* 28 (1952) 5–23.

Zeller, Eduard
"Noch ein Wort über den Ausspruch Jesu bei Justin, Apol 1.61 über die Wiedergeburt." *Theolo-gische Jahrbücher* 14 (Tübingen, 1855) 138–40.

Zimolong, B.
"Die Nikodemus-Perikope nach dem syrosinai-tischen Text." Dissertation, Breslau, 1919.

B. Dualism in John

Achtemeier, Elizabeth R.
"Jesus Christ, the Light of the World. The Biblical Understanding of Light and Darkness." *Int* 17 (1963) 439–49.

Baaren, T. Van
Some Reflections on the Symbolism of Light and Dark-ness, in honor of Harald Biezais (Stockholm, 1979) 237ff.

Barrett, Charles Kingsley
"Paradox and Dualism." In his *Essays on John* (London: S. P. C. K., 1982) 98–115.

Baumbach, Günter
Qumran und das Johannesevangelium, Aufsätze und Vorträge zur Theologie und Religionswissenschaft 6 (Berlin: Evangelische Verlagsanstalt, 1958).

Becker, Jürgen
Das Heil Gottes. Heils- und Sündenbegriffe in den Qumrantexten und im Neuen Testament. SUNT 3 (Göttingen: Vandenhoeck & Ruprecht, 1964) 217–37.

Becker, Jürgen
"Beobachtungen zum Dualismus im Johannes-evangelium." *ZNW* 65 (1974) 71–87.

Bergmeier, Roland
Glaube als Gabe nach Johannes. Religions- und theologie geschichtliche Studien zum prädestinatiani-schen Dualismus im vierten Evangelium, BWANT 112 (Stuttgart: W. Kohlhammer, 1980).

Bergmeier, Roland
"Studien zum religionsgeschichtlichen Ort des prädestinat Dualismus in der johanneischen Literatur." Dissertation, Heidelberg, 1974.

Böcher, Otto
Der johanneische Dualismus im Zusammenhang des nachbiblischen Judentums (Gütersloh: Gerd Mohn, 1965).

Bultmann, Rudolf
"Zur Geschichte der Lichtsymbolik im Altertum." In his *Exegetica. Aufsätze zur Erforschung des Neuen*

Testaments, ed. E. Dinkler (Tübingen: Mohr-Siebeck, 1967) 323–55.

Charlesworth, James H.
"A Critical Comparison of the Dualism in 1 QS 3,13–4,26 and the 'Dualism' Contained in the Gospel of John." In *John and Qumran*, ed. J. H. Charlesworth (London: Chapman, 1972) 76–106.

Coetzee, J. C.
"Christ and the Prince of this World in the Gospel and the Epistles of St. John." *Neot* 2 (1968) 104–21.

Dibelius, Martin
"Die Vorstellung vom göttlichen Licht. Ein Kapitel aus der hellenistischen Religionsgeschichte." *Deutsche Literaturzeitung* 36 (1915) 1469–83.

Goetz, H.
"Der theologische und anthropologische Heilsuniveralismus bei Johannes in seiner exegetischen Begründung." Dissertation, 1896.

Hélou, C.
Symbole et langage dans les écrits johanniques: lumière—ténèbres (Paris: Mame, 1980).

Hilgenfeld, Adolf
"Das Johannes-Evangelium alexandrinisch oder gnostisch?" *ZWT* 25 (1882) 388–435, esp. 422–28.

Huppenbauer, H. W.
Der Mensch zwischen zwei Welten. Der Dualismus der Texte von Qumran (Höhle I) und der Damaskusfragmente. Ein Beitrag zum Vorgeschichte des Evangeliums, ATANT 34 (Zurich: Zwingli Verlag, 1959).

Johnson, Thomas Floyd
"The Antitheses of the Elders: A Study of the Dualistic Language of the Johannine Epistles." Dissertation, Duke University, 1980 [DissAbstr 80–08189].

Klein, F. N.
"Die Lichtterminologie bei Philon von Alex. und in den hermetischen Schriften." Dissertation, Leiden, 1962.

Malmede, H. H.
"Die Lichtsymbolik im Neuen Testament." Dissertation, Bonn, 1960.

Onuki, Takashi
Gemeinde und Welt im Johannesevangelium. Ein Beitrag zur Frage nach der theologischen und pragmatischen Funktion des johanneischen Dualismus (Stuttgart: W. Kohlhammer, 1983).

Osten-Sacken, Peter von der
Gott und Belial. Traditionsgeschichtliche Untersuchungen zum Dualismus in den Texten aus Qumran, SUNT 6 (Göttingen: Vandenhoeck & Ruprecht, 1969).

Preisker, Herbert
"Jüdische Apokalyptik und hellenistischer Synkretismus im Johannes-Evangelium dargelegt am Begriff 'Licht.'" *TLZ* 77 (1952) 673–78.

Preisker, Herbert
"Zum Charakter des Johannesevangeliums." In *Luther, Kant, Schleiermacher in ihrer Bedeutung für den Protestantismus. Forschung und Abhandlungen Georg Wobbermin zum 70. Geburtstag (27 Oktober 1939) dargebracht von Kollegen, Schülern und Freunden,* ed. D. F. W. Schmidt et al. (Berlin: Verlag Arthur Collignon, 1939) 379–93, esp. 387–92.

Schottroff, Luise
Der Glaubende und die feindliche Welt. Beobachtungen zum gnostischen Dualismus und seiner Bedeutung für Paulus und das Johannesevangelium, WMANT 37 (Neukirchen: Neukirchener Verlag, 1970).

Schottroff, Luise
"Johannes 4:5–15 und die Konsequenzen des johanneischen Dualismus." *ZNW* 60 (1969) 199–214.

Schweizer, Eduard
"Jesus der Zeuge Gottes." In *Studies in John Presented to Professor J. N. Sevenster on the Occasion of his Seventieth Birthday* (Leiden: E. J. Brill, 1970) 161–68.

Segal, A. F.
"Two Powers in Heaven." Dissertation, Yale University, 1975.

Stemberger, Günter
La symbolique du bien et du mal selon saint Jean, Parole de Dieu (Paris: Editions du Seuil, 1970).

Thomas, Richard W.
"The Meaning of the Terms 'Life' and 'Death' in the Fourth Gospel and in Paul." *SJT* 21 (1968) 199–212.

Wetter, Gillis Petersson
"*Phōs.* Eine Untersuchung über hellenistische Frömmigkeit, zugleich ein Beitrag zum Verständnis des Manichäismus." *Skrifter utgifna af (k.) Humanistiska Vetenskapssamfundet i Uppsala* 17:2 (Leipzig: Harrassowitz; Uppsala: A.-B. Akademiska Bokhandelung, 1917).

3

1 **Now there was a man of the Pharisees, named Nicodemus, a ruler of the Jews. 2/ This man came to Jesus by night and said to him, "Rabbi, we know that you are a teacher come from God; for no one can do these signs that you do, unless God is with him." 3/ Jesus answered him, "Truly, truly, I say to you, unless one**

is born from above, he cannot see the kingdom of God." 4/ Nicodemus said to him, "How can a man be born when he is old? Can he enter a second time into his mother's womb and be born?" 5/ Jesus answered, "Truly, truly, I say to you, unless one is born of water and the Spirit, he cannot enter the kingdom of God. 6/ That which is born of the flesh is flesh, and that which is born of the Spirit is spirit. 7/ Do not marvel that I said to you, 'You must be born from above.' 8/ The wind blows where it wills, and you hear the sound of it, but you do not know whence it comes or whither it goes; so it is with every one who is born of the Spirit." 9/ Nicodemus said to him, "How can this be?" 10/ Jesus answered him, "Are you a teacher of Israel, and yet you do not understand this? 11/ Truly, truly, I say to you, we speak of what we know, and bear witness to what we have seen; but you do not receive our testimony. 12/ If I have told you earthly things and you do not believe, how can you believe if I tell you heavenly things? 13/ No one has ascended into heaven but he who descended from heaven, the Son of man. 14/ And as Moses lifted up the serpent in the wilderness, so must the Son of man be lifted up, 15/ that whoever believes in him may have eternal life." 16/ For God so loved the world that he gave his only Son, that whoever believes in him should not perish but have eternal life. 17/ For God sent the Son into the world, not to condemn the world, but that the world might be saved through him. 18/ He who believes in him is not condemned; he who does not believe is condemned already, because he has not believed in the name of the only Son of God. 19/ And this is the judgment, that the light has come into the world, and men loved darkness rather than light, because their deeds were evil. 20/ For every one who does evil hates the light, and does not come to the light, lest his deeds should be exposed. 21/ But he who does what is true comes to the light, that it may be clearly seen that his deeds have been wrought in God.

In this segment, questions regarding the use of sources, the historical value, the composition, and the theology of the Gospel of John are intertwined and overlap to a greater degree than previously. The divergence of the commentaries demonstrates that. In 1893 B. Weiss[1] could still write: "There is nothing at all against the view

---

1   *Das Johannes-Evangelium*, 106.

that John was a witness to this dialogue." In 1954 Strathmann[2] believed it to be "a mistake . . . to raise at all the question of the external historicity of a dialogue that takes the course this one does." In the judgment of Bultmann[3] the discourse is "the primary element in the composition with respect to both content and literary analysis;" the Evangelist took it "from his source, the 'revelation discourses'." This raises the question of the relation of source and style. Verses 19–21 presuppose a fearless openness for Jesus, who is the light, and this ensues from the works done by man previously; but this cannot be reconciled with the Johannine doctrine of the witness of the Spirit, "from above." This discrepancy shows that the text has been reworked. The first half of the segment, the dialogue of Jesus with Nicodemus, is a doctrinal statement, transposed into dialogue form, concerning the significance (or lack of significance) of the miracles of Jesus; it is of decisive importance for understanding the entire gospel.

■ **1** "Man" = "a certain one" (ἄνθρωπος = τίς) is not a Semitism, but is Koine[4] and is already attested in classical Greek. Νικόδημος (cf. 7:50, 19:39): a very popular name in Greek that also is found among Jews.[5] "Of the Pharisees" (ἐκ τῶν Φαρισαίων): that Pharisees believed in Jesus as a result of his miraculous deeds is contradicted by what is said of the Pharisees elsewhere in the Gospel of John.[6] "Ruler" (ἄρχων) is indeterminate; in 7:48 there are "rulers" (ἄρχοντες) alongside the Pharisees. Presumably the word here means a member of the Sanhedrin. It thus becomes evident that the Gospel of John took over a tradition, according to which a highly placed man by the name of Nicodemus was numbered among the followers (secret?) of Jesus in Jerusalem.

■ **2** "By night" (νυκτός): why does Nicodemus come at night? According to Billerbeck,[7] the rabbis carried on their disputations until well into the night. But that explanation does not fit this passage: Nicodemus does not come during the day and then converse with Jesus into the night. Another possibility would be that his "fear

of the Jews" (cf. 19:38) determined the kind of visit he made to Jesus. But that does not fit the picture well either. For Nicodemus appears as the spokesman for a group (s. οἴδαμεν, "we know," 3:2). He could belong to "the many" of which 2:23 speaks; Jesus' miracles allegedly led them to faith, but of course not of the right kind. Bultmann puts things together differently.[8] Nicodemus gives Jesus the honorific title, "rabbi," and testifies to a conviction shared by many ("we know") that Jesus is a divinely inspired teacher. His basis for so doing: no one can do such wonders ("miracles" in the plural) as Jesus does unless God is with him. The belief that a miracle legitimated a teaching was not self-evident throughout late Judaism.[9] On the other hand, John 3:2 agrees with Acts 2:22, where Peter says: "Jesus of Nazareth, a man attested to you by God (ἀποδεδειγμένον) with mighty works and wonders and signs which God did through him in your midst, . . ." and the Gospel of Mark is scarcely to be understood apart from the assumption that the many miracles of Jesus are narrated as proof that he is the Son of God. Yet in the Gospel of John itself there are also passages which make sense only as a positive evaluation of miracles (as legitimation or as divine attestation). An incomprehensible example of this is the healing of the blind man in chapter 9. Here the one party argues—the Christians—that a man born blind could only be healed by a divine miracle and a divine worker of miracles, while the opposition—the authorities—respond with a light or a less light touch (the man healed was excommunicated from the Jewish synagogue) and with the objection, admittedly not demonstrable, that the miracle had not been proved. Was it really this very same man? Was he really blind from birth? His parents are ready only to assert that he was blind from birth, but they do not know how he came to be healed. He is old enough to speak for himself. Windisch has attempted to represent that in series of scenes that certainly might be very effective in the theatre. But for the Evangelist this story, which he has taken over from

---

2   *Das Evangelium nach Johannes*, 67.

3   *John*, 132 [93].

4   Bultmann, *John*, 133 n. 3 [94 n. 2] with reference to BDF §301 (2).

5   On a "*Naqdimon ben Gorjon*" in the time of Jesus, cf. Billerbeck, 2: 413–19.

6   See on 9:13.

7   2: 420.

8   *John*, 133f. [94f.].

9   Billerbeck, 1: 127f. points to *B. Mes.* 59b.

his source, can be used only as evidence that Jesus is the light of the world. The blind man, now healed, makes this general assertion in 9:31: "We know that God does not listen to sinners." Then in verses 32f.: "Never since the world began has it been heard that any one opened the eyes of a man born blind. (33) If this man (Jesus) were not from God, he could do nothing." The Evangelist can endorse his source in this passage, but only in an entirely different sense: If Jesus were not the word of God becoming audible, he could do nothing.

■ **3** It is all the more important that Jesus' response to Nicodemus (introduced with an especially emphatic "Truly, truly, I say . . .") decisively contradict the assertion of Nicodemus that he, Jesus, will be incontestably legitimized by miracles for everyone who sees his works. In so doing, Jesus makes use of an expression that permits various interpretations: "to be begotten from above," and "to be born again." The first is what is intended: to receive a new, heavenly existence. But Nicodemus understands it in the second sense: "to be born again." With this misunderstanding he makes it clear that he does not comprehend Jesus. Jesus therefore says: "Whoever does not receive from God a new, unearthly existence, cannot see the kingdom of God," which means, "cannot see the works of God." Nicodemus has seen miraculous deeds of Jesus, perhaps healing miracles, and thought that he saw God at work in them. But the "kingdom of God" ($\beta\alpha\sigma\iota\lambda\epsilon\iota\alpha\ \tau o\hat{v}\ \theta\epsilon o\hat{v}$) —in the Gospel of John, the expression occurs only here and in verse 5—does not admit of perception in the same way as does an earthly event, like the anointing of the eyes of the blind man with clay. If one is to perceive the kingly rule of God (which occurs as an earthly event but is not identical with it), then he must have become a new being, a new existence, indeed, he must have acquired new eyes, in order to discern the hand of God at work. Nothing further is said about that. This much only is clear: the divine rule is not an earthly event that everyone can perceive.

■ **4** Nicodemus, however, understands Jesus' words to mean that man must experience the process of his birth anew. In that connection he inquires: how is that possible? As an old man he cannot enter a second time into the womb of his mother and be born again. So understood the answer of Nicodemus is foolish and grotesque. And one can scarcely explicate it as being anything else.

The Evangelist thus paints the lack of understanding on the part of Nicodemus (= the man without faith) in the most lurid colors. One knows well what the Johannine Jesus would answer to the question: By what sort of process do I become a new man? How can an old man begin life anew? He is determined by what he has received from his parents and by his own experience and it is therefore prescribed, by and large, that he shall become what he is. He not only carries his past around with him as a part of his life, but also as a basic element of his existence. Birth implies such a total beginning that it already contains the dominant lines of one's future life. To be sure, man is still a bundle of possibilities; he is not just a process to be played out. But he can no more become a new man than he can become a bird, or a bunny, or a palm tree. Nor can he jump out of his own time and suddenly be transformed from an Amenophis to a Heidegger. The Evangelist could really only answer the question if he were to depict exactly what it means to be "born from above" in its own peculiarity and in its absolute diversity for all earthly becoming and all earthly change. But he appears to be ready with another answer.

■ **5** Jesus appears to repeat his answer once again with only slight modification. But one thing is new: he now mentions as the precondition that one must be born of water and the spirit. That can only refer to Christian baptism. It is described in somewhat greater detail in Acts 19:5f. where those who were disciples of John are baptized by Paul: "On hearing this, they were baptized in the name of the Lord Jesus. And when Paul had laid his hands upon them, the Holy Spirit came on them; and they spoke with tongues and prophesied." Baptism in John 3:5, as in Acts 19:5f., is thought of as Spirit combined with an earthly vehicle, or even several vehicles (Acts): in every case it is connected with water baptism and possibly with a laying on of hands. Further, the gift of "ecstasy" and prophecy are visible expressions of the new life. Jesus indicates nothing of that in verse 5: he mentions only water for baptism. However, the connection of the gift of the Spirit with baptism contradicts the conviction of the Evangelist. His understanding is indicated in 20:22 (with allusion to Gen 2:7): "And when he had said this, he breathed on them, and said to them, 'Receive the Holy Spirit.'" Moreover, in 3:5 the phrase "enter the kingdom of God" occurs in place of "see the kingdom of God" (in view of v 3). That is also a figure:

the kingdom of God is an invisible realm into which one cannot therefore enter at all; it is simply not accessible. This does not have to do with water baptism, as in verse 3. This kingdom is not visible like a stone that lies on the path; it is no earthly object. It is "visible" only to the one who exists in it. Only for the one who loves and is loved—to use another figure—is love (given and received) a reality.

■ **6** "That which is born of the flesh is flesh, and that which is born of the Spirit is spirit." Here "flesh" denotes the earthly reality, "Spirit" the divine reality. Even if one has extraordinarily gifted and pious parents, one does not, on that account, belong to the divine reality. One must have a new life from God (the gnostics also attempted to say that in their own way), a reality that does not stem from earthly heirs. Paul's expression in 2 Cor 4:18 is related to what is being said here: "For the things that are seen are transient, but the things that are unseen are eternal." "Eternal" does not mean unlimited duration, but something qualitatively different from all earthly things.

■ **7** Jesus admonishes Nicodemus not to marvel—perhaps one could even translate not to stumble—at his words: you must be born from above. The plural "you" that pops up here shows that it is not really Nicodemus as an individual who is addressed, but Nicodemus as a representative of all those Jews who stand on the threshold of Christian faith, but without crossing over. We will meet this same construction in 5:28: "Do not marvel at this; for the hour is coming when all who are in the tombs will hear his voice and come forth, those who have done good, to the resurrection of life, and those who have done evil, to the resurrection of judgment." These words are preceded by verse 27: "And he has given him authority to execute judgment, because he is the Son of man." This entire section, 5:27–29, is an insertion of the redactor, who has earlier inserted verses 22–24, which likewise assign all judgment to the Son. As a consequence, one is to honor him as one does the Father. It is clear that in both of these passages the redactor considered the "resurrection" in the here and now as an unsatisfactory doctrine of the resurrection and therefore, by means of the two insertions, sought to reinstate again the customary futuristic eschatology, with the judgment at the end of time. It then becomes a question whether the "do not marvel" in 3:7 is not likewise an

indication that the redactor attempted to effect his understanding by means of an interpretive overlay. This may involve the figure of the wind in 3:8.

■ **8** This verse returns to the singular, so far as the speaker is concerned. Jesus next employs the word "pneuma" ($\pi\nu\epsilon\hat{\upsilon}\mu\alpha$), which has a double meaning, in order to overcome the surprising lack of comprehension on the part of his dialogue partner. It may mean wind, but it can also mean the divine Spirit that God breathed into man at the time of the creation. The point of comparison lies in the observation that one can indeed hear the wind, but does not know whence it comes or whither it goes. So it is with every one who is born from above. Two things are to be noted in this connection: first, one can not only hear the rushing of the wind, but one can also immediately perceive whence the wind comes and whither it goes. One can determine, for example, that a wind blows out of the west and blows toward the east. The comparison with that which is born from above is thus not appropriate. In the second place, in the gnostic movement of that era there was the view that the true gnostic was able to say on his behalf: I know whence I have come (viz., from God) and whither I go (to God). On the other hand, it is difficult to say to what extent one can say of the one born from above that he hears his voice.

Verse 8 is perhaps intended to assert that one cannot understand one who is born from above. In that case, verse 9 would follow on very well.

■ **9** Nicodemus immediately confesses to a complete lack of understanding. But although Jesus warned him not to marvel, it is precisely his question, "How can this be?" that indicates such a misunderstanding. In any case, the warning of Jesus that Nicodemus is not to marvel if he meets one born from above and does not understand him leaves his dialogue partner without consolation. It does not make much sense that Nicodemus is chided because he does not comprehend the speech of one born of the Spirit. One can throw some light on the matter by saying that Jesus attempts to make it clear to him that he, Nicodemus, cannot understand one born of the Spirit, and to that Nicodemus surprisingly responds: how can there be a distinction among men whereby those born of the flesh cannot understand those born of the Spirit? Such a dualism, such an unbridgeable distinction among men is, in fact, alien to Jewish teaching, although a student frequently did not immediately understand what his rabbi said.

■ **10** Verse 10 now introduces a harsh reprimand of Nicodemus, to whom is ascribed a position that he did not in fact hold and which was unknown in contemporary Judaism: "Are you a teacher of Israel, and yet you do not understand this?" Jesus himself has just made it clear that one born of the Spirit cannot understand one born of the flesh. Had he at any point assumed that Nicodemus was perhaps born of the Spirit? The reader is probably meant to conclude that, even in its highest moment, Israel remains closed to the Christian mystery.

■ **11** Once again, a statement that sounds strange in the mouth of Jesus is introduced with a double ἀμήν ("truly, truly"): "I say to you, we speak of what we know, and bear witness to what we have seen; but you do not receive our testimony." Precisely this last clause shows that it is the Christian congregation that is speaking and mounting a polemic against the Jewish community, which has apparently closed itself off finally to the Christian community. Just as the individual Nicodemus was earlier represented as the spokesman for Israel, so Jesus now appears as the speaker for all those who (like himself) are "born from above." That same intrusive "we" also shows up in the midst of a speech of Jesus in 4:22 and evidently represents the church speaking: "You (the Samaritans) worship what you do not know; we worship what we know, for salvation is from the Jews." John 3:11 evidently looks back on a time when the Jews had decisively rejected all efforts on the part of the Christian community. The Jewish agreement to put everyone who confesses Christ out of the synagogue is mentioned in 9:22; this amounts to excommunication. That happens to the man born blind in 9:34. Around 200 CE,[10] a petition to God was inserted in the eighteen benedictions with the result that in every synagogue service every Jew had to say: may God annihilate the heretics, that is, the Christians. A Christian could not participate in such a prayer without betraying his faith in Christ. In effect, in the long run, it was essentially christology that led to the break with the Jews. There are expressions in the Gospel of John that lead to the conclusion that there was still a fellowship between Jews and Jewish Christians, albeit an endangered one; in other passages it is evident that the break is already complete. The attempt of Jesus in the first half of the Gospel of John to win the Jews proves futile. The Fourth Gospel is not an evangelistic work directed at Israel.

■ **12** Verse 12 apparently turns again to the dialogue between Jesus and Nicodemus, although the dialogue has become a monologue of Jesus: in verse 9 Nicodemus is dumbfounded. Verses 12–21, if they are conceived as a part of a conversation of Jesus with Nicodemus at all, represent Jesus preaching to Nicodemus, who is no longer capable of asking questions. But exegetes have not been able to agree on what Jesus or the Evangelist really intends to say in verse 12. What is meant by the "earthly things" (ἐπίγεια)? By the "heavenly things" (ἐπουράνια)? What earthly things has Jesus said to Nicodemus that he did not believe? Bultmann[11] interprets: "The phrase has been taken from the source,[12] where its meaning was unambiguous: ἐπίγεια ['earthly things'] referred to the earthly world as understood in Gnosticism; the Revealer sheds light on its origins and nature, and consequently on the nature of man, who is called on to see the earthly world as alien to himself. Ἐπουράνια ['heavenly things'] referred to the heavenly world which, according to the Revealer's teaching is to be seen as the home of souls, to which he opens the way back." For Gnosticism, however, the earthly things are always understood in their demonic essence. Gnostic cosmology is by no means the doctrine of earthly things, but a doctrine of the fall of a portion of the divine spirit, and thus a "negative soteriology," so to speak. These problems were especially difficult for the gnostic: How can such a fall have taken place? Of course, there were gnostic sects which reckoned with the presence of good and evil from the beginning. But Gnosticism presupposes, for the most part, the inviolate existence of the divine spirit.[13] Gnostic thought endeavored to solve this puzzle in various ways. Since it did not view man as a creation of evil from the beginning and therefore was not inclined to despair of him, by some sort of maneuver it came to the following view: a part of the primordial essence became detached and was enclosed in a world that came into being as a result of that detachment; its

---

10   Cf. *Ber.* 28b.
11   *John,* 147f. [105].
12   That is, from the revelation discourse source conjectured by Bultmann.
13   Cf. Haenchen, "Das Johannesevangelium und sein Kommentar," 211f.

encapsulation was in the form of divine sparks, which continued their life in all or at least many human beings; as a consequence, man understood human existence as an imprisonment among evil powers. It then became a matter of recalling that these sparks in man really belonged to the primordial essence and that they must be prepared for the return journey to the heavenly realm of light; this journey could be achieved only by the strictest possible internal and external detachment from the evil world, in an ascetic mode of existence, which was not to be forgotten for a moment. Consistent Gnosticism was put into practice actually only in small groups, like the Manicheans, to which the young Augustine belonged. Augustine's later doctrine of sin still retained visible traces of his past in this regard. Only the *electi* ("elect") (living as entirely withdrawn ascetics), who were nourished only by food deposited in designated places by the *auditores* ("auditors") (Augustine was one before he became a Christian), practiced this asceticism. Supplying the *electi* with food constituted a good deed on the part of the *auditores,* so that they, too, perhaps would be rewarded with the return journey to the heavenly realm of light. The mission of the gnostic redeemer consisted in enlightening the divine sparks in man regarding the world drama, reminding them of their heavenly home, and leading them to it. That the gnostic redeemer was a fallen spark of light who perceived the truth (*salvatore salvandus,* "a redeemer in need of redemption") had by no means become an unavoidable part of all gnostic interpretation, as theologians earlier thought. The basic human experience to which the emerging gnostic system of thought attached itself was, on the one hand, man's sense that he had fallen into a world in which he was an alien and which was ruled by demonic powers (an abbreviated expression of this experience could perhaps be: πόθεν τὰ κακά "whence comes evil?"). On the other hand, the gnostic system was based on the dreadful discovery that evil not only lurks around outside to mislead man, but also has deep roots inside man.

The Gospel of John may well use gnostic-sounding words and phrases, but it is to be basically distinguished from gnostic doctrine: the redeemer in the Gospel of John, Jesus, is not one of those fallen divine sparks, but the "Son," who existed from eternity in perfect harmony with the Father. Among men there is no "man who is saved by nature" (φύσει σωζόμενοι), nor is there the man who merits the return journey to the realm of light by virtue of good deeds; there are only those for whom salvation is opened up through the inscrutable divine will, through faith in the grace proclaimed by the redeemer. Judas is the type of the "sons of perdition," who are excluded from election by grace. The Christian owes his salvation not to his own good works, but to the divine gift, which provides him with faith in the redeemer.

What, then, are the earthly things that Jesus has already taught and that the Jews rejected? To say that one does not know whence the wind comes and whither it goes is simply not suitable. As a consequence, the double meaning of "spirit" (πνεῦμα) does not fit at all. The theologian Thüsing[14] takes everything that the earthly Jesus says as "earthly things," and limits "heavenly things" to the risen Christ. He thereby discloses a fundamental difficulty that is concealed here. Although the Evangelist strives to have Jesus proclaim a heavenly message on earth, his words nevertheless remain—as do his miracles—merely pointers to something that is accessible to us only in dark and fragmentary form. The apostle Paul was of the opinion (1 Cor 13) that he could speak in ecstasy with the tongues of angels. But such utterances of the Spirit are not understandable by the hearer if he or she does not possess the gift of interpretation, and even this remains forever inadequate in some way or another. The Fourth Gospel intimates this when Jesus speaks constantly of an invisible Father, with whom the Son once sojourned, and to whom he will return in heavenly glory at the end of his earthly life. John 17:5 speaks of the glory that Jesus had with the Father before the world was made, in the love of the Father (17:24), and which he will receive again following his earthly life. But this language of Jesus participates in metaphoricality, which is a representation that is always ambiguous. Wellhausen[15] attempts to help with this suggestion: "A new paragraph begins with 3:9, which stems from a later continuator. Verse 9 does not go with verse 8. For Jesus has just said that man does not understand the way of the

---

14 *Erhöhung,* 225f.
15 *Das Evangelium Johannes,* 18.

Spirit. Verses 10ff., however, suit verse 8 even less well: Nicodemus is reproached because he does not understand what, according to verse 8, is not supposed to be understood. . . . Further, the second birth . . . through baptism . . . as something elemental . . . is set in contrast with higher matters." In 3:11 Jesus speaks in the plural and subsequently speaks of himself in the third person, and views "the earthly course of his life as already ended" in 3:19; "he is no longer thinking of Nicodemus." Wellhausen considers the possibility of explaining 3:9–21 as an addition. But he hesitates to adjudge 3:1–8 as the original text. The separation into sources thus appears to be fruitless. Does it help to suggest that this passage represents a composition of the Evangelist? The attempts to understand the section as a report of an event (today met mostly among Catholic authors) are—*sit venia verbo,* "if I may say so"—antiquated. Strathmann[16] is quite right: the dialogue is only a form. "For the focus is only on" Jesus and not Nicodemus . . . ; "the latter tacitly disappears in the course of the conversation." He is only "the occasion of Jesus' discourse on the topic," viz., the true way of salvation. The discourse of Jesus in verses 14–21 passes imperceptibly over into testimony about Jesus. Strathmann[17] continues: "This wavering transition, without notice, from a discourse of Jesus to Christian talk about him . . . is made possible only by virtue of the fact that the entire Gospel . . . is an evangelistic witness on behalf of Jesus." The individual events are only "forms of the Evangelist's proclamation." It has not been said that the Evangelist is an especially brilliant author. The especially well-articulated and interesting narration of the story of Lazarus' resurrection, for example, is taken over from a tradition with a different theological aim. But we can attempt to conceive the work of the Evangelist as a literary composition that makes use of traditions directed to other ends. Perhaps that is the case also with verse 12. Schnackenburg[18] recalls Wis 9:16: "We can hardly guess at what is on earth, and what is at hand we find with

labor; but who has traced out what is in the heavens?" He also refers to *Sanh.* 39a, where Rabbi Gamaliel says to the emperor: "You do not know what is on earth; is it possible for you to know what is in heaven?" Is it not possible that a Jewish proverb is taken up in verse 12 in order to introduce a comparison? Thus the gift of the Spirit can be called something earthly insofar as it takes place on earth, while the continuation, verses 13–21, can be called something heavenly insofar as the subject of the discourse is the Son of man descending from heaven and returning again to heaven. Verse 12 therefore underscores the complete lack of understanding of the Christian message on the part of a well-intentioned Judaism, and permits the reader to sense that now the most important part of this message is to be indicated, a message that only now explains how that endowment with Spirit is possible.

■ **13** The "ascension into heaven" is already a past event (and of course so is the "descent from heaven"). The speaker's perspective is thus that of the Christian, post-Easter community. We will learn that the Evangelist often interchanges the perspective of the earthly Jesus with that of the exalted Jesus and thus combines the latter with the perspective of the community. Treated in verse 13 are basically two themes. In the first place, it is recalled that there is really only one who came down from heaven and will return there, viz., the Son of man.[19] That implies that he alone has brought the true message, the correct gospel from God and has thereby opened up access to God.

■ **14f.** Verses 14f. develop the second theme in greater detail: Moses lifting up the serpent in the wilderness (Num 21:8f.) and the salvation of those who looked on it is an image and precursor of what must happen to Jesus (at this point the narrator returns again to the perspective of the earthly Jesus). The Son of man must be "exalted," crucified, "that whoever believes in him may have eternal life."[20] In this way it becomes evident that the presupposition for being born from above is the

16 *Das Evangelium nach Johannes,* 66.

17 *Das Evangelium nach Johannes,* 67.

18 *John,* 1: 391.

19 A self-designation of Jesus especially favored in the Gospel of John: 1:51; 3:13–14; 5:27; 6:27, 53; 8:28; 12:23, 34; 13:31; cf Schnackenburg, *John,* 1: 529–42.

20 John avoids mention of the crucifixion, which is named only in the passion narrative, and refers instead to its divine meaning, the exaltation; on this point cf. 19:30.

death of Jesus on the cross (not a pre-understanding of man). In fact, the risen Lord first gives the Holy Spirit to the disciples, according to John 20:22, and 7:39 expressly says that the Spirit had not been given during Jesus' earthly life because Jesus was not yet glorified. In this reference to Num 21:8f. one sees how the Evangelist has conceived the witness of the OT for Jesus (cf. John 5:39).

■ **16** Verse 16 expands on the last part of verse 15: God so loved the world that he gave up his only Son (incarnation and crucifixion are included in this giving up), that whoever believes in him should not perish. The all-encompassing love of God for the entire human domain and the sending of Jesus to save only those who have faith are connected in a peculiar way. The Evangelist in fact is thinking in dualistic and predestinarian terms, if one may make use of later concepts.[21] He knows that not everyone who hears the proclamation becomes a Christian, that it is not the fault of the messenger when someone rejects the message, that God has not given all men over to the Son, as it is remarked subsequently (17:9). He nevertheless understands the Christian message as a demonstration of God's grace.

■ **17** For God has not sent his Son into the world to hold court, but "to save the world." For a moment it appears that the Evangelist intends to teach the ultimate salvation of all men. But that is not the case, as verse 18 immediately makes clear.

■ **18** Whoever believes in Jesus does not come into judgment (meaning: is not condemned); whoever does not believe has already come into judgment, been condemned, because he does not believe "in the name of the only Son of God." Since there is no salvation apart from faith in him, judgment of the non-believers, whom the Gospel of John does not describe more precisely, is inevitable. Yet this judgment, which simply sets in with logical necessity, is not the purpose in sending Jesus.

■ **19** Like the preceding one, this verse reveals the secret of Johannine eschatology: the final judgment is not one coming at some time in the future, something yet outstanding, but takes place in whether one believes the proclamation or not. The judgment is the division between the good and the evil. But it does not take place

merely in disclosing who each one is; the decisive determination of man occurs only in the encounter with God's revelation. Whoever does not want to come to God and the one sent by God, the light, suffers judgment because he is filled with anxiety before the all-seeing eyes of God.

■ **20f.** As it is put in these verses, it appears that the light reveals only what is already good and evil: whoever is good is not afraid of God and therefore comes to Jesus; whoever is bad is afraid and stays away. Yet this moralizing statement, in which everything depends solely on the quality of man already present, cannot be the meaning of the Evangelist. Rather, the character of man is determined only in the encounter with Jesus: whoever opens himself to Jesus in spite of, or with, his sins is good. That one falls completely under God's mercy, along with his deeds.

Overview

As it lies before us, John 3:2–21 is a fine torso. Its beginning still permits us to surmise what the Evangelist intended to convey to his reader: the correct faith. He selected a night scene for that purpose: the great Nicodemus, member of the Sanhedrin, comes to Jesus and conveys to him the good news that he has found disciples in Jerusalem, among them Nicodemus himself. And since he is a forthright man, he states candidly why he and his friends acknowledge Jesus as a teacher sent from God: it is not the content of Jesus' teaching (to this there is only indirect reference), but Jesus' miracles that have convinced Nicodemus and his associates. Such miracles as Jesus performs demonstrate that God stands behind him. Again, it is not the kind of miracle that is so convincing, but its absoluteness: no human can perform such acts in and of himself. It is thus not that Jesus heals the sick and thus proves himself to be the savior that is important, but that Jesus is able to make the incurable well; this irresistible power to persuade owes to the absoluteness of his power to perform miracles.

And so the first scene, which is meant to be a profession of affection, if one may put it so, now comes, tragically, to rejection. Faith that arises from the miracles of Jesus is not the way to Jesus nor to the right kind of faith in him. For this faith, the kind that is awakened by the

---

21   Cf. Schnackenburg, *John*, 1: 543–57.

sight of the miraculous, is so certain of itself that it determines one's relationship to God: God is not disclosed in the way earthly things and relationships are disclosed. For God is not a thing among other things. We have already quoted 2 Cor 4:18 earlier: God is not visible, so that man cannot make sure of him by looking around and by taking logical possession of him, so to speak. And because that is the way it is with God, the one who wants to catch sight of the reign of God must acquire new eyes. It does nothing for one's relationship to God—to cite a later example—to see the spectre of the resurrected Lazarus hovering before one's eyes. That God makes the spiritually dead alive—and that all we humans are—is the decisive thing; the raising of Lazarus can help indirectly by pointing to something quite different. Jesus does not speak here, of course, of "new eyes," but uses another expression that describes the totality of the one who must become new for God: such a person must be born from above. "From above" means the same thing as "from God" in Jewish parlance of that time.

These words of Jesus are conceived and intended as a mild correction that ought to keep Nicodemus from perceiving God as a stone. But Nicodemus does not understand what was said to him, and because he is an honorable man who does not conceal the limits of his spirit in conversation, he not only says what he does not understand, but why it seems to him not to be comprehensible. He understands Jesus' words along these lines: an old man (as he probably is, being a member of the Sanhedrin) has to be born a second time and yet that cannot be expected of him: he cannot enter a second time into the womb of his mother and then be reborn. In our judgment, a second hand commences at this juncture, and if we are not mistaken, it is the hand of the redactor, who sounds an ecclesiastical note. At first glance, Jesus' second answer in verse 5 is distinguished only in non-essentials from his answer in verse 3. But that is deceptive. In verse 3 the kingdom of God is "the reign of God," but in verse 5 it is the domain of God into which one may enter only if one has been baptized (i.e., has received "water and Spirit"). In the latter the realm of God is the community, to which one only has access when one becomes a member through baptism. For that reason, "to see the kingdom" is replaced in verse 5 by "enter into." That now means: whoever is born anew has

become a "Christian," has been taken into the congregation. The concerns of the Evangelist are thereby misrepresented and obscured. The text of the Evangelist could resume in verse 6, if these words mean a transformation of one's being by God. However, if one interprets this verse in the sense of the redactor, then it emphasizes the sharp contrast between the Christian community and those who are not Christians. An attempt on the part of the redactor to clarify the relation between Christianity and Judaism with the help of an everyday experience and a word with a double meaning ($\pi\nu\epsilon\hat{v}\mu\alpha$: "wind; spirit") follows in verse 7 ("Do not marvel that . . . "). The reality of the wind is something everyone recognizes because we all hear the voice of the wind, its rushing, its whisper, its howling. But man does not know whence the wind comes and whither it goes. Of course, all that is not exactly correct. Everyone knows whence the west wind, the khamsin, comes and whither it blows. The attempt to distinguish something double in the wind, something perceivable from something imperceptible, is not successful. The figure of the wind is really not usable, if $\pi\nu\epsilon\hat{v}\mu\alpha$ is taken in the sense of "Spirit," and especially if it is understood as the redactor understands it: one can hear the Christian proclamation but not understand it, unless one is baptized. Just what the redactor wants to express by the question of Nicodemus in verse 9 is quite unclear: "How can this be?" To what does "this" refer? Nicodemus began with the point that everyone could acknowledge: God stands behind the miracle worker. Jesus contests the view that everyone is able to come to this acknowledgment. To be sure, the redactor has interpreted Jesus' answer differently than the Evangelist, but he has retained the view that one cannot understand the Christian message without baptism (of course, together with the Spirit connected with it). If verse 9 (understood as the formulation of the redactor) refers to the possibility of a knowledge communicated in baptism and therefore only accessible to Christians, it may then appear to be entirely plausible to modern man. But this is the way the matter appeared to the redactor: Nicodemus deserves to be reprimanded for his lack of understanding, on the one hand, and that is evidence, on the other, that the "teacher of Israel" also had to capitulate in the face of Christian teaching (of course, Nicodemus was not necessarily a "teacher of Israel" as a mere member of the Sanhedrin). In any case, we Christians tell the things we know and bear witness to what we have seen, and the Jews do not accept this testimony. Up to this point, the redactor has Jesus speak only of "earthly things," elementary Christian doctrine, so to speak, but not yet of "heavenly things," which appear to go together with Jesus' coming from heaven and with his departure to heaven, according to the following verses, and which completely transcend Nicodemus' ability to understand. But the redactor at least suggests some of the elements of this higher knowledge: Jesus has gone to heaven (the redactor who reasons in this fashion is a post-Easter Christian and therefore views some of the temporal relationships differently than Jesus would have represented them in his speech to Nicodemus), and that was possible only because he came down from heaven previously as the "Son of man." In so doing, the redactor employs one of the christological titles that appears to be especially favored by him (one may refer only to 5:27, which is also a verse belonging to the redactor). In this context the speaker now provides something like a proof-text: Just as Moses raised up the serpent in the wilderness (Num 21:8), so that everyone who looked up to it was saved, so must the Son of man be raised up (on the cross), so that all who look up to him will be saved and have eternal life—elevation on the cross and exaltation to heaven are thus related to each other. The redactor does not appear to know that there are Christian *electi,* whom the Father has chosen and who alone have been given to Jesus. Basically, for the redactor, the possibility is open for everyone to be received into the community by means of Christian baptism and thus to be saved. "For God so loved the world that he gave his only Son (over to death), that whoever believes in him should not perish but have eternal life. For God sent the Son into the world, not to condemn the world, but that the world might be saved through him." Of course, not everyone desires to be saved. Whoever believes in Jesus will not be condemned; whoever does not have faith is already condemned because he has not believed in the name of God's only Son. The decisive sentences come in verses 19–21: "And this is the judgment, that light has come into the world, and men loved darkness rather than light. For their deeds were evil. For every one who does evil

hates the light, and does not come to the light, lest his works be exposed. But he who does what is true comes to the light, that his works may be evident, because they have been wrought in God." How the redactor sees these relationships thus becomes clear: the good men whose works are not so bad become Christians because it becomes evident that their works are good in the penetrating light of Jesus. Whoever refuses to become a Christian has his or her reasons for that, viz., wickedness, which would come to light in the encounter with Christ. When one pursues the logic of this line of thought, it follows that the world wants to know nothing of Christ and Christians: it is not a mysterious act of grace that holds sway; rather, human freedom keeps evil men away from Christ. The Christian community is made up of good, upstanding men; the enemies of Christians are inferior folk. That, of course, has nothing to do with the teaching of the Evangelist, and also has nothing in common with the doctrine of *justificatio impii* ("the justification of the godless"). What is being expressed here in all innocence is a doctrine of *justificatio piorum* ("the justification of the godly"), if a name derived from categories of the Reformation is permitted.

And what about Nicodemus? The redactor has lost sight of him in his eagerness to develop a Christian apologetic. This is, of course, a defense against hostile attacks on Christians, according to which Christians are homeless riff-raff: "not many of you were wise by worldly standards, not many were rich in influence, not many of noble birth, but God chose what was foolish in the world" (1 Cor 1:26). These philippic invectives against Nicodemus would scarcely have come to the lips of the Evangelist as easily as they did to the lips of the redactor. In any case, he not only has the rich old man appear on behalf of Jesus and the Christians in the council in 7:50f., but he also has him help with the burial of Jesus in 19:39f. in person, without a thought to the cost.

207

10. John's Humble Acknowledgment of Jesus

Bibliography

Beutler, Johannes
Martyria. Traditionsgeschichtliche Untersuchungen zum Zeugnisthema bei Johannes, Frankfurter theologische Studien 10 (Frankfurt: Verlag Josef Knecht, 1972).

Billerbeck, Paul
"Zu Mt 1,18" and "zu Mt 9,15." 1: 500–17.

Boismard, Marie-Emile
"Aenon, près de Salem: *Jean,* III,23." *RB* 80 (1973) 218–29.

Boismard, Marie-Emile
"Les traditions johanniques concernant le Baptiste." *RB* 70 (1963) 5–42, esp. 25–30.

Boismard, Marie-Emile
"L'amie de l'époux (Jo. III,29)." In *A la rencontre de Dieu. Mémorial Albert Gelin,* Bibliothèque de la faculté Catholique de Théologie à Lyon 8 (Le Puy/Paris: Xavier Mappus, 1961) 289–95.

Bussche, Henri van den
"Les paroles de Dieu: Jean 3, 22–36." *BVC* 55 (1964) 23–28.

Cambe, Michel
"Jésus baptise et cesse de baptiser en Judée (Jean 3,22–4,3)." *ETR* 53 (1978) 97–102.

Hauck, Friedrich
"Καθαρός." *TDNT* 3: 425–26.

Huppenbauer, H. W.
Der Mensch zwischen zwei Welten. Der Dualismus der Texte von Qumran (Höhle I) und der Damascusfragmente. Ein Beitrag zum Vorgeschichte des Evangeliums, ATANT 34 (Zurich: Zwingli Verlag, 1959), esp. 68f., 104f.

Kundsin, Karl
Topologische Überlieferungsstoffe im Johannes-Evangelium, FRLANT, n.s., 22 (Göttingen: Vandenhoeck & Ruprecht, 1925), esp. 25–27.

Lindars, Barnabas
"Two Parables in John." *NTS* 16 (1969/1970) 318–29.

Linnemann, Eta
"Jesus und der Täufer." In *Festschrift für Ernst Fuchs,* ed. G. Ebeling et al. (Tübingen: Mohr-Siebeck, 1973) 219–36.

Payot, Christian
"L'interprétation johannique du ministère de Jean Baptiste." *Foi et vie* 68 (1969) 21–37.

Richter, Georg
"Zum gemeindebildenden Element in den johanneische Schriften." In his *Studien zum Johannesevangelium,* ed. Joseph Hainz. BU 13 (Regensburg: F. Pustet, 1977), esp. 387–91.

Schnackenburg, Rudolf
"Die 'situationsgelösten' Redestücke in Joh 3." *ZNW* 49 (1958) 88–99.

Selms, A. van
   "The Best Man and the Bride—from Sumer to St.
   John with a new interpretation of Judges, Chapters
   14 and 15." *JNES* 9 (1950) 65–75.
Wilson, Jeffrey
   "The Integrity of John 3:22–36." *JSNT* 10 (1871)
   34–41.

3

22 **After this Jesus and his disciples went into
the land of Judea; there he remained
with them and baptized. 23/ John also
was baptizing at Aenon near Salim,
because there was much water there;
and people came and were baptized. 24/
For John had not yet been put in prison.
25/ Now a discussion arose between
John's disciples and a Jew over puri-
fying. 26/ And they came to John, and
said to him, "Rabbi, he who was with you
beyond the Jordan, to whom you bore
witness, here he is, baptizing, and all are
going to him." 27/ John answered, "No
one can receive anything except what is
given him from heaven. 28/ You yourselves bear me witness, that I said, I am
not the Christ, but I have been sent
before him. 29/ He who has the bride is
the bridegroom; the friend of the bridegroom, who stands and hears him,
rejoices greatly at the bridegroom's
voice; therefore this joy of mine is now
full. 30/ He must increase, but I must
decrease. 31/ He who comes from above
is above all; he who is of the earth
belongs to the earth, and of the earth he
speaks; he who comes from heaven [is
above all]. 32/ He bears witness to what
he has seen and heard [, yet no one
receives his testimony;] 33/ he who
receives his testimony sets his seal to
this, that God is true. 34/ For he whom
God has sent utters the words of God, for
it is not by measure that he gives [the
Spirit]; 35/ the Father loves the Son, and
has given all things into his hand. 36/ He
who believes in the Son has eternal life;
he who does not obey the Son shall not
see life, but the wrath of God rests upon
him."**

In this segment John once more gives testimony on behalf of Jesus: an indication that it was necessary to take the wind out of the sails of the contemporary rival baptist group;[1] John himself expresses his renunciation of such rivalry and gives the reason for his rejection. In support of the view that this segment contains a historical remi-niscence, one points to the place-names of Aenon and Salim; these places must lie west of the Jordan, according to verse 26; this is supported by verse 25. So Bultmann imagines an apophthegm stemming from the Baptist tradition, to which verse 27 and verse 29a, "at most," also belong.[2] In it the Baptist invokes his authority (v 27), which the Evangelist has reinterpreted to refer to Jesus—as in the Prologue. But this view is as dubious as

1   Editor: Haenchen would probably not have empha-
     sized the existence of the baptist groups for the
     Gospel of John in his final version.

2   *John*, 169 [123].

the relocation of 3:22–30 after 3:31–36, in which, to be sure, even Schnackenburg concurs. The two exegetes have taken no notice of Strathmann's observation[3] that to "attribute Christian proclamation to the Baptist" on the sly fits the style of the Evangelist. If one assumes that the redactor had the work of the Evangelist before him in form of a roll or codex, such a rearrangement is impossible and becomes a further argument against the hypothesis. All speeches and events of this Gospel are basically only forms of the Christian kerygma that make use of this or that tradition; however, tradition is dispensable for some subsections.

■ **22** "After these things" (μετὰ ταῦτα) again provides an indefinite introduction to a new segment: Jesus and his disciples leave the capital city and tarry "in the Judean countryside" to baptize. We do not learn where Jesus baptized. That he himself baptized is contested in 4:2. Since for the Gospel of John the Spirit is imparted only by the risen Christ, such baptisms would have been water baptisms like those of John.[4] The Evangelist does not claim that any one was baptized in Jesus' name.

■ **23** However, John is also baptizing, although not in the Jordan but at Aenon (Αἰών) near Salim (Σαλίμ). The reason given is that "there was much water there" (ὕδατα πολλά), which might mean "many springs." It is unclear how these places are to be located more precisely. Eusebius[5] locates the two places eight Roman miles south of Scythopolis; which would place them "in the northernmost part of Samaria."[6] But, as a starting point, Aenon is no better than "Salim," which is mentioned in Joshua (LXX B 19:22). What is more important to the Evangelist is that the unconditional superiority of Jesus becomes all the more conspicuous precisely in a comparable situation, viz., baptism.

■ **24** The notice that John had not yet been imprisoned is frequently interpreted as a polemic against the Synoptics or against a synoptic traditon, which implied that Jesus did not appear until the Baptist had been confined in Machaerus. But the Johannine narrator wishes to establish how it was possible that Jesus and John appeared side by side.

■ **25** It must be admitted that verse 25 poses an unsolved riddle: it speaks of a dispute between some of John's disciples and a Jew about purification. The dispute is to be understood as a one between some disciples of John and a Jew baptized by Jesus. But in the context of what follows, verse 25 can only affirm that a dispute took place between the disciples of John and Jesus' disciples. The oldest extant text of course reads "with a Jew" (μετὰ Ἰουδαίου), but efforts were soon made to correct the difficult passage. Perhaps O. Holtzmann[7] has made the right suggestion in "with the disciples of Jesus" (μετὰ τῶν Ἰησοῦ). In any case, the disciples of John observed the baptism of Jesus. It is understandable in all probability that the dispute is only about a "cleansing" (καθαρίσμα) and not about baptism: the attention of the reader is not called to such a conflict, to such a doubt about the efficacy of Christian baptism.

■ **26** "They," that is, the disciples of John, who were present at the events in 1:19–34 and have now learned first-hand of Jesus' baptism, come now with a report to John, which is basically a complaint, an accusation. They address their master as rabbi, that is, with the honorific title that Nicodemus gave Jesus, and tell him: that man, whose name we will not mention, who was with you (John the Baptist) beyond the Jordan and to whom you bore witness–that man is now baptizing and all are going out to him. Jesus' name is not spoken because the disciples of John must not bring an audible charge against Jesus. That Jesus performs with great success what was hitherto reserved to John alone comes through, nevertheless, in their surprising and incomprehensible statement. In spite of the overtones of the accusation, it becomes evident in their statement that John himself now defends Jesus' activity and success.

■ **27** "The man" (ἄνθρωπος) once again substitutes for "anyone" (τις; negated "no one"): no one can receive anything unless it is given to him by God. What is meant by anything is religious authority; it is not a matter of human endowment or pretension, but of a gift from heaven, i.e., from God.

■ **28** John now makes his declaration but not for the first time. The complaint now lodged with him must bear witness of what he himself has already declared: I am not the Christ, but was sent before him. The success of Jesus

---

3   *Das Evangelium nach Johannes,* 82

4   Contrary to Schnackenburg, *John,* 1: 411.

5   *Onomasticon* 40.1

6   Bauer, *Das Johannesevangelium,* 62.

7   *Das Johannesevangelium,* 210.

is thereby conceived in its real essence, and that is now stated in verse 29.

■ **29** The image of the bride, bridegroom, and friend of the bridegroom (perhaps he delivered the proposal to the bride and so prepared the way for the wedding) is first of all to be assessed as a figure. At a later time the church was considered the bride. But the Evangelist John himself, who does not use the concept "church" (ἐκκλησία), uses this image graphically to indicate that John the Baptist is able to greet, and does greet, the success of Jesus with a pure, selfless joy. Since Jesus has "the bride," since all flock to him, John's joy is complete. Put differently, John's preparation for Jesus was successful, on the one hand, and, on the other, his own task has thereby come to its conclusion. Hirsch[8] has rightly emphasized two things: John has overcome life's anxiety and lust for position, and one senses that "these are words of one upon whom the shadow of death has already fallen." The Evangelist does not need to depict the imprisonment and execution of John in detail; the hint he provides is sufficent, even if one does not overhear his soft voice.

■ **30** The relation of the Baptist to Jesus is reduced in this verse to the briefest maxim: he must increase, while I must decrease. However, this is not merely a pronouncement over John, whose departure is hinted at here, but a pronouncement that applies to all Christians. The kerygmatic proclamation basically begins here and its formal subject is John the Baptist.

■ **31** He who comes from above is over all: that is an assertion about Jesus that also applies to John and his subordination. It is pointed out to the reader that the Baptist is designated as one from the earth who speaks of earthly things: the line between the divine and the human runs between Jesus and John. He who comes from heaven, comes from God, can bear witness to this.

The second "is above all" is lacking in 𝔓[75] ℵ* *pc* it sy[c]; in spite of strong attestation, it might be the error of an early copyist.

■ **32** *Only he who has come down from heaven* is able to bear witness to what he has seen and heard. The text does not pass on to specific revelations of how things look in heaven and what transpires there. Rather, only he who comes from God is able to tell us what God has planned for us, how God is disposed to us—thus what Paul sketched in his doctrine of grace. However, the clause, "yet no one receives his testimony," creates difficulties, especially since it was just said that all the people flocked to Jesus. There is undoubtedly a tension here. That everybody flocks to Jesus belongs to the view that sanctions Jesus over against John. When no one–this no doubt refers to the Jews–hears the testimony of Christ, the bitter experience of the post-Easter community is in evidence, the experience of the second or even the third generation, which was confounded by the Israel's rejection and consequently experienced disappointment.

■ **33** Whoever accepts the message of Christ confirms that God is true and that he does not deceive men about his real intentions by means of this message. This provides the connection to verse 34.

■ **34** He who is sent by God speaks the word of God. The Gospel of John is often perceived as a gospel dominated by christology. That is not true. Everything in the Gospel of John is about God and only about God and therefore about Jesus. God gives Jesus his own words to speak and has given him the Spirit in full measure.

■ **35** This assertion is repeated in different language: God loves the Son–the terms "Son" and "he whom God has sent" denote the same person–and he has given all things into the hand of the Son. That does not mean that everybody becomes a Christian. The Evangelist thinks more realistically, as one often says, and precisely for that reason he is at the same time "dualistic," as verse 36 corroborates.

■ **36** He who believes in the Son has eternal life; he who refuses obedience to the Son will not see life, because the wrath of God rests upon him. This saying about the wrath of God, which bears down on the unbelievers, stands in shocking contrast and tension with the resounding words, given earlier, that God loves the world. But in 3:16, too, it is not concealed that God's love does not extend to everyone, but only to those who believe on Jesus. Universalism and particularism are not to be neatly separated from each other in these passages. God is not simply the "God of love," and although the picture of Christ in the Sistine Chapel does not reflect the

---

8   *Das vierte Evangelium*, 144.

Johannine Gospel, it nevertheless contains a profound truth. One must not forget: only he would escape this dilemma who takes the will of God to be completely indeterminate.

Overview

Wohlenberg[9] asserts that the first four disciples were called not on the basis of a cursory acquaintance with Jesus alone. This fact is obvious. "The Gospel of John in part fills out the gaps in the Gospel of Mark in this connection" (John 1:35ff., 2:2–12, 17, 3:22–26, 4:4ff.). Wohlenberg does not appear to have considered why Mark omits precisely what Wohlenberg thinks is necessary for understanding, and why John supplies only what is lacking (if not completely lacking). Rather, the Gospel of John pushes the baptism of John as far as possible into the background. The Baptist offers humble testimony on behalf of Jesus, who has been sent by God. The saying of Jesus in 3:34 is not a self-assertion, as it is not in 7:16, 14:10, 24. Although $\dot{\rho}\hat{\eta}\mu\alpha$ appears insead of $\lambda\acuteo\gamma o\varsigma$ (both terms mean "word"), the meaning of the verse is the same: "For he whom God has sent utters the words of God." Jesus appears in the Gospel of John as the one sent by God, and not as a revealer. He stands as the one sent by the Father on the Father's behalf in the world. He is—to use the words of Col 1:15 once again—the visible image of the invisible Father. As Jesus explains time and again in the Fourth Gospel, he does not speak his own words, but the words of his Father (3:34, 7:16, 8:26, 38, 40, 14:10, 24, 17:8), he does not do his own works, but the works of his Father (4:34, 5:17, 19ff., 30, 36, 8:28, 14:10, 17:4, 14), he does not fulfill his own will, but the will of his Father (4:34, 5:30, 6:38, 10:25, 37). If we might formulate pointedly what is being said, we could say: according to the Gospel of John, all signficance attaches to Jesus precisely because he does not want to be anything else and is the voice and the hands of his Father. Jesus demands honor for himself for this reason alone: whoever does not honor him, does not honor the Father who sent him (5:23, 44, 7:18, 8:50, 54). The Jews are therefore completely in error when they accuse Jesus of blasphemy: he makes himself equal to God (5:18). Jesus actually stands in God's place as the one who is completely taken up into God's sovereignty.

---

9   *Das Evangelium des Markus,* KNT 2 (Leipzig: A. Deichert, 1910) 55.

Bibliography

Argyle, A. W.
"A Note on John 4:35." *ExpTim* 82 (1971) 247–48.

Bligh, John
"Jesus in Samaria [Jn 4:1–42]." *HeyJ* 3 (1962) 329–46.

Boers, Hendrikus
"Discourse Structure and Macro-Structure in the Interpretation of Text: John 4:1–42 as an Example." SBLASP (Chico, CA: Scholars Press, 1980) 159ff.

Bonneau, N. R.
"The Woman at the Well: John 4 and Genesis 24." *Bible Today* 67 (1973) 1252–59.

Bousset, Wilhelm
Kyrios Christos. A History of the Belief in Christ from the Beginnings of Christianity to Irenaeus, tr. John E. Steely (Nashville: Abingdon Press, 1970), esp. 315f. = *Kyrios Christos. Geschichte des Christusglaubens von den Anfängen des Christentums bis Irenaeus* (Göttingen: Vandenhoeck & Ruprecht, ⁵1965), esp. 245.

Bowman, John
"Early Samaritan Eschatology." *JJS* 6 (1955) 63–72.

Bowman, John
"Samaritan Studies." *BJRL* 40 (1957/1958) 298–329.

Brandenburger, Egon
"Joh 4,31–38: Exegese und Anregungen zur Meditation und Predigt." *Kirche im Dorf* 22 (1971) 203–9.

Braun, François-Marie
"Avoir soif et boire: Jn 4,10–14; 7,37–39." In *Mélanges bibliques en hommage au R. P. Béda Rigaux,* ed. A. Descamps and A. De Halleux (Gembloux: Duculot, 1970) 247–58.

Brown, Raymond E.
"The Problem of Historicity in John." *CBQ* 24 (1962) 1–14, esp. 13f.

Bull, Robert J.
"An Archaeological Context for Understanding John 4:20." *BA* 38 (1975) 54–59.

Cahill, Peter Joseph
"Narrative Art in John IV." *Religious Studies Bulletin* 2 (1982) 41–48.

Cantwell, L.
"Immortal Longings in Sermone Humili. A Study of John 4,5–26." *SJT* 36 (1983) 73–86.

Carmichael, C. M.
"Marriage and the Samaritan Woman." *NTS* 26 (1980) 332–46.

Chappuis, Jean-Marc
"Jesus and the Samaritan Woman. The Variable

Geometry of Communication." *Ecumenical Review* 34 (1982) 8–34.

Cullmann, Oscar
"Samaria and the Origins of the Christian Mission." In his *The Early Church*, ed. A. J. B. Higgins; tr. A. J. B. Higgins and S. Godman (London: SCM Press; Philadelphia: Westminster Press, 1956) 183–92.

Cullmann, Oscar
The Christology of the New Testament, tr. Shirley C. Guthrie and Charles A. M. Hall (Philadelphia: Westminster Press, 1959), esp. 238–48 = *Die Christologie des Neuen Testaments* (Tübingen: Mohr-Siebeck, 1957 ²1958), esp. 245–52.

Dagonet, P.
Selon saint Jean une femme de Samarie, Epiphanie (Paris: Editions du Cerf, 1979).

Daube, David
"Jesus and the Samaritan Woman: The Meaning of συγχράομαι." *JBL* 69 (1950) 137–47 = "Samaritan Women." In his *The New Testament and Rabbinic Judaism* (University of London: Athlone Press, 1956) 373–82.

Dehn, G.
Jesus und die Samariter. Eine Auslegung von Jo 4,1–12 (Neukirchen: Neukirchener Verlag, 1956).

Dibelius, Martin and Conzelmann, Hans
The Pastoral Epistles: A Commentary on the Pastoral Epistles, ed. Helmut Koester; tr. Philip Buttolph and Adela Yarbro. Hermeneia—A Critical-Historical Commentary on the Bible (Philadelphia: Fortress Press, 1972), esp. 100–103 = *Die Pastoralbriefe*, ed. Günther Bornkamm. HNT 13 (Tübingen: Mohr-Siebeck, ⁴1966), esp. 74–77.

Dölger, Franz Josef
"*Soter*." *PW* 2, 3rd series, 1211–21.

Freed, Edwin D.
"The Manner of Worship in John 4,23." In *Search the Scriptures* [Festschrift for R. T. Stamm], ed. J. M. Meyers et al. (Leiden: E. J. Brill, 1969) 33–48.

Friedrich, Gerhard
Wer ist Jesus? Die Verkündigung des vierten Evangelisten dargestellt an Johannes 4, 4–42, Biblisches Seminar (Stuttgart: Calwer Verlag, 1967).

Galbiati, Enrico
"Nota sulla struttura del 'libro dei segni' (*Gv.* 2–4)." *Euntes docete* 25 (1972) 139–44.

Gärtner, Bertil
The Temple and the Community in Qumran and the New Testament. A Comparative Study in the Temple Symbolism of the Qumran Texts and the New Testament, SNTSMS 1 (London: Cambridge University Press, 1965), esp. 44f., 119f.

Hahn, Ferdinand
"Die Worte vom lebendigen Wasser im Johannesevangelium. Eigenart und Vorgeschichte von Joh 4,10.13f; 6,35; 7,37–39." In *God's Christ and His People. Studies in honor of Nils A. Dahl*, ed. Jacob Jervell and Wayne A. Meeks (Oslo: Universitets-forlaget, 1977) 51–70.

Hahn, Ferdinand
"Das Heil kommt von den Juden." In *Wort und Wirklichkeit. Studien zur Afrikanistik und Orientalistik. Eugen Ludwig Rapp zum 70. Geburtstag.* Vol. 1, *Geschichte und Religionswissenschaft-Bibliographie*, ed. B. Benzing, O. Böcher, and G. Mayer (Meisenheim am Glan: Anton Hain, 1976) 67–84.

Hall, David R.
"The Meaning of *synchraomai* in John 4:9." *ExpTim* 83 (1971/1972) 56–57.

Hatch, William H. P.
"An Allusion to the Destruction of Jerusalem in the Fourth Gospel." *Expositor*, 8th ser., 17 (1919) 194–97.

Hauck, Friedrich
"Κόπος" and "Κοπιάω." *TDNT* 3: 827–30.

Hauck, Friedrich
"Καρπός." *TDNT* 3: 614–16.

Hogan, M. P.
"The Woman at the Well (Jn 4,1–42)." *Bible Today* 82 (1976) 633–69.

Horst, J.
Proskynein. Zur Anbetung im Urchristentum nach ihrer religionsgeschichtlichen Eigenart (Gütersloh: C. Bertelsmann, 1932), esp. 306.

Hudry-Clergeon, C.
"De Judée en Galilee. Etude de Jean 4,1–45." *NRT* 113 (1981) 818–30.

Kilpatrick, George D.
"John iv,41: *pleion* or *pleious*?" *NovT* 18 (1976) 131–32.

Kilpatrick, George D.
"John 4:9." *JBL* 87 (1968) 327–28.

King, J. S.
"Sychar and Calvary: A Neglected Theory in the Interpretation of the Fourth Gospel [Jn 4]." *Theology* 77 (1974) 417–22.

Leidig, E.
"Jesu Gespräch mit der Samariterin." Dissertation, Basel, 1980.

Lietzmann, Hans
Der Weltheiland (Bonn: Markus and Webers Verlag, 1909).

Loewe, R.
"'Salvation' is Not for the Jews." *JTS* 32 (1981) 341–68.

Lohmeyer, Ernst
Christuskult und Kaiserkult, Sammlung gemeinverständlicher Vorträge und Schriften aus dem Gebiet der Theologie und Religionsgeschichte 90 (Tübingen: Mohr-Siebeck, 1919).

Macdonald, J.
The Theology of the Samaritans, NTL (Philadelphia: Westminster Press, 1965), esp. 362–71.

Marshall, I. Howard
"The Problem of New Testament Exegesis [John 4:1–45]." *Journal of the Evangelical Theological Society* 17 (1974) 67–73.

Mussner, Franz
"ZΩH" *Die Anschauung vom "Leben" im vierten Evangelium unter Berücksichtigung der Johannesbriefe. Ein Beitrag zur biblischen Theologie,* Münchener Theologische Studien 1,5 (Munich: Zink, 1952).

Neyrey, Jerome H.
"Jacob Traditions and the Interpretation of John 4:10–26." *CBQ* 41 (1979) 419–37.

Niccacci, Alviero
"Siracide 6,19 e Giovanni 4,36–38." *BeO* 23 (1981) 149–53.

Olsson, Birger
Structure and Meaning in the Fourth Gospel. A Text-Linguistic Analysis of John 2:1–11 and 4:1–42, tr. Jean Gray. ConBNT 6 (Lund: C. W. K. Gleerup, 1974).

Pamment, Margaret
"Is There Convincing Evidence of Samaritan Influence on the Fourth Gospel?" *ZNW* 73 (1982) 221–30.

Potter, R. D.
"Topography and Archaeology in the Fourth Gospel." *SE* 1 = TU 73 (Berlin: Akademie-Verlag, 1959) 329–37.

Purvis, James D.
"The Fourth Gospel and the Samaritans." *NovT* 17 (1975) 161–98.

Rengstorf, Karl Heinrich
Die Anfänge der Auseinandersetzung zwischen Christusglaube und Asklepiosfrömmigkeit, Schriften der Gesellschaft zur Förderung der Westfälischen Landesuniversität zu Münster 30 (Münster: Aschendorff, 1953), esp. 15 n. 45.

Robinson, J. A. T.
"The 'Others' of John 4,38: A Test of Exegetical Method." *SE* 1 = TU 73 (Berlin: Akademie-Verlag, 1959) 510–15.

Roustang, F.
"Les moments de l'Acte de Foi et ses conditions de possibilité." *RSR* 46 (1958) 344–78.

Sabugal, S.
"El título Messías-Christos en el contexto del Relato sobre la Actividad de Jesús en Samaría: Jn 4,25.29." *Augustinianum* 12 (1972) 79–105.

Schenke, Hans-Martin
"Jakobsbrunnen—Josephsgrab—Sychar. Topographische Untersuchugen und Erwägungen in der Perspektive von Joh 4,5.6." *ZDPV* 84 (1968) 159–84.

Schmid, Lothar
"Die Komposition der Samaria-Szene in Joh 4, 1–42." *ZNW* 28 (1929) 148–58.

Schnackenburg, Rudolf
"Die 'Anbetung in Geist und Wahrheit' (Joh 4, 23) im Lichte von Qumrantexten." *BZ* 3 (1959) 88–94.

Schnackenburg, Rudolf
"Die Messiasfrage im Johannesevangelium." In *Neutestamentliche Aufsätze. Festschrift für Prof. Josef Schmid zum 70. Geburtstag,* ed. J. Blinzler, O. Kuss,

F. Mussner (Regensburg: F. Pustet, 1963) 240–64, esp. 264.

Schottroff, Luise
"Johannes 4:5–15 und die Konsequenzen des johanneischen Dualismus." *ZNW* 60 (1969) 199–214.

Schweizer, Eduard
"Πνεῦμα." *TDNT* 6: 436–38.

Segalla, Giuseppe
"Tre personaggi in cerca di fede: un guideo, una samaritana, un pagano (Gv 3–4)." *Parole di Vita* 16 (1971) 29–49.

Staerk, Willy
Der biblische Christus. Vol. 1 of *Soter, die biblische Erlösererwartung als religionsgeschichtliches Problem; eine biblisch-theologische Untersuchung.* BFCT, 2nd series: Sammlung wissenschaftlicher Monographien 31 (Gütersloh: C. Bertelsmann, 1933).

Steinmeyer, F. L.
Beiträge zum Verständniss des johanneischen Evangeliums. Vol. 2, *Das Gespräch Jesu mit der Samariterin* (Berlin: Wiegandt & Grieben, 1887).

Taylor, W. M.
Jesus at the Well: John IV, 1–42 (New York: A. D. F. Randolph & Co., 1884).

Thyen, Hartwig
"Das Heil kommt von den Juden." In *Kirche. Festschrift für Günther Bornkamm zum 74. Geburtstag* (Tübingen: Mohr-Siebeck, 1980) 163–84.

Ullmann, C.
"Bemerkungen zu Joh IV 13,14 und VI,35." *TSK* 1 (1828) 791–94.

Unnik, W. C. van
"A Greek Characteristic of Prophecy in the Fourth Gospel." In *Text and Interpretation: Studies in the New Testament presented to Matthew Black,* ed. E. Best and R. McL. Wilson (London: Cambridge University Press, 1979) 211–30.

Vellanickal, M.
"Drink from the Source of the Living Water." *Biblebhashyam* 5 (1979) 309–18.

Vries, E. de
"Johannes 4:1–42 in geest en hoofdzaak." *Gereformeerd theologisch tijdschrift* 78 (1978) 93–114.

Walker, Rolf
"Jüngerwort und Herrenwort. Zur Auslegung von Joh 4,39–42." *ZNW* 57 (1966) 49–54.

Watson, Wilfred G. E.
"Antecedents of a New Testament Proverb." *VT* 20 (1970) 368–70.

Wedel, Alton F.
"John 4,5–26 (5–42)." *Int* 31 (1977) 406–12.

Wendland, Paul
"Σωτήρ." *ZNW* 5 (1906) 335–53.

Wilson, J.
"The Integrity of John 3:22–36." *JSNT* 10 (1981) 34–41.

Windisch, Hans
"Der johanneische Erzählungsstil." In

ΕΥΧΑΡΙΣΤΗΡΙΟΝ. *Studien zur Religion und Litera-tur des Alten und Neuen Testaments Hermann Gunkel zum 60. Geburtstag, dem 23 Mai 1922, dargebracht von seinen Schülern und Freunden*, ed. Hans Schmidt. FRLANT, n.s., 19 (Göttingen: Vanden-hoeck & Ruprecht, 1923), 174–213, esp. 178–81.

4

1 Now when the Lord knew that the Phar-isees had heard that Jesus was making and baptizing more disciples than John 2/ (although Jesus himself did not bap-tize, but only his disciples), 3/ he left Judea and departed again to Galilee. 4/ He had to pass through Samaria. 5/ So he came to a city of Samaria, called Sychar, near the field that Jacob gave to his son Joseph. 6/ Jacob's well was there, and so Jesus, wearied as he was with his journey, sat down beside the well. It was about the sixth hour. 7/ There came a woman of Samaria to draw water. Jesus said to her, "Give me a drink." 8/ For his disciples had gone away into the city to buy food. 9/ The Samaritan woman said to him, "How is it that you, a Jew, ask a drink of me, a woman of Samaria?" For Jews have no dealings with Samaritans. 10/ Jesus answered her, "If you knew the gift of God, and who it is that is saying to you, 'Give me a drink,' you would have asked him, and he would have given you living water." 11/ The woman said to him, "Sir, you have noth-ing to draw with, and the well is deep; where do you get that living water? 12/ Are you greater than our father Jacob, who gave us the well, and drank from it himself, and his sons, and his cattle?" 13/ Jesus said to her, "Every one who drinks of this water will thirst again, 14/ but whoever drinks of the water that I shall give him will never thirst; the water that I shall give him will become in him a spring of water welling up to eternal life." 15/ The woman said to him, "Sir, give me this water, that I may not thirst, nor come to here to draw." 16/ Jesus said to her, "Go, call your husband, and come here." 17/ The woman answered him, "I have no husband." Jesus said to her, "You are right in saying, 'I have no husband'; 18/ for you have had five husbands, and he whom you now have is not your husband; this you said truly." 19/ The woman said to him, "Sir, I per-ceive that you are a prophet. 20/ Our fathers worshiped on this mountain; and you say that in Jerusalem is the place where men ought to worship." 21/ Jesus said to her, "Woman, believe me, the hour is coming when neither on this mountain nor in Jerusalem will you wor-

ship the Father. 22/ You worship what you do not know; we worship what we know, for salvation is from the Jews. 23/ But the hour is coming, and now is, when the true worshipers will worship the Father in spirit and truth, for such the Father seeks to worship him. 24/ God is spirit, and those who worship him must worship in spirit and truth." 25/ The woman said to him, "I know that Messiah is coming (he who is called Christ); when he comes, he will show us all things." 26/ Jesus said to her, "I who speak to you am he." 27/ Just then his disciples came. They marveled that he was talking with a woman, but none said, "What do you wish?" or, "Why are you talking with her?" 28/ So the woman left her water jar, and went away into the city, and said to the people, 29/ "Come, see a man who told me all that I ever did. Can this be the Christ?" 30/ They went out of the city and were coming to him. 31/ Meanwhile the disciples besought him, saying, "Rabbi, eat." 32/ But he said to them, "I have food to eat of which you do not know." 33/ So the disciples said to one another, "Has any one brought him food?" 34/ Jesus said to them, "My food is to do the will of him who sent me, and to accomplish his work. 35/ Do you not say, 'There are yet four months, then comes the harvest'? I tell you, lift up your eyes, and see how the fields are already white for harvest. 36/ He who reaps receives wages, and gathers fruit for eternal life, so that sower and reaper may rejoice together. 37/ For here the saying holds true, 'One sows and another reaps.' 38/ I sent you to reap that which you did not labor; others have labored, and you have entered into their labor." 39/ Many Samaritans from that city believed in him because of the woman's testimony, "He told me all that I ever did." 40/ So when the Samaritans came to him, they asked him to stay with them; and he stayed there two days. 41/ And many more believed because of his word. 42/ They said to the woman, "It is no longer because of your words that we believe, for we have heard for ourselves, and we know that this is indeed the Savior of the world."

This pericope is a veritable tangle of difficulties. Verses 1–3 form a transition, of which there are many in the first chapters. These transitional verses lead from Jesus' activity in Jerusalem (2:12–3:21) and Judea (3:22ff.) to the scene set in Samaria, 4:4–42. It is easy to see how 3:22–36 prompted the transition: in 3:26 and 4:1ff., the fact that Jesus has had greater success than John produces a reaction: in 3:26 John's disciples complain that everyone is going to Jesus, and John has to make it clear to them that Jesus' success is to be expected; in 4:1 the Pharisees have problems with Jesus' success, which exceeds that of John, who is already under suspicion.

They threaten persecution. For this reason Jesus has to quit Judea and return to Galilee. On the way Jesus meets the Samaritan woman and converts her and her fellow villagers. Thus far the compositional arrangement is transparent.

■ **1** The problem, however, lies in the detail, as is often the case. The introductory sentence is complicated and clumsy: "Now when Jesus" (or "the Lord") "knew that the Pharisees had heard that Jesus. . . ." Prior to chapter 20, the reading "the Lord" appears in the Gospel of John only in two dubious places, 6:23 and 11:2. Although some noteworthy manuscripts preserve this reading ($\mathfrak{P}^{66}$ and $\mathfrak{P}^{75}$), it is by no means certain. In the Gospel of John when Jesus is spoken of in the third person the phrase "the Lord" ($\delta \kappa\acute{\upsilon}\rho\iota\sigma\varsigma$) is not used. The common designation "Jesus" is supported by a series of respectable witnesses (D *al* ℵ Θ sy^{cp} bo, among others), but it can also be an attempt at an early "Western" correction, which suddenly pops up here, in an effort to improve the reading "the Lord," which is uncommon in John. Where ℵ and D are in agreement in the Gospel of John, that only shows that the text of ℵ was influenced early on by D, and not only in the opening chapters. Bultmann[1] proposes excising the words "the Lord knew that" as a "clumsy gloss, which makes the structure of the sentence cumbrous." But the resulting sentence, "when the Pharisees heard that Jesus, . . . Jesus left, . . ." is not convincing. Perhaps the difficulty arises from the fact that the Evangelist or his source wanted to serve two purposes at the same time. First, Jesus ought to appear as the acting subject from the beginning, so he belongs at the head of the sentence. Second, because of his great success, the Pharisees intend to proceed against him, causing him to leave Judea quickly for fear of the impending persecution. This context, however, appeared to the narrator to violate the respect due Jesus; he therefore only cautiously suggests it. The expression "the Lord knew" ($\acute{\epsilon}\gamma\nu\omega$) refers to Jesus' supernatural knowledge.

■ **2** Critics have attacked this verse particularly sharply. Yet this verse retracts the baptismal activity of Jesus just mentioned. Moreover, the word "although" ($\kappa\alpha\acute{\iota}\tau\sigma\iota\gamma\epsilon$), which is otherwise unknown to John, appears here.

According to Bultmann,[2] this verse is a redactional gloss. In that case, it is difficult to see why the redactor did not make his correction earlier in 3:22. But an internal difficulty presents itself: it is precisely the emphasis on the exceptional success of Jesus in baptizing that creates difficulties. Baptism by the earthly Jesus is meaningless for the Evangelist: before the risen Lord breathes the Spirit into the disciples (20:22), his baptism and the baptism of his disciples would be merely a baptism with water, like that of John. The correction is therefore made at 4:2, where a special emphasis is placed on baptismal activity: Jesus himself did not baptize, only his disciples. A reflective reader could more readily accept the baptism of the disciples as a forerunner of later church practice.

■ **3** To this verse it has been objected: there were also Pharisees in Galilee. That is historically accurate, since the Pharisees were a lay movement diffused throughout the country. Yet the Fourth Gospel thinks of the Pharisees rather as officials residing in Jerusalem alongside the high priests (so John 1:24, 7:32 [twice], 45–48, 8:13, 9:13, 15, 11:46f., 57, 12:19, 42).

■ **4** The expression "He had to . . ." may be explained in part on the view that the divine will played a role, since it was possible to go around by way of the Jordan valley, through the gap at Beth-shan, and thus arrive in Galilee without going through Samaria. But Jesus took the shortest way, according to the Gospel of John, as Josephus indicates.[3] In this way he could forestall persecution by leaving dangerous Judea by the quickest route. The reader thus learns how Jesus really happened to be in Samaria: he was not there as the result of a planned mission. It came about for reasons other than a humanly planned "journey"—as is often the case in Paul's journeys.

■ **5** The Samaritan village—$\pi\acute{\sigma}\lambda\iota\varsigma$ is often used in the sense of village[4] —by the name Sychar is mentioned neither in the OT nor in the rabbinic literature; it is used for the first time by the pilgrim from Bordeaux in 333, and thus in a time when Christian pilgrims, then becoming numerous, longed to see and also got to see every village mentioned in the NT. Sychar is now identified for the most part with Askar,[5] which lies 1.5 kilometers

---

1   *John*, 176 n. 2 [128 n. 4].
2   *John*, 176 n. 2 [128 n. 4].
3   *Vita*, 269.

4   Zahn, *Das Evangelium des Johannes*, 233; Schlatter, *Der Evangelist Matthäus: Seine Sprache, sein Ziel, seine Selbständigkeit* (Stuttgart: Calwer Verlag, 1929,

northeast of Jacob's well. Shechem, which was then only a small settlement, lies closer to Jacob's well. The well at Sokher[6] mentioned in *Menaḥ.* 10.2 is of course closer to the "piece of land" that Jacob gave to Joseph. In just such a way the two places mentioned in Gen 33:19 and 48:22 were confused as early as Josh 24:32.

■ **6** "Jacob's well"—as a name it appears not only in Aramaic but also in Greek without the article—is mentioned for the first time by the Bordeaux pilgrim (following this reference; the name does not appear in the OT). The tradition speaks simply of the fatigue and thirst of Jesus. The Evangelist adopts that description without permitting Jesus either to eat (v 28) or to drink (v 32). The "everyday, human" is used only as a transition to the religious.

Οὕτως ("and so") means about the same thing, according to Ammonius, as ὡς ἔτυχε ("just, simply"):[7] Jesus simply sits on the ground. In fact, $\mathfrak{P}^{66}$ and 1201 read "the earth" (τῇ γῇ) instead of "the well" (τῇ πηγῇ). But that may well owe to haplography. Of course, the brink of the well was probably surrounded by a round stone wall that functioned as a seat. The well shaft, over 30 meters deep, was walled with stone and penetrated an underground spring at the bottom. The opening was 2.40 meters in diameter and covered with a large lid to protect the well against dirt and other forms of contamination. There was no windlass to raise the (leather) pail to the surface, as was the case with all Palestinian wells of the period. It was necessary to bring along a leather vessel with its own rope; two openings in the well cover had been provided for the purpose of drawing water. It would not have been possible to use a clay jar, such as the Samaritan woman might have carried on her head or shoulder, to draw water; in lowering it into the well and raising it again, one would have damaged it on the stone lining. The Evangelist, or perhaps his source, no longer knew that or perhaps did not want to deal with that detail. Because in the scene at the cross Jesus' cry "I thirst" (19:28) comes at the same time, at midday, Lightfoot[8]

was prompted to posit a connection between the two scenes. But the thirst motif can play a role in each story without there being an inner relationship between them. "About the sixth [hour]" (ὡς ἕκτη): "about" (ὡς) appears before all designations of time in the Gospel of John.

■ **7** "The woman of Samaria" (γυνὴ Σαμαρῖτις, v 9): Hirsch[9] attributes the words to the redactor because only someone outside of Samaria could have said this. The woman comes to draw water: that is a typical scene in the Near East.[10] The fact that she wanders out to Jacob's well in the midday heat prompts Zahn[11] to think of "some sort of popular belief or superstition" regarding the powers of that water; however, the explanation lies in the nature of the literary composition. Bengel asserts that John also records as reliable authority conversations that he did not hear, but that were dictated to him by the spirit (*dictante spiritu*). In pointing this out, B. Bauer[12] is silently critical of Bengel.

■ **8** Jesus turns to the woman because the disciples have all gone away to buy food. One or two disciples would have been sufficent to carry some pieces of pita bread, plate-shaped, about 3 cm thick, and perhaps something to eat with it. But the conversation of Jesus with the woman, which was to be revelatory in character, required privacy, undisturbed by the disciples. Moreover, Jesus now had to ask the woman for water and thus was able to strike up a conversation with her. Since the woman had brought with her only a (clay) water jug, but not a leather vessel for drawing water and no rope, she was unable to draw water or to give it away. But the reader, who seeks edification, is not disturbed by things like that.

■ **9** The woman wonders why a Jew—in the Gospel of John Jesus is designated a Jew only in this passage— addresses a Samaritan woman. This indicates indirectly to the reader that Jesus' request breaks down the wall of partition erected by the Jewish law (cf. Gal 3:28). The sentence "For Jews have no dealings with Samaritans" (οὐ ... Σαμαρίταις; omitted in ℵ* D it) explains the point to the reader. Daube translates the sentence: "The Jews do

6 1963) 48.
5 Schnackenburg, *John,* 1: 422f. and Brown, *John,* 1: 164f.
6 Billerbeck, 2: 432f.
7 *Catenae graecorum patrum in Novum Testamentum,* 8 vols. Vol. 2, *Catenae in evangelia s. Lucae et s. Johannis,* ed. John Anthony Cramer (Oxford, 1838–1944; reprint Hildesheim: G. Olms, 1967) 216, 21.

8 *St. John's Gospel,* 122.
9 *Studien,* 53.
10 Cf. Jos. *Ant.* 2.275f.
11 *Das Evangelium des Johannes,* 238.
12 *Kritik der evangelischen Geschichte des Johannes* (Bremen: C. Schünemann, 1840) x.

not use vessels together with Samaritans";[13] Barrett follows suit.[14] That may reflect a regulation enacted first around 65 CE, which declared that Samaritan women were unclean, and thus all food and drink handled by them were likewise unclean.[15] According to Barrett, the Evangelist did not add this sentence to the Gospel until his old age. But the relation of the Jews to the Samaritans was not uniform until the time of Rabbi Aqiba (died 135).[16] Since the word "vessel" does not appear in this sentence, one can simply translate: "The Jews have no dealings with the Samaritans."

■ **10** Jesus' request for a drink is understood from now on only as the occasion for further conversation. Actually, the woman (so Jesus responds) should have asked him for a drink, had she known who he was (in the last analysis Jesus is the gift of God) and what he was able to give: "living water." The reader is alerted to the fact that the woman does not understand: man is unable to understand the revelation without further help. In Judaism "spring water" (living water) is primarily a figure for Yahweh himself and the salvation that proceeds from him (cf. Jer 2:13, 17:13, Sir 24:21, Prov 13:14, 18:4). It is then interpreted to refer to the Torah (in the Damascus Document [CD 6.4] Num 21:18 is interpreted thus: "The 'well' in question is the law") and finally with reference to the teaching of the wise. Philo calls God "the spring of living" ($\pi\eta\gamma\grave{\eta}$ $\tauο\hat{\upsilon}$ $\zeta\hat{\eta}\nu$),[17] by which he understands concretely the law and the God who teaches virtues through the law. In the gnostic book of Baruch, the passage "which is to them a bath . . . a spring of living water welling up" ($\ddot{ο}\pi\epsilon\rho$ $\dot{\epsilon}\sigma\tau\grave{\iota}$ $\lambdaο\upsilon\tau\rhoό\nu$ $\alpha\dot{\upsilon}\tauο\hat{\iota}\varsigma$ . . . $\pi\eta\gamma\grave{\eta}$ $\zeta\hat{ω}\nu\tauος$ $\ddot{\upsilon}\delta\alpha\tauος$ $\dot{\alpha}\lambda\lambdaο\mu\acute{\epsilon}\nuο\upsilon$) shows how the notions of "baptism" and "drinking" are intermingled:[18] a drink functions as baptism in living water.

On the other hand, the Gospel of John was not influenced by Odes of Solomon 6:11–18: "all the thirsty on earth drank of it [viz., gnosis] and their thirst was assuaged and put to rest . . . and they have life eternal on account of the water." Bultmann[19] and Goppelt[20] pre-

sent much comparative material.[21]

■ **11** The woman herself gathers from Jesus' word that he is able to offer more than well water. That astounds her. She objects that he has no vessel with which to draw and the well is deep. Whether the Evangelist and his source were aware that the shaft of Jacob's well intersected a spring below, or whether they overlook such details, remains an open question. For "well" and "spring" are used interchangeably without affecting the meaning.

Ο$\ddot{\upsilon}\tau\epsilon$ . . . $\kappa\alpha\grave{\iota}$ (correlation of negative and positive terms) is not common in classical Greek: Bauer[22] and BDF[23] point to 3 John 10.

■ **12** The woman is under the impression that Jesus is claiming that he has more to offer than her ancestor Jacob, who gave them this great well with its deep, walled shaft, and who drank from it along with his family and his herds, and who was evidently satisfied with its water.

■ **13** Jesus responds in a solemn manner: "Every one who drinks from Jacob's well will thirst again." That means: everything that the world has to offer man will not satisfy him in the long run. His appetite directs him constantly to something new. Man therefore needs "more," viz., what the text now hints at enigmatically.

■ **14** The water that Jesus will give (when he is "raised up") satisfies man's thirst forever because it is that for which man really yearns. Negatively expressed, that means: man is relieved of his restlessness, of his lack of peace, of the desire that drives him. That is expressed positively by means of a new enigmatic figure: in him who receives it, the water that Jesus gives becomes a spring of water welling up into everlasting life. This saying is understood for the most part as referring to water that leads him who receives it to eternal life. The preposition $\epsilon\dot{\iota}\varsigma$ ("unto, to") is thus understood in a final sense.[24] But strictly speaking the text says: this water becomes a spring of water. This suggests another meaning: whoever is led to God by Jesus through his Spirit becomes himself a spring, a bearer of salvation for others. This is in fact fulfilled by the Samaritan woman:

13   "Jesus and the Samaritan Woman: The Meaning of $\sigma\upsilon\gamma\chi\rho\acute{\alpha}ο\mu\alpha\iota$," *JBL* 69 (1950) 139 = "Samaritan Women," in *The New Testament and Rabbinic Judaism* (University of London: Athlone Press, 1956) 375.

14   *John*, 232f.

15   Billerbeck, 1: 540.

16   Billerbeck, 1: 538f.

17   *De fuga*, 198.

18   Hippolytus, *Ref.* 27.2 [ANL 5.22].

19   *John*, 181–86 [133–36].

20   *TDNT* 6: 135–45.

21   Goppelt, however, thinks of participation in the sacrament in connection with this passage (especially on 143f.), as do many other scholars.

22   *Das Johannesevangelium*, 67.

23   §445.3.

having come to faith herself, she now leads the Samaritans to faith (cf. 7:38). Gnosticism had a field day with this verse,[25] without of course taking over "to eternal life" along with the rest of the verse.

■ **15** The conversation continues with a fresh misunderstanding on the part of the woman: she would like to have some of that water which would relieve her of the arduous daily task of coming to draw water. If Jesus were to ease her task in this way, he would supercede Jacob in her eyes. There is involved in this misunderstanding, even if obscured, a genuine, deep desire for salvation on the part of humankind. That humankind aspires to be "high" today makes no difference to the Samaritan woman.

■ **16** The further conversation does not connect up with the preceding, but makes an abrupt transition to a new theme that only gradually becomes evident. Jesus' request to the woman to return to him with her husband catches her by surprise. His surprising request takes on meaning by virtue of the fact that the woman must give a response that permits Jesus to exhibit his supernatural knowledge.

■ **17** Many exegetes are of the opinion that the woman seeks to free herself from her painful situation by uttering a "half-truth."[26] But one should not inquire after the psychology of the woman but after the intention of the author. He has Jesus ironically affirm that she has not told a lie.

■ **18** He then exposes the larger untruth: she has had five husbands (from whom she was separated by death or a bill of divorce), and now lives "in sin," as they say. According to Billerbeck,[27] a woman was permitted to remarry three times at most; but the question of the Sadducees in Mark 12:18–27 presupposes the remarriage of a woman six times (for a total of seven) as commanded by the law, if only as a piece of theological speculation. A married Jewish woman could only enter into a new marriage if the old ended in the death of her spouse or if he gave her a bill of divorce. How the woman came to be married five times holds no significance for the story; the Evangelist chooses not to speak of "lawless and vulgar" matters. What he wants to show is the uncanny knowledge of Jesus. Those exegetes who took the text literally were correct. However, that was not enough for most of them. Whoever asserts that Jesus wishes to lay bare her morals misunderstands the text.[28] In the original form from which the Evangelist took it over, it was designed to show only that Jesus discerned a fate that could not otherwise be divined. Other exegetes prefer an allegorical interpretation—also in opposition to the sense of the scene: the woman is the Samaritan people, as it were, her five husbands are the five gods whom the Samaritans revere according to 2 Kgs 17:24ff., and her present paramour is Jahweh. Schnackenburg[29] has rightly put an end to this allegorizing.[30] Brown, too, finds such an allegorical aim indeed possible, but not intimated by the Evangelist.[31] In spite of that, he surprises the reader by reporting how Bligh[32] interprets the response of the woman: she is unmarried and has matrimonial designs on Jesus.[33]

The allegorical interpretation of 2 Kgs 17 fails because the text does not lend itself to that reading. The foreign colonists, whom the king of Assyria settled in Samaria following the fall of the northern kingdom, worshiped seven deities, not five, and these seven not in succession. This passage, which has been reworked by the Deuteronomist, does not make it clear whether or not they worshiped Jahweh in addition. Here again "edifying" scholarship has elicited something more and different from the text than it intends.

---

24   Cf. Schnackenburg, *John,* 1: 431; Braun, *La Sainte Bible,* 342; Brown, *John,* 1: 171.

25   Cf. Hippolytus, *Ref.* 5.9.18, 5.13, 5.27.2.

26   E.g., Holtzmann, *Das Evangelium des Johannes,* 66; B. Weiss, *Das Johannes-Evangelium,* 142; Büchsel, *Das Evangelium nach Johannes,* 64; Strathman, *Das Evangelium nach Johannes,* 85.

27   2: 437.

28   Zahn (*Das Evangelium des Johannes,* 244) speaks of "revealing her immoral life, which has exhibited profligacy and unbridled passions for a long time."

29   *John,* 1: 433.

30   The ghost lingers in Hirsch (*Studien,* 146), who understands the woman as symbol of the Samaritan people and as individual at the same time.

31   *John,* 1: 171.

32   "Jesus in Samaria," *HeyJ* 3 (1962) 335f.

33   [Brown reports this as a "curiosity"—Translator.]

■ **19** How the woman comes to her answer has been much discussed. Zahn continues to psychologize: "She turns the conversation from her personal situation to a question concerning the national cult."[34] Edwards is bolder yet.[35] He believes that the woman regards Jesus as a mind reader, a religious phenomenon, and when he wants to speak, one should let him speak about matters of his own and about a local religious controversy. Such behavior that seems almost cynical, according to Büchsel, is not to be attributed to the woman: "From the perspective of his greatness and the consciousness of her depravity, she has discovered the position in relation to him that is appropriate to her."[36] B. Weiss[37] and Strathman[38] found a simpler solution: her recognition of him as a prophet is the consequence of his incomprehensible wisdom. The response of W. Bauer[39] is even closer to the mark: the recognition of Jesus as a prophet is only a verbal allusion to the theme that is really closest to the Evangelist's heart: the theme of the correct form of worship. It is decisive for his judgment that the question of guilt, consciousness of sin, and forgiveness plays no role at all. If one conceives verses 17f. as evidence of Jesus' omniscience, it is possible to understand the curious reaction of the woman, her question regarding true worship, as an attempt on the part of the Evangelist to provide a literary transition, which presents the occasion to elaborate on the question of true worship. The real continuation of verse 18 in the Evangelist's source is verse 28, where Jesus' complete knowledge of her life allows her to surmise that he is the messiah. In verse 25 Jesus reveals who he is to the woman, but this fact is ignored in verse 28. In order to clarify the connections between the source and the development of the "Johannine doctrine" of true worship, we must first analyze verses 20–28 more closely.

■ **20** Which—the woman asks of the stranger she has acknowledged as a prophet—is really right: the Samaritan practice of worshiping on Gerizim ("on this mountain"), or the Jewish custom of worshiping in Jerusalem (the word "Zion" is not even used)?

■ **21** The conviction that the deity was to be worshiped at a specific place signified by an epiphany is old: it extends from the burning bush to Lourdes. Instead, the Samaritan woman says: Jerusalem or "this mountain." Jesus answers the woman—he addresses her as he does his mother at the wedding at Cana and at the cross (20:15) "woman" ($\gamma\acute{v}\nu\alpha\iota$): "The hour is coming when neither on this mountain nor in Jerusalem will you worship the Father." In the time of Jesus' earthly life the temple still stood on Zion, while the sanctuary on Gerizim had long since been destroyed (128 BCE). He thus speaks here as a prophet. To be sure, only in verse 23 does it become evident how revolutionary are his pronouncements concerning true worship. When the Evangelist wrote, the Jewish temple had long lain in ruins. The prophesy has been fulfilled.

■ **22** Verse 22 ruptures the context: he reproaches the Samaritans because they do not know what they worship, while "we," the Christians and Jews, know that "salvation comes from the Jews." In contrast to many conservative interpreters, Bauer[40] and Bultmann[41] correctly point out that for the Gospel of John salvation comes only from God and Jesus Christ who has been sent by him. In the Gospel of John the Jews predominantly represent the unbelieving world. Verse 22 is therefore a later correction (cf. the same process in 5:22–23, 27–29, 30b), part of an ecclesiastical redaction, without which, of course, the Fourth Gospel would never have been widely disseminated.

■ **23** It is only with this verse that we come again to the genuine Johannine train of thought. The Evangelist intentionally combines two different temporal aspects in the phrase, "the hour comes and now is": the time of the earthly Jesus (for whom "the hour" lay still in the future) and the time of the resurrected Jesus and the post-Easter congregation (for whom the hour had already arrived). This hour could not arrive during the earthly life of Jesus "for as yet the Spirit had not been given, because

34   *Das Evangelium des Johannes*, 244; cf. his remarks on v 18.

35   *John*, 45.

36   *Das Evangelium nach Johannes*, 64.

37   *Das Johannes-Evangelium*, 143.

38   *Das Evangelium nach Johannes*, 84f.

39   *Das Johannesevangelium*, 69.

40   *Das Johannesevangelium*, 70.

41   *John*, 189f n. 6 [139 n. 6].

Jesus was not yet glorified" (7:39). For that reason, the disciples are always depicted in the Gospel of John as without understanding (see 4:32f.). On the other hand, the Fourth Gospel nevertheless describes Jesus—and this complicates the matter initially for the reader—as faith understands him, the faith made possible (only) by the Spirit (cf. 16:12), after "the hour" has come (20:22). The correlary of this is that the Lord who wanders about on earth has already been designated as the one who awakens faith, the faith that only the risen Lord finds (see below on v 38). The true worshiper will worship neither in Jerusalem nor on Gerizim, but will worship the Father in Spirit and truth. True worship is thereby denied to Jews and Samaritans alike, since they think of him as connected with a holy place. But true worship is that which sees the Father (14:9) through the "Spirit of truth" (15:26) in Jesus, who is the truth (14:6). The theme of true worship appears also in the OT, in Qumran, and in Hellenism. The inadequacy of the sacrificial cult is attested already in Isa 1:11–20, 29:13; Joel 2:13; Amos 5:1–25; Micah 6:6–8; Psalms 40:7, 50:7–23, 51:18f. and other passages. 1 Kgs 8:27ff., Isa 66, and Mal 1:11[42] do not break through the limits of a piety connected with a place of worship, as Bultmann claims.

The Qumran community expected that the Holy Spirit would cleanse some men of all evil deeds in the end time (1QS 4.20f.); according to CD this has already transpired in the Qumran community (CD 2.12f., 1QS 3.4–6, 8.5f.). Their conviction that "atonement will be made for the earth more effectively than by any flesh of burnt-offerings or fat of sacrifices" is demonstrated by 1QS 9.4f. But not only can the community as a whole receive the Spirit but also the individual member: 1QH 7.6f., 11f., 13.18f., 14.25, 16.6f., 11f., 17.26.

From the Hellenistic world, cf. Cicero, "But the best and also the purest, holiest and most pious way of worshiping the gods is ever to venerate them with purity, sincerity and innocence both of thought and of speech."[43] Philo, "No, for this man, like those others, has gone astray from the road that accords with true piety (εὐσέβεια), deeming it to be ritual (θρησκεία) instead of holiness (ὁσιότης), and offering gifts to Him who cannot be bribed and will not accept such things, and flattering Him who cannot be flattered, who welcomes genuine worship of every kind, but abhors all counterfeit approaches. Genuine worship is that of a soul bringing simple reality as its only sacrifice."[44]

■ **24** As "spirit" God is of course not confined to a particular place. However, when the Evangelist uses the term "spirit" he does not have in mind a fine, luminous material diffused throughout all unformed matter, as in Stoicism, nor does he have in mind, as in Hebrew thought, the notion that God has a πνεῦμα ("spirit").[45] Rather, πνεῦμα ("spirit"), like ἀλήθεια ("truth"), concerns the reality of God. To be sure, "spirit" is beyond everything earthly, but for the believers it is manifest in Jesus and they come to experience it through the gift of the Spirit which enables them to know the revelation. For the Evangelist, therefore, Jerusalem and Gerizim, when they are correctly understood, are replaced by Jesus and his word, which in turn become the gift of the Spirit to the church.

■ **25** Verse 25 serves as the transition to a loftier subject; the woman does not yet grasp what Jesus is talking about. But her reference to the messiah prepares for Jesus' word of self-revelation that now follows.[46] Later sources report that the Samaritans expected a *Ta'eb* ("he who returns," or, probably more accurately, "he who restores"). Zahn: "He will bring the extinct tabernacle with all its paraphernalia to light and restore the cult to its original purity."[47] The Evangelist probably built this sentence on his own conception of the messiah: the messiah—this non-Greek word is put on the lips of the Samaritan woman to give the scene some local color— will decide finally which is the true worship.

"We know" (οἴδαμεν), a correction in 𝔓⁶⁶, read by G L φ 33 *al* sy^hmg, would presuppose the perspective of the

---

42   Cited by Bultmann, *John*, 190 n. 4 [140 n. 3].
43   *De Natura Deorum Academica* 2.28.71, tr. H. Rackham, LCL, 193.
44   *Quod Deterius Potiori insidiari solet* 7.21, tr. F. H. Colton and G. H. Whitaker, LCL, 217.
45   Bauer, *Das Johannesevangelium*, 71.
46   Bauer, *Das Johannesevangelium*, 71.
47   *Das Evangelium des Johannes*, 253.

Samaritans generally, but it probably crept into the text through copyists who were influenced by the οἴδαμεν in verse 22. Ἀναγγέλλω is a hellenistic replacement for ἀπαγγέλλω.[48]

■ **26** "I am" (ἐγὼ εἰμι) simply means: "I am he," i.e., the messiah of whom the Samaritan woman had just spoken. Stauffer[49] of course sees in this a play on the secret name of God, which, according to him, is represented by אני והוא ("I am he"). That would have been completely incomprehensible for the woman. But it is likewise improbable that the Evangelist intends to refer the reader to that formula. At most one can say: he has Jesus use a known hellenistic revelation formulation. The Evangelist has the woman's perception of Jesus grow steadily (Jew, lord, prophet, christ) and does not introduce an expression that overpowers everything else into the midst of this development. Jesus' judgment regarding the true form of worship is legitimized by the fact that he is the Christ and is to be recognized as such, precisely on the basis of the presupposition expressed in verse 25.

■ **27** The Evangelist skillfully intertwines the conversation with the woman with that of the disciples (it is uncertain whether the disciples played a role in the Evangelist's source). Jesus' exchange with the woman has reached its goal in substance. The disciples are puzzled by the fact that Jesus converses with a woman (not with a Samaritan woman). Billerbeck quotes Aboth Rabbi Nathan 2 (1d): "One does not speak with a woman on the street, not even his own wife, and certainly not with another woman, on account of gossip."[50] But the disciples dare not ask the master about it.

■ **28** Originally, verse 28 probably followed immediately on verse 18: in verse 29 the woman alludes to verse 18, not to verse 26. Why the woman leaves her jug behind then becomes more understandable: she is eager to proclaim her message in the village. According to Daube,[51] she leaves the jug behind so that Jesus could drink from it.[52] But Jesus could not draw water from the deep well with this jug. That Jesus surprised the woman with his friendly request[53] lies outside the intention of the Evangelist. In the judgment of Edwards,[54] the woman forgets the jug in her excitement.

■ **29** Jesus' extraordinary knowledge serves here to suggest that he could perhaps be the messiah. The narrative does not stipulate that Jesus permits the woman to recognize him as such at that moment. The distinction between verses 38 and 42 is thereby anticipated.

■ **30** The Samaritans leave the city (aorist tense) and head toward (imperfect) Jesus: The call of the woman has had its effect. While they are on their way, there is time for Jesus' conversation with the disciples, which the Evangelist inserts here.

■ **31** The disciples offer Jesus some food which they had purchased in the village (v 8). Just as the request for water earlier served to lead into a speech of Jesus, so now the offer of food functions only to introduce a lecture directed to the disciples and the reader. The disciples appear here to be a unified group, without individualization. Both of these things—the absence of individualization (which appears not just here) and of the every day with its obvious needs, but not to the extent that a "spiritual" perspective comes into play—contributes to the impression that the Gospel of John is remarkably colorless. The earthly does not possess its own value. Whoever attempts to make the Fourth Gospel into an especially realistic book of reminiscences, as Edwards does, is on the wrong track.

■ **32** Once again we have a Johannine enigmatic saying that immediately invites misunderstanding. Because the disciples have not yet received the Spirit, the food to which Jesus alludes is simply denied to them. However, the perspective of the Evangelist is fixed on Jesus. The important thing is that Jesus has this food.

■ **33** As one expects, the disciples misunderstand the remark of Jesus, just as the woman does in verses 11 and 15, and for the same reason: they take the remark about food in a realistic or literal sense.

---

48 Bauer, *Das Johannesevangelium*, 71.
49 *Jesus and His Story*, tr. Dorothea M. Barton (London: SCM Press, 1960) 152.
50 2: 438.
51 "Jesus and the Samaritan Woman: The Meaning of συγχράομαι," *JBL* 69 (1950) 138 = "Samaritan Women," in *The New Testament and Rabbinic Judaism* (University of London: Athlone Press, 1956) 374.
52 Barrett (*John*, 240) concurs.
53 So Daube, "Jesus and the Samaritan Woman: The Meaning of συγχράομαι," *JBL* 69 (1950) 137 = "Samaritan Women," in *The New Testament and Rabbinic Judaism* (University of London: Athlone Press, 1956) 373.
54 *John*, 47.

■ **34** One must not interpret this verse in a psychological-realistic fashion, as Zahn does:[55] just as Jesus loses his thirst in his conversation with the Samaritan woman, so here he loses his appetite: "One sees into what a state of suspense and elation Jesus was thrown by his unintended conversation with this non-Jewish woman." Zahn's generation did not anticipate the interrogation of a text with a view to the mode of composition that underlay it. They were convinced that with the demonstration of Johannine authorship the most important piece of exegetical work had been done. Here the Evangelist means that man lives out of what he lives for. Since Jesus lives entirely for the fulfillment of the divine will, he lives out of it. The man who has nothing for which to live, is starving to death spiritually. Because the disciples have not yet come to see the Father (14:8f.), they do not recognize this food. Whoever interprets verse 34 as a variation of Zahn's realistic interpretation will naturally have to have recourse to the diagnosis "docetism."

■ **35** The contrast between the perspective of Jesus and that of his disciples takes a fresh turn with this verse.

One customarily reasons: in Palestine it takes six months from sowing to harvest, on average. But the time varies with the land and the type of grain sown. One needs only to compare the data provided by Hirsch,[56] Barrett,[57] Schnackenburg,[58] and Brown[59] to see how differently this verse is interpreted. We prefer to think that the words of the disciples ("There are yet four months, then comes the harvest") are intended to mean: there is yet time before the harvest is ready. Jesus here uses the word "harvest" of the Samaritan mission in a figurative sense: Jesus sees the field already white for harvest.

■ **36** The reaper already receives his wages (not: reward); from here on the figure has only a non-literal sense: "and gathers fruit for eternal life." That refers to Jesus, the missionary, and the Samaritans who are pouring out to him in faith. The word ἵνα ("in order that") is here scarcely to be distinguished from ὥστε ("so that"), i.e.,

purpose is scarcely to be distinguished from result. It is not entirely clear who the sower and the reaper are because the Evangelist again maintains a double perspective: on the one side, he has Jesus speak in Samaria from the perspective of his earlier situation, in which he both begins and completes the mission;[60] on the other side, he has Jesus speak from the standpoint of the Christian mission in Samaria generally, with reference to which every generation is dependent on the labor of preceding generations.

■ **37** "For here the saying . . ." reflects only the second perspective. The proverb (λόγος, "word"), which alludes to that perspective, means: the sower often does not get to enjoy the fruits of his labor; cf., for example, Job 31:7f. "and if any spot has cleaved to my hands, then let me sow, and another eat"; and Aristophanes, *Equites* 392: "You reap an alien harvest."

■ **38** Verse 38 is clearly expressed from the point of view of the resurrected Jesus: in 20:21 he sends the disciples out. A sending out like that in the synoptic tradition (Mark 6:7 pars.) does not make sense for the Evangelist, because the disciples only receive the Spirit after Jesus' exaltation.[61] Since the work of F. C. Baur a reference is often assumed here to the mission of Philip and that of Peter and John to Samaria as narrated in Acts 8. Others think that ἄλλοι ("others") refers to OT prophets (including John the Baptist). The one suggestion is as alien to the Evangelist as the other; and an allusion to Simon Magus[62] is out of the question. The Evangelist writes of the Christian mission, which he proleptically has Jesus found, and he teaches the Christian missionaries to insert themselves unpretentiously and gratefully into the unity of the Christian missionary work that extends over generations. With this goes a second observation: Gentile Christianity was friendlier to the Samaritan mission to a much greater degree than was Jewish Christianity (Matt 10:5f.), and was thereby conscious of acting in accord-

---

55   *Das Evangelium des Johannes*, 256.
56   *Studien*, 54, and *Das vierte Evangelium*, 152.
57   *John*, 241.
58   *John*, 1: 482f.
59   *John*, 1: 182.
60   Cf. τελειώσω ("to complete, finish") in verses 34 and 19:30.
61   Bultmann, *John*, 200 n. 1 [147 n. 6].

62   Cf. Holtzmann, *Das Evangelium des Johannes*, 85.

ance with Jesus' intention. The Evangelist gives expression to this by ascribing the beginning of the Samaritan mission to Jesus himself.

■ 39 Verse 39 resumes the story of the Samaritans, which had been interrupted at the end of verse 30. Verse 29 is directly cited: the testimony of the woman regarding the miracle-worker, Jesus, leads many to faith in Jesus.

■ 40 He accedes to the request of the Samaritans and stays with them two days. It goes without saying that during these two days he was active as a teacher; the results so indicate.

■ 41f. Butmann[63] thinks that in these verses he has discovered something akin to Kierkegaard's problem of "second-hand disciples" in the *Philosophical Fragments* (especially chapter 5). But that is eisegesis: the woman has certainly told the Samaritans of Jesus only as an all-knowing miracle-worker; thus, what they initially experienced was faith in Jesus as a miracle-worker. When they had Jesus with them, they modified their faith in hearing his own words; verses 41f. therefore represent an important insight into faith for the Evangelist: faith is then genuine when the auditor perceives the Lord speaking in the words of the proclamation. Λαλία ("words, speech, talk") has a disdainful connotation: the speech of the missionary witnesses is certainly not prattle. Yet they do remain insignificant human words, if the Lord himself does not come to expression through them. The Samaritans thus come to confession of Jesus as the "Savior of the world."

Pre-Christian Judaism thought God the real redeemer of Israel. In Hellenism, Zeus and Asclepius, Isis and Serapis, were venerated as "saviors." The designation of the Roman Emperor as "savior of the world" (σωτὴρ τοῦ κόσμου) was quite common from Hadrian on.[64]

The recognition of Jesus as the savior of the world on the part of the Samaritans includes the other expressions of Jesus' significance and functions as their unsurpassable term: a Jew—more than Jacob—a prophet—the messiah—the savior of the world.

Overview

Older investigators read this story as a historical report. In so doing, they ran into all sorts of difficulties. Why do the disciples go together to do the shopping? Two, or at most three, would have been sufficient to get some pita bread and other provisions. Or was Jesus being accompanied by only two or three disciples? Why did the disciples not refresh their master and themselves beforehand with a drink from the well? Were they perhaps traveling through the countryside without a leather bucket and rope to draw water? The woman, too, did not have an ἄντλημα, a leather bucket, and a rope. How does she intend to draw water? She cannot draw water from the deep well with the water jug (ὑδρία) that she carries. Why does she come out to Jacob's well at midday, in the heat, when there is a spring in Sychar? From whom did the narrator learn about Jesus' conversation with the woman? The thought that he questioned Jesus or the woman after the fact is as modern as it is absurd. A suggestion occasionally employed by exegetes to the effect that not all of the disciples went into the "city," but John, perhaps, remained with Jesus, is flatly contradicted by the text.

But neither can the conversations of Jesus with the woman and with the disciples be conceived as reflections of actual discourse. There are constant disjunctions in the text. The attempt was made initially to account for them psychologically. Since the woman does not grasp Jesus' riddle about living water (which would not have been so difficult for a contemporary Jew to understand), Jesus attempts, by revealing her personal life, to make her "subconscious" audible. How did he come to know about her five husbands? According to Lange,[65] "the psychic effect of the five husbands on the woman . . . left traces in her appearance." But to read such numbers exactly requires more than "a penetrating human glance"; Büchsel wants to make use of this idea.[66] Since the woman's reputation was known in the entire region and Jesus and his disciples would have picked up the

63 *John*, 200f. [148f.].
64 Cf. Barrett, *John*, 244; on the title σωτήρ, "savior," cf. Conzelmann in M. Dibelius and H. Conzelmann, *The Pastoral Epistles. A Commentary on the Pastoral Epistles*, ed. Helmut Koester; tr. Philip Buttolph and Adela Yarbro. Hermeneia—A Critical-Historical Commentary on the Bible (Philadelphia: Fortress Press, 1972) 100–103.
65 Cited by B. Weiss, *Das Johannes-Evangelium*, 142.
66 *Das Evangelium nach Johannes*, 64.

village gossip along the way, this rationalistic solution also leads nowhere. Can Jesus and his disciples have discussed scandal with her in a school of meditation? For the woman suddenly to begin speaking of the place of true worship is not an "ordinary woman's ploy" (with which one exegete is apparently familiar), by means of which she "hopes to avoid further unpleasant discussion of her relationships," but neither is it "the beginning of an understanding of Jesus' significance." It is worth noting that the woman bases her supposition (v 29) that Jesus is the messiah, not on Jesus' self-testimony in verse 26, but on his miraculous knowledge (v 18). That also suggests that the Evangelist inserted verses 19–26 into an older text, in order to express his own concerns. It is more than a dubious psychological interpretation to suggest that Jesus rejects food and drink because he is sated with missionary success; Zahn paints this picture: "One sees into what a state . . . of elation Jesus was thrown by this conversation."[67] Wellhausen,[68] prompted by Schwartz,[69] finds it problematic that Jesus says nothing to the Samaritans (verse 41). For that reason, Wellhausen recasts the story so that Jesus' speech about sowing and harvest was originally directed not to the disciples but to the Samaritans when they offered him food. That shows how easily satisfied even great scholars like Wellhausen could be in exegeting the Gospel of John.

Some exegetes were of course uncomfortable with such historical-psychological interpretations. They then had recourse to a typological understanding. Thus Strathmann: "The woman is not a flesh and blood figure at all. She is a type, but not that of a deplorable, degenerate woman, who lives in a 'maximum of matrimonial bewilderment and error,' but a symbol of Samaritanism, a personification of the Samaritan community."[70] The Evangelist therefore "preaches in the form of a freely inventive author."[71] With this one can concur to a great extent. On the other hand, one cannot say of John (Strathmann believes John, the son of Zebedee, to be the author of the Gospel of John) what he further asserts: "A very reflective spirit has represented his faith in Jesus in the form of a consummate, brief work of art, deliberate even in detail."[72] In his enthusiasm, Strathmann thereby passes over the difficulties we indicated above. It is precisely in this pericope that one can see that it was not a matter of the Evangelist creating a "consummate, brief work of art." Bultmann[73] therefore does greater justice to this story when he indicates that the Evangelist joined a tradition (the wording of which we can no longer reconstruct [?]) to his own message only with difficulty.[74] Precisely because the Evangelist uses the tradition with little alteration, the speeches he inserts also have the effect of being sprinkled here and there.

Hirsch[75] goes along with Strathmann for the most part. But his solution is more elegant than his Erlangen colleague. He writes, "The careful depiction of the scene" is "a sign that the author has applied special skill to the entire story of the Samaritan woman. The dialogue is the most detailed and liveliest of the entire work. Whoever does not see traces of the poet here is beyond help. The Samaritan woman is simultaneously an individual woman living in lawless vulgarity and the personification of her people."[76] Hirsch then adopts the thesis that the five husbands correspond to the five gods from 2 Kgs 17.[77] "The story weaves into an indivisible unity the coming to Jesus of a lawless woman and the overcoming of the Samaritan religion by the Christian. . . . In the Fourth Gospel everything is at once history and interpretation. . . . We have here the best and purest example, encountered by Jesus, of the analytical depths of the author's view of the movements of the human heart—a view that forsakes reality. The spiritual event in which the faith of the woman arises is as transparent as crystal. And yet a real conversation with a libertine Samaritan woman might not go just this way now or anytime." If one examines the narrative more closely, it can be shown (in opposition to Hirsch): recourse to the five Samaritan gods in 2 Kgs is not correct—there were seven; and the

67   *Das Evangelium des Johannes*, 256.
68   *Das Evangelium Johannes*, 21.
69   "Aporien," 4: 509.
70   *Das Evangelium nach Johannes*, 82.
71   Strathman, *Das Evangelium nach Johannes*, 83.
72   *Das Evangelium nach Johannes*, 89.
73   *John*, 175f. [127f.].
74   Contrast Hirsch, *Studien*, 43, 53–55.

75   *Das vierte Evangelium*, 146–48.
76   Hirsch, *Das vierte Evangelium*, 146.
77   *Das vierte Evangelium*, 147.

spiritual event in which the faith of the woman comes into being is not clear as crystal. In fact, only Jesus' knowledge of things that no one outside her circle of acquaintances could have known, and thus a supernatural knowledge, made an impression on the woman and prompted her to announce to her neighbors that Jesus was possibly the messiah. That might be the text of the source, which treats Jesus as a "divine man" ($\theta\epsilon\hat{\iota}os$ $\dot{\alpha}\nu\acute{\eta}\rho$) and precipitates faith. But at bottom this pericope does not have to do with the woman and her new faith, in the view of the Evangelist, as Hirsch assumes, but with Jesus himself and his message. All other persons win life to the extent that they help underscore the message of Jesus. The Evangelist does not report that the woman has had five husbands and now has a sixth lover in order to illustrate that she has fallen into sin. If that were the case, her reaction to Jesus' revelation of her life would be incomprehensible. This fate was therefore deliberately selected (already by the source) because it falls so completely outside the rule that it does not give itself away. Even the most seasoned psychologist could not read it in the countenance of the woman. When Jesus nevertheless perceives it, he thereby reveals a superhuman knowledge. The Evangelist thus corrects the theology of his source: a magical knowledge of all possible innerworldly matters is not what makes Jesus the "son"; what makes him the son is that he is the way to the Father. The Jewish cult had no more claim to be true worship because it required worship on Zion than did the Samaritans because they advocated worship on Gerizim. The Father is not a being bound to a space that belongs to the innerworldly. In this respect, Johannine doctrine approximates Pauline: "There is neither Jew nor Greek . . ." (Gal 3:28).

Bultmann has found in verses 39–42 "a symbolic representation of the problem of those who hear the message at 'second-hand',"[78] which Kierkegaard discusses in detail in his *Philosophical Fragments*.[79] About this passage, 4:39–42, Bultmann writes: "[The woman]

symbolizes mediatory proclamation which brings its hearers to Jesus. . . . That is to say, the believer must not base his faith on the authority of others, but must himself find the object of faith; he must perceive, through the proclaimed word, the word of the Revealer himself."[80] It is doubtful that this is an adequate interpretation of verses 39–42. What the woman proclaims to her neighbors is indeed the message of the prophet-messiah Jesus. What the hearers perceive on the basis of Jesus' own message is that Jesus is the "savior of the world." The conception of Jesus as "savior" ($\sigma\omega\tau\acute{\eta}\rho$), which basically runs through the entire source, is thereby also corrected, just as the designation of the woman as a "first-hand hearer" is corrected by Jesus' own message: he himself is the way.

The situation is perceived differently in the case of Kierkegaard's distinction between disciples firsthand and disciples secondhand, and thus between the Christian community that was contemporary with Jesus and the current community of faith: "There is no disciple at second hand," he says.[81] "If the contemporary generation had left nothing behind them but these words: 'We have believed that in such and such a year God appeared among us in the humble figure of a servant, that he lived and taught in our community, and finally died,' it would be more than enough. The contemporary generation would have done all that was necessary; for this little advertisement, this *nota bene* on a page of universal history, would be sufficient to afford an occasion for a successor, and the most voluminous account can in all eternity do nothing more."[82] The testimony of a believer can provide the occasion for another or later person to decide for or against Christ; John has indicated that already in 20:22.[83] Since, however, in the end everything depends on discerning God in the testimony, the distinction between disciples firsthand and disciples secondhand becomes insignificant.

Finally, the composition of John 4:1–42 may be addressed. We intend to proceed in such a way that the

---

78 *John,* 200 [148].

79 Tr. David F. Swenson (Princeton: Princeton University Press, 1936) 74–93.

80 *John,* 201 [148].

81 *Philosophical Fragments,* tr. David F. Swenson (Princeton: Princeton University Press, 1936) 88.

82 *Philosophical Fragments,* tr. David F. Swenson (Princeton: Princeton University Press, 1936) 87.

83 Cf. H. Gerdes, *Das Christusbild Sören Kierkegaards* (Dusseldorf/Köln: Diederichs, 1960).

sequence of the verses is examined in order to discover the reasons or bases for aporias or problematic transitions in the text. We will thereby point out where the theology of the Evangelist compelled him to alter the text transmitted to him.

If one reflects on the real inner sequence of verses 1–3, one becomes aware that the text is no longer being composed in accordance with the logic of the context. That is manifest immediately in verses 1f. The first sense unit must actually have been: Jesus had more success than John in teaching and baptizing (E 3).[84] E = event. The note in verse 2 belongs to this remark as a correction (E 2): although Jesus himself did not baptize, only his disciples. This remark has nothing to do with the strained relationship between Jesus and the Pharisees; it is intended only to correct the expression "Jesus baptized." Since, however, the expression appears to belong in the context of verse 1, this verse is constructed so that the words "Jesus baptized more disciples than John" come last. The twice repeated use of the word "baptize" in close succession appears to connect verse 2 more closely to verse 1 than it really is. Actually, there must have followed immediately on E 3 (Jesus baptized more disciples than John) E 4: the Pharisees heard. This statement is so briefly expressed that an important communication to the reader is suppressed: "and intended to persecute Jesus." The reader must now deduce that from the context. It is doubtful that the effort of the author to achieve brevity is what prompted this succession of items; it is at least also possible that he did not want to introduce the notion of "persecution" so early (see 5:16). The suggestion of a threat to Jesus on the part of the Pharisees has as its consequence: "Jesus knows of it" (E 5). An assertion about Jesus (he makes more disciples than John) would stand at the beginning of such a sequence of statements in 4:1f. But in that case the contrast between Jesus and John would have been excessively emphasized–especially in relation to 3:26– and would have obscured the real opposition between Jesus and the Pharisees, which is what matters to the author. That could also explain why the author prefers an awkward sequence of sentences in verses 1f. in spite of everything. Following on E 5 (Jesus knew of it), verse 3

presents the description of how Jesus reacts to the alleged danger (as E 6): he quits Judea and again journeys to Galilee. The story proper begins with verse 4 (E 8): the journey to Galilee which leads through Samaria. Following immediately on this is the mention of Sychar (E 10), which lies close to the well of Jacob (E 11). The note inserted between these two items, with reference to the field that Jacob gave to Joseph (verse 5b), alleviates the abruptness with which Jacob's well is introduced in verse 6, on which almost all the following action turns. Water is easily drawn from a "spring" ($\pi\eta\gamma\dot\eta$), but not from a "well" ($\phi\rho\dot\epsilon\alpha\rho$), as Jacob's well is called in verse 14. We have already contested the view (supra, ad loc.) that Jacob's well is both, a well above but a spring at the bottom. The author employs the term "spring" ($\pi\eta\gamma\dot\eta$) first, which—in combination with the "water jug" ($\dot\upsilon\delta\rho\dot\iota\alpha$) of the woman—initially obscures the difficulty connected with drawing water (it is certainly not to be eliminated). In any case, it is evident that the author is an adroit story teller who endeavors to report a coherent story. In verse 6 (= E 12) Jesus arrives at the site of the first scene: in an entirely human manner, tired from the journey, he simply sits down beside the well. The time of day–noon– makes his exhaustion more understandable. Up to this point, beginning in verse 3, the talk is always limited to Jesus, and then only in the third person, because he is, so to speak, alone on the scene. But a second person nows appears on the scene in verse 7 (= E 14), a Samaritan woman, who has come to draw water. The conditions for a dialogue are thereby provided, a dialogue that continues until verse 26. The weariness of Jesus and the water that the woman has come to fetch anticipate the theme of the coming dialogue: Jesus requests (v 7:b = E 15) a drink of water. That he addresses this remark to the woman is explained by verse 8 (= E 16): the disciples have gone away into the village to buy food. This bit of information comes rather late, if one views the sequence of sentences in relation to the ideal order of events (i.e., if one compares the order of the discourse with story time). For the disciples have been accompanying Jesus on

---

84 The abbreviation scheme follows the analysis of Birger Olsson, *Structure and Meaning in the Fourth Gospel. A Text-Linguistic Analysis of John 2:1–11 and* *4:1–42*, tr. Jean Gray, ConBNT 6 (Lund: C. W. K. Gleerup, 1974) 124–33.

his journey. The last opportunity to mention the disciples would have been between verses 5 and 6, perhaps in this fashion: "The disciples now went into, . . . but Jesus being exhausted, . . ." The narrator refers to persons present only at the time they become necessary for the composition. He was obliged to mention the disciples in verse 8 in order to provide the motivation for Jesus to turn to the woman. In this way a pause transpires between Jesus' request and the woman's response: this is the price the narrator must pay. That is all the more possible since the woman does not respond to the request immediately (indeed, she cannot respond to the request), but surprisingly inquires (v 9a) how it is possible for him, a Jew, to make a request of a Samaritan woman. Verse 9b provides the necessary explanation for the reader who does not know of the hostile relationship of Jews and Samaritans: the two groups have no dealings with each other. A secondary theme is thus introduced, alongside the theme of water, which has prevailed up to this point: Jews/Samaritans. The two themes are henceforth intertwined as far as verse 42, although not with equal emphasis and clarity.

In verse 10, Jesus extends the dialogue in a surprising direction. He does not directly address her question (there is of course no one else present whom he could ask for a drink other than the woman with her water jug). Rather, Jesus responds with a conundrum: the roles of the requester and the responder would actually have to be reversed, if the woman really understood her situation: For, if she knew who it was before whom she stands and what he is able to give her, she would ask him to give her living water. With this answer the word "water" takes on a new, metaphorical sense, which is suggested by the phrase "living water." But the term is ambiguous, so that the woman understands "living water" to mean "spring water," while Jesus understands it to refer to "water of life." The woman understands (verse 11) Jesus' promise to mean that he will give her spring water, and she doubts that he is in a position to do that. For Jacob's well (the woman speaks accordingly in v 11 of "well" [φρέαρ]) leads to a spring, it is true, but that is beyond the reach of Jesus because he does not possess a vessel for drawing water, as she immediately observes. If this possibility is ruled out, does he then possess greater powers than her ancestor Jacob, who nevertheless gave them the well and was evidently content with it since he

and his sons and his cattle drank from it (v 12)? The counter of the woman presupposes, if only as a tentative probe, the possibility that the stranger could perhaps be in possession of special powers; one is not to think here of demonic gifts—could the Lord also be a water witcher? Jesus' answer (vv 13f.) at first permits the woman her convictions, but he calls her attention to a deficiency in Jacob's well that she has previously not noticed: when she has drunk of this water, it is not long until she is thirsty again and must go to fetch water. If, however, she drinks from the water that he is able to give her, then she will never be thirsty again. Jesus refers here to the heavenly gift of union with God, which, unlike all earthly gifts, does not at once awaken a new appetite in man. In Judaism one had, in fact, also reflected on and discussed the wisdom of God as such a spring dispensing peace to humankind. But in her attachment to the earthly the woman has never achieved such thoughts; rather, she asks for that magical water (v 15) that can spare her so much labor and effort and which the stranger appears to offer her. Up to this point the course of the dialogue has progressed smoothly, although each is speaking of something different than the other. But with verse 16 Jesus breaks out of the train of thought—at least to the woman that appears to be the case—with the request that she should call her husband. The narrator shows, in verses 17f., that the woman instinctively evades the issue with her rejoinder: "I have no husband," and then she is confronted with Jesus' answer, which confronts her in detail with the life she thought could not be divined. The conversation ends here, because an insertion of the Evangelist begins with verse 19, in which he asserts with gentle insistence what is very important to him. The actual continuation of the story is in verse 28 (= E 20): The woman leaves her jug (but not so that Jesus can now get a drink from it, as one exegete conjectures) and hurries to her village with the news: I met a man who has told me everything I ever did; is he perhaps the Messiah (vv 28–30)? The Samaritans come and he remains with them for two days (vv 39f.). The story of the first mission to the Samaritans, which Jesus himself initiated, has reached its goal. Verses 19–27 stem from the Evangelist (except for v 22, which was added by a reader friendly to the Jews), as do verses 31, 38 and verse 40 in part. *The events in the presumed source would have come, consequently, in the following sequence:*

Verse 4: He had to pass through Samaria.

5: So he came to a city of Samaria,
called Sychar, near the field that
Jacob gave to his son Joseph.

6: Jacob's well was there, and so
Jesus, wearied as he was with his
journey, sat down beside the well.

7: There came a woman of Samaria to
draw water. Jesus said to her,
"Give me a drink."

9: The Samaritan woman said to him,
"How is it that you, a Jew, ask a
drink of me, a woman of Samaria?"

10: (reworked) Jesus said to her,
"If you knew who it is that is
saying to you, 'Give me a drink,'
you would have asked him, and he
would have given you living water."

11: The woman said to him, "Sir,
you have nothing to draw with, and
the well is deep; where do you get
this living water?

12: Are you greater (mightier) than our
father Jacob, who gave us this well,
and drank from it himself, and his sons,
and his cattle?"

13: Jesus said to her, "Every one who drinks
of this water will thirst again.

14: Whoever drinks of the water that I shall
give him will never thirst again."

15: The woman said to him, "Sir, give me
this water, that I may not thirst,
nor (have to) come here to draw."

16: He said to her, "Go, call your husband,
and come here."

17: The woman answered him, "I have no husband."
Jesus said to her, "You are right in
saying, 'I have no husband.'

18: For you have had five husbands,
and he whom you now have is not your husband."

28: So the woman left her water jar,
and went away into the city,
and said to the people:

29: "Come, see a man who told me all
that I ever did."

30: They went out of the city and came
to him.

39: Many believed on him because of the
woman's testimony, "He told me all that
I ever did."

40: . . . They asked him to stay with them;
and he stayed there two days.

41: And many more believed because of his word.

42: They said to the woman, "It is no longer
because of your words that we believe,
for we have heard for ourselves, and we
know that this is indeed the Savior of
the world."

The last section of the Overview permits us to draw an important conclusion: the narrator whose work is used by the Fourth Evangelist knew how to write. Jesus' conversation with the woman at the well proves that. At the same time, it becomes evident here that he represents Jesus more or less as miracle worker ($\theta\epsilon\hat{\iota}os$ $\dot{a}v\acute{\eta}\rho$). In this case Jesus does not perform a miracle, as he does in 4:43–54; but he does legitimate himself as messiah by his supernatural knowledge. The use of ambiguous words or double entendres, often thought to be specifically Johannine, was already familiar to the narrator of the source.

12. The Son of the Royal Official

Bibliography

Bacon, Benjamin Wisner
"'Native Place' in John." *Expositor*, 8th ser., 23 (1922) 41–46.

Boismard, Marie-Emile
"Saint Luc et la rédaction du quatrième évangile (Jn iv, 46–54)." *RB* 69 (1962) 185–211.

Boismard, Marie-Emile
"Guérison du fils d'un fonctionnaire royal." *AsSeign* 75 (1965) 26–37.

Busse, Ulrich
Die Wunder des Propheten Jesus. Die Rezeption, Komposition und Interpretation der Wundertradition im Evangelium des Lukas, Forschung zur Bibel 24 (Stuttgart: Katholisches Bibelwerk, 1977 ²1979), esp. 141–60.

Colwell, Ernest Cadman
John Defends the Gospel (New York: Willett, Clark & Co., 1936).

Cribbs, F. Lamar
"A Study of the Contacts that Exist between St. Luke and St. John." SBLASP 2 (Missoula: Scholars Press, 1973) 1–93.

Cribbs, F. Lamar
"St. Luke and the Johannine Tradition." *JBL* 90 (1971) 422–50.

Erdozáin, Luis
La función del signo en la fe según el cuarto evangelio. Estudio crítico exegético de las perícopas Jn IV,46–54 y Jn XX,24–29, AnBib 33 (Rome: Pontifical Biblical Institute, 1963), esp. 9–35.

Feuillet, André
"La signification théologique du second miracle de Cana (*Jo.* IV,46–54)." *RSR* 48 (1960) 62–75.

Fortna, Robert T.
The Gospel of Signs (Cambridge: Cambridge University Press, 1970), esp. 38–48.

Fortna, Robert T.
"Source and Redaction in the Fourth Gospel's Portrayal of Jesus' Signs." *JBL* 89 (1970) 151–66, esp. 153–61, 164.

Freed, Edwin D.
"Jn IV, 51: παῖς or υἱός?." *JTS* 16 (1965) 448–49.

Gardner-Smith, Percival
Saint John and the Synoptic Gospels (Cambridge: Cambridge University Press, 1938), esp. 22–24.

Haenchen, Ernst
"Johanneische Probleme." *ZTK* 56 (1959) 19–54. Also in his *Gott und Mensch. Gesammelte Aufsätze* 1 (Tübingen: Mohr-Siebeck, 1965) 78–113.

Hahn, Ferdinand
"Sehen und Glauben im Johannesevangelium." In *Neues Testament und Geschichte. Historisches Geschehen und Deutung im Neuen Testament. Oscar Cullmann zum 70. Geburtstag,* ed. H. Baltensweiler and B.

Reicke (Zurich: Theologischer Verlag; Tübingen: Mohr-Siebeck, 1972) 125–41.

Harnack, Adolf von
New Testament Studies. Vol. 2, *The Sayings of Jesus, the Source of Matthew and St. Luke,* tr. J. R. Wilkinson (New York: G. P. Putnam's Sons; London: Williams & Norgate, 1908) 74–77 = *Beiträge zur Einleitung in das Neue Testament.* Vol. 2, *Sprüche und Reden Jesu. Die zweite Quelle des Matthäus und Lukas* (Leipzig: J. C. Hinrichs, 1907), esp. 54–56.

Heer, Josef
"Johanneische Botschaft XI: Der Glaube des Königlichen (Jo 4,43–54)." *Sein und Sendung* 33 (1968) 147–64.

Kilpatrick, George D.
"Jn IV,51: παῖς or υἱός?" *JTS* 14 (1963) 393.

Martyn, J. Louis
"We have found Elijah." In *Jews, Greeks, and Christians. Religious Cultures in Late Antiquity. Essays in Honor of William David Davies,* ed. Robert Hammerton-Kelly and Robin Scroggs. SJLA 21 (Leiden: E. J. Brill, 1976), esp. 192f.

Neirynck, Frans
"John and the Synoptics." In *L'Evangile de Jean. Sources, rédaction, théologie,* ed. M. de Jonge. BETL 44 (Gembloux: Duculot; Louvain: University Press, 1977) 73–106.

Neirynck, Frans et al.
"L'Evangile de Jean. Examen critique du commentaire de M.-E. Boismard et A. Lamouille." *ETL* 53 (1977) 363–478, esp. 451–78.

Nicol, W.
The Sēmeia in the Fourth Gospel. Tradition and Redaction, NovTSup 32 (Leiden: E. J. Brill, 1972), esp. 41–48, 55f., 73f.

Reim, Günter
"John iv, 44—Crux or Clue?" *NTS* 22 (1975/1976) 476–80.

Schnackenburg, Rudolf
"Zur Traditionsgeschichte von Joh 4,46–54." *BZ* 8 (1964) 58–88.

Schulz, Siegfried
Q—die Spruchquelle der Evangelisten (Zurich: Theologischer Verlag, 1972), esp. 236–46.

Schweizer, Eduard
"Die Heilung der Königlichen: Joh 4, 46–54." *EvT* 11 (1951/1952) 64–71.

Siegman, Edward F.
"St. John's Use of the Synoptic Material." *CBQ* 30 (1968) 182–98.

Silva, Rafael
"Dos casos de exégesis evangélica de difícil solución (Mt 8,5–13; Lc 7,1–10; Jo 4,46–54)." *Compostellanum* 13 (1968) 89–107.

Temple, S.
"The Two Signs in the Fourth Gospel." *JBL* 81 (1962) 169–74.

Tenney, Merrill C.
"Topics from the Gospel of John. Part II: The Meaning of the Signs." *BSac* 132 (1975) 145–60.

Willemse, Johannes
"La patrie de Jésus selon Saint Jean iv. 44." *NTS* 11 (1965) 349–64.

Windisch, Hans
Johannes und die Synoptiker. Wollte der vierte Evangelist die älteren Evangelien ergänzen oder ersetzen? UNT 12 (Leipzig: J. C. Hinrichs, 1926).

4

43 After the two days he left there for Galilee. **44/** For Jesus himself testified that a prophet has no honor in his own country. **45/** So when he came to Galilee, the Galileans welcomed him, having seen all that he had done in Jerusalem at the feast, for they too had gone to the feast. **46/** So he came again to Cana in Galilee, where he had made the water wine. And at Capernaum there was an official whose son was ill. **47/** When he heard that Jesus had come from Judea to Galilee, he went and begged him to come down and heal his son, for he was at the point of death. **48/** Jesus therefore said to him, "Unless you see signs and wonders you will not believe." **49/** The official said to him, "Sir, come down before my child dies." **50/** Jesus said to him, "Go; your son is well." The man believed the word that Jesus spoke to him and went his way. **51/** As he was going down, his servants met him and told him that his son was living. **52/** So he asked them the hour when he began to mend, and they said to him, "Yesterday at the seventh hour the fever left him." 53/ The father knew that was the hour when Jesus had said to him, "Your son is well"; and he himself believed, and all his household. 54/ This was now the second sign that Jesus did when he had come from Judea to Galilee.

Verses 43–45 form a transition created by the Evangelist. He does not permit the second Cana miracle to follow immediately upon the first; verses 46–54 are concerned with the healing and with faith, and there are traces of a polemic against another kind of faith and tradition. Whether the situation was different in a source and whether that source consisted entirely of "signs" is another question.

■ 43 "After the two days" resumes verse 40. Following "thence" ℵ Θ insert "and went to" to smooth the construction ("After two days he departed thence [and went to] Galilee"). But 4:3 is also resumed here following the Samaritan intermezzo.

■ 44 Verse 44 provides a Johannine form of the saying of an itinerant sage in Mark 6:4 pars.: "A prophet is without honor only in his own country etc." The "own country" (ἰδία [in spite of 1:11 unemphatic] πατρίς) is not Judea or Jerusalem,[1] but Galilee (see on 1:46 and 7:41f.). The Evangelist has in mind that Jesus has found genuine faith in alien Samaria in contrast to the faith depending solely on signs that he found in Jerusalem (2:23), in which, of course, the Galileans also participate (v 45).

■ 45 Verse 45 refers to the many signs—they are mentioned in 2:23 (cf. 7:31, 12:37) but not described—that the Galilean pilgrims had witnessed. This poses the question: do these many miracles belong to the same tradition as the two Cana miracles reported in detail? The question is subsequently further complicated by the healing of the lame man in Jerusalem in chapter 5, which appears to be a singular event (7:21). The Overview will have to go into these matters.

■ 46 Verse 46 expressly refers to 2:1–11. The story of the believing centurion from Capernaum, which Matt 8:5–13 and Luke 7:1–10 locate in Capernaum, reads very differently here. In place of the centurion, a "royal"

officer or government administrator appears, and it is uncertain whether he is in the service of "King" Herod Antipas. It becomes even less apparent that he is a pagan with an unusually strong, exemplary faith in Jesus' power; here the Johannine account diverges most acutely from the synoptic tradition.

The reading βασιλίσκος, which can mean the "petty king," found in D a bo, probably originated with a back translation of the Latin word regulus, which was then rendered as βασιλίσκος.

■ 47 This man is indeed stationed in Capernaum, as in the Synoptics. But when he hears that Jesus is again sojourning in Galilee, he comes to Cana and asks Jesus to heal his son. With that is given the necessity of healing at a distance. Ἐρωτᾶν in the sense of "ask, request" is not "incorrect" but hellenistic usage. The supposition that Luke 7:3 lies behind this passage thus becomes superfluous. John is independent of the Synoptics here also. If John has actually made use of Luke, the almost total divergence from the Lukan account would become completely incomprehensible.

■ 48 Verse 48 is surprising. The man had not made his faith in Jesus dependent upon getting to see Jesus perform a miracle first. Rather, he believes that Jesus can heal at a distance. The Gospel of John only uses the Old Testament "signs and wonders" (LXX in Exod 7:3, Deut 4:34, Isa 8:18, 20:3, Jer 39:20, Wis 8:8, 10:16) at this point. The Evangelist has inserted verses 48f. only in order to express his own understanding of the traditional story by chiding faith based on miracle. Beyond that, he manifests here his peculiar intermediate position between Paul on the one hand and the synoptic tradition on the other: according to Paul (Phil 2:6ff.), in his incarnation the son of God divested himself of his divine powers so that none of the demonic rulers of this age

---

1   As many exegetes from Schwegler to Barrett (*John*, 246) and Tasker (*John*, 83) conceive it.

recognized him (1 Cor 2:8); according to Mark, it is precisely the demons who recognize Jesus in his true status and are made dumb by his powerful words. These miracles legitimate Jesus. John teaches the incarnation of the logos, but understands the miracles, of which he relates seven in detail, only as pointers to something entirely different (Jesus the light of the world, the way to the Father, etc.); he does not understand them as credentials to be discovered by every man.

■ **49** Verse 49 is necessary to restore the connection to the underlying story. It is not the most satisfactory style to repeat the request of the father, but it was the shortest way. The word παιδίον does not prove that the story has to do with a "little boy, lad," as Zahn believes;[2] diminutives are favored in Koine, although there is scarcely a trace of their diminutive sense. For παιδίον א substitutes παῖδα ("servant"), following Matthew, while A φ retain the υἱὸς ("son") of verse 47. The struggle in the tradition over whether it had to do with a servant or a son is decided decisively in the Gospel of John in favor of "son." Originally the story concerned a sick servant of the centurion.[3] Thus, Luke is correct in 7:2 with his "a servant . . . who was dear to him" (δοῦλος . . . ὅς ἦν αὐτῷ ἔντιμος).

■ **50** Jesus now fulfills the request of the official with the word: "Go; your son is well" (ζῆν is found in this sense in the LXX and corresponds to Hebrew היה). The man believes the word of Jesus and departs for Capernaum, which was 33 km away. Hirsch is of the opinion that the narrator understood Matt 8:7ff. as a successful test of faith for the father: "This man, although rebuffed, is able to recognize the powerful and true word that demands trusting obedience."[4] But verse 49 fulfills the request; it is not "a harsh rejection," and the text of Matthew, which was not used by John, is not a rebuff.[5] Joüon meets the difficulty in having the man reach Capernaum on the same day—in view of "yesterday" in verse 52—by pointing out that the Jewish day begins with sunset.[6]

■ **51** The genetive absolute alongside αὐτῷ (dative) is a grammatical flaw of the common language. The news of the servants coming to meet him—in Matthew 8:9 it is soldiers—proves that Jesus' promise has been fulfilled. The same phrasing from verse 50 is purposely used here ("Your son is well") (D Θ 𝔎 33 sy quote literally ὁ υἱός [σου], "your son"). Thus on his way home the father receives the good news.

■ **52** When the man inquires at what hour his son took a turn for the better, he learns that it was about the seventh hour (1:00 P.M.) that the fever left him. The inquiry about the hour is the most precise time designation that was possible at that time.

■ **53** The answer of the servants shows the father that the word of Jesus was instantly effective. The parallel from *Ber.* 34b is striking:[7] When a son of Rabbi Gamaliel II (ca. 90 CE) got sick, the father sent two men of learning to Rabbi Chanina ben Dosa to beg for mercy from God. After praying, Rabbi Chanina sent the two petitioners back with the message: "Go, the fever has left him." The messengers took note of the time and returned. In response to this news Rabbi Gamaliel said: "That's just the way it happened; in that moment the fever left him." It is improbable that the rabbinic tradition is dependent upon John. With the confirmation of the miracle, the man and his entire "house"—family and servants—believed. The Evangelist understands the tradition thus: in the first place, the man only believed that Jesus would heal his son. Then, the second, enhanced statement about belief betokens the beginning of true faith in Jesus as the dispenser of eternal life. The Evangelist repeatedly uses the word ζῆν, "to be well, live," yet he permits the reader to recognize the deeper significance it has for the Evangelist himself: "I am the resurrection and the life" (11:25). In the source 4:53 corresponds to the statement in 2:11.

■ **54** The miracle is here reckoned as the second (without reference to the many miracles mentioned in 2:23). Πάλιν δεύτερον ("again, a second") is a colloquial form of

---

2 *Das Evangelium des Johannes,* 270.
3 Brown (*John,* 1: 193) interprets differently.
4 *Das vierte Evangelium,* 154.
5 Cf. Schnackenburg, *John,* 1: 471f. n. 30; Haenchen, *Der Weg Jesu,* 97.
6 "Notes philologiques sur les évangiles," *RSR* 18 (1928) 358.
7 Billerbeck, 2: 441; D. R. Cartlidge and D. L. Dun-gan, *Documents for the Study of the Gospels* (Cleveland: Collins, 1980) 158.

the expression; we meet it again in 21:16 and it does not indicate a reworking.

Overview

The second miracle performed in Cana, like the first, is not provided with commentary in the form of a discourse. The discourses of Jesus attached to miracles are directed to the "Jews" (᾿Ιουδαῖοι); they are not present here, just as they were not present at the wedding. That is not to say that these two miracles are not "signs" in the Johannine sense; they are presented here expressly in their character as signs. Further, this story is related to the account of the wedding in Cana in 2:11—referred to as the beginning of the signs—by virtue of the fact that Jesus is now at the middle point of his action. That probably indicates the essence of the "source" utilized by John: it reports miracles of Jesus that reveal and demonstrate that he is the son of God.

The relationship of this pericope to the story in Matt 8:5–13//Luke 7:1–10 shows how widely a narrative may vary, not only through the redactional work of an evangelist, but also in the oral tradition.[8] It can be safely said that the story of the "royal official" and that of the centurion from Capernaum go back to the same event. Catholic exegetes, as recently as Mollat[9] and Braun,[10] and the older Protestant exegetes[11] have not progressed beyond observing the "considerable differences" between the two stories. Of course, there is no reason to view the Johannine story as a free recasting of the Synoptic.[12] Bultmann has also incorrectly concluded that verses 48f. have displaced a synoptic dialogue and John has inserted the healing at a distance.[13] The clumsiness in style with which the Evangelist gives his own meaning to the story, except for verses 48f., demonstrates rather that he took the story over without alteration. An insertion in the

context such as we have here is possible only when the context is already fixed. It is precisely the way in which John treats the story here that proves that this is not the first time the Evangelist has brought the flow of the oral tradition to a halt. The pericope of the royal official, as we now read it at the hands of John, is comprehensible only on the presupposition that a fixed text was already familiar to the Evangelist. This story has thus not only undergone a considerable development before it reached the Evangelist, but it has also achieved a firm form that he did not disturb. But he no doubt took the liberty to interpret what had been transmitted to him at a new and deeper level. To be sure he did not always do this by the insertion of a verse as he does here. Such instances are relatively rare. As a rule, he interprets the gospel tradition by means of Jesus' discourses, which he either appends, or, in the case of the passion, prefixes.

The differences between this story and the synoptic parallels are admittedly large: now only the royal official's son, who is seriously ill, is found in Capernaum; the official himself comes to Jesus in Cana. There is no mention of the fact that he is a heathen. His famous expression of faith has also disappeared, and it is this expression that forms the focal point of the synoptic accounts. Precisely for this reason the tradition has undergone modification: it is no longer human behavior that is in focus—be it ever so exemplary—but a miraculous deed of Jesus: it is a second sign. But it then becomes a matter of indifference whether it is a Jew or a heathen who turns to Jesus; the form of the story that the Evangelist has taken over is more important: a healing at a distance unequivocally demonstrates the power of Jesus. In any case, it is precisely this element of the miraculous demonstration in the story of Rabbi Chanina (see above on verse 52) that constitutes an astonishing parallel, and

---

8   On which see Haenchen, "Johanneische Probleme," 82–90, where the matter is discussed in detail.

9   *Le quatriéme évangile,* 89.

10 *La Sainte Bible,* 350; a change cannot be detected until Schnackenburg (*John,* 1: 195), and Brown (*John,* 1: 193), who is even clearer.

11 Beyschlag, Hengstenberg, Godet, *John,* 204, and Zahn, *Das Evangelium des Johannes,* 273: ". . . On the basis of certain superficial similarities, it has wantonly been decided that John has formed his narrative 'out of the Synoptic' for want of a creative impulse of his own."

12 So, for example, Hirsch, *Das vierte Evangelium,* 154, and Strathmann, *Das Evangelium nach Johannes,* 93: "One is . . . compelled to take the view that John reworked the report of the same event to suit his purposes most effectively."

13 *John,* 206 [152].

it is also here that the healing at a distance is combined with the control of a specific time reference. It is possible that a Jewish motif has influenced the tradition here; that Schnackenburg finds my analysis of the Lukan parallel "not completely convincing"[14] is distressing.

The tradition taken over here by John attempts to bear immediate witness once again, through this miracle, to the majesty and power of Jesus. The Evangelist, however, wants the reader to know, by means of verses 48f., what is to be retained as Christian from such faith in miracles. The royal official does not request a miracle, of course, because he is not otherwise prepared for faith in Jesus. He simply requests that his son recover. For the Evangelist, this is, of course, only a modification—even if an astonishing one—in earthly relationships, but does not alter the relationship of man to God. If one believes that Jesus can preserve earthly life, one has still not grasped the notion that he is able to give true life, life out of and in God.

As the Evangelist understands the tradition, the petitioner in fact only believes, in the first instance, that Jesus will make his son well. He comes to true faith, however, when the exact minute of the miracle is confirmed: this the Evangelist finds described in the final statement of the story: "And he himself believed, and all his household." There thereby transpires exactly what Jesus had predicted in verse 48: the father first believed that he saw "signs and wonders." The authentic Christian example is, however, described in 20:29, in Jesus' words to Thomas: "Blessed are those who have not seen and yet believe."

This pericope also makes it necessary to call Käsemann's interpretation of the Fourth Gospel, in *The Testament of Jesus,* into question. The opening statement, unaltered in all three editions, takes courage: "I would like to begin this study with the unusual confession that I shall be discussing a subject which, in the last analysis, I do not understand."[15] We would like to pose the same question that Käsemann directs to his readers: "In what sense is he flesh, who walks on the water and through closed doors, who cannot be captured by his enemies, who at the well of Samaria is tired and desires a drink, yet has no need of drink and has food different from that which his disciples seek?"[16] When carefully considered, the texts to which allusion is here being made already help us to answer these questions (for the texts that Käsemann lists are actually very different), of which we have cited only the first. The story of Jesus walking on the water is told not only in John 6:16–21, but also—in slightly different form, to be sure—in Mark 6:45–52 and Matt 14:22–33. The early congregation found it said in their sacred book of the Lord: he walks over the sea like he is walking on firm ground, and, in accordance with their way of doing exegesis, they made this refer to Jesus. How little inclined they were to deny walking on the water to humankind as such is shown by the variants in Matthew: Peter is also permitted to walk on the waves—to the extent that his faith allows. In short, not everything that Käsemann attributes to the Johannine Christ is specifically Johannine; neither is the Christ's practice of walking through closed doors attributed to him prior to his resurrection. One must handle the evangelists circumspectly and must not jumble their statements.

Käsemann does concede, in view of chapter 21, that a redactor, too, has attempted to complete and correct the Fourth Gospel. But if one reflects closely on the Gospel of John, it becomes evident that the situation is not as simple as Käsemann is prepared to accept: the pericope presently being analyzed shows, for example, that the Evangelist took over traditions that he could fit into his own scheme only with difficulty, as modern research has shown to be the case at numerous points in the Gospel. The Evangelist was only able to make use of the story of Thomas by providing in the last verse what was for him an indispensable theological correction.

It becomes evident in chapter 5 that the redactor has added a futuristic eschatology at two important points in order to "improve" the text. At the very least there are actually three hands that one can distinguish in the Gospel of John: a "gospel of miracles," whose $\sigma\eta\mu\epsilon\hat{\iota}\alpha$ the Evangelist takes up as signs that point to an entirely different dimension of God. The Evangelist has taken over considerable material from this source. But neither is the redactor confined to chapter 21. If one does not distinguish all three "evangelists," it is not surprising that everything remains incomprehensible.

---

14 *John,* 1: 275 n. 37.

15 *The Testament of Jesus,* 1.

16 *The Testament of Jesus,* 9.

By way of summary, what Gardner-Smith[17] and others have affirmed may be repeated: Points of contact with the Synoptic Gospels are few and concern only certain motifs. Of longer verbal parallels there are none. Often only the isolated word or phrase is reminiscent of the Synoptics. These conclusions do not point to the use of the Synoptic Gospels, but to the utilization of a tradition that has points of contact with the tradition taken up by the Synoptics. In these cases, the Gospel of John exhibits the later, often already obviously "hackneyed" form.

As a consequence, the props have been pulled out from under the earlier view, taken as obvious, that the Gospel of John "made use of" the Synoptics or at least part of them. The concept of an author appears to have played a role in this popular assumption: the author had the works of his predecessors at least in his head, perhaps even on his desk. But the Gospel of John certainly did not know the Synoptics. He did not intend to supplement them, to improve them, or to replace them.

There is nothing to be said in favor of the view that he was the first to crystalize the flow of oral tradition. The Gospel of John rather presupposes a tradition that has already become fixed, indeed, already "hackneyed." The apologetic consequences thereby disappear: as "first" Evangelist he may be as early as Mark and of the highest historical worth. His tradition, like his theological message, exhibit clear traces of progressive development. The Fourth Gospel is no doubt a mature work, but it is no early harvest hothouse plant.

---

17 *Saint John and the Synoptic Gospels* (Cambridge: Cambridge University Press, 1938).

13. The Miracle at the Pool

Bibliography

A. On 5:1–30

Abelson
  The Immanence of God in Rabbinical Literature
  (London, 1912), esp. on John 5:17ff.
Bacchiocchi, Samuele
  "John 5:17: Negation or Clarification of the
  Sabbath?" *AUSS* 19 (1981) 3–19.
Benoit, Pierre
  "Découvertes archéologiques autour de la piscine
  de Béthesda." In *Jerusalem through the Ages,* ed. P.
  W. Lapp (Jerusalem: Israel Exploration Society,
  1968) 48–57.
Bernard, Jacques
  "La guérsion de Bethesda. Harmoniques judéo-
  hellénistiques d'un récit de miracle un jour de
  sabbat (suite et fin)." *MScRel* 33 (1976) 3–34.
Bernard, Jacques
  "Jean V et le Jésus de l'histoire." Dissertation,
  Université de Lille III, 1978.
Bertling, D.
  "Eine Transposition im Evangelium Johannis."
  TSK 53 (1880) 351–53.
Bligh, John
  "Jesus in Jerusalem [Jn 5]." *HeyJ* 4 (1963) 115–34.
Boismard, Marie-Emile
  "L'évolution du thème eschatologique dans les
  traditions johanniques." *RB* 68 (1961) 507–24,
  esp. 514–18.
Bowman, John
  "The Identity and Date of the Unnamed Feast of
  John 5,1." In *Near Eastern Studies in Honor of
  William Foxwell Albright,* ed. Hans Goedicke
  (Baltimore: Johns Hopkins University Press, 1971)
  43–56.
Bröse, Ernst
  "Noch einmal: der Teich Bethesda." *TSK* 76
  (1903) 153–56.
Buse, Ivor
  "John v, 8 and the Johannine-Marcan Relation-
  ship." *NTS* 1 (1954/1955) 134–36.
Bussche, Henri van den
  "Guérison d'un paralytique à Jerusalem le jour du
  sabbat. Jean 5, 1–18." *BVC* 61 (1965) 18–28.
Chazel
  "Essai d'interpretation de jean v,26–30." *Revue de
  théologie et de questions religieuses* 2 (1893) 199–210,
  295–305.
Cullmann, Oscar
  "Sabbat und Sonntag nach dem Johannesevan-
  gelium: Joh 5,17." In his *Vorträge und Aufsätze
  1925–1962,* ed. K. Fröhlich (Tübingen: Mohr-
  Siebeck; Zurich: Zwingli Verlag, 1966) 187–91.

Dodd, Charles Harold
"Une parabole cachée dans le quatrième Evangile [Jn 5:20a]." *RHPR* 42 (1962) 107–15. In his *More New Testament Studies.* (Grand Rapids: Wm. B. Eerdmans, 1968) 30–40.

Dodd, Charles Harold
"John 5,19–35 in Christian History and Interpretation." In *Christian History and Interpretation: Studies Presented to John Knox,* ed. W. R. Farmer, C. F. D. Moule, and R. R. Niebuhr (Cambridge: Cambridge University Press, 1967) 183–98.

Dodd, Charles Harold
"Notes from Papyri: Joh 5,5." *JTS* 26 (1924/1925) 77–78.

Duprez, A.
Jésus et les dieux guérisseurs. A propos de Jean V, Cahiers de la Revue Biblique 12 (Paris: J. Gabalda, 1970).

Eltester, Walther
Eikon im Neuen Testament, BZNW 23 (Berlin: A. Töpelmann, 1958).

Ferraro, Giuseppe
"Il senso di *heos arti* nel testo di Gv 5,17." *RivB* 20 (1972) 529–45.

Fitch, W. O.
"The Interpretation of St. John 5,6." *SE* 4 = TU 102 (Berlin: Akademie-Verlag, 1968) 194–97.

Gaechter, Paul
"Zur Form von Joh 5,19–30." In *Neutestamentliche Aufsätze. Festschrift für Prof. Josef Schmid zum 70. Geburtstag,* ed. J. Blinzler, O. Kuss, F. Mussner (Regensburg: F. Pustet, 1963) 65–68.

Gaffron, Hans-Georg
"Studien zum koptischen Philippusevangelium unter besonderer Berücksichtigung der Sakramente." Dissertation, Bonn, 1969.

Gryglewicz, Feliks
"Die Aussagen Jesu und ihre Rolle in Joh 5,16–30." *Studien zum Neuen Testament und seiner Umwelt* 5 (1980) 5–17.

Haenchen, Ernst
"Johanneische Probleme." *ZTK* 56 (1959) 19–54; Also in his *Gott und Mensch. Gesammelte Aufsätze* 1 (Tübingen: Mohr-Siebeck, 1965), esp. 105–9.

Haenchen, Ernst
"Literatur zum Codex Jung." *TRu* 30 (1964) 39–82.

Jeremias, Joachim
The Rediscovery of Bethesda; John 5:2, New Testament Archaeology 1 (Louisville, KY: Southern Baptist Theological Seminary, 1966) = *Die Wiederentdeckung von Bethesda, Joh 5,2.* FRLANT, n.s., 41 (Göttingen: Vandenhoeck & Ruprecht, 1949).

Jeremias, Joachim
"Die Bedeutung des Fundes vom Toten Meer (3 Q 15 bestätigt Jo 5,2)." *Informationsblatt für die Gemeinden der niederdeutschen lutherischen Landeskirchen* 9 (1960) 193–94.

Jeremias, Joachim
"Die Kupferrolle von Qumran und Bethesda." In his *Abba. Studien zur neutestamentlichen Theologie und Zeitgeschichte* (Göttingen: Vandenhoeck & Ruprecht, 1966) 361–64.

Jervell, Jacob
Imago Dei. Gen 1,26f. im Spätjudentum, in der Gnosis und in den Paulinischen Briefen, FRLANT, n.s., 58 (Göttingen: Vandenhoeck & Ruprecht, 1960), esp. 132–70.

Johnson, Daniel B.
"A Neglected Variant in Gregory 33 (John v,8)." *NTS* 18 (1971/1972) 231–32.

Langbrandtner, Wolfgang
Weltferner Gott oder Gott der Liebe. Der Ketzerstreit in der johanneischen kirche. Eine exegetisch- religionsgeschichtliche Untersuchung mit Berücksichtigung der koptisch-gnostischen Texte aus Nag-Hammadi, Beiträge zur biblischen Exegese und Theologie 6 (Frankfurt: P. Lang, 1977), esp. 11–14.

Lohse, Eduard
"Jesu Worte über den Sabbat." In his *Die Einheit des Neuen Testaments. Exegetische Studien zur Theologie des Neuen Testaments* (Göttingen: Vandenhoeck & Ruprecht, 1973) 62–72.

Malinine, M. et al., eds.
De resurrectione. Codex Jung. (Zurich and Stuttgart: Rascher Verlag, 1963), esp. 28f, 43–50.

Maurer, Christian
"Steckt hinter Joh 5,17 ein Übersetzungsfehler?" *Wort und Dienst,* n.f., 5 (1957) 130–40.

Moreton, M. J.
"Feast, Sign and Discourse in Joh 5." *SE* 4 = TU 102 (Berlin: Akademie-Verlag, 1968) 209–13.

Norris, J. P.
"On the Chronology of St. John V. and VI." *The Journal of Philology* 3 (1871) 107–12.

Pronobis, C.
"Bethesda zur Zeit Jesu." *TQ* 114 (1933) 181–207.

Sell, Jesse
"A Note on a striking Johannine Motif found at CG VI:6, 19." *NovT* 20 (1978) 232–40.

Sundberg, Albert C.
"*Isos tō Theō*: Christology in John 5.17–30." *BR* 15 (1970) 19–31.

Thompson, J. M.
"Accidental Disarrangement in the Fourth Gospel." *Expositor,* 8th ser., 17 (1919) 47–54.

Vanhoye, Albert
"La composition de Jn 5,19–30." In *Mélanges bibliques en hommage au R. P. Béda Rigaux,* ed. A. Descamps and A. de Halleux (Gembloux: Duculot, 1970) 259–74.

Vardaman, E. J.
"The Pool of Bethesda." *BR* 14 (1963) 27–29.

Wieand, David J.
"John v. 2 and the Pool of Bethesda." *NTS* 12 (1966) 392–404.

B. On Johannine Eschatology

Aebert, B.
"Die Eschatologie des Johannesevangeliums."
Dissertation (Breslau: Teildruck Würzburg, 1936).

Barrett, Charles Kingsley
"Unsolved New Testament Problems—The Place
of Eschatology in the Fourth Gospel." *ExpTim* 59
(1947/1948) 302–5.

Beasley-Murray, George R.
"The Eschatology of the Fourth Gospel." *EvQ* 18
(1946) 97–108.

Beck, M. M.
*Die Ewigkeit hat schon begonnen. Perspektiven johan-
neischer Weltschau* (Frankfurt: Verlag Josef Knecht,
1965).

Blank, Josef
*Krisis. Untersuchungen zur johanneischen Christologie
und Eschatologie* (Freiburg: Lambertus-Verlag,
1964).

Blank, Josef
"Die Gegenwartseschatologie des Johannes-
evangeliums." In *Vom Messias zum Christus. Die Fülle
der Zeit in religionsgeschichtlicher und theologischer
Sicht,* ed. K. Schubert (Vienna: Herder, 1964)
279–313.

Boismard, Marie-Emile
"L'évolution du thème eschatologique dans les
traditions johanniques." *RB* 68 (1961) 507–24.

Bultmann, Rudolf
"Die Eschatologie des Johannes-Evangelium."
Zwischen den Zeiten 6 (1928) 4–22.

Cassien, Bishop
"Kirche oder Reich Gottes? Zur johanneischen
Eschatologie." In *Extremis* 6–8 (1939) 186–202.

Collins, Adela Yarbro
"Crisis and Community in the Gospel of John."
CurTM 7 (1980) 196–204.

Corell, Alf
*Consummatum est. Eschatology and Church in the
Gospel of St. John* (London: S. P. C. K., 1958; New
York: Macmillan, 1959).

Dodd, Charles Harold
"The Epistle of John and the Fourth Gospel." *BJRL*
21 (1937) 129–56, esp. 142–44.

Grimm, Carl Ludwig Wilibald
"Ueber den ersten Brief des Johannes und sein
Verhältniß zum vierten Evangelium." *TSK* 22
(1849) 269–303, ep. 287–89.

Groos, Dr.
"Der Begriff der κρίσις bei Johannes, exegetisch
entwickelt, ein Beitrag zur neutestamentlichen
Lehre vom Gericht." *TSK* 41 (1868) 244–73.

Hilgenfeld, Adolf
"Die johanneische Theologie und ihre neueste
Bearbeitung." *ZWT* 6 (1863) 214–28, esp. 223–28.

Holwerda, David Earl
*The Holy Spirit and Eschatology in the Gospel of John; A
Critique of Rudolf Bultmann's Present Eschatology*
(Kampen: Kok, 1959).

Kittel, Rudolf
"Zur Eschatologie des Johannesevangelium."
Deutsches Pfarrerblatt 65 (1965) 716–20.

Köstlin, Karl Reinhold
*Der Lehrbegriff des Evangeliums und der Briefe
Johannis* (Berlin: G. Bethge, 1853), esp. 278–83.

Kümmel, Werner Georg
"Die Eschatologie der Evangelien. Ihre Geschichte
und ihr Sinn." *Theologische Bücherei* 5 (1936) 225–
41.

Kysar, Robert
"The Eschatology of the Fourth Gospel—A
Correction of Bultmann's Hypothesis." *Perspective*
13 (1972) 23–33.

Linton, Olaf
"Johannesevangeliet og eskatologien." *SEÅ* 22–23
(1957/1958) 98–110.

Martin, J. P.
"History and Eschatology in the Lazarus Narrative,
John 11.1–44." *SJT* 17 (1964) 332–43.

Meyer, Paul W.
"The Eschatology of the Fourth Gospel." Dissertation, Union Theological Seminary, 1955.

Moule, C. F. D.
"A Neglected Factor in the Interpretation of
Johannine Eschatology." In *Studies in John Presented
to Professor J. N. Sevenster on the Occasion of his
Seventieth Birthday* (Leiden: E. J. Brill, 1970) 155–
60.

Pancaro, Severino
"A Statistical Approach to the Concept of Time
and Eschatology in the Fourth Gospel." *Bib* 50
(1969) 511–24.

Ricca, P.
Die Eschatologie des Vierten Evangeliums (Zurich and
Frankfurt: Gotthelf-Verlag, 1966).

Richter, Georg
"Präsentische und futurische Eschatologie im
vierten Evangelium." In *Jesus und der Menschensohn.
Für Anton Vögtle,* ed. R. Pesch and R. Schnacken-
burg (Freiburg: Herder, 1975) 117–52. In his
Studien zum Johannesevangelium, ed. Josef Hainz.
BU 13 (Regensburg: F. Pustet, 1977) 346–82.

Stählin, Gustav
"Zum Problem der johanneischen Eschatologie."
ZNW 33 (1934) 225–59.

Stauffer, Ethelbert
"Agnostos Christos. Joh 2,24 und die Eschatologie
des vierten Evangeliums." In *The Background of the
New Testament and its Eschatology* [in honor of
Charles Harold Dodd], ed. W. D. Davies and D.
Daube (Cambridge: Cambridge University Press,
1956) 281–99.

Summers, Ray
"The Johannine View of the Future Life." *RevExp*
58 (1961) 331–47.

Thompson, J. D.
"An Analysis of Present and Future in the Eschatology of the Fourth Gospel." Dissertation, Emory University, 1967.

Turner, William
"Believing and Everlasting Life—A Johannine Inquiry." *ExpTim* 64 (1952/1953) 50–52.

Wanke, Joachim
"Die Zukunft des Glaubenden. Theologische Erwägungen zur johanneischen Eschatologie." *Theologie und Glauben* 71 (1981) 129–39.

Watts, D. J.
"Eschatology in the Johannine Community. A Study of Diversity." Dissertation, Edinburgh, 1980.

Weiß, Josef
Die Predigt Jesu vom Reiche Gottes, ed. F. Hahn (Göttingen: Vandenhoeck & Ruprecht, ³1964), esp. 60–65.

5

1 After this there was a feast of the Jews, and Jesus went up to Jerusalem. 2/ Now there is in Jerusalem by the sheep (gate) a pool, in Hebrew called "Bethzatha," which has five porticoes. 3/ In these lay a multitude of invalids, blind, lame, paralyzed (lame, who waited on the stirring of the waters. 4/ For from time to time an angel of the Lord would come down to the pool and stir up the waters. Whoever got into the pool first after the troubling of the waters was cured of whatever sickness he had.) 5/ One man was there, who had been ill for thirty-eight years. 6/ When Jesus saw him and knew that he had been lying there a long time, he said to him, "Do you want to be healed?" 7/ The sick man answered him, "Sir, I have no man to put me into the pool when the water is troubled, and while I am going another steps down before me." 8/ Jesus said to him, "Rise, take up your pallet, and walk." 9/ And at once the man was healed, and he took up his pallet and walked.

Now that day was the sabbath. 10/ So the Jews said to the man who was cured, "It is the sabbath, it is not lawful for you to carry your pallet." 11/ But he answered them, "The man who healed me said to me, 'Take up your pallet, and walk.'" 12/ They asked him, "Who is the man who said to you, 'Take up your pallet, and walk'?" 13/ Now the man who had been healed did not know who it was, for Jesus had withdrawn (unnoticed), as there was a crowd in the place.

Afterward, Jesus found him in the temple, and said to him, "See, you are well   Sin no more, that nothing (still) worse befall you." 15/ The man went away and told the Jews that it was Jesus who had healed him. 16/ And this was why the Jews persecuted Jesus, because he did this on the sabbath. 17/ But Jesus answered them, "My Father is working still, and I am working." 18/ This was why the Jews sought all the more to kill him, because he not only broke the sabbath but also called God his Father,

making himself equal with God.
19/ Jesus said to them, "Truly, truly, I say
to you, the Son can do nothing of his own
accord, but only what he sees the Father
doing; for whatever he does, that the Son
does likewise. 20/ For the Father loves
the Son, and shows him all that he himself is doing; and greater works than
these will he show him, that you may
marvel. 21/ For as the Father raises the
dead and gives them life, so also the Son
gives life to whom he will. 22/ The Father
judges no one, but has given all judgment
to the Son, 23/ that all may honor the
Son, even as they honor the Father. He
who does not honor the Son does not
honor the Father who sent him. 24/
Truly, truly, I say to you, he who hears my
word and believes him who sent me, has
eternal life; he does not come into judgment, but has passed from death to life.
25/ Truly, truly, I say to you, the hour is
coming, and now is, when the dead will
hear the voice of the Son of God, and
those who hear will live. 26/ For as the
Father has life in himself, so he has
granted the Son also to have life in himself, 27/ and has given him authority to
execute judgment, because he is the Son
of man. 28/ Do not marvel at this; for the
hour is coming when all who are in tombs
will hear his voice 29/ and come forth,
those who have done good, to the resurrection of life, and those who have done
evil, to the resurrection of judgment."
30/ "I can do nothing on my own authority;
as I hear, I judge; and my judgment is
just, because I seek not my own will but
the will of him who sent me."

■ 1 "After these things" ($\mu\epsilon\tau\grave{\alpha}\ \tau\alpha\hat{v}\tau\alpha$) again introduces a new section (see above on 2:12). $\mathfrak{P}^{66}$, $\mathfrak{P}^{75}$, A B D W *pm* read "feast" ($\acute{\epsilon}o\rho\tau\acute{\eta}$) without the article, while ℵ C ℜ place an article before the word. They presumably imply the Passover, as do many exegetes, and as do Tatian[1] and Irenaeus.[2] Bernard[3] and Strathman[4] decide in favor of Tabernacles. Braun[5] among others supports the Feast of Pentecost, while Weiss[6] takes it to refer to the Feast of Purim, as do many of his predecessors.

But the feast is mentioned only in order to get Jesus to Jerusalem for the purpose of making an important

speech. The "Johannine festival pilgrimages" are only a literary medium (with the exception of the last), without historical or chronological value. Jesus must go up to Jerusalem because for the narrator "the Jews" live there (1:19, 2:13, 5:1, 7:14, 9:13, 10:22, 11:18f., 55). They are the representatives of the "world" and enemies of Christ and Christians (9:22, 34). The healing story which follows is assigned by Bultmann[7] and Fortna[8] to the "Signs Source," in which this was originally the seventh and last miracle, according to Fortna. In any case, it was already set in Jerusalem in the tradition utilized by the

1   Cf. Zahn, *Geschichte des neutestamentlichen Kanons* 2
     (Leipzig: A. Deichert, 1890–1892) 544f., 555.
2   *Adv. haer.* 2.22.3.
3   *John*, 1: 226.
4   *Das Evangelium nach Johannes*, 94.
5   *La Sainte Bible*, 351.
6   *Das Johannes-Evangelium*, 193.
7   *John*, 238 n. 1 [177 n. 4].
8   *Gospel of Signs*, 48–54, 107f.

Evangelist. Bultmann places 5:1–47 after 6:1–71.[9]

■ **2** Verse 2 contains several difficulties. (1) The present tense of the verb to be ($\check{\epsilon}\sigma\tau\iota\nu$) appears to convey the idea that the structure mentioned in what follows was still standing at the time the source was composed. But it is doubtful that at that time one knew of the five porticoes, four of which enclosed the double pool, and the fifth of which stood between them. The text only refers to one pool. The excavations of the White Fathers show that there were two pools, a smaller one on the north and a larger one on the south, divided by a rock partition 6.5 meters wide. On top of this stood the fifth portico.[10] Josephus mentions neither the pool nor the porticoes, but only the northerly suburb of Bezetha. He reports that the Syrian Legate Cestius burned this town in his attack on Jerusalem in October 68.[11] Further, he reports that the Romans razed not only the greater part of the first wall but also the north suburb in May of 70, which had been "previously destroyed by Cestius."[12]

(2) The construction in verse 2 is disputed (the Gospels were originally written without accents, iota subscripts, and word division). Jeremias translates:[13] "There is in Jerusalem by the Sheep Pool a place called Bethesda in Aramaic that has five porticoes . . ." The difficulty thereby arises that there is no antecedent for "the one called" ($\dot{\eta}\,\dot{\epsilon}\pi\iota\lambda\epsilon\gamma o\mu\acute{\epsilon}\nu\eta$). The antecedent "town" must then be supplied. Bauer[14] and Bultmann,[15] among others, advocate another construction. They take $\kappa o\lambda\upsilon\mu\beta\acute{\eta}\theta\rho\alpha$ ("pool") as a nominative and supply the word $\pi\acute{\upsilon}\lambda\eta$ ("gate") to go with $\pi\rho o\beta\alpha\tau\iota\kappa\hat{\eta}$ ("sheep"). The result is: "There is in Jerusalem by the Sheep Gate[16] a pool called Bethseda in Aramaic with five porticoes." Jeremias objects that a pool could not have been called a "house" (in Hebrew *beth*). But the Evangelist takes the Hebrew name Bethesda (whose components he did not under-

stand) to refer to the entire complex: the pool with the five porticoes. Origen writes in his commentary on John: "In Jerusalem by the Sheep Gate is a pool . . . For this reason He (Jesus) goes to the pool by the Sheep Gate . . ."[17] and exegetes the passage with the second meaning given above in view. On the other hand, exegetes since Eusebius have understood the text in the sense of the first possibility given above. It then becomes necessary to explain the name "Sheep Pool." Origen had already mentioned that the water in the pool was regarded as having healing powers in his time because the viscera of the lambs (offered to God) were thrown into the pool.[18] Pilgrims who later went to the Holy Land report other legends regarding the "Sheep Pool."[19]

(3) The final difficulty is occasioned by the various forms of the "Hebrew" name in verse 2. The diverse forms in the manuscripts presuppose an original "Bezetha."[20] That might be an old reference to the "fosse" that separates that part of the city from the tower of Antonia.[21] From that the northern suburb of Jerusalem probably received its name, which exhibits a similar array of variants in the manuscripts of Josephus (*BJ* 2.328, 530, 5.149–151), as it does in John 5:2.

■ **3** Verse 3 was subsequently expanded and elucidated in a variety of ways (early form: $\mathfrak{P}^{66}$, $\mathfrak{P}^{75}$, $\mathfrak{H}$ A* q sy[c] sa). A Θ Ψ 063 078 have further increased the number of sick seeking a cure by the addition of "great" ($\pi o\lambda\acute{\upsilon}$) after "multitude." D a b j l f[1] have added the "paralytics" ($\pi\alpha\rho\alpha\lambda\upsilon\tau\iota\kappa o\acute{\iota}$) as a fourth group of sick; how these are to be distinguished from "crippled" ($\chi\omega\lambda o\acute{\iota}$) is not made clear. Finally, Ψ A[corr] D W Θ λ φ *pl* lat sy[p] bo Chr have added the explanatory comment: "who were waiting on the movement of the waters." In the old form of the text the sick wait in all five porticoes and not just in the fifth portico between the two pools, as in the later form. It is

---

9 *John*, 209f. [154f.]. Cf. §4 of the Introduction, "Disorder and Rearrangement."

10 Cf. Cyrillus of Jerusalem, *Hom.* MPG 33.1133; Theodor of Mopsuestia, *Commentary on John*, ed. J. B. Chabot (Paris, 1897) I 108.3f.; Joachim Jeremias, *Rediscovery of Bethesda*, 18 nn. 38 and 39.

11 *BJ* 2.530.

12 *BJ*, tr. H. St. John Thackeray, LCL, 5.302.

13 *Rediscovery of Bethesda*, 9.

14 *Das Johannesevangelium*, 79.

15 *John*, 240 n. 5 [179 n. 5].

16 Cf. Neh 13:1, 32, 33:39.

17 Fragment 61.

18 *Commentary on John*, Fragment 61.

19 Cf. *Itinera Hierosolymitana saeculi IIII–VIII*, ed. P. Geyer. Corpus Scriptorum Ecclesiasticorum Latinorum 39 (Vienna—Prague—Leipzig, 1898) 21.5f., 177.14ff.

20 Cf. Barrett, *John*, 251ff.

21 Cf. Dalman, *Sacred Sites and Ways*, 274.

clear, however, that healing powers were not attributed to the water in the pools as such. Otherwise the sick would have spent as much time as possible in the water. The reader will receive more exact information only in verse 7.

■ **4** Verse 4 is not found in $\mathfrak{P}^{66}$, $\mathfrak{P}^{75}$, and the oldest manuscripts. It was first present in the Byzantine text in various forms and gives a vivid account of how the reader is to understand the cause of the stirring of the water, which is what gives the water its curative powers. Although these additions are found only in later manuscripts, they might not be entirely foreign to the original story of the curative pool.[22] Why the Evangelist reports nothing of this kind beyond the indications given in verse 7 will be discussed in the Overview.

■ **5** The multitude of sick fades away and the scene focuses on one of them alone—in modern terms: we have a closeup. He has been sick for thirty-eight years. It is not said that he spent this entire time there in the portico.[23] But the narrator has probably imagined the situation. The duration of the illness (cf. Luke 13:11, Acts 4:22, John 9:1) is a way of emphasizing the magnitude of the healing to follow.[24] Verse 5 paves the way for verse 6: the spotlight is turned on Jesus, who suprisingly and masterfully alters the situation from the ground up.

■ **6** Verse 6 describes how Jesus comes to notice just this man: he sees him lying there and recognizes that he has been ill for so long a period, thanks to his supernatural knowledge,[25] and not to an exchange with the sick man.[26] His healing is therefore an especially great miracle. Jesus begins the conversation by asking whether the sick man wants to be healed. Even the modern reader is surprised by this since one presupposes that a sick man desires to be healed. But the narrator intends for the sick man to depict the situation; that is a livelier form of presentation than when the information in provided in the third person (as in vv 3 and 5). On the other hand, the narrator wants Jesus to seize the initiative. He must then insert a word of Jesus that establishes his contact with the sick man and at the same time permits the sick man to depict his deplorable situation. The words of Jesus, "Do you want to be healed?" serve this purpose. This question also permits the reader to anticipate that Jesus will now effect a miraculous cure.

■ **7** The sick man then depicts his situation, which is as good as hopeless. He does not ask Jesus to heal him—how could he do that? Strathmann, however, observes: "The sick man does not remark at all the invitation concealed in Jesus' question."[27] But it can only be understood as such by the Christian reader. The sick man does not know who is it that is speaking to him; he is therefore unable to perceive that Jesus is offering him the prospect of healing. He knows only one possibility, viz., the healing powers of the pool, and that possibility has eluded him repeatedly for many years. For he has no one to put him in the pool when the waters are disturbed.[28] So someone else always beats him to the pool. If one reflects on what kind of answer is implied in the words of the sick man, it runs something like this: "Of course I want to be well. I have continually sought to be healed for many years. But it has always turned out to be impossible." Brown understands the situation in exactly the opposite sense.[29] He believes the representation of the man's obtuseness to be so true-to-life that it could have belonged to the original tradition, and thus interprets: If his illness were not so tragic, one could almost be bemused by his unimaginative behavior in relation to the curative waters. "His crotchety grumbling about the 'whippersnappers' who outrace him to the water betrays a chronic inability to seize opportunity." Here psychological fancies play a trick on the exegete and prompt him to see a character there full of life, while the narrator merely depicts the bleak situation, from which the word of Jesus alone saves the sick man. Dodd[30] affirms that the Torah was beneficent, but how could it be for those who refuse to make use of the means of grace? This leads to a peculiar bit of exegesis: "The man might have been healed long ago, perhaps, if he had

22 Jeremias, *Rediscovery of Bethesda*, 25f. and n. 2 and Mark 5:30; Acts 5:13f., 19:11f.

23 In agreement with Brown, *John*, 1: 207.

24 Bultmann, *History of the Synoptic Tradition*, 221.

25 Cf. Strathman, *Das Evangelium nach Johannes*, 97, and Brown, *John*, 1: 207.

26 Weiss, *Das Johannes-Evangelium*, 197.

27 *Das Evangelium nach Johannes*, 97.

28 Βάλλω, "put, bring" in Koine: cf. Mark 2:22, John 18:11, 20:25, 27.

29 *John*, 1: 209.

30 *Interpretation of the Fourth Gospel*, 319f.

stepped down into the pool. Precisely; and that is why the first word of Jesus is, 'Have you the will to be become a healthy man?' The reply is a feeble excuse. The man has not the will. The law might show the way to life; it was powerless to create the will to live. The will to live, together with the power to live, is given in the word of Christ." This contrast between Torah and the word of Christ is imported into the story without basis and does not throw light on the story, but in fact obscures it. The thought that the sick ought to participate in the cure is foreign to the Evangelist.

■ **8** Jesus' word now follows unexpectedly. It is at once command and gift, which produces the miracle: "Rise, take up your pallet and walk." This saying is reminiscent of Mark 2:11, where Jesus says to the lame man: "Rise, take up your pallet and go home." Dodd has shown that the Evangelist does not make use of the corresponding synoptic traditions.[31] It is likely, however, that "wild" details from the oral tradition were taken up, perhaps even by the Evangelist himself.[32] The parallel command in Mark 2:11 is more natural: the one who is healed is dispatched to his "house," to his own people. That he carries his pallet shows that the miracle has been effective. The command in John 5:8 "take your pallet and walk" goes together with the transformation the miracle story has undergone: it becomes the occasion for a conflict over the sabbath (cf. vv 9ff.). The Johannine version of the story thereby gains its peculiarities: the conflict does not unexpectedly befall Jesus; rather, he provokes it. He causes the man who was healed to get up and walk about on the sabbath with his pallet by way of demonstration and thus precipitates the conflict with the Jews and their sabbath prescriptions.[33] Wellhausen conceives of a literary dependence of this verse on Mark 2:11 and so raises this objection: the sick man was not brought to the pool on a stretcher but was able to get around himself, "however not to the extent that he could get into the pool first."[34] The command borrowed from Mark 2:11 would therefore be out of place. But the scene in John 5:1–7 is not depicted in exhaustive detail. It is of course self-evident that the sick man could not have lain on the stone pavement in the porticoes the entire day; it is just as clear that he would hardly have come each morning with his pallet and limped home each evening, as he is depicted as doing. One can therefore only concede to Wellhausen that the narrator merely took from the tradition the details that were important to him. In so doing, he probably did not ask himself how the sick man came to be in the porticoes at all, any more than he inquired how the sick man got something to eat. The narrator is not concerned to paint a complete picture of the sick man, who is only of interest as an object of Jesus' healing act. "He is only an object that Jesus selects in order to demonstrate his divine power on the sabbath—a demonstration that produces conflict": this is the way Strathmann describes this type of scene.[35]

■ **9** Some exegetes have reproached the man now cured for not first thanking Jesus before picking up his pallet and departing. That shows that they do not agree with the narrator. For the narrator everything turns on Jesus and the success of his word. He therefore not only relates that the man was "immediately" made well, but that he carried out the instructions of Jesus at once and went around carrying his "burden." The narrator does not intend to depict the rise of a personal, emotionally charged relationship between Jesus and the one cured. Verse 21 will reveal that "get up" (ἔγειρε) is the pronouncement that produces healing for the Evangelist. Jesus does not heal the man–so the Evangelist sees matters–out of compassion, but he makes him well in order to have the occasion to do something that was for him incomparably more important: a revelatory discourse concerning his relationship to the Father. The Evangelist does not wish to represent Jesus as moved by emotions. The love about which the Gospel of John speaks is not sentimental love. Jesus is able to react surprisingly sharply to a worldly demand, even when well intended (cf. 2:3f., 7:3ff., 19:26), and is thereby able to indicate his distance from the "world." Of course, the sabbath conflict is again basically only a transitional motif, leading to a christological theme that the Evangelist deliberately approaches.

■ **10** It is astonishing that the Jews are unmoved by the miracle, either at this point or in what follows. They are concerned only with the observance of the sabbath law.

---

31   *Tradition,* 178f.
32   Bultmann (*John,* 237f. [177]) holds a comparable view.
33   Contrary to Bultmann, *John,* 242 n. 3 [181 n. 2].
34   *Das Evangelium Johannes,* 24.
35   *Das Evangelium nach Johannes,* 99.

But the Evangelist does not refract the theme of the sabbath healing in the same way that the Synoptics do (which are not, to be sure, entirely unanimous: cf. Mark 1:29–31; 3:1–5, Luke 13:10–17, 14:1–6). It only helps him to emphasize, in a preliminary way, Jesus' relation to the Father. That becomes clear, of course, only from verse 17 on. First the difficulties that establish Jesus as the one who has caused the sabbath prohibition to be transgressed (by carrying a burden from one location to another) are to be described—as a moment in the narrative that slows the pace and heightens the tension. The man comes immediately to the attention of the Jews: he is the one carrying his pallet about on the sabbath (that he himself is also a Jew is bracketed out). They make him aware–and the reader along with him–that he is doing something unlawful. For it is forbidden to carry a burden on the sabbath in Jer 17:21f. in these words: "Thus says the Lord: Take heed for the sake of your lives, and do not bear a burden on the sabbath day or bring it in by the gates of Jerusalem. And do not carry a burden out of your homes on the sabbath or do any work, but keep the sabbath day holy, as I commanded your fathers."

■ **11** The man who had been healed does not yield entirely to the Jewish demand (in that event there would have been no conflict between Jesus and the Jews), but appeals to the instructions he received from the one who had made him well. That is reminiscent of chapter 9, where this form of argument is used throughout. The Evangelist could not make use of the same method twice with the same effect, at least not to the same extent. It is likewise clear that in both cases a literary device is employed in order to indicate a contradiction between the sabbath law and a command of Jesus. Moreover, the sabbath question serves here only as a skirmish, as preparation for the real concerns of the Evangelist.

■ **12** Now the interest of the Jews begins to intensify. They do not inquire about the miracle that has taken place (in chapter 9 the reality of the miracle is first established in each instance), but they want to know who it was that actually commanded him to break the sabbath. A contrast between law and gospel is not intended (on this point see the Overview).

■ **13** Verse 13 introduces an element into the narrative that suddenly arrests the action and heightens the tension: with the best of good intentions the man who has been healed cannot answer their question. For Jesus, who did not reveal who he was (should he not perhaps have introduced himself to the lame man?), has meanwhile disappeared into the crowd which presses about. Were this situation to obtain, the action would be at an end. The inner logic of the narrative therefore requires that the man who was cured and Jesus meet somewhere else, so that the lame man can tell the Jews who made him well. Jesus will thereby become known as the one who ordered him to break the sabbath.

■ **14** For such a meeting the temple is the appropriate place, by literary standards. Every reader has heard of the temple. Jesus often makes speeches there in the Gospel of John, and so it is no contradiction for the lame man to go there. But the word that Jesus now speaks to the man who was cured of course surprises both the interpreter and the attentive reader: "See, you are well." Jesus could have said that earlier. But the composition of the narrative required that conversation be avoided initially. Only by having the lame man pick up his pallet and walk, in accordance with the instruction of Jesus, and only by having Jesus depart, could an exchange take place between the man now healed and the Jews. The word, "well," which has appeared now for the fourth time (vv 7, 9, 11, 14), holds the scene together formally. But with the affirmation that the healing has taken place matters cannot come to an end. So the further warning of Jesus is added: "Sin no more, that nothing worse befall you." Exegetes have expended a great deal of effort on this saying. In John 9:2 Jesus rejects the explanation that illness is retribution for sin. The Evangelist must therefore have taken over this saying from his source. But that does not explain everything. Of what did the sin that struck the lame man 38 years earlier and laid him low for so long consist, and how young must he have been at that time? Perhaps the original form of the story ended with the word to the man who was cured to return to his home, and an editor decided to insert a moralistic ending. That of course does damage to the present form of the composition.

■ **15** Verse 15 sounds like this: the man who was cured, of all people, went directly to the Jews after Jesus' warning and denounced him. That leads not only to the question of how he now suddenly comes to know the name of Jesus, but makes him appear to be a super ingrate and crassly malicious. We ought not therefore to be surprised when the heavy artillery of moralizing typology and psychology are trotted out. Yet it is the case that the report to the Jews causes the action to resume. That seems to be the interest of the Evangelist. Earlier he manipulated the man almost like a marionette by having him immediately pick up his pallet and walk about; in a similar way, he now causes him to blurt out the name of his savior in response to the question of the Jews. In addition, it remains unclear whether he has now given a report to those Jews at the pool (who had questioned him). But the Evangelist does not concern himself with such details.

■ 16 One must also be wary here of attributing an aim to the Evangelist that is alien to him. For example, on the basis of this sabbath healing, one should not attempt to demonstrate Jesus' power over the sabbath, as it is depicted in Mark 2:23–28 and as it is likewise worked out in special detail in the tradition underlying chapter 9. At this point, the conflict over the sabbath is only a prelude that permits the development of the real conflict, the christological discourse. The word ἐποίει ("he used to do, he kept doing") does not, in all probability, refer to the healing, but to Jesus' instruction to the man who was cured. 𝔓⁶⁶ reads ἐποίει, 𝔓⁷⁵ and 579 ἐποίησεν, by contrast. Both readings are attested very early. The second seems to us to be subject to the difficulty that applies also to the imperfect. According to BDF,[36] the imperfect can be understood as the expression of "relative time" and would then be represented in German or English as the pluperfect. Bauer[37] would like to understand the imperfect here as the expression of repetition, so that it corresponds to the regular activity of Jesus. But this one healing on the sabbath is represented in the Fourth Gospel as a singular and characteristic deed of Jesus (7:23). In the tradition used by the Gospel of John, the controversy appears to have played a greater role than in the Gospel of John itself, where the Pauline battle against the Jewish law lies in the past as a decisive event. The narrator does not specify the form of persecution more closely. He does not have the Jews take up stones to kill Jesus. That would divert the attention of the reader too much to these sideshows. For that reason, the simple word ἐδίωκον ("persecuted, kept persecuting") is suffi-

cient. The imperfect might be understood as iterative.[38] The Evangelist, who is here very abrupt and vague in order to come to his real christological theme quickly in a single train of thought, appears to be thinking of repeated activity on the part of the Jews. However, he does not want to describe it more closely, since for him everything turns on the reaction of Jesus to his opponents, and not on the depiction of Jewish aggression in detail.

■ 17 Jesus' "answer" does not refer to a question directed to him or to accusations hurled against him. Rather, in response to an unexpressed reproach (that the reader knows), Jesus calls upon God and his own relation to him in majestic tranquility (only in vv 19–21 will this be made more explicit): "My Father works up to the present moment,[39] and I am working." By this enigmatic word he means: "Because my Father works up to the present moment, I am also working (without the sabbath pause)." The narrator has the Jews perceive immediately that by "my Father" he means "God." The notion that God cannot stop working and that, consequently, the notion of the sabbath rest of God (Gen 2:2) stands in tension with this working led to various attempts on the part of the rabbis[40] and Philo to reconcile the two. Two considerations of the rabbis may be especially emphasized: God's activity as physical creation indeed came to an end on the sabbath, but not his moral activity, which comes to fruition in both good and evil (in that the good people are rewarded in their earthly estate and the evil resisted). This view is expressed in *Gen. Rab.* 8ᶜ.

Exod. Rab. 30 (89ᵃ) gives a different view: according to rabbinic exegesis, the sabbath commandment does not forbid one to carry something about in one's house on the sabbath. But God's homestead is the upper and the lower worlds. He may thus create within it without coming into conflict with the sabbath.

The information of Philo seems to us to be less tortured.[41] Philo explains flatly on one occasion: "For God never leaves off making, but even as it is the property of fire to burn and of snow to chill, so it is the property of God to make: nay more so by far, inasmuch as He is to all besides the source of action." This proof is supported by the thought: "True being is creating, not

---

36 §330.
37 *Das Johannesevangelium*, 82.
38 BDF §325.

39 Cf. Bauer, *Greek-English Lexicon*, s.v. ἄρτι.
40 Cf. Billerbeck, 2: 461f.
41 In *Leg. all.* 1.3f., *Det. Pot. Ins.* §161 and 18, and *De*

suffering." But now, as a pious Jew, Philo must make sense out of the rest of God as that rest is attested by Genesis. For that reason he equates the sabbath rest of God with ἀνάπαυσις ("a ceasing"), with ἀναπαύεσθαι ("to cease, rest"), also understood as an attribute of God by Gnosticism. This rest he interprets as immutable, as vitality undiminished by activity. "But a being that is free from weakness, even though he be making all things, will cease not to all eternity to be at rest."[42] Of course this thought in fact leads to another that is entirely alien to Genesis: The sabbath rest of God lasts forever, not just for the seventh day, just as his creativity endures forever. The sabbath as the necessity to rest from work makes sense only for man, who gets fatigued from work and needs a day of rest. The notion that God works continually is not unknown in pagan thought. Cicero[43] speaks of philosophers who think of God as constantly acting and always setting something in motion. If God is the "prime mover" (primum movens), he is not conceivable apart from his activity as the mover of everything. On the other hand, the correlative thought is that the prime mover is not himself moved, but "as unmoved he moves all things" (ἀκίνητον πάντα κινεῖ). The (imagined) axis remains unmoved.[44] Maximus Tyre says, "If Hercules had wanted to rest, no one would have ventured to call him a son of Zeus."[45]

■ 18 The Evangelist does not really permit the Jews to go into the first part of Jesus' "answer"—which is difficult to contest—but he does go into the second part: "and I am working." Up to this point they have persecuted Jesus because he violated the sabbath—with his instruction to the man who was healed. However, we learn only in verses 19–21 that the word "rise" (ἔγειρε) was the most important expression among Jesus' words. Now the Jews seek to kill him because he compares his works with those of his "Father," and thus makes himself equal to God. We thus come to the point that is central for the Evangelist. From this point he unfolds a special doctrine that is gradually made clear in what follows.

■ 19 In a certain sense, this christology is the real theme of the Gospel of John, but in its relationship to the earthly life of Jesus. The question of how Jesus comports himself to God is posed and answered in all four canonical Gospels, albeit it in diverse ways. The fourth Evangelist gives a response that scarcely anyone before him had given thought to. The history of doctrine did not seize upon it in the way peculiar to the Gospel of John, as is attested by the evidence down to and including Käsemann's *The Testament of Jesus*. Käsemann retains the "liberal" understanding of the Johannine Jesus as the "God who goes about on earth" and does not take into account the dialectic developed in John 5:19–21 and 5:24–26 (cf. the Overview). That statement is valid, although the one side of Johannine christology has deeply influenced the history of doctrine.

Jesus' "answer" begins with the formula, ἀμήν, ἀμήν ("truly, truly"). It is a solemn expansion of the simple ἀμήν used in the Synoptics to introduce important sayings of Jesus. In the Gospel of John this formula appears twenty-five times from 1:51 to 21:28,[46] with the meaning: "That's the way it is."

Jesus' discourse proper begins with a sentence in lapidary style: "the son can do nothing of his own accord." Jesus indeed claims—the Jews understood this correctly—the title of son and the position of son, but he here gives them a new and unexpected sense. In his claim to the name of son the Jews heard him claim equality with God. But this is exactly what the name "the son" does not mean in the mouth of Jesus. He is not thereby expressing his own power and authority. He is not demanding the place for himself depicted by Matt 11:22 and 28:19ff. How, then, are Jesus' words rightly to be understood?

Jesus is not without deeds. His work, however, is bound to that of the Father in a peculiar way: "the Son can do nothing of his own accord, but only what he sees the Father doing; for whatever he does, the Son does likewise." A correlation of this kind between two sets of

---

cher. 87–90.

42 *De cher.* 90, tr. F. H. Colson and G. H. Whitaker, LCL.

43 *De off.* 3.28.102.

44 "Imagined" here does not refer to a subsisting subject, but to the assertion that the reposing one is not spatially palpable.

45 *Diss.* 15.6.2.

46 Cf. *TDNT* 1: 335–38.

actions is known to us from everyday experience, at least to a certain degree. A glance in the mirror shows us that every movement we make corresponds to the movement of our mirror image (we can ignore the reversal of sides for the moment). Of course, this experience cannot be used to explain verse 19 completely. The mirror image does indeed mimic what the person standing before the mirror performs, but it is not a living person that performs in the mirror, and the text of John does not attest the word that corresponds approximately to our phrase, "mirror image": the word εἰκών is lacking in the Gospel of John. Paul uses it in 2 Cor 4:4 and it appears in Col 1:15. In both passages Jesus is designated as "image of God" (εἰκὼν τοῦ θεοῦ), but in order to emphasize his power and glory. That is especially evident in the hymn in Colossians. But that is not the thing expressed in John 5:19. Rather, in this passage it is that the son can do nothing of his own accord, that he is completely dependent on the work of the Father. The concept of the "icon" ("image") is thus not relevant here. Perhaps something quite different plays a role here: the concept of the image or icon may have too strong a gnostic flavor for the taste of the Evangelist. The term does indeed turn up in the Gospel of Thomas,[47] and especially often in the Gospel of Philip.[48]

Above all, it was probably advisable not to use this term because the relation between a living Person and his or her mirror image does not correspond to the intention of the Evangelist. If Jesus were only a mirror image of the Father, then the reality would belong entirely to the Father and the mirror image of Jesus would not be "true man" (vere homo, to use the terminology of the later Fathers). At the same, he would also not be "true God" (vere deus). On the contrary, the Evangelist sought, in his own way, to emphasize both assertions in their true and genuine sense. Jesus is not, for him, a mirror image that automatically reacts; rather, Jesus sees what the Father does and acts accordingly. With Käsemann, one could conceive this as the obedience of

Jesus.[49] But "to obey, obedience" (ὑπακούω, ὑπακοή, and ὑπήκοος) do not appear in the Gospel of John. These words do not have the right ring in this context.

■ **20** Verse 20 therefore supplements the preceding verse in a personal sense: "The Father loves the Son, and shows him all that he himself is doing." It thus becomes clear that Jesus is not merely a copy or mirror image. The Evangelist compares the relationship of the Father to Jesus with that of an old, experienced handcraftsman to his son. Then one day the son would be instructed—in their family business—when the father shows him how to do everything. The Evangelist thus makes use of a scene that for the reader of that day was very graphic. It is now important to recognize that the Evangelist is not speaking here of a process that goes on within the divine domain but of Jesus' activity on earth. These earthly deeds of Jesus are the work of him whom the Father loves and who does what he sees the Father doing. This "on earth," however, includes the notion that for Jesus' contemporaries his earthly life and his earthly activities were dialectical. Because this process imitates the activity of the Father, it has a double effect, one positive and one negative. The negative consists in the fact that Jesus' words and deeds are also ambiguous "signs," and that they can therefore fall on deaf ears. That is true of the whole of Jesus' activity, as John represents it, up to the resurrection: Jesus' message is still not understood. This feature makes it clear that there is only one who appears below the invisible line that separates us from the invisible Father. The condition of "the being who is born from above" is not fulfilled until the resurrection (cf. 7:39 and 20:22). Since the Spirit did not come until after Easter, the entire earthly life of Jesus has not yet produced true faith. The Samaritans who believed and the man born blind who was excommunicated from the synagogue can only be cited by the Evangelist as true believers because he—consciously—telescopes the times before and after Easter ("The hour comes and now is," 5:25). Only after Easter is the situation altered. The

---

47 Cf. sayings 50 (90:1) and 83 (95:20, 22, 25).

48 Cf. sayings 26 (106:14), 60 (112:37), 61 (113:24), 67 (115:11, 13, 14, 15, 16f.), 69 (115:35), 72 (116:37), 76 (117:37), 86 (120:13), 121 (129:27, 32), 124 (132:21), 127 (134:13); cf. the dissertaion of Hans-Georg Gaffron on the Gospel of Philip, "Studien zum koptischen Philippusevangelium unter unter besonderer Berücksichtigung der Sakramente," Bonn,

1969.

49 *The Testament of Jesus*, 18.

earthly life of Jesus is not reduced to a minimum in the Gospel of John (as it is in Gal 4:4); it can be effective—at least in a certain way. For the Evangelist writes his gospel, one that depicts this earthly life, for the post-Easter congregation. This congregation perceives the message of Jesus, thanks to the Spirit, and believes that he was sent by the Father. The Spirit is the key that opens up the message of Jesus and makes it effective.

■ **21** How does the Gospel of John concretize the task of the son, which follows from his unity with the Father? The answer is provided by the assertion: "For as the Father raises the dead and gives them life, so also the Son gives life to whom he will." It will repay us to read these words (continued in vv 24–26) with care. The decisive term is ἔγειρε ("rise"). It reminds the reader of verse 8, where Jesus says to the sick man: "rise" (ἔγειρε). A relationship between two events thus emerges: between the "rising" of the lame man, which Jesus effects by his word of command, and the "rising" ("resurrection") of the (spiritual) dead, in which the Father allows Jesus to participate. The healing at the pool was thus not only an event within the concrete world (it was of course that, too, and the Evangelist does not by any means doubt that it really took place). But as such an earthly event it was also a pointer to something entirely different, something that Jesus was capable of bringing to pass in any case, but which was no longer a graphic earthly event: Jesus, too, could "give life."

The words "to whom he will" stand in contradiction to the statement that Jesus does not do his will, but the will of his Father (4:34, 5:30, 6:38, 6:40). That applies to his awakening of the (spiritual) dead. The alien insertion in verses 22f. and 27ff., of which we will speak momentarily, attributes to Jesus a position quite different from the one to which "to whom he will" corresponds.

In this way the earthly life of Jesus, as the Evangelist depicts it with the help of his source, is an ever new allusion to Jesus' real aim and his genuine authority. Of course, it is always in the form merely of an allusion, an indirect communication, as it touches the deeds of Jesus. But the Evangelist attempts, in the speeches of Jesus, to press the limits of indirect communication as far as possible. At all events, these discourses must also make use of earthly words and figures. The limits of the code are not overridden here either, although the Evangelist is confident that the Spirit will unlock this code for post-Easter readers. Bultmann[50] has rightly emphasized these inner limits also of the speeches of Jesus. They of course threaten to make the speeches as ineffective as the miracle at the pool, which leaves the cured man in "spiritual" death (it turns out differently in the healing of the man born blind in chapter 9). It can happen that the "dead" to whom Jesus spoke in the Gospel of John remain dead; it can also happen that the reader will not understand the speeches of Jesus and thus remain "dead," viz., without true life in communion with God. Election is involved, about which verses 24–26 will have more to say.

■ **22–23** These verses introduce a completely new idea, which cannot be combined with either verses 19–21 or with verses 24–26. Up to this point it has been affirmed that the son does only what he sees the Father doing; he can do nothing of his own accord. That stipulates that the Father is and remains the one who makes the determinations, and the son only carries out the will of the Father. On the other hand, in these verses the complete authority for the judgment is attributed to the son; the Father has transferred it to the son. The son is thus no longer the one who lives only for the will of the Father. Rather, the Father here waives his right to judgment in favor of the son. Verse 23 gives the reason for this: everyone ought to honor the son as they honor the Father; if the son is the almighty world judge, then Christians will take care not to withhold appropriate honor to this powerful figure. This idea is reinforced by the statement: "He who does not honor the son does not honor the Father who sent him." The Johannine formula "who sent him" comports poorly with the style of the Evangelist, but not with his message. For verses 22f. contradict John 3:17f: "Whoever believes on him (i.e., the son), is not to be judged." These verses also contradict what is said in 5:24 (see below). Bultmann is blinded by the fact that in verses 19–21 the office of judge is depicted only in one aspect, that of giving life.[51]

From verse 23 Bultmann infers that God is not to be relieved by another judge, viz., the son; rather, the

50   *Theology of the New Testament*, 2: 398 [13f.] and 412 [45f.].

51   *John*, 256 n. 2 [192 n. 2].

equality of the working of the Father and of the son is being described. The Father thus remains judge, just as the correlation "just as . . . so also" (ὥσπερ—οὕτως) in verse 21 indicates; both, Father and son, exercise the office of judge. But there is nothing in verse 21 about the office of judge; that comes only in verse 22 (where the insertion begins). That the Father executes his office as judge through the son is denied in verse 23: the Father has given judgment entirely over to the son, "that all may honor the Son, even as they honor the Father." The "mythological formulation" is by no means open to misunderstanding, but contradicts the interpretation that attempts to understand a verse that is alien to Johannine thought as though it were Johannine.

Moreover, the concept of "judgment" (κρίσις), which Bultmann takes as his point of departure, is not that of the Evangelist. For him, "the judgment," as verse 24 indicates, is condemnation and not a "decison" between "life" and "death." The insertions in the Johannine text, on the other hand, conceive the "judgment" (κρίσις) in the sense of the future judgment of the world at the end of time, as verse 27ff. immediately demonstrate. The redactor missed the mention of the future last judgment in the Johannine text; for him, it is through this judgment that Jesus' great power will be demonstrated. From this perspective on the situation, he has also added the words "to whom he will" (οὓς θέλει) in verse 21. Jesus only gives life to those whom the Father has given to him, and the same holds for Jesus' disciples. The words οὓς θέλει would be acceptable whether "he will" is referred to the Father or whether in its place the words "whom the Father wills" (οὓς ὁ πατὴρ θέλει) were to appear.

■ 24–26 These words connect up directly with verse 21 and elucidate that passage. The double "truly, truly" (ἀμὴν ἀμὴν) again calls attention to the fact that a pronouncement of decisive importance follows. The assertion, "He who hears my words and believes him who sent me," should not be interpreted too narrowly. As will become clear in verse 25, the Evangelist is speaking not only of the earthly life of Jesus; rather he has the entire message of Jesus before and after Easter in mind. In John 20:21 we will learn that the disciples, who proclaim the message of Jesus, participate in his authority and providential significance. In this passage, then, it is a question of the encounter of man with the message of Jesus in general, as that message is represented precisely in the Gospel of John. To him who hears this message and is certain that it is the divine truth—to him is communion with God promised and given.

Verse 21 asserted that Jesus is able to make the dead alive, that he causes those who are spiritually dead to come to life. This resurrection takes place in the midst of mortal life. Although one remains in the world (17:15), one is transposed into another kind of existence. Such a person enters into communion with the Father of whom Jesus is the representative, but whom no one has ever seen. More is said of this communion in 14:23. Such a person "does not come into judgment" (here the Evangelist employs an expression drawn from the received tradition concerning the future expectation of the endtime), which is already taking place within the existing world. Such a person, rather, has passed over from the realm of death (the world for whom God is dead) to the realm of life.

When the Evangelist says "give life," "resurrect," he does not have in mind a corpse rising again from the grave (the resurrection of Lazarus is important only as an indirect allusion to something entirely different). But neither does he mean a mere sense of oneness with a higher power, a sense of being attuned subjectively. He is speaking, rather, of a new life that takes its rise mysteriously within the old, bodily/spiritual existence, and therefore within real existence, not one that is dreamed. Insofar as it is visible in the activity of man, it remains ambiguous (the ultimate form of this ambiguity is the "exaltation of Jesus" as crucifixion and return to the Father). Such a person overcomes the anxiety in which even he is caught up before the powers, the powers that threaten him in his environment and seek to bring him under their sway. He learns to live in the world without succumbing to the world. He overcomes restlessness, although what threatens him does not disappear. The community of the Evangelist might have been very conscious of the threat of persecution that hung over them every moment. But they lived in the peace they had received from Jesus (14:27, 16:33). For such a person the distinction between earthly life and earthly death has also become unimportant, at the end. This new existence in communion with God is also not effaced by being transposed from the mystery of time to the mystery of eternity. He who comes into contact with God "will never taste death" (8:52).

There appears to be a doctrine quite analogous to this in the Coptic *Treatise on Resurrection* from Nag Hammadi. This treatise sets out the idea, especially in 48.15, that the resurrection is no illusion ($\phi\alpha\nu\tau\alpha\sigma\iota\alpha$), but that the world is simply an illusion. The one who has faith knows that he is already redeemed, already resurrected, although he continues to see and hear, etc., within the world. When the hour of death draws near to him, he will be drawn upwards by the redeemer like the sun draws its rays back to itself when it sets.[52] At that moment the illusion of the world comes to an end.

The distinction between the Gospel of John and Gnosticism becomes evident at two points precisely in this apparent parallel: in the first instance, the Gnostic already knows that his true self was always in existence; in the second, he views the world as a mere illusion, which ceases upon the death of the conceiving subject. The Evangelist, by contrast, takes the world seriously. In the high priestly prayer of Jesus, it is said, "I do not pray that thou shouldst take them out of the world, but that thou shouldst keep them from the evil one" (John 17:15). The world is no mere appearance, is not made up of illusory soap bubbles that burst in the hour of death. Furthermore, the Evangelist takes the world so seriously that he knows that he belonged to the world before Jesus chose him. He who is tempted to reckon the Gospel of John among gnostic documents must take note of these differences between the Gospel of John and Gnosticism.

The reader whose eyes have been opened comes to know, in verse 24, that in causing the lame man "to rise up" there is merely an allusion to the real resurrection. That is made clear in the example given: here is a man who could indeed "rise up bodily" but who had not the slightest premonition of the true resurrection into communion with God. This shows how the Evangelist interprets the miracle stories which came down to him in the tradition and how he thus appropriates them in a new sense. In Jesus' discourse, it is especially important to observe the distinction between present and future and yet their coalescence: "the hour comes and now is." "The hour" still lay in the future of Easter morning from the standpoint of the earthly Jesus. But from the perspective of the Evangelist, "the hour" has become the present, although not for everyone. The time of the resurrection—now coalesced with the moment when one comes to faith—is no longer connected with a cosmic catastrophe of a near or remote future, as it was expected in late Judaism and also in the primitive Christian community, although with waning urgency.[53] The new life begins, for the Evangelist, wherever one opens oneself up to the Christian message and begins to live out of it. But the real goal is the "invisible Father" (that becomes evident to the one who attends carefully to what the Evangelist has to say). The significance of Jesus is that he is the way to the Father, and that we can "see" and "hear" the Father in him: his words are the words of his Father, and his deeds are the deeds of his Father.

■ **27–29** Not all Christians who were contemporary with the Evangelist were happy with this message. Most of them held onto the older notions of a judgment at the end of time, which the Son of man (as in Daniel) would carry out. The transformation of a futuristic eschatology into a "now" eschatology, into the moment when one comes to faith, was not satisfactory. Verses 27–29 were inserted, consequently, as a codicil to supply what was sorely missed.[54] Verse 27 first assures the reader that God has given the Son authority to execute judgment, "because he is the Son of man" (Dan 7:13). The futuristic and mythological expectations connected with the endtime are again introduced with this apocalyptic title. The Son of man is understood here as the judge of the world and identified with Jesus, as may be deduced from verse 28: "Do not marvel at this; for the hour is coming" (the dialectic of the times, the "now" and the "then," is here deliberately corrected in that what had been said earlier is interpreted in a traditional sense) "when all who are in the tombs will hear his voice and come forth," and indeed "those who have done good, to the resurrection

52 On the "sun theology," cf. F. L. Cross, *The Jung Codex: A Newly Recovered Gnostic Papyrus. Three Studies by H. C. Puech, G. Quispel and W. C. van Unnik* (London: A. R. Mowbray, 1955) 28f.

53 Cf. 1 Thess 4:13–17, 1 Cor 15:20–29, 50–55; Mark 9:1, 13:24–27, 14:62; Rom 13:11ff.; Matt 16:28, 24:26f., 30f., 34, 26:64, 28:18; Luke 9:26f., 21:32f., 22:69f.; Acts 1:9–11, 3:20f.

54 Cf. Bultmann, *John*, 260f. [195f.].

of life, and those who have done evil, to the resurrection of judgment."

The expression "to the resurrection of judgment" shows that the redactor has created a difficulty: to a resurrection to life there must really correspond a "resurrection to death." But what is the meaning of a resurrection of those who have done evil if they are then to be annihilated? It probably has to do with eternal torture, like that described in Isa 66:24. But in that case, the expression "judgment" (v 29) does not fit with the conception of the redactor, who has in mind a division between the good and the bad, which he appropriately calls "judgment" in verses 22 and 27.

The Evangelist has made it clear in 11:25 that Jesus sharply rejects this doctrine of the last judgment. In its place the Gospel of John advocates a resurrection that takes place in the encounter of the one who believes with God and that can be realized in any moment of life. The essential thing occurs in the believing acceptance of the message of Jesus: the man of faith enters into communion with God. There is nothing greater that man can receive. But verses 27–29 are not satisfied with that, but look for a cosmic turn of events in which the graves will open, the good will be rewarded, and the evil condemned. What is being proclaimed in this passage is not the justification of the sinners but of the justified,[55] and the gruesome vision of Isa 66:24 turns up again.

The redactor overlooks the fact that Jesus judges no one (8:15). The phrase, "Do not marvel at this" (viz., that Jesus will hold judgment as the Son of man) labors to create a transition. Of course, the Evangelist also knows of a judgment, viz., the abiding remoteness of God. This judgment takes place now, when anyone rejects the message of Jesus and thereby blocks access to the Father. This judgment imparts to life its seriousness, but also permits it a further final hope.

■ **30** Verse 30 connects up with verse 26: Jesus can do nothing of himself, "for I seek not my own will but the will of him who sent me." The redactor has inserted the further words, "as I hear, I judge," in order to maintain the connection with his insertion in verses 27–29; but he does not notice that the Father has given judgment entirely over into the hands of the Son, according to

verse 27. But what the Evangelist really intends to say is expressed in the assurance that Jesus can do nothing of himself, which reverts to verse 19. Therein lies, of course, the one great problem connected with Johannine christology: we are so easily tempted (as are the Jews in the Gospel of John) to see in Jesus a god who actually strides over the earth seeking his own. That would be blasphemy for the Evangelist: only because Jesus is here solely on behalf of God, because he raises no claim on his own behalf, does he offer an undistorted image of the Father. The Jews claim that he makes himself equal with God. He makes himself of equal rank with God, and since there can be only one God, Jesus replaces him. Such a misunderstanding appears in various manifestations of Christian piety. But the Evangelist has other ideas. Since Jesus does what he sees the Father doing and only that, believers are able to see the Father in him. It follows that "I and the Father are one" (10:30) and "the Father is greater than I" (14:28). That is the dialectic of Johannine christology.

Overview

These thirty verses contribute an unusual amount to deciphering the Gospel of John. They show how the Evangelist permits an action to unfold and thus exhibit the height and breadth of his compositional ability; they serve as an excellent introduction to the peculiarities of his christology; and finally, they permit us to make the source problem of the Gospel of John transparent in its manifold aspects.

The first segment forms a healing miracle story set in Jerusalem. The place where the healing took place was probably indicated by the source used here (today we know it to have been a series of porticoes constructed by Herod, four of which enclosed two large pools and the fifth of which divided the two pools). The Evangelist might not have seen the former magnificent building himself. Weiss' assertion that "the buildings serving charitable purposes were spared destruction"[56] is merely a friendly assumption that conflicts with the facts known to us. It cannot be verified on the basis of the present tense of the verb "to be" (ἔστιν, v 2). The Evangelist has omitted the old legend of the healing powers of the

---

55   Cf. the insertion in John 3:19–21.
56   Weiss, *Das Johannes-Evangelium*, 194.

waters when troubled; Jesus does not compete with an angel not as a winner. The confrontation of Jesus with the sick man stands out all the more because the narrator has omitted everything that seemed to him to be dispensable. The odd question of Jesus, "Do you want to be healed," is not intended to determine whether the lame man has the desire to become well again (the Johannine Jesus is not trained to practice psychology), but permits the reader to divine that the story of a healing is to follow. Further, the contrast to the hopeless situation the sick man had experienced now for decades, and the healing power of Jesus, which is easily overshadowed, as it were, by the infrequency of the gifts of healing dispensed by the pool, are so little emphasized that we cannot know for sure that the narrator intends to underscore it, even indirectly. Finally, one must not forget that the healing is not reported for its own sake, but is only the means of producing a sabbath conflict between Jesus and the Jews. Form criticism has prompted the presumption that the notice appended as verse 9c, "Now that day was the sabbath," as though it were an afterthought, did not belong originally to the healing story, but was added to it in the course of the tradition. This verse forms the transition to the next narrative unit.

This healing narrative gave rise in the nineteenth century to allegorical interpretations. In his commentary, H. J. Holtzmann comments on his predecessors with the words: "On the one hand, . . . the Christian experience takes the form of a biblical narrative, according to which he who is redeemed by the savior also knows himself to be free from legal compulsions,"[57] but in that same salvation there is motivation "to sin no more" ($\mu\eta\kappa\acute{\epsilon}\tau\iota$ $\dot{\alpha}\mu\alpha\rho\tau\acute{\alpha}\nu\epsilon\iota\nu$; Gal 5:1, 13, Rom 6:1–18).[58] On the other hand, the question in verse 6 is correctly understood only when it is taken as a question put to Jerusalem, indeed, to the entire nation, when the sick man is understood as the type of the latter.[59] In that case the thirty-eight years in verse 5 require some sort of interpretation, preferably with reference to the duration of

the sojourn in the wilderness in accordance with Deut 2:14.[60]

Hirsch, who takes H. J. Holtzmann as his model, has interpreted the story of the healing at the pool correlatively: "Since the author never created the signs of Jesus out of whole cloth, but freely remodelled something that was already part of the tradition, the story is presumably best to be taken as a story circulating outside the three Gospels. The thirty-eight years of the man's illness does not, in that case, depend on tradition. That is an allusion to Deut 2:14 and denotes the years of the sojourn in the wilderness. It is scarcely too bold to interpret the story as follows: the sick man, whom Jesus restores to free movement and health after thirty-eight years of immobility, and who does not thank Jesus for it but makes common cause with the disciples of Moses against Jesus, is the embodiment of law-bound Judaism, in the same way as the Samaritan woman represents the Samaritan people and religion. That means that he is at once an individual person viewed poetically (and is supplied as such with an unmistakable trace of baseness) and as a symbol. The warning Jesus issues against the offense that something worse befall him thereby gains its significance: it is the separation from Jesus, who wants to free Judaism from bondage to the law, that will deliver Judaism over to judgment. To view the event as 'parable' scarcely goes beyond what Paul says in Gal 4 . . . It is Paul's point of view, expressed in Gal 4:10 and appropriated by the Gentile church for itself, that it would be an inappropriate encroachment on the freedom that Jesus gives us to adhere in any way to the Sabbath commandment. . . . in Paul's most profound thought: Christ is the end of the law."[61]

Strathmann repeats this exposition in brief.[62] He finds in the narrative of the healing "a stylized story in the service of preaching, whose basic motif we have before us in another variation in the synoptic story of the healing of the paralytic." According to Bultmann,[63] "Neither the source nor the Evangelist has in mind an

57 Hausrath, *Neutestamentliche Zeitgeschichte* (Heidelberg: Bassermann, ²1874) 4: 418.

58 Thoma, *Die Genesis des Johannes-Evangeliums* (Berlin, 1882) 470; O. Holtzmann, *Das Evangelium des Johannes*, 60, 102, 217.

59 Luthardt, *Das johanneische Evangelium*, 1: 439.

60 Baumgarten, *Geschichte Jesu* (1859) 139f.

61 Hirsch, *Das vierte Evangelium*, 156–58.

62 *Das Evangelium nach Johannes*, 100.

63 *John*, 241f. n. 7 [180 n. 7].

allegorical interpretation of the 38 years," with reference to Deut 2:14. The miracle story is presumably derived from the signs source.[64] Fortna believes that the healing story was the last of the seven stories derived from the signs source.[65] Perhaps following "and he walked" ($\pi\epsilon\rho\iota\epsilon\pi\acute{\alpha}\tau\epsilon\iota$) in chapter 5 there stood something like: "And Jesus said to him, 'Sin no more lest something worse befall you,'" and then perhaps a further sentence to this effect: "This Jesus did as the seventh (last) sign."[66]

This survey of research contains a series of questions that ought to be noted by current scholarship. In the first place, it is not a matter of casually lining up, one after another, marks of synoptic, Pauline, and Johannine theology. If one invokes any kind of "unity of Scripture," one must not misuse that unity by doing away with patent contradictions between and among NT writings; we have learned meanwhile to make such distinctions. Hirsch's interpretation of the Gospel of John is further threatened because he sees John as the great follower of Paul and does not distinguish the external and internal situations of the two with sufficient care. Furthermore, because he assesses the poetic potential of the fourth Evangelist extraordinarily highly, he is prompted to overlook the question whether a picture that is successful from a literary point of view—if that is what it is—but alien to the Evangelist theologically could not have been derived from a source (e.g., in the healing of the man born blind in chapter 9). When carefully considered, his exposition of the healing story as an artistic delineation of the destiny of an individual, and of the Jewish people at the same time, can no more be supported than can his correlative interpretation of the Samaritan woman in chapter 4 (see the commentary *ad loc.*). The sick can indeed once again move about freely, but the Jewish people have by no means been brought back "to health and restored mobility." In general, one ought first to check Johannine assertions regarding the Jewish law to see whether they have anything to do with the Pauline problem of the law before one undertakes to interpret Johannine pronouncements on the law in a Pauline sense. The way in which Jesus speaks of "your law" in John 8:17, 10:34, 15:25, for example, indicates to what extent "Johannine Christianity" felt itself to be removed

from the Jewish law. Basically, only prooftexts are derived from the law in support of Jesus or the law is employed apologetically. When Jesus breaks the sabbath, it is not so much to show that he is above the law as to prepare for an account of his relation to the Father. Oddly enough, neither Hirsch nor the other exegetes have seen that the term "well, healed" runs through the entire healing story and holds it together linguistically (vv 6, 9, 11, 14, and 15). The striking formulation of Jesus' question in verse 6 has been influenced by this term ($\acute{v}\gamma\iota\acute{\eta}s$), which probably belonged to the source. Its reappearance in 7:23 (where the healing at the pool is mentioned again) is not warrant for attributing this passage to the source also. For the apologetic advanced in 7:23 presupposes that Jesus' healing on the sabbath, and not his command to the man who had been healed to take up his pallet and walk, constituted breaking the sabbath. The brevity of the expression in 5:16 perhaps created the misunderstanding, especially since the Synoptics presume that Jesus' infringement of the sabbath was his healing on the sabbath (e.g., Luke 13: 10–14).

Holtzmann[67] and other scholars of his time still viewed the healing story in John 5:2ff. as a free use of synoptic materials. Hirsch rightly did not trace the healing narrative back to the Synoptics, but neither did he take it as a pure invention of the Evangelist.[68] Bultmann and Fortna go further; both assume that the story contains a component of a "signs source." But here one must make distinctions. The story is valued by the Evangelist because of the word "rise" ($\check{\epsilon}\gamma\epsilon\iota\rho\epsilon$) in verse 8, which he took to point to something entirely different: to the resurrection of the (spiritually) dead through the Father and the Son. It is not thereby demonstrated that this narrative belonged to a "signs source" (conjectured on the basis of 2:11 and 4:54; Fortna even conjectures that it was the seventh and last sign). It is a question whether the great miracles of chapters 9 and 11 did not form the conclusion of a "signs source," if it really belonged to such a source in spite of considerable formal differences.

It becomes especially evident in this review how strongly conscious and unconscious exegetical methods have influenced the understanding of the composition. It

---

64   Bultmann, *John*, 237f. [177].
65   *Gospel of Signs*, 102–9.
66   Fortna, *Gospel of Signs*, 53.

67   *Das Evangelium des Johannes*, 3f., 76.
68   *Das vierte Evangelium*, 156.

was once taken for granted that the Gospel of John was the work of a single author, viz., of the beloved disciple, John the son of Zebedee. There were theologians whose faith hung on this hypothesis of genuineness. The contradictions and tensions that gradually made themselves felt were at first shoved on the reader, who dared to want to penetrate the mystery of this the deepest of all the Gospels. Very gradually and hesitatingly the insight emerged that perhaps the author also shared the blame for these difficulties. This supposition may be stated with the greatest consideration of hindsight in this way: here lay a work behind which stood the life long meditation of its author. Later criticism became bolder: Perhaps the author died before he could put the finishing touches on his work. It then would have owed its unsatisfactory form to the disciples of the Evangelist; they could not always find their way around in the various versions and sketches. So it appeared that apostolic authenticity and the recognition of aporias were reconciled with each other. Brown has advanced a modern form of this hypothesis in his commentary.[69] Meanwhile, a much more severe form of this type of criticism was developed:[70] to the original document were added ever more layers, which owed their existence to all sorts of editors. There was not yet the slightest inkling that the time for these alleged revisions was very limited: $\mathfrak{P}^{52}$ and the Egerton Papyrus each in its own way made it impossible to push the Fourth Gospel down deep into the second century, as was common earlier. It was probably published as early as the end of the first century. That excludes the possibility of a whole series of revisions. Since textual criticism allows us to be certain of only two small additions (5:3f. and the pericope of the woman taken in adultery, 7:53–8:11), it is best to assume that an unpublished version of the Gospel was made useable successfully by a single editor, although it still required decades before the Gospel of John was generally recognized in this form alongside the three Synoptics. Accordingly, a tripartite divison of the components of the Gospel of John commends itself.

Chapter 5:1–30 offers the reader an especially good opportunity to learn to distinguish these three voices that come to expression in the Fourth Gospel:

1. The voice of the materials employed by the Evangelist;

2. The voice of the Evangelist himself;

3. The voice of the redactor. At the same time, it will be evident that the possibility of making these distinctions has its limits.

Following an introductory first verse, a healing story begins with verse 2 and extends as far as the words "took up his pallet and walked" in verse 9. The balance of this verse turns the healing into a breach of the sabbath, which in verse 16 finally threatens to produce a persecution of Jesus on the part of the Jews. Jesus' reply is understood by the Jews as a blasphemous making-himself-equal with God. This misunderstanding in the end elicits a longer discourse of Jesus about his true relation to the Father.

At first glance, we thus have before us in this chapter a consistently developed unity. Upon closer examination, however, it is so filled with "aporias" that Schwartz can say of it: "The story of the healing of the sick man at the pool of Bethesda . . . belongs to those segments of the Fourth Gospel that become the more difficult the more one pores over them."[71] Of what does the conflict over the sabbath—the one that breaks out in verse 9c—really consist? The first answer must be: it consists of the man who was healed taking up his pallet and walking around. As the Jews immediately instruct him (v 10), that is work that is forbidden on the sabbath. The man who was healed responds, however, that the performer of miracles, who has just healed him, told him to do just that. If one examines verse 8 more closely, it then becomes apparent that Jesus does not give the man who was healed an order like he does in Mark 2:11: the man is not to go home, but is to parade around defiantly with his pallet. That is intended not only to serve as proof that the lame man was healed, but also that he thereby violated the sabbath, in accordance with the order given him. Viewed in this context, the entire healing event can therefore only mean that the sabbath law has been abrogated––and what prodigious significance that had for Judaism. But when we reflect further on the matter, it turns out that the Evangelist himself did not intend to sustain this meaning as he continues the story.

---

69   *John*, 1966.

70   One thinks above all of Schwartz, "Aporien," and Wellhausen, *Das Evangelium Johannes.*

71   "Aporien," 3: 152.

He makes use of the tradition in order to make his own point; better put, in order to bring out in the tradition what, on his own perception, is contained therein. As a consequence, the Evangelist does not handle the text arbitrarily. His "composition" is intended to liberate the right message of Jesus, nothing more. In so doing, he does not entertain the slightest doubt about the "reality" of the tradition that has come down to him, but he does have questions, in all probability, about the clarity of the transmitted report and this is where his own interpretation comes into play.

The tradition of the healing at the pool that he here takes up already has a history behind it. We are still able to observe that, although we cannot reconstruct it word for word in its earliest form. That owes, in part, to the fact that this tradition was not valued by the Evangelist for itself, but only for the correct significance attached to the Christ. He did not concern himself to transmit the tradition that had come down to him with solicitious exactitude, and he was not an artist with a desire to paint. That of course protected him from becoming lost in details, but sometimes, as a consequence, particulars are lost that were necessary for the understanding of earlier readers. That is demonstrated by the amplification of verse 3 and the addition of a new verse 4.

The healing story offers many possibilities of colorful and vivacious narration. However, the Evangelist hurries to come as quickly as possible to what is important because Jesus appears. The old tradition of the pool with the curative powers, in which an angel stirred the waters upon occasion—on this verse 4 would have given correct advice—and which then enabled a single individual to be cured, would have permitted it to be made clear, for example, how superior Jesus was to this Jewish Lourdes. He effects with a single word what the sick man had been waiting in vain for thirty-eight years to obtain. But the Evangelist has something more important to say. The command of Jesus that effects the miracle, "Rise, take up your pallet, and walk," is the point of departure for what has to be narrated as the real event.

In this instance Jesus provokes a breach of the sabbath. This feature, which was already embedded in the tradition, could have been exploited to show Jesus' power over the sabbath. But the Evangelist does not proceed along those lines. He indicates that there is no sabbath rest for God—in spite of Gen 2:2—and thus not

for Jesus either. To understand this "thus" correctly is the aim of Jesus' discourse in verses 19–21, 24–26, and 30a.

The Jews could understand Jesus' claim that he acts exactly like his Father, God, only as blasphemy: Jesus arrogates to himself what belongs to God alone. He appears to want to steal divinity for himself. But the contrary is true. He can do nothing of himself. He is not a "second God" or even the one true God. He exists only for God. The term "obedience" is not suitable. That suits a servant, but not a son, as the Evangelist understands this sonship. The son looks only to the Father, and does here on earth what he sees the Father do. The Father has no secrets from him. He reveals everything to him. The Father has life in himself and thus has the ablility to bestow it. Involved is not this earthly life, which invariably ends in the grave, but real life—it is called "eternal life" here. Jesus also possesses this true life and the ability to bestow it on others: he can do what he sees the Father doing, and will do nothing else. Like the Father, he can cause the dead to rise and can make them alive. A suggestion that he is able to perform such things is given in the healing story with the word, "rise" ($\check{\epsilon}\gamma\epsilon\iota\rho\epsilon$). The Evangelist exploits the feature of the sabbath breach: such an act is always possible. The real purpose of the entire earthly life of Jesus is to give such life. Everything that he performs in his miracles points to that.

However, in spite of everything, this divine act remains a mystery. It occurs in living man, who is nevertheless actually dead in his earthly existence that is alienated from God. This divine act of Jesus permits man, here and now, to pass over from death to life, the life that deserves the name. Of what it consists is not further described. Later, the Evangelist will now and again remind the reader what this life is: "My Father and I will come and make our home with him" is the way one of these hints runs (14:23). Jesus has overcome the separation of God and man (1:14), so runs the promise. That promise is fulfilled wherever a man hears the message of Jesus and sees the Father in him—the Father who is so dismayingly invisible (1:18, 6:46). As a consequence, because Jesus has so thoroughly emptied himself on behalf of God, God is present here in all his fullness (1:16).

Since the Evangelist has eyes only for this event as a whole, his narration of earthly events often seems flat and colorless. He has only one passion (as Käsemann correctly observes on occasion) and that is the one in which the Father can become visible for us (for it really does depend on the Father: 14:28). As a result, in this Gospel, much more than in the Synoptics, the everyday world is short-changed and Jesus comes perilously close to being misunderstood docetically. He goes from "sign" to "sign." His life consists of nothing but allusions to the Father, is a continuous allusion to the Father. And yet no one can understand this allusion prior to the coming of the Spirit (7:39). But for the Evangelist the Spirit has already come. He can therefore speak of the allusion and lift the veil of the mystery in the discourses of Jesus just a bit.

One can understand that this picture of Jesus appeared to the redactor of the Gospel to be in need of augmentation (vv 22f., 27–29, 30b). He therefore added as much as he could of what the "church"[72] said in its confession that differed from or went beyond what the Evangelist proclaimed, and he did so in a style that conformed as much as possible to that of the Evangelist. And so the redactor paints over the Johannine picture of Jesus, without really being aware of it, and represents Jesus as the "Son of man," who will execute judgment on the world as such at the end of time, when the graves open and the dead rise up, some to the resurrection of life, others to the resurrection of judgment. Consequently, because Jesus will be the judge to whom God has given over all judgment, one must honor Jesus as one honors the Father, and one must fear him as one fears the Father. For this Father, whom Jesus, as the son of man, will make evident, has become unlike the Father proclaimed by the Evangelist. Jesus himself has become like the Jesus in the Sistine Chapel. Before him those condemned, those who have done evil, will be cast into hell. With this doctrine of judgment the moral demand has been inserted into the Gospel of John as what is really essential. And there arises a furtive struggle between the Johannine picture of Jesus and God and that of the redactor. The reader, as well as the learned exegete, will therefore easily become bewildered and will often not know how he or she is to forge a unity out of everything that nevertheless appears in this Gospel.

The segment, 5:1–30, is an especially important specimen of Johannine composition. The healing story admits of restructuring as a story about breaking the sabbath. The conflict that arises as a result is retarded because the one who was healed does not know who Jesus is. Exegetes have complained in part that the reader does not learn how the man who was healed learns the name of Jesus in the temple.[73] But the Evangelist leaves it to the reader to puzzle out things not essential for himself. A sentence like: "Then the man who was healed learned that the name of his healer was 'Jesus'" would have been extremely awkward. In that case, the one healed would really appear to be an ungrateful and wicked individual; as it is, that is only an auxiliary hypothesis of Hirsch. Now, finally, the conflict with the Jews breaks out. It leads to Jesus' haughty words about his relationship to his Father (v 17). It is erroneous to conclude[74] that Jesus makes himself equal to God. The Evangelist can now develop his particular christology in 5:19–21, 24–26, 30a, c. It is genuinely new. Precisely because Jesus renounces his own willfulness in its entirety and exists only for the Father is there due him the "glory" ($\delta\acute{o}\xi\alpha$) of the sovereign who sent him.[75] Because men can see only in him the Father who remains invisible (14:9), an encounter with him and with his word possesses that decisive character that goes back to the "drawing power" (6:44) of the Father. The determination of the eternal destiny of man is decided in the here and now of this encounter (5:24). The word of Jesus plays such a role only in the Gospel of John. To that extent it corresponds to the theology of the Reformation, although this characteristic, viewed purely formally, may appear to be gnostic also. This encounter is made possible only after Easter by the coming of the Spirit (7:39). The expression, "The hour comes and now is," is

---

72 Editor: The problem of "an ecclesiastical redactor" no longer presented itself to the author in his last years in the form in which Bultmann proposed it.

73 So Schwartz, "Aporien," 3: 157; Wellhausen, *Das Evangelium Johannes*, 25.

74 As Holtzmann (*Das Evangelium des Johannes*, 77) does.

75 Cf. Haenchen, "Der Vater," 208–16.

therefore very important to and characteristic of the Evangelist. It explains at once why the Evangelist can relate earthly works, although they still remain incomprehensible. Like the Gospel of Mark, he is concerned to show the identity of Jesus with the exalted Lord in a time when the companions of the earthly Jesus and the witnesses of his resurrection had died. That identity cannot be made visible from the standpoint of the exalted Lord. In opposition to the gnostic movement,[76] the attempt was made to assure the reality of the resurrected Lord by heightening his miracles and by giving evidence that he had partaken of food and drink. When the Gospel of John is understood aright, all this apologetic becomes unnecessary. In the opinion of the Fourth Evangelist, the identity of Jesus with the exalted Lord can be guaranteed only on the basis of the earthly Jesus, although his true being was not perceived by the faithful until after Easter. Since, however, the Gospel was read by the post-Easter community, to which the Spirit had opened up these hints ("signs") that those who listened to Jesus did not yet understand, this message of a hidden revelation was now entirely meaningful. John 5:25 contains this peculiar dialectic between the uncomprehended revelation in the earthly life of Jesus and his exalted existence. The believing hearing of the word of Jesus was the eschatological moment for the Evangelist. He did not anticipate a cosmic catastrophe, in which everything would be made right. The way to the Father was open here and now for the believers. But because the "church" did not understand this Gospel and therefore held doggedly to what appeared to the Fourth Gospel to be unimportant, its theology of the word was again obscured by renewed emphasis on miracle, sacrament, office, parousia. The identity of the earthly Jesus with the exalted Lord could be guaranteed only on the basis of the earthly Jesus, although he was not understood until after Easter. This peculiar tension between the uncomprehended revelation in the earthly life of Jesus and the office of the exalted one underscores both the attraction and the repulsion of the Fourth Gospel. Paul developed his message on the basis of his vision of the risen Lord; Mark labored unsuccessfully, in effect, with the "mysterious revelation" of the messianic secret.

Since Bultmann used the concept of "crisis"—crisis understood as the crisis of decision—he had not yet discovered that verses 22–23 also derive from the redactor and not just verses 27–29 (and 30b). In chapter 5 there are thus relatively long insertions in the text of the Evangelist made by the redactor. That supports our earlier surmise that the Gospel of John was subjected to considerable modification prior to its publication. That long hindered the recognition that there were three, not two, different hands to be distinguished in the Gospel of John, and that each of these was theologically unique:

1. The source, which put the greatest possible emphasis on the great miracles as proof that Jesus was the son of God;

2. The Gospel proper, which represented a theological breakthrough and interpreted the miracles only as signs of the relationship to God;

3. The redactor, who enriched the Gospel of John with a theology of the sacraments and a primitive ethic, as well as with the disciple whom Jesus loved, whom he employed apologetically.

That the source, above all, contains the pericopes that are most strikingly narrated makes it even more difficult to discern the theology and evolution of the Fourth Gospel.

The faith that the Johannine Jesus demands is not actually related to him, but is referred to the Father, who sent him (5:24). Jesus speaks "only" the revelatory word that is necessary for faith. Yet this word really only repeats the words of the Father (3:34, 7:16, 8:26, 38, 40, 14:10, 24, 17:8), and so 5:24 corresponds entirely to this basic notion. It follows from this that the preaching of the disciples (and of course of the Evangelist) possesses this decisive character following the outpouring of the Spirit (20:22). We have attempted, in the exegesis of verses 21 and 24–26, to shed light on how the Evangelist understands the process of passing over into life. The fact that verses 31–47 follow upon this pericope in the text demonstrates that there are as yet unresolved difficulties.

---

76   In the gnostic movement, the incarnation of the redeemer threatened to become a fall into the demonic material world and thus to prompt a docetic explanation (cf. 1 John 4:2).

14. Testimony for Jesus

Bibliography

Bell, H. Idris
"Search the Scriptures" [Joh 5,39]. *ZNW* 37 (1938)
10–13.

Bernard, Jacques
"Témoignage pour Jésus-Christ: Jean 5:31–47."
MScRel 36 (1979) 3–55.

Boismard, Marie-Emile
"A propos de Jean V,39. Essai de critique textuelle." *RB* 55 (1948) 5–34.

Bruce, F. F.
"'It is they that bear witness to me.'" In his *The
Time is Fulfilled. Five Aspects of the Fulfilment of the
Old Testament in the New* (Grand Rapids: Wm. B.
Eerdmans, 1978) 33–53.

Charlier, Jean-Pierre
"L'exégèse johannique d'un précepte légal: Jean
VIII, 17." *RB* 67 (1960) 503–15.

Duprez, A.
Jésus et les dieux guérisseurs. A propos de Jean V,
Cahiers de la Revue Biblique 12 (Paris: J. Gabalda,
1970).

Giblet, Jean
"Le témoignage du Père (Jean 5, 31–47)." *BVC* 12
(1955/1956) 49–59.

Haenchen, Ernst
"Zum Text der Apostelgeschichte." In his *Gott und
Mensch. Gesammelte Aufsätze* 1 (Tübingen: Mohr-
Siebeck, 1965) 172–205.

Magaß, Walter
"11 Thesen zum Bibelleser- und zum ʺSuchenʺ in
der Schrift (Joh 5, 39)." *Linguistica Biblica* 47
(1980) 5–20.

Mayeda, Goro
*Das Leben-Jesu-Fragment Papyrus Egerton 2 und seine
Stellung in der urchristlichen Literaturgeschichte* (Bern:
P. Haupt, 1946).

Mees, M.
"Textverständnis und Varianten in Kap. 5 des
Johannesevangeliums bei Epiphanius von Salamis."
Lateranum 46 (1980) 250–84.

Neugebauer, Fritz
"Miszelle zu Joh 5,35." *ZNW* 52 (1961) 130.

Vanhoye, Albert
"Opera Jesu donum Patris [Jo 5,36; 17,4]." *VD* 36
(1958) 83–92.

Vanhoye, Albert
"L'oeuvre du Christ, don du Père (Jn v,36 et
xvii,4)." *RSR* 48 (1960) 377–419.

Wahlde, Urban C. von
"The Witnesses to Jesus in John 5:31–40 and
Belief in the Fourth Gospel." *CBQ* 43 (1981) 385–
404.

5

31 "If I bear witness to myself, my testimony is not true; 32/ there is another who bears witness to me, and I know that the testimony which he bears to me is true. 33/ You sent to John, and he has borne witness to the truth. 34/ Not that the testimony which I receive is from man; but I say this that you may be saved. 35/ He was a burning and shining lamp, and you were willing to rejoice for a while in his light. 36/ But the testimony which I have is greater than that of John; for the works which the Father has granted me to accomplish, these very works which I am doing, bear me witness that the Father has sent me. 37/ And the Father who sent me has himself borne witness to me. His voice you have never heard, his form you have never seen; 38/ and you do not have his word abiding in you, for you do not believe him whom he has sent. 39/ You search the scripture because you think that in them you have eternal life; and it is they that bear witness to me; 40/ yet you refuse to come to me that you may have life.

41/ I do not receive glory from men. 42/ But I know that you have not the love of God within you. 43/ I have come in my Father's name, and you do not receive me; if another comes in his own name, him you will receive. 44/ How can you believe, who receive glory from one another and do not seek the glory that comes from the only God? 45/ Do not think that I shall accuse you to the Father; it is Moses who accuses you, on whom you set your hope. 46/ If you believed Moses, you would believe me, for he wrote of me. 47/ But if you do not believe his writings, how will you believe my words?"

■ 31 Jesus admits that his self-testimony would have no value if he bears witness to himself. The author of the gospel must have known what kind of offense it was when Jesus constantly speaks of himself in his relation to the Father as the one whom the Father had sent. Is that not a form of self-testimony to which one need not pay attention? Is it not a human claim pure and simple that expresses an extreme form of arrogance? How can one require faith in such a claim? These responses correspond precisely to Jewish logic, which was taken over by the early community.

■ 32 Now, however, Jesus asserts that there is really another who bears testimony on his behalf. When he, Jesus, emphasizes that he knows this witness to be true,

that is of course a peculiar continuation of the same line of thought. To invoke a witness of whose veracity one was not persuaded would indeed be senseless.

Consequently, the reading attested by ℵ D a e q sy^c "you know" ($o i \delta a \tau \epsilon$) is understandable: it implies that the Jews recognize the truth of this witness on behalf of Jesus. However, since the Jews have neither heard the voice of God nor seen his form, according to verse 37, and since his word does not abide in them, they do not know the testimony of the Father and know nothing about his truth. Whoever conceived the conjecture "you know" ($o i \delta a \tau \epsilon$) most likely thought of John the Baptist as that "other witness," who is mentioned in verse 33. But for Johannine thought it was self-evident that God alone could really be the witness, and it is further self-evident that this witness is true.

■ **33** The Jews turned to John the Baptist and he bore witness for "the truth" (1:19–27). That could mean simply that the Baptist proclaimed Jesus as "the coming one" and testified that he was the lamb of God and the bearer of the Spirit (1:29–34). But the expression used in verse 33 perhaps has a further and higher sense. Jesus refers to himself in 14:6 as "the truth." In that case, the sentence implies that the Baptist is bearing witness to Jesus as "the truth," who was sent by God into the world (cf. 18:37).

■ **34** But Jesus does not accept human testimony. He cannot seriously invoke it. For the Baptist, too, is a mere man; he is "of the earth" (3:31). As a consequence, his testimony, too, has limited value. Had Jesus called on this testimony, he would have admitted that God can be guaranteed by human testimony. In that case, God would be subject to human judgment. Accordingly, God and he whom God has sent would become part and parcel of the world. Why then does Jesus mention the testimony of the Baptist at all? The answer, "that you may be saved," could then imply that the response of the Baptist made it possible for some to reflect on the matter and to pose seriously the question whether Jesus was not really who he claimed to be.

■ **35** Verse 35 appears to belittle the Baptist and to chide the Jews with respect to their behavior toward John. John of course was not that "light" (Jesus alone is the "light"; cf. 1:9), but he was a lamp that was lighted and is burning. The image that comes to mind is that of the small lamp in antiquity that was filled with oil and fitted with a wick and that gave a weak light. F. Neubauer has conjectured that there is an allusion to Ps 132:17 in this figure: "I have prepared a lamp for my anointed." At all events, such allusions do not belong to the style of the Evangelist. On the other hand, one might accept such an allusion were Christian scribalism at work. It comports with the conviction of the Evangelist that the Baptist made reference to Jesus. The Evangelist also reports that everyone was leaving John and going over to Jesus (3:26). But evidence provided by the continuation of verse 35 to the effect that the Baptist was not taken

seriously and his reference to Jesus was ignored, would not have been put into the record as yet. Had people been glad just to have "a man of God" in their midst? That is not, as Lohmeyer claims,[1] "merely an artful hint" that "John was a messianic figure to them [the Jews]." It could well recall the acclaim with which the preaching and baptism of John was received in his day. But that interpretation is not certain.

■ **36** Jesus, however, has a better witness than the Baptist (that is probably what is meant by "greater than John," μείζω τοῦ Ἰωάννου), viz., the works that the Father gave him to do. From the perspective of Johannine theology, this can be understood only by taking the "works" as "signs." In that case, they would of course not be accessible to everyone and would not be compelling in the sense in which the world would prefer it. They would have something to say only to the one "who is born from above." If one understands "works" in this way, then the Evangelist is true to his message. God and the one whom he sent, accordingly, cannot be established "objectively," like a high pressure zone. Easter is of course a date on the calendar, but when Easter occurs for the individual, it cannot be dated.

■ **37** In addition to these "works," the Father is now also mentioned as witness. That is not suitable to the context. The Father is indeed the sole witness that really must be considered, but the Jews have never caught sight of him and have never heard his voice. It is difficult for the interpreter to account for the fact that God is mentioned as a witness alongside the Baptist, the works, and Scripture. That is to say nothing of the fact that the elders saw God on Mt. Sinai, along with Moses, according to Exod 24:11. Verse 37 knows nothing of that. The Jews who are being addressed have never heard the voice of the Father nor seen his form. Strictly speaking, for the Jews the Father was the unknown God. Of course it helps to observe that the Jews represent the unbelieving world.

■ **38** The statement that the Jews do not have God's word abiding in them has to be interpreted to mean that they have only tentatively decided for Jesus (2:23–25). Yet in the present segment they do not decide for Jesus and the Father at all, but do not believe the one whom the Father has sent, as is expressly emphasized. To what does

---

1   *Das Urchristentum.* Vol. 1, *Johannes der Täufer* (Göttingen: Vandenhoeck & Ruprecht, 1932) 29.

"word" (λόγος) refer? To Jesus, the Logos of the Prologue, or to the OT?

■ **39** Verse 39 is an especially controversial passage. The original form of the text is probably "search" (ἐραυνᾶτε) attested by 𝔓⁶⁶ 𝔓⁷⁵ PEger 2 (ca. 150 CE) and B. Later manuscripts have restored the classical form, ἐρευνᾶτε. The meaning is not affectd by the vowel change.

Papyrus Egerton 2 contains material from the synoptic, Johannine, and apocryphal traditions. Its author was presumably familiar with several gospels and created his own gospel out of them for his community. Barrett quotes the text that is parallel to the text of John (lines 5–10) and discusses the two.[2] He goes into Black's thesis (see further below) that an Aramaic form of the saying of Jesus lies behind this passage and the variants attested in a b syᶜ. Jeremias has reconstructed the text and translated it as follows: ". . . <to> the lawyer<s '. . . e>very one who act<s contrary to the l>aw, but not me! . . . (5) . . . what he does, as he does it.' <And> having turn<ed> to <the> rulers of the people he <sp>oke the following saying; '(Ye) search the scriptures in which ye think that ye have life; these are they (10) which bear witness of me.[3] Do not think that I came to accuse <you> to my Father! There is one <that ac>cuses <you>, even Moses, on whom ye have set your hope.'[4] And when they sa(15)<id>: 'We know that God <hath> spok<en> to Moses, but as for thee, we know not <whence thou art>,'[5] Jesus answered and said unto them: 'Now (already) accusation is raised[6] against <your> unbelief. (20) <No one o>therwise . . .'"[7]

Mayeda provides a full apparatus.[8] He conjectures that the Papyrus made use of a source that was also known to the Gospel of John. We share Jeremias' judgment that the author freely quoted fragments of the gospel tradition (from memory), combined them, and then revised

them. Black conjectures that both the Gospel of John and Papyrus Egerton 2 have an Aramaic source with the wording: dᵉ, disᵉbhirin 'attun bᵉhon.[9] The Gospel of John represents the ambiguous Aramaic ד with ὅτι, while Papyrus Egerton 2 more correctly by the relative pronoun. The old Latin witness b transmits part of verse 39 in doubled form: *quoniam putatis vos in ipsis vitam aeternam habere, in quibus putatis vos vitam habere.* The Latin witnesses a ff² and both Armenian versions also offer the relative pronoun. The Aramaic term סבר, which Black conjectures here, can mean both "to think, imagine" and "to hope."[10] On the other hand, Barrett emphasizes that the hypothesis of an Aramaic original is indeed possible but not essential. He understands the verb "search" (ἐραυνᾶτε) not as an imperative but as an indicative: "You search the Scriptures with the motive of gaining eternal life, and it is they that bear witness to me." Papyrus Egerton 2, on the other hand, must be translated as: "You search the Scriptures in which you suppose you have eternal life." Barrett believes this "smoother" reading is secondary.[11]

We prefer to translate ἐρυαννᾶτε ("search") as an indicative. The theme of Scripture is taken up again in verse 45, with which Payprus Egerton 2 also continues (see above). But the Paprus does not provide us with an original text of the Gospel of John; rather, it combines various Scriptural texts on the principle of word association.

Hirsch is of the opinion that the words "because you think that in them you have eternal life" (ὅτι ὑμεῖς δοκεῖτε ἐν αὐταῖς ζωὴν αἰώνιον ἔχειν) are an additon of the redactor.[12] They are intended to explain why the study of the Scriptures does not lead the Jews to Jesus: the Jews believe that they already have life in the Law and the Prophets. But in that case it is not the study of Scripture

---

2   *John*, 268.

3   John 5:39.

4   John 5:45.

5   John 9:29.

6   Cf. John 12:31.

7   Jeremias, *NTApoc* 1: 96; *Unknown Sayings of Jesus*, tr. Reginald H. Fuller (London: S. P. C. K., 1958) 18–20.

8   *Das Leben-Jesu-Fragment Papyrus Egerton 2 und seine Stellung in der urchristlichen Literaturgeschichte* (Bern: P. Haupt, 1946).

9   *An Aramaic Approach to the Gospels and Acts* (Oxford:

10   Clarendon Press, ²1954) 54f.

10   *An Aramaic Approach to the Gospels and Acts* (Oxford: Clarendon Press, ²1954) 181f.

11   *John*, 268. On the subject of an Aramaic ד in NT texts, see Haenchen, "Zum Text der Apostelgeschichte," in his *Gott und Mensch. Gesammelte Aufsätze* 1 (Tübingen: Mohr-Siebeck, 1965) 172–205, esp. 196.

12   *Studien*, 57f.

that alienates them from Jesus, but the prejudice with which they conduct their study. It is not the redactor who has introduced something foreign into the text; it is the exegete who imports an alien meaning using these words as the occasion.

■ **40** The text does not say that the Jews do not want to come to Jesus because they believe they already have salvation in the Law and the Prophets.[13] Rather, the Jews are reproached because they do not want to come to Jesus for life, although the Scriptures bear witness to Jesus.

■ **41** Verse 41 is reminiscent of verse 34 with its "I do not receive glory from men," which seems rather abrupt. Jesus makes no use of the testimony of the Baptist. He seeks the glory of God, i.e, the glory that is given by God, as indicated by verse 44, which picks up the thread again.

■ **42** The connection between verses 41 and 42 is difficult (but cf. 2:23–25). Some manuscripts have sought to smooth the text by rearrangement: "that you do not have the love of God."[14] This rearrangement is attested by (א*) D b e q. Boismard points to this passage as another one of those passages where Sinaiticus and D concur. We are of the opinion, however, that a special text-type is not manifest in these cases, but that, in the Gospel of John, Sinaiticus has been strongly influenced in a "Western" direction.

■ **43** Verse 43 again lacks a good connection with the preceding and its content is unclear: Who is the one who comes in his own name and is acknowledged by the Jews? Hirsch has judged that to be an allusion to Bar Kochba,[15] which was written, of course, by a redactor and not the Evangelist. All our manuscripts admittedly contain the verse. However, the Gospel of John appeared prior to Bar Kochba, as one must now agree in view of 𝔓52 and Papyrus Egerton 2. Spitta sees a reference to Deut 18:20 in this verse.[16] But there reference is to a prophet who presumes to speak in God's name when God has not authorized him to speak, or to a prophet who speaks in the names of other gods. The verse thus remains obscure.

■ **44** A new thought is again introduced in this verse: the one who seeks glory from men and does not strive for the glory that comes from the only God is unable to come to faith. That could be a development of the thought in verse 42.

■ **45-57** These verses are related to verse 39 in content: the Scriptures bear witness to Jesus. Moses has already written of Jesus. Luke 24:44 shows that the later community appropriated the OT for this form of persuasion. It does not suit the theology of the Evangelist, but it probably comes close to Luke 16:31. Judgment follows, for the Evangelist, in the moment in which man rejects the message of Jesus. To hold that the Jews should already have acknowledged Jesus on the basis of the OT, and therefore that the Jews are actually guilty of disobedience to Moses, is a form of apologetic that is foreign to the Evangelist; it comes very close to identifying the real guilt of the Jews as their lack of faith with respect to Moses.

Overview

A break comes between verses 30 and 31. The themes of the resurrection of the dead and the relation of the Father and Son are not carried further, and the tightly woven train of thought is broken off. These difficulties show up in almost all modern commentaries (on this, more below). What follows is only a makeshift. In accordance with the possibilities, it is presupposed that we are moving in the thought world of the Evangelist. That Jesus speaks of himself and of his authority as the one sent by the Father belongs to the peculiarities of the Gospel of John. Is that not testimony to himself? Is that not then worthless in the eyes of the Jews? Is that not purely and simply a human claim reflecting the greatest possible arrogance? Does the claim of Jesus not demand an unexceptional witness, a μαρτυρία? It is possible that the Evangelist had already faced this question. The answer he gives in the farewell discourses appears to

---

13 Contrary to Bultmann, *John*, 267f. [201].
14 [Rather than: "that the love of God you do not have."—Translator.]
15 *Studien,* 58; Wellhausen, *Das Evangelium Johannes,* 27, had already suggested this interpretation.
16 *Das Johannesevangelium als Quelle der Geschichte Jesu* (Göttingen: Vandenhoeck & Ruprecht, 1910) 133.

point to the Spirit, which puts all the questions of the disciples to rest. It is not out of the question, however, that the entire segment, verses 31–47, which treat the problem of "witness" (μαρτυρία) and of "glory" (δόξα), is a redactional addition; it is designed to indicate that there were, nevertheless, valid witnesses for Jesus.

Brown makes evident what internal difficulties have to be faced in verses 31–47. In his opinion, verse 31 pre-supposes the silent objection, which is articulated in 8:13: "No one can be his own witness."[17] In fact, the principle is enunciated in the Mishnah, *Ketub.* 2.9.[18] Jesus enumerates four witnesses who speak on his behalf. However, according to Brown, they are only four aspects of the "other" witness (the "Father"), who is mentioned in verse 32: (1) John the Baptist (see 1:19–34); (2) Jesus' miracles;[19] (3) the Father himself (who, in Brown's interpretation of verse 38, provides internal testimony within the hearts of men); (4) the sacred Scriptures (which come from God).

A saying of Jesus with such an apologetic tendency is unknown to the Synoptics. As a consequence, Brown believes that this entire segment could derive from the apologetic of the Christian community in the face of Jewish objections; indeed, the whole of chapter 5 is intended to move Jewish Christians to leave the synagogue and profess their faith in Jesus.

According to Brown, verses 41–47 are directed against the roots of Jewish disbelief.[20] Jesus is angry with the Jews not on the basis of personal ambition, but because they reject God's presence in him. Verses 45–47 attack the Jews at their most sensitive point: they hope that Moses will be their advocate before God,[21] but he is their prosecutor.

Granted that verses 31–40 stem from the apologetic of the Christian community, then the tensions that exist between and among these verses had not yet become evident, let alone explained. The identity of the "other" (ἄλλος) in verse 32, who is different from Jesus, was already contested in ancient times. Because of verses 34

and 36, Cyril of Alexandria and the Latin Church Fathers saw the "Father" here (as do Bultmann and Brown himself today). Chrysostom and most of the Greek Fathers, however, interpreted the "other" to refer to the Baptist.[22] If the reference is to the "Father," the subsequent reference to the Baptist does not fit the context. Even if John's testimony has come from God (see 1:29–36), it is here rejected as the testimony of man (v 34). The implication, moreover, is that the four categories of testimony recognized by Brown are not to be understood as four aspects of God. If the "works" (ἔργα) refer to the miracles of Jesus, as Brown believes, then this verse runs counter to the theology of the Evangelist, as it was expounded earlier. On the other hand, it would conform to the theology of the narrative material of which he has made use. But such an assessment of the miracles can also have suited the redactor very well. That is not unimportant for the question of sources. Bultmann's interpretation of the "works" (ἔργα) as referring to the whole activity of Jesus as revealer arouses the suspicion that it is intended to avoid the "most obvious" reference to the miracles of Jesus, which is more immediately plausible. God cannot really be introduced as the third witness, since "the witness" is not an aspect of God. Consequently, it is puzzling why the Father is introduced as a third witness in his own right, alongside the Baptist and the miracles. Brown interprets verse 37 as internal testimony evidently in order to undergird his "four aspect" theory. The reference to Scripture in the text, i.e., in verse 39, has not been clearly marked off from what precedes.

All of this creates the impression that the entire segment, verses 31–47, is really an attempt, not thought through, to protect Jesus from the charge that his assertions about himself are of no value, by introducing "objective" witnesses. That applies also to verses 45–47. These verses are not really connected with verses 43f., but come closer to verses 39f., without simply being united thematically with them.

---

17   *John,* 1: 227–29.
18   Billerbeck, 2: 446; cf. J.-P. Charlier, "L'exégèse johannique d'un précepte légal: Jean VIII, 17," *RB* 67 (1960) 503–15.
19   This is how Brown understands the "works" [ἔργα], which Bultmann, however, takes to mean the whole of Jesus' activity as revealer (*John,* 265f. [190f.]).
20   *John,* 1: 228f.
21   See Billerbeck, 2: 561.
22   *In Joh.* 11.1; MPG 59, p. 230.

Now that suggests the conclusion that the redactor played a greater role in the transmitted text of the Gospel of John than has hitherto been accepted. If the verses identified by us as insertions (vv 5, 22f, 27–29, 30b) are intended to supplement the Johannine doctrine of the resurrection of the "dead" in the present encounter with the message of Jesus; and if they are intended to supplement that doctrine with the older expectation embedded in futuristic eschatology and the doctrine of the last judgment by the Son of man at the end of days; we could then say that the redactor has made the attempt here to supplement the Johannine doctrine of Jesus' self-witness, left unguarded in a way peculiar to him, and to undergird it with arguments evidently created to meet Jewish objections.

Furthermore, the tradition of the witness of the Baptist for Jesus, taken over by the Evangelist, emerges as not entirely suitable to the doctrine of the Evangelist: The "Father" is visible only in Jesus, and so only those who participate in the Spirit after Easter can see him.

15. The Feeding of the Five Thousand

Bibliography

Barrett, Charles Kingsley
"John and the Synoptic Gospels." *ExpTim* 85 (1973/1974) 228–33.

Berrouard, M.-F.
"La multiplication des pains et le discours du pain de vie (*Jean*, 6)." *Lumière et vie* 18 (1969) 63–75.

Bligh, John
"Jesus in Galilee." *HeyJ* 5 (1964) 3–26.

Boismard, Marie-Emile
"Le papyrus Bodmer II." *RB* 64 (1957) 363–98.

Braun, François-Marie
"Quatre 'signes' johanniques de l'unité chrétienne." *NTS* 9 (1962/1963), esp. 147f. on 6:12–13.

Charlier, Jean-Pierre
"La multiplication des pains." *AsSeign* 32 (1967) 31–45.

Cribbs, F. Lamar
"St. Luke and the Johannine Tradition." *JBL* 90 (1971) 422–50, esp. 435–37.

Cribbs, F. Lamar
"A Study of the Contacts that Exist between St. Luke and St. John." SBLASP 2 (Missoula: Scholars Press, 1973) 1–93, esp. 39–43.

Dunkerley, R.
"The Sign of the Meal (Jn 6)." *London Quarterly and Holborn Review* 32 (1963) 61–66.

Gärtner, Bertil
John 6 and the Jewish Passover, ConNT 17 (Lund: C. W. K. Gleerup; Copenhagen: Ejnar Munskgaard, 1959).

Haenchen, Ernst
"Johanneische Probleme." *ZTK* 56 (1959) 19–54. Also in his *Gott und Mensch. Gesammelte Aufsätze* 1 (Tübingen: Mohr-Siebeck, 1965), esp. 90–93.

Heising, A.
"Exegese und Theologie der alt- und neutestamentlichen Speisewunder." *ZKT* 86 (1964) 80–96.

Johnston, Edwin D.
"The Johannine Version of the Feedings of the Five Thousand—an Independent Tradition?" *NTS* 8 (1961/1962) 151–54.

Lee, Edwin Kenneth
"St. Mark and the Fourth Gospel." *NTS* 3 (1956/1957) 50–58.

Leenhardt, F. J.
"La structure du chapitre 6 de l'évangile de Jean." *RHPR* 39 (1959) 1–13.

Léonard, Jeanne-Marie
"2 Rois 4 42–44 et Jean 6 1–13." *ETR* 55 (1980) 265–70.

Martyn, J. Louis
"We have found Elijah." In *Jews, Greeks, and Christians. Religious Cultures in Late Antiquity. Essays*

in Honor of William Daivd Davies, ed. Robert Hammerton-Kelly and Robin Scroggs. SJLA 21 (Leiden: E. J. Brill, 1976) 181–219, esp. 193–97.

Mendner, Siegfried
  "Zum Problem 'Johannes und die Synoptiker.'" *NTS* 4 (1957/1958) 282–307.

Mollat, D.
  "Le chapitre VI³ de Saint Jean." *Lumière et vie* 31 (1957) 107–19.

Moule, C. F. D.
  "A Note on Didache IX.4." *JTS,* n.s., 6 (1955) 240–43.

Norris, J. P.
  "On the Chronology of St. John V and VI." *The Journal of Philology* 3 (1871) 107–12.

Ponthot, J.
  "Signification générale et structure du chapitre VI de S. Jean." *Revue Diocésaine de Tournai* 11 (1956) 414–19.

Preiss, Théo
  "Etude sur le chapitre 6 de l'Evangile de Jean."

ETR 46 (1971) 143–67, esp. 144–56.

Quiévreux, François
  "Le récit de la multiplication des pains dans le quatrième Evangile." *RSR* 41 (1967) 97–108.

Shorter, Mary
  "The Position of Chapter VI in the Fourth Gospel." *ExpTim* 84 (1973) 181–83.

Smith, Morton
  "Mark 6:32–15:47 and John 6:1–19:43." SBLASP 2 (Missoula: Scholars Press, 1978) 281–87.

Smith, Morton
  "Collected Fragments: On the Priority of John 6 to Mark 6–8." SBLASP 1 (Missoula: Scholars Press, 1979) 105–8.

Wilkens, Wilhelm
  "Evangelist und Tradition im Johannesevangelium." *TZ* 16 (1960) 81–90.

6

1 After this Jesus went to the other side of the sea of Galilee, which is the sea of Tiberias. 2/ And a multitude followed him, because they saw the signs which he did on those who were diseased. 3/ Jesus went up into the hills, and there sat down with his disciples. 4/ Now the Passover, the feast of the Jews, was at hand. 5/ Lifting up his eyes, then, and seeing that a multitude was coming to him, Jesus said to Philip, "How are we to buy bread, so that these people may eat (and be satisfied)?" 6/ This he said to test him, for he himself knew what he would do. 7/ Philip answered him, "Two hundred denarii would not buy enough bread for each of them to get a little." 8/ One of his disciples, Andrew, Simon Peter's brother, said to him, 9/ "There is a lad here who has five barley loaves and two fish; but what are they among so many?" 10/ Jesus said, "Make the people sit down." Now there was much grass in the place; so the men sat down, in number about five thousand. 11/ Jesus then took the loaves, and when he had given thanks, he distributed them to those who were seated; so also the fish, as much as they wanted. 12/ And when they had eaten their fill, he told his disciples, "Gather up the fragments left over, that nothing may be lost." 13/ So they gathered them up and filled twelve baskets with fragments from the five loaves, left by those who had eaten. 14/ When the people saw the sign which he had done, they said, "This is indeed the prophet who is to come into the world " 15/

Perceiving then that they were about to come and take him by force to make him king, Jesus withdrew again to the hills by himself.

■ **1** "After this" (μετὰ ταῦτα) is one of the little connectives used in the Gospel of John.[1] According to the present text of the Gospel, Jesus had been speaking prior to this time in Jerusalem. The transition is difficult. For this reason, many exegetes have placed chapter 6 before chapter 5. Bultmann arranges the text as follows: after chapter 4 comes 6:1–59, then chapter 5; 7:15–24 and 8:13–20 follow in that order. The title for the whole section is "Revelation as Κρίσις [Judgment]."[2] These rearrangements are impossible.[3] The outline based on these rearrangements, consequently, also does not stand up. Brown rightly concludes that placing chapter 6 before chapter 5 has some advantages, but he does not think it absolutely necessary.[4] Other arguments speak for the traditional order, which is what we also prefer. The Evangelist has no interest in reproducing exactly the itinerary of Jesus. He presumably did not have the possibility of doing so. "The other side of the sea" appears to locate the following event on the east shore. The identification of the sea is overdone. This problem was recognized at an early date and attempts were made to eliminate it. While (G) N *pc* sy[2] omit τῆς Γαλιλείας ("of Galilee"), D (Θ) *pc* b c r[1] eliminate the double designation by inserting εἰς τὰ μέρη ("the regions of") before τῆς Τιβεριάδος ("of Tiberias"). The phrase εἰς τὰ μέρη appears in Mark 8:10 and Matt 2:22, 15:21, 16:13. Hirsch incorrectly holds the view that the reading of D is "the point of departure for all manuscript variants."[5] 𝔓[75] reads the text as it appears in Greek New Testaments today, while 𝔓[66], which Hirsch did not yet know, inserts τῆς Τιβεριάδος into the text. Josephus[6] uses the name Tiberias to designate the sea in question; Tiberias, the city, was founded 26 CE.[7] Pausanias[8] refers to λίμνην Τιβεριάδα ὀνομαζομένον ("the lake called Tiberias"). In John 21:1, the editor who supplements the Gospel refers to "the sea of Tiberias." He also supplemented the text here by adding the new name to the old.

■ **2** The context does not make comprehensible why a multitude of people was following (imperfect of duration) Jesus. This feature belongs to the tradition of this story (which is secondary in relation to the synoptic account). "They saw" is a *constructio ad sensum*.[9] The reading of 𝔓[66], ἐθεώρουν ("they used to see," imperfect), is an improvement on the imperfect ἑώρουν, which corresponds to the participle ἑώρων read by ℵ 𝕽 *pm*; 𝔓[75] reads ἐθεώρων. The forms of θεωρέω replace the present and imperfect of ὁράω, which is not common.[10] The crowd gathers because people saw the healings of Jesus. That note is derived from the theology of the source. The Evangelist contests taking the signs in their literal sense in verse 26. Mark is also not entirely successful in introducing the crowd.[11]

■ **3** Manuscripts ℵ and D again concur; ℵ in the entire Gospel of John often shows "Western" influence.[12] Mark knows nothing of a mountain (6:30–44, 8:1–10), although Matthew probably does in Matt 15:29 (feeding of the 4,000), but not in 14:33 (feeding of the 5,000).[13] That Jesus first sees the multitude coming to him in verse 5 but does not escape to the hills until verse 15,[14] betrays a secondary development, which was probably found already in the source.[15]

■ **4** Wellhausen regards verse 4 as one of those "mile-

---

1 See further on 2:12.
2 *John*, 203–84 [149–214]. Cf. Schnackenburg, *John*, 2: 7–11; Barrett, *John*, 271f.
3 See the Introduction §4, "Disorder and Rearrangement."
4 *John*, 1: 235f.
5 Hirsch, *Studien*, 59.
6 *BJ* 3.57 and 4.456.
7 Billerbeck, 2: 467–77; Dalman, *Sacred Sites and Ways*, 274.
8 5.7.3.
9 BDF §134(1).

10 BDF §101, *s.v.* ὁράω.
11 See Haenchen, *Der Weg Jesu*, 245.
12 Contrary to Boismard, "Le Papyrus Bodmer II," *RB* 74 (1957) 366.
13 Cf. Gardner-Smith, *St. John and the Synoptic Gospels* (Cambridge: Cambridge University Press, 1938) 27–33.
14 Wellhausen, *Das Evangelium Johannes*, 28.
15 Contrary to Bultmann, *John*, 211 n. 5 [156 n. 4].

stones of chronology" introduced at random into the narrative and only subsequently tacked on to the text;[16] such chronological notices extended the duration of Jesus' activity by several years. Hirsch conjectures,[17] correctly in my judgment, that the editor at least indicated the institution of the Lord's Supper with this verse, since he remarked its absence in the narrative.[18]

■ 5 Verse 5 opens the narrative proper with a certain solemnity.[19] Unlike Matt 15:29f., there is no mention here of the healing of the sick or of Jesus teaching people. The fact that Jesus sits down with his disciples is not intended as an analogy to a rabbi who sat and taught. Rather, the thought of the miracle that Jesus will perform subsequently dominates the whole story. The question addressed to Philip[20] may suggest that Jesus himself did not know what he intended to do and so sought advice and counsel from others.

■ 6 There follows the assurance that the question was meant to test (not tempt). Jesus knew everything in advance and already had the miracle in mind. This is not to say that Jesus' omniscience turns his human form into a mere appearance, any more than Mark 2:8 and Matt 9:4 are meant to do that; one must not, therefore, infer docetism from such remarks in the Gospel of John.

■ 7 Verse 7 is not intended to paint Philip as particularly faithless, but to make clear to the reader that the sum of 200 denarii (already mentioned in the tradition) would not be nearly enough.[21] The heightening of the miracle as the tradition develops is especially evident here. The size of the crowd, the number of which is first mentioned in verse 10, is therefore quite large.

■ 8 Hirsch wants to attribute Andrew to the redactor since an "author parsimonious with words"—is that what the author of the source was?—would not have said, "one of his disciples," and then given his name afterwards.[22]

But "Andrew, the brother of Simon" appeared earlier in 1:40 and is mentioned in 1:45, 6:8, 12:22 (twice) in addition. Peter himself is skipped over in this passage. One might conjecture that Peter is spared in this way from the faithlessness that Andrew naively and involuntarily confesses. But the Evangelist does not intend to say that. Peter simply does not play a conspicuous role in the Gospel of John.

■ 9 The observation of Andrew that there was a lad[23] there with five barley loaves and two fish is intended only to show the reader that in this case human possibilities have failed. How the lad came to be there is not a question to be raised. The story is reminiscent of 2 Kgs 4:42ff.: A man brought to the prophet Elisha twenty barley loaves (like poor people eat) and fresh ears of corn in a sack. Then the prophet commanded: "Give to the people that they may eat." But his servant objected: "How am I to set this before a hundred men?" Then he replied: "Give them to the men so that they may eat, for thus says the Lord, 'They shall eat and have some left.'" When he had set the food before the men, they ate and had some left, as the Lord had promised.

While B. Weiss rashly asserts that there is nothing against the view that the Evangelist was an eyewitness,[24] Bauer holds the view, probably correctly, that the Elisha story probably served as "the model for our story";[25] Bultmann, on the other hand, is of the opinion that there is no proof that 2 Kgs 4:43f. had any influence on this

---

16 *Das Evangelium Johannes*, 28.

17 *Studien*, 60.

18 Cf. Bultmann, *John*, 212 n. 2 [156 n. 6]: the relationship to the Eucharist is produced by the redactorial addition in 6:51–58.

19 Bultmann views the matter differently, *John*, 212 n. 3 [156 n. 7], and he also resists such solemnity in 4:35.

20 Philip is mentioned twelve times in the Gospel of John.

21 Cf. the Overview.

22 Hirsch, *Studien*, 60.

23 On the forms παιδάριον ("lad") and ὀψάριον ("morsel"), cf. D. C. Swanson, "Diminutives in the Greek New Testament," *JBL* 77 (1958) 134–51, with tables of diminutives in -ιον, -άριον, -ίδιον, -άρδιον, -ιδάριον, -ίσκος,-ίσκη, -ίς. Altogether, the NT uses thirty-three forms of diminutives, so popular in Koine; they actually have no diminutive meaning. Matthew and Luke have the greatest number of different forms, although Mark and John run a close second. Accordingly, the German edition of Blass-Debrunner is to be corrected, but not the English.

24 *Das Johannes-Evangelium*, 236.

25 *Das Johannes-Evangelium*, 92.

narrative.[26] But the agreements are simply too great: a supply of barley bread that is much too small is presupposed, with the thought: "What is this for so many?" And men are sated and yet there is food left over. Barrett believes that 2 Kgs 2:42–44 may have influenced this story.[27] It is remarkable that Wellhausen does not discuss the OT parallel. Nevertheless, it is especially important for the history of the development of traditional segments.

■ 10 Verse 10 of course recalls Mark 6:39ff. But there people are made to sit down on the green grass in groups of fifty and one hundred, thus making the count reported in 6:44 possible. Perhaps John has reproduced the tradition utilized by him in a somewhat abbreviated form. In any case, his interpretation does not hang on the miracle story as such, but on its character as a sign, which he later reveals (v 35).

■ 11 Jesus himself distributes the bread and fish, without the help of the twelve apostles. It is of course true that the picture is not thereby made clearer. The Evangelist pushes the apostles into the background elsewhere. The decisive thing is what Jesus does. Each person receives not merely a morsel, but as much as he wants. The redactor has presumably read an allusion to the Lord's Supper into "when he had given thanks" ($\varepsilon\dot{v}\chi\alpha\rho\iota\sigma\tau\dot{\eta}\sigma\alpha s$), which he does not find reported in the Gospel of John. The head of every Jewish household, however, said a blessing over the bread: "Blessed be you, Yahweh, our God, King of the world, . . . who causes the bread to issue from the earth."[28] The word "morsel" ($\dot{o}\psi\dot{\alpha}\rho\iota o\nu$) is a diminutive of $\ddot{o}\psi o\nu$, which means something cooked, to be eaten with bread; what is meant is fish to be eaten with bread.

■ 12 All were satisfied. In Mark 6:43, those who had eaten their fill themselves gathered up the uneaten scraps or crumbs of bread ($\kappa\lambda\dot{\alpha}\sigma\mu\alpha\tau\alpha$). In the Gospel of John, Jesus has the disciples do the gathering—perhaps a feature derived from the source. Only through this feature do the dimensions of the miracle become evident: the leftovers gathered together are more, much more, than the amount with which they began. Nothing is said of remnants of fish. According to a rabbinic tradition,[29] only those scraps that were smaller than an olive were not retrieved. It was also a Jewish custom to collect the scraps of bread. In this case, however, the leftovers serve to confirm the miracle.

■ 13 The disciples collect twelve basketfuls—one for each disciple. How these baskets came to be there all of a sudden is a question not to be asked of such a story: they are intended to lend vividness without resorting to realism. The twelve baskets and the five loaves are tellingly contrasted with each other: the whole miracle can be seen in this one picture. The narrative originally closed with this picture. But in this version it moves beyond the climax.

■ 14 When the people have seen the miracle that Jesus has performed, they declare that he is the prophet who has come into the world. Acts 3:22f (Deut 18:15) indicates that the relation of this prophet to Jesus was also known and recognized outside Johannine Christianity.

In Qumran "the prophet" was expected as one of three messianic figures (along with the two messiahs): 4QTestim 5, 1QS 9.10 (also cf. *T. Benj.* 9.2, *T. Levi* 8.15, 1 Macc 4:46, 14:21).

This passage permits the conjecture that the tradition underlying the source used in the Gospel of John was also influenced by Jewish Christianity.

■ 15 Verse 15 introduces a thought that is fundamentally different from verse 14: Jesus perceives that the crowd is going to take him, because of the miracle of the loaves, and make him king. That Jesus escapes this desire of the crowd by beating a hasty retreat to the hills[30] is contradicted by verse 3, where he is already in the hills. However, this withdrawal is entirely appropriate, since Jesus emphasizes the unpolitical character of his kingdom before Pilate in 18:36: "My kingdom is not of this world." It is of decisive importance for the christology of the Evangelist that Jesus, as the one sent by the Father, does not pursue any political goal, which in any case would be "of the world."

The addition in D, "and he prayed there," does not take into consideration that Jesus withdrew into the hills for an entirely different reason. Perhaps whoever added this gloss was thinking of Mark 6:46.

The two last verses contain many difficulties. Schnackenburg[31] thinks they can be solved only by accepting the view that verse 14, "the choral response,"

---

26 *John*, 212 n. 6 [157 n. 3].
27 *John*, 229.
28 Billerbeck, 2: 685.

29 Billerbeck, 4: 2, 626.
30 The witness of ℵ* lat sy^c make that clear by substituting "flees" for "withdraws."

was formulated by the Evangelist in accordance with his own theological judgment. It is the case that some miracle stories have "choral conclusions," in praise of the miracle worker, as, for example, Mark 4:41b, where, following the stilling of the storm, the disciples say: "Who then is this, that even wind and sea obey him?" The synoptic accounts of the feeding end differently, however: in Mark 6:44 and 8:9 and Matt 14:21 and 15:38 by giving the large number of persons who were fed; in Luke 9:17 and in the Gospel of John by giving the number of baskets, twelve, filled with scraps of bread. John 6:13 likewise ends with the mention of the baskets. A further choral conclusion to the miraculous feeding is unnecessary in the Johannine narrative. If one considers verse 14 in and of itself, it does have the effect of a choral conclusion made up of Johannine material. "The prophet" is mentioned in 1:21 as the third eschatological figure after the Messiah and Elijah. In 7:40 some Jews in Jerusalem say of Jesus: "This is really the prophet"; others regard him as the messiah; a third group contests this because the messiah is supposed to come from the village of Bethlehem. "The prophet" refers properly to the promise given in Deut 18:15 that God will send a prophet like Moses, whose instructions all have to obey. John 6:14 gives the impression that it is intended to form an edifying transition to an unedifying continuation. For now comes something for which there is no synoptic counterpart: Jesus—the action now moves over to him— perceives that those who were miraculously fed are coming to take him by force and make him king. Since in those days, in the eastern part of the Roman empire, Caesar was often called "king" ($\beta\alpha\sigma\iota\lambda\epsilon\dot{\upsilon}s$), like the Seleucids before him, that would be a proclamation of Jesus as Caesar, and with that the Romans would have immediately intervened. For the Evangelist, however, the proclamation of Jesus as a (worldly) king would have been an intolerable thought. In the temptation narratives, Matthew and Luke regard the invitation to world rulership as a temptation of the devil. Whoever wrote verse 15 wanted to make it clear that the Christian movement was not political. The Jews accuse Paul and his companions and the whole Christian mission of being an anti-Roman political movement in Acts 17:7: they are

turning the entire empire upside down and assert that there is another Caesar ($\beta\alpha\sigma\iota\lambda\epsilon\dot{\upsilon}s$), viz., Jesus. The post-Easter sect, which spread quickly, was maligned as an anti-Roman political movement, and John 6:15 belongs to this context as a piece of Christian apologetic: Jesus avoids the senseless demand of the crowd by withdrawing quickly into the hills. But verse 15 has yet a further function: it separates Jesus from the disciples, who had not participated in the miraculous feeding in the Johannine version and in whom the crowd therefore has no further interest. Verse 15 therefore connects the story of the feeding with that of the walking on the water in that it prepares for the latter.

Relevant to the entire scene of the miracle of the bread and its effect is what the Grand Inquisitor says to the Christ who has returned in Dostoyevsky's novel, *The Brothers Karamazov*: "Thous didst promise them the bread of Heaven, but, I repeat again, can it compare with earthly bread in the eyes of the weak, every sinful and ignoble race of man? And if for the sake of the bread of Heaven thousands and tens of thousands shall follow Thee, what is to become of the millions and tens of thousands of millions of creatures who will not have the strength to forego the earthly bread for the sake of the heavenly? Or dost Thou care only for the tens of thousands of the great and strong, while the millions, numerous as the sands of the sea, who are weak but love Thee, must exist only for the sake of the great and strong? No, we are for the weak too."[32]

■ **Overview**

The Christian community was very fond of the feeding stories. As a consequence, they appear five times in the Gospels, aside from the occurrence in John 6: Mark 6:34–44, Matt 14:13–21, Mark 8:1–10, Matt 15:32–39, Luke 9:10–17. That permits us, in connection with our passage, to track more precisely the development of the tradition that lies behind the Johannine source and the Gospel of John as a whole. The first thing that is evident is this: There is general agreement regarding the context in which the feeding stories appear: in Mark 6 there follows on the feeding of the 5,000 (vv 34–44) the account of the walking on the water (vv 45–52) and the

---

31   *John*, 2:20–24.

32   Fyodor Dostoyevsky, *The Brothers Karamazov*, tr. Constance Garnett (New York: Modern Library, 1950), 300f.

crossing to Gennesaret (vv 53–56). Mark 7:1–23 indeed depicts a controversy with the Pharisees and thus appears to address a new theme, but 7:24–30 contains the story of the Syrophoenician woman, in which the children's bread plays the decisive role, and a healing story in 7:31–37 brings the whole segment to a close. The feeding of the 4,000 in Matt 8:1–9a parallels the feeding of the 5,000 very closely, although it is not recognized as a parallel as such by Mark. There is no analogue to the walking on the water, although there is a crossing (8:9f.), which leads this time to Dalmanutha. There follows a controversy with the Pharisees in 8:11f., in which the Pharisees demand a sign. In 8:13–21 there is a discourse on bread (leaven) and in 8:22–26 a healing story. The Johannine version comes very close to this complex: the feeding of the 5,000 is depicted in 6:5–13, the walking on the water in 5:16–20. A crossing is reported briefly in verse 21, which ends this time in Capernaum. To this is joined a controversy with the crowd in 6:26–31, which demands a sign. Then in 6:32–51a, the Evangelist achieves his ultimate purpose with the interpretive discourse of Jesus on himself as the true bread from heaven.

What is of interest here is the fact that, in spite of all the differences, there is agreement not only in the "shorter segments," but also a striking concurrence in themes over a longer segment of the tradition. That leads to the question whether longer sequences of tradition were not formed earlier than is commonly thought, sequences that turn out to have been gathered around a single theme. It could be that particularly impressive single pieces, "small units," exercised a cohesive power that generated more extensive blocks of tradition. These consisted of individual units of tradition; such units of course occasionally could also be exchanged with others. The question to what extent the individual evangelists participated in this process should be investigated.

The Johannine version, consequently, has not been created out of one or several synoptic texts.[33] It is simply not conceivable that the Evangelist had the Synoptics before him and selected a word from this, a usage from that, and a feature from the other in composing his account. On the one hand, this view assumes that all three Gospels—or at least the Gospel of Mark—had at that time been widely circulated and were at the disposal of the fourth Evangelist; on the other, it assumes that this was not sufficient to account for all the features of the Johannine account. Rather, the solution to be preferred is this: the story of the miraculous feeding was already being told prior to Mark in various versions, among which no absolute priority can be assigned. John 6:1–13 is another version of the same story, and it is not dependent on the synoptic accounts. That is not to say that the Johannine version is as old or even older and more original than the Markan account. Various features, for example, the naming of Philip and Andrew and the omission of Peter, exhibit later, novelistic coloring, and the relation of Jesus to his disciples appears to be a later and at the same time Johannine perspective.

The introduction is briefer than in Mark 6 and the parallel because, as in Mark 8, the connection of the feeding with the story of Herod and the Baptist, on the one hand, and with the mission of the Twelve, on the other, is lacking. In Mark 8 the immediate commencement of the feeding is to be explained on the basis that a repetition only requires a new frame of reference (although only hinted at). The relation of Jesus to his disciples (the Twelve are not mentioned) is altered in John 6:1–13. The initiatives all lie with Jesus, who knows from the outset what he intends to do. The question put to Philip only indicates that the needs of the people cannot be met by natural means; the same is true of Andrew's remark in 6:9b. Verse 9a, on the other hand, functions as the transition to the miracle story to follow. The collection of the fragments of leftover bread demonstrates that the bread was more than enough for the original number of people present and brings to light the miraculous multiplication of loaves. The mention of barley loaves was probably influenced by 2 Kgs 4:42f. (LXX); Christians steeped in scriptural lore found the miracle of Jesus prefigured already in the OT. The fish, which were also multiplied, are appropriate to a location by the sea, but they frustrate the eucharistic significance often sought for the feeding. Jesus prays prior to the distribution of food, and this belongs to the realm of Jewish custom, according to which the head of the house-

33   So Hirsch, *Das vierte Evangelium*, 170; Strathmann,
    Das Evangelium nach Johannes, 111.

hold pronounced a blessing prior to the beginning of the meal.

In the synoptic account, the miracle makes no impression on the disciples (who are excluded from the action itself) and none on the crowd. In the Johannine version, on the other hand, the crowd wants to take him as the promised prophet and make him king (vv 14f.); this indicates that the miracle in its Johannine sense has not been understood as an allusion to Jesus and the true bread from heaven.

The pericope contains the text of the source only lightly reworked by the Evangelist (except for vv 14f.?). It is a variant of the story of a miraculous feeding found several times in various forms in the Synoptics.

It is now appropriate to carry out a comparison of details. If one assumes that the miraculous element in a story is not lessened during the process of transmission, but rather increases, then the version in Mark 8:1–9a is the earliest in the series of those preserved: instead of 5,000, "only" 4,000 are sated; and this number is satisfied with seven rather than five loaves of bread. To the seven loaves there corresponds seven basketfuls of leftover fragments. Matt 15:32–38 is very closely related to Mark 8:1–9a, although the number of those miraculously fed has risen from 4,000 to: "Those who ate were four thousand men, besides women and children" (Matt 15:38). In the Markan version, walking on the water is missing from chapter 8. The crossing takes place without an additional miracle. One can of course ask whether Mark has left one miracle out, since otherwise the two narratives would have been very nearly identical. But this speculation is erroneous, in my judgment. Mark was firmly persuaded, as Mark 8:19–21 demonstrates, that two different feedings had taken place. The fact that the miracle of walking on the water does not occur in Mark 8 shows that the miraculous element has not been heightened to the same extent as in Mark 6:34–44 and in the even more developed form preserved by Matthew in 14:13–31 (Peter walking on the water). The number of baskets in Mark 6, Matthew 14, and Luke 9 does not correspond to the number of loaves that were divided. The reason for that is the assimilation of the number of baskets to the number of disciples who participated in the distribution. But that also results in an exaggeration of the miracle.

The Johannine version concurs with that of Mark 6:34–44 on many points: five loaves (John 6:9), 5,000 filled, and twelve baskets are presupposed. The fragments, the κλάσματα, have been interpreted by F. C. Synge as referring to the eucharist, at least in Mark 8:19f.:[34] the κλάσματα are not uneaten fragments, but portions that remained undistributed. The disciples (who do not participate in the distribution in John) are to distribute the eucharistic meal of the body and blood of Christ, of which nothing may perish. But that does not fit the picture being drawn in John. There the κλάσματα are the fragments that have been distributed, of which none is to perish.

C.F.D. Moule,[35] like A. Robinson[36] before him, finds an echo of John 6 and 11 in the Didache: The sentence, "As this κλάσμα ("broken bread") was scattered upon the mountains, but was brought together and became one,..." (Did. 9.4) is an echo of John 6:12, "gather up" (συναγάγετε) and of John 11:52, "but to gather into one the children of God who are scattered abroad," with reference to the story of the feeding. What is correct in this interpretation, in my opinion, is that "broken bread" (κλάσμα) in Did. 9.3 (which corresponds to the "cup," ποτήριον) is an allusion to the eucharistic meal of the community. But that has nothing to do with the "fragments of bread" (κλάσματα) in John 6: these fragments were never scattered on the mountains.

Let us return to the Johannine version: there follows the story of the walking on the water in a form, to be sure, that deviates from that of Mark. That indicates that the Gospel of John is not dependent on Mark. Other indications support the same conclusion: in Mark 6:37 two hundred denarii are sufficient to provide each person with a morsel of bread, but in John 6:7 they are not enough to do that. According to Mark 6:35, the feeding takes place toward evening; in John 6:15f. dusk does not fall until he has withdrawn to the hills. John's mention of the barley loaves, in which the influence of 2 Kgs 4:42–44 is evident, is new. That could be a piece of later Christian scribalism; but it may also be that an older

---

34   "Studies in Texts," *Theology* 50 (1947) 263f.

35   "A Note on Didache IX.4," *JTS*, n.s., 6 (1955) 240–43.

36   *Theological Studies* 13 (1911/1912) 547f.

feature of the story is (again) being honored. More on this point subsequently.

The character of the Johannine representation vis-à-vis the synoptic tradition, however, becomes especially evident at another point: in Mark 6 the disciples make Jesus aware of the hunger of the crowd. In Mark 8, on the other hand, the initiative passes to Jesus: he points out to the disciples how isolated they are and how impossible it would be to buy bread. There is no mention in the Gospel of John of any need. When Jesus sees the crowd gathering, it is already certain for him that he will now perform the miracle of the feeding (6:5f.). The question put to Philip and the observation of Andrew (persons not mentioned in the synoptic accounts) only emphasize that the possibility does not exist for men to solve the problem. The Johannine source aims ultimately at the magnificently miraculous, as Strathmann has well put it: "The miracle as such and therefore a demonstration of power" is "the purpose at which the action of Jesus is exclusively aimed."[37] This goes together with the fact that in the Johannine version the "human" trait disappears that is present in Mark 6 and 8 (although in different ways): the compassion of Jesus for the poor. This miracle story as a whole, which he did not doubt really took place, is only a hint for the Fourth Evangelist that Jesus is the true bread from heaven. We will speak of that later, since the discourse on bread in 6:26–51a develops this theme in detail.

On this basis, the Johannine version, compared with the synoptic accounts, is to be understood as cold and colorless. The concentration on Jesus and his miracle causes the "human" element to recede. If one may briefly describe the modification in the tradition, one can perhaps say: the primitive community combined a memory of a meal of Jesus and his disciples beside the Sea of Galilee with the OT story of Elijah and in so doing proclaimed that whatever proceeded and proceeds from the miraculous power and the richness of the Lord's blessing excels by far the miracle of the OT convenant. For Albert Schweitzer the feeding was a report of the first "supper" of Jesus, who expected the imminent end of the age.[38] The memory of this meal, which was at the same time freighted with the highest eschatological

tension, was retained, but now transformed into a miracle story. Schweitzer's interpretation made an enormous impression. But it is only a hypothesis, which was hastily historicized, with the result that Schweitzerian imminent eschatology was attributed to Jesus; this eschatology of course was corrected just as quickly as a consequence of the delay of the persecutions connected with the last days.

The source for the Gospel of John offers a pure miracle story without any eschatological symbolic content. The Evangelist takes it up with a view to what he himself has in mind to say regarding the manna of Moses and Jesus and the true bread from heaven. How little he altered the heart of the report that came down to him is indicated by the fact that he took over the story of the walking on the water along with it, because the two had become connected at one stage of the tradition (but not yet in Mark 8). That is characteristic of the style of composition of the Evangelist: He takes over relatively large blocks of narrative material whose real meaning he develops only later in a discourse of Jesus (in our case in 6:26). It would therefore be wrong to seek something of that mysterious sense, the real message of the Evangelist, in any single feature of the Johannine narrative material. It is characteristic of this method of composition that many features of the narrative material cannot really be exploited.

If one attempts, as does Bultmann, to interpret the story of the feeding as a part of a "signs source," such an attempt has both positive and negative features. It is correct, in my opinion, to hold that this pericope contains a segment of tradition that the Evangelist found in his source and which he reproduces relatively accurately; this piece of tradition reported a miracle that awakened faith. But one is thereby in danger of overlooking the fact that this piece of tradition does not represent the earliest form of the feeding story, but a developed and, at the same, abbreviated late form, by virtue of the evolution of the tradition. One must not think of the evolution of the tradition like the growth of a spruce or fir. It is much more like the growth of a mighty oak with a great crown extending in all directions. The conception of the signs source, as Bultman appears to hold it,

---

37 *Das Evangelium nach Johannes*, 108.
38 *The Mysticism of Paul the Apostle*, tr. William Montgomery (London: A. and C. Black, [2]1953) 362–66 = *Die Mystik des Apostels Paulus* (Tübingen: Mohr-Siebeck, 1930, [3]1981) 352–56.

tempts one to view the form of the source used by the Gospel of John as the original form and, at the same time, to forget the history of its tradition. The complex relationships between and among the original form of specific narrative material, the late form found in the source that the Evangelist employed, and the authentic message of the Evangelist must constantly be kept in mind by the exegete, without overlooking possible intrusions on the part of the redactor. Moreover, the Evangelist often altered, abbreviated, or expanded his source (cf., for example, 4:48f., 5:1–7). There is also the danger that one will view John 6:1–13 in the wrong perspective, viz., in its relation to the synoptic narratives of the feeding. One must rather read this story—indeed, the whole of chapter 6—in comparison with chapter 5. The two chapters are constructed in comparable ways. In both cases, a miracle of Jesus is first related: the healing of the lame man in chapter 5, the feeding of the 5,000 in John 6:1ff. A kind of interlude then follows in both instances. In chapter 5 it begins basically with the concluding sentence in verse 9b: "Now that day was a sabbath." Here the fuse for the explosion to follow is lighted. The real argument with the Jews opens with verse 17; that argument culminates in the great discourse of Jesus on his relation to the Father, which provides the principal contribution to the comprehension of Johannine christology. In John 6, a miracle story again sets up the larger unity of the chapter. The redeeming moment—almost imperceptible— is the story of the feeding. It does not appear at first to provide the occasion for a conflict, as in 5:9b. An interlude begins in 6:14, that runs internally parallel to 5:9bff. Since, however, it contains diverse material, it is not so perspicuous as 5:9b–18. The long discourse of 6:25–71 is as important as the discourse of Jesus in 5:19–47, if it does not surpass it on account of the immediate consequences it evokes. For an enthusiastic crowd no longer follows Jesus after chapter 6. The "great crowd" sought by Jesus has disappeared. In 8:30 it appears that many new believers are won: this is an illusion which Jesus himself immediately dispels. The excommunication of the man born blind from the synagogue (John 9:34f.) forms the external dividing line. The decline of the Jesus movement has evidently taken place; it had begun with 6:14. The raising of Lazarus, which appears once again to bring in many believers (11:45), is really the beginning of the end.

16. Jesus Walks on Water

Bibliography

Anonymous
"Noch ein Versuch über das Wandeln Jesu auf dem Meere nach Mt 14,24–33; Mk 6,45–51 und Joh 6,16–21." *Magazin für Religionsphilosophie, Exegese und Kirchengeschichte* 12 (1802) 310–33.

Bleek, Friedrich
"Verhältniss der johanneischen Darstellung zur synoptischen in der Erzählung vom Wandeln Jesu auf dem Meere." In his *Beiträge zur Einleitung und Auslegung der heiligen Schrift.* Vol. 1, *Beiträge zur Evangelien-Kritik* (Berlin: G. Reimer, 1846) 102–5.

Giblin, Charles Homer
"The Miraculous Crossing of the Sea (Jn 6,16–21)." *NTS* 28 (1983) 96–103.

Gieseler, J. K. L.
"Vermischte Bemerkungen: Zu Joh 6,22." *TSK* 2 (1829) 137–38.

Gifford, George
"'Ἐπὶ τῆς θαλάσσης (Joh 6,19)." *ExpTim* 40 (1928/1929) 236.

Heil, J. P.
Jesus Walking on the Sea. Meaning and Gospel Functions of Matt 14:22–23, Mark 6:45–52 and John 6:15b–21, AnBib 87 (Rome: Pontifical Biblical Institute, 1981).

Holtzmann, Heinrich Julius
"Das schriftstellerische Verhältnis des Johannes zu den Synoptikern." *ZWT* 12 (1869) 62–85, 155–78, 446–56; esp. 163–64, 170.

Roberge, Michel
"Jean VI, 22–24: Un problème de critique textuelle." *Laval Théologique et Philosophique* 34 (1978) 275–89.

Roberge, Michel
"Jean VI, 22–24: Un problème de critique littéraire." *Laval Théologique et Philosophique* 35 (1979) 139–51.

Zarella, Pietro
"Gesú cammina sulle acque. Significato teologico di Giov 6,16–21." *Scuola Cattolica* 95 (1967) 146–60.

6

16 When evening came, his disciples went down to the sea, 17/ got into a boat, and started across the sea to Capernaum. It was now dark, and Jesus had not yet come to them. 18/ The sea rose because a strong wind was blowing. 19/ When they had rowed about three or four miles, they saw Jesus walking on the sea and drawing near to the boat. They were frightened. 20/ But he said to them, "It is I; do not be afraid." 21/ Then they were glad to take him into the boat, and immediately the boat was at the land to which

they were going. 22/ On the next day the
people who remained on the other side of
the sea saw that there had been only one
boat there, and that Jesus had not
entered the boat with his disciples, but
that his disciples had gone away alone.
23/ However, boats from Tiberias came
near the place where they ate the bread
after the Lord had given thanks. 24/ So
when the people saw that Jesus was not
there, nor his disciples, they themselves
got into the boats and went to Capernaum, seeking Jesus. 25/ When they
found him on the other side of the sea,
they said to him, "Rabbi, when did you
come here?"

■ **16** As night fell (this happens suddenly in the south), the disciples went down to the sea. They thus did not "retreat" with Jesus. That supports the view that verses 14f. did not belong originally to the story of the feeding of the 5,000. Nevertheless, verse 16 can be understood from the point of view of verse 3. Since Jesus had gone up on the mountain (v 3)—to the top of the mountain?—the disciples who had been left alone must now take a decision. They do not stay at the place where the feeding took place. There is no further mention of the crowd, although the people remained at the location of the feeding (v 22). Mark had not really been able to make clear why the disciples had departed without Jesus (6:45). Originally the separate narrative of the feeding was not designed to be followed by a story of Jesus walking on the sea.

■ **17** The disciples get into a boat (the boat in which they came to the feeding?) and go across the lake toward Capernaum. The story does not indicate precisely why they want to go there. It was reported in 2:12 that Jesus and his relatives stopped a short time there. But that does not explain why Capernaum is now the destination. The tradition of some teaching activity of Jesus in Caper-naum (Matt 11:23, Luke 10:15), accompanied by miracles, presumably dictated that at this point Caper-naum would be the scene of further activity (note 6:59).

The second part of the verse is quite remarkable: "It

was now dark ($\sigma\kappa\sigma\tau\iota\alpha$), and Jesus had not yet come to them." The correction of ℵ D could have been in-fluenced by 12:35.[1] This reading avoids the pluperfect "had fallen" ($\dot\epsilon\gamma\epsilon\gamma\dot\sigma\nu\epsilon\iota$), which indicates, according to Bauer,[2] that the disciples had waited until night fell. On the view of Wikenhauser,[3] verse 17b gives the reason the disciples had gotten into the boat. Brown conjectures that the disciples could have sailed along the shore in the expectation that Jesus would come to them on the beach.[4] Brown takes $\ddot\eta\rho\chi\sigma\nu\tau\sigma$ ("began") as a conative imperfect (attempted action). The translation, "they began to cross, . . ." seems to us to be more nearly correct. In the primitive tradition verse 17 perhaps had the function of preparing for the trouble to which the disciples, now left alone, were coming. That trouble now sounds remote.

■ **18** Bultmann proposes to strike verse 18 as a gloss,[5] in company with Heitmüller,[6] because the stilling of the storm is not narrated in what follows and the genitive absolute appears rarely in the Gospel of John and is thus out of place. Wendland had already observed that the motif of danger plays no part in this account.[7] If, how-ever, a storm does not threaten, Jesus' walking across the lake is emptied of any real meaning (he cannot be of help). As OT precursors for walking on the sea, one usually cites Job 9:8 ("and trampled the waves of the sea"), Isa 43:16 ("Thus says the Lord, who makes a way

1 Bultmann, *John*, 215 n. 3 [159 n. 9].
2 *Das Johannesevangelium*, 93.
3 *Das Evangelium nach Johannes*, 121.
4 *John*, 1: 251.
5 *John*, 215 n. 4 [159 n. 1].
6 "Das Evangelium des Johannes," 773.
7 *Die urchristlichen Literaturformen*, HNT 1, 3 (Tübingen: Mohr-Siebeck, 1912) 276.

in the sea, a path in the mighty waters"), and Ps 77:19 ("Thy way was through the sea, thy path through the great waters"). But only Job 9:8 LXX is a real parallel: the Lord "walks on the sea as on firm ground" ($\pi\epsilon\rho\iota\pi\alpha\tau\hat{\omega}\nu$ $\dot{\omega}s$ $\dot{\epsilon}\pi'$ $\dot{\epsilon}\delta\dot{\alpha}\phi\sigma\nu s$ $\theta\alpha\lambda\dot{\alpha}\sigma\sigma\eta s$).

■ **19** "After they had rowed" or "after they had gone (sailed) twenty-five or thirty stadia" ($\dot{\epsilon}\lambda\eta\lambda\alpha\kappa\acute{o}\tau\epsilon s$), which means to about the middle of the lake. According to Josephus,[8] the lake was forty stadia wide and one hundred forty stadia long. But these figures are in fact too small: at its widest point the lake is 12 kilometers (about 7 miles), and at its longest point about 21 kilometers (about 12 miles).[9] The narrator did not of course have modern geographical data at his disposal. The entire story is narrated not from the perspective of Jesus, but from the standpoint of the disciples (unlike Mark 6:48): they see Jesus suddenly come towards them over the lake and draw near the boat. This sight fills them with fear. As a consequence, Jesus speaks to them.

■ **20** His words reassure them: "It is I; do not be afraid." The phrase "I am" ($\dot{\epsilon}\gamma\acute{\omega}$ $\epsilon\dot{\iota}\mu\iota$) does not function at this point as a divine revelation formula. Yet scholars have seen a divine ephiphany in the Markan parallel. Hirsch proposes to reconstruct the first appearance of Jesus to Peter out of John 21, Mark 6, and Matt 14:30f.,[10] and confesses that he would regard this story, "if it had perhaps gone as conjectured here, as a very accurate report of a personal experience." That of course could be to overrate the fanciful possibilities of reconstruction.

■ **21** The disciples want to take Jesus into the boat with them. In this regard Bultmann asks:[11] "Should one assume that they carried out their intention? Or should one imagine that 'Jesus, going before the ship, drew it to land.'"? We must respond negatively to both questions, in my judgment. Both perspectives miss the singularity of the new miracle that occurs here: the boat with the disciples and with Jesus on board are suddenly at the shore to which the disciples were heading. In interpreting the sense of the passage, Chrysostom writes: "He did not, however, get into the boat, in order that the effect of the miracle ($\theta\alpha\hat{\nu}\mu\alpha$) might be greater."[12] Origen is of the same opinion: "by divine power" ($\theta\epsilon\dot{\iota}\alpha$ $\delta\nu\nu\dot{\alpha}\mu\epsilon\iota$) they suddenly come to land. A new miracle is appended to that of the walking on the water.

In the hymn to Pythian Apollo,[13] a ship miraculously arrives at its destination swiftly after the god comes on board: this has no bearing on our passage.

■ **22** Today scholars think of "on the next day" ($\tau\hat{\eta}$ $\dot{\epsilon}\pi\alpha\acute{\nu}\rho\iota\sigma\nu$) as a segment marker rather than as a chronological datum.[14] The following verses probably ought to produce the objective "proof" for the reality of the miracle. But the impression they leave is unclear, as though the story were poorly narrated or as though various traditions have coalesced. The crowd is still located at the site of the feeding,[15] which is now described as "on the other side of the sea" from the standpoint of the disciples and Jesus on the west shore. "Saw" ($\epsilon\hat{\iota}\delta\sigma\nu$)[16] expresses the matter from the standpoint of the past.[17] What is meant is that on the next day the people remember that they had seen only one boat on the shore, in which the disciples alone, without Jesus, had departed. The hellenistic diminutive $\pi\lambda\sigma\iota\dot{\alpha}\rho\iota\sigma\nu$ ("little boat") interchanges with $\pi\lambda\sigma\hat{\iota}\sigma\nu$ ("boat") without any difference in meaning.[18]

■ **23** The word $\alpha\lambda\lambda\alpha$ is not to be taken to mean "but" ($\dot{\alpha}\lambda\lambda\dot{\alpha}$), but is to be understood as "other" ($\check{\alpha}\lambda\lambda\alpha$). Ships from Tiberias come to the site of the feeding—the author could not get the crowd to Jesus again without the help of additional ships. The words "after the Lord had given thanks" ($\epsilon\dot{\nu}\chi\alpha\rho\iota\sigma\tau\acute{\eta}\sigma\alpha\nu\tau\sigma s$ $\tau\sigma\hat{\nu}$ $\kappa\nu\rho\acute{\iota}\sigma\nu$) are

---

8   *BJ* 3.506.

9   These figures are derived from Gerber, *Biblisch-historisches Handwörterbuch,* vol. 3, ed. B. Reicke and L. Rost (Göttingen: Vandenhoeck & Ruprecht, 1966); Denis Baly, *The Geography of the Bible,* revised edition (New York: Harper & Row, 1974) 196, gives the figures as 12 and 18 km., respectively; the figures given by K. W. Clark in *IDB* 2, s.v. "Galilee, Sea of," are 13 miles by 8 miles.

10   *Frühgeschichte,* 1: 182–86.

11   *John,* 216 n. 3 [159 n. 7].

12   *Hom.* 43.1, t. VIII, p. 255e/256a.

13   *Homeric Hymns,* 394ff., tr. Hugh G. Evelyn-White, LCL, 352ff.

14   For example, Brown, *John,* 1: 257.

15   Against Bultmann, *John,* 216 n. 5 [160, n. 1].

16   א D: $\epsilon\hat{\iota}\delta\epsilon\nu$ ("he saw").

17   Cf. Brown, *John,* 1: 257.

18   א* D and (ℜ Θ) attempted to improve the text at an early date.

omitted by D 091 *pc* a e sy^{sc}. They are present, on the other hand, in 𝔓^{75} and in ℵ A B K L W Δ Θ f^{13}. In 𝔓^{66}, unfortunately, a quire containing John 6:11–35 is missing. We may be confronted here with an addition of the redactor, who recalls his conception of the feeding as a eucharistic meal and speaks of Jesus as the Kyrios.

■ **24** Verse 24 repeats, in part, what was said in verse 22. However, it is probably intended to make clear to the reader the logical conclusion that the crowd had drawn: since Jesus and his disciples were no longer there, they get into the boat and cross the lake to Capernaum, seeking Jesus. This phrase, "seeking Jesus," prepares for Jesus' saying in verse 26: "You seek me . . ." Why the crowd proceeds to Capernaum is as mysterious as why the disciples do so in verse 17. The narrator probably already has in mind the long discourse that he locates in Capernaum (a certain tradition may lie at its base). Dodd is of course of the opinion that the transformation of a dangerous mob into a synagogue congregation obscures the danger that existed in getting Jesus involved politically in a messianic movement. Jesus avoided this by his retreat into the hills, while the disciples escaped across the lake in a flight at night (with the danger of a shipwreck). The difficulty with this interpretation, however, is that a messianic insurrection would have been a threat only in the event that Jesus had really fed 5,000 persons with five barley loaves. Instead of this, we are of the opinion that Dodd has confused the later suspicion of Christians as an underground political movement with the situation in the time of Jesus.

■ **25** When the people find Jesus again on the other side of the lake (this time viewed from the perspective of the site of the feeding, which they had just left), they ask him: "Rabbi, when did you come here?" One might really have expected them to ask: "How did you get here (so quickly)?" But the form of the question used is also intended to call attention only to the miracle: Jesus got to Capernaum earlier from the mountain of feeding than did the crowd which traveled the next day by boat. It is of course scarcely credible that there were enough ships in Tiberias to transport 5,000 people. The number 5,000 was of course a part of the tradition of the feeding. But the narrator probably no longer had the larger number in mind; he may now have thought only of "a crowd" that could have consisted of as few as 100 persons. This question points once more to the miracle of the crossing and the walking on the water (of course, only the reader knows that; the crowd does not); it also serves as the point of departure for the discourse of Jesus to follow.

Overview

The written source used by the Evangelist evidently combined the story of the feeding of the 5,000 with the sketch of the walking on the sea, as in Mark 6:45–52 and Matt 14:22–27. He also took over the story of the walking on the water, although that story did not serve his purposes to the same degree as the narrative of the feeding. The walking on the water is therefore an old miracle story that had undergone more than one development. Its best known form is in Mark 6:45–52. Yet that version is not original either. For the feeding and the departure of the disciples are artificially connected: Jesus requires the disciples to leave, yet no obvious reason is given for it.

Albert Schweitzer holds this opinion about the feeding: "From Jesus' point of view it was a sacrament of salvation."[19] He continues: "This meal must have been transformed by tradition into a miracle, a result which may have been in part due to the references to the wonders of the Messianic feast which were doubtless contained in the prayers, not to speak of the eschatological enthusiasm which then prevailed universally. Did not the disciples believe that on the same evening, when they had been commanded to take Jesus into their ship at the mouth of the Jordan, to which point he had walked along the shore—did they not believe that they saw Him come walking towards them upon the waves of the sea?"[20] One sees here how Schweitzer unhesitatingly takes over an old rationalistic explanation of this miracle because he wants to be able to understand it psychologically on the basis of his presumption of acute eschatological tension.

There is nothing of this in the Markan account itself: Jesus sees the disciples in distress—at night! He passes them by in the fourth watch of the night. Exegetes who

---

19   *The Quest of the Historical Jesus,* 377.
20   *The Quest of the Historical Jesus,* 379f.

have calculated the distance and time exactly have come to the conclusion that Jesus was walking on the waves with the alacrity of a pedestrian. That is behavior meant to be contrasted with the Schweitzerian explanation, and yet it is related to it in its rationalism. Mark sees matters quite differently. The disciples cry out because they take Jesus for an apparition (that indicates to the reader that an event occurred that was humanly impossible); then Jesus gets into the boat with them. The wind abates; but they still do not comprehend anything. It is possible, indeed, even probable, that the story of the stilling of the storm has played a role here (Mark 4:35–41). Again, in the Markan version the text reads: "and the wind ceased" (Mark 4:39). The Matthean version in 14:22–27 essentially reflects the Markan text.[21] However, a second expansion then follows. Peter also attempts to walk on the water. Jesus rescues him when he begins to doubt and starts to sink, and he then worships Jesus as the Son of God. When they came to shore many sick were healed.

Things are quite different in the second version of the feeding story recorded in Mark 8:1–10 and Matt 15:32–39. In this version, Jesus boards ship with his disciples following the feeding and journeys to a place, the name of which has been corrupted in the tradition (perhaps Magdala). In our judgment, the older text lacked an account of a miracle on the return journey from the feeding.

The Johannine account resembles that of Mark, although it has its own peculiarities. As the author represents it (6:14f.), Jesus stood in danger of being proclaimed Caesar, and when he saw that danger unfolding, he avoided it by a rapid retreat to the mountains. This is the way Jesus left the scene of the feeding. The crowd of people spent the night at the site of the feeding. At dusk the disciples had already departed and started for Capernaum in the boat, without having received appropriate instructions from Jesus for such occasions. They had to act on their own resolution. There is a difficulty at this point in the Markan account also: Jesus requires the disciples to travel to Bethsaida without him, while he repairs to the mountain to pray. The difficulty is of a compositional sort: Jesus must somehow get up on the mountain in order to be able to see the distress of the disciples on the lake and to come to them over the swells. John distributes the emphases somewhat differently: the disciples journey on their own in the direction of Capernaum; it is indeed briefly reported that a high wind came up and the sea became rough, but no mention is made of a real danger for the disciples; Jesus simply comes across the waves from the mountain: that is not extolled as a great rescue effort. In its place appears a new miracle which has eluded scholarly attempts to give a rational explanation: at the moment when the disciples want to take Jesus into the boat in the middle of the lake, the disciples, the boat, and Jesus are suddenly at their destination, the shore at Capernaum. Since the enormous crowd likewise reaches Capernaum by means of ships from Tiberias, the earlier constellation of the three groups appears to be reconstituted here, except that the synagogue at Capernaum appears in place of the wilderness. These peculiarities demonstrate that the Evangelist is here following a written source of his own. The feature that Jesus came to the aid of his disciples who were distressed at sea had disappeared from this source. The story that is narrated in the text of John makes it evident to the reader that the crowd seeking Jesus did catch sight of the miraculous in the earthly sense, but no more. When they address him as "rabbi"— their aim to make him king has been forgotten— that proves that they do not have the slightest premonition of his true position. And so the Evangelist can append the long discourse of Jesus on the true manna, the manna that Moses did not give. Rather, Jesus is himself the bread of life. When Jesus makes these pronouncements, the crowd becomes rebellious, and the people who had just wanted to make him king depart disappointed and embittered. Basically, only the Twelve remain loyal to him and even their fidelity appears to be in doubt: in response to his confession of loyalty, Peter receives the reply that one of the Twelve chosen by Jesus is a devil. The catastrophe of Jesus' Galilean ministry has set in.

Scholars like Hirsch but also Kümmel,[22] who presuppose some use of the synoptic Gospels, have not sufficiently taken it into account, in my judgment, that the synoptic Gospels were by no means available at that

---

21 Luke does not have a corresponding story, because in the copy of Mark used by Luke the great omission had already begun; it extends to 8:26. On this point, cf. Haenchen, *Der Weg Jesu*, 303f.; in line 18 Luke 18:18–22 is to be read instead John 6:11–35.

22 *Introduction*, 201ff.

time—between 80 and 90 CE—in every community. The Gospel of Mark especially might not have been easily procured; Matthew was presumably in the process of dissemination. But above all, the community in which the Evangelist lived appears to have been outside the mainstream of the Christian tradition. If our conjecture is correct that the Evangelist found a written gospel in that community, a gospel that depicted Jesus as attested by many and impressive miracles, that is no reason to assume that the Evangelist looked for other traditional material in the synoptic style.

17. Jesus' Discourse
on the True Bread from Heaven

Bibliography

A. On 6:26–59

Aletti, J.-N.

"Le discours sur le pain de vie (Jean 6). Problèmes de composition et fonction des citations de l'Ancien Testament." *RSR* 62 (1974) 169–97.

Andersen, Axel

"Zu Joh 6,51bff." *ZNW* 9 (1908) 163f.

Barrett, Charles Kingsley

"Das Fleisch des Menschensohnes (Joh 6,53)." In *Jesus und der Menschensohn. Für Anton Vögtle*, ed. R. Pesch and R. Schnackenburg (Freiburg: Herder, 1975) 342–54.

Barth

"Nähere Beleuchtung des 6. Kapitels des Ev. Johannes." *Magazin für christliche Prediger* 2.1 (1824) 43–63.

Beauvery, R.

"Le fils de Joseph   Manna descendue du ciel? Jn 6,41–52." *AsSeign* 50 (1974) 43–49.

Bergmeier, Roland

"Glaube als Werk? Die 'Werke Gottes' in Damaskusschrift II, 14–15 und Johannes 6, 28–29." *RevQ* 6 (1967) 253–60.

Blank, Josef

"Die johanneische Brotrede. Einführung: Brotvermehrung und Seewandel Jesu: Jo 6,1–21." *BibLeb* 7 (1966) 193–207.

Blank, Josef

"'Ich bin das Lebensbrot' Jo 6,22–50." *BibLeb* 7 (1966) 255–70.

Borgen, Peder

Bread from Heaven. An Exegetical Study of the Concept of Manna in the Gospel of John and the Writings of Philo, NovTSup 10 (Leiden: E. J. Brill, 1965).

Borgen, Peder

"Observations on the Midrashic Character of John 6." *ZNW* 54 (1963) 232–40.

Borgen, Peder

"The Unity of the Discourse in John 6." *ZNW* 50 (1959) 277–78.

Bornkamm, Günther

"Die eucharistische Rede im Johannes-Evangelium." *ZNW* 47 (1956) 161–69. In his *Geschichte und Glauben,* part 1. *Gesammelte Aufsätze,* vol. 3. BEvT 48 (Munich: Chr. Kaiser Verlag, 1968) 60–67.

Bornkamm, Günther

"Vorjohanneische oder nachjohanneische Bearbeitung in der eucharistischen Rede Joh 6?" In his *Geschichte und Glauben,* part 2. *Gesammelte Aufsätze,* vol. 4. BEvT 53 (Munich: Chr. Kaiser Verlag, 1971) 51–64.

Croatto, J. Severino

"Riletture dell'Esodo nel cap. 6 di San Giovanni."

BeO 17 (1975) 11–20.

Crossan, John Dominic
"It is Written: A Structuralist Analysis of John 6." SBLASP 1 (Missoula: Scholars Press, 1979) 197–214.

Dunn, James D. G.
"John VI—An Eucharistic Discourse?" *NTS* 17 (1971) 328–38.

Feuillet, André
"Les thèmes bibliques majeurs du discours sur le pain de vie (Jn 6). Contribution à l'étude des sources de la pensée johannique." *NRT* 82 (1960) 803–22, 918–39, 1040–62.

Feuillet, André
"Note sur la traduction de Jér xxxi 3c." *VT* 12 (1962) 122–24.

Feuillet, André
Le discours sur le pain de vie (Jean, chapitre 6) (Paris: Desclée de Brouwer, 1967).

Finkel, Abraham
The Pharisees and the Teacher of Nazareth. A Study of their Background, their Halachic and Midrashic Teachings, the Similarities and Differences, AGJU 4 (Leiden: E. J. Brill, 1964), esp. 149ff.

Fortna, Robert T.
"Source and Redaction in the Fourth Gospel's Portrayal of Jesus' Signs." *JBL* 89 (1970) 151–66, esp. 155–61.

Gambino, G.
"Struttura, composizione et analisi letterario-teologica di Gv 6,26–51b." *RivB* 24 (1976) 337–58.

Gärtner, Bertil
John 6 and the Jewish Passover, ConNT 17 (Lund: C. W. K. Gleerup; Copenhagen: Ejnar Munskgaard, 1959).

Ghiberti, G.
"Il c[ap] 6 di Giovanni e la presenza dell'Eucarestia nel 4° Vangelo." *Parole di Vita* 14 (1969) 105–25.

Giblet, Jean
"The Eucharist in St. John's Gospel (John 6)." *Concilium* (GB) 4 (1969) 60–69.

Goguel, Maurice
The Eucharist from the Beginning to the Time of Justin Martyr, tr. Charles Porter Coffin (Evanston, IL, 1933) = *L'Eucharistie des origines jusqu'à Justin Martyr* (Paris: G. Fischbacher, 1910).

Hofius, Otfried
"Erwählung und Bewahrung. Zur Auslegung von Joh. 6,37." *Theologische Beiträge* 8 (1977) 24–29.

Howard, J. K.
"Passover and Eucharist in the Fourth Gospel." *SJT* 20 (1967) 329–37.

Jeremias, Joachim
"Joh 6, 51c–58—redaktionell?" *ZNW* 44 (1952/1953) 256–57.

Jonge, Heik Jan de
"Caro in spiritum." In *De Geest in het geding. Opstellen aangeboden aan J. A. Oosterbaan ter gelegen-*heid van zijn afscheid als hoogleraar, ed. I. B. Horst et al. (Alphen/Rijn: Willinck, 1978) 145–68.

Kieffer, René
Au delà des recensions? L'évolution de la tradition textuelle dans Jean VI, 52–71, ConBNT 3 (Lund: C. W. K. Gleerup, 1968).

Kilmartin, Edward J.
"Liturgical Influence on John VI." *CBQ* 22 (1960) 183–91.

Kilmartin, Edward J.
"The Formation of the Bread of Life Discourse (John 6)." *Scr* 12 (1960) 75–78.

Kittel, Gerhard
"Die Wirkungen des christlichen Abendmahls nach dem Neuen Testament." *TSK* 96/97 (1925) 214–37.

Klos, Herbert
Die Sakramente im Johannesevangelium. Vorkommen und Bedeutung von Taufe, Eucharistie und Busse im vierten Evangelium, SBS 46 (Stuttgart: Katholisches Bibelwerk, 1970).

Köster, Helmut
"Geschichte und Kultus im Johannesevangelium und bei Ignatius von Antiochien." *ZTK* 54 (1957) 56–69.

Kuzenzama, K. P. M.
"La préhistoire de l'expression 'pain de vie' (Jn 6,35b.48)." *Revue Africaine de Théologie* 4 (1980) 65–83.

Leal, Juan
"De realitate eucharistia panis vitae." *VD* 31 (1953) 144ff.

LeDéaut, Roger
"Une aggadah targumique et les 'murmures' de Jean 6." *Bib* 51 (1970) 80–83.

Leenhardt, F.-J.
"La structure du chapitre 6 de l'évangile de Jean." *RHPR* 39 (1959) 1–13.

Léon-Dufour, Xavier
"Le mystère du Pain de Vie (Jean 6)." *RSR* 46 (1958) 481–523.

Luthardt, Christoph Ernst
"Ἔργον τοῦ θεοῦ und πίστις in ihrem gegenseitigen Verhältniß nach der Darstellung des johanneischen Evangeliums." *TSK* 25 (1852) 333–74.

Malina, B. J.
The Palestinien Manna Tradition. The Manna Tradition in the Palestinian Targums and its Relationship to the New Testament Writings, AGSU 7 (Leiden: E. J. Brill, 1968), esp. 94–106.

McPolin, J.
"Bultmanni theoria litteraria et Jo 6,51c–58c." *VD* 44 (1966) 243–58.

Mees, Michael
"Sinn und Bedeutung westlicher Textvarianten in Joh 6." *BZ* 13 (1969) 244–51.

Menoud, Philippe-Henri
"'Le fils de Joseph.' Etude sur Jean I, 45 et VI, 42." *RTP* 18 (1930) 275–88.

Mollat, D.

"Le chapitre VIᵉ de Saint Jean." *Lumière et vie* 31 (1957) 107–19.

Moloney, Francis J.

"John 6 and the Celebration of the Eucharist." *Downside Review* 93 (1975) 243–51.

Mondula, N.

La puissance vivificatrice de la chair du Christ selon l'évangile de S. Jean (Rome, 1978).

Moore, F. J.

"Eating the Flesh and Drinking the Blood: A Reconsideration." *ATR* 48 (1966) 70–75.

Nearon, J. R.

"My Flesh for the World." An Essay in Biblical Theology (Rome, 1973).

Pahk, S. S.

"The Meaning of Bread: A Structuralist Analysis of John VI, 1–58." Dissertation, Vanderbilt University, 1980.

Preiss, Théo

"Etude sur le chapitre 6 de l'Evangile de Jean." *ETR* 46 (1971) 143–67.

Richter, Georg

"Die Alttestamentlichen Zitate in der Rede vom Himmelsbrot: Joh 6,26–51a." In his *Studien zum Johannesevangelium*, ed. Josef Hainz. BU 13 (Regensburg: F. Pustet, 1977) 199–265.

Richter, Georg

"Zur Formgeschichte und literarischen Einheit von Joh VI, 31–58." *ZNW* 60 (1969) 21–55. In his *Studien zum Johannesevangelium*, ed. Josef Hainz. BU 13 (Regensburg: F. Pustet, 1977) 88–119.

Roberge, Michel

"Le discours sur le pain de vie (Jean 6,22–59). Problèmes d'interprétation." *Laval Théologique et Philosophique* 38 (1982) 265–300.

Ruager, Søren

"Johannes 6 og nadveren." *TTKi* 50 (1979) 81–92.

Ruckstuhl, Eugen

"Literarkritik am Johannesevangelium und eucharistische Rede (Jo 6, 51c–58)." *Divus Thomas* 23 (1945) 153–90, 301–33.

Rusch, Frederick A.

"The Signs and the Discourses: The Rich Theology of John 6." *CurTM* 5 (1978) 386–90.

Schenke, Ludgar

"Die formale und gedankliche Struktur von Joh 6,26–58." *BZ*, n.f., 24 (1980) 21–41.

Schlatter, Adolf

"Der Bruch Jesu mit der Judenschaft." In *Aus Schrift und Geschichte. Theologische Abhandlungen und Skizzen Herrn Prof. D. Conrad von Orelli zur Feier seiner 25-jährigen Lehrtätigkeit in Basel von Freunden und Schülern gewidmet* (Basel: B. Reich, 1898) 1–23.

Schlier, Heinrich

"Joh 6 und das johanneische Verständnis der Eucharisitie." In his *Das Ende der Zeit. Exegetische Aufsätze und Vorträge*, 2 (Freiburg and Vienna: Herder, 1971) 102–23.

Schnackenburg, Rudolf

"Zur Rede vom Brot aus dem Himmel: Eine Beobachtung zu Joh 6, 52." *BZ* 12 (1968) 248–52.

Schnackenburg, Rudolf

"Das Brot des Lebens." In *Tradition und Glaube. Das frühe Christentum in seiner Umwelt. Festgabe für Karl Georg Kuhn zum 65. Geburtstag*, ed. J. Jeremias, H.-W Kuhn, and H. Stegemann (Göttingen: Vandenhoeck & Ruprecht, 1971) 328–42.

Schneider, Johannes

"Zur Frage der Komposition von Jo 6,27–58." In *In Memoriam Ernst Lohmeyer*, ed. W. Schmauch (Stuttgart: Evangelische Verlagswerk, 1951) 132–42.

Schürmann, Heinz

"Joh. 6, 51c—ein Schlüssel zur johanneischen Brotrede." *BZ* 2 (1958) 244–62.

Schürmann, Heinz

"Die Eucharistie als Repräsentation und Applikation des Heilsgeschehens nach Joh 6, 53-58." *TTZ* 68 (1959) 30–45, 108–18. In his *Ursprung und Gestalt. Erörterungen und Besinnungen zum Neuen Testament*, Kommentare und Beiträge zum Alten und Neuen Testament (Düsseldorf: Patmos Verlag, 1970) 167–84.

Schweizer, Eduard

"Das johanneische Zeugnis vom Herrenmahl." *EvT* 12 (1952/1953) 341–63.

Segalla, Giuseppe

"La struttura circolare-chiasmatica di Gv 6,26–58 e il suo significato teologico." *BeO* 13 (1971) 191–98.

Škrinjar, A.

"De terminologia sacrificiali in J 6,51–56." *Divus Thomas*, Piacenza (1971) 189–97.

Springer, E.

"Die Einheit der Rede von Kaphernaum (Jo 6)." *BZ* 15 (1918–1921) 319–34.

Stanley, David M.

"The Bread of Life." *Worship* 32 (1957/1958) 477–88.

Steinmeyer, F. L.

Die Rede Jesu in der Schule von Capernaum (Berlin: Wiegandt & Grieben, 1892).

Temple, Patrick J.

"The Eucharist in St. John 6." *CBQ* 9 (1947) 442–52.

Temple, Sydney

"A Key to the Composition of the Fourth Gospel." *JBL* 80 (1961) 220–32, esp. 224–30.

Thomas, J.

"Le discours dans la synagogue de Capharnaum. Note sur Jean 6,22–59." *Christus* 29 (1982) 218–22.

Thompson, J. M.

"The Interpretation of the John VI." *Expositor*, 8th ser., 11 (1916) 337–48.

Thyen, Hartwig

"Aus der Literatur zum Johannesevangelium (4.

Fortsetzung)." *TRu* 43 (1978) 328–59.

Ullmann, C.
"Bemerkungen zu Joh IV,13.14 und VI.35." *TSK* 1 (1828) 791–94.

Vanneste, A.
"Le pain de vie descendu du ciel (Jn 6,55–58)." *AsSeign* 54 (1966) 41–53.

Wilckens, Ulrich
"Der eucharistische Abschnitt der johanneischen Rede vom Lebensbrot (Joh 6,51c–58)." In *Neues Testament und Kirche. Für Rudolf Schnackenburg,* ed. J. Gnilka (Freiburg and Vienna: Herder, 1974) 220–48.

Wilkens, Wilhelm
"Das Abendmahlszeugnis im vierten Evangelium." *EvT* 18 (1958) 354–70.

B. Sacraments in the Gospel of John

Baker, J. A.
"The 'Institution' Narratives and the Christian Eucharist." In *Thinking about the Eucharist. Essays by Members of the Archibishop's Commission on Christian Doctrine,* with a preface by Ian T. Ramsey (London: SCM Press, 1972) 38–58.

Braun, François-Marie
"Le baptême d'après le quatrième Evangile." *RevThom* 48 (1948) 347–93.

Braun, François-Marie
"L'eucharistie selon saint Jean." *RevThom* 70 (1970) 5–29.

Brooks, O. S.
"The Johannine Eucharist. Another Interpretation." *JBL* 82 (1963) 293–300.

Brown, Raymond E.
"The Eucharist and Baptism in John." Proceedings of the Society of Catholic College Teachers of Sacred Doctrine 8 (1962) 14–37. In his *New Testament Essays* (Milwaukee: Bruce, 1965) 77–95.

Brown, Raymond E.
"The Johannine Sacramentary Reconsidered." *TS* 23 (1962) 183–206. In his *New Testament Essays* (Milwaukee: Bruce, 1965) 51–76.

Costa, M.
"Nota sul simbolismo sacramentale del IV Vangelo." *RivBib* 13 (1965) 239–54.

Craig, Clarence Tucker
"Sacramental Interest in the Fourth Gospel." *JBL* 58 (1939) 31–41.

Cullmann, Oscar
Urchristentum und Gottesdienst, ATANT 3 (Zurich: Zwingli Verlag, ²1950).

Evans, C. F.
"The Eucharist and Symbolism in the New Testament." In *Thinking about the Eucharist. Essays by Members of the Archibishop's Commission on Christian Doctrine,* with a preface by Ian T. Ramsey (London: SCM Press, 1972) 59–66.

Feuillet, André
Le sacerdoce du Christ et de ses ministres d'après la prière sacerdotale du quatrième évangile et plusieurs données parallèles du Nouveau Testament (Paris: Editions de Paris, 1972).

Fritschel, T. C.
"The Relationship between the Word and the Sacraments in John and in Ignatius." Dissertation, Hamburg, 1962/1963.

Ghiberti, G.
"Il c[ap] 6 di Giovanni e la presenza dell' Eucaristia nel 4° Vangelo." *Parole di Vita* 14 (1969) 105–25.

Holtzmann, Heinrich Julius
"Sakramentliches im Neuen Testament." *ARW* 7 (1904) 58–69.

Howard, J. K.
"Passover and Eucharist in the Fourth Gospel." *SJT* 20 (1967) 329–37.

Klos, Herbert
Die Sakramente im Johannesevangelium. Vorkommen und Bedeutung von Taufe, Eucharistie und Busse im vierten Evangelium, SBS 46 (Stuttgart: Katholisches Bibelwerk, 1970).

Koehler, T.
"The Sacramental Theory in John 19,26f." *University of Dayton Review* 5 (1968) 49–58.

Köster, Helmut
"Geschichte und Kultus im Johannesevangelium und bei Ignatius von Antiochien." *ZTK* 54 (1957) 56–69.

Lindars, Barnabas
"Word and Sacrament in the Fourth Gospel." *SJT* 29 (1976) 49–64.

Lindijer, C. H.
De sacramenten in het Vierde Evangelie (Haarlem: Bohn, 1964).

Lohse, Eduard
"Wort und Sakrament im Johannesevangelium." *NTS* 7 (1960/1961) 110–25.

MacGregor, George Hogarth Carnaby
"The Eucharist in the Fourth Gospel." *NTS* 9 (1962/1963) 111–19.

Michaelis, Wilhelm
Die Sakramente im Johannesevangelium (Bern: Buchhandlung der Evangelischen Gesellschaft, 1946).

Naish, J. B.
"The Fourth Gospel and the Sacraments." *Expositor,* 8th ser., 23 (1922) 53–68.

Niewalda, P.
Sakramentssymbolik im Johannesevangelium. Eine exegetisch-historische Studie (Limburg: Lahn-Verlag, 1958).

Philips, T.
Die Verheissung der heiligen Eucharistie nach Johannes; eine exegetische Studie (Paderborn: F. Schöningh, 1922).

Proudman, C. L. J.
"The Eucharist in the Fourth Gospel." *CJT* 12 (1966) 212–16.

Raney, W. H.
The Relation of the Fourth Gospel to the Christian

Cultus (Giessen: A. Töpelmann, 1933).

Ruckstuhl, Eugen

"Wesen und Kraft der Eucharistie in der Sicht des Johannesevangeliums." In *Das Opfer der Kirche. Exegetische, dogmatische und pastoraltheologische Studien zum Verständniss der Messe,* ed. R. Erni. Luzerner theologische Studien 1 (Lucerne: Rex-Verlag, 1954) 47–90.

Schnackenburg, Rudolf

"Die Sakramente im Johannesevangelium." *Sacra Pagina. Miscellanea biblical congressus internationalis catholici de re biblica,* 2 vols., ed. J. Coppens, A. Descamps, and E. Massaux. BETL 12–13 (Paris: J. Gabalda; Gembloux: Duculot, 1959) 2: 235–54.

Schweizer, Eduard

"Das johanneische Zeugnis vom Herrenmahl." *EvT* 12 (1952/1953) 341–63.

Smalley, Stephen S.

"Liturgy and Sacrament in the Fourth Gospel." *EvQ* 29 (1957) 159–70.

Stöger, Alois

"Das österliche Sakrament der Taufe. Meditation zu Joh 3,1–21." *BibLeb* 52 (1979) 121–24.

Tragan, P. R., ed.

Segni e sacramenti nel Vangelo di Giovanni. Sacramentum 3, Studia Anselmiana 66 (Rome: Editrice Anselmiana, 1977).

Vawter, Bruce

"The Johannine Sacramentary." *TS* 17 (1956) 151–66.

Worden, T.

"The Holy Eucharist in St. John—I." *Scr* 15 (1963) 97–103.

Worden, T.

"The Holy Eucharist in St. John—II." *Scr* 16 (1964) 5–16.

6

26 Jesus answered them, "Truly, truly, I say to you, you seek me, not because you saw signs, but because you ate your fill of the loaves. 27/ Do not labor for the food which perishes, but for the food which endures to eternal life, which the Son of man will give to you; for on him has God the Father set his seal." 28/ Then they said to him, "What must we do, to be doing the work of God?" 29/ Jesus answered them, "This is the work of God, that you believe in him whom he has sent." 30/ So they said to him, "Then what sign do you do, that we may see, and believe you? What work do you perform? 31/ Our fathers ate the manna in the wilderness; as it is written, 'He gave them bread from heaven to eat.'" 32/ Jesus then said to them, "Truly, truly, I say to you, it was not Moses who gave you the bread from heaven; my Father gives you the true bread from heaven. 33/ For the bread of God is that which (he who) comes down from heaven, and gives life to the world." 34/ They said, "Lord, give us this bread always." 35/ Jesus said to them, "I am the bread of life; he who comes to me shall not hunger, and he who believes in me shall never thirst. 36/ But I said to you that you have seen me and yet do not believe. 37/ All that the Father gives me will come to me; and him who comes to me I will not cast out. 38/ For I have come down from heaven, not to do my own will, but the will of him who sent me; 39/ and this is the will of him who sent me, that I should lose nothing of all that he has given me, but raise it up at the last day. 40/ For this is the will of my Father, that every one who sees the Son and believes in him should have eternal life; and I will raise him up at the last day." 41/ The Jews then murmured at him, because he said, "I am the bread which came down from heaven." 42/ They said, "Is not this Jesus, the son of Joseph, whose father and mother we know? How does he now say, 'I have come down from heaven'?" 43/ Jesus answered them, "Do not murmur among yourselves. 44/ No one can come to me unless the Father who sent me draws him; and I will raise him up at the last day. 45/ It is written in the prophets, 'And they shall be taught by God.' Every one who has heard and learned from the Father comes to me. 46/ Not that any one has seen the Father except him who is from God; he has seen the Father. 47/ Truly, truly, I say to you, he who believes has eternal life. 48/ I am the bread of life. 49/ Your fathers ate the manna in the wilderness, and they died. 50/ This (one) is the bread which comes down from heaven, that a man may eat of it and not die. 51a/ I am the living bread which came down from heaven; if any one eats of this bread, he will live for ever;

51   and the bread which I shall give for the life of the world is my flesh." 52/ The Jews then disputed among themselves, saying, "How can this man give us his flesh to eat?" 53/ So Jesus said to them, "Truly, truly, I say to you, unless you eat the flesh of the Son of man and drink his blood, you have no life in you; 54/ he who eats my flesh and drinks my blood has eternal life, and I will raise him up at the last day. 55/ For my flesh is food indeed, and my blood is drink indeed. 56/ He who eats my flesh and drinks my blood abides in me, and I in him. 57/ As the living Father sent me, and I live because of the Father, so he who eats me will live because of me. 58/ This (one) is the bread which (who) came down from heaven, not such as the fathers ate and died; he who eats this bread will live forever." 59/ This he said in the synagogue, as he taught at Capernaum.

■ **26** Jesus does not respond to the question directed to him in verse 25, which is in fact intended only to call the reader's attention to the miracle of walking on the water. Rather, he refers to the conclusion of verse 24, to an expression used by the Evangelist: "seeking Jesus."

It thus becomes evident that the Evangelist does not intend to reproduce a discourse of Jesus transmitted to him in the tradition, but proposes to plead the cause of Jesus himself by having Jesus say what the Evangelist takes to be the truth—in his consciousness of possessing the Spirit. That applies to the earlier discourses as well as to those that are to follow.[1] Introduced with a solemn double "amen," Jesus assures them that they did not really seek him because they saw "signs" ($\sigma\eta\mu\epsilon\hat{\iota}\alpha$ does not

---

1   On this point, see the commentary on 16:13.

mean "miracles" here, but "pointers"), but because they ate their fill of bread. It is not even mentioned that Jesus had miraculously multiplied the loaves. This miracle is important for the Evangelist only to the extent that it points to the true bread from heaven: Jesus. As in 4:15, the crassest possible misunderstanding is thereby presupposed, viz., that man seeks Jesus only in the hope that he may be satiated by him in an earthly sense. On this view, those before whom Jesus stands think only of their material existence and the victuals required for that existence, "the bread of life."

■ **27** Jesus therefore admonishes his hearers not to procure perishable food, but to seek the food that endures to eternal life, a food which is given by true fellowship with God.

Another point is much more important: the words, "which the Son of man will give you; for on him has God the Father set his seal," have been inserted by the redactor. He understood the narrative of the feeding as the inauguration of the eucharist and wanted to recall that meaning here. He therefore introduces the Son of man as the one who administers the eucharist and represents Jesus as the one "sealed" by the Father. That implies in this context that Jesus is attested by means of his miracles.[2] The redactor has thought it necessary to clarify the expression "the Father," which is a favorite of the Evangelist, by adding "God" (ὁ θεός).

That ℵ 28 *al* lat Cl omit the second mention of "the food" (τὴν βρῶσιν) is to explained by haplography: the eyes of an aged scribe slipped from the τὴν before βρῶσιν to the τὴν following the second βρῶσιν.

■ **28** Verse 28 relates to Jesus' admonition that his hearers should procure the food that is eternal. In response, the hearers inquire: What should we do in order to be doing the works of God? The expression "do the works of God" appears in Num 8:11 LXX. There it denotes the work of the Levites, who are obligated to fulfill the liturgical tasks set them by God. In the passage in John, it probably depicts the Jewish-legal mentality of the hearers: they are asking what they should do in order to do the works intended by God.

The verb ἐργάζομαι passes from the meaning "to procure (for oneself)" over to the sense "work, perform."

But one should not make too much of that and attribute some sort of wordplay to the hearers.[3] In any case, we do not have to do with the auditors and their probable reaction, but with the Evangelist and his train of thought.

■ **29** Verse 29 clarifies the Jewish question: this religion of doing is abrogated. For, the solitary "work" that God intends man to do is to have faith in Jesus, whom God has sent. It is the conviction of the Evangelist that the whole of the Christian religion is summed up in this point. Further, this dialogue reflects the contrast between the Jews and the Christian community in which the Evangelist lived and worked. The problem for exegesis is to give the formula, "have faith in Jesus," the content that it possessed at that time and must have today, if it is not to be discarded like a disposable container. This expression has just one meaning for the Evangelist: Jesus is the one sent from God, and in him God is represented and made present.[4]

■ **30** This verse often surprises exegetes and induces them to exercise their critical powers. Jesus' hearers have just experienced the impressive miracle of the feeding of the 5,000. How then could they demand a sign that legitimizes Jesus? The Evangelist, however, is not offering a deep psychological analysis of the reaction of the hearers. The Jewish demand for a sign shows, on the one hand, how difficult it is for men to understand the signs they have witnessed as such. On the other hand, the Evangelist thereby creates the transition to the real theme at which he is aiming: the bread from heaven.

■ **31** The hearers assist the transition by making reference to what the fathers had experienced: "they ate manna in the wilderness," and then as Jews they add the scriptural reference. The primary reference is to Ps 77:24 LXX: "And he caused manna to fall on them, and he gave them bread from heaven." This verse is given here in abbreviated and contracted form, which serves the following line of argument. Additional OT references are Ex 16:4 LXX, where the Lord says to Moses: "Behold, I rain bread from heaven for you," and Ps 104:40 LXX, "and he satisfied them with bread from heaven." Later Wis 16:20 puts it thus: "Instead of these things thou didst give thy people the food of angels, and without their toil thou didst supply them from heaven

---

2   Against Bauer, *Das Johannesevangelium*, 95.
3   Bultmann, *John*, 220 n. 3 [162 n. 8].
4   See 14:9; cf. Haenchen, "Der Vater," 68–77.

with bread ready to eat." These passages indicate how popular this theme was in Judaism. That applies also to the rabbinic period.[5] The *Apocalypse of Baruch* attests the expectation that the miracle of the manna will be repeated in the last days (29:8): "And it shall come to pass at that self-same time that the treasury of manna shall again descend from on high, and they will eat of it in those years, because these are they who have come to the consummation of time."[6] The Evangelist of course does not share this future eschatological expectation; that is demonstrated by Jesus' reply in verse 32.

■ **32** Again introduced by a double "amen," Jesus affirms two things, one negative and one positive. He contests that it was Moses who gave them bread from heaven, but he promises with equal emphasis that his Father will give them the true bread from heaven. The contrast to Jewish tradition and Jewish religious claims is thus put in its sharpest form. Verse 34 now explains what this true bread from heaven is.

■ **33** The Evangelist employs a linguistic device that is not accessible to us in English. The word for "bread" in Greek (ὁ ἄρτος) is masculine in gender. As a consequence, "that which comes down from heaven" can be taken to refer either to "bread" or to Jesus in Greek. The Evangelist uses this double possibility to illustrate once again the world's lack of understanding of the Christian message.

■ **34** In verse 34 the people request that Jesus give them this bread always. We have already met this technique of misunderstanding in 4:15. The Evangelist is thus indifferent to the request they have just made for a sign before they acknowledge the claim of Jesus. The theme is now changed—superficially, at least—but also the mood of the people: of course they request the gift of bread that they misunderstand.

■ **35** Verse 35 now provides the flat answer: Jesus tells them plainly that he is the bread of life. This answer certainly does not yet make it clear in what sense he is the bread of life. Instead of that explanation, there follows this assertion: "Whoever comes to me will never again hunger, and whoever believes in me shall never again thirst." This claim assumes that the world can never satisfy man. Everything that the world has to offer (in modern terms: fast cars, beautiful women) is unsatis-

fying, alienating, or better, makes one restless. Man is afflicted with dissatisfaction, boredom, anxiety, and care. He is unable to find that authentic rest, that true peace, that goal for which it is rewarding to live and strive. But that would be too obvious: the matter has not yet been discussed in such terms. Instead, a new theme is introduced, which is treated in verses 36–38 and 40.

■ **36** Verse 36 recalls that Jesus had already said that the people have indeed seen but have not believed him. Because this seeing was not the true "seeing," ℵ A *pc* it sy^sc have omitted the word "me" (με), so that "seeing" refers only to the sign Jesus performed. What the Evangelist means by true seeing is made clear by 14:9.

■ **37** Verse 37 sounds comforting. Nevertheless, it has not been said that the Father gives everyone and everything to Jesus. He whom the Father gives Jesus is destined for salvation, and of course comes to faith and will not be rejected by Jesus. For Jesus desires to fulfill the will of his Father.

■ **38** It is once more emphasized that Jesus is he who has not come down from heaven to do his own will, but the will of him who sent him. But what is this will? Verse 39 appears to provide the answer.

■ **39** Verse 39 appears to say that, in accordance with God's will, Jesus will not lose anything of what God has given him. However, "but" (ἀλλά) introduces a sentence that completely contradicts the message of the Evangelist: "but raise him up on the last day." It is precisely this futuristic eschatology that is foreign to the Evangelist (11:24). He has replaced that notion with the ever present possibility of an encounter with the message of Jesus and thus salvation. One could attempt to salvage the contradiction by saying that the Evangelist here calls this moment of encounter "the last day," or "the judgment day." In that case, he is taking up and reinterpreting a traditional expression.

■ **40** The literal repetition in the beginning of verse 40, "For this is the will of my Father," however, shows that verse 39 is a correction, one that introduces futuristic eschatology into this passage, as in many other verses in this segment. Such an insertion also occurs at the end of verse 40 with the words: "and I will raise him up at the last day." This addition and the whole of verse 39 stem

---

5   Cf. Billerbeck, 2: 481 and Schlatter, *Der Evangelist Johannes*, 172.
6   *APOT* 2: 498.

from the redactor. But there is something further to be considered in connection with these and comparable statements in the Gospel of John: it is not said that the Father has given everyone to Jesus and it is not said that everyone will come to him. Rather, the Evangelist knows about the deep mystery touching the message of Jesus: no matter how persuasively and scintillatingly it is presented, it still seizes some while leaving others cold. For the one it is the word of God; for the other, it is merely a human word that is not convincing. Why that is so and why God has not given all people into the hands of Jesus, the Evangelist does not know either. He can only determine that it is so and respect the inscrutable will of God. To the extent that God remans the *Deus absconditus*, and to the extent that he does not reveal himself in his Son (and the mere hearing of the proclamation is not yet a reception of the revelation), we can ask no further questions, but must fall silent.

■ **41** The message of Jesus is now elaborated and vindicated in verses 41–51a and 59. The Jews—this term shows up wherever Jesus' auditors are hostile—murmur at Jesus. It is obvious, however, that verse 41 does not follow directly on verse 40, but refers instead to verse 35: "I am the bread of life." That could prompt the conjecture that the whole section, verses 36–40, is an addition of the redactor. On the other side of that question, however, the repetitions found in verses 39 and 40 clearly indicate that verse 39 is an insertion, and we have no firm basis for assuming that an insertion has been made inside an insertion. This passage, verses 36–38 and 40a, b, concerns the problem of how men who have seen, that is, who have heard the proclamation, can remain without faith, a condition that comes to light in their contact with Jesus. The Jews murmur against Jesus on account of his claim that he is the bread that has come down from heaven.

■ **42** They give a reason for their objection: Jesus is of course the son of Joseph. They know his father and his mother (א* W b sy^sc omit "his mother" "because in the eyes of Christians the existence of Jesus' mother did not preclude his heavenly origin").[7] However, the birth of Jesus from a virgin was not "an article of faith" for the Evangelist.[8] He assumes, rather, that Jesus as true man

had an earthly father and mother; he further assumes that this does not deny that he came from God. It is not said that one encountered this opinion only among "Jews"; it is possible that the Evangelist also knew Christians for whom the acceptance of a human father for Jesus was not compatible with their christology, as, for example, those represented in Matthew and Luke.

■ **43f.** In these verses Jesus admonishes the Jews to desist from their murmuring. It is again not said that everyone will come to faith. Luther one time expressed the matter in this way: *Non enim absolute pro omnibus mortuus est Christus.* The Evangelist says the same thing in a different way: "No one can come to me unless the Father who sent me draws him." That reminds the reader that he who is sent does not have his own authority. He is always dependent upon his Lord. It goes without saying that the words, "and I will raise him up at the last day," again stem from the redactor, who is ever desirous of expressing his futuristic eschatology. The expression "The Father draws the elect to Jesus" means the same thing as "The Father has given the elect to Jesus."

■ **45** Verse 45 provides a prooftext taken from Jer 31:34: "And no longer shall each man teach his neighbor and each his brother, saying, 'Know the Lord,' for they shall all know me," and from Isa 54:13 LXX: "I shall make ... all your sons taught by God" (καὶ θήσω ... πάντας τοὺς υἱοὺς διδακτοὺς θεοῦ). These texts appear to have led Bultmann's exegesis astray: "It is now perfectly clear what is meant when it is said that the Father 'draws' men to him. The πᾶς ['everyone'] already indicates that it does not refer to the selection of a chosen few, but that any man is free to be among those drawn by the Father. ... Moreover verse 45b shows that this 'drawing' is not a magic process, nor is it governed by rigid laws like the laws of nature. It occurs when man abandons his own judgement and 'hears' and 'learns' from the Father, when he allows God to speak to him. The 'drawing' by the Father occurs not, as it were, *behind* man's decision of faith but *in* it."[9] The interpretation that hangs everything finally on the free decision of man turns the sense of the text into its opposite. The words "everyone who hears and learns" certainly does not imply that everyone hears and learns. One could also say, as an alternative: "If

---

7   Cf. Bauer, *Das Johannesevangelium*, 97.
8   Bauer, *Das Johannesevangelium*, 97.
9   *John*, 231f. [172].

292

anyone hears and learns." The "laws" or "powers of nature"—a modern concept that is wholly inappropriate to this passage—have nothing to do with God's "determination" of man's destiny. Bultmann's statements in his *Theology* do not get much further either: "Inasmuch as the assertion that no one can come to Jesus whom the Father does not 'draw' (6:44) is followed by the statement, 'Every one who has heard and learned from the Father comes to me,' the πᾶς by itself ['every one'] indicates that everyone has the possibility of letting himself be drawn by the Father (and also the possibility of resisting)."[10] Further: "Man cannot act otherwise than as what he is, but in the Revealer's call there opens up to him the possibility of *being* otherwise than he was. He can exchange his Whence, his origin, his essence, for another; he can 'be born again' (3:1ff.) and thus attain to his true being."[11] But man does not take a decision to be born, any more than he can take a decision to be "born from above." On the first passage quoted from Bultmann above, it is to be said: the text does not say that "everyone can hear and learn from the Father." On the contrary, the quotation "and everyone will be taught by God" has been taken up into the Johannine context and thereby reinterpreted. In the thought of the Evangelist not everyone has the possibility of hearing the Father; only those hear the Father whom the Father has given to Jesus. In other words, for the Evangelist the determination of eternal life and death does not lie with the decision of man, but with the decision of the Father, which lies beyond our conceptual powers. It makes no difference whether one chooses to call that determinism or not. And it is also not true that the cosmological dualism of Gnosticism has been replaced, in the Fourth Gospel, by a dualism of decision.[12] Although some Valentinians taught that the Pneumatics are "saved by nature" (φύσει σωζόμενοι), as Clement of Alexandria reports, and therefore redeemed in advance by virtue of their divine sparks, that is not simply "the Gnostic doctrine." The Gospel of Thomas shows in saying 21[13] that not everything was settled even when the Gnostic discovered his divine spark and was thereby separated from the world. The world is more like a thief lurking in ambush, awaiting the occasion to break and enter. The

Gnostic of the Gospel of Thomas must therefore be on guard every moment of his life, right up to the end, against the possibility of being engulfed by the world again; that is, to be on guard against understanding oneself again from the perspective of the world as a part of the world, with worldly hopes and aims and anxieties. If the Gnostic relapses into this corruption, a life full of decisions taken previously will not help him in the least. If the Gospel of John represents a dualism of decision, it would not be possible to distinguish it from Gnosticism proper. The Evangelist represents neither a dualism of decision nor a dualism of essence. If he were to see a *prima causa* in the "Father," then the Father would belong to the world.[14]

■ **46** Verse 46 seeks to make clear that no one can claim to have seen God. Only he who was with the Father, and now, after Easter, is with him again, has seen God. We are all therefore dependent on Jesus, who makes the Father visible for the faithful, according to 14:9.

■ **47** This verse emphasizes the decisive significance of faith: whoever believes has eternal life (by doing just that). Eternal life does not wait until "beyond the grave," but breaks in here and now in the encounter with Jesus and his message. True existence begins at this point. Prior to this time man is actually dead.

■ **48** On the one hand, verse 48 once again definitively formulates Jesus' claim that he is the bread of life. On the other, the claim that the Jews make on behalf of Moses and the sacred story connected with him (the manna in the wilderness) is thereby put down.

■ **49** "Your fathers": were they not also the fathers of Jesus? Evidently that is not the judgment of the Evangelist. For those fathers lacked faith. And the manna did not alter the case: it was not the "bread of life" for them. The people who ate that bread have died. But will not those who believe in Jesus also die? According to 11:25, the Evangelist does not deny that, but he expects that the relationship to God through faith will not thereby be affected.

■ **50a** Verse 50a again makes use of the fact that "bread" (ὁ ἄρτος) is masculine in Greek (unlike German and English). "This is . . ." (οὗτος) of course refers to Jesus in this context. He is the bread that comes down from

---

10 *Theology of the New Testament*, 2: 23.
11 *Theology of the New Testament*, 2: 25.
12 *Theology of the New Testament*, 2: 21.
13 *The Nag Hammadi Library*, 120f.; also cf. sayings 70 and 97.
14 See the remarks above on 3:1ff.

heaven. He who eats of this bread will not die, will not be severed from his union with God. Because fellowship with Jesus is depicted as an eating of bread—the figure of the bread of life is presupposed—the redactor is permitted to introduce his own doctrine of the eucharist in verse 51b. A new segment thus commences, which extends to verse 59.

■ **51b** This verse appears to be an explanation. Bultmann, who often attributes such explanatory notes to the Evangelist, disregards his customary view here and finds the redactor at work in verses 51b–58.[15] The redactor sees the life that Jesus gives in the eucharist: "and the bread which I shall give [after Easter] for 'the life' of the world is my flesh." For the redactor that means that Jesus' flesh on the cross has been sacrificed for the salvation of the world. Everything now depends on whether man has a share in this flesh. The subject of Jesus' discourse is no longer bread but flesh.

■ **52** Verse 52 makes clear what sort of an objection the doctrine of the eucharist being developed here will provoke among the Jews. The body and blood of Jesus ($\sigma\hat{\omega}\mu\alpha$, $\alpha\hat{\iota}\mu\alpha$) are distinguished in the accounts of the last supper in Mark 14:22, 24, Matt 26: 26,28, Luke 22:19f.; they are also distinguished in 1 Cor 11:24f. and 10:16f. The contrast between $\sigma\hat{\omega}\mu\alpha$ and $\alpha\hat{\iota}\mu\alpha$ is now replaced by that between $\sigma\acute{\alpha}\rho\xi$ $\kappa\alpha\grave{\iota}$ $\alpha\hat{\iota}\mu\alpha$ ("flesh and blood"). Ignatius provides parallel usages. Although Ignatius is conducting a polemic against the docetic gnostics, who hold that Jesus' passion was in appearance only, this man—who is facing martyrdom, who wants to imitate Jesus' passion by so doing—appears to spiritualize the eucharist. In his letter to the Ephesians, Ignatius speaks of breaking bread, "which is the medicine of immortality" ($\phi\acute{\alpha}\rho\mu\alpha\kappa\sigma\nu$ $\dot{\alpha}\theta\alpha\nu\alpha\sigma\acute{\iota}\alpha\varsigma$), "the antidote that we should not die" ($\dot{\alpha}\nu\tau\acute{\iota}\delta\sigma\tau\sigma\varsigma$ $\tau\sigma\hat{\nu}$ $\mu\grave{\eta}$ $\dot{\alpha}\pi\sigma\theta\alpha\nu\epsilon\hat{\iota}\nu$).[16] Yet one ought, as *Trall.* 6:1 admonishes, to live on Christian fare and avoid the strange food of heresy, which in 6:2 is a "deadly poison" ($\theta\alpha\nu\acute{\alpha}\sigma\iota\mu\sigma\nu$ $\phi\acute{\alpha}\rho\mu\alpha\kappa\sigma\nu$) alongside honeyed wine. The passages that mention "flesh" ($\sigma\acute{\alpha}\rho\xi$) in connection with

the eucharistic are *Rom.* 7:3: "I desire the 'bread of God,' which is the flesh of Jesus Christ, . . . and for drink I desire his blood, which is incorruptible love"; *Phld.* 4, in which the true eucharist is designated as the "one flesh" ($\mu\acute{\iota}\alpha$ $\sigma\acute{\alpha}\rho\xi$) of our Lord Jesus Christ and as the one cup for union with his blood. In *Smyrn.* 7:7, he says of the heretics: they abstain from eucharist and prayer because they do not confess the eucharist "to be the flesh" ($\sigma\acute{\alpha}\rho\kappa\alpha$ $\epsilon\hat{\iota}\nu\alpha\iota$) of our Savior Jesus Christ, "who suffered for our sins" ($\tau\grave{\eta}\nu$ $\acute{\nu}\pi\grave{\epsilon}\rho$ $\tau\hat{\omega}\nu$ $\dot{\alpha}\mu\alpha\rho\tau\iota\hat{\omega}\nu$ $\pi\alpha\theta\sigma\hat{\nu}\sigma\alpha\nu$). The expression in *Trall.* 8:1, "in faith, which is the flesh of the Lord, and in love, which is the blood of Christ" ($\dot{\epsilon}\nu$ $\pi\acute{\iota}\sigma\tau\epsilon\iota$, $\acute{o}$ $\dot{\epsilon}\sigma\tau\iota\nu$ $\sigma\acute{\alpha}\rho\xi$ $\tau\sigma\hat{\nu}$ $\kappa\nu\rho\acute{\iota}\sigma\nu$, $\kappa\alpha\grave{\iota}$ $\dot{\epsilon}\nu$ $\dot{\alpha}\gamma\acute{\alpha}\pi\eta$, $\acute{o}$ $\dot{\epsilon}\sigma\tau\iota\nu$ $\alpha\hat{\iota}\mu\alpha$ $^{\prime}I\eta\sigma\sigma\hat{\nu}$ $X\rho\iota\sigma\tau\sigma\hat{\nu}$) reminds one of the spiritualization found in the Gospel of Philip.[17] There the text says: while our flesh will not inherit, the flesh of Jesus and his blood will inherit. "Because of this he said: 'He who shall not eat my flesh and drink my blood has no life in him.' What is it? His flesh is the logos, and his blood is the Holy Spirit."[18] The matter is treated differently in Justin, *First Apology* (66.1ff.): "This food we call Eucharist, of which no one is allowed to partake except one who believes that the things we teach are true, and has received the washing for forgiveness of sins and for rebirth, and who lives as Christ handed down to us. For we do not receive these things as common bread or common drink; but as Jesus Christ our Saviour . . . took [$\check{\epsilon}\sigma\chi\epsilon\nu$] flesh and blood for our salvation, so also we have been taught that the food consecrated by the word of prayer which comes from him, from which our flesh and blood are nourished by [$\kappa\alpha\tau\acute{\alpha}$] transformation, is the flesh and blood of that incarnate Jesus. . . . This also the wicked demons in imitation handed down as something to be done in the mysteries of Mithra; for bread and a cup of water are brought out in their secret rites of initiation, with certain invocations which you either know or can learn."[19] Consequently one is tempted to assume that the mystery religions have influenced the understanding of the eucharist in the time of Justin. However, one recognizes

15   *John,* 234–37 [174–77].

16   *Eph.* 20:2.

17   105: 1–7, p. 33, in the edition and translation of R. McL. Wilson, *The Gospel of Philip. Translated from the Coptic Text, with an Introduction and Commentary* (New York: Harper & Row, 1962).

18   Ménard, *L'Evangile selon Philippe. Introduction— texte—traduction—commentaire* (Paris: Letouzey &

Ané, 1967) 142, cites Apollinaris of Hierapolis, Fragment IV on the Passover: $\acute{o}$ $\dot{\epsilon}\kappa\chi\acute{\epsilon}\alpha\varsigma$ $\dot{\epsilon}\kappa$ $\tau\hat{\eta}\varsigma$ $\pi\lambda\epsilon\acute{\nu}\rho\alpha\varsigma$ $\alpha\dot{\nu}\tau\sigma\hat{\nu}$ $\tau\grave{\alpha}$ $\delta\acute{\nu}\sigma$ $\pi\acute{\alpha}\lambda\iota\nu$ $\kappa\alpha\theta\acute{\alpha}\rho\sigma\iota\alpha$, $\check{\nu}\delta\omega\rho$ $\kappa\alpha\grave{\iota}$ $\alpha\hat{\iota}\mu\alpha$, $\lambda\acute{o}\gamma\sigma\nu$ $\kappa\alpha\grave{\iota}$ $\pi\nu\epsilon\hat{\nu}\mu\alpha$ ("What poured out of his side was the two elements that again cleanse, water and blood, word and spirit").

19   Tr. E. R. Hardy, *Early Christian Fathers,* 286f.

even in the Gospel of Luke itself something that approaches this new understanding. In Luke's account of the last supper, Luke 22:19f., "body" ($\sigma\hat{\omega}\mu\alpha$) and "blood" ($\alpha\hat{\iota}\mu\alpha$) are still distinguished, in accordance with the old tradition. Yet in Luke 24:39, the risen Christ says that he has "flesh and bones" ($\sigma\acute{\alpha}\rho\kappa\alpha$ $\kappa\alpha\grave{\iota}$ $\mathring{o}\sigma\tau\acute{\epsilon}\alpha$). This crass way of putting the matter, in contrast, perhaps, to Pauline terminology, can be attributed to the opposition to the gnostic Docetics (although that does not have to be the only reason; the expression "appeared" [$\mathring{\omega}\phi\theta\eta$] in the early tradition found in 1 Cor 15 could have aroused the suspicion that the disciples had only seen an "apparition" [$\phi\acute{\alpha}\nu\tau\alpha\sigma\mu\alpha$]). If, however, one conceives the reality of the resurrection in this way, then one must also conceive participation in the eucharist in a corresponding way. The redactor therefore imports a later form of the doctrine.

■ **53** Verse 53 does not soften the offense, but solemnly repeats and sharpens what has already been said. In the view of the redactor, the Christian eucharist is a mystery that is not to be made rationally accessible to those outside. He sticks rather to the formulation: whoever desires eternal life must eat the flesh of the Son of man and "drink my blood." To the pious Jew it was blasphemy to demand them to drink blood. With this expression the redactor risked giving credence to charges of cannibalistic (Thyestean)[20] meals among Christians. At the same time, this expression contains an antignostic polemic. In the mouth of the redactor, "to have life in oneself" means the prospect of being raised up at the last judgment. The "eternal life" that the Evangelist attributes to those who have faith is not conceived here as a union of the individual with God that begins here and now and is not interrupted by death. The term "son of man" in the mouth of Jesus is used simply in the sense of "I." Strictly speaking, the redactor can only have anticipated a resurrection of the faithful; those without faith abide in death.

■ **54** Verse 54 now continues this line of thought with further explanatory comments in which the Greek verb

$\tau\rho\acute{\omega}\gamma\omega$ is used for "to eat." BDF §101 designates this verb as the colloquial replacement for $\mathring{\epsilon}\sigma\theta\acute{\iota}\omega$; it does not yet appear in the Septuagint. In Ps 40:10 (LXX) the Hebrew phrase אוֹכֵל לַחְמִי is translated by $\mathring{o}$ $\mathring{\epsilon}\sigma\theta\acute{\iota}\omega\nu$ $\mathring{\alpha}\rho\tau o\nu$ $\mu o\nu$ ("the one eating my bread"). Bauer may be right that an expression closer to chewing, crunching (of morsels of bread) is deliberately chosen here.[21] As Ps 40:10 shows, $\mathring{\epsilon}\sigma\theta\acute{\iota}\omega$ is possible throughout. Since the expression in John 13:18 is $\mathring{o}$ $\tau\rho\acute{\omega}\gamma\omega\nu$ $\mu o\nu$ $\tau\grave{o}\nu$ $\mathring{\alpha}\rho\tau o\nu$ ("he who ate my bread"), this raises the suspicion that verses 13:18f. are an insertion of the redactor; these verses are not suitable precursors of verse 21.[22]

■ **55** Verse 55 gives the basis of what was said previously: Jesus' flesh is therefore true food and his blood is true drink because those who partake of them will be raised up on the last day. Futuristic eschatology and conviction about the sacraments are thus closely connected for the redactor: only he who has partaken of the eucharist can hope for the resurrection. Manuscript D omits the words "and my blood is drink indeed" ($\kappa\alpha\grave{\iota}$ $\tau\grave{o}$ $\alpha\hat{\iota}\mu\acute{\alpha}$ $\mu o\nu$ $\mathring{\alpha}\lambda\eta\theta\acute{\eta}s$ $\mathring{\epsilon}\sigma\tau\iota\nu$ $\pi\acute{o}\sigma\iota s$), perhaps because the eye of the copyist jumped from ($\beta\rho\hat{\omega}$)$\sigma\iota s$ ("food") to ($\pi\acute{o}$)$\sigma\iota s$ ("drink"). D is rich in scribal errors of the most varied sort. (א*) א (D) Θ lat sy read $\mathring{\alpha}\lambda\eta\theta\hat{\omega}s$ instead of $\mathring{\alpha}\lambda\eta\theta\acute{\eta}s$. Brown explains this variant as follows: $\mathring{\alpha}\lambda\eta\theta\iota\nu\acute{o}s$ would be impossible here, because it denotes the heavenly reality, "the only real," in contrast to its natural counterpart, and that does not fit this context because Jesus is not here contrasting his flesh and blood with a natural counterpart, but is emphasizing the genuine value of his flesh and blood as food and drink.[23] The "Western" reading with the adverb $\mathring{\alpha}\lambda\eta\theta\hat{\omega}s$ catches the meaning of the verse better. $\mathfrak{P}^{66}$ and $\mathfrak{P}^{75}$ B C L W 565 892 *pl* read $\mathring{\alpha}\lambda\eta\theta\acute{\eta}s$.

■ **56** Verse 56 repeats the phrase of the redactor used earlier, $\tau\rho\acute{\omega}\gamma\epsilon\iota\nu$ $\tau\grave{\eta}\nu$ $\sigma\acute{\alpha}\rho\kappa\alpha$ ("eat my flesh"), and sets it in tension with a favorite phrase of the Evangelist, "abides in me and I in him."[24] That the one who partakes of the eucharist abides in Jesus and Jesus in him is what precisely cannot be said of the eating and drinking of "the

---

20 Thyestes was a Greek legendary figures who is supposed to have eaten, unwittingly, the flesh of his own sons at a banquet.

21 *Das Johannesevangelium*, 98.

22 See the commentary on this passage.

23 Brown, *John*, 1: 283.

24 Cf. 15:5.

elements of the eucharist," bread and wine. Rather, Jesus will really be reunited with the faithful only at the last day. Jesus has already been raised from the dead, of course, but the believers have not yet been raised. The Evangelist has an entirely different view of these matters.[25] For the redactor the eucharistic bread and wine are mysteriously identical with Jesus' body and blood. For that reason, it can be said that Jesus abides in those who have eaten him. The mystical ring of the words should not be allowed to obscure the fact that the redactor actually thinks in a very rationalistic way. The long addition offered by D (a ff²) mitigates the offense by retrieving the concept of the "body": "If you do not receive the body of the Son of man as the bread of life, you do not have life in him." Hirsch of course regards this addition of D as "the most beautiful paradox, precisely what the Jews shortly hereafter refer to as a 'hard saying': If you do not receive the body of the Son of man that has been given over to death (this is how $\sigma\hat{\omega}\mu\alpha$ is to be translated in John), you do not have life in him."[26] This interpretation is possible only if one accepts with Hirsch that a discourse in the third person is here interwoven with a discourse in the first person. The second derives from the redactor, the first from the Evangelist, who shuns having Jesus speak of the eating of his own flesh by the hearers.

■ **57** The expressions occurring in this verse that have a Johannine ring have absolutely nothing to say against redactorial activity. It is interesting, however, that the expression, "the living Father," only occurs here. It corresponds to the phrase, "the living bread," in verse 51.

"As is shown by the context $\delta\iota\acute{\alpha}$ cannot mean 'on account of,' 'for the sake of,'" writes Bultmann.[27] He therefore translates "because of the Father" and in his note gives the meaning as "to owe one's life to." Radermacher says: "Generally this preposition manifests a remarkable variation in construction and meaning."[28] It often has an instrumental sense when used with the accusative. That appears to us to be the case in this passage. Just as the Father has life and gives life to the son, so will he who partakes of the eucharist live through him—in the resurrection on the last day.

■ **58** "This" ($o\hat{\upsilon}\tau o s$) refers not only to the bread of the last supper but also to Jesus. The "fathers" have not partaken of the Christian eucharist and so died (cf. 6:49). But whoever eats the Christian eucharist will therefore live forever, because he will be raised on the day of judgment. In this sense the Christian eucharist means a "medicine of immortality" ($\phi\acute{\alpha}\rho\mu\alpha\kappa o\nu$ $\grave{\alpha}\theta\alpha\nu\alpha\sigma\acute{\iota}\alpha s$) for the redactor. In this verse the redactor reaches the same conclusion that the Evangelist had reached in verse 51a. And he has not written without skill.

■ **59** Bultmann[29] takes this verse to be the original conclusion to the scene. In 1:28 and 8:20, however, a mention of the locale marks the close of the scene. But in this case it is questionable whether there was a tradition that reported alleged activity of Jesus in Capernaum. The woes against Capernaum (Matt 11:23//Luke 10:15) also permit us to think that the founding of a Christian community in Capernaum had not been successful. Yet it is surprising that the discourse of Jesus all of a sudden becomes a sermon in the synagogue. Brown seeks to confirm the possibility that behind 6:35–50 stands a sermon preached by Jesus in the synagogue at Capernaum during Passover time and he does so with the help of the lectionary theory of A. Guilding.[30] But that appears to us to exceed the realm of possibility, in spite of the caution exercised by Brown in his work. The introduction in verse 25 leads one to expect that the discourse of Jesus took place in the open. Loisy attributes verse 59 to the redactor and in that he is correct.[31]

Overview

In a certain sense verses 51b–59 are the most decisive for the investigation of this section. On Bauer's view they stem from the hand of the Evangelist: "Just as he treats baptism in 3:5, so he speaks here of that other mystery of

---

25 Cf. 5:24f.
26 *Studien*, 65.
27 *John*, 236 n. 8 [176 n. 7].
28 *Neutestamentliche Grammatik. Das Griechisch des Neuen Testaments im Zusammenhang mit der Volkssprache dargestellt*, HNT 1 (Tübingen: Mohr-Siebeck, ²1925) 142.
29 *John*, 234 [174].
30 Brown, *John*, 1: 278–80. Aileen Guilding, *The Fourth Gospel and Jewish Worship. A Study of the Relation of St. John's Gospel to the Ancient Jewish Lectionary System* (Oxford: Clarendon, 1960).
31 *Le quatrième évangile*, 244.

Christianity, likewise in an anticipatory fashion. The constant repetition and ever sharper formulations of the paradox in verses 52–57 in opposition to his opponents can be understood only on this assumption. The horror of the world in the face of the Thyestean meals of the Christians is reflected here . . . horror which has its ultimate basis in eucharistic practices."[32] Käsemann concedes: "To be sure, the presence of redactional work in John may be demonstrated on the basis of chapter 21 and can hardly be denied for texts such as 6.51b–58."[33] But he then adds: "Yet undoubtedly the Evangelist not only knew of Jesus' baptism, but also presupposed the practice of Christian baptism and of the Lord's Supper in his community. If there are allusions to the sacraments in John 3.3ff.; 6.32ff. and in other texts, they are hardly surprising at the end of the first century. On the contrary, one would expect to find a multitude of sacramental allusions in a Christian document of that time."[34] Brown, for whom the editor of the first and second editions of the Gospel of John is the Evangelist himself, regards verses 51–59 as an addition of the editor of the third edition, that is, of the redactor; these verses belonged originally to the Johannine account of the inauguration of the eucharist at the last supper. Finally, Bultmann's opinion of verses 51b–58 may be epitomized as follows: "Thus we must inevitably conclude that verses 51b–58 have been added by an ecclesiastical redactor; it is the same editor who has added . . . the refrain: ['I will raise him up at the last day']. . . . It has been added in an attempt by the editor to make the whole discourse reflect the views of verses 51b–58."[35]

There is a note of uncertainty in most of these exegetes. Brown,[36] for example, takes verses 51–58 to be derived from Johannine material and wonders seriously whether one could not accede to the thesis of A. Guilding to the effect that in his preaching Jesus himself followed the scriptural texts that were part of the lectionary cycle of the Jewish synagogue during that period (in which, of course, there was reference to the

eating of the forbidden fruit of the tree of life). He of course sees that this thesis has very little persuasive power. Bauer recognizes the contradiction between verses 51b–59 and what follows and also the consequences that Wellhausen[37] and others have drawn from that contradiction, viz., that these verses represent a reworking of the text. But, Bauer adds: "That is not absolutely necessary. The author holds fast to sacramental practice, but he knows that the supernatural effect does not proceed from such things. For him these sentences can stand alongside each other: he who has faith has eternal life . . . and: only he who partakes of the Lord's Supper has eternal life."[38] Käsemann also advocates such juxtapositions in the last analysis.[39] Yet he goes further and asks: why did John not forecast the institution of the sacraments and why did he even substitute the narrative of the foot-washing for the institution of the Lord's Supper? He answers: "This implies that the peculiar relationship of our Gospel to the sacraments and the cult may not be investigated and determined in isolation. . . . The debate really centers upon John's conception of history."[40] That means for Käsemann that not only is the primacy of christology at stake, but in the last analysis "Incarnation rather means, as the prologue unmistakably indicates, the encounter of the Creator with his creature."[41]

Now of course that is to overlook the fact, as it appears to us, that the cosmos and man are not viewed as creations in the Gospel of John, as one can assume on the basis of some sentences in the Prologue and isolated references in the narrative preceding Jesus' ministry. Whoever wants to come to Jesus must be born from above, must be "drawn" by God. And that does not happen to all men, but only to a select group. Jesus does not pray for the cosmos. The saying taken over by the Evangelist and used in 1:29 has only limited application. Käsemann's formulation, the logos "overcomes or increases the world's resistance to its Creator," does not do justice to the Gospel of John. For this emphasis on the

---

32   *Das Johannesevangelium*, 99f.
33   *The Testament of Jesus*, 32.
34   *The Testament of Jesus*, 32.
35   *John*, 219f. [162].
36   *John*, 1: 278ff.
37   *Das Evangelium Johannes*, 32.
38   *Das Johannesevangelium*, 101f.
39   *The Testament of Jesus*, 32.
40   *The Testament of Jesus*, 33.
41   *The Testament of Jesus*, 34.
42   *The Testament of Jesus*, 35.

creator[42] appears to us to have been read into the Fourth Gospel. The christology that in fact dominates everything has to do with the one who was sent, who saves those whom the Father has given him. Here Käsemann has to pay for his statement: "The formula 'the Father who sent me' is, lastly, neither the only nor the most typical christological formula in the Gospel."[43] Jesus is never designated as "the revealer" in the Gospel of John, although Bultmann constantly calls him that (and Käsemann agrees):[44] that should give one pause.

But first let us stay with the question whether John could really countenance a sacramental theology alongside a completely different christology. What, then, do verses 51b–59 really imply? For, an insertion begins with v. 51b. While the Evangelist sees the present of the exalted one in the word of the proclamation (kerygma), that does not satisfy the redactor. He has not grasped that Jesus made the Father present in his word and deed and that the preaching of the disciples continues that making present of the Father—they thus proclaim that in which the Father was and is to be seen. This "is" occurs, however, only in the word.

The redactor, on the other hand, wants more "palpability"; he wants what the sacrament appears to provide. His doctrine of the sacrament, however, is not easy to comprehend. His basic presupposition is that the exalted one has taken his humanity with him into heaven, so to speak. Contact with him depends on that humanity. But how can one conceive of the humanity of the exalted one and the elements of the lord's supper as bound together in such a way that we can partake of these elements and simultaneously partake of the humanity of the exalted one and thus of the exalted one himself? The redactor does not propose to understand the matter in such a way that Jesus as a whole is present in microform, so to speak, in every morsel of the eucharistic bread. His points of departure are the two passages 1:14 ("and the Logos became flesh") and 13:18 ("He who ate my bread," a quotation from Ps 41:10). While the second passage establishes that Jesus' bread is eaten in the eucharist, the first passage, by contrast, appears to confirm that Jesus, the Logos, became flesh. Since man consists of flesh and blood, as the matter was conceived in antiquity, there

was a tendency to understand the "elements" of the eucharist—following models in pagan meals in the mystery religions, in which the god is eaten and the power of the god thereby transferred to the initiates— the bread and wine, as representatives of Jesus' flesh and blood. Just how they are that is not contemplated; the fact of it appears to be sufficient. The believing Christian acquires communion with the humanity of Jesus—so the redactor appears to intend his doctrine of the eucharist: the Christian literally takes that humanity into himself and thus Jesus also. That is a complete misunderstanding on the view of the Evangelist: the humanity of Jesus is important for him only because it makes possible the "becoming visible" of the invisible Father—in suggestive deeds and words. This humanity of Jesus is of course retained following Good Friday because the proclamation does not fall silent. Since the Gospel of John does not pass the synoptic sayings material on, but has the earthly Jesus already announce his significance himself, the humanity of Jesus is preserved for the fourth Evangelist in the words of Jesus that are transmitted. Nothing depends on the flesh and blood of Jesus; his flesh and blood, isolated from his word and the Spirit that is imparted with those words, lack significance. For that reason, the Evangelist has not preserved a tradition of the institution of the lord's supper.

For the redactor, on the other hand, much more weight lay on the palpability of the connection with Jesus in the present. For him the reality of the connection of the believer with his heavenly savior is alone important because this believer no longer understood himself as "spirit," but as a person of flesh and blood. The situation is comparable with respect to the reality of the resurrected one in Luke 24 and in the Thomas story, which the Fourth Gospel has taken over—in a corrected form, of course. It becomes evident on the basis of the letters of Ignatius why such weight was placed on the tangibility of the eating and drinking of the resurrected Christ: only in this way did one guard against the gnostic heresy that Jesus' body was only an apparition. Gnosticism held the view it did because for it an incarnation already signified an entry into the sinful material world. For Christians, on the other hand, such a doctrine was unacceptable,

43   *The Testament of Jesus*, 11.
44   *The Testament of Jesus*, 31.

because on this view Jesus would be only an appearance, a phantom, which was not a revelation of the Father. That the redactor's conception of the eucharist contained grave difficulties (which were then ascribed to the Evangelist) is brought to light by the further development of the doctrine of the eucharist.

The sacraments were not simply unimportant for the Evangelist, so that an allusion to them would have been sufficient to bring them to mind, but they actually contradict the heart of his proclamation. Whether the community in which he lived thought just as he did and therefore was unacquainted with the sacraments of the "great church," or whether he was a loner and designed his own picture of the Christ, cannot be determined. Yet the Fourth Gospel, in its original form (before it was made acceptable to the church at large by a redactor), appears to be evidence of a peculiar Christian development on the fringe of the Christianity of the "great church," a development that led its own isolated life (not in Ephesus, of course, where the revised form of the Gospel of John was perhaps published).

The individual verses can now readily be understood on the basis of the redactor's conception of the eucharist sketched above. Verse 51 is to be distinguished from what precedes in that the expression, "the living bread," appears in the place of "the bread of life." The "bread of life" corresponds to 11:25 ("I am the resurrection and the life") and 14:6 ("I am the way, the truth, and the life"). To the extent that Jesus brings the faithful to the Father is he the life. But the same thing can be expressed in other words: he provides the water of life. On the other hand, in 8:12 and 9:5 he can say of himself that he is the "light of the world." Both ways of expressing the matter are correct from the perspective of the theology of the Evangelist. To the extent that the believer can perceive the Father in him is Jesus the light of the world and the water of life. To the extent that Jesus makes the (invisible) Father visible to the believer does he provide the water of life; but he is not that water. Thus, the expression, "the living bread," would be entirely possible. But that expansion now facilitates the reinterpretation of the word by reference to the sacrament: one can eat bread, and, correspondingly, it can then be said: "if any one eats of this bread, he will live forever." That is now clarified in verse 51b, where the sacramental meaning clearly emerges: "and the bread which I shall give" (future since the death of Jesus has not yet taken place) "for the life of the world is my flesh."

One can construe the words as follows: "the bread that I will give for the life of the world." But he probably intended it to be taken as: "my flesh for the life of the world." That implies: as the redactor conceives it, Jesus' flesh is sacrificed on the cross for the life of the world, for the salvation of the world. But it now depends on man getting a share in this redemptive flesh. They salvage the eucharistic doctrine by means of the futuristic expectation of a resurrection on the last day. Whoever partakes of the Christian sacrament, and only he, will be resurrected on the day of judgment: for the redactor, that is the life that Jesus dispenses. And he arrives at this view because he, like the more or less contemporary expression in Luke 24:39, conceives the resurrected Christ as having "flesh and bones." Even if that does not sound so coarse as it does in Luke, but implies a kind of "heavenly flesh" (a notion that shows up later in the history of dogma), one can only share in this Christ by means of the elements of the eucharist.

There is no internal space for such a doctrine of the eucharist in the Gospel of John, any more than there is space for a futuristic eschatology, and never alongside his "authentic" doctrine. It can indeed be the case, as Käsemann puts it,[45] that the Gospel of John "is the relic of a Christian conventicle existing on, or being pushed to, the Church's periphery." If, however, our assumption turns out to be right that the Evangelist has made use of and reinterpreted a very different, wonderfully joyful gospel, it is not at all out of the question that the Evangelist was a loner, a reformer, or even a revolutionary, who did not flit off to just any fanciful future, but caught sight of the sole important thing, the thing that gave meaning to life, in the present encounter with the message of Jesus. It is not at all out of the question that the Evangelist understood the conclusion of the story of walking on the sea—they came suddenly to land from the middle of the lake—in its deeper sense, as a pointer to the fact that the encounter with Jesus and his message burst the

---

45   *The Testament of Jesus*, 39.

bounds of time and space. Then the two thousand years that had meanwhile passed for Kierkegaard, a period he sought ardently to bridge, would already have been noted and overcome in the Gospel of John.

A. Guilding's thesis that Jesus always constructed his discourses on themes that were related to the lections appropriate to various feasts can be connected with 6:4. In my judgment, the redactor has inserted this verse in order to pave the way for a eucharistic interpretation. Quite apart from that, however, the OT text in question, Genesis 3, with its warning not to eat from the tree of life, is not at all appropriate to this discourse of Jesus. Rather, the contrary trend of the discourse of Jesus becomes evident precisely in view of this apologetic attempt to represent Jesus as a pious Jew vis-à-vis the observance of festivals. Jesus puts the matter sharply in verse 32: Moses did not give you bread from heaven. Judaism and the Jewish religon cannot claim to mediate salvation. Rather, the true giver of the manna from heaven is God, who now sends Jesus as the bread from heaven. Faith in Jesus is therefore the only deed well pleasing to God. This faith in Jesus is equated, in verse 40, with seeing Jesus. This seeing of Jesus of course has to do with the one about whom 14:7ff. speak: the one who sees the Father in Jesus.

In this pericope, the questions that go together with Johannine christology are especially pressing. Dodd[46] has correctly pointed out that in the first part of the Gospel of John a miracle is narrated first; then follows a discourse in which a Johannine interpretation of the miracle is given. In this case, a miracle is taken over from the tradition, probably from a non-canonical gospel, and narrated in detail as such; the Evangelist does not begin his interpretation until verse 26. How are the preceding twenty-five verses now to be conceived? Two possibilities appear to present themselves: the one is that the Johannine Jesus is represented as 'a God walking around on the earth.' Käsemann seems to us to have opted for this possibility not only because he himself employs the expression just quoted,[47] but also because he writes: "The presence of miracles narrated by John cannot be explained by John's faithfulness toward the tradition. John took up the tradition freely. . . . he selected the

most miraculous stories of the New Testament. He would hardly have done so had he wanted to use them as mere illustrations in the speeches of Jesus and thus been disinterested in the miracle itself. . . . No Christian at the end of the first century could have come to the idea that God could enter the human scene without miracles, or that rebirth should be the sole miracle appropriate to him. The Johannine criticism of miracles begins and ends where Jesus himself is sought or forgotten for the sake of his gifts. On the other hand his glory cannot be without miracles and the greater and the more impressive they are the better. . . . There is no reductionism about the miracles in the Fourth Gospel."[48]

The counterpart to such a conception as Käsemann's is found in Bultmann. He accepts the view that 20:30f. concluded the gospel of which the Evangelist made use, and then continues: "Now if the Evangelist dared to use this ending as the conclusion of his book, it shows not only that the σημεῖον ['sign'] is of fundamental importance for him, but at the same time—if he can subsume Jesus' activity, as he portrays it, under the concept of σημεῖον!—that this concept is more complex than that of the naive miracle story. Rather it is clear—and it will be made perfectly clear by the exegesis—that the concepts σημεῖα and ῥήματα (λόγοι [both mean 'word']) both qualify each other: σημεῖον is not a mere demonstration, but a spoken directive, a symbol; ῥήμα is not teaching in the sense of the communication of a set of ideas, but is the occurrence of the Word, the event of address. . . . Yet this raises the question how far the Evangelist has put a new interpretation on the traditional material, and whether he has brought this out by editing his source."[49] Bultmann later adds this note: "The question whether the Evangelist believed the miracle to have been an actual historical occurrence may not, it seems to me, be answered so obviously in the affirmative as usually happens; but here we may leave it aside."[50]

These, then, appear to constitute the possibilities of how the Evangelist conceived the miracles: as actual events which demonstrate that the divine is at work, that God is walking about on the earth; or as symbols, and as symbols only, but not as events actually occurring.

Critical biblical scholarship among liberal theologians

---

46 *Interpretation of the Fourth Gospel*, 290.
47 *The Testament of Jesus*, 27.
48 *The Testament of Jesus*, 22.

49 *John*, 113f. [78f.].
50 *John*, 119 n. 3 [83 n. 4].

around the turn of the century intended to discover a picture of Jesus in the Fourth Gospel that could be reduced exactly to the formula used by Käsemann: Jesus is God walking about on the earth. For that reason, Käsemann cites F. C. Baur, G. P. Wetter, W. Heitmüller, and W. Bousset with approval,[51] and emphasizes that "all miracles remain signs pointing beyond themselves to the revelation occurring in the Logos himself. Nevertheless, for John the miracles are also 'proofs' of divine power in the sphere of the transitory." Yet it holds true that: "the miracles in John are primarily meant to be manifestations of the glory of Jesus."[52] "We must not forget that Thomas is referred to the faith which does not see, only after he has seen and touched."[53]

In my judgment, Käsemann thereby overlooks the fact that the Evangelist continually corrects the miracle stories transmitted to him; these corrections are turned into mere allusions to something entirely different, something that cannot be directly observed. The assertion that the Evangelist has sought out the most miraculous of the stories can be made only on the supposition that he had before him the entire gospel tradition from Mark on, and not just the canonical gospels. However, the situation is seen in an entirely different light if he did not have all these gospels before him on his desk, but had only a single "gospel of miracles" par excellence before him, a gospel that he found in his community, and on which he then built his Gospel. And the situation takes on a different cast if one does not perceive in John a scintillating author such as Windisch and Hirsch celebrated in him (and they were not alone in this). Thus, if he chose to utilize this gospel, he was compelled to use individual corrective glosses (as, for example, in 4:48f.) and the discourses of Jesus to bear witness to his own christology. That he made such a Gospel depicting the earthly life of Jesus serviceable goes together with his view that this earthly life, perceived entirely as something Jesus really lived through, was at the same time an indirect communication of the revelation (of course understood by neither the Jews nor the disciples). It is indirect insofar as all these miracles, including even the resuscitation of Lazarus who was already decomposing (apart from individual healings such as 5:9 and 9:7),

remain within the realm of earthly events: once revived, Lazarus can of course continue his earthly existence for a time, until the high priests have put him to death for a second and final time (12:10).

The decisive thing, however, is that the relation of Lazarus to God is not altered by his resuscitation any more than is that of the lame man in Chapter 5. Passages that imply that the disciples came to faith on the basis of miracles belong to material that was taken over, as, for example, 2:11, 23–25. Yet this faith is put in question as early as 2:24. It follows from 7:39 that a confession of faith was not possible prior to the coming of the Spirit, and the Spirit is imparted only after Easter (20:22). On this point the difference between perceptions of the gospel used by the Evangelist and the perceptions of the Evangelist himself are especially clear. Käsemann's remarks about miracles in the Gospel of John are therefore to be corrected in three respects: (1) the list of miracles given by Käsemann go beyond the miracles narrated by the other canonical Gospels only relatively speaking (to the extent that they concern the earthly Jesus; only the risen Jesus goes through closed doors).[54] (2) All the miracles of John do not break the earthly frame of reference: the five thousand who are fed get hungry again, etc. (3) The significance of the miracles as signs ($\sigma\eta\mu\epsilon\hat{\iota}\alpha$) is not recognized. To this extent Jesus remains as unrecognized and as incomprensible during his earthly life as he does in Mark. His earthly existence becomes comprehensible only after Easter, and even then not as God walking about on the earth and being accredited by miracles. Käsemann does not take into consideration the dialectical nature of what Jesus says about his relationship to the Father: he does not do his own will, he does not speak his own words, he does not do his own deeds. He exists only for the Father and thus is one with the Father. That by no means precludes, however, that the Father is greater than he, and his prayer in chapter 17 is by no means a sham. Käsemann continually perceives a docetic impression in the face of the Johannine Jesus, a perception that Baldensperger already shared;[55] this perception stems from a conviction that all four Evangelists presuppose, viz., that the man Jesus was also a divine being. However, the fourth

---

51 *The Testament of Jesus*, 9 n. 6, 27 n. 1, 66 n. 14.

52 *The Testament of Jesus*, 53.

53 *The Testament of Jesus*, 22.

54 *The Testament of Jesus*, 9; cf. *Jesu lezter Wille nach Johannes 17* (Tübingen: Mohr-Siebeck, [3]1971) 51ff.

55 *Der Prolog des vierten Evangeliums. Sein polemisch-*

Evangelist, who does not take offense at Jesus as the progeny of Joseph and Mary, gives greater room to the humanity of Jesus than do Matthew and Luke.

Our arguments respecting the theses of Käsemann make it a matter of course that we cannot agree with Bultmann's solution either. If the Evangelist made extensive use of a gospel foreign to him (of course not without heavy corrections and long insertions, especially in chapters 4 and 11), he did so, by all appearances, not just because he knew the gospel and was perhaps familiar with it for some time. He was opposed not to the details of the miracles as they are narrated, but to the way in which the miracles were understood. The Evangelist did not take the miracles merely in their symbolic sense, in our opinion, but took them as real events. But as miracles they pointed to something different, and this a symbol cannot do. So nothing contradicts the view that the Evangelist objected to the miracles that were narrated in detail by his source, or are only suggested by way of summary, as in 2:23, 7:31, or 20:30. He did not conceive them solely as miracles—that they were is in a certain sense incidental, not to say, irrelevant to him; it is important to him that the "raising up" ($\dot{\epsilon}\gamma\epsilon i\rho\epsilon\iota\nu$) of the lame man in 5:8 points to the raising up of the (spiritually) dead, as the Father and therefore also the son are able to effect.

Earlier we called the "signs" ($\sigma\eta\mu\epsilon i\alpha$) indirect forms of communication. It is a question whether the discourses of Jesus go beyond this "indirectness." What then is really being said when Jesus refers to himself as the true bread from heaven? Does the Evangelist go beyond his use of "raise up" ($\dot{\epsilon}\gamma\epsilon i\rho\epsilon\iota\nu$) in chapter 5? When Jesus, speaking in the name of the Father, calls himself the true bread from heaven, or the water of life, the light of the world, the truth and the life, what does he really mean? Käsemann answers: "They speak of what enables man to live," and then he supplements this remark with another: "He can do this only as creator."[56] The logos is of course not the creator, but the mediator of creation, through which everything came into being that came into being. However, the concept of "creator" is not the central idea, is not the key idea, in the Fourth Gospel (apart from the fact that the term "creator" does not appear in the

Gospel of John). Indeed, Jesus does not give what is necessary for earthly life, like the Samaritan woman and the audience in Capernaum hoped he would. What he does give is perhaps indicated most clearly by the self-designation "the way." It is the new union with God that he brings, and that is precisely what cannot be directly described. In his farewell discourses, Jesus speaks of the peace he gives his own, the peace that the world cannot give, and of the perplexing questions that will cease for the believers (16:23). That is of course something that makes no impression in the modern world because constant questioning and probing is taken as genuine human behavior, while unquestioning confidence is prohibited. If the content of what John says about God appears to us to be minimal, we must not of course forget that in the picture he draws everything that he says elsewhere stands in the background and can be invoked to fill out the picture. In general, we may well say: if God is the bread of life and the water of life for us, then that is a proclamation of grace, although Pauline concepts are almost entirely lacking. That Jesus limits himself to the message that he, the mere man, is the revealer, and the mere "that"—or rather the claim that the Evangelist has said everything there is to say on that score—squares with Bultmann's understanding of the Johannine proclamation: a decison is demanded of man. But Bultmann's understanding does not give sufficient weight to the fact that it is God who gives the true bread from heaven, and not man's decision. And it does not take into account the difficulty that we can speak of God only in earthly terms; those terms are never adequate. That in part has led to the reproach of backwardness, which the computer has overrun and to which it has put an end. If, however, one also takes into account all the information the computer is able to store and reproduce, one must not forget that all that information has been input by man. If the Evangelist is monosyllabic with respect to the assertions he makes about God (whom no one has ever seen, except the son), one should not reproach him for a shortage of information for which he remains obligated to us. John has withheld much in his assertions, which the fantasy of the Apocalypse provides in such plentitude, and is also silent about "the deep things of God," which Paul thinks

---

apologetischer Zweck (Tübingen: Mohr-Siebeck, 1898) 171.

56 *The Testament of Jesus,* 51.

he knows by virtue of the OT statement and the interpretive power of the Spirit (Rom 11:25–36; 1 Cor 2:16). It is true: because the Evangelist is taciturn—one can also complain about the abstractness of his language—much of Jesus' humanity does not come to expression, which is the case in the Synoptics also. But we must not forget that to a great extent his source describes a "divine man" (θεῖος ἀνήρ). If the Evangelist rules that out, then he retains very little of the "material" in hand. But this "little"—for example, his words about the bread from heaven—was related at the same time to our life here in an anxiety-laden world. Of course not in such a way that his statements can be understood by everyone—and this raises a possible objection against the Evangelist. In our world, in the scientific age, of course only what can be basically repeated by everyone can claim to be the truth. The Evangelist has rejected the repeatability of his statements by everybody when he refers to the fact that Jesus can only come to the one whom the Father "draws." The bread from heaven is not explained on every guarantee found on merchandise in the department store.

18. Jesus and the Resolution of Relationships

Bibliography

Beauvery, R.
"Voulez-vous partir, vous aussi? Jn 6,60–69."
AsSeign 52 (1974) 44–51.

Boccali, Giovanni
"Spirito e vita (Gv 6,63)." *Parole di vita* 13 (1968)
118–31.

Boccali, Giovanni
"Un maschal evangelico e la sua applicazione [Gv
6,63]." *BeO* 10 (1968) 53–58.

Bornkamm, Günther
"Die eucharistische Rede im Johannes-Evangelium." *ZNW* 47 (1956) 161–69, esp. 165–68. In his
Geschichte und Glauben, part 1. *Gessamelte Aufsätze*,
vol. 3. BEvT 48 (Chr. Kaiser Verlag, 1968) 60–67.

Cipriani, Settimio
"La confessione di Pietro in Giov 6,69–71 e suoi
rapporti con quella dei Sinottici." In *San Pietro. Atti
della XIX settimana Biblica, Associazione Biblica
Italiana* (Brescia: Paideia, 1967) 93–111.

Dekker, C.
"Grundschrift und Redaktion im Johannesevangelium." *NTS* 13 (1966/1967) 66–80, esp.
67–70, 77f.

Ferraro, Giuseppe
"Giovanni 6,60–71. Osservazioni sulla struttura
letteraria e il valore della pericope nel quarto
vangelo." *RivB* 26 (1978) 33–69.

Hilgenfeld, Adolf
"Noch ein Wort über Joh 6,71." *ZWT* 9 (1866)
336.

Joubert, H. L. N.
"'The Holy One of God' (John 6:69)." *Neot* 2
(1968) 57–69.

Leal, Juan
"Spiritus et caro in Joh 6,64." *VD* 30 (1952) 257ff.

Michael, J. Hugh
"The Actual Saying behind St. John vi. 62."
ExpTim 43 (1931/1932) 427–28.

Pascher, J.
"Der Glaube als Mitteilung des Pneumas nach Joh
6,61–65." *Theologische Quartalschrift* 117 (1936)
301–21.

Phillips, G.
"This is a Hard Saying: Who Can be a Listener to
It?" SBLASP 1 (Missoula: Scholars Press, 1979)
185–96.

Temple, Sydney
"A Key to the Composition of the Fourth Gospel."
JBL 80 (1961) 220–32, esp. 230–32.

Worden, T.
"'Seigneur, à qui irions-nous?'" *Concilium* 50 (Paris,
1969) 105–81.

60 Many of his disciples, when they heard it,
said, "This is a hard saying; who can
listen to it?" 61/ But Jesus, knowing in
himself that his disciples murmured at it,
said to them, "Do you take offense at
this? 62/ Then what if you were to see
the Son of man ascending where he was
before? 63/ It is the spirit that gives life,
the flesh is of no avail; the words that I
have spoken to you are spirit and life. 64/
But there are some of you that do not
believe." For Jesus knew from the first
who those were that did not believe, and
who it was that should betray him. 65/
And he said, "This is why I told you that
no one can come to me unless it is
granted him by the Father." 66/ After
this many of his disciples drew back and
not longer went about with him. 67/
Jesus said to the twelve, "Will you also
go away?" 68/ Simon Peter answered
him, "Lord, to whom shall we go? You
have the words of eternal life; 69/ and
we have believed, and have come to
know, that you are the Holy One of God."
70/ Jesus answered them, "Did I not
choose you, the twelve, and one of you is
a devil?" 71/ He spoke of Judas the son
of Simon Iscariot, for he, one of the
twelve, was to betray him.

■ **60** Verse 60 begins a new scene and question. They
basically dominate the balance of the chapter. Verse 66
does not begin an entirely new section. Following verse
60, many disciples of Jesus begin to desert him because
of his speech (it is a simplification to say that all of them
were present in the synagogue at Capernaum). Many
disciples declare themselves unable to listen further to
such a "hard saying"; as verse 66 will make still clearer,
this ends their relationship to Jesus as disciples.

■ **61** The Evangelist permits Jesus to respond to this
opposition (which is rooted in non-understanding), without having anyone tell him about it: Jesus simply "knows"
that they are murmuring, although this murmuring
against him has not been expressed (cf. Mark 2:8). In
view of the offense, the Evangelist provides the reader of
the Gospel with interpretive help; this explanation is
designed to reduce the stumbling block (σκανδαλίζω) as
much as possible. It is so brief, however, as to require
interpretive help itself.

■ **62** Verse 62 indicates what one must reckon as decisive:
whoever takes offense in the face of Jesus' claim that this
man sets himself over against the entire tradition and

represents himself as the one who alone makes "eternal
life" possible, should not forget that Jesus is indeed more
than a "mere man": he has come from God and will
return to him again.

■ **63** What makes him important and gives him his authority is thus not his existence as a mere man, as "flesh."
The "flesh," his earthly existence, merely presents him
with the possibility of spreading his message in word and
deed, the possibility to make God visible in this message.
"Spirit" is therefore not ecstasy but the knowledge of
God: it alone brings one into relationship with the Father
and thereby creates life. That "the flesh is to no avail"
does not mean that it could therefore have gotten along
just as well without assuming human form. It is intended
to prevent one from seeking the center of gravity where
it does not lie. The redactor's doctrine of the sacraments,
which contradicts every attempt at apologetic reconcil-
iation and leveling of the two points of view, is thus
pointedly rejected.

■ **64f.** In these verses the effort is made to adduce proof
that the desertion on the part of the disciples was not
unexpected: Jesus knew about it all along and had

spoken of it. Accordingly, this state of affairs and Jesus himself are spoken of in the third person; in contrast, in verse 65, Jesus' own words are introduced (or appended) with the phrase, "and he said." The whole has the effect of two glosses, which put a different interpretation on the prediction that one would betray him: Jesus knew beforehand who would not believe in him. It thus becomes unwittingly evident that man is a nonentity; it has been determined in advance who has been selected to believe and who not. The early Christian problem of the fall from faith thereby announces itself: the matter is not settled when one comes to faith in Jesus; one must also abide in this faith. The cause of the desertion, however, in distinction from Mark 18:31–38, is not persecution, which leaves men weak with its terrors, but the content of the teaching itself. For the redactor it is the Christian doctrine of the sacraments; for the Evangelist, on the other hand, it is the absolute claim of Jesus, which is also turned against the OT.

In this context, one should go further into the language of verse 63b: "the words that I have spoken to you are spirit and life." That can be understood and misunderstood finally as a theory about God that has become detached from the historical figure of Jesus and that is really the point; the man Jesus is only the fortuitous bearer of the message.[1] For this man has come down from heaven—although that is not visible—and therefore alone brings the right message. More exactly: he is the true message in word and in deed. That raises the question for us whether this is not a mystical conception that must be made to disappear by means of interpretation or exposition. Our situation is such that many messages reach us and these point in various directions; which direction should we take? For John the knowledge that Jesus' words are "spirit and life" and that they alone bring us into a new relation with God is therefore a divine gift, and not a perception that is accessible to us. It is then not the case that Jesus' words have the character of a mathematical formula that compels our assent. It is possible that those words will leave some cold and a Christian does not have the right to look on such persons with contempt. It is always possible that tomorrow morning he will come to recognition: that is basically the way it is with me. I do not know how it happens, but today these words no longer make an impression on me. The word "decision" does not help us escape the dilemma of this situation. We have to accept the fact that some of us will not pass Jesus by, others will do so easily, without difficulty. Paul once spoke of non-Christians as those who have no hope (for life after death; 1 Thess 4:13). Whoever seeks to become a Christian in order to acquire such a hope should desist at once. That hope can be the consequence of becoming a Christian, but it cannot serve as the impulse to become a Christian. And the form of the Pauline expectation of last things is not accessible to us, in any case. Many indeed long to have the graves open and earthly life continued in a form of existence altered only in part; the Evangelist, however, if he is the author of 5:25, did not share that hope.

■ **66** Verse 66 basically begins again just where verse 60 began. Except that this time it is not a question of the "many" who no longer want to follow Jesus, but of the narrower circle of disciples, which does not appear elsewhere in John: how do matters stand with them? Will they survive the offense that the many found intolerable?

■ **67** Jesus himself provokes the decision that has already devolved upon them with the question: do they also want to go away? The twelve appear only here in a decisive passage in the Gospel of John and so the passage appears to have been intended as something like an exemplary picture of a loyal disciple. However, we should follow the scene to its end before we pretend to understand what it is about.

■ **68** As spokesman for the twelve ("we"), Simon Peter—who is solemnly introduced by name and a name of honor among Christians—answers by alluding to Jesus' words "go away": "Lord to whom shall we go (away)?" There is no one in sight who could challenge the disciples to become his disciples. But the response turns not only on this negative: of Jesus it must be said that he alone has the words of life. For the Evangelist that means: Jesus' words are full of eternal life, for they lead us to the Father; the Father speaks to us in them.

■ **69** What was just said in the previous verse is now uttered with a solemn epithet: "we have believed, and have come to know, that you are the Holy One of God."

---

1   Cf. Bultmann, *John*, 443ff. [340ff.]: "It is irrelevant to the message who bears it." John certainly does not mean that.

"The Holy One of God" is one of those titles that designates Jesus' position. "The messiah" or "the Son of man" would do just as well. At all events, what is meant is the one who has come from God as redeemer, who himself belongs to the divine sphere, and who therefore can make the claim to be a bearer of an authoritative message from God. The words "we have believed and have come to know" stand amicably beside each other as though they could not designate two different and mutually hostile certainties. But for John they really express one and the same certainty and subject matter. For him, the one who believes really knows God, who remains closed, inaccessible, unrecognized to the one who lacks faith. But this knowing is not concurrence in some mathematical, logical proposition. It is rather faith: the surrender of the whole man to the one who is known and to his will, love (but without wild passion), and peace. In a real sense the Jesus that John delineates is himself the model of such faith, although John never says that he believes.

■ **70f.** The concluding verses demonstrate that the Evangelist was never given to a glorification of the twelve. Following immediately on the solemn declaration "we have believed and have come to know," of all times, Jesus gives a twofold response that stands in sharp contrast to the words and confession of Peter. First of all, Jesus insists that he is the one who chose the twelve. The disciples did not come to Jesus and abide with him by virtue of some human determination. To the contrary, Jesus created the circle of disciples by his own decision. Whatever authority the circle has, it has from him. The disciples, or the Christians, are once again reminded of their limits. It was not their decision, but the decision of Jesus that turned them into disciples, into Christians.

This decision does not, however, curtail Jesus' freedom. It is therefore not the case that calling is also election at the same time. Paul writes in Rom 8:30: "And those whom he predestined he also called; and those whom he called he also justified; and those whom he justified he also glorified." The acts of God thus hew to an unwavering line that brings consolation to the individual Christian. One could put it in a nutshell: *In ecclesia certa salus.* But John has Jesus say something different: he chose the twelve and one of them is a devil. In verse 71b it said that Judas Iscariot is the one meant. One might think that Jesus' foreknowledge is again being documented. But that is not what is at issue for John. Rather, he wants to make something clear to his readers with this case: although faith is not in the hands of man, is not a possibility to which man has access from the start, and although the believer should know that he has been chosen by God, he must not entertain the thought that his salvation is thereby assured: nothing more could happen to him now (as a chosen one). Judas is one of the twelve chosen by Jesus, and he became the betrayer. Indeed, perhaps the Evangelist could even have said: he was chosen by Jesus to be the betrayer.

Overview

In this passage we may observe: the Evangelist has here introduced the twelve, who play a major role in primitive Christian tradition, to illustrate how little a person may boast and feel himself or herself assured of salvation, even though he or she has been chosen by Jesus. The true bread has of course come down from heaven to give life to the world. But that does not imply that everyone will be saved, that everyone will find his or her way to the Father. The tremendous tension in which the believer exists is not relieved precisely because everything depends on the will of the Father. The Fourth Gospel is anything but primitive and undialectical. To be a disciple does not mean to have certainty (cf. vv 60 and 66). The simple language employed by the Evangelist serves to mislead the reader to expect simple thoughts and to fail to see the farther horizons that lie hidden in the scene following the discourse at Capernaum. It goes without saying that the twelve have no authority in the eyes of the Evangelist.

There are no passages in the Gospel of John, except for 6:67–70, where Jesus speaks with the twelve alone as he does in the Synoptics. But that owes to the fact that the twelve play no role in John—again apart from 6:67–70—which is not a particularly good recommendation for the twelve. Yet these verses in the Gospel of John make contact with the confession of Peter in Mark 8:27ff. Following the "hard saying" in the synagogue at Capernaum, many of his disciples forsake Jesus. When he now asks the twelve, "Will you also go away?" Simon Peter answers (also as a spokesman for the disciples): "Lord, to whom shall we go? You have the words of eternal life. And we have believed and have come to know that you are the Holy One of God." Here Jesus also provokes a confession on the part of the disciples, in which, to be sure, a messianic title does not appear. To this Jesus responds: "Did I not choose you, the twelve, and one of you is a devil?" The Evangelist explains that Jesus means Judas, son of Simon Iscariot (Σίμωνος Ἰσκαριώτου). The tradition that is here being used no longer has Peter as a "Satan," but turns Judas into a devil. But another difference is even more significant: the confession of Peter (who speaks for the twelve) is depicted here basically in its dubiousness: one of the twelve who allegedy knew and believed in Jesus is not a believer but a devil. According to Bultmann, "The intention of these verses is to show that even for those who emerged out of the circle of the unbelievers and penetrated into the circle of the 'disciples' (μαθηταί), who also overcame the offence that diminished this circle down to the Twelve, no certainty is given."[2] But for the Gospel of John Judas was lost as "the son of perdition, that the scripture might be fulfilled" (17:12). The betrayer—and indeed the future betrayer—was chosen by Jesus. In the Gospel of John man is not lost or redeemed through his own decision, as he is in the gnostic Gospel of Thomas, but through the determination of God, before whom the hearts of men are like rivulets. The opinion that a dualism of decision is characteristic of the Gospel of John, while in Gnosticism, on the other hand, one is persuaded that the pneumatics are "saved by nature" (φύσει σωζόμενοι), is mistaken on both counts.

2 *John*, 450f. [345].

Ο ΙΟΥ ΔΑΙ . . ΤΩ . . .

ΟΥ ΔΕΝ Α Ι ΗϹΑ . . .

ΠΕΝ ΕΙΩΘΕ Ν . .

ΘΡΗ Κ Ϲ Κ Ϲ Ι Α . .

Ρ Ι ΟΡ ΙΟΝ . .

ΙΚ Α ΕΙΤϹ